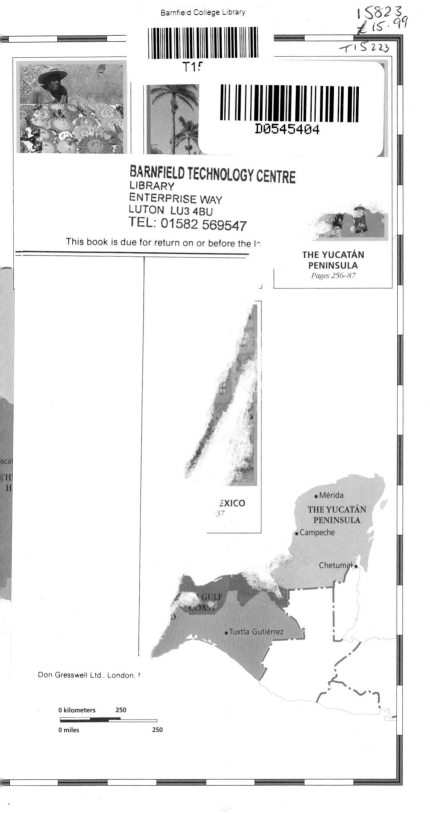

THE YUCATÁN
PENINSULA
Pages 256–87

EXICO
37

• Mérida
THE YUCATÁN
PENINSULA
• Campeche

Chetumal •

GULF
COAST

• Tuxtla Gutiérrez

0 kilometers   250

0 miles   250

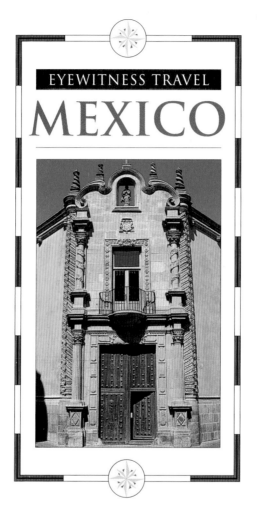

EYEWITNESS TRAVEL

MEXICO

EYEWITNESS TRAVEL
MEXICO

DK

DK

LONDON, NEW YORK,
MELBOURNE, MUNICH AND DELHI
www.dk.com

PROJECT EDITOR Nick Inman
ART EDITORS Stephen Bere, Marisa Renzullo
EDITORS Elizabeth Atherton, Claire Folkard, Emily Green,
Freddy Hamilton, Jane Oliver, Sophie Warne, Lynda Warrington
US EDITOR Mary Sutherland
DESIGNERS Gillian Andrews, Jo Doran, Paul Jackson,
Tim Mann, Nicola Rodway
MAP CO-ORDINATOR David Pugh
RESEARCHER Eva Gleason
PICTURE RESEARCHERS Monica Allende, Ellen Root
DTP DESIGNER Maite Lantaron, Pamela Shiels

MAIN CONTRIBUTORS
Nick Caistor, Maria Doulton, Petra Fischer, Eduardo Gleason, Phil
Gunson, Alan Knight, Felicity Laughton, Richard Nichols, Chloë Sayer

CONSULTANTS
Antonio Benavides, Simon Martin, Lourdes Nichols

Reproduced by Colourscan (Singapore)
Printed and bound by South China Printing Co. Ltd.

First published in Great Britain in 1999
by Dorling Kindersley Limited
80 Strand, London, WC2R 0RL

Reprinted with revisions 2001, 2002, 2003, 2006, 2008, 2010

Copyright © 1999, 2010 Dorling Kindersley Limited, London
A Penguin Company

ISBN 978-1-40535-380-9

*Front cover main image: Church of Nuestra Señora de los
Remedios and Popocateptl, Cholula, Puebla*

MIX
Paper from
responsible sources
FSC
www.fsc.org   **FSC™ C018179**

Produced with the generous help of the Proyecto México, Dirección
de Divulgación, Coordinación Nacional de Difusión, Instituto Nacional
de Antropología e Historia, Córdoba 45, Col. Roma, Delegación
Cuauhtémoc, CP 06700, Mexico

⌁CONACULTA • INAH ❀

◁ The Maya site of Tulum in the Yucatán Peninsula

Plaza Santo Domingo in Oaxaca

CONTENTS

HOW TO USE
THIS GUIDE **6**

**Statue of Tlaloc in Xalapa
Museo de Antropología**

INTRODUCING
MEXICO

MEXICO CITY

Monumento a la independencia

MEXICO REGION
BY REGION

Maya village in Xcaret theme park
on the Yucatán Peninsula coast

TRAVELERS'
NEEDS

Carne asada, a classic Mexican dish
of barbecued spicy steak

SURVIVAL GUIDE

Temple of the Inscriptions
at the ancient Maya site
of Palenque

HOW TO USE THIS GUIDE

This guide helps you to get the most from your visit to Mexico. It provides detailed practical information and expert recommendations. *Introducing Mexico* maps the country and sets it in its historical and cultural context. The six regional sections, plus *Mexico City*, describe important sights, using maps, photographs, and illustrations. Features cover topics from food and wine to fiestas and native wildlife. Restaurant and hotel recommendations can be found in *Travelers' Needs*. The *Survival Guide* has tips on everything from making a telephone call to using local transportation.

MEXICO CITY

This is divided into three areas, each with its own chapter. A final chapter, *Farther Afield*, covers peripheral sights. All sights are numbered and plotted on the chapter's area map. Information on each sight is easy to locate as it follows the numerical order on the map.

A locator map shows where you are in relation to other areas of the city center.

All pages relating to Mexico City have red thumb tabs.

Sights at a Glance lists the chapter's sights by category: Churches and Cathedrals, Museums and Galleries, Streets and Squares, Historic Buildings, Parks and Gardens.

1 Area Map
For easy reference, sights are numbered and located on a map. City center sights are also marked on the Mexico City Street Finder (pages 118–25).

A suggested route for a walk is shown in red.

2 Street-by-Street Map
This gives a bird's-eye view of the key areas in each chapter.

Stars indicate the sights that no visitor should miss.

3 Detailed information
The sights in Mexico City are described individually. Addresses, telephone numbers, and opening hours are provided along with information about admission charges, photography, guided tours, wheelchair access, and public transportation.

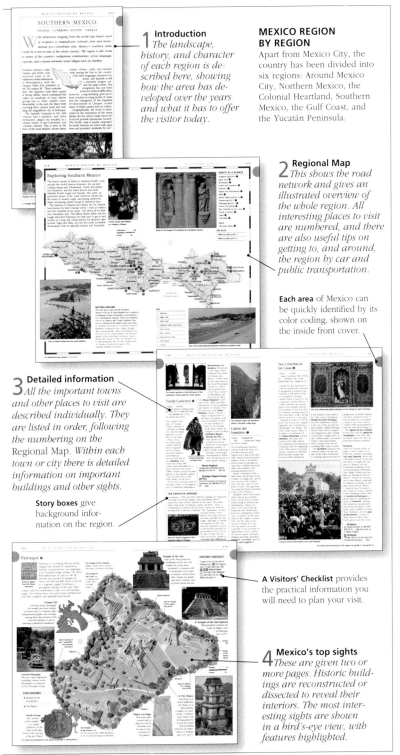

1 Introduction
The landscape, history, and character of each region is described here, showing how the area has developed over the years and what it has to offer the visitor today.

MEXICO REGION BY REGION

Apart from Mexico City, the country has been divided into six regions: Around Mexico City, Northern Mexico, the Colonial Heartland, Southern Mexico, the Gulf Coast, and the Yucatán Peninsula.

2 Regional Map
This shows the road network and gives an illustrated overview of the whole region. All interesting places to visit are numbered, and there are also useful tips on getting to, and around, the region by car and public transportation.

Each area of Mexico can be quickly identified by its color coding, shown on the inside front cover.

3 Detailed information
All the important towns and other places to visit are described individually. They are listed in order, following the numbering on the Regional Map. Within each town or city there is detailed information on important buildings and other sights.

Story boxes give background information on the region.

A Visitors' Checklist provides the practical information you will need to plan your visit.

4 Mexico's top sights
These are given two or more pages. Historic buildings are reconstructed or dissected to reveal their interiors. The most interesting sights are shown in a bird's-eye view, with features highlighted.

INTRODUCING MEXICO

DISCOVERING MEXICO

Mexico is a wonderfully varied country – ranging from rocky deserts to tropical forests, and mountain valleys to superb Pacific and Caribbean beaches. There are the spectacular ruins of ancient cities, and elegant Spanish colonial towns which still adhere to the traditional customs of Indian communities, while also embracing the hectic life of modern cities. No two regions of the country are alike; each has its own colorful traditions in food, music, and dress.

Wooden mask from Tocuaro

(left photo)

Traditional dancers in the Zócalo

MEXICO CITY

- **The historic hub of Zócalo**
- **Chapultepec**
- **Artists' district of Coyoacán**
- **Xochimilco floating gardens**

One of the world's largest cities, Mexico's capital can seem overwhelming, yet offers a wealth of things to see and do. Its historic heart, packed with streetlife, revolves around the **Zócalo** *(see pp62–3)* – the spectacular giant square with centuries of history in one place: the Aztec ruins of the Templo Mayor, the Spanish Cathedral, and the 20th-century murals of Diego Rivera.

To the west is the shady park of **Chapultepec** *(see pp88–9)*, with the Museo de Antropología (Museum of Anthropology), a fabulous showcase for Mexico's pre-Columbian cultures.

Even hectic Mexico City has its quiet corners, like **Coyoacán** *(see pp104–105)*, south of the center, with charming old streets and the homes of artists Diego Rivera and Frida Kahlo. Farther south are the spectacular colorful water gardens of **Xochimilco** *(see p112)*, a uniquely Mexican experience.

AROUND MEXICO CITY

- **Ancient Teotihuacán**
- **Stone guardians of Tula**
- **Crafts in Taxco and Puebla**

Within a short distance of the capital, the central plateau has some of the most dramatic relics of ancient Mexico, in the awesome city of **Teotihuacán** *(see pp134–7)*, with its avenue of massive pyramids and palaces dating back nearly 2,000 years, and enigmatic **Tula** *(see p144)*,

with its giant Toltec stone warriors. The centuries of Spanish rule are reflected in charming colonial towns like the mountain city of **Taxco** *(see pp146–7)*, famed for its silversmiths, and lovely **Puebla** *(see pp150–53)*, its buildings beautifully decorated with locally made, colorful tiles.

Rock formations in Cabo San Lucas

NORTHERN MEXICO

- **Beaches of Baja California**
- **Whale watching**
- **Sierras & Cañón del Cobre**

The long desert peninsula of Baja California is lined by idiosyncratic little towns and stunning beaches leading down to the stylish resort of **Cabo San Lucas** *(see p169)*. Offshore, the waters of the Sea of Cortés are rich in marine life and especially whales, and a trip to see them is a real treat.

On the mainland east of "Baja," the thinly populated northern states are marked by empty plains, giant cacti,

Well-preserved pyramids of the ancient city of Teotihuacán

◁ Scenes from a religious ceremony in a reconstruction of a Mayan fresco from Bonampak

Traditional textiles for sale at a market stall in Zinacantán, Chiapas

gaunt crags, vast horizons, and bright desert flowers. Some of Mexico's busiest cities are located here, including **Monterrey** *(see p179)* and **Chihuahua** *(see p172)*. The desert is broken up by high sierras with spectacular mountain scenery, above all in the vast **Cañón del Cobre** (Copper Canyon) *(see pp176–7)*.

THE COLONIAL HEARTLAND

• **Unique colonial cities**
• **Stylish Puerto Vallarta**
• **Lake Pátzcuaro**
• **Monarch butterfly migration**

The states to the north and west of Mexico City are rich in Spanish colonial architecture, Indian traditions, and coastal and mountain landscapes. Their colonial cities have a special atmosphere: Baroque **Zacatecas** *(see pp192–3)*, vibrant **Guadalajara** *(pp188–9)*, timeless **Guanajuato** *(pp202–205)*, and exquisite **San Miguel de Allende** *(pp198–9)*. Guadalajara and its state of Jalisco are home to Mexico's famous *mariachis, charros* (cowboys), and *tequila*.

On the coast, fashionable **Puerto Vallarta** *(see p185)* is flanked by smaller resorts. The islands of **Lake Pátzcuaro** *(see p207)* are the scene of Day of the Dead fiestas.

The remote high mountains east of Morelia witness the winter mass migration of monarch butterflies *(see p211)*.

SOUTHERN MEXICO

• **Beautiful Pacific beaches**
• **Magnificent colonial cities**
• **Greatest Mayan sites**

Mexico's finest Pacific beaches line the coasts of Guerrero and Oaxaca. Brash **Acapulco** *(see pp218–19)* is the most celebrated attraction, but for visitors who prefer more relaxed resorts, **Zihuatanejo** or **Puerto Escondido** *(see p216)* fit the bill, with miles of empty beaches lying between them.

Oaxaca and Chiapas states have large Indian populations, and the colors and traditions of indigenous peoples are all around. Gracious colonial **Oaxaca** city *(see pp222–5)* has Mexico's most fascinating handicrafts. To the east in the Chiapas highlands, the unique city of **San Cristóbal de las Casas** *(see p231)* is surrounded by villages where the Mayans' way of life survives to this day.

In the north of Chiapas, the landscape drops precipitously into tropical rain forest. Sparsely populated today, some 1,500 years ago this was a thriving area of Mayan culture, and contains some of the best sites, in **Yaxchilán** *(see p232)*, **Bonampak** *(p232)*, and the jungle city of **Palenque** *(see pp234–7)*.

Olmec sculpture in La Venta

THE GULF COAST

• **Languid but lively Veracruz**
• **El Tajín – ancient Totonac city**
• **Olmec sculptures**

Hot and humid, this region centers on the great port of **Veracruz** *(see p250)*, one of Mexico's liveliest cities. It is rich in pre-Columbian relics, especially the pyramid-city of **El Tajín** *(see pp242–3)*, once capital of the Totonacs. Farther southeast, Parque La Venta in **Villahermosa** *(see p255)* is home to the powerful sculptures of ancient Mexico's Olmec culture.

THE YUCATÁN PENINSULA

• **Chichén Itzá and Uxmal**
• **Mérida and Campeche**
• **Stunning beaches**

The Yucatán remains slightly apart from the rest of Mexico. Its inhabitants, the Maya, were the most sophisticated pre-Columbian culture, leaving superb monuments and architecture in **Chichén Itzá** *(see pp274–7)* and **Uxmal** *(pp262–4)* and hundreds of lesser-known sites. Later, the Spanish built elegant cities in **Mérida** *(see pp270–71)* and **Campeche** *(p260)*. On the fabulous Caribbean coast is **Cancún** *(see p279)*, Mexico's most popular resort. To the south is the **Mayan Riviera** *(see p280)*, with idyllic white-sand beaches and coral reefs.

Mayan rain forest city of Calakmul

Putting Mexico on the Map

Geographically, Mexico is considered to be part of North, rather than Central, America. It covers an area of almost 2 million square kilometers (760,000 square miles) and has a population of 111 million. Administratively, the country is divided into 31 states and a Federal District, in which stands the vast, sprawling capital, Mexico City.

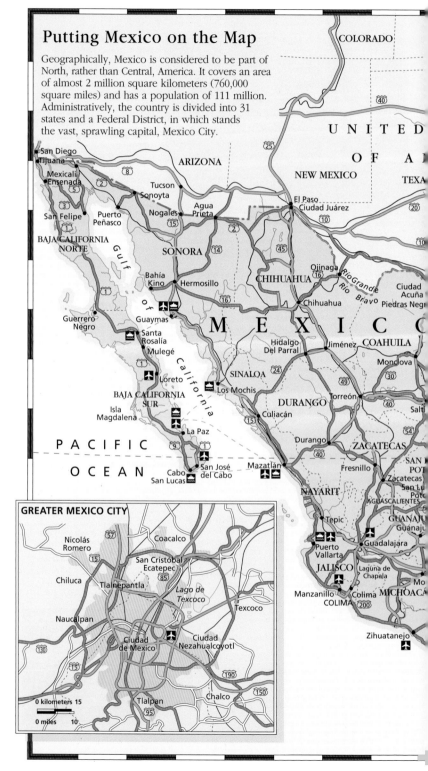

COLORADO

UNITED
OF A
ARIZONA
NEW MEXICO   TEXA

San Diego
Tijuana
Mexicali
Ensenada
San Felipe
Puerto Peñasco
BAJA CALIFORNIA NORTE

Tucson
Sonoyta
Nogales
Agua Prieta

El Paso
Ciudad Juárez

SONORA

Ojinaga
Río Grande
Río Bravo
Ciudad Acuña
Piedras Negr

Bahía Kino
Hermosillo
CHIHUAHUA
Chihuahua

Guerrero Negro
Guaymas
Santa Rosalía
Mulegé

Hidalgo Del Parral
Jiménez   COAHUILA

Monclova

M E X I C O

Loreto
BAJA CALIFORNIA SUR
Isla Magdalena
La Paz

SINALOA
Los Mochis

DURANGO
Culiacán
Torreón

Salt

PACIFIC
OCEAN

Durango
ZACATECAS

Cabo San Lucas
San José del Cabo
Mazatlán
Fresnillo

SAN POT
Zacatecas
San Lu
Poto
AGUASCALIENTES

NAYARIT

Tepic

GUANAJU
Guanaju

Puerto Vallarta
Guadalajara

JALISCO   Laguna de Chapala

Manzanillo   Colima   MICHOACA
COLIMA

Mo

Zihuatanejo

GREATER MEXICO CITY

Nicolás Romero
Coacalco
San Cristóbal Ecatepec
Chiluca
Tlalnepantla
Lago de Texcoco
Texcoco
Naucalpan
Ciudad de Mexico
Ciudad Nezahualcoyotl
Chalco
Tlalpan

0 kilometers 15
0 miles 10

NORTH, CENTRAL, AND SOUTH AMERICA

CANADA

UNITED STATES OF AMERICA

ATLANTIC OCEAN

MEXICO

Mexico City

CUBA
DOMINICAN
REPUBLIC
HAITI

GUATEMALA
EL SALVADOR
BELIZE
HONDURAS
NICARAGUA
COSTA RICA
PANAMA

VENEZUELA
GUYANA
SURINAME
FRENCH
GUIANA
COLOMBIA

PACIFIC OCEAN

ECUADOR

PERU

BRAZIL

BOLIVIA

CHILE

PARAGUAY

0 kilometers 1,000

0 miles 500

KEY

✈ International airport

⛴ Ferry port

═ Highway

▬ Major road

— Railroad

▬ International border

- - State line

ARKANSAS

MISSOURI

OKLAHOMA

Arkansas

ARKANSAS

40

STATES

Red

LOUISIANA

RICA

20

35

Dallas

45

Houston

10

San Antonio

Corpus Christi

Nuevo Laredo

McAllen

Brownsville

Reynosa

Matamoros

rrey

NUEVO LEÓN

101

Ciudad Victoria

Tropic of Cancer

180

TAMAULIPAS

35

Tampico

GULF OF MEXICO

QUERÉTARO

105

étaro

HIDALGO

Pachuca

Río Pánuco

Tuxpan

Poza Rica

VERACRUZ

MEXICO CITY

TLAXCALA

Xalapa

Tlaxcala

Veracruz

ernavaca

Puebla

MORELOS

PUEBLA

Balsas

Chilpancingo

OAXACA

175

GUERRERO

125

Oaxaca

200

pulco

Puerto
Escondido

Bahías de
Huatulco

CHIAPAS

190

200

Tuxtla
Gutiérrez

San Cristóbal
de las Casas

Tapachula

Guatemala

EL SALVADOR

Mérida

180

YUCATÁN

Campeche

261

CAMPECHE

307

QUINTANA
ROO

Chetumal

186

TABASCO

Villahermosa

Río Usumacinta

Belize

BELIZE

Lago de
Izabal

GUATEMALA

HONDURAS

Cancún

Isla
Cozumel

0 kilometers 200

0 miles 100

A PORTRAIT OF MEXICO

*A*t once orderly and chaotic, Mexico assaults the senses with the sights and sounds, tastes and smells of a unique mix of cultures and landscapes. Nowhere else in the Americas are ancient history and magic rituals so inextricably entwined with the routines of modern daily life.

Mexico's arid north abuts the US along a 3,140-km (1,950-mile) border. This frontier is the only place on the planet where the so-called "first" and "third" worlds come face-to-face. To the south, Mexican territory ends amid tropical forest on the banks of the Usumacinta river, the border with Guatemala. North and south Mexico are starkly different. The northern states are wealthier, whiter, more urban, and industrialized. Although there are indigenous communities in the north, the southern states are home to the vast majority of the country's Indians, most of whom remain peasant farmers.

La Catrina, a Days of the Dead figure

Between these extremes there are many Mexicos to be seen. Modern agribusiness exists alongside pre-Columbian farming techniques. Rural Indian groups maintain their ancestral rites while many urban Mexicans are swayed by Western consumerism.

This is also a populous country. Of a total population of more than 111 million, one fifth is crammed into the Valley of Mexico, around 2,100 m (7,000 ft) above sea-level. The country is dominated by Mexico City. The vast, sprawling capital is one of the biggest cities in the world and its growth shows no sign of slowing down.

Fishermen preparing their nets on a beach in the Yucatán

◁ The hilltop archaeological site of Monte Albán near Oaxaca

Decorative tiles in the city of Puebla

THE MEXICAN WAY OF LIFE

The traditional Mexican view of the world can be thought of in terms of concentric circles. First comes the family, at the center of which is the venerated matriarch. Mother's Day is one of the most important dates in the Mexican calendar, and it is no coincidence that some of the harshest slang words and insults in Mexican Spanish incorporate variations on the word *madre*. Yet with the family under assault, as elsewhere in the world, from the forces of modernity, today this social fabric is being subjected to

Cycling, an inexpensive way of getting around town

unprecedented strain. Loyalties outside the family are traditionally confined to an immediate circle of friends, who may be *compadres* or *comadres* (godparents to one's children), or simply *cuates* ("pals").

Wider society, as well as authority figures, tend to be regarded with suspicion, and although confrontations are usually avoided, compliance is often no more than lip service. Mexicans have a tendency (particularly in the south) to say "yes" even when they mean "no," and to regard rules as an unwarranted constraint. Yet Mexican society is far from homogeneous.

Despite centuries of interbreeding between European settlers and native Mexican "Indians," 20 percent of Mexicans still consider themselves to be purely indigenous. The common culture of Mexico, as can be seen in the national cuisine, fiestas, and the arts and crafts, blends contributions from all quarters. Even so, in some regions pre-Columbian traditions, untouched by European influences, still survive.

Stalls in the market of San Cristóbal de las Casas

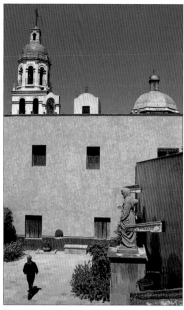

The Convento de la Santa Cruz in Querétaro

RELIGION

Almost nine out of ten Mexicans regard themselves as Catholic, but Mexican Catholicism has incorporated many elements of pre-Christian religion. The most venerated figure, especially among the poor, is the Virgin of Guadalupe, the country's patron saint. Said to be one of the three "untouchable" institutions (the others are the army and the presidency), the dark-skinned Virgin appeared, according to legend, in 1531 on a site once dedicated to the pagan mother-goddess Tonantzin. Shrines to the Virgin are to be found all over Mexico, even in remote places.

The state has had an uncomfortable relationship with the Catholic Church, as a result of the latter's support first for the Spanish colonial authorities and later for the Emperor Maximilian. Until the Salinas reforms of the 1990s, priests were forbidden to appear in public in their vestments and

Mexico had no diplomatic relations with the Vatican. Paradoxically, the two great heroes of Mexican independence, Hidalgo and Morelos, were both priests.

In opposition to the Catholics, the influence of evangelical protestants is growing rapidly in Mexico. The evangelicals tend to be highly enthusiastic and regular practitioners of their religion.

THE ARTS AND SPORTS

Mexico has a rich artistic tradition in the fields of painting, architecture, literature, and film.

Many of the murals of Diego Rivera, José Clemente Orozco, and David Alfaro Siqueiros and the canvases of Frida Kahlo and Rufino Tamayo are acknowledged masterpieces. Octavio Paz, the great contemporary interpreter of *mexicanidad* ("Mexican-ness") won a Nobel prize for literature, and the novelist Carlos Fuentes is world renowned. Mexican film had a heyday in the 1940s–

Traditional mask

50s, and the industry still produces international hits regularly, such as *Like Water for Chocolate* (1992), *Amores perros* (2000), *Y tu mamá también* (2001), and *Pan's Labyrinth* (2006).

Festival in honor of the Virgin of Guadalupe, December 12

Charreria, a popular spectator sport, particularly in the north

Almost more interesting than formal works of art are the expressions of folk art for which Mexico can be justifiably proud. Mariachi music has gained adherents as far away as Belgium and Japan. Mexican crafts, meanwhile, are testament to a limitless creativity.

Mexicans are sports mad. The most popular sports – soccer, boxing, bullfighting, and baseball – have been imported from other countries. Wrestling, *lucha libre*, is also an import but with a distinctive Mexican stamp on it, in the form of masks worn by the combatants. A uniquely Mexican sport is *charrería*, which is somewhat akin to rodeo. It centers on competitions to test skills of horsemanship but has a whole culture of bright costume and festivity surrounding it.

Masked wrestlers in lucha libre

POLITICS AND ECONOMICS

Since the upheaval of the Revolution between 1910 and 1920, Mexico has been the most politically stable country in Latin America. With the collapse of the Soviet Union, the Institutional Revolutionary Party (PRI) inherited the title of the world's oldest political regime. Peruvian novelist Mario Vargas Llosa once described Mexico's system as "the perfect dictatorship" for its ability to change presidents – and even modify its ideology – every six years, while retaining an iron grip on power. The government of Carlos Salinas de Gortari (1988–94) swept away much of the economic control the PRI had formerly championed. His successor, Ernesto Zedillo, pursued the neoliberal recipe with equal enthusiasm. The cost, however, was a widening gap between rich and poor. As a consequence, challenges to the regime, both from within the PRI and from an increasingly active opposition, grew steadily, leading to PRI's defeat in the 2000 elections, the first time it has been out of power since 1929. Changes are expected under the government of Vicente Fox and the National Action Party (PAN). So

Mariachis performing in Zacatecas

far, however, political competition has done little to eradicate the endemic corruption for which Mexico, sadly, has a deserved reputation. With roots at least as old as the Spanish colonial era, corruption flourished during the PRI's bureaucratic monopoly. It was further boosted by the 1970s oil boom and the growth of crime syndicates who were able to buy political and police protection.

In 1994 the Zapatista National Liberation Army (EZLN) burst onto the scene with the seizure of six towns in the state of Chiapas. Although formal hostilities lasted less than two weeks, negotiations failed

Mexico City's futuristic stock exchange building

to prosper, and tension has remained high. Other small guerrilla groups have emerged, with more radical agendas.

The EZLN's uprising coincided with Mexico's entry into the North American Free Trade Agreement (NAFTA) with the US and Canada, a treaty the guerrillas – almost all of them Maya peasants – saw as inimical to their interests. NAFTA was a bold

Cadets at the military medical school on parade

attempt to overcome almost two centuries of suspicion between Mexico and its northern neighbor. But while the two economies are increasingly interlinked, the relationship remains delicate. The thousands of undocumented migrants who annually cross the border in search of a better life – and the drug traffickers who exploit the same routes – are major sources of friction. Mexico's rapid transformation

from an agricultural to an industrial economy has failed to resolve the employment problems of its growing population: one million jobs per year are needed to keep pace with the new entrants to the market, with the shortfall is provided by the precarious "informal" economy.

Partly as a legacy of the struggle for independence and the Revolution, and partly as a result of living next door to a super-power, Mexicans are enthusiastically patriotic. Their nationalism reaches its height each September 15. On this date Father Hidalgo's call or cry ("*El Grito*") for Mexican independence is repeated everywhere, from the Palacio Nacional in Mexico City to the humblest town hall. Nonetheless, tradition is under threat. Younger Mexicans are as likely to celebrate Hallowe'en (a European/US festival) as they are to honor their ancestors on the Days of the Dead at the same time of year.

A political rally in the capital

The Landscape and Wildlife of Mexico

The volcano Pico de Orizaba, Mexico's highest mountain

Despite serious threats to its environment, Mexico remains one of the three richest nations on earth in terms of the variety of its flora and fauna. With more than 30,000 plant species, almost 450 different mammals, and over 1,000 types of bird – many of which are unique to Mexico – it is a naturalist's paradise. The reason for this natural wealth is the range of habitats, from snow-capped volcanoes to mangroves, deserts, and tropical forests, not to mention part of the world's second-longest barrier reef.

Resplendent quetzal

DESERTS AND SCRUBLANDS

Over half of Mexico's land is classified as arid, and another 30 percent as "semi-arid." The only true desert – where the annual rainfall is less than 25 cm (10 inches) – is the Desierto de Altar in northwest Sonora. The dry scrublands that cover much of northern Mexico, particularly Chihuahua, Sonora, and Baja California, conceal a surprising abundance of wildlife.

The desert tortoise *is threatened with extinction because of the trade in wild animals. A recovery program has begun in Mapimí in northern Mexico (see p173).*

Cactuses (see p171) *have adapted to the harsh conditions of life in deserts.*

Rattlesnakes *of several different species are among the many reptiles found in Mexico. They are typical of arid zones.*

WETLANDS

These habitats, which range from ponds to mangrove swamps and coastal lagoons, are fast disappearing through land reclamation, pollution, and urbanization. They are home to wading birds such as herons or egrets. The saline lagoons of the Yucatán Peninsula support colonies of flamingos (see p272).

The leopard frog *and its innumerable relatives fill the air of the wetlands with their chorus of croaking.*

The sora, *a member of the rail family, is a winter visitor found in reed beds across the country.*

Mangroves *grow along tropical coastlines in brackish water. They provide a habitat for wading birds and other fauna.*

COASTS

Mexico's coastline totals over 10,000 km (6,250 miles) in length. On the Pacific, promontories and islets are common, while on the Atlantic side the coastline is sandy. A magnificent coral reef lies off the coast of Quintana Roo. Isolated beaches provide nesting grounds for species of sea turtle.

The sea fan *is one of many fascinating species found on the coral reef (see p283).*

Whales, *including the world's biggest, the blue whale, are seen off Baja California (see p164).*

MOUNTAINS AND CANYONS

Mexico is a land of mountains: more than half the country is over 1000 m (3,200 ft) above sea level. Mountainsides are typically clad in pine or pine-oak forest. There are also arid mountains in the North, including the haunt of the endangered Mexican bighorn sheep, and areas of cloud forest and montane rainforest in the south.

Bighorn sheep, *sacred to some pre-Columbian people, roam the remote, arid northwest mountains.*

The bobcat *is a medium-sized feline, sometimes glimpsed amid the thornscrub of northern Mexico.*

Yellow-eyed junco *is one of the most familiar birds of the Mexican mountains.*

TROPICAL FORESTS

Rainforest is the earth's richest habitat in terms of the number of species it supports. Mexico's rainforest is on the Atlantic slope south of the isthmus of Tehuantepec, with isolated remnants in northern Oaxaca and southern Veracruz. These areas' rich wildlife includes jaguars, parrots, and the extraordinary quetzal, a bird sacred to the Maya *(see pp46–7)*.

The jaguar *is Mexico's biggest cat, but it has suffered from the loss of its jungle habitat in the south and west.*

The keel-billed toucan *is unmistakable because of its huge, multicolored bill.*

Armadillos *defend themselves from predators by rolling into a ball.*

The Indigenous Peoples of Mexico

Mexico's indigenous inhabitants are probably more numerous today than at the time of the Spanish Conquest. However, the precise definition of "indigenous" is debatable. Official statistics show that more than one in ten of the population of 111 million belongs to one of the 62 Indian language groups. Some, like the Tarahumara, Huichol, and Lacandón *(see p232)*, retain much of their pre-Columbian way of life. Most, however, have abandoned traditional dress (at least in public) and ways of life, and are often indistinguishable from mixed-race Mexicans.

The Yaqui *of Sonora perform their evocative Danza del Venado (Deer Dance) during Easter Week and on the Day of the Dead.*

The Trique *of Oaxaca are among the less numerous indigenous peoples. Here a woman is using a traditional loom, one end of which is fastened to a tree while the other is tied around her back to maintain the tension.*

A string of shamans' baskets form the tail of the serpent.

Eight ancestors inhabit the second level of creation. They have no legs and cannot speak.

A creator god in the form of a serpent is at the heart of creation.

The Maya *civilization (see pp46–7) went into decline before the arrival of the Spanish. The descendants of the Maya, who inhabit the state of Chiapas and the Yucatán Peninsula, speak a large number of mutually unintelligible languages. These women belong to the Tzotzil Maya.*

The mockingbird carries people's memories from the past to the present.

The Tarahumara *(see p174), who live in the area around Copper Canyon in Chihuahua state, play a tough endurance game called rarajipari, in which two opposing teams kick wooden balls around an improvised mountain course. The game can last for several days.*

The Huichol *(see p184) are known in Mexico for their dazzlingly colored handicrafts, especially beadwork. They cling precariously to the lands of their ancestors on the border of Jalisco and Nayarit states.*

WHERE MEXICO'S INDIGENOUS PEOPLE LIVE

The indigenous population is concentrated mainly in the south, although some large groups – the Yaqui, Mayo and Tarahumara – are in the north. The states of Oaxaca and Chiapas have the largest proportion of indigenous inhabitants. The five most widely spoken indigenous languages are Nahuatl (the language of the Aztecs), peninsular Maya, Zapotec, Mixtec, and Otomí.

Mayo
Tarahumara
Yaqui
Chihuahua

Cora
Huichol
Huastec
Totonac
Otomí
Mérida
Guadalajara
Tarascan
Mexico City
Maya
Nahua
Mixtec Trique
Zapotec

The third or outer level of creation is the realm of plants, animals, and all other natural phenomena.

An open flower symbolizes life rising from the earth.

The Shaman is a cross between a priest and a healer, with a vast knowledge of medicinal plants. There is no easy dividing line between magic, ritual, and traditional medicine in indigenous culture. However, all are rapidly being supplanted by "western" science and medicine.

HUICHOL YARN PAINTING

Mexico's indigenous people make an extraordinary variety of crafts *(see pp348–9)*, usually in bright colors and based on striking, symbolic designs. This painting depicts the Huichol view of creation as divided into three phases or levels, each inhabited by different beings.

Catholicism in Mexico is for many a mixture of Christianity, brought by the Spanish, and lingering beliefs from ancient Mexico. The indigenous inhabitants of Mexico adapted their religion to that of their rulers without abandoning belief in their ancient gods.

The sun is shown with a snake beneath it, which symbolizes its path across the sky.

An earth mother has a seed of corn in her chest and ears of corn to either side.

The tortilla (see p320), *a flat corn (maize) pancake, is the staple food of both indigenous and mixed-race Mexicans. Here an Indian woman prepares tortillas the way it has been done for generations.*

Corn (maize) was unknown to Europeans before the conquest of the Americas. Along with beans, it is still the essential crop grown by Mexican peasants, although the agricultural way of life is increasingly threatened by the globalization of the world economy.

Architecture in Mexico

Waterspout on Casa de los Muñecos, Puebla

Most colonial houses in Mexico were highly functional, with an interior courtyard for privacy and wrought-iron grilles to protect the windows. The Baroque age introduced flamboyance, while local materials, such as Puebla tiles, led to the growth of regional styles. Neo-Classicism, fashionable after 1785, favored austerity, but French influence in the 1800s brought a return to ornamentation. In the 20th century, Modernism was embraced with enthusiasm.

Façade tiles on the Casa del Alfeñique, Puebla (see p150)

EARLY COLONIAL (1521– C.1620)

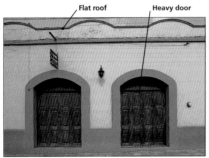

Flat roof · Heavy door

These houses in San Cristóbal de las Casas (see p231) have courtyards, flat roofs, and simple doorways.

Casa de Montejo (1543–9) in Mérida (see p270) has a Plateresque façade showing two conquistadors in full armor.

THE PLAZA MAYOR

Mexican town-dwellers take pride in their *plaza mayor* (main square). Under Spanish rule, urban planning was strictly controlled, and towns were modeled on the capital. Straight streets led to a large plaza with civic and religious buildings, plus *portales* (arcades) for the merchants. Urban renewal in the late 1800s equipped the squares with statues, bandstands, and cast-iron lamps and benches.

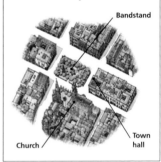

Bandstand

Church · Town hall

BAROQUE (C.1630 – C.1800)

Wrought-iron balcony

Ornamental details carved in limestone include the coat of arms of the Marqués de Jaral de Berrio.

Palacio de Iturbide in Mexico City (see p79) was designed in about 1780 by Francisco Guerrero y Torres. The sumptuous former residence has an exuberant façade.

Outer wall of red stone

Finely carved pilasters flank the high doorway, which admitted carriages to the central patio.

These figures are thought to depict inhabitants of nearby Tlaxcala.

Figures from classical mythology

Casa de los Muñecos (House of the Figures; late 18th century), in Puebla (see p150), has a façade adorned with locally made azulejos (glazed tiles).

NEO-CLASSICAL (1785–C.1880)

Stone statues portray eight of the nine Muses.

Upper balustrade

The portico has two rows of fluted columns.

Teatro Juárez *in Guanajuato (see p203) was commissioned in 1873 and built by Antonio Rivas Mercado. It combines Neo-Classicism with lavish French styles of decoration.*

PORFIRIAN (1876–1911)

This late 19th-century stained-glass window *showing a coat of arms is from the Museo Bello in Puebla (see p152).*

French-influenced ornamental stonework

Islamic-style window

This eclectic mansion *in Guadalajara was completed in 1908. The era (see p53) freely combined Rococo, Neo-Classical, Neo-Baroque, and other styles.*

RURAL ARCHITECTURE

Many Indian populations use local materials to build houses in styles particular to their region. Depending on geography and climate, houses may be square, rectangular, apsidal, or round. In regions with heavy rainfall, roofs are steep and often thatched with palm or grass, while overhanging eaves protect walls of poles or wattle-and-daub. Where trees are plentiful, wooden houses are common. In areas with low rainfall, builders use stone, bricks, or adobe (mud bricks).

Nahua house in Hidalgo, with log walls and a roof of *zacate* (grass)

Thatched Maya house of rubble masonry and plaster, in the Yucatán

MODERN (C.1920–PRESENT)

The outline emulates New York skyscrapers on a smaller scale.

Luis Barragán's Casa Gilardi, *in Mexico City, has a ground floor characterized by broad, intersecting planes of color. The 1970s design incorporates water as an architectural element.*

Innovative vertical windows

Indoor pool

Imposing angular doorway

Yellow-painted glass panes admit shafts of light.

The Loteria Nacional *(see p85) was built around 1936 by José A. Cuevas. Formality and symmetry give it an Art Deco appearance.*

Church Architecture

Figure in Santo Domingo, Oaxaca

After the conquest, new towns were dominated by churches and cathedrals. Throughout the 16th century, missionary friars acted as architects, using Renaissance, Plateresque, and Mudejar styles. Native carvers added details, and the result was *tequitqui*, a blend of Indian and European elements. The Baroque style of the 1600s became even more ornamented after 1750, with the Ultra-Baroque, or Churrigueresque.

Domes of Mitla church
(see pp226–7)

EARLY MONASTERIES

As Spanish friars took their conversion work into remote territories, they established a network of missions. Each colonial monastery, with its church, was virtually self-sufficient, incorporating living quarters for the friars, a school, hospital, library, wells, and orchards. Crenellated stone walls and other defensive characteristics gave many missions a fortress-like appearance.

The Plateresque portal of San Agustín Acolman (see p138), *finished in 1560, contrasts with the monastery's overall severity. Beside the door are two pairs of garlanded columns on angel pedestals, with a saint set between each pair.*

The mission church at Mulegé in Baja California (see p168) *was built by the Jesuits in the 18th century. The simple, functional design is characteristic of remote missions.*

Atrium

Izamal's Convento de San Antonio de Padua (see p273) *was built on the site of a Maya religious center by the Franciscans between 1553 and 1561. The colonnade enclosing the large atrium was added in about 1618, the wall belfry in the 1800s.*

The façade *has detailed, exuberant carving. This scene shows the Baptism of Christ, surrounded by cherubs, spirals, and foliage. It is flanked by statues of St. Sebastian and St. Prisca.*

Richly decorated *retablos* (altar-pieces) line the nave, adding to the cumulative splendor. This *retablo*, dedicated to St. Joseph, is adorned with cherubs, ears of corn, shells, and fruit.

The dome *is covered with glazed tiles, probably from Puebla, and inset with eight rectangular windows. The dome's frieze reads "Gloria a Dios en las alturas" ("Glory to God in the Highest"). External ribs lead to a tile-domed lantern, surmounted by a cross.*

The sacristy is reached by a door beside the high altar.

Finials

The main retablo, *conceived in high Churrigueresque style by Isidoro Vicente de Balbás, depicts the glory of the Christian Church. Heavily gilded, the carved wood conveys richness and splendor. Estípite (inverted) pilasters (see p143) replace the Classical columns of earlier times.*

South entrance

Baptistery

IGLESIA DE SANTA PRISCA, TAXCO

Begun in 1751, and finished in just seven years, the parish church of Taxco *(see pp146–7)* exemplifies the Churrigueresque style of Mexican architecture. The style is characterized by dazzling surface ornament that conveys flowing movement and obscures the form beneath. The huge costs of this church were borne by wealthy silver magnate José de la Borda.

POPULAR BAROQUE

Rural churches of the Baroque period often display enormous exuberance and charm. These eclectic, imaginative creations are aptly classified as *barroco popular*. In Puebla, the popular passion for ornamentation found expression in the glistening tiles that cover church façades with vivid patterning. Interiors exhibit a profusion of plaster figures, such as clusters of angels, cherubs, saints, animals, flowers, and fruit. These were accentuated with brilliant gold leaf and color.

San Francisco Acatapec *(see p149)*

Music and Dance

Across Mexico, celebrations are accompanied by music that owes its variety to a fusion of musical traditions. Pre-Conquest musicians played wind and percussion instruments. Today the reed-flute, conch shell, and *huehuetl* drum evoke the sounds of ancient Mexico. The Spanish introduced stringed instruments. Over time, Mexican music evolved into the *sones* (strains) of Jalisco, Veracruz, and other states. Mexico has also absorbed influences from the rest of Europe, and Africa, Cuba, and the US.

Man with accordion

MARIACHIS

Mariachi music originated in the state of Jalisco during the 19th century, when *mariachi* musicians (from the French word *mariage*) played music for weddings and balls. Suitors still often engage *mariachi* bands to serenade their girlfriends at home.

A *mariachi* band can consist of between three and 15 musicians.

The violin leads the *mariachi* melody.

Trumpets are a modern addition to *mariachi* music.

The guitar was introduced to Mexico by the Spanish.

Mariachi **musician in traditional costume**

Mariachi **bands** *can be seen in the Plaza Garibaldi in Mexico City, playing songs about love, betrayal, and revolutionary heroes.*

TRADITIONAL DANCES

Mexico has a vast range of regional dances performed only in their specific areas. During religious celebrations, they take place in squares and in front of churches. Dancers, who are usually male, communicate the story-line through dance steps, sign language, and sometimes words. Some dances hark back to pre-Columbian times and ancient rituals; others were introduced by Spanish friars and show European influence.

Tlaxcala Carnival dancers *wear elaborate garments embroidered with sequins, and carved wooden masks with pale skin tones. Carnival is a time for revelry when dancers parody their ancient oppressors.*

Quetzal dancers *in Cuetzalan wear headdresses of reeds and colored paper, tipped with feathers. The steps of this Nahua dance relate to the passage of the sun.*

VOLADORES

During this ancient Nahua and Totonac ritual, five men climb to the top of a pole often reaching as high as 30 m (100 ft). While one plays a drum and a reed-pipe on a tiny platform at the top, the other four "fly" to the ground, suspended on ropes.

*Each **volador** circles the pole 13 times before reaching the ground, making a total of 52 turns. This symbolizes the 52-year cycles of the Mesoamerican calendar (see p47). The central pole represents a vertical connection between the Earth, the heavens above, and the underworld below.*

Totonac voladores wear velvet panels decorated with sequins and beads.

Headdresses are adorned with mirrors and plastic flowers.

Voladores can be seen performing regularly at El Tajín (see pp242–3) and outside the National Anthropology Museum in Mexico City (see pp90–95).

Devil Mask with real horns from Michoacán

Male Mask from Puebla

Tiger Mask with animal teeth from Guerrero

MASKS

Masks were worn for a range of dances in ancient Mexico and Spain. Today, Mexican masks represent men and women, supernatural beings, and birds and animals, and can be realistic or stylized. Wood is the most common material, but some mask-makers rely on leather, clay, paper, cloth, gourds, and even wax. Dancers look through slits above or below the painted eyes.

Tiger dancers perform during festivals in the state of Guerrero. These ancient dances reflect the preoccupations of farming communities and once featured jaguars or ocelots.

A conchero dancer *performs for the Virgin of Guadalupe in Mexico City. Traditional instruments are used by concheros. Dance steps are also accompanied by the rattle of seed pods worn on the ankles.*

Dancehalls *in the capital and Mexico's other major cities attract devotees of danzón, merengue, mambo, cumbia, salsa, rock, and other musical styles. Events in Salón México (1995), a remake of a classic movie, took place at the famous dancehall of the same name in Mexico City (see p117).*

MEXICO THROUGH THE YEAR

I n the words of Mexican poet Octavio Paz, "Fiestas are our only luxury." Indeed, every day is a saint's day or other cause for celebration somewhere in Mexico, with fireworks exploding, a band playing, and the population dancing. Some traditional fiestas derive from indigenous celebrations, while others were brought by the Christian Spanish conquistadors. Many now blend the two influences.

Radishes sculpted for Oaxaca's *Noche de los Rábanos*

Most events are localized, but a few occasions are celebrated throughout the country – particularly Independence Day, the Day of the Dead, and the day honoring the Virgin of Guadalupe *(see p109)*. Visitors should be warned that many fiestas include cockfights, but these take place in separate arenas and are visible only to those who choose to enter.

The weather is an important factor determining when to visit. For combining a beach and inland vacation consider autumn; the weather is glorious, but cooler for visiting archaeological sites. There are also fewer tourists at this time of year. Winter is a good time to see wildlife.

Indigenous and Christian traditions mixed in an Easter procession

SPRING

The temperate weather conditions of spring, just before the start of the rainy season, make this a perfect time to visit the coast. However, Easter Week is one of the busiest times, and transportation gets booked up in advance. At this time of year jacaranda and flame trees blossom in a riot of color in town squares all over the country. In late spring the weather is hot, and fruits such as mangos, mameys, pineapples, and papayas fill the markets. Migratory birds, particularly birds of prey, can be seen on the Gulf Coast as they fly along it when making their way north to their summer habitats.

Easter Week *(Semana Santa; Mar/Apr)* is celebrated all over Mexico but is particularly beautiful in the southern states and in the Colonial Heartland. Passion plays are performed in most regions, notably in Taxco (Guerrero), Pátzcuaro (Michoacán), San Cristóbal de las Casas (Chiapas), Ixtapalapa in greater Mexico City, and throughout Oaxaca state.

On Palm Sunday there are processions, and palm crosses are sold outside churches. Good Friday sees parades of women swinging incense holders and carrying flowers in front of images of Christ and the Virgin Mary. They are accompanied by solemn singing, torchbearers, and hooded penitents. On this day the steps of Christ along the route to his crucifixion are re-enacted. Participants include self-flagellating sinners, robed children, and Roman soldiers. Realistic re-enactments of the whipping and crucifixion of Christ may also be staged. In the evening and on Easter Saturday cardboard "Judases" are burned and fireworks let off. On the Saturday, it is also customary in some towns to throw water at passers-by.

The Tarahumara Indians *(see p22)* have evolved their own version of the Easter story featuring an annual running battle between wicked "pharisees" and "soldiers" guarding the Virgin.

Natalicio de Benito Juárez *(Mar 21)*. Wreaths are laid at monuments to the reforming president on his birthday, notably in Guelatao, near Oaxaca, where he was born.

A Cinco de Mayo parade, which celebrates the Battle of Puebla

One of the *voladores* taking part in a Corpus Christi display

Sol a Sol Regatta *(mid-Apr)*, Isla Mujeres (Quintana Roo). Fireworks, a basketball match, and parties mark the end of a boat race from St. Petersburg, Florida to the island.

Feria de San Marcos *(Apr/May)*, Aguascalientes. Cultural, sporting, and other events combine at this important fair *(see p185)*.

Labor Day *(Día del Trabajo; May 1)*. Marches organized by trade unions and political parties culminate with speeches in town squares.

Cinco de Mayo *(May 5)*. The commemoration of the Battle of Puebla, a Mexican victory over the invading French army in 1862, is celebrated with particular enthusiasm in Puebla state *(see p153)*.

Mother's Day *(Día de la Madre; May 10)*. Every *mamacita* in Mexico is honored on this day and, finances permitting, taken out to lunch, regaled with flowers, or serenaded by mariachis *(see p28)*.

St. Isidore's Day *(May 15)*. Seeds, agricultural implements, ox yokes, and animals are blessed before planting begins in rural Mexico.

Corpus Christi *(May/Jun)*. Church services and parades take place all over Mexico. In Papantla (Veracruz), there is a special performance by the *voladores*, or "flyers" *(see p29)*, whose ritual invokes fertility, communicating with the heavens, and honoring the sun.

SUMMER

With the arrival of the rains, summer is usually considered the off season in Mexico. However, the rain tends to fall in the afternoon, and the mornings are bright and clear. The high precipitation ensures the countryside is verdant, making this a good time to tour inland. The air in Mexico City is also at its cleanest. Markets everywhere are bursting with fruit and vegetables; and only in these months can visitors taste fresh *cuitlacoche* corn fungus *(see p323)*, Mexico's answer to truffles, and the elaborate *chiles en nogada*, green chilies stuffed with ground meat and almonds.

Navy Day *(Día de la Marina; Jun 1)*. Port towns organize events to honor the navy. Official festivities take place in Guaymas (Sonora) and include uniformed processions, regattas, and fleet parades.

Horseman competing in the Lienzo Charro

Lienzo Charro *(Jun)*, Mexico City. There are displays of horsemanship *(charrería, see p74)* by riders in costumes and huge sombreros on most Sundays at the Lienzo Charro in the third section of Chapultepec Park *(see p88–9)*. The main event is in June, when a national *charro* exhibition is held.

Guelaguetza *(late Jul)*, Oaxaca. Regional dances are performed in a variety of costumes in the beautiful main fiesta of Oaxaca state *(see p225)*.

Feast of the Assumption *(Día de la Asunción; Aug 15)*. Church services and processions take place everywhere. In many towns, the streets are decorated with carpets of flowers, over which the procession of the statue of the Virgin passes. The most lively celebrations take place in Huamantla (Tlaxcala), where the Fiesta de la Virgen de la Caridad *(see p139)* lasts for nearly two weeks and ends with bulls being let loose in the streets of the town.

PUBLIC HOLIDAYS

Año Nuevo (New Year's Day; Jan 1)

Día de la Constitución (Constitution Day; Feb 5)

Natalicio de Benito Juárez (Birthday of Benito Juárez; Mar 21)

Jueves Santo (Easter Thursday)

Viernes Santo (Good Friday)

Día del Trabajo (Labor Day; May 1)

Cinco de Mayo (May 5)

Día de la Independencia (Independence Day; Sep 16)

Descubrimiento de América (Columbus Day; Oct 12)

Día de la Revolución (Revolution Day; Nov 20)

Día de la Virgen de Guadalupe (Festivity of the Virgin of Guadalupe; Dec 12)

Noche Buena (Christmas Eve)

Navidad (Christmas Day)

Costumed dancer at the Guelaguetza

Costumed horsemen in an Independence Day celebration

AUTUMN

As the rainy season ends, the countryside is still green, the weather is warm, and days are long. Rivers are full, so the white-water rafting season begins in Veracruz and San Luis Potosí. Autumn is a good time to travel in-land, especially with the added attraction of cultural events during the Festival Internacional Cervantino. The luxuriant vegetation of the Gulf Coast and Chiapas can also best be appreciated at this time of year, without heavy rains. In early and late autumn respectively, Mexico celebrates its two principal fiestas, Independence Day and the Days of the Dead.

Presidential Address *(Sep 1)*. During the afternoon on this day people watch the president's speech on television or listen to it on the radio.
El Grito/Independence Day *(Día de la Independencia; Sep 15–16)*. Father Miguel Hidalgo's "cry" to arms *(Grito)* to free Mexico of Spanish rule in 1810 *(see p49)* is commemorated all over Mexico, particularly in

A packed crowd witnesses a bullfight at Plaza México in Mexico City *(see p110)*

Hidalgo, Morelia, and Guana-juato. Fiestas take place in every town square on the evening of September 15, including fireworks, music, and the throwing of eggshells filled with confetti. Later, local officials repeat Hidalgo's shout, while in Mexico City the president himself makes the cry from the balcony of the Palacio Nacional *(see p67)*. The next day is an occasion for parades. Child-ren in particular dress in national costume or as Inde-pendence heroes.
Descubrimiento de América *(Oct 12)*. Originally the celebration of the discovery of the Americas, this day is now more of a hom-age to the peoples of ancient Mexico.
Festival Internacional Cervantino *(Oct)*, Guanajuato. Music, dance, and theater groups from all over the world gather in Guanajuato *(see pp202–5)* for the highlight of Mexico's cultural calendar. The festival is dedicated to the Spanish writer Miguel Cervantes, crea-tor of *Don Quixote*. It began in the 1950s with Cervantes-inspired one-act plays staged by students here. Col-onial buildings blend into stage settings for performances which may feature period costumes and even horses.

Days of the Dead decoration

Bisbee International Marlin Fishing Tournament *(last week of Oct)*, Cabo San Lucas (Baja California Sur). A large cash prize for the biggest catch is on offer at this international event.
Tecate Mexicali Surf Festival *(Oct)*, Ensenada (Baja California Norte). The surfing fraternity hits Mexico for wave-riding competitions.
Days of the Dead *(Días de Todos Santos; Oct 31–Nov 2)*. Mexico's most colorful fiesta *(see pp34–5)*.
Baja Mil Off Road Race *(1st week of Nov)*, Baja California, from Ensenada to La Paz or vice-versa depending on the year. Hundreds of motor-cycles, beach buggies, and pickups from around the world take up the challenge of this grueling off-road race.
Bull-fighting season *(Nov–Mar)*. The grandest bullrings include those in Mexico City, Aguascalientes, San Luis Potosí, and Zacatecas.
International Silver Fair *(Feria de la Plata; Nov/Dec)*, Taxco *(see pp146–7)*. Stun-ning displays of silverwork can be admired, and prizes are awarded to the best silversmiths.
Revolution Day *(Día de la Revolu-ción; Nov 20)*. Small boys have black moustaches painted on them and wear red kerchiefs and boots. The girls are decked out as *lupitas* (female revolutionaries) in frilly skirts and loop earrings. There are also parades by sportsmen and women.
Día de Santa Cecilia *(Nov 22)*. The patron saint of musicians is feted with much gusto. There are celebrations in the Plaza Garibaldi in Mexico City, Querétaro, and Pátzcuaro (Michoacán).
Puerto Escondido Inter-national Surf Tournament *(last week of Nov)*, Puerto Escondido (Oaxaca). Surfers from all over Mexico and the US congregate in the sun to compete on Oaxaca's waves.

WINTER

In all areas, temperatures drop at night in December, but, with the exception of Northern Mexico, the weather is still good enough for beach vacations. Over Christmas and the New Year, Mexicans and foreigners alike flock to the coastal resorts. In Mexico City, December brings the extravagant celebrations for Mexico's patron saint, the Virgin of Guadalupe. This is also the season when the first whales (see p164) reach Baja California, and migratory monarch butterflies (see p211) arrive in Michoacán. In the markets, citrus fruit is in plentiful supply.

Día de la Virgen de Guadalupe

(Dec 12). The appearance of Mexico's patron saint in 1531 on the Cerro del Tepeyac hill is remembered in every town and village. Thousands of pilgrims flock to her shrine in Mexico City (see p109) to view her from a crowded moving walkway. In the rest of the country las mañanitas (an early-morning birthday song) is sung at dawn, and special church services are attended. Boys dress up as Juan Diego, the Indian who encountered the Virgin's apparition.

A piñata, filled with a mixture of sweets and fruit

Posadas (Dec 16–24). These parties re-enact the nativity story of Mary and Joseph seeking lodging, and take place over the course of nine nights in all parts of Mexico. The participants carry candles and lanterns and sing the posadas song. Each night culminates in a party at a different house. An essential part of any posada is the piñata, a clay pot filled with mandarin oranges, sugar cane, and candy and decorated with crepe paper, sometimes in the shape of comic heroes or animals. This is suspended overhead on a rope, and blindfolded children take turns swinging at it with a stick. In the end they crack it open and unleash a shower of candy and fruit.

Day of the Holy Innocents (Día de los Inocentes; Dec 28). A day for practical jokes.

Epiphany (Día de los Santos Reyes; Jan 6). Mexican children receive their Christmas presents from the Three Kings in the morning and eat the traditional rosca de reyes, a ring-shaped cake filled with dried fruits and containing a hidden image of the baby Jesus. Most cities have processions to celebrate the arrival of the Kings. There are spectacular ones on Avenida Juárez and Xochimilco in Mexico City, in Querétaro, and in Campeche,

An Indian in a headdress for the Día de la Virgen de Guadalupe

Mérida, and Tizimín in the Yucatán Peninsula.

Candlemas (Día de la Candelaria; Feb 2). Baby Jesus is lifted out of the nativity scenes. Streets are decorated with paper lanterns; in some villages there are bull runs and bullfights. Most towns have an outdoor fiesta in the main square with music, sideshows, fireworks, and dancing.

The Night of the Radishes (Noche de los Rábanos; Feb 24), Oaxaca. Radishes carved into fantastic shapes, including nativity figures, are put on display and offered for sale amid general festivities in the zócalo (see p222).

Feria Artesanal del Mundo Maya (Feb), Mérida (Yucatán). This fair offers a good opportunity to see a variety of Maya handicrafts.

Flag Day (Día de la Bandera; Feb 24). School children parade and pay homage to the flag. There are official ceremonies in the main squares of most towns.

Carnival (Feb/Mar). The days preceding the rigors of Lent are celebrated nationally with extravagant parades, floats, confetti, dancing, and the burning of effigies. The most spectacular partying takes place in port towns such as La Paz and Ensenada in Baja California, Acapulco, Mazatlán (Sinaloa), Campeche in the Yucatán, and, most famously, in Veracruz on the Gulf Coast.

A colorful carnival parade in the Yucatán Peninsula

The Days of the Dead

Skeleton candle-holder

According to popular belief, the dead have divine permission to visit friends and relatives on Earth once a year. During the Days of the Dead, the living welcome the souls of the departed with offerings of flowers, specially prepared foods, candles, and incense. This is not a morbid occasion, but one of peace and happiness. Celebrations vary from region to region but in general the souls of children are thought to visit on November 1, in the evening, and those of adults on November 2, before departing for another year.

Skull masks *and clothing painted with bones are sometimes worn by city children during the Days of the Dead. Carnival dancers may also take the role of Death, a familiar presence during Mexican festivals.*

A photo of the dead person is a common focal point for Days of the Dead altars.

Sugar figures, *bread, and other foodstuffs are temptingly displayed. The dead are believed to take the essence or the aroma of the offerings, which are themselves later consumed by the living.*

Candle sticks and incense burners

ALTARS FOR THE DEAD

Many families keep holy pictures and images of saints on a shelf or table. For All Saints' and All Souls' Days (November 1 and 2) these home altars carry offerings for the dead. In towns and cities, offerings may also be displayed in public places. Shown here is an altar in the Museo del Anahuacalli *(see p111),* evoking the life and work of muralist Diego Rivera.

The marigold (cempasúchil), *often referred to in Mexico as "the flower of the dead," is used in profusion. Here Diego's name is spelled out among scattered marigold petals.*

WHERE TO SEE THE DAYS OF THE DEAD

Celebrations occur virtually everywhere in central and southern Mexico. Before the festival, market stalls sell an abundance of sugar figures, pottery, flowers, and skeleton toys. In Toluca *(see p144)* trestle tables are piled high with sweets. Most Mexicans visit cemeteries during the morning of November 2, but Purépecha villagers living around Lake Pátzcuaro hold a vigil on the night of November 1 *(see p207).* In Tzintzuntzán *(see p206),* masked villagers perform dances.

Isla Janitzio, an island in Lake Pátzcuaro, where the celebrations are particularly colorful

Personalized altars *are set up in homes and adorned with the dead person's favorite foods and drinks, and other objects, such as children's toys.*

Hand-made paper cuts, with the delicacy of lace, decorate many altars.

Papier-mâché skeletons *are often displayed in public places. Like Posada's skeletons, they perform everyday activities.*

Portrait of José Guadalupe Posada, from a mural by Diego Rivera *(see p81).*

Fine textiles and articles of new clothing are sometimes set out on altars.

Calla lilies, which feature in many of Rivera's paintings, are included here among the offerings.

This child's grave *in San Pablito, Puebla, with brightly colored flowers among the images painted on it, is typical of the highly personal style of decoration often used. Before the Days of the Dead, cemeteries throughout Mexico are tidied and graves repainted.*

ARTS AND CRAFTS FOR THE DAYS OF THE DEAD

Death is portrayed with humor and even affection by craftspeople and artists. Skulls and skeletons are fashioned from sugar, tin, wood, paper, clay, and bone. Skeletons shown as bishops and shoe-cleaners participate side by side in the modern equivalent of the medieval dance of death. In the words of poet and essayist Octavio Paz, "The Mexican is familiar with death, jokes about it, caresses it, sleeps with it, celebrates it ..." Many objects are made especially for the Days of the Dead; others are sold year round in galleries and craft shops.

This papier-mâché and wire skull, *sporting skeletons and angels, was created by Saulo Moreno. The green growths of the apple tree stress the idea of regeneration.*

Sugar skulls *may be inscribed with the name of a person living or dead or, as here, with a fitting sentiment: "Amor Eterno" ("Everlasting Love").*

Humorous miniature scenes, *peopled with spectral figures, are made for the occasion. In this example skeleton gamblers of painted clay are depicted playing poker in a wooden, mirror-lined room.*

La Catrina, *by the engraver José Guadalupe Posada (see p80), is widely associated with the Days of the Dead, and her image often appears in works by craftspeople.*

The Climate of Mexico

Coastal influences and sharp variations in altitude both have an impact on Mexico's climate. The cold Californian current lowers temperatures and rainfall on the Pacific coast, and, along with the North Pacific anticyclone, contributes to the arid nature of northwestern Mexico. In sharp contrast, the Caribbean coast in the southeast, which faces warm waters, has a tropical climate. Inland, temperatures are much cooler in the central mountains.

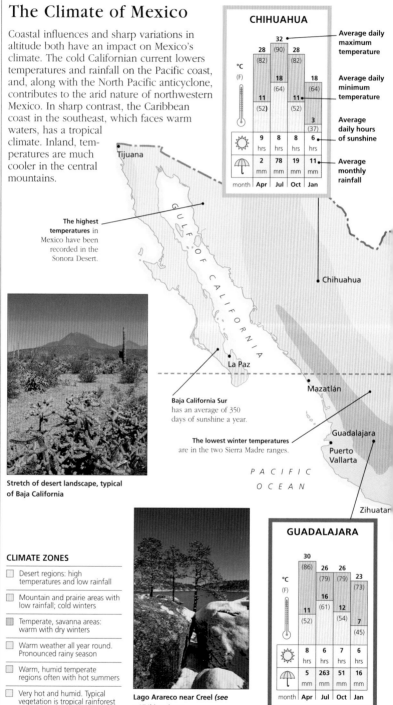

CHIHUAHUA

32			
28 (82)	(90)	28 (82)	
°C (F)			
	18 (64)	18 (64)	
11 (52)		11	
			3 (37)
9 hrs	8 hrs	8 hrs	6 hrs
2 mm	78 mm	19 mm	11 mm
month Apr	Jul	Oct	Jan

- Average daily maximum temperature
- Average daily minimum temperature
- Average daily hours of sunshine
- Average monthly rainfall

The highest temperatures in Mexico have been recorded in the Sonora Desert.

Tijuana

GULF OF CALIFORNIA

Chihuahua

La Paz

Mazatlán

Baja California Sur has an average of 350 days of sunshine a year.

The lowest winter temperatures are in the two Sierra Madre ranges.

Guadalajara

Puerto Vallarta

PACIFIC OCEAN

Zihuatan

Stretch of desert landscape, typical of Baja California

CLIMATE ZONES

- Desert regions: high temperatures and low rainfall
- Mountain and prairie areas with low rainfall; cold winters
- Temperate, savanna areas: warm with dry winters
- Warm weather all year round. Pronounced rainy season
- Warm, humid temperate regions often with hot summers
- Very hot and humid. Typical vegetation is tropical rainforest

Lago Arareco near Creel (see p174) in winter

GUADALAJARA

30 (86)			
	26 (79)	26 (79)	23 (73)
°C (F)			
	16 (61)		
11 (52)		12 (54)	
			7 (45)
8 hrs	6 hrs	7 hrs	6 hrs
5 mm	263 mm	51 mm	16 mm
month Apr	Jul	Oct	Jan

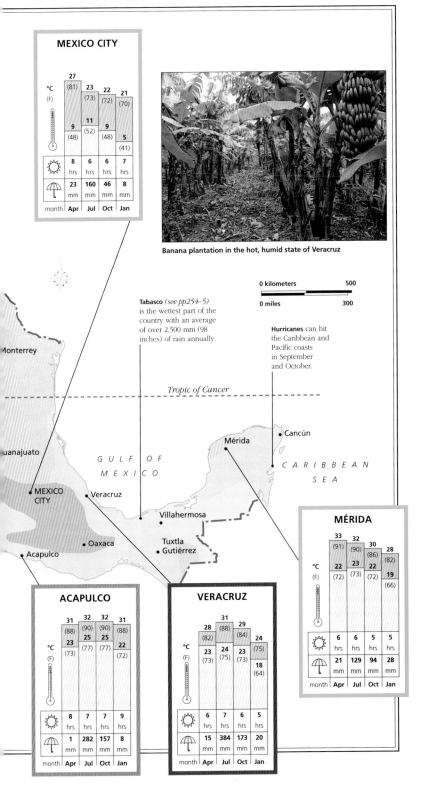

MEXICO CITY

27 (81)	23 (73)	22 (72)	21 (70)
9 (48)	11 (52)	9 (48)	5 (41)
8 hrs	6 hrs	6 hrs	7 hrs
23 mm	160 mm	46 mm	8 mm
Apr	Jul	Oct	Jan

°C (F)

month

Banana plantation in the hot, humid state of Veracruz

0 kilometers — 500
0 miles — 300

Tabasco *(see pp254–5)* is the wettest part of the country with an average of over 2,500 mm (98 inches) of rain annually.

Hurricanes can hit the Caribbean and Pacific coasts in September and October.

Monterrey

Tropic of Cancer

• Cancún

Mérida

uanajuato

*G U L F   O F
M E X I C O*

*C A R I B B E A N
S E A*

• MEXICO CITY

• Veracruz

• Villahermosa

• Oaxaca

Tuxtla
• Gutiérrez

• Acapulco

MÉRIDA

33 (91)	32 (90)	30 (86)	28 (82)
22 (72)	23 (73)	22 (72)	19 (66)
6 hrs	6 hrs	5 hrs	5 hrs
21 mm	129 mm	94 mm	28 mm
Apr	Jul	Oct	Jan

°C (F)

month

ACAPULCO

31 (88)	32 (90)	32 (90)	31 (88)
23 (73)	25 (77)	25 (77)	22 (72)
8 hrs	7 hrs	7 hrs	9 hrs
1 mm	282 mm	157 mm	8 mm
Apr	Jul	Oct	Jan

°C (F)

month

VERACRUZ

28 (82)	31 (88)	29 (84)	24 (75)
23 (73)	24 (75)	23 (73)	18 (64)
6 hrs	7 hrs	6 hrs	5 hrs
15 mm	384 mm	173 mm	20 mm
Apr	Jul	Oct	Jan

°C (F)

month

THE HISTORY OF MEXICO

Modern Mexico is the product of a collision of two cultures that occurred when the Spanish conquistadors defeated the Aztecs in 1521. In the following centuries, the ancient civilizations of Mexico fused with the Catholic European culture of Spain. After gaining its independence in the 19th century, Mexico set about forging its own identity, a process that continues today.

Mesoamerica, a region of which ancient Mexico formed a large part, had a history stretching back three millennia by the time the Spanish arrived. Although powerful imperial states – especially that of the Aztecs – had developed, they were no match for the superior arms of the Spanish conquistadors, who overran the country and imposed their rule and religion on the indigenous population.

Statue of Benito Juárez

For the next 300 years Mexico was a colony of Spain. Hungry for silver, the Spaniards pushed into the arid north, founding new cities. In central and southern Mexico they lorded it over a subjugated Indian population, who worked on Spanish estates, paid tribute to the Crown, and worshiped the Christian God – albeit without completely abandoning old religious beliefs and practices. During the 18th century, however, Spain's grip on its colony weakened as it confronted rival imperial powers in the Americas and disgruntled colonial subjects in Mexico itself.

The Napoleonic Wars in Europe triggered a struggle for independence in Mexico that was finally accomplished in 1821. In the mid-19th century, however, the US expanded its territory southward, squeezing Mexico into its present-day borders.

Not until the mid-20th century, following the Revolution launched in 1910, did the country at last achieve stability and sustained economic growth. Nevertheless, social problems, some of them deriving from the colonial past, remain serious.

Map of the island city of Tenochtitlán (modern Mexico City), drawn by Alonso de Santa Cruz in 1560

◁ A well-preserved mural from Teotihuacán *(see p41)*

THE OLMECS

Settlers arrived in Mexico having crossed the Bering landbridge from Asia to Alaska some 20 millennia ago. By the second millennium BC farming villages were springing up. Sometime around 1500 BC the first notable culture, that of the Olmecs, was established on the hot and humid Gulf coast, principally at San Lorenzo (see p253) and later at La Venta (see p254). The Olmecs built ceremonial centers rather than cities, and their earthen pyramids suggest that they were

Olmec stone figure governed by a central authority capable of mobilizing extensive manpower. They rafted heavy basalt blocks downriver and carved them into massive heads and other sculptures with stylized or feline ("were-jaguar") features. They also produced ceramics and exquisite jade figurines. During the first millennium BC, however, the Olmec centers declined. San Lorenzo was the scene of systematic destruction and desecration in around 900 BC – although by whom is uncertain – and Olmec civilization faded into obscurity.

THE CLASSIC MAYA

The Olmec "mother culture" inspired a series of successor cultures in the lowlands to the east and the highlands to the west. In the lowlands dense Maya settlements, grouped around massive ceremonial centers, began to form in the Mexico-Guatemala border region by about 500 BC. Maya civilization reached its greatest flowering in the "Classic Period" of AD 200–900. Numerous cities developed in which elaborate temples were surrounded by elite residential quarters, and cultivated fields. The Classic Maya pursued a vigorous ritual life and practiced sophisticated art (see p233). They also acquired remarkable mathematical and astronomical knowledge. This made it possible for them to do the elaborate calculations needed for the "Long Count" of their calendar, which spanned millennia (see p47).

Once thought of as pacific, the Maya actually engaged in regular and ruthless intercity warfare. Glyphs (see pp46–7) on their stelae – carved stone obelisks – record the victories of great rulers, who warred, allied, intermarried, and patronized the arts in the same way as the princely families of

Carving in the palace of Palenque, one of the greatest cities of the Classic Maya

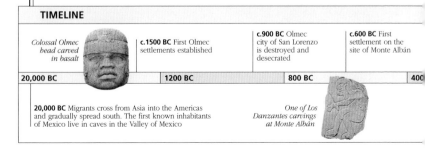

TIMELINE

Colossal Olmec head carved in basalt	**c.1500 BC** First Olmec settlements established	**c.900 BC** Olmec city of San Lorenzo is destroyed and desecrated	**c.600 BC** First settlement on the site of Monte Albán
20,000 BC	**1200 BC**	**800 BC**	**400**

20,000 BC Migrants cross from Asia into the Americas and gradually spread south. The first known inhabitants of Mexico live in caves in the Valley of Mexico

One of Los Danzantes carvings at Monte Albán

Wall painting in Tomb 105 at Monte Albán, the center of Zapotec civilization

Renaissance Italy. By around AD 800, however, the Classic Maya faced crisis: the population had outstripped available resources, and several centers were destroyed and abandoned, the victims, perhaps, of epidemics or peasant revolt.

THE RISE AND FALL OF TEOTIHUACÁN

In the central highlands, meanwhile, other cities flourished. The population of the hilltop Monte Albán *(see pp220–21)*, for instance, climbed from 5,000 in 500 BC to around 25,000 in AD 700. When the city declined, Mitla *(see p226)* and other lesser towns sprang up to contest its power in the area around Oaxaca.

All these cities were overshadowed, however, by the great Classic metropolis of Teotihuacán *(see pp134–7)*, built on an imposing site in an open valley to the north of what is now Mexico City.

Teotihuacán rose to prominence around 200 BC and reached the height of its power in AD 400–500, when it dominated the valley and a wider hinterland beyond. Its influence stretched far to the south, into the Maya region. By this time it had become a vast city of some 125,000 inhabitants, making it one of the largest cities in the world.

During the 7th century disaster struck. Like the cities of the Classic Maya, Teotihuacán may have overstretched its resources. Poverty and discontent appear to have increased, and nomads from the arid north began to threaten the city. Around 650 the city was attacked and partially burned by these northern invaders, or local rebels, or both. It did not disappear suddenly but entered a long decline, as its population was leached away. The fall of Teotihuacán sent shockwaves throughout Mesoamerica.

Funerary mask from Teotihuacán

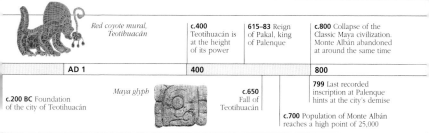

Red coyote mural, Teotihuacán

Maya glyph

	c.400 Teotihuacán is at the height of its power	**615–83** Reign of Pakal, king of Palenque	**c.800** Collapse of the Classic Maya civilization. Monte Albán abandoned at around the same time

| **AD 1** | | **400** | | **800** |

c.200 BC Foundation of the city of Teotihuacán

c.650 Fall of Teotihuacán

799 Last recorded inscription at Palenque hints at the city's demise

c.700 Population of Monte Albán reaches a high point of 25,000

THE TOLTECS

The collapse of Teotihuacán and decline of Monte Albán resulted in a phase of fragmentation and militarization in central Mexico. A series of successor states such as Cacaxtla *(see p156)*, and Xochicalco *(see p145)* carved out local fiefs. One, the Toltec state, built a loose hegemony between about 900 and 1100. Probably northern migrants, the Toltecs settled in the north of the Valley of Mexico. Here they built the city of Tula *(see p144)*, which may have had a population of 40,000. The Toltecs, who were keen traders dealing especially in obsidian, exacted tribute from dependent communities. They also developed a militarist culture, evident in the serried ranks

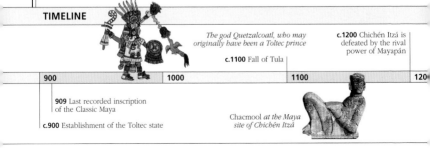

Atlante statue at Tula

of their Atlantes (stone warriors), gruesome friezes depicting war and sacrifice, skull racks, *chacmools* (reclining sacrificial statues), and military orders such as the Eagle and Jaguar Knights.

Tula collapsed and was torched and desecrated around AD 1100, but its influence lived on. Some Toltecs are thought to have migrated to the Yucatán in the 10th century, where their influence is evident. Among them may have been a prince or leader called Quetzalcoatl (meaning the "Feathered Serpent"), who was later transformed into a god. Since the collapse of the Classic Maya cities, power had shifted to the northern part of the Yucatán Peninsula, especially Uxmal and the other cities of the Puuc hills. Around AD 1000 Toltec motifs – feathered serpents, Atlantes, and *chacmools* – began to appear, notably at Chichén Itzá. This city headed a regional confederacy until, in about 1200, it was overthrown by the nearby Mayapán, and Izamal, and by other rivals on the coasts of the Yucatán Peninsula.

THE AZTEC EMPIRE

The last great Mesoamerican empire, that of the Aztecs (often called the Mexica), also arose in the Valley of Mexico, from where it went on to dominate much of the Mexican heartland. The Aztecs arrived as a poor, ill-equipped band, who had trekked overland from their distant northern homeland, Aztlán (the location of

The Aztec legend of the eagle perching on a prickly pear cactus, illustrated in the Codex Mendoza

TIMELINE

The god Quetzalcoatl, who may originally have been a Toltec prince

c.1200 Chichén Itzá is defeated by the rival power of Mayapán

c.1100 Fall of Tula

| 900 | 1000 | 1100 | 120◄ |

909 Last recorded inscription of the Classic Maya

c.900 Establishment of the Toltec state

Chacmool at the Maya site of Chichén Itzá

which is unknown). They initially served as the menials and mercenaries of established cities. In around 1325, however, they were advised by their tribal god, Huitzilopochtli, to pitch their tents where they saw an eagle perched on a cactus, devouring a snake. This omen (depicted on Mexico's national flag) was seen on a lake-island, which thus became the site of the city of Tenochtitlán. Ruthless fighters with a sense of providential mission, the Aztecs gradually expanded their territory. At the same time they boosted agriculture by creating fertile *chinampas*, irrigated fields, to feed the urban population.

By the 1420s they had emerged as the dominant power in the Valley of Mexico. Their loose tribal organization gave way to an imperial system based on strict hierarchy, a warrior ethic, and a despotic emperor. Soon, their conquests spread to the rich lowlands of the south and east. Tribute poured in. At the same time, constant warfare provided prisoners, feeding the demand for human sacrifice to appease their gods – for only by feeding palpitating hearts to the gods could the fragile cosmos be maintained in place. Mass sacrifices – like that which took place to mark the dedication of the rebuilt Templo Mayor *(see pp68–70)* in 1487, when 20,000 prisoners were said to have been immolated – served to terrorize enemies and bolster the empire.

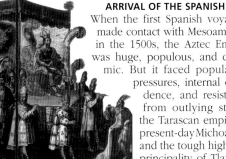

The Meeting of Cortés and Moctezuma, attributed to Juan Correa (c.1645–1716)

ARRIVAL OF THE SPANISH

When the first Spanish voyagers made contact with Mesoamerica in the 1500s, the Aztec Empire was huge, populous, and dynamic. But it faced population pressures, internal dissidence, and resistance from outlying states: the Tarascan empire in present-day Michoacán, and the tough highland principality of Tlaxcala *(see p156)*, to the east.

Hernán Cortés landed on the coast of what is now Veracruz in 1519 and marched to Tenochtitlán. But first he defeated, then joined forces with, the Tlaxcalans who proved invaluable allies in the Spaniards' destruction of Aztec power. By means of such alliances, Cortés was able to confront and finally defeat the Aztec empire of Moctezuma II (1502–20). After a bloody and destructive siege, Tenochtitlán was conquered.

The Conquest of Mexico as depicted in a mural by Juan O'Gorman (1905–82)

Carving of the Aztec goddess Coyolxauhqui in the Templo Mayor, in Mexico City

1500s Aztec wars with Tlaxcala, to the east, which later becomes a Spanish ally

1520 On July 1, the so-called Noche Triste ("Sad Night"), the Spanish are defeated by the Aztecs

1300 | **1400** | **1500**

c.1325 The Aztecs found Tenochtitlán (modern Mexico City) on a lake-island

1426–40 The Aztecs take control of the Valley of Mexico under Emperor Itzcoatl

1502 Accession of Moctezuma II as Aztec emperor

1519 Cortés lands on the coast of Veracruz

1521 The Spanish capture Tenochtitlán and the Aztec Empire falls

Mesoamerica

The term Mesoamerica refers to a geographical region whose people shared a broadly similar culture before the arrival of the Spanish *(see p43)*. It covers what is now central and southern Mexico, Belize, Guatemala, and parts of Honduras and El Salvador. The people of Mesoamerica had many things in common, including gods, a calendar, and building practices, but had different languages and customs. The civilizations are normally divided into "highland" (especially the Valley of Mexico) and "lowland," such as the Maya.

Chacmool
These carved reclining figures can be seen at central Mexican and Maya archaeological sites. The stone dishes often found on their stomachs are said to have held sacrificial offerings, but there is no evidence for this.

Ballgame
The ballgame, played with a rubber ball (see p277), was a feature of most civilizations of Mesoamerica. This stone disk shows a Maya player.

MAP OF MESOAMERICA
The civilizations shown on the map did not always exist at the same time. Often, as in the case of the Mixtecs and the Zapotecs, one group would take over the territories of its predecessors.

TARASCANS
TOLTECS
El Tajín
CLASSIC VERACRUZ
Tula
Teotihuacán
Tenochtitlán
Cholula
Xochicalco
AZTECS
Monte Albán
Mitla
ZAPOTECS

Pyramids
Mesoamerican pyramids are stepped and, like this one at Edzná (see p261), crowned with a temple. The Aztecs used them for human sacrifices, while for the Maya they were usually funerary buildings. They were often built on top of earlier pyramids.

Human Sacrifice
The need to appease gods with human blood was a strong belief in ancient Mexico, particularly to the Aztecs. This codex illustration shows Aztec priests killing victims, whose bodies are then thrown down the steps of the temple.

Obsidian
A hard, glassy volcanic stone, obsidian was fashioned into domestic items, weapons, and sacrificial knives such as this one. Metals were not used until the late Classic period and never for functional objects.

Jade
This green stone was more highly prized than gold in Mesoamerica. The Zapotecs, in particular, used it to make objects such as this fearsome-looking bat-god pendant.

Food
Many foods now eaten all over the world originated in Mesoamerica. They include tomatoes, chilies, chocolate, and corn (maize). This scene from an Aztec codex shows a granary being filled with corn.

Chichén Itzá · Cobá

Uxmal

Tulum

· Edzná

GULF OF MEXICO

M A Y A

L MECS

San Lorenzo

· La Venta

Palenque

· Tikal

· Bonampak

I X T E C S

C A R I B B E A N   S E A

P A C I F I C   O C E A N

Technology
Although the wheel was known, it was used only for nonfunctional objects such as this Huastec toy dog in Xalapa Museum (see pp248–9). Most burdens were carried by human porters or by canoe.

KEY

☐ Highland areas

☐ Lowland areas

PERIODS OF MESOAMERICA

PRECLASSIC						CLASSIC		POSTCLASSIC		
	Olmecs					Classic Veracruz		Totonacs		
					Maya					
								Tarascans		
					Teotihuacán		Toltecs		Aztecs	
			Zapotecs					Mixtecs		
1500 BC	1200 BC	900 BC	600 BC	300 BC	0	AD 300	AD 600	AD 900	AD 1200	AD 1500

The Maya

Unlike the other peoples of Mesoamerica, the Maya did not develop a large, centralized empire. Instead they lived in independent city-states. This did not impede them in acquiring advanced knowledge of astronomy and developing sophisticated systems of writing, counting, and recording the passing of time. The Maya were once thought to have been a peaceful people, but they are now known to have shared the lust for war and human sacrifice of other pre-Columbian civilizations.

LOCATOR MAP

☐ Extent of Maya Territory

Mural from Bonampak
The Maya were the finest artists of Mesoamerica. Their talent for portraiture can be seen especially in the extraordinary series of murals painted in a temple at Bonampak (see p232).

In the Tzolkin or Sacred Round
20 day names were combined with 13 numbers to give a year of 260 individually named days.

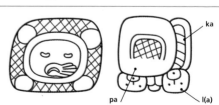

Architecture
Pyramids, palaces, and other great works of Maya architecture can be seen at such sites as Palenque (see pp234–7), Chichén Itzá (see pp274–6), Cobá (see p284), and Tulum (see pp284–5). This detail is from Uxmal (see pp262–4).

20 named days

GLYPHS

Other Mesoamerican civilizations developed writing systems, but none was as complete or sophisticated as that of the Maya. They used about 800 different hieroglyphs (or simply "glyphs"), some representing whole words, others phonetic sounds. Some glyphs were understood as early as the 1820s, but the major advances in decipherment really began in the 1950s.

ka

pa

l(a)

A Maya glyph can represent either a whole word, or the sounds of which it is composed. Some words were written in several ways. Above are two ways of writing the name Pakal, the ruler of Palenque. Pakal means "shield," depicted by the left glyph.

ASTRONOMY

The Maya had a knowledge of astronomy that was very advanced for their time. They observed and predicted the phases of the moon, equinoxes and solstices, and solar and lunar eclipses. They knew that the Morning and Evening Star were the same planet, Venus, and calculated its "year" to be 584 days, within a fraction of the true figure (583.92 days). It is almost certain that they calculated the orbit of Mars as well. Remarkably, they achieved all this without the use of lenses for observing distant objects, instruments for calculating angles, or clocks to measure the passing of seconds, minutes, and hours.

The Observatory at Chichén Itzá

THE MAYA CALENDAR

The Maya observed the 52-year "Calendar Round." This resulted from two calendar cycles, the Haab and the Tzolkin, which acted simultaneously but independently. For periods longer than 52 years the Maya used a separate system called the Long Count.

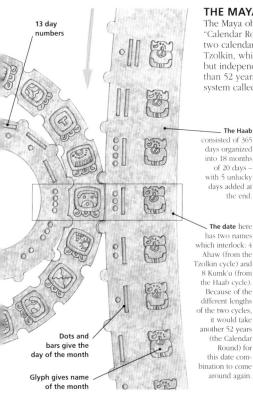

13 day numbers

The Haab consisted of 365 days organized into 18 months of 20 days – with 5 unlucky days added at the end.

The date here has two names which interlock: 4 Ahaw (from the Tzolkin cycle) and 8 Kumk'u (from the Haab cycle). Because of the different lengths of the two cycles, it would take another 52 years (the Calendar Round) for this date combination to come around again.

Dots and bars give the day of the month

Glyph gives name of the month

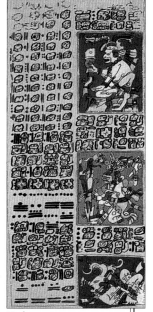

Codex
Maya books, codices, were created by writing on both sides of a thin sheet of bark, which was then folded like a concertina. Only four have survived, including the Dresden Codex, a replica of which is shown above.

NUMBERS

Mesoamerica used a vigesimal counting system, that is they worked to base 20 rather than base 10. The Maya represented numbers with dots (units) and bars (fives).

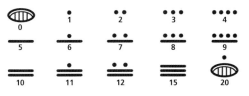

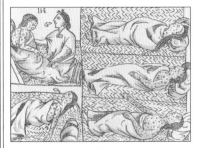

Indians suffering from smallpox, a disease introduced to Mexico by the Spaniards

COLONIAL MEXICO

Following their defeat of the Aztecs, the conquistadors entrusted the Indian population to Spanish *encomenderos*. These quasi-feudal seigneurs were expected to protect and convert their charges, who, in return paid them tribute. Spanish expeditions probed the outer reaches of Mesoamerica – Oaxaca, Chiapas, and the Yucatán Peninsula. Lured by the promise of silver, they also penetrated the Gran Chichimec, the region to the north, beyond the boundaries of Aztec and Tarascan domains, to reach distant Zacatecas and beyond. Hand in hand with this military conquest in search of booty went a spiritual conquest. Franciscan and Dominican friars tirelessly preached to, converted, and baptized the Indians. European diseases such as smallpox produced massive Indian mortality.

MEXICO IN THE 17TH CENTURY

During the 17th century, the institution of the hacienda *(see pp50–51)* was established by rich Spaniards looking for the good life of the hidalgo in the colonies. The distant Crown, represented by the Viceroy, managed to exert only a loose control over these settlers who came to farm and mine, and the colony enjoyed a measure of independence. Nevertheless, "New Spain" remitted huge quantities of bullion to its European overlord.

As the colonial economy matured, the settlers produced a Mexican-born, Creole elite, proud of their new homeland. Indians, whose numbers had begun to recover, learned how to cultivate European crops and raise cattle. The mixing of Spanish-born settlers with Indians created intermediate castes. The wealthy white elite financed grandiose haciendas, great town residences, and lavish churches *(see pp26–7)*. Creole accomplishments were also evident in Mexico City's flourishing University (the oldest in the Americas) and the literary output of the Baroque age, notably the plays and poems of Sor (Sister) Juana Inés

A gathering of administrators and clerks at the Hacienda Peotildas in the Yucatán

TIMELINE

The Virgin of Guadalupe

1531 An apparition initiates the cult of the Virgin of Guadalupe *(see p108)*

1546 Zacatecas *(see p192)* founded following the discovery of silver deposits

1571 The Spanish Inquisition arrives in Mexico. The first auto-da-fé is held three years later

1629 A major flood hits Mexico City and takes five years to subside

1651 Birth of Sor Juana Inés de la Cruz

Sor Juana Inés de la Cruz

| 1550 | 1600 | 1650 |

de la Cruz. Compared to Europe, 17th-century Mexico was a tranquil place. The authority of the Church, combined with the lack of a regular army, created an underlying stability for the colony.

THE COMING OF INDEPENDENCE

In the 18th century, however, the new Bourbon dynasty in Spain sought to emulate French colonialism in clawing back Mexico's partial autonomy, centralizing royal power, weakening the Church, creating a regular army, boosting bullion remittances, and extracting more taxes. Relations between Spain and Mexico worsened as Creoles increasingly resented the interference of Spanish officials. Indians and lower castes suffered from higher taxes and – as the population grew and shortages of basic goods recurred – lower living standards. The old alliance between Crown and Church weakened: in 1767 the Jesuits were expelled.

International events compounded these tensions. Repeatedly involved in European wars, Spain was short of cash and incapable of controlling the sea-lanes to Mexico. To the north, the French and British threatened the colony's far-flung frontiers, which embraced the present southern United States, from Florida to California. The American Revolution of 1776 afforded an example of colonial rebellion, and Napoleon's overthrow of the Bourbon monarchy in 1808 provoked a crisis in the colonial government. On September 16, 1810, a parish priest, Miguel Hidalgo, gave his famous call to arms in the cause of independence,

Hidalgo shown in a mural by Juan O'Gorman in Castillo de Chapultepec *(see p88)*

El Grito ("The Cry"). The revolt failed, however, and Hidalgo was executed. A second revolt four years later, lead by another priest, José María Morelos, was similarly crushed. But repression could not shore up a tottering empire. Guerrilla resistance continued. In 1821, shortly after the army had seized power in Spain, Mexico's Creole elite proclaimed the country's independence. Spain lacked the will or ability to fight on, and its principal American colony became the independent nation of Mexico.

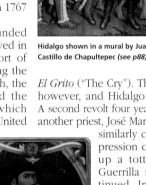

Independence leader José María Morelos (1765–1815)

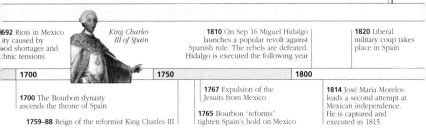

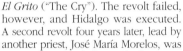

1692 Riots in Mexico City caused by food shortages and ethnic tensions	*King Charles III of Spain*	1810 On Sep 16 Miguel Hidalgo launches a popular revolt against Spanish rule. The rebels are defeated. Hidalgo is executed the following year	1820 Liberal military coup takes place in Spain
1700		**1750**	**1800**
1700 The Bourbon dynasty ascends the throne of Spain		1767 Expulsion of the Jesuits from Mexico	1814 José María Morelos leads a second attempt at Mexican independence. He is captured and executed in 1815
1759–88 Reign of the reformist King Charles III		1765 Bourbon "reforms" tighten Spain's hold on Mexico	

The Hacienda

Mexico's haciendas, or country estates, evolved during the colonial and post-colonial era. Production was determined by what the land and climate could offer. Some estates were given over to cattle, or to corn and wheat; others grew sugar cane or agave for making the alcoholic drink *pulque*. Landowners in the Yucatán grew rich cultivating henequen (sisal), whereas those in mountainous areas, such as Zacatecas, often ran silver mines. The 1910 Revolution brought about the destruction of many haciendas, but some have been preserved or restored, and a few now serve as hotels *(see p290)*.

Laborers on a Porfirian hacienda where, by 1910, many rural Mexicans lived and worked

A TYPICAL HACIENDA

This illustration shows an idealized 19th-century hacienda. Under Porfirio Díaz, many estates experienced their most prosperous phase. To make up for their isolation, haciendas were often self-sufficient, with dairies, brick-kilns, orchards, and other facilities.

Lookout and defensive tower

Gardens offered an escape for the landowner from the working life of the hacienda.

Casa Grande (Main House)
This spacious and comfortably furnished building lay at the heart of the hacienda. During the Porfirian era, houses were often remodeled to resemble European castles or English stately homes. Landowners rarely lived on their estates, preferring to make brief visits from the city.

Worksheds
Each hacienda incorporated special buildings and work areas. The men shown above are breaking ore at a mining estate in Guanajuato.

Stable for horses and mules
*The art of horsemanship (*charrería, *see p74) was crucial to life on the hacienda. Horses were needed for agriculture, for transporting produce, and to aid the laborers on mining estates.*

A private railroad station allowed landowners to transport their produce rapidly through difficult terrain.

Cattle were kept in sheds on the estate and provided a constant supply of meat and dairy products.

Protective outer wall

Granaries
Grain was usually stored in immense barns, but in Guanajuato and Zacatecas it was stored in conical silos. Landowners hoarded grain and sold it in lean times.

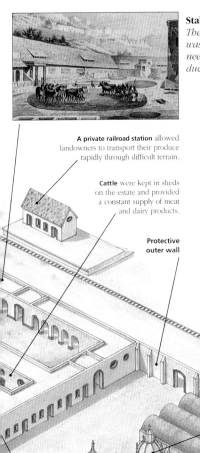

Church
Landowners were responsible for the spiritual welfare of their workforce. Shown here is the church at Santa María Regla, near Huasca (see p139).

Cemetery

Servants' quarters were usually in a poor condition. Laborers lived with their families in a single, cramped room.

Entrance gate
Some haciendas resembled fortresses, with high walls and lookout towers. This Moorish-style double archway is from the sisal hacienda at Yaxcopoil in the Yucatán (see p271).

THE NEW NATION

Mexico achieved its independence at great cost. The economy was ravaged, and Spanish capital fled the country. After a brief imperial interlude – when Agustín de Iturbide made himself Emperor Agustín I (1821–3) – Mexico became a republic. But political consensus proved elusive. Mexico's elites were roughly divided into liberals, who favored a progressive, republican, free-trading secular society, and conservatives, who preferred a centralized, hierarchical state, backed by Church and army, possibly capped by a monarchy. Administrations came and went: 30 presidents governed in the 50 years after 1821. The army absorbed the bulk of revenue and generated a host of *caudillos* who built up their retinues and contested for power, often without principle or ideology. Prominent among them was Antonio López de Santa Anna, whose slippery opportunism and shifting alliances with Church, army, and financiers enabled him to attain the presidency no fewer than 11 times.

Monumento a los Niños Héroes *(see p89)*

WAR WITH TEXAS

Texas broke away from the rest of Mexico in 1836. Victorious at the Alamo, Santa Anna's forces were crushed by the Texans a month later at San Jacinto. Ten years after this, Texas' decision to join the US sparked a war in which the US invaded Mexico by land and sea. Mexican resistance, though dogged, was ill-coordinated.

The capital fell after fierce fighting, during which a group of cadets (the Niños Héroes – Boy Heroes) died defending Chapultepec Castle rather than surrender. The war ended with the Treaty of Guadalupe Hidalgo (1848), in which Mexico lost nearly half its territory – the vast area stretching from Texas to California – to the US.

LOCATOR MAP

▨ *Mexican territory before 1848*

☐ *Modern Mexico*

THE REFORM

Defeat in the war against the US provoked political reassessment and polarization. A new generation of liberals, led by the Indian lawyer Benito Juárez, advocated radical reforms to modernize the country. In 1854 they ousted Santa Anna and embarked on a radical

Benito Juárez, the popular leader who steered Mexico through the period of the Reform

TIMELINE

General Antonio López de Santa Anna

| 1824 Federal republic created | 1840–46 War of the Castes: Maya revolt in the Yucatán | 1862 May 5: Mexican forces defeat French invaders at Puebla |
| | 1846–8 Mexican-American War | 1860 Reform laws |

| 1820 | 1830 | 1840 | 1850 | 18● |

1821 Mexican independence declared under Agustín de Iturbide

1836 Rebellion of Texas. Santa Anna victorious at the Alamo but defeated at San Jacinto

1848 In the Treaty of Guadalupe Hidalgo, Mexico loses nearly half its territory, and the present-day border along Río Grande to the north is established

1857 Liberal democratic constitution

1858–61 War of the Reform: liberal victory under Juárez

The Execution of Emperor Maximilian by the French painter Édouard Manet

program, known as La Reforma (The Reform). In the 1857 democratic constitution they separated Church and state; sold off Church and other corporate-owned lands; and made all citizens equal before the law.

The Church and the army resisted these measures, but in the ensuing War of the Reform (1858–61) the liberals were victorious. In 1864, however, the conservatives struck a deal with Maximilian of Hapsburg, who assumed the Mexican throne, backed by the French bayonets of Napoleon III. Maximilian, a liberal, humane, but naive ruler, found himself depending on repression to maintain his crown. The liberals wore down the French and their conservative allies in a guerrilla struggle. In 1866 Napoleon III withdrew his troops and a year later, Maximilian was cornered at Querétaro, captured, and executed by a firing squad. Mexico's last monarchy had fallen; the republic under the national hero, Juárez, was restored.

PORFIRIO DÍAZ

After Juárez's death in 1872 the liberal leaders jockeyed for succession. A young general, Porfirio Díaz, hero of the war against the French, seized power in 1876. A canny politician, Díaz placated the Church and marginalized or eliminated his rivals. Consolidating his hold on government in the 1880s, he ruled as an authoritarian president until 1911. During the so-called *porfiriato*, Mexico prospered and became more centralized than ever before. Communications improved; cities expanded. But by the 1900s the elderly dictator had alienated the peasantry, who had lost their fields to commercial haciendas. The middle class, meanwhile, chafed under the political restrictions of the regime and yearned for genuine democracy. The scene was set for the Revolution of 1910.

Detail of a mural by Juan O'Gorman showing Porfirio Díaz (seated) and some of his ministers

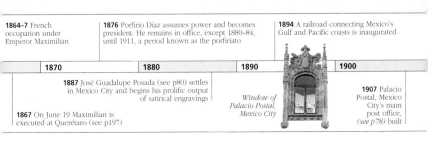

1864–7 French occupation under Emperor Maximilian

1876 Porfirio Díaz assumes power and becomes president. He remains in office, except 1880–84, until 1911, a period known as the porfiriato

1894 A railroad connecting Mexico's Gulf and Pacific coasts is inaugurated

1870 **1880** **1890** **1900**

1887 José Guadalupe Posada (see p80) settles in Mexico City and begins his prolific output of satirical engravings

Window of Palacio Postal, Mexico City

1907 Palacio Postal, Mexico City's main post office, (see p78) built

1867 On June 19 Maximilian is executed at Querétaro (see p197)

General Francisco "Pancho" Villa, the great northern revolutionary leader

championing the cause of villagers who – like his own family – had lost land to the sugar plantations. Madero, however, was not ousted by such popular movements but by the military, who assassinated him in February 1913. The ruthless Victoriano Huerta formed a new regime so unpopular that the opposition united against it. Zapata allied with the great northern revolutionary leader Pancho Villa *(see p173)*, who had built up a formidable army on the prairies of Chihuahua, and in a second period of civil war (1913–14), these and other supporters of the constitution defeated Huerta and destroyed the regular army.

Villa and Zapata could not stomach the authority of their nominal chief, the dour provincial landlord Venustiano Carranza. A revolutionary convention, at Aguascalientes, failed to broker a peace. In a third and final bout of civil war, in 1915, Carranza's leading general, Álvaro Obregón, defeated Villa, reducing him to an outlaw. Zapata and others fought on, but it was clear that Carranza's faction had won, and in 1917 they promulgated a radical new constitution.

THE REVOLUTION

In 1910 Francisco I. Madero, an idealistic young landlord, opposed Díaz's seventh reelection to the presidency and called for a national uprising. The ensuing revolution, which brought together disaffected peasants and urban middle-class progressives, induced the aged dictator to negotiate and resign. Madero was elected president, but he could not meet popular demands for agrarian reform and greater democratization and at the same time satisfy conservatives who preferred Díaz's authoritarian rule. In Morelos, south of Mexico City, Emiliano Zapata led a fresh rebellion,

AFTERMATH OF REVOLUTION

Mexico was exhausted after the Revolution. Over a million people had died during it, or emigrated because of it. The currency had collapsed, and the country's infrastructure was in tatters. Carranza's coalition, dominated by reformers

Poster of the revolutionary leader Emiliano Zapata

TIMELINE

1919 Assassination of Zapata

1917 Mexico's current liberal, revolutionary constitution is passed

1923 Pancho Villa is assassinated

1928 Assassination of Obregón

1929 Partido Nacional Revolucionario formed

1941–5 Mexico allies with the US during World War II

1910

1930

1950

1910 Mexican Revolution is launched by Madero

1911 Madero becomes president but is assassinated in 1913

Venustiano Carranza

1920 Military revolt ousts and kills Carranza

1938 Nationalization of the oil industry

1934 Cárdenas becomes president

1940 Assassination of Trotsky in Mexico City *(see p103)*

1956 The Torre Latinoamericana is built in Mexico City *(see p75)*

such as Obregón and Plutarco Elías Calles, was shaky. Carranza was ousted and killed in 1920. In the following years, the infant revolutionary regime battled to survive against pressures from the Church, fearful of its anticlericalism, and from the US, which disapproved of such a radical constitution. In 1928, Obregón was assassinated. Calles responded to the crisis this caused by organizing a new national party, the Partido Nacional Revolucionario (PNR), the forerunner of the party which, under different names (PRM, PRI), governed Mexico until ousted in the 2000 elections.

Union poster in support of the reforms instituted by President Cárdenas

MODERN MEXICO

President Cárdenas (1934–40), confronting the depression, implemented a sweeping agrarian reform, boosted the rights of organized labor, and, in 1938, nationalized the foreign-owned oil industry. Subsequent political leaders, typified by President Alemán (1946–52), favored industry and the private sector, which became the motor of an "economic miracle" – the sustained, low-inflation growth of the 1950s and 60s.

The miracle eventually ended. In 1968, on the eve of the Mexico City Olympics, student protests were bloodily repressed, tarnishing the regime's legitimacy. Seeking to recoup prestige, while reorienting the economy, the governments of the 1970s borrowed and spent, partly on the basis of Mexico's second oil boom. Inflation quickened and, in 1982, the economy slumped. President Salinas (1988–94) opted for "neo-liberal" reform, privatizing state enterprises, cutting protective tariffs, and concluding the North American Free Trade Agreement with the US and Canada. Shortly after Salinas left office, Mexico suffered a recession. Mexico's problems in the 1990s were compounded by an armed rebellion in the state of Chiapas (see p230). Despite intermittent government repression and negotiation, the situation in Chiapas remains unsettled. Economic woes combined with social unrest led to victory for the center-right Partido Acción Nacional (PAN) in the 2000 elections, raising hopes for change under president Vicente Fox. In 2006, Felipe Calderón, of the same party, was elected president.

Parade during the opening ceremony of the 1968 Olympic Games, staged in Mexico City

1985 On September 19 an earthquake hits Mexico City, killing an estimated 9,000 people

1988 President Salinas begins a series of neo-liberal reforms

2000 PAN wins presidential elections

2005 Yucatán Peninsula hit by Hurricane Wilma

1970	1990		2010	2030

1968 Olympic Games in Mexico City. Student protest repressed

President Salinas

1994 Zapatistas overrun San Cristóbal de las Casas (Chiapas). In 12 days of fighting, 145 people die

2009 Swine flu outbreak

2007 Chichén Itzá is one of the New Seven Wonders of the World

INTRODUCING MEXICO CITY

Mexico City at a Glance

Mexico City is a huge, hectic, overpopulated, and often smog-ridden metropolis, as well as the center of commerce and government for the country. Yet despite the problems of modern city life, the oldest capital of the New World is rich in both indigenous and colonial history. The aptly named Historic Center was the site of the Aztec capital, while the elegant Reforma district mixes colonial architecture with striking contemporary buildings. Allow at least two or three days to explore the city in full.

LOCATOR MAP

The National Anthropology Museum (see pp90–95) *is considered one of the finest museums of its kind in the world. It explores Mexico's prehistory; the lives and beliefs of the Maya, Aztecs, and other great civilizations; and the ways of life of the country's present-day indigenous people.*

REFORMA AND CHAPULTEPEC *(See pp 82–95)*

Bosque de Chapultepec (see pp88–9) *is Mexico City's largest park. Once a summer vacation spot for the Aztecs, it still offers a relaxing respite from the bustling city.*

SAN ÁNGEL AND COYOACÁN
(See pp 96–105)

San Ángel *(see pp98–101)* is a lively district that preserves some of the finest colonial architecture in the capital. It is also known for its Saturday craft fair.

0 meters 200

0 yards 200

Coyoacán *(see pp104–5)* has an atmosphere distinct from the rest of the city, with peaceful plazas and charming streets.

◁ The colorful domes of Museo del Carmen in San Ángel district

Palacio de Bellas Artes (see p80), *the city's concert hall, is a grand early 20th-century building overlooking the Alameda Central. Inside, it is decorated with works by Mexico's greatest muralists. It is home to the popular dance group, Ballet Folklórico.*

Templo Mayor (see pp68–70) *is the site of the Aztec teocalli (sacred city) that formed the heart of Tenochtitlán, their capital. The first stone was discovered in 1978; later digs uncovered spectacular finds.*

THE HISTORIC CENTER *(See pp 60–81)*

0 meters	500
0 yards	500

Monumento a la Revolución (see p86) *is dedicated to the 1910 Revolution. Intended as the start of a new senate building, in 1932 it was made into a monument, and revolutionary heroes were buried beneath the pillars. A museum of the Revolution is housed at its base.*

Catedral Metropolitana (see pp64–5) *was completed in 1813 after almost 300 years construction. Latin America's largest church, it dominates the main square of the city. Its Baroque altars and side chapels are magnificently ornate.*

THE HISTORIC CENTER

W hen Hernán Cortés led his army into the Aztec capital of Tenochtitlán it stood on an island in Lake Texcoco. After conquering the city the Spanish razed it to the ground, reusing much of the stonework in their own constructions, and gradually filling in the lake. The buildings of the Historic Center – which

Stained glass in the Colegio de San Ildefonso

stands on the site of the Aztec city – date mainly from the colonial and post-independence eras. In a patchwork of architectural styles, they range from colonial churches and mansions to an Art Nouveau/Art Deco theater-cum-gallery and a 1950s skyscraper. A prominent exception is the excavated remains of the great Aztec temple.

SIGHTS AT A GLANCE

Historic Buildings
Antiguo Colegio de San Ildefonso ❹
Casa de los Azulejos ⓯
Palacio de Bellas Artes ⓱
Palacio de la Antigua Escuela de Medicina ❾
Palacio Nacional ❷
Secretaría de Educación Pública ❼
Templo Mayor ❸
Torre Latinoamericana ⓰

Museums and Galleries
Laboratorio Arte Alameda ⓴
Museo de Arte Popular ㉒
Museo de la Caricatura ❺
Museo de la Charrería ⓬
Museo de la Ciudad de México ⓫
Museo del Ejército y Fuerza Aérea ⓭
Museo Franz Mayer ⓳
Museo José Luis Cuevas ❿
Museo Mural Diego Rivera ㉑
Museo Nacional de Arte ⓮
Museo Nacional de la Estampa ⓲

Churches
Catedral Metropolitana ❶
Templo de la Enseñanza ❻

Squares
Plaza de Santo Domingo ❽

GETTING AROUND
The main metro stations are in the two large squares, the Zócalo and Alameda. Walking is the best way to get around, although the streets between the Alameda and the Plaza Garibaldi (to the north, *see p109*) are considered unsafe to stroll through.

KEY

▨	Street-by-Street map *pp62–3*
▨	Street-by-Street map *pp78–9*
Ⓜ	Metro station
ℹ	Tourist information

0 meters	250
0 yards	250

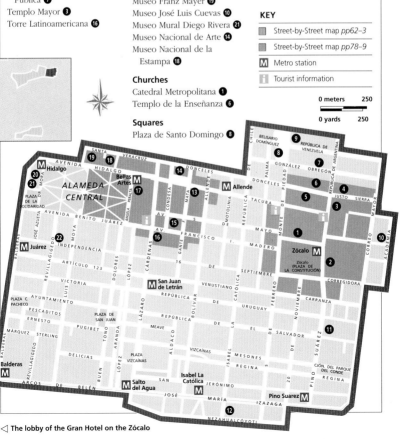

◁ **The lobby of the Gran Hotel on the Zócalo**

Street-by-Street: Zócalo

Indian dancer performing in the Zócalo

The Plaza de la Constitución, invariably known as the Zócalo, is one of the biggest public squares in the world. A giant national flag flies in the middle of this vast paved space, which is dominated by two buildings, the cathedral and the Palacio Nacional. On the square stand other public buildings, restaurants, shops, and hotels. At one corner are the sunken remains of the Aztecs' principal temple complex. A good view of the Zócalo can be had from the terrace of the Hotel Majestic.

Museo de la Caricatura
A caricature of singer David Bowie is among the works of cartoon art in this 18th-century building ❺

Templo de la Enseñanza
A dazzling gold altarpiece is the main feature of this late 18th-century Baroque church, which was built as a convent chapel ❻

Fuente de la Zona Lacustre
is a water monument that incorporates a relief map of the Aztec city of Tenochtitlán.

Nacional Monte de Piedad, a government-run pawn shop, occupies a historic building dating from the 16th century.

★ **Catedral Metropolitana**
Although damaged by the subsidence affecting the center of Mexico City, this is still one of the greatest religious buildings in Latin America ❶

Hotel Majestic (see p292)

Alameda

Gran Hotel (see p292)

Sagrario Metropolitano

0 metres   75
0 yards   75

For hotels and restaurants in this region see pp292–4 and pp326–30

Colegio de San Ildefonso
Great murals, stained glass, and other decorative details can be seen in this former seminary ❹

★ Templo Mayor
Pathways lead through the excavated remains of this Aztec temple unearthed in the 1970s ❸

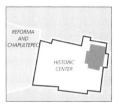

LOCATOR MAP
See Street Finder map pp124–5

The former archbishop's palace

The first printing press in the Americas was set up in this house in 1536.

Museo Nacional de las Culturas has displays on major civilizations of the world.

Palacio Nacional
This Renaissance palace houses the offices of the President of Mexico. Inside is a collection of murals by Diego Rivera ❷

KEY

– – – Suggested route

STAR SIGHTS

★ Catedral Metropolitana

★ Templo Mayor

ZÓCALO
PLAZA DE LA CONSTITUCIÓN

PINO SUÁREZ

20 DE NOVIEMBRE

SEMINARIO

Supreme Court

Former city hall

Mexico's main square is used as a venue for state ceremonial occasions and military parades. It is seen here with the Palacio Nacional in the background.

Catedral Metropolitana ●

Hymn book on view in the choir

The biggest church in Latin America, Mexico City's cathedral is also at the heart of the world's largest Catholic diocese. Its towers rise 67 m (220 ft) above the Zócalo, and it took almost three centuries – from 1525 to 1813 – to complete. This extraordinarily long period is reflected in the multiple styles of its architecture and internal decoration, ranging from Classical through Baroque and Churrigueresque to Neo-Classical. It has five principal altars, and 16 side chapels containing a valuable collection of paintings, sculpture, and church furniture.

Sacristy
The sacristy contains 17th-century paintings and items of carved furniture such as this decorated cabinet.

Kings and Queens
The sculptures adorning the Altar de los Reyes are of kings and queens who have been canonized.

The high altar is a block of white marble carved with images of saints.

Side entrance

★ Altar de los Reyes
The two oil paintings on this Baroque masterpiece are the Adoration of the Kings *and the* Assumption of the Virgin, *both by Juan Rodríguez Juárez.*

Capilla de San José
This side chapel is one of 16 dedicated to saints and manifestations of the Virgin, all exquisitely decorated with statues and oil paintings.

STAR SIGHTS

★ Altar de los Reyes

★ Choir

For hotels and restaurants in this region see pp292–4 and pp326–30

The Sinking Cathedral

The cathedral is sinking into the soft clay of what was once the bed of Lake Texcoco. Restoration work, mostly carried out underground, has prevented its collapse.

VISITORS' CHECKLIST

Zócalo. **Map** 4 E2. Ⓜ *Zócalo.*
⬜ *8am–8pm daily.* ♿ **Choir**
⬜ *10am–3pm.* **Sacristy** *Tel* 55 21 77 37. ⬜ *11am–2pm.*

Sagrario Metropolitano

Built in the mid-18th century as the parish church attached to the cathedral, the Sagrario has a sumptuous high Baroque façade adorned with sculpted saints.

The clocktower is decorated with statues of Faith, Hope, and Charity.

The façade is divided into three and flanked by monumental bell towers.

Main entrance

★ Choir
With its gold-alloy choir-rail imported from Macao, superbly carved stalls, and two magnificent organs, the choir is a highlight of the cathedral.

Architecture of the Catedral Metropolitana

The building of this vast cathedral took over 240 years, from the first decades after the conquest to the last years of Spanish rule, including long periods when construction virtually came to a halt. The result is the work of many different architects, artists, and sculptors at different times, incorporating a variety of styles, mostly from Spain but also elements that were distinctly Mexican. Despite this mixture, it all combines to form an enormously impressive whole.

THE EARLY COLONIAL CHURCH

Mexico City's first cathedral, begun by Cortés in 1525, was just south of the modern one, near Avenida 5 de Mayo (the remains of some columns can still be seen). It was soon determined to be too small, however, and orders to build a new cathedral were issued in 1536 and 1552, though work did not actually begin until 1573. The basic plan, with three huge vaulted naves, was the work of Claudio de Arciniega, but his design was altered by other architects. Much of the first walls were built by Juan Miguel de Agüero, who was principal architect of Mérida cathedral in the Yucatán. Only after the sacristy was finished, in 1626, was the first cathedral demolished.

BAROQUE ARCHITECTURE

The greater part of the cathedral was completed in the mid-17th century, and consecrated in 1656. The oldest sections, such as the sacristy, are in the restrained Spanish Baroque style known

as Plateresque, so named because its sculptors were said to reproduce the effects of silverware *(plata)* in stone. The three portals of the main façade, from 1670-90, are grander, with elegant columns framing statues of saints.

Carved estípites on the façade of the Sagrario Metropolitano

CHURRIGUERSQUE

Spanish late Baroque architecture was dominated by the ornate style named after the Churriguera family of architects. A hallmark was the use of estípites – square-sided relief columns, like upturned

Bell tower, built between 1660–1813

obelisks, used as bases for elaborate designs. They are prominent in the choir, chapels, and the extraordinary Altar de los Reyes by Jerónimo de Balbas, built between 1710–37, which inspired similar designs throughout Mexico. Outside, the foremost example of Churrigueresque is the Sagrario Metropolitano's façade, built by Lorenzo Rodríguez in 1740-68.

NEOCLASSICAL

In the 1780s the task of completing the still-unfinished upper levels was given to José Damién Ortiz de Castro – the only Mexican-born architect to work on the cathedral. He added the bell towers and upper stories of the façade. Final touches, though, were made by another Spaniard, Manuel Tolsá, who in 1813 added the clocktower and rebuilt the dome in a more austere Neo-Classical style.

SUBSIDENCE

The cathedral's huge weight has caused it to sink into the soft subsoil since it was first built, but this problem became acute after the 1985 earthquake. A massive rescue project to stabilize the structure was completed in 2000. This has ensured the cathedral will not fall down, and the now erratic angles of its columns, and the slope of the floor, are among its most striking features.

Elaborate altar inside the Capilla de las Reliquías

Palacio Nacional ❷

Av Insurgentes Sur & Periférico.
Tel 56 06 97 58. ⬜ 9am–4:45pm
daily. 🎫 book in advance.

Filling the whole east side
of the Zócalo, this imposing
building occupies the site of
the palace of Aztec emperor
Moctezuma, and later the
home of the Conquistador
Cortés *(see p43)*. The present
palace was begun in 1562
in an austere Baroque style
typical of Spanish architecture
of the time, as the residence
of Mexico's Viceroys and the
center of government.

The main courtyard of the Palacio Nacional

It has had an eventful
history, and was attacked by
rebels in 1624 and 1692. After
independence in 1821 it
became the residence of the
presidents of Mexico, and
the offices used by President
Juárez in the 1860s are open
to the public. In the 1920s a
third story was added, in har-
mony with the original style.

Today the Palacio Nacional
still contains the offices of the
President of Mexico and the
Finance Ministry, but its
greatest attractions are the
extraordinary murals around
the staircase of the main
patio. These were painted
by Diego Rivera in 1929–35,
in the aftermath of the 1910
Revolution. His aim was to
celebrate Mexico's turbulent
history, from its ancient past
to the potential future
released by the Revolution,
including an astonishing
gallery of portraits of

historical figures. The main
murals above the great
staircase present a dynamic
panorama of Mexican history.
On the right-hand wall is an
idealized vision of ancient
indigenous Mexico before the
arrival of the Spaniards.
Filling the bottom of the
central panel are the bloody
battles of the Conquest, with
Cortés rearing up on a white
horse, and Cuauhtémoc, the
last Aztec emperor, shown
holding a spear. The
horrors of the Conquest
are also depicted just
above to the left, with
priests torturing
heretics, but across to
the right priests
such as Bartolomé
de Las Casas, who
protected Indians,
are also shown.

Independence forms
the centerpiece of the main
panel, with heroes like
Hidalgo and Morelos. Foreign
invasions, by the United

**Statue in the
palace gardens**

States in 1847 and France in
the 1860s, are shown in the
far right and left panels of the
main wall respectively. The
inner right panel refers to
Juárez's Reform laws of 1857,
while the 1910 Revolution
appears on the upper left,
with Porfirio Díaz, Madero,
and a host of other
identifiable faces. The
Revolution also crowns the
central panel with peasant
hero Zapata (with
moustache) behind
a banner demanding
Tierra y Libertad ("Land
and Liberty"). On the left
wall is the astonishing
*Mexico Today and
Tomorrow*, an exuber-
ant portrayal of the
promise of the
Revolution. Further
murals with idealized
images of life in
pre-conquest Mexico and
Aztec Tenochtitlán from
1941-51 continue around
the first floor.

PLAN OF THE MURAL BY DIEGO RIVERA

KEY

① Quetzalcoatl and the
Ancient Indian World

② The Foundation of
Tenochtitlán (c.1325)

③ The Conquest of Mexico (1521)

④ The Colonial Era

⑤ Mexican Independence (1821)

⑥ The US Invasion of Mexico (1847)

⑦ The Reform Laws (1857–60)

⑧ The French Occupation and Execution
of Maximilian (1867)

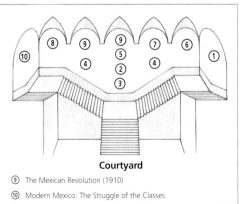

Courtyard

⑨ The Mexican Revolution (1910)

⑩ Modern Mexico: The Struggle of the Classes

Templo Mayor ●

This Great Temple, built by the Aztecs in the 14th and 15th centuries, stood at the heart of Tenochtitlán. The temple complex was almost completely destroyed by the Spaniards after their conquest of the Aztec capital. The chance discovery of the extraordinary Coyolxauhqui carving in 1978 prompted excavations that uncovered the remains of superimposed temples denoted by the stage of construction to which they belong. Stage I is not visible as it is buried beneath Stage II.

View of the Templo Mayor archaeological site

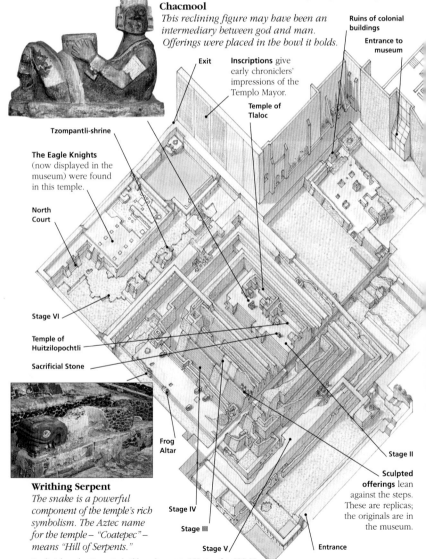

Chacmool
This reclining figure may have been an intermediary between god and man. Offerings were placed in the bowl it holds.

Ruins of colonial buildings

Entrance to museum

Inscriptions give early chroniclers' impressions of the Templo Mayor.

Exit

Temple of Tlaloc

Tzompantli-shrine

The Eagle Knights (now displayed in the museum) were found in this temple.

North Court

Stage VI

Temple of Huitzilopochtli

Sacrificial Stone

Frog Altar

Stage II

Sculpted offerings lean against the steps. These are replicas; the originals are in the museum.

Writhing Serpent
The snake is a powerful component of the temple's rich symbolism. The Aztec name for the temple – "Coatepec" – means "Hill of Serpents."

Stage IV

Stage III

Stage V

Entrance

SIDE ELEVATION OF THE MUSEUM

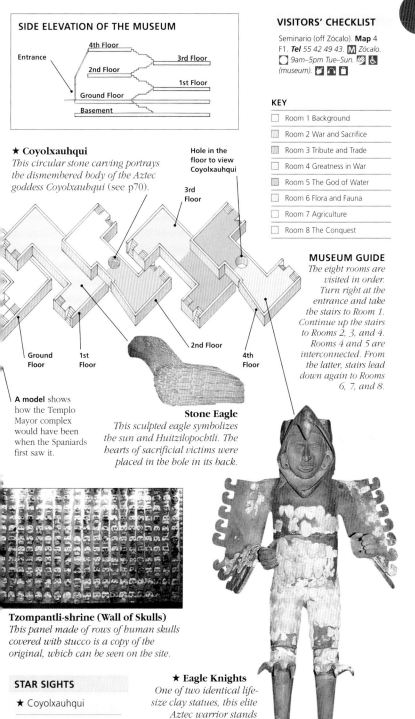

Entrance

4th Floor
3rd Floor
2nd Floor
1st Floor
Ground Floor
Basement

VISITORS' CHECKLIST

Seminario (off Zócalo). **Map** 4
F1. **Tel** 55 42 49 43. M Zócalo.
○ 9am–5pm Tue–Sun.
(museum).

KEY

☐ Room 1 Background

☐ Room 2 War and Sacrifice

☐ Room 3 Tribute and Trade

☐ Room 4 Greatness in War

☐ Room 5 The God of Water

☐ Room 6 Flora and Fauna

☐ Room 7 Agriculture

☐ Room 8 The Conquest

★ Coyolxauhqui
This circular stone carving portrays the dismembered body of the Aztec goddess Coyolxauhqui (see p70).

Hole in the floor to view Coyolxauhqui

3rd Floor

MUSEUM GUIDE
The eight rooms are visited in order. Turn right at the entrance and take the stairs to Room 1. Continue up the stairs to Rooms 2, 3, and 4. Rooms 4 and 5 are interconnected. From the latter, stairs lead down again to Rooms 6, 7, and 8.

Ground Floor

1st Floor

2nd Floor

4th Floor

A model shows how the Templo Mayor complex would have been when the Spaniards first saw it.

Stone Eagle
This sculpted eagle symbolizes the sun and Huitzilopochtli. The hearts of sacrificial victims were placed in the hole in its back.

Tzompantli-shrine (Wall of Skulls)
This panel made of rows of human skulls covered with stucco is a copy of the original, which can be seen on the site.

STAR SIGHTS

★ Coyolxauhqui

★ Eagle Knights

★ Eagle Knights
One of two identical life-size clay statues, this elite Aztec warrior stands proudly in his eagle feather costume.

The Building of the Templo Mayor

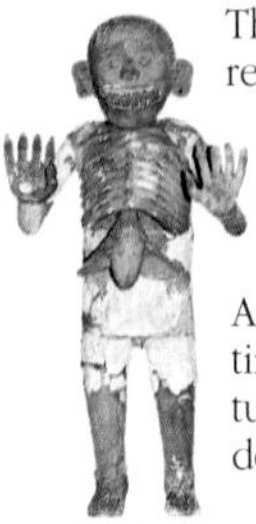

The Aztecs erected their most important religious building on the spot where – in fulfilment of a prophecy *(see p43)* – they had seen an eagle perched on a cactus devouring a snake. The first temple was built some time after 1325, according to Aztec sources, but it was enlarged many times over the course of the next two centuries. The twin temples on its summit were dedicated to the god of war, Huitzilopochtli, and the god of rain and water, Tlaloc. Aztec chronicles tell that both deities were frequently appeased with human sacrifices.

Statue of Mictlantecuhtli *(see p265)*

The ruins of the temples today

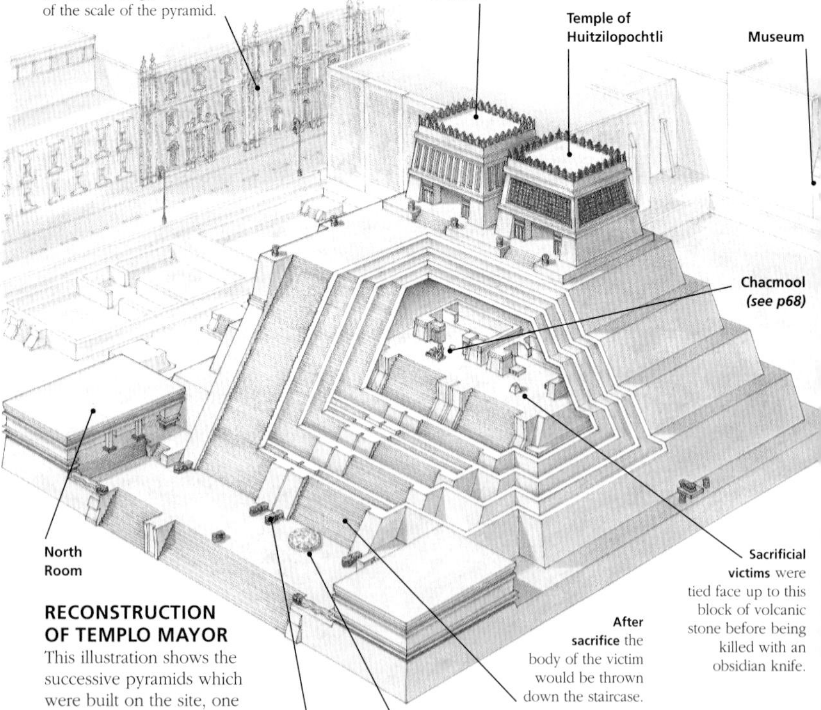

Present-day buildings are shown here to give an idea of the scale of the pyramid.

Temple of Tlaloc

Temple of Huitzilopochtli

Museum

Chacmool *(see p68)*

North Room

RECONSTRUCTION OF TEMPLO MAYOR

This illustration shows the successive pyramids which were built on the site, one on top of the other.

After sacrifice the body of the victim would be thrown down the staircase.

Sacrificial victims were tied face up to this block of volcanic stone before being killed with an obsidian knife.

Two snake heads *guard the foot of the main staircase. They indicate that the temple was built as a symbolic re-creation of Coatepec – "the Hill of the Serpent" – a sacred place in Aztec mythology.*

A carved round stone *shows the separated head, limbs, and torso of the Aztec goddess Coyolxauhqui. According to legend she was slain and dismembered by Huitzilopochtli, her brother, because she had killed their mother, Coatlicue. The stone is now in the museum (see p69).*

The colonial Antiguo Colegio de San Ildefonso, now home to an impressive collection of Mexican murals

Antiguo Colegio de San Ildefonso **4**

Justo Sierra 16. **Map** 4 F1. **Tel** 57 02 63 78. Ⓜ Zócalo, Allende. ⬤ 10am–5:30pm Tue–Sun. 🎫 Tue free. 🎫 reserve in advance. ♿ 📷 🔲 **www**.sanildefonso.org.mx

This 16th-century building, originally a Jesuit seminary, is an outstanding example of Mexican civil architecture from the colonial era. It was remodeled in the 18th century, and the greater part of the present-day building dates from 1770–80. The façade on Calle San Ildefonso, however, which combines Baroque and Neo-Classical styles, is original.

Today the building belongs to the national university and serves as a museum. Its star attraction is the collection of murals from the earliest years of the Mexican muralist movement – including masterful works by Rivera, Siqueiros, and Orozco. In fact, San Ildefonso is regarded as the birthplace of the movement. The first murals commissioned included those of David Alfaro Siqueiros, who in 1922–4 painted four works around the stairwell of the Colegio Chico, the oldest of the three patios which make up the San Ildefonso complex. Perhaps the best-known of these is *The Funeral of the Sacrificed Worker*. At around

the same time, José Clemente Orozco was painting a series of murals on the north wall of the Patio Grande with equally universal themes – among them motherhood, freedom, and justice and the law. These include *Revolutionary Trinity* and *The Strike*. Arguably the most dramatic piece, however, is *The Trench*. The Orozco works to be found on the staircase – including a nude study of Cortés and his indigenous mistress La Malinche – relate mostly to the theme of *mestizaje*, or the mixing of the races that formed the Mexican nation. The Anfiteatro Simón Bolívar contains an early work by Diego Rivera, *The Creation*. The other murals in this hall

Courtyard of the Museo de la Caricatura, formerly the Colegio de Cristo

were painted by Fernando Leal between 1930 and 1942. The conference room to the north of the Patio Grande, known as El Generalito, is furnished with 17th-century carved wooden choir stalls.

Museo de la Caricatura **5**

Donceles 99. **Map** 4 E1. **Tel** 5 704 04 59. Ⓜ Zócalo. ⬤ 10am–6pm daily (5pm Sat, Sun). 🎫 🎫 reserve in advance.

With its intricately adorned and finely preserved Baroque façade, the former Colegio de Cristo is one of the best examples in Mexico City of an upper-class 18th-century dwelling. Originally conceived in 1610 as an educational foundation for poor students, it was rebuilt in the 1740s, and later became a private house. The tiny patio and the broad staircase with its low, stone archway are among the highlights. In the 1980s, the building was restored to house the collection of the Mexican Society of Cartoonists. This includes contemporary cartoons and works by the influential early 20th-century artist, José Guadalupe Posada.

The gold main altarpiece of the
Templo de la Enseñanza

Templo de la Enseñanza **❻**

Donceles 104. **Map** 4 E1.
Ⓜ *Allende.* ⏰ *7:30am–8pm
Mon–Sat, 10am–2pm Sun.*

One of the most remarkable
churches in Mexico City, the
Templo de la Enseñanza has
an extremely narrow and
ornate façade sloping back-
ward slightly from ground
level. The atrium is tiny and
the interior decoration the
height of late 18th-century
"ultra-Baroque."

Built as a convent church,
La Enseñanza was vacated by
the nuns as a result of the 19th-
century anti-clerical Reform
Laws. It was later used by
government bodies, including
the Ministry of Education.

The dazzling gold main
altarpiece is studded
with the sculpted fig-
ures of saints. It rises
up to the roof of the
church, its height
enhancing its vertical
dimensions, and it is
flanked by huge paint-
ings. The vault above
is adorned with a
fresco of the Virgin of
El Pilar, to whom the
church is dedicated. In
the lower choir, which
is situated to either
side of the altar, are
lattice-work screens
intended to hide the
nuns from the gaze
of other worshipers.

Secretaría de Educación Pública **❼**

República de Argentina 28. **Map**
4 E1. *Tel 30 03 10 00.* Ⓜ *Zócalo,
Allende.* ⏰ *9am–6pm Mon–Fri.*

This former convent building, dating from 1639, is
renowned for its large series
of murals by Diego Rivera.
Painted between 1923 and
1928, they reflect Rivera's
diverse influences: Italian
frescoes, French cubists,
and pre-Columbian Mexico.

The ground floor of the first
patio is dedicated to the glori-
fication of labor, a highlight
being a mural showing a
country schoolmistress giving
a lesson. On the staircase is
a series of landscapes from
regions of Mexico, while
on the third floor, in a
panel called *The Painter,
The Sculptor and the
Architect*, is a well-
known self-portrait.
The first floor walls
contain monochrome
grisailles depicting
scientific, artistic, and
intellectual labor, and
on the top floor are
portraits of workers'
heroes, such as
Zapata. The second
patio, on the ground
floor, features a series
of panels depicting
popular fiestas, of
which *The Day of the Dead* is
particularly noteworthy. The
third floor draws on revolutionary songs (*corridos*) for its

Tower of the
church of Santo
Domingo

subject matter and includes a
panel, *The Arsenal*, in which
the artist Frida Kahlo hands
out guns to revolutionaries.

In stark contrast to the style
of Rivera is a striking mural
by David Alfaro Siqueiros,
Patriots and Parricides. This
is located on the staircase in
a part of the building which
used to be a customs house
(the Ex-Aduana), near the
República de Brasil entrance.

Plaza de Santo Domingo **❽**

Map 4 E1. Ⓜ *Allende.*

Second only in importance to
the Zócalo itself, the Plaza de
Santo Domingo (officially
called Plaza 23 de Mayo)
is steeped in history. The
Dominicans built a con-
vent here – the first in
New Spain – in 1527, of
which all that remains
today is a restored
chapel, the Capilla de
la Expiación. Most of
the other buildings
that flank the square
date from the 18th
century. The church
of Santo Domingo,
with its sober façade
partly covered in red
volcanic *tezontle*
stone, was erected
between 1717 and
1737. Its tower is
capped by a pyrami-
dal pinnacle covered with
Talavera tiles. The interior of
the church contains statues
of saints thought to date from

Siqueiros mural of *Patriots and Parricides* in the Secretaría de Educación Pública

Façade of the Capilla de la Expiación in the
Plaza de Santo Domingo

the 16th century, as well as oil paintings by Juan Correa and Alonso López de Herrera. The antique organ and the 18th-century cedar-wood choir stalls with carved images of the saints are among the treasures. The side altars are impressive for their gold embellishments.

The uneven subsidence that led to the demolition of previous churches on this site is widely evident in the square. From the door of the church, the undulation of the Tuscan-style *portales*, or arcade, which runs down the west side of the square, is noticeable. Under the arcade sit scribes, who, for a small fee, will fill out official documents using old manual typewriters.

Palacio de la Antigua Escuela de Medicina ❾

Brasil 33, cnr of Venezuela. **Map** 4 E1. *Tel* 55 29 75 42. Ⓜ *Zócalo, Allende.* ⭘ *9am–6pm daily.* **www**.palaciomedicina.unam.mx

Now home to the Museum of Medicine of the National University (UNAM), the Palacio de la Inquisición

stands on the site of the building in which the Holy Inquisition carried out its fearsome interrogations from the late 16th century onward. The building today dates from the 18th century and underwent restoration in the 1970s. It is notable for its Baroque façade – unusually set on the corner of the building – and for its graceful main courtyard. There are "hanging" arches in each corner of the courtyard, with the supporting pillars set into the wall behind. A typical 19th-century apothecary's store, transferred in its entirety from Oaxaca, is one of the museum's more unusual features. It has displays on the history of Mexican medicine from pre-Columbian times, including sacred and medicinal plants and their uses.

Museo José Luis Cuevas ❿

Academia 13. **Map** 4 F2. *Tel* 55 42 61 98. Ⓜ *Zócalo.* ⭘ *10am–6pm Tue–Sun.* 🎫 *Sun free.* 📷 *reserve in advance.* 💻 📱 **www**.museojose luiscuevas.com.mx

Formerly the cloisters of the Santa Inés convent, this 17th-century jewel was converted to private dwellings in the 19th century and declared a national monument in 1932. Since 1988 it has housed an art gallery reflecting the personal tastes of Mexican painter and sculptor José Luis Cuevas.

The exquisite patio is dominated by the massive bronze sculpture of *La Giganta* (*The Giantess*), which Cuevas created specifically for this space. A number of smaller bronzes by the artist are dotted around the ground floor. The galleries contain paintings by Cuevas and other Mexican artists, including a number of portraits of him and his wife Bertha.

Statue of *The Giantess* in the patio
of the Museo José Luis Cuevas

There are also temporary exhibits by foreign artists. At the entrance to a small "dark room" dedicated to Cuevas' works of erotica, visitors are warned, tongue-in-cheek, of the dangers they pose to those of a puritan upbringing.

The doors of the ex-convent church of Santa Inés, next door to the museum, are carved with reliefs showing scenes from the life of the saint (including her beheading) and portraits of the founders of the convent kneeling in prayer.

Nearby, on the corner of La Santísima and Moneda, is the 18th-century Iglesia de la Santísima Trinidad (Church of the Holy Trinity), worth a visit for the paintings of the martyrs in the nave, two wooden sculptures representing the Trinity, and a crucifix inlaid with bone and precious woods.

Doorway of the Iglesia de la
Santísima Trinidad

Façade of the Museo de la Ciudad de México

Museo de la Ciudad de México ⓫

Pino Suárez 30, cnr of República del Salvador. **Map** 4 E3. **Tel** 55 42 00 83. Ⓜ Zócalo. ☐ 10am–5:30pm Tue–Sun. 🎫 🎫 Wed free. 🎫 🚫

The palace of the counts of Santiago de Calimaya, long renowned for their ostentatious lifestyle, is regarded as one of the most outstanding 18th-century buildings in the city. Built in 1781, the palace is faced with red volcanic *tezontle* stone. Its Baroque portal and magnificent carved wooden doors convey the social standing of its former inhabitants. At the foot of the southwest corner, the builders incorporated a stone serpent's head, which was taken from a wall made up of similar heads that surrounded the Aztecs' ceremonial center.

The first courtyard is noteworthy for the fountain with its carving of a mermaid holding a guitar, and for the trilobate arches near the staircase. Also outstanding is the richly carved stone doorway to the first-floor chapel.

In the early 20th century, the painter Joaquín Clausell lived in the building. The walls of his studio, on the third floor, are covered with an unusual mural, consisting of a collage-like set of scenes influenced by the Impressionists that Clausell met when he was in France.

The building has been occupied by the Museum of Mexico City since 1960. However, at present the collection is limited mostly to furniture and carriages associated with the house and temporary exhibits.

Museo de la Charrería ⓬

Isabel la Católica 108, cnr of José María Izazaga. **Map** 4 D3. **Tel** 57 09 47 93. Ⓜ Isabel la Católica. ☐ 11am–5pm Mon–Fri. 🎫 reserve in advance. ♿ 🍴 🚫

Dedicated to the Mexican art of horsemanship, this museum is located in what was once a Benedictine chapel dedicated to the Virgin of Monserrat. The remains of the chapel date from the 18th century, and its façade is still intact.

Inside, the museum displays the fancy, silver-trimmed costumes of the *charro* and his female equivalent, along with a wide variety of artifacts associated with the culture of *charrería*. Included in the collection are ornate saddles, spurs, and guns, as well as several of the impressive competition trophies awarded to the most successful *charros*. Watercolors of *charrería* events, a model of a *charro* stadium (*lienzo*), and brief historical descriptions of the development of the art help to put the collection in context.

Museo del Ejército y Fuerza Aérea ⓭

Filomeno Mata 6, cnr Tacuba. **Map** 4 D1. **Tel** 55 12 32 15. Ⓜ Allende, Bellas Artes. ☐ 10am–6pm Tue–Sat, 10am–4pm Sun. ♿ 🎫 reserve in advance. 🖥 🎫 🚫

Housed in what was once the chapel of a 17th-century Betlemitas hospital, this museum is notable for the three dramatic relief sculptures in metal on the wall facing Calle Filomeno Mata. They were created for the Paris Exposition of 1889 by Jesús F. Contreras and represent the indigenous chieftains Izcóatl, Nezahualcóyotl, and Totoquihuatzin.

Inside the museum is another statue worthy of note, depicting the last Aztec emperor, Cuauhtémoc. The museum itself is dedicated to the long and eventful history of the Mexican armed forces from the Conquest to the 20th century. Exhibits include chain mail, horse armor, and a fascinating array of weapons.

Nearby, on Calle Tacuba, is the Café Tacuba (*see p326*), a restaurant renowned for its excellent Mexican cuisine.

CHARRERÍA

Charrería is the Mexican art of horsemanship and the culture associated with it. The *charro* is akin to a US cowboy. He dresses in traditional costume and proves his skill and daring in the saddle at *charreadas* (rodeos), wielding a lasso on horseback. But *charros* are seldom working cowboys. More often they are well-off landowners who can afford their fancy costumes. *Charrería* is more than a display of equestrian talent, however, and a *charro* event is a social occasion in which food, drink, and music also play an important role.

Saddle in Museo de la Charrería

Museo Nacional de Arte ⑭

Tacuba 8. **Map** 4 D1. *Tel 51 30 34 00.* Ⓜ *Allende.* ◯ *10:30am–5:30pm Tue–Sun.* 🎫 *Sun free.* 🖥 🖊 *reserve in advance.* 🔲 ♿ **www.**munal.com.mx

Created in 1982, the Museo Nacional de Arte is worth a visit for the building alone. An imposing, Neo-Classical piece of architecture, it was completed in 1911 as the Ministry of Communications and Public Works. Its double staircase, in bronze and marble, is enclosed by a semicircular window three stories high. The interior, with its intricate ironwork and many candelabra, is sumptuous.

The museum's galleries encompass Mexican art from the 16th century to 1954. The collection includes commercial engravings, political cartoons, and folk art, as well as paintings. Much of the collection of religious art from the 16th to early 19th century resulted from confiscations following anti-clerical reform laws in the 1800s *(see p53).* As well as works by the great muralists – Rivera, Siqueiros, and Orozco – the outstanding pieces include a series of landscapes by 19th-century painter José María Velasco. One room is devoted to portraits, including a depiction of the art-lover María Asúnsolo by David Alfaro Siqueiros.

Right in front of the museum is the Plaza Manuel Tolsá, centering on one of the city's favorite monuments – *El Caballito* (The Little Horse) is in reality a massive equestrian statue of Charles IV of Spain by Manuel Tolsá (1802).

Window of Casa de los Azulejos

Casa de los Azulejos ⑮

Francisco I. Madero 4. **Map** 4 D2. *Tel 55 12 78 24.* Ⓜ *Bellas Artes, Allende.* ◯ *7am–1am daily.* ♿

The 16th-century "House of Tiles" was originally the palace of the counts of Orizaba. The blue-and-white tiled exterior is attributed to a 1737 remodeling by the 5th countess, who is said to have imported the style from the city of Puebla, where she had been living previously. Now occupied by the Sanborn's store *(see p114)* and restaurant *(see p326)* chain, the lovingly restored building conserves much of its original Mudéjar interior. The main staircase is decorated with waist-high tiling, and there is a mural on the first floor landing by José Clemente Orozco, entitled *Omniscience,* which was painted in 1925. On the upper floor it is worth taking note of the mirrors surrounded by elaborate gold frames containing the figures of angels and cherubs.

Across the street is the Iglesia de San Francisco, once part of the largest convent in New Spain, which had been built on the site of the Aztec Emperor Moctezuma's zoo. The church is entered via the Capilla de Balvanera, a chapel with a Churrigueresque façade and a decorated interior, but there is little left of interest inside.

Torre Latinoamericana at dusk

Torre Latinoamericana ⑯

Eje Central Lázaro Cárdenas and Francisco I. Madero. **Map** 4 D2. *Tel 55 18 74 23.* Ⓜ *Bellas Artes.* ◯ *9am–10pm daily.* 🎫 ♿ 🖥 🅿

This skyscraper rises 44 floors and its 182-m (600-ft) height boasts the best view of Mexico City – smog permitting. Completed in 1956, the steel-framed structure has survived a number of earthquakes, notably that of 1985. In 30 seconds, its express elevators whisk visitors to the 37th floor. On the 38th floor is an aquarium claiming to be the highest in the world. A second elevator rises to a 42nd-floor viewing platform and a cafeteria. From here a spiral staircase leads to the open-air cage below the TV mast.

Staircase in the Museo Nacional de Arte

Street-by-Street: The Alameda Central

The Alameda takes its name from the *álamos*, or poplar trees, planted here in the late 16th century by the Viceroy Luis de Velasco. Originally only half the size, the park assumed its present dimensions only in the 18th century. Its many statues date mainly from the 1900s, although the central Baroque fountain has been there since the expansion of the Alameda under Viceroy Carlos Francisco de Croix (1766–71). The most imposing monument is the Hemiciclo a Juárez, a semi-circular monument with Doric pillars of Carrara marble, by the sculptor Lazanini.

A balloon seller in the park

Museo Franz Mayer
This museum houses what is probably the finest collection of applied and decorative arts in Mexico. Exhibits date from the 16th to the 19th century ⓳

Palacio Postal, the main post office, has an elegant interior of wrought iron and marble, and houses a postal museum.

Iglesia de San Juan de Dios is an 18th-century church with an unusual concave façade.

LAZARO CARDENAS

AVENIDA MIGUEL HIDALGO

Reforma

Museo Nacional de la Estampa
The exhibits in this small but interesting gallery explain the history of the graphic arts in Mexico ⓲

Hemiciclo a Juárez was inaugurated in 1910 when Mexico celebrated the centenary of its independence struggle.

AVENIDA JUÁREZ

Alameda Central

★ **Palacio de Bellas Artes**
The Art Nouveau façade of this theater is equalled only by its impressive Art Deco interior, with murals by some of the greatest Mexican artists of the 20th century ⓱

0 meters	100
0 yards	100

◁ Façade of the Palacio de Bellas Artes

Statue of Charles IV

Museo Nacional de Arte

An equestrian statue of Charles IV guards the entrance to this collection of modern Mexican art. The building was constructed between 1904 and 1911 **⓮**

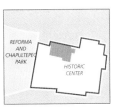

LOCATOR MAP
See Street Finder pp124–5

Café Tacuba
(see p326)

Zócalo

Museo del Ejército

Housed in a 17th-century monastery chapel, this army museum displays a collection of weaponry and military memorabilia dating from the conquest up to the 20th century **⓭**

Palacio de Minería is one of the city's finest 19th-century Neo-Classical buildings.

Palacio de Iturbide, named after the Emperor Agustín de Iturbide (*see p52*), is a superb example of colonial architecture.

TACUBA

FILOMENO MATA

FRANCISCO I MADERO

GANTE

STAR SIGHTS

★ Palacio de Bellas Artes

★ Torre Latinoamericana

★ Casa de los Azulejos

KEY

– – – Suggested route

★ Casa de los Azulejos

Talavera tiles cover the outside of this 18th-century mansion. Inside is an Orozco mural **⓯**

★ Torre Latinoamericana

Mexico City's first skyscraper was built in the 1950s and has survived many major earthquakes **⓰**

Bar La Ópera is an old-fashioned restaurant on 5 de Mayo. A legend says that a bullet hole in the ceiling was made by Pancho Villa (*see p54*).

Palacio de Bellas Artes ⑰

Eje Central & Ave Juárez. **Map** 3 C1.
Tel 55 12 25 93. Ⓜ Bellas Artes.
⭘ 10am–5:45pm Tue–Sun. ♿
⭧ reserve in advance. 🎟 Sun free.
▢ 🅿 www.inba.gob.mx

Arguably the most beautiful building in the Historic Center, the Palacio de Bellas Artes was conceived in 1905 as a new national theater. Italian architect Adamo Boari designed an innovative building around a steel frame, incorporating Neo-Classical and Art Nouveau elements together with pre-Columbian decorative details.

The exterior of the building is clad in Italian marble and its cupolas are covered in tiles. The largest, central dome is surmounted by a Mexican eagle surrounded by figures representing the dramatic arts.

Interrupted by the revolution, the work was completed by Federico Mariscal in 1934. This accounts for the contrasting Art Deco interior, with its geometric shapes in colored marble and eyecatching illumination, especially the vertical lamps flanking the entrance to the auditorium.

The theater has a curtain that is a glass mosaic by Tiffany Studios of New York. Said to comprise a million pieces of glass, it represents the Valley of Mexico with its volcanoes

Pinoncelly's stained-glass skylight in the Museo Nacional de la Estampa

in the background and is based on a design by Gerardo Murillo ("Dr Atl"). On the second floor are two murals by Rufino Tamayo: *Birth of our Nationality* and *Mexico Today*, painted in 1952–3. The third floor includes David Alfaro Siqueiros' masterpiece of the same period, *New Democracy*. On the right-hand wall José Clemente Orozco painted *Catharsis*, whose theme is war and bourgeois decadence. With his work known as *Man, the Controller of the Universe*, Diego Rivera took his revenge on John D. Rockefeller, who had ordered the destruction of a similar mural at the Rockefeller Center in New York on ideological grounds. He portrays Rockefeller among the debauched rich at a nightclub, with the germs of venereal disease above them. The building also houses the Museo de Arquitectura.

The impressive Art Deco interior of the Palacio de Bellas Artes

Museo Nacional de la Estampa ⑱

Av Hidalgo 39. **Map** 3 C1.
Tel 55 21 22 44. Ⓜ Bellas Artes.
⭘ 10am–6pm Tue–Sun. 🎟 Sun free. ⭧ reserve in advance.

Dedicated to the history of the graphic arts, from pre-Columbian to modern times, this museum has an extensive collection, only part of which is on show at any one time.

Probably the best-known of the artists whose work is on display is José Guadalupe Posada (1852–1913). His enduring image of *La Calavera Catrina* – a well-dressed skeleton – is among the most familiar representations of the Mexican fascination with death. Posada's work featured in the popular satirical newspapers of his day.

In the Sala de Técnicas is a range of works illustrating the different techniques used by print artists. The building itself has a 1986 stained-glass skylight by Salvador Pinoncelly.

Museo Franz Mayer ⑲

Av Hidalgo 45. **Map** 3 C1. **Tel** 55 18 22 66. Ⓜ Hidalgo, Bellas Artes. ◐ 10am–5pm Tue–Sun. 🎫 Tue free. 📷 reserve in advance. 🖵 🛈 www.franzmayer.org.mx

This is the richest collection of applied art to be found in Mexico City. Assembled by German financier and art collector Franz Mayer, it is housed in a two-storey, 16th-century building which for most of its existence was a hospital. The museum has what is perhaps the most beautiful courtyard in the Historic Center, featuring a delightful fountain.

The collection – which contains more than 8,000 pieces (as well as about 20,000 antique tiles) from Europe, the Far East and colonial Mexico – is highly varied. Exhibits include tapestries, high-relief wooden carvings of religious scenes, ceramics, and over 1,000 pieces of silverwork, and furniture. Among the most beautiful objects are a number of inlaid wooden chests. There are also some impressive wooden screens, one of which has a rendering of the conquest of Mexico City on one side and a partial view of the city in the colonial period on the reverse.

Talavera vase in the Museo Franz Mayer

This impressive collection of applied and decorative arts also has a number of outstanding examples of Mexican colonial-era paintings.

The attractive, leafy courtyard of the Museo Franz Mayer

Laboratorio Arte Alameda ⑳

Doctor Mora 7. **Map** 3 B1. **Tel** 55 10 27 93. Ⓜ Hidalgo. ◐ 9am–5pm Tue–Sun. 🎫 Sun free. 📷 reserve in advance. 🖵 www.artealameda. inba.gob.mx

This museum of contemporary art is located in the former convent and church of San Diego de Alcalá, built in the 16th century. From 1964 to 1999, the building housed the Pinacoteca Virreinal, a collection of religious art now displayed in the Museo Nacional de Arte (see p75). In 2000 the doors opened to the Laboratorio Arte Alameda. This art space is dedicated to showing major works by Mexican and international artists, and focusing on transdisciplinary, temporary exhibits and events. With its cutting-edge shows, it hopes to interest new audiences in contemporary art and to raise the profile of Mexican artists.

Museo Mural Diego Rivera ㉑

Corner of Colón and Plaza Solidaridad. **Map** 3 B1. **Tel** 55 12 07 54. Ⓜ Hidalgo, Juárez. ◐ 10am–6pm Tue–Sun. 🎫 Sun free. ♿

This small gallery is built around one of muralist Diego Rivera's masterpieces, *Dream of a Sunday Afternoon in the Alameda Central*. Painted in 1947 for the dining room of the nearby Hotel Prado, the mural combines the history of Mexico with the dreams of its protagonists and the recollections of Rivera himself. He includes two self-portraits, and an image of his wife, the painter Frida Kahlo.

The three-sectioned colorful painting caused a stir when first unveiled. The phrase "God does not exist" was removed by Rivera after a Christian group defaced the mural.

Museo de Arte Popular ㉒

Revillagigedo 11. **Map** 3 C2. **Tel** 55 10 22 01. Ⓜ Juárez. ◐ 10am–5pm Tue–Sun. 🎫

Located one block south of Parque Alameda inside an Art Deco building, the Museo de Arte Popular brings together folk art from all over Mexico. It includes contemporary and traditional pieces made from many different materials, reflecting the country's cultural and geographical diversity. Colorful indigenous costumes and religious art are especially well represented.

The Museo Mural Diego Rivera – home to the artist's great *Dream of a Sunday Afternoon in the Alameda Central*

PASEO DE LA REFORMA AND BOSQUE DE CHAPULTEPEC

El Caballito, a sculpture on the Paseo de la Reforma

In the 1860s, during the short-lived reign of the Emperor Maximilian (*see p53*), a grand avenue was laid out between the city of Mexico and the Bosque de Chapultepec. This broad, elegant, tree-lined boulevard, the Paseo de la Reforma, is now flanked by tall modern office buildings. Little evidence remains of the mansions with which it was lined at the turn of the century. But the statues and fountains that adorn Reforma, including the golden Angel of Independence that is the city's symbol, maintain a link with the glories of the past. South of the Paseo is the triangle of streets called

the Zona Rosa, which is filled with shops, hotels, restaurants, and cafés. Beyond this are Roma, a district of offices and shops, and La Condesa, popular for its many informal restaurants. The Bosque de Chapultepec, at the western end of the avenue, was a sacred site in pre-Columbian times. Once the residence of the Aztec emperors, it has been a public park since 1530. The castle on the top of the steep hill at its northeastern end was also Maximilian's home. Today, with its boating lakes, zoo, and cafés, the Bosque de Chapultepec is a very pleasant place to escape the hustle and bustle of the city.

SIGHTS AT A GLANCE

GETTING AROUND
Auditorio, Chapultepec, and Constituyentes are the best metro stations for the Bosque de Chapultepec. Hidalgo station is situated at the opposite end of Reforma from Chapultepec.

KEY

Ⓜ	Metro station
🛈	Tourist information

0 kilometers 1
0 miles 1

◁ **A bar in the Zona Rosa, south of the Paseo de la Reforma**

Paseo de la Reforma ●

The 3.5-km (2-mile) stretch of Reforma, which links the center of the city with Chapultepec, was once lined with beautiful houses. These have now given way to less stately hotels and office blocks, as well as to the Torre Mayor skyscraper, the tallest building in Latin America. Paseo de la Reforma remains, however, an outstanding city street. The monuments that adorn its *glorietas*, or traffic circles, have a special place in the affection of the locals. Between the Caballito and the Angel is a series of smaller statues, commissioned in the 19th century, which commemorate prominent Mexicans from each state. The road continues to the southwest across the Bosque de Chapultepec.

Bronze statue of couple

Monumento a la Independencia
Popularly known as the Angel of Independence, this figure was created by Antonio Rivas Mercado, and was erected in 1910. It commemorates the heroes of the struggle against Spanish colonial rule (see p49).

Diana Cazadora
The bronze figure of Diana the huntress, by Juan Fernando Olaguíbel (1896–1971), was once thought to offend public decency. At the request of the city authorities she was covered up, but only temporarily.

Hotel Sheraton

Torre Mayor

RÍO RHIN
RÍO SENA
RÍO TIBER
RÍO VOLGA
RÍO GUADALQUIVIR
RÍO NILO
RÍO MISSISSIPPI
RÍO ATOYAC
MARIANO ESCOBEDO
PASEO DE LA REFORMA
PASEO DE LA REFORMA
GENOVA
AMBERES
HAMBURGO
AMBERES
LIVERPOOL
LONDRES
FLORENCIA
HAMBURGO
PRAGA
OXFORD
TOKIO
SEVILLA
TOKIO
HAMBURGO
LIEJA
JOSÉ VASCONCELOS

US Embassy

Monumento a los Niños Héroes & Chapultepec Park

Japanese Embassy

Bolsa de Valores
Mexico City's stock exchange is in a futuristic building which has a glass-domed dealing floor. This is flanked by a pencil-slim glass tower which houses offices.

| 0 meters | 250 |
| 0 yards | 250 |

For hotels and restaurants in this region see pp292–4 and pp326–30

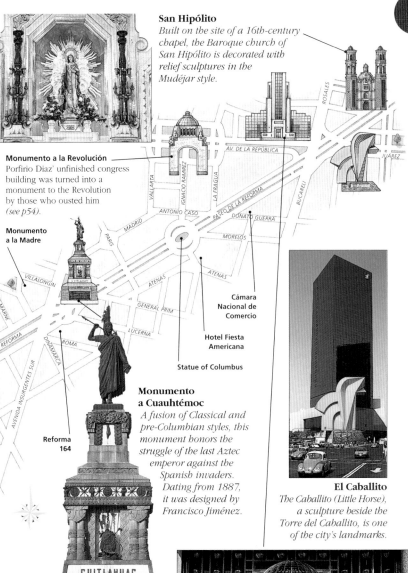

San Hipólito
Built on the site of a 16th-century chapel, the Baroque church of San Hipólito is decorated with relief sculptures in the Mudéjar style.

Monumento a la Revolución
Porfirio Diaz' unfinished congress building was turned into a monument to the Revolution by those who ousted him *(see p54).*

Monumento a la Madre

Cámara Nacional de Comercio

Hotel Fiesta Americana

Statue of Columbus

Reforma 164

Monumento a Cuauhtémoc
A fusion of Classical and pre-Columbian styles, this monument honors the struggle of the last Aztec emperor against the Spanish invaders. Dating from 1887, it was designed by Francisco Jiménez.

El Caballito
The Caballito (Little Horse), a sculpture beside the Torre del Caballito, is one of the city's landmarks.

Zona Rosa
The "Pink Zone" is a triangle of partly pedestrianized streets to the south of Reforma, with shops and cafés. Sadly, the area is not what it was and is not considered to be completely safe.

Lotería Nacional
The National Lottery building, designed by José A. Cuevas and completed around 1936, includes details of Art Deco craftsmanship (see p25).

Museo Nacional de San Carlos ❷

Puente de Alvarado 50. **Map** 3 A1.
Tel 55 66 83 42. Ⓜ *Hidalgo,*
Revolución. ◯ *10am–6pm Wed–Mon.*
🏛 *Sun free.* 🎫 *reserve in advance.*
Ø 🖥 🎦 www.mnsancarlos.com

Occupying an imposing Neo-Classical edifice completed in the early 19th century, this museum has the largest collection of European art in Mexico. The bulk of the collection consists of paintings spanning the 14th to the early 20th century, including notable examples of the Flemish, French, Italian, and Spanish schools. Among the highlights are engravings by Goya and sculptures by Rodin. The origin of these riches is to be found in the collections assembled by the San Carlos Academy of Mexico, established by the Spanish King Charles III in 1783.

Seven galleries on the upper floor house the permanent collection. Pride of place at the entrance is given to *La Encarnación*, a stunning gilded altarpiece dating from 1465, by Pere Espallargues.

At one time the building was home to a "museum of strange objects," but this was later moved to the Museo del Chopo, a twin-towered Art Nouveau structure. Built between 1903 and 1905, toward the end of the dictatorship of Porfirio Díaz *(see p53)*, this steel-framed museum was

The impressive Monumento a la Revolución in the Plaza de la República

known for many years as the "crystal palace," because of its resemblance to the famous London building of that name.

Monumento and Museo de la Revolución ❸

Plaza de la República. **Map** 3 A1.
Tel 55 46 21 15. Ⓜ *Revolución.*
◯ *9am–5pm Tue–Sun (to 6pm Sat,*
Sun). ♿ 🏛 *Sun free.* 🎦 🎟

The striking dome-topped cube that is the Monumento a la Revolución was originally

designed as part of a new parliament building under the dictator Porfirio Díaz. Due to unanticipated problems with the marshy ground, it was never completed. Then, in 1932, as an alternative to demolishing it, the architect Carlos Obregón Santacilia proposed that it be converted into a monument celebrating the 1910 revolution that put an end to the *porfiriato*. Stone cladding and sculptures were added, and the remains of revolutionary heroes such as Francisco Villa were interred at the base of the columns. The austerity of the monument's functional and Art Deco styling is relieved by details in bronze. The statues, sculpted by Oliverio Martínez de Hoyos, represent independence, the 19th-century liberal reform, and the post-revolutionary agrarian and labor laws.

At the base of the monument is a museum dedicated to the 50-year period from the expulsion of the French in 1867 to the 1917 revolutionary constitution. The exhibits on display range from photographs, documents, and reproductions of period newspapers to carriages, clothing, and contemporary artifacts.

Rear façade and gardens of the Museo Nacional de San Carlos

Museo de Cera and Museo Ripley ④

Londres 4. **Map** 2 F3. *Tel 55 46 37 84.* Ⓜ *Insurgentes, Cuauhtémoc.* ◯ *11am–7pm daily.* 🎦 ▣ 🛈 🚫

Housed in a striking Art Nouveau mansion that was designed by architect Antonio Rivas Mercado, the Museo de Cera (wax museum) is an entertaining trip through Mexican history and culture. One room contains effigies of every Mexican president since 1920. Other rooms feature personalities as diverse as Emiliano Zapata, the comedian Mario Moreno (Cantinflas), and soap opera star Verónica Castro. A robot of tenor Plácido Domingo sings an operatic aria, while in the dungeons below the torture victims groan and scream.

Adjacent is the Ripley's Believe it or Not! museum of the bizarre, containing everything from a copy of the Mona Lisa made from pieces of toast to the ever-popular calf-with-two-heads. Those of a delicate disposition should avoid the tunnel that imitates the physical effects of an earthquake.

A sports car covered in coins and flag in the Museo Ripley

Sala de Arte Público Siqueiros ⑤

Tres Picos 29. **Map** 1 A3. *Tel 55 31 33 94.* Ⓜ *Auditorio, Polanco.* ◯ *10am–6pm Tue–Sun.* 🎦 *Sun free.* ♿ 🎦 *reserve in advance.* 🚫 **www**.siqueiros.inba.gob.mx

This was the home and studio of the celebrated Mexican muralist David Alfaro Siqueiros. Just weeks before his death in 1973 he bequeathed it, with all its contents, to the nation. The painter's life and work are represented here by a collection that includes finished works as well as drawings, plans, models, and

Modern interior of the Museo Rufino Tamayo

photo-montages of his many murals. There is also a selection of photographs and documents charting the events of Siqueiros' life, which was singularly eventful. It included two prison terms, one of which was for his part in a plot to kill León Trotsky *(see p103)* – Siqueiros had been a supporter of Stalin. In spite of this, his painting was popular, and in the 1940s and 1950s the state commissioned him to produce several works.

The ground-floor gallery is the site of the 1970's mural entitled *Maternity*, which was originally designed for a school. A ramp leads to the upper floor and the galleries which contain paintings by Siqueiros. The second-floor gallery is devoted to the work of other artists, both foreign and contemporary Mexican.

Façade of the Sala de Arte Siqueiros, the artist's former home

Museo Rufino Tamayo ⑥

Cnr of Paseo de la Reforma & Gandhi. **Map** 1 B4. *Tel 52 86 65 19.* Ⓜ *Chapultepec.* ◯ *10am–5:40pm Tue–Sun.* 🎦 *Sun free.* ♿ 🎦 *reserve in advance.* ▣ 🛈 **www**.museotamayo.org

The outstanding collection of modern painting and sculpture assembled by one of Mexico's foremost 20th-century artists, Rufino Tamayo, and his wife Olga, occupies a stunning futuristic, concrete-and-glass building which is set among the trees of Chapultepec park *(see pp88–9).* The building was designed by architects Teodoro González de León and Abraham Zabludovsky, and was awarded the national prize for architecture in 1981.

Sculpture at the Museo Rufino Tamayo

Housed within this light and airy gallery are some 800 paintings in all, as well as drawings, sculptures, and graphic art. There are also a number of paintings by Rufino Tamayo himself. Among the many other modern artists in the collection are de Kooning, Warhol, Dalí, and Magritte. The museum also has a variety of temporary exhibitions.

Museo de Arte Moderno **7**

Cnr of Paseo de la Reforma & Gandhi. **Map** 1 B4. *Tel* 55 53 62 33. 🚇 *Chapultepec.* ⬜ *10am–5:30pm Tue–Sun.* 🈚 *Sun free.* 🎫 🏠 www.bellasartes.gob.mx

A wide range of 20th-century Mexican painting and sculpture is housed in this gallery of modern art. The collection includes works by all the well-known figures – Rufino Tamayo, Diego Rivera, David Alfaro Siqueiros, and Frida Kahlo – as well as artists who do not belong to the mainstream established by the muralists and others since the Revolution. Foreign artists, such as Leonora Carrington, who have worked in Mexico, are also represented.

The museum has a fine array of oils by Tamayo and several works by Francisco Toledo, his fellow Oaxacan. Among the other highlights are Frida Kahlo's *The Two Fridas*, Diego Rivera's portrait of Lupe Marín, and *Las Soldaderas* by José Clemente Orozco. Contemporary artists in the collection include Alberto Castro Leñero, Irma Palacios, and Emilio Ortiz.

Sculptures are exhibited in the gardens, and the adjacent circular gallery has temporary exhibitions of modern Mexican and international art.

Castillo de Chapultepec **8**

Bosque de Chapultepec. **Map** 1 A5. *Tel* 52 41 31 00. 🚇 *Chapultepec.* ⬜ *9am–5pm Tue–Sun.* 🈚 *Sun free.* 🎫 🚫 www.mnh.inah.gob.mx

The hill which forms the highest point of the Bosque de Chapultepec once stood on the lake shore across the water from Tenochtitlán *(see p94)*. On its summit stands this 18th-century castle, now housing the Museo Nacional de Historia. A crucial battle was fought here in 1847, when army cadets died trying to defend the fortress against invading US troops. In the

Bosque de Chapultepec **9**

A favorite weekend recreational spot for residents of Mexico City, Chapultepec has been a public park since the 16th century. Its tree-shaded paths are lined with vendors selling everything from Mexican snacks to balloons and cotton candy for children. Its attractions include a zoo, a boating lake, a number of museums and galleries, and often, live, open-air entertainment. There is also a botanical garden that dates from the earliest days of the republic. It is well worth making the climb up to the castle terrace, from which the view across the city is stunning.

Auditorio Nacional ①
Mexico's national concert hall is a favored venue for arts events. In front of it stands this contemporary sculpture by Juan Soriano.

Boaters on Lago Chapultepec

"Papalote" Museo del Niño ⑨
This children's museum has over 400 interactive exhibits, organized into five themes: the human body, expression, the world, "Con-science," and communication. A giant video screen shows educational movies. There is also an internet room.

0 meters	500
0 yards	500

Fuente de Tláloc ⑧
This fountain was designed by muralist Diego Rivera. Tlaloc was the central Mexican rain deity (see p265), and one of the most important gods in the pantheon.

Fuente de Petróleos

BOULEVARD PRESID

Fuente de Física Nuclear

Fuente de la Juventud

Monumento a Nicolás Copérnico

Museo Nacional de Historia Natural ⑨

Lago Menor

View from the castle of Monumento a los Niños Héroes and Reforma

1860s, the castle became the palace of Emperor Maximilian *(see p53)*. Subsequently it served as an official residence for presidents of the republic.

The museum covers Mexican history from the Conquest to the Revolution. Exhibits include period artifacts and paintings, and items relating to historical figures. A tailcoat that once belonged to Francisco I. Madero, the eyeglasses of Benito Juárez, and the rifles used in the execution of Maximilian are all on display.

The walls of the museum are decorated with large murals showing historical events. The most striking of these is Siqueiros' *From the Porfiriato to the Revolution*.

In the castle's grounds is the Galería de Historia, known as the Museo del Caracol (the "Snail Museum") because of its shape. In it, the visitor is guided through a series of dioramas illustrating scenes from the struggle for independence up to the Revolution.

Sala de Arte Público Siqueiros ②
The house of muralist David Alfaro Siqueiros is now a museum displaying his paintings, and documents relating to his life *(see p87)*.

VISITORS' CHECKLIST

Map 1 B4. **M** *Chapultepec, Microbus La Feria, Papalote Museo del Niño.* **"Papalote" Museo del Niño Tel** 52 37 17 73. ☐ *9am–6pm Mon–Wed & Fri, 10am–7pm Sat, Sun.* **& ⭘** www.papalote.org.mx

Museo Nacional de Antropología ③
One of the city's main attractions, this museum has a world-famous collection of ancient relics. Several hours are needed to do it justice (see pp90–95).

Museo Rufino Tamayo ④
Works by Tamayo himself and other painters are on show in this gallery *(see p87)*.

Castillo de Chapultepec ⑦
Once the residence of Mexican rulers, including the Emperor Maximilian and the president Lázaro Cárdenas, this castle enjoys views of the park and of the Paseo de la Reforma.

Museo de Arte Moderno ⑤
Opened in 1964, this museum has a collection of works by 20th-century Mexican artists.

Monumento a los Niños Héroes ⑥
This honors the army cadets ("boy heroes") who died defending the castle in 1847 *(see p52)*.

Museo Nacional de Antropología ⑩

Stucco head from Palenque

Inaugurated in 1964, the vast and airy National Museum of Anthropology by Pedro Ramírez Vázquez is a just setting for a world-renowned collection of finds from Mexico's pre-Columbian cultures. The museum's large, central patio is almost entirely covered by an 84-meter (275-ft) long canopy which is balanced on an 11-meter (36-ft) pillar. This canopy is thought to be the largest concrete structure in the world to be supported by a single pillar.

The courtyard with bronze conch shell sculpture beside the pond

★ Olmec Heads

Two of the massive, basalt heads for which the Olmecs (see p254) are best known stand close together in the Gulf Coast gallery. Found at San Lorenzo (see p253), they may be portraits of high-ranking people.

Stairs to reconstruction of Tomb 104 at Monte Albán *(see pp220–21)*

Monte Albán Tomb 7 reconstruction

Reconstructions of Maya temples

Maya stela

Stairs to reconstruction of Palenque's royal tomb *(see p236)*

A giant statue of a rain deity, either Chalchiuhtlicue or Tlaloc *(see p264)*, stands near the museum's entrance.

Restaurant

Head of a young man from Palenque

This distinctive, life-size carved head was found among offerings in the tomb at the base of the Temple of the Inscriptions at the Classic Maya site of Palenque.

Entrance

Bosque de Chapultepec & Voladores

Steps to taxis and bus stop

The pillar supporting the canopy is decorated with bas reliefs of European and ancient Mexican civilizations.

Stela de la Ventilla

This carved pillar from Teotihuacán served as a movable marker in the ballgame (see p276).

For hotels and restaurants in this region see pp292–4 and pp326–30

The Ethnology collections on the upper floor of the museum show aspects of the traditional lifestyle of the major indigenous groups of Mexico *(see pp20–21).*

★ **Sun Stone**
This intricately carved stone is the highlight of the Aztec room. The earth or sun god at the center is surrounded by signs for the 20 days of the Aztec ritual calendar.

Concrete canopy

VISITORS' CHECKLIST

Cnr of Gandhi and Paseo de la Reforma. **Map** 1 A3. **Tel** 55 53 63 81. M Chapultepec, Auditorio. ◯ 9am–7pm Tue–Sun. 🗱 🕭 🖋 reserve in advance. 🚻 🚭 🍴 🖾
www.mna.inah.gob.mx

Toltec Coyote-Headed Warrior
This head of a warrior wearing a coyote headdress was found at Tula (see p144). It was made by covering a clay base in mother-of-pearl.

Giant Atlante sculpture from Tula *(see p144)*

Model of Teotihuacán

Tarascan house

★ **Funerary Mask**
This stone mask, encrusted with shell, turquoise, pyrite, and jade, is among the finest of the many priceless pre-Columbian treasures that the museum contains.

KEY

☐	Introduction and Prehistory
☐	Preclassic Era
▦	Teotihuacán
☐	Toltecs
▦	Aztecs *(see pp94–5)*
▦	Oaxaca
▦	Gulf Coast
▦	The Maya
☐	Northern and Western Mexico
▦	Ethnology collection
☐	Temporary exhibitions
☐	Nonexhibition space

STAR EXHIBITS

★ Sun Stone

★ Olmec Heads

★ Funerary Mask

GALLERY GUIDE
The ground floor is dedicated to archaeological finds from ancient Mexico, each room dealing with a particular civilization or region of the country. Doors lead out to structures built within the grounds of the museum. The upper floor displays ethnology collections.

Exploring the Museo Nacional de Antropología

The twelve galleries on the ground floor are all accessible from the central patio, so that a tour can begin wherever the visitor likes. Although the first seven galleries are in chronological order, covering the history of the central plateau, the following five galleries visit the various regions of Mexico, including one dedicated to the great civilization of the Maya. The upper floor is devoted to a collection of costumes, houses, and artifacts of the 56 surviving indigenous cultures in Mexico as well as exploring aspects of their religion, social organization, and festivals.

Totonac stone carving

Detail from the reconstruction of the Temple of Quetzalcoatl façade

INTRODUCTORY GALLERIES

The first three galleries present an introduction to the study of anthropology, and an outline of the historical development of Mesoamerica *(see pp44–5)*, which ran from what is now northern Mexico down to western Honduras and El Salvador. An account of the prehistoric origins of the indigenous Mesoamerican cultures helps set the rest of the museum in context.

PRECLASSIC ERA

Beginning with the earliest agricultural settlements in the central plateau around 1700 BC, the Preclassic gallery illustrates the rise of more complex cultures, shown in particular detail through the development of the ceramic arts. Outstanding among the collection are a number of figures influenced by the Olmecs *(see p254)* from the Gulf of Mexico, including the "jaguar-boy" found at Tlapacoya in Mexico state. There is also a reconstruction of an intact burial site from Tlatilco in Mexico state, in which the skulls exhibit the cranial deformation and filed teeth that are typical of that period.

TEOTIHUACÁN

Centered on the mysterious, ancient city that the Aztecs dubbed "the place where men became gods," the culture of Teotihuacán *(see pp134–6)*

Geometric sculpture of the water-goddess Chalchiuhtlicue

was among the most important of the Classic era in Mesoamerica. The gallery is dominated by the huge stone statue of the water-goddess, Chalchiuhtlicue. Along one wall a reconstruction of the façade of the Temple of Quetzalcoatl, reproduces the original blues and reds with which it was painted. Colorful murals of Teotihuacán adorn the gallery's side walls.

Some of the finest pieces are less monumental. They include a wide variety of pottery vessels for domestic use, such as grain and water storage urns, figurines, and funerary masks showing a talent for lapidary, and obsidian carvings. The inhabitants of Teotihuacán, whose culture reached its height between 100 BC and AD 800, were experts in fashioning shiny

black obsidian knives. There are also statues that illustrate aspects of the religious way of life in Teotihuacán.

TOLTECS

As Teotihuacán declined, other cities of the central plateau, Tula in particular, rose to prominence. The founders of Tula *(see p144)* were the Chichimecas from the north, who adopted the name Toltecs, meaning "artists." They soon acquired a reputation as specialists in the military arts. The most noticeable exhibit is a gigantic stone warrior figure known as an Atlante, with which the Toltecs are most commonly associated. These figures were used as pillars in their temples.

The Toltec gallery also includes items from other cities of the Postclassic period, including Xochicalco in

One of the original Atlantes sculptures from Tula *(see p144)*

Crude Toltec pottery work

Morelos, which more properly belong to the Teotihuacán tradition. Notable among them are stone carvings dedicated to the god Quetzalcoatl, and the stylized head of a macaw, which was perhaps used as a ball-court marker. Xochicalco's most famous monument, the serpent frieze around the base of the temple of Quetzalcoatl, is illustrated with a photographic mural.

OAXACA

Following on from the Aztec Hall (see pp94–5), this is the first gallery dedicated to the regions of Mexico. It presents the artifacts of the two great peoples of Oaxaca: the Zapotecs, builders of the hilltop city of Monte Albán, and their neighbors and successors the Mixtecs, who created Mitla, with its stone friezes.

On display are polychrome ceramic pieces from both cultures. In the garden is a reconstruction of a Monte Albán tomb. Both peoples were skilled in the art of jewelry, and there are many examples here.

GULF OF MEXICO

Among the most spectacular, and the best-known of all the museum's exhibits are the extraordinary colossal stone heads from the Preclassic Olmec culture, which flourished from 1200 to 600 BC. The Olmecs also produced smaller, but equally remarkable, sculptures of heads and figures in a variety of types of stone, most of them with the characteristic Olmec features of

Huastec sculpture of the god Xilonen

broad, flat-nosed faces and thick lips, curled downward.

The Olmecs share this gallery with the Totonacs from central Veracruz and the Huastecs from the northern shores of the Gulf. The best-known creations of the Totonacs are the carved stone "yokes," the purpose of which is still not fully understood. The Huastecs were some of the finest artists of Mesoamerica, particularly in their use of clay, bone, and shell.

Stela from Yaxchilán showing a Maya ruler, circa AD 800

THE MAYA

There is no doubting the special hold of the Maya on the imagination of visitors to Mexico, whether because of the intricate beauty of their great stone cities in the jungle, such as Palenque in Chiapas (see pp234–7), or the continuing mystery of their sudden decline, before the arrival of the Spanish conquistadors.

Among the highlights of the Maya gallery are carved stelae, such as the one from Yaxchilán, lintels from the Classic period, and a particularly outstanding carved head of a young man, found at Palenque. A small, underground gallery contains a reconstruction of the royal tomb of Pakal found beneath Palenque's Temple of the Inscriptions. It also displays artifacts from the site, including

high-quality stucco heads. The outside garden features several reconstructions of Maya ceremonial buildings, together with a group of other sculptures and stelae.

NORTHERN AND WESTERN MEXICO

The sparsely inhabited northern deserts never produced the great civilizations characteristic of central and southern Mexico. Nonetheless, the ceramic art from Paquimé (see p170) – the most notable of the so-called Oasis cultures – has a distinctive elegance, with its geometric patterns, smooth-polished surfaces and adornments such as copper or turquoise. The gallery also contains examples of metalwork, and models of the unique multi-story adobe houses of Casas Grandes.

At the height of the Aztec (Mexica) empire, the Tarascans (Purépechas), the dominant culture of the Pacific coast, retained their independence, and with it a distinctive artistic tradition. This gallery provides evidence of their skill in metalworking (they were among the first in the region to use gold, silver, and copper for jewelry and utensils), and in pottery.

Other items of particular note include the polished earthenware from Classic-era Colima, and the ceramics of the cloisonné technique using different colored clays, which is thought to have originated there.

Colima earthenware

ETHNOLOGY COLLECTION

The eleven interconnected galleries on the top floor of the museum, beginning with Gallery 13, are devoted to all aspects of Mexican ethnology, including housing, costumes, artifacts, religions, social structures, and the festivals of the 58 surviving indigenous cultures of Mexico.

The Aztec Hall

The largest gallery in the museum displays the treasures of the Mexica culture – better known as the Aztecs. When Hernán Cortés and his conquistadors arrived in 1519 *(see p49)*, the Aztecs ruled most of what is now Mexico, either directly or indirectly. This gallery gives the visitor a strong sense of the everyday culture of the Aztec people, the power and wealth of their theocratic rulers, and their enormous appetite for blood, sacrifice, war, and conquest.

Model of the Templo Mayor (see pp68–70)

Realistic stone head, possibly representing the common man

LARGE SCULPTURES

The entrance landing and central section of the gallery are devoted to large stone sculptures. Near the entrance is the Ocelotl-Cuauhxicalli, a 94-cm (3-ft) high stone vessel in the form of a jaguar-eagle. It was used as a receptacle to hold the hearts of human sacrificial victims. A statue of Coatlicue, the mother of Coyolxauhqui and later of Huitzilopochtli *(see p70)*, is one of the few representations of the goddess in Aztec art. This statue shows her with eagle's claws, a dress made of snakes, and a necklace of hearts and hands. She has been decapitated, and two serpents emanate from her neck to symbolize blood. Other large sculptures here are the goddesses Coyolxauhqui and Cihuateteo, a small-scale representation of a *teocalli* or temple, and a *tzompantli*, an altar of skulls from the Templo Mayor. On the wall opposite the door, dominating the gallery, is the Sun Stone.

THE AZTEC PEOPLE AND THEIR HISTORY

The section to the right of the entrance describes the Aztec people, their physical appearance and their history. The most conspicuous piece here is a carved round stone, known as the Stone of Tizoc, which records the victories of Tizoc, the seventh ruler

THE LAKE CITY OF TENOCHTITLÁN

The Aztecs' capital city, Tenochtitlán, was built on an island in a shallow lake. Stone causeways connected the city to the shore of the lake, and an aqueduct brought fresh water. Temples and other civic and ceremonial buildings stood at the center of the city (sacred precinct), around what is now the Zócalo *(see pp62–3)*. This area was surrounded by a great wall.

Tlatelolco and the Plaza de las Tres Culturas *(see p108)*.

Causeways connected the city to the lake shore.

Bosque de Chapultepec *(see pp88–9)*

Ceremonial center and Templo Mayor

The old city square, is now the Zócalo.

Canals were used for everyday transport of goods and people around the lake city.

Coyoacán *(see pp104–5)*

of the Aztecs (1481–6). This trachyte stone was found in the Zócalo. Another object of interest is a stone head with inset teeth and eyes to add to its realism. It is thought to represent the common man. Other sculptures represent everyday Aztec people, including a statue of a Mexica noble dressed in robes appropriate to his rank.

This part of the museum includes a model of the temple complex that stood at the center of Tenochtitlán. Surrounded by a wall, the complex focused upon the Templo Mayor topped by its twin shrines. The rounded temple in front of the Templo Mayor was dedicated to the god Quetzalcoatl. Above the model hangs a large painting by Luis Covarrubias showing the city as it may have looked when first seen by the Spanish.

Polished obsidian statue of a monkey god

SACRED OBJECTS

The display cases to the left of the entrance show items used for religious purposes by the Aztecs. One of the most interesting pieces is a vase in the form of a pregnant monkey, carved out of obsidian, a hard black, volcanic stone akin to glass. This vase symbolizes the wind loaded with black rain clouds which will engender growth and fertility. Also on display here is the stone altar on which human sacrificial victims were stretched in order to remove their hearts. Other items include solar disks, sacrificial knives, and representations of various deities.

THE SUN STONE

Often mistakenly referred to as the Calendar Stone, this basaltic disk was unearthed in the Zócalo in 1790. The carvings describe the beginning of the Aztec world and foretell its end. The Aztecs believed they were living in the fifth and final "creation" of the world. Each creation was called a sun. The stone is 3.6 m (12 ft) in diameter and weighs 24 tonnes.

The central god could be the sun god Tonatiuh or the earth god Tlaltecuhtli.

The 20 days of the Aztec month are shown on the inner band.

Two fire serpents run around the rim of the stone, their tails meeting at the date of creation.

Four square panels around the center indicate that the previous suns (creations) were destroyed by jaguars, wind, rain, and water.

OTHER EXHIBITS

Aspects of Aztec daily life are described in other parts of the hall. There are notable collections of craft objects. The ceramics section shows plates, vases, masks, and other items, many with decorative work. Pieces of Aztec jewelry made out of bone, gold, wood, crystal, and shells are displayed, while their clothing includes animal skins and feathers. The musicality of the Aztecs is shown with a range of instruments, such as flutes and whistles. A wooden drum (*huehuetl*) is finely carved with a warring eagle and vulture.

Along the back wall are documents and drawings explaining the system of tribute that sustained the Aztec economy. Here there is also a diorama of the market in Tlatelolco, part of Tenochtitlán, showing a scene of pots, food, and other goods being bought and sold.

Aztec shield made out of animal hide and feathers

SAN ÁNGEL AND COYOACÁN

At the time of the Spanish conquest, Coyoacán ("place of the coyotes") was a small town on the shore of Lake Texcoco. It was connected to the Aztec capital of Tenochtitlán, an island in the lake, by a causeway. After conquering Tenochtitlán, Hernán Cortés set up his headquarters here in 1521 while the city was rebuilt along Spanish lines.

Monumento a Álvaro
Obregón, San Ángel

Nearby San Ángel was then a village called Tenanitla, where Dominican and Carmelite friars chose to settle after the conquest. It became known as San Ángel in the 17th century, after the foundation of the convent-school of San Angelo Mártir. Its official name today is Villa Álvaro Obregón, but this is rarely used.

Until this century both San Ángel and Coyoacán were rural communities well outside Mexico City. The growth of the metropolis has since swallowed them up, but both retain a good deal of their original colonial architecture. Much favored as a place of residence by artists and writers, many of whom prefer the relative tranquillity of San Ángel and Coyoacán to the bustle nearer the city center, they are also popular with families for weekend day trips.

Some of the area's famous inhabitants in the past have included Diego Rivera, Frida Kahlo, and Russian revolutionary León Trotsky. The latter was assassinated in Coyoacán in August, 1940. The former homes of all three are among the area's attractions, along with a number of museums and art galleries. Restaurants and specialty shops abound, and there are popular weekend craft markets in the Jardín Centenario (in Coyoacán) and the Plaza San Jacinto (in San Ángel).

SIGHTS AT A GLANCE

Museums and Galleries
Casa/Museo León Trotsky ❿
Museo de la Acuarela ❽
Museo de Arte Carrillo-Gil ❺
Museo del Carmen ❸
Museo Estudio Diego Rivera ❹
Museo Frida Kahlo ❾

Churches
Iglesia de San Antonio
 Panzacola ❻

Streets and Squares
Avenida Francisco Sosa ❼
Coyoacán see pp104–105 ⓫
Plaza San Jacinto ❷

Walks
*San Ángel to Coyoacán
 see pp98–9* ❶

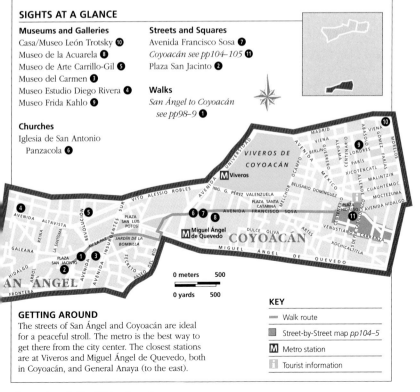

KEY

— Walk route

▨ Street-by-Street map *pp104–5*

Ⓜ Metro station

ℹ Tourist information

GETTING AROUND

The streets of San Ángel and Coyoacán are ideal for a peaceful stroll. The metro is the best way to get there from the city center. The closest stations are at Viveros and Miguel Ángel de Quevedo, both in Coyoacán, and General Anaya (to the east).

◁ Tree sculpture in Plaza Hidalgo, Coyoacán

A Walk from San Ángel to Coyoacán ❶

Few parts of Mexico City can boast a domestic architecture of the colonial and pre-revolutionary eras as
well-preserved as that of Coyoacán and San Ángel. This
walk connects the two squares at the heart of these
districts, both of which are well-known in the city for
their weekend craft fairs. The walk often follows tree-
lined, cobbled streets. Along the way are churches,
museums, art galleries, and monuments, as well as
some picturesque places to stop for a meal.

The domes of the Museo del Carmen in San Ángel

SIGHTS ON WALK

Plaza San Jacinto ①
Museo del Carmen ②
General Álvaro Obregón ③
Plaza Federico Gamboa ④
San Antonio Panzacola ⑤
Avenida Francisco Sosa ⑥
Museo Nacional de la
   Acuarela ⑦
Plaza Santa Catarina ⑧
Jardín Centenario ⑨

Iglesia de San Jacinto, on the main square of San Ángel

San Ángel

Leave Plaza San Jacinto ①
(*see p100*), a pleasant square
with numerous restaurants,
by Calle Madero. At the end
of this road you will pass the
Centro Cultural de San Ángel
on your right. On reaching
Avenida Revolución, turn
right and cross over to reach
the Museo del Carmen ②
(*see p100*). The church of this
former monastery has three
tiled domes that are the symbol of San Ángel. The museum

contains
some fine religious
paintings by Cristóbal
de Villalpando, as well
as furniture from the
colonial era. In the
crypt, mummified
bodies disinterred by
troops during the
Revolution (*see p54*)
can be seen. On leav-
ing the church, turn
right and walk along
Revolución then right
again into the cobbled
street of Avenida La
Paz where there are
some good but rather
pricey restaurants.

Chimalistac

Cross Avenida
Insurgentes and will you come
to the Jardín de la Bombilla,
the small, wooded park that
surrounds the monument to

Detail of Monumento a Álvaro Obregón

General Álvaro Obregón ③,
assassinated nearby in July
1928, before he could assume
the presidency for the second
time (*see p55*). The rather severe obelisk, erected in 1935,
no longer contains
the general's arm,
which he lost at the
battle of Celaya. The
granite sculptures
that flank the
monument are the
work of Ignacio
Asúnsolo (1890–
1965). Cross Calle
Chimalistac and
walk along a lane
to Plaza Federico
Gamboa ④. This
square (which is
also known as
Plaza Chimalistac) is named
after a writer and politician
of the *porfiriato* (*see p53*).
The chapel of San Sebastián

Chimalistac, dating from the 17th century, sits crosswise in the square. It is notable, among other things, for a stunning Baroque altarpiece with 18th-century religious paintings. San Sebastián was one of the few open chapels in Mexico City. The atrial cross which stands in front of it is a relic of the days when mass was celebrated in the outdoors.

On leaving the square, turn left and walk along Ignacio Allende, a narrow street, until you reach Miguel Angel de Quevedo. Cross this to stroll in Parque Tagle. Once through the park, bear right into

Jazz by Angel Mauro Rodriguez in Museo de la Acuarela

Calle Arenal. Walk along this quiet street until you reach the bustling Avenida Universidad.

Avenida Francisco Sosa

Directly across Universidad stands the chapel of San Antonio Panzacola ⑤ *(see p101)*, a tiny jewel of a church dating from the 17th century. Next to the chapel is an old stone bridge over a tributary of the Río Magdalena. Cross this and you come to one of the prettiest streets in the city. Avenida Francisco Sosa ⑥ *(see p102)* is also one of the oldest colonial streets in Latin America. Take the

TIPS FOR WALKERS

Starting point: Plaza San Jacinto, San Ángel. *Length:* 3.5 km (2 miles). *Places to eat:* Plaza San Jacinto, Avenida La Paz, Plaza Santa Catarina, Jardín Centenario. *Metro station:* Miguel Ángel de Quevedo.

Archway on Jardín Centenario, in the center of Coyoacán

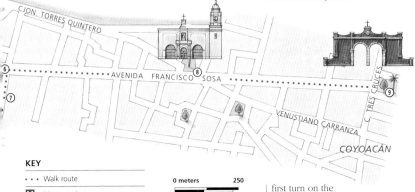

KEY

• • • Walk route

Ⓜ Metro station

0 meters 250
0 yards 250

first turn on the right down Calle Salvador Novo for a short detour to visit a gallery of watercolor paintings, the Museo Nacional de la Acuarela ⑦ *(see p102)*. Halfway along Francisco Sosa you come to the enchanting Plaza Santa Catarina ⑧ where story-tellers gather on Sunday lunchtimes. The main building on the square is a lovely yellow church with a triple-arched façade. Opposite the chapel is the Casa de la Cultura Jesús Reyes Heroles, a university arts center with a beautiful, leafy garden. At the end of Francisco Sosa you arrive at the twin arches of what was once the gateway into the convent of San Juan Bautista. This then leads into the pleasant square of Jardín Centenario at the heart of Coyoacán ⑨ *(see pp104–5)*.

The charming Iglesia de Santa Catarina on the square of the same name

Plaza de San Jacinto ❷

San Ángel. Ⓜ *Miguel Ángel de Quevedo.*

On Saturdays this square, which forms the center of San Ángel, is an excellent place to shop for Mexican handicrafts, either at the outdoor stalls or in the Bazar del Sábado, which is located in a 17th-century house in the northwest corner.

The 16th-century Iglesia de San Jacinto, just off the square, was originally annexed to a Dominican monastery of the same name. The church has a fine dome. In the interior, the carved wooden screen, and the onyx font in the nave are both worth seeing.

The most impressive building on the north side of the square is the Casa del Risco, also known as the Casa del Mirador, a well-preserved, 18th-century house built for the Marqués de San Miguel de Aguayo and donated to the nation in 1963. Constructed around an interior courtyard with an extravagant fountain, the house contains a wealth of colonial furniture and decor.

On the square's west side is a plaque commemorating the soldiers of the Irish-American San Patricio batallion who died fighting for Mexico against the United States in 1846–7.

Courtyard of the Museo del Carmen

Museo del Carmen ❸

Avenida Revolución 4. **Tel** 56 16 28 16. Ⓜ *Miguel Ángel de Quevedo.* ◔ *10am–5pm Tue–Sun.* 🖼 *Sun free.* ✍ www.museodelcarmen.org

The Carmelite monastery-school of San Angelo Mártir, built in the early 17th century, gave its name to the San Ángel district. The three beautiful domes that rise above it, elaborately decorated with colorful tiles, are still a symbol of the area. Later the monastery and its church became known as El Carmen. Today it serves as a museum of furniture, paintings, and

Dazzling main altarpiece in the church of the Museo del Carmen in San Ángel

other artistic and historical objects from the colonial period. Much of the original interior is preserved, including the monks' cells. In the crypt a dozen mummified bodies, which were disinterred by troops during the Revolution *(see p49)*, are displayed in glass-topped coffins. Decorative details include Talavera tiles from Puebla and carved, painted ceilings. The chapel on the first floor contains an 18th-century gold-painted altarpiece inset with oil paintings of

saints. Other highlights to look out for in the museum are a series of religious paintings by the 18th-century master Cristóbal de Villalpando and a richly carved door with symbols representing the Virgin Mary.

Diego Rivera's workshop, surrounded by a cactus hedge

Museo Estudio Diego Rivera ❹

Corner of Calle Diego Rivera and Altavista. **Tel** 55 50 15 18. Ⓜ *Viveros, Barranca del Muerto.* ◔ *10am–6pm Tue–Sun.* 🖼 *Sun free.* 🚻 📷 *for a fee.* www.bellasartes.gob.mx

One of Mexico's most outstanding 20th-century architects, Juan O'Gorman, built these twin houses in 1931–2 for two of the country's most distinguished painters, Diego Rivera and Frida Kahlo. Surrounded by a cactus hedge, the houses are connected by a rooftop bridge, over which Frida used to take Diego his meals. *The Two Fridas* and several other of her most well-known works were painted here. Behind her house is a building her father used as a photographic studio.

The large living room/studio in Rivera's house contains an assortment of his personal belongings, from paintbrushes to huge, papier-mâché skeletons and pre-Columbian pottery. Other rooms are devoted to temporary exhibitions.

Across the street is the San Ángel Inn *(see p330)*, an elegant restaurant, with a beautiful garden popular with Mexico's elite. Built in 1692, it was originally a Carmelite monastery. After 1915 it was turned into a restaurant and today it is known for its excellent cuisine and its string of famous patrons, among them Brigitte Bardot, Henry Kissinger, and Richard Nixon.

Museo de Arte Carrillo-Gil ❺

Avenida Revolución 1608. *Tel 55 50 62 60.* Ⓜ Miguel Ángel de Quevedo. ◷ 10am–6pm Tue–Sun. Sun free. 🚻 📷 reserve in advance.
www.museodeartecarillogil.com

This light and airy gallery on three floors has temporary exhibitions and sometimes shows the collection of art that embraces some of the finest 20th-century Mexican artists. Founded in 1974, the collection was assembled by Dr. Alvar Carrillo and his wife and includes works by Diego Rivera, José Clemente Orozco, and David Alfaro Siqueiros. Among the Rivera canvases are a number of works from the artist's Cubist period. Less well-known, but equally interesting, are paintings by Austrian Wolfgang Paalen (1905–1959) and German Gunther Gerzso, a contemporary artist.

Dr. Carrillo, who studied medicine in Paris, began supporting avant-garde artists in his native Mexico from the late 1930s onward, by purchasing their works and through

published criticism. He was himself a painter of some note, and a close friend of Orozco.

Not far from the museum, near the corner of Revolución and La Paz, is the well-known San Ángel flower market. You can pick up anything here, from an extravagant arrangement to a single rose at any time of the day or night. It is an especially fine sight at night, when the flowers glow under the artificial lights.

The red façade of the Capilla de San Antonio Panzacola

Capilla de San Antonio Panzacola ❻

Corner of Avenida Universidad and Avenida Francisco Sosa. Ⓜ Miguel Ángel de Quevedo, Viveros.

This tiny 17th-century chapel originally belonged to the nearby parish church of San Sebastián Chimalistac *(see p99)*. It sits next to a miniature stone bridge over a stream at the end of Avenida Francisco Sosa *(see p102)*. Painted a striking dark red color, with reliefwork in a contrasting creamy white, its façade includes a niche containing a statue of St. Anthony. Above the arched entrance is a relief sculpture of St. Sebastian the martyr. The arch is flanked by pilasters supporting a molded entablature. The undulating roofline ends in twin towers and has a cross in its center.

Colorful display of blooms on a stall in the San Ángel flower market

The frontage of Casa Alvarado, one of the residences on Avenida Francisco Sosa

Avenida Francisco Sosa 🕖

Between San Ángel and Coyoacán.
Ⓜ Miguel Ángel de Quevedo.

Mexico City's most attractive street is also one of the oldest colonial streets in Latin America. Running approximately 1.5 km (just under a mile) between Avenida Universidad and the Jardín Centenario in Coyoacán (*see pp104–105*), it is lined with handsome residences.

At the beginning of it stands the quaint, 17th-century chapel of San Antonio Panzacola (*see p101*). A short way farther along the avenue, soldiers stand guard outside the imposing city residence of the former Mexican president, Miguel de la Madrid. Continuing down the street there are a number of very attractive residences including the Casa de la Campana (No. 303) and No. 319, which has a replica Atlante (*see p144*) outside it. No. 383 is another interesting colonial house, thought to have been constructed in the 18th century by Pedro de Alvarado, the Spanish conqueror of Mexico and Guatemala. The house next door belonged to his son. About halfway along the avenue is the pleasant Plaza Santa Catarina. On this square stand a church and the Casa de la Cultura Jesús Reyes Heroles, an arts center. A short way farther along is the cultural department of the Italian embassy. At the end of the street, on the corner of Jardín Centenario in Coyoacán, is the 18th-century Casa de Diego de Ordaz.

Museo Nacional de la Acuarela 🕗

Salvador Novo 88. **Tel** 55 54 18 01
Ⓜ Miguel Ángel de Quevedo.
🕙 10am–6pm Tue–Sun. 🚫
📷 reserve in advance. 🖥

Dedicated primarily to some of the finest works by Mexican watercolor artists from the 19th century to the present day, this museum is located in a small, two-story house set in a pretty garden.

The larger part of the collection consists of works by contemporary artists, including many winners of the Salón Nacional de la Acuarela annual prize for watercolors. Embracing a wide range of styles and subject matter, it may surprise those who think of watercolors primarily in terms of delicate landscapes. Two outstanding canvases are *La Carrera del Fuego* and *Jazz*, both by Ángel Mauro Rodríguez, which can be seen on display on the ground floor of the museum.

There is an international room containing a selection of paintings by artists from all over the Americas, as well as Spain and Italy, including US artists Robert Wade and Janet Walsh. A separate gallery in the garden outside houses temporary exhibitions.

The Museo Nacional de la Acuarela, home to a collection of watercolors

---

FRIDA KAHLO (1907–54)

Arguably Mexico's most original painter, Frida Kahlo led a troubled life. A childhood bout of polio left her right leg slightly withered. Then, when she was 18, she broke her back in a traffic accident which rendered her incapable of having children. The pain she suffered for much of her life is reflected in many of her often violent and disturbing paintings, particularly her self-portraits. In 1929 she married the muralist Diego Rivera. Rivera was a notorious womanizer but Frida too had affairs, with both women and men – including León Trotsky. She and Rivera divorced in 1939, remarried the following year but thereafter lived separately.

Bronze statue of Frida Kahlo

Museo Frida Kahlo ❾

Londres 247. *Tel 55 54 59 99.*
Ⓜ *Coyoacán.* ◯ *10am–5:45pm Tue–Sun.* 🈸 ♿ *ground floor only.*
🈸 *reserve in advance.* 📷 🚫 📷
www.museofridakahlo.org

This is the house where the painter Frida Kahlo was born, lived for much of her life, and eventually died. She painted some of her famous works here, many of them inspired by the pain she suffered as a result of breaking her back.

This house is a treasure trove, not only of Frida's paintings, but also of many artifacts associated with her life and that of her lover Diego Rivera, with whom she shared the house. Donated to the nation by Rivera in 1955, not long after Frida's death, it is preserved much as it was when they lived there.

On display are letters and diaries as well as ceramics and other everyday items. A handwritten accounts book shows the couple's earnings and outgoings for March/April 1947, including the fee earned by Frida Kahlo for the famous painting *The Two Fridas*. One wall is covered with Rivera's collection of "*retablos*": small paintings created as religious offerings in gratitude for prayers answered. There are also giant paper "Judas" figures, burned on Easter Saturday as a symbolic destruction of evil forces *(see p30)*, as well as pre-Columbian art collected by Rivera. Frida's wheelchair and one of the corsets she had to wear constantly because of her disability are also on display.

Casa/Museo León Trotsky ❿

Avenida Río Churubusco 410.
Tel 56 58 87 32. Ⓜ *Coyoacán.*
◯ *10am–5pm Tue–Sun.* 🈸 📷 ♿

León Trotsky, the Russian revolutionary, lived in this house from 1939 until his assassination in 1940. Before moving here he lived with the muralists Diego Rivera and Frida Kahlo.

To frustrate would-be assassins, Trotsky fitted the windows and doors with armor-plating, raised the height of the surrounding wall, and blocked off most of the windows that overlooked the street, among other things. All this foiled one attempt on his life: about 80 bullet holes can still be seen in the outer walls.

However, these precautions did not stop Ramón Mercader, a regular visitor to the house, who had won his victim's confidence. The room where the murder took place is just as it was, complete with the chair and table where Trotsky was sitting when he died.

Trotsky's typewriter, books, and other possessions can be seen where he left them. One of the photographs on display shows him on his arrival in Mexico in 1937, standing on the quay in Tampico with his wife Natalia and Frida Kahlo.

THE ASSASSINATION OF TROTSKY

The intellectual, León Trotsky, was born Lev Davidovitch Bronstein, in Russia, in 1879. He played a leading role in the Bolshevik seizing of power in 1917 and in forming the Red Army to fight the Russian Civil War of 1918–20. But Lenin's death in 1924 led to a power struggle within the ranks of the victorious revolutionaries, and in 1927 Trotsky was forced into exile by his rival, Joseph Stalin. He was granted asylum in Mexico in 1937 but even across the Atlantic he was not safe from Stalin's purge of all his opponents. His house was assaulted in May 1940 by Mexican Stalinists led by the muralist David Alfaro Siqueiros and machine-gunned for 20 minutes. Then on August 20, 1940, he was fatally wounded by another assassin, Ramón Mercader, who pierced his skull with an icepick.

León Trotsky

Frida Kahlo's brightly colored kitchen with pottery on display

Street-by-Street: Coyoacán ⑪

Once the haunt of conquistador Hernán Cortés and his Indian mistress "La Malinche," the atmospheric suburb of Coyoacán is an ideal place for a stroll, especially on the weekend, when a lively craft fair operates in its two main squares, Jardín Centenario and Plaza Hidalgo. Packed with cafés, restaurants, and cantinas, its narrow streets retain much of their colonial-era charm. Calle Felipe Carrillo Puerto, heading south out of the plaza, is a good place to shop for curios. Coyoacán is also known in Mexico City for its delicious ice cream.

Casa de Cortés
The north side of Plaza Hidalgo is taken up by this distinctive 15th-century building, now used as government offices.

Indoor craft bazaar (open at weekends)

Cantina La Coyoacana (*see p116*)

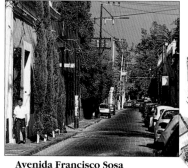

Avenida Francisco Sosa
This narrow, pretty street (see p102) leading to nearby San Ángel is a delight to stroll along. It is lined with handsome, well-maintained mansions which were built by wealthy families in colonial times.

Gateway of former monastery

Casa de Diego de Ordaz
While named after the conquistador Diego de Ordaz, the house dates only from the 18th century. At one corner is this ornate niche with a statue of the Virgin Mary.

Jardín Centenario
was once the atrium of the monastery of San Juan Bautista, of which only the church remains.

Plaza Hidalgo
The Casa de Cortés faces the church of San Juan Bautista across this spacious square centering on a bandstand.

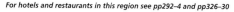

Iglesia de San Juan Bautista
Once part of a convent dedicated to St. John the Baptist, this church was originally built in the 16th century. Though much altered, it still has a number of interesting relief sculptures on its façade.

Plaza de la Conchita
This quiet colonial square shaded by trees, and with a stone cross in the middle, is the prettiest spot in Coyoacán.

LOCATOR MAP

COYOACÁN
SAN ÁNGEL

HIGUERA
SAN FRANCISCO
VALLARTA
FERNÁNDEZ LEAL
CARRANZA
VENUSTIANO

Meditation (1980), a statue by Rocío Peredo

Casa del Teatro

0 meters   50
0 yards   50

Iglesia de la Conchita
This tiny church, officially the Capilla de la Concepción, has an intricately carved, Mudejar-style façade. The interior contains a Baroque altarpiece and some outstanding colonial paintings.

Casa de la Malinche
Traditionally associated with Cortés' mistress "La Malinche," this 16th-century house was probably built for Ixtolinque, a local chieftain. Today it is the home of two well-known Mexican artists, Rina Lazo and Arturo García Bustos.

KEY

– – – Suggested route

FARTHER AFIELD

There is plenty worth discovering in this massive, sprawling city beyond the Historic Center. Head north to the Plaza Garibaldi and you can be serenaded by mariachis or explore the nearby ruins of Tlatelolco, Tenochtitlán's twin city. The Basílica de Guadalupe, the largest shrine to the Virgin Mary in all of the Americas, is even farther north, on the site where legend says she appeared in 1531. In the south, Xochimilco preserves the only remnant of Lake Texcoco and its pre-Columbian floating gardens. Boatmen will ferry you around its tree-lined canals. The 2,500-year-old pyramid of Cuicuilco, meanwhile, is thought to be the oldest structure in the city.

SIGHTS AT A GLANCE

Museums and Galleries
Museo Anahuacalli **7**
Museo Dolores Olmedo Patiño **12**
Museo Nacional de las Intervenciones **6**

Public buildings
Universidad Nacional Autónoma de Mexico **8**

Squares and Markets
Mercado de La Merced **4**
Plaza Garibaldi **3**

Churches
Basílica de Guadalupe **1**

Historic Sites
Pirámide de Cuicuilco **9**
Tlatelolco and Plaza de las Tres Culturas **2**

Suburbs
Tlalpan **10**
Xochimilco **11**

Streets
Avenida Insurgentes Sur **5**

KEY

▨ Main sightseeing areas
☐ Parks and open spaces
☐ Greater Mexico City
✈ Airport
🚉 Train station
🚌 Bus station
═ Highway
▬ Major road
═ Minor road

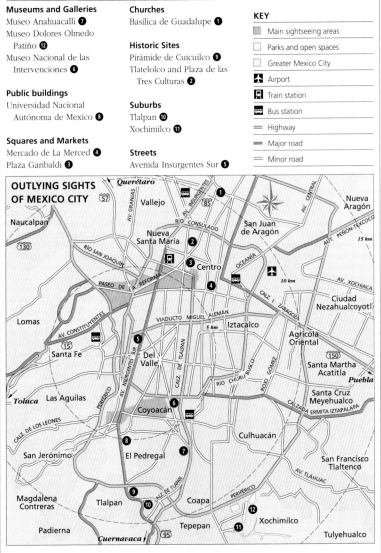

OUTLYING SIGHTS OF MEXICO CITY

Colorfully decorated punts in the floating gardens of Xochimilco

The beautiful Antigua Basílica de Guadalupe, with its Baroque twin towers

Basílica de Guadalupe ❶

Plaza de las Americas 1. **Tel** 55 77 60 22. Ⓜ La Villa. ◯ 6am–9pm daily. ♿ 🏠 www.virgendeguadalupe.org.mx

The richest and most visited Catholic shrine in all the Americas is a complex of buildings at the foot of a hill, the Cerro del Tepeyac. According to legend it was here in 1531 that a brown-skinned Virgin Mary miraculously appeared to the Indian Juan Diego in 1531. She is named after the Virgin of Guadalupe in Extremadura, Spain.

The Antigua Basílica was built in the early 18th century. Twin towers flank its Baroque façade, which features relief carvings of the Virgin. It is overshadowed by the circular, modern church that now stands beside it, which can accommodate up to 10,000 worshipers. An object of veneration inside it is Diego's tunic on which the image of the Virgin was supposedly imprinted as proof of the miracle he witnessed. There is also an interesting museum.

The impressive Capilla del Pocito is a late 18th-century chapel regarded as one of the finest achievements of Mexican Baroque architecture. The Virgin is supposed to have appeared four times in all. This chapel was constructed on the site of her fourth appearance. It is roughly elliptical in shape and its domed roof is faced with dazzling blue and white Talavera tiles (see p153).

Next door to another chapel, the Capilla de Indios, is a house in which Juan Diego is said to have lived after the Virgin's first appearance until his death in 1548.

Each year on December 12 an estimated 50,000 people assemble at the shrine to celebrate the anniversary of the appearance of the Virgin.

Tiles on the Capilla del Pocito, near the Basílica de Guadalupe

Plaza de las Tres Culturas ❷

Eje Central & Ricardo Flores Magón. Ⓜ Tlatelolco, Garibaldi. ◯ 9am–6pm Tue–Sun. ♿

The remains of the ceremonial center of Tlatelolco form a major part of the Plaza de las Tres Culturas. The square gets its name ("The Three Cultures") from the mix of modern, colonial, and pre-Columbian architecture that have developed around it

Tlatelolco, the "twin city" of the Aztec capital, Tenochtitlán, was the most important commercial center of its day. The site here has a "templo mayor" similar to that of Tenochtitlán (see pp68–9). There are also smaller temples including the "calendar temple", dedicated to the god of the wind. It owes its name to the glyphs adorning three of its sides, which represent dates in the Aztecs' ritual calendar. In the northwest corner of the archaeological zone, the remains of the carved "wall of serpents" can be seen, which marked the boundary of the ceremonial center.

The Spanish erected their own temples on the site, particularly the Templo de Santiago, a Catholic church in a severe, almost militaristic, style. Built by the Franciscan order, and finished in 1610, the church has twin towers flanking the main door. Over the side door are statues of the apostles. The original font, in the form of a shell, can still be seen inside. It is said that Juan Diego, who witnessed the appearance of the Virgin of Guadalupe, was baptized here. Beside the church is a Franciscan monastery, built in 1660.

The modern era is conspicuously represented by several buildings, particularly the concrete-and-glass foreign ministry tower. Scattered around the plaza are sculptures by Federico Silva. Between the monastery and the nearby residential tower block is a 1944 mural by David Alfaro Siqueiros. Entitled *Cuauhtémoc Against the Myth*, it combines sculpture with alfresco painting. Cuauhtémoc was the last Aztec emperor, killed by the Spanish under Hernán Cortés. In front of the Templo de Santiago is a plaque that reads: "On 13 August 1521, heroically defended by Cuauhtémoc, Tlatelolco fell into the hands of Cortés. It was neither triumph nor defeat, but the painful birth of the *mestizo* nation that is Mexico today."

In October, 1968, the Plaza de las Tres Culturas was the scene of another painful moment in Mexican history, when the military opened fire on student protesters, killing several hundred.

The entrance of the Templo de Santiago in the Plaza de las Tres Culturas

Plaza Garibaldi ❸

N of the Alameda, off Lázaro Cárdenas.

The Plaza Garibaldi is the home of mariachi music. Dressed in their tight-trousered costumes, mariachi musicians can be seen scouting for work among the heavy traffic of the nearby Eje Central at most times of the day and night. Mariachi music was born in Jalisco on the Pacific Coast. In the first two decades of the 20th century there was heavy migration from Jalisco to the capital, and the Plaza del Borrego (later renamed the Plaza Garibaldi) became the mariachis' home from around 1920 onward. Today the area abounds with bars and restaurants serving a staple fare of tacos and tequila.

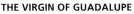

Mariachi statue in the Plaza Garibaldi

A mariachi (the term refers to the band, not the individual musician) can be hired per song or per hour. Rates vary, according to the number of musicians and their ability.

Visitors are warned that the streets between the Alameda and the Plaza Garibaldi can be dangerous to walk through and are advised to reach the square by taxi.

Mercado de La Merced ❹

Anillo de Circunvalación & Calle Callejón de Carretones. Ⓜ *Merced.* ◯ *daily.* ♿

Said to be one of the biggest markets in the Americas, La Merced has 5,514 separate stalls. It occupies the spot on which an Aztec market stood prior to the conquest by the Spanish.

La Merced is divided into seven sections, six of which specialize in different types of merchandise, while the seventh is a traditional market. The market is particularly good for food, especially chilies, fruits, and fresh vegetables.

The northern section of the market used to be occupied by the Convento de la Merced. The restored 17th-century Moorish-style cloister of the monastery can still be seen on the other side of the Anillo de Circunvalación at República de Uruguay 170. It is particularly noted for the richness of its carved stonework.

The Virgin of Guadalupe, patron saint of Mexico

THE VIRGIN OF GUADALUPE

On December 12 each year, thousands of pilgrims flock to the Basílica de Guadalupe to commemorate the apparition of Mexico's patron saint on the Cerro del Tepeyac. Acts of veneration also take place in every town and village throughout the country. Birthday songs, *las mañanitas*, are sung at dawn. Special services are then held, followed by dancing and music in town squares, with children dressed in local costumes. As often in Mexico, a Catholic tradition has merged with pre-Columbian influence: the cult of the Virgin of Guadalupe has distinct parallels with that of Tonantzin, a Mesoamerican mother-goddess.

Spectators watching the action at the enormous Plaza México – Mexico City's bullring

Avenida Insurgentes Sur ❺

South from Glorieta de Insurgentes.
Ⓜ *San Antonio, Barranca del Muerto.*

The Avenida de los Insurgentes runs just over 30 km (18 miles) from the capital's border with Mexico State in the north to the start of the highway to Cuernavaca in the south, and is said to be the longest street in Latin America.

Its southern (Sur) stretch has several sights of interest. Just a few blocks south of its junction with the Viaducto Miguel Alemán stands the World Trade Center, formerly the Hotel de México. This is without doubt one of the most prominent buildings on the Avenida. Its slim, glass tower is surmounted by a huge circular section that has a revolving floor.

The Polyforum Siqueiros, one of Mexico City's most audacious works of modern architecture, is next door to the World Trade Center. Its upper floor, which is reached by twin, circular staircases, is topped by an octagonal dome. This is decorated by one of David Alfaro Siqueiros' finest works, *March of Humanity*, one of the largest murals in the world.

At Eje 6 Sur and Insurgentes is the Ciudad de los Deportes, which includes a football stadium and the Plaza México, reputedly the world's largest bullring. It seats up to 60,000 people and is surrounded by statues commemorating the great bull-

fighters, including Manuel Rodríguez ("Manolete"), who was in the arena's inaugural program in 1946.

Just before the junction with Barranca del Muerto is the Teatro de los Insurgentes, built in the early 1950s by architect Alejandro Prieto. The curved façade is adorned with an allegorical mural by Diego Rivera on the theme of theater in Mexico. Completed in 1953, the mural centers on a huge pair of hands holding a mask, around which are gathered significant revolutionary and independence heroes.

Museo de las Intervenciones ❻

Cnr of General Anaya & Calle 20 de Agosto. ***Tel*** *56 04 09 81.* Ⓜ *General Anaya.* ◯ *9am–6pm Tue–Sun.* 🎟 *Sun free.* 🛈

This former convent still bears the bullet holes from a battle that took place here between US and Mexican forces in 1847. Today it is a museum dedicated to the foreign invasions of Mexico since its independence in 1821. The collection consists of

Cloister in the Museo de las Intervenciones

The carriage of Benito Juárez in the Museo de las Intervenciones

weapons, flags, and other artifacts, including a throne and saber belonging to Agustín de Iturbide (see p52) and a death mask of the Emperor Maximilian (see p53), as well as paintings, maps, and models.

Adjoining the museum is the former convent church, which has some superb gilded altarpieces, as well as religious paintings from the 16th to the 18th century. These include *La Asunción* by the 16th-century painter Luis Juárez and the 17th-century work *La Virgen y San Ildefonso* by Manuel de Echave.

Rear façade of the unusual Museo del Anahuacalli

Museo del Anahuacalli ❼

Museo 150. **Tel** 56 17 43 10.
◯ 10am–6pm Tue–Sun.
⬤ public hols. 🖼 🚹 ground floor.
🖼 reserve in advance. 🚹 🏛
www.anahuacallimuseo.org

This museum was conceived and created by muralist Diego Rivera to house his collection of pre-Columbian art. It was completed after his death by architects Juan O'Gorman, and Heriberto Pagelson, and

Rivera's own daughter, Ruth. Built of black volcanic stone, it takes the form of a pyramid. The collection consists of some 2,000 pieces, representing most of the indigenous civilizations of Mexico. There are funerary urns, masks, and sculptures from the ancient culture of Teotihuacán. The studio, although never actually used by Rivera, has been set up as if it were, with his materials and half-finished works on display. A smaller gallery next to the pyramid contains an exhibition of papier mâché sculpture relating to the Days of the Dead, celebrated October 31–November 2 (see pp34–5).

Image of the Goddess of Maize in the Museo del Anahuacalli

Universidad Nacional Autónoma de México (UNAM) ❽

Ciudad Universitaria. **Tel** 56 22 64 70. Ⓜ Universidad, Ciudad Universitaria. ◯ 7am–9:30pm daily. ⬤ public hols. ♿ www.unam.mx

Latin America's largest university is also a UNESCO World Heritage site. It occupies a vast campus in the south of the city. Many of the most interesting buildings are concentrated in a relatively small area close to Avenida Insurgentes. To the west of the avenue is the striking Olympic stadium, the symbol of the 1968 Mexico Olympics. Over the main entrance is a high-relief painting by Diego Rivera. Facing the stadium, on the east side of Insurgentes, is the rectory tower, adorned with dramatic murals by David Alfaro Siqueiros. The theme of the

mural on the south wall is the recurring struggle of the Mexican people to forge an independent identity, while on the north wall is a mural of glass mosaic tiles depicting the functions of the university. The adjacent Museo Universitario has changing exhibitions of contemporary art. Nearby is the Biblioteca Central, one of the university's most spectacular buildings. Its tower is covered with mosaics by Juan O'Gorman. Each wall illustrates a period of Mexican history and the scientific achievements it produced.

A separate complex of buildings farther south on Insurgentes includes one of the city's major centers for performance arts, the Sala Nezahualcóyotl (see p117) and the Hemeroteca (a newspaper library). The Espacio Escultórico, a huge concrete circle, contains some modern sculpture. However the remarkable natural sculpture of the twisted volcanic rock on which the campus is built is even more impressive.

Close to the Olympic stadium is the university's Jardín Botánico. As well as its cactus collection, the garden has an arboretum and a section devoted to jungle plants. Located in the Pedregal ecological reserve, home to a unique volcanic ecosystem, the garden is also noted for its collection of Mexican medicinal plants.

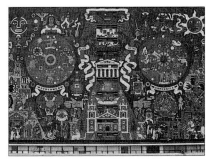

Mosaic on the Biblioteca in the University, depicting the scientific achievements of Mexican history

Unusual remains of the circular Pirámide de Cuicuilco

Pirámide de Cuicuilco ❾

Av Insurgentes Sur & Periférico.
Tel 56 06 97 58. ⬤ 9am–4:45pm
daily. 🎫 reserve in advance.
www.inah.gob.mx

This pyramid belongs to the earliest known urban civilization in the Valley of Mexico, founded around 600 BC. It is all that is left of the ceremonial center of a settlement thought to have comprised as many as 20,000 inhabitants at its peak. The surviving structure is a truncated, layered cone, just 25 m (82 ft) high but 100 m (328 ft) across. The eruption of a nearby volcano, Xitle, forced the inhabitants of the area to flee around 100 AD. The solidified lava, which can be as much as 8 m (26 ft) deep, makes excavation of the area difficult. However, a museum on the site exhibits the pottery, tools, and spearheads that have been found.

Another pre-Columbian ceremonial site within the urban area is the Cerro de la Estrella (southeast of the city), which was inhabited from AD 1000 until the arrival of the Spanish.

Tlalpan ❿

Mex 95. 25 km south of city center.

In the age of the Spanish viceroys, Tlalpan was a favorite country retreat both for ordinary Mexicans and the nobility. As a result, a large number of elegant mansions and haciendas were built here from the early 18th century onward.

Visitors to the old town, now the seat of Mexico City's largest *delegación* (suburban area), can stroll along narrow streets and admire the beautiful architecture, which dates from the 17th to the 20th century. The 18th-century Casa Chata, the Casa del Marqués de Vivanco, and the Casa del Conde de Regla are among some of the outstanding buildings here.

In the central Plaza de la Constitución, with its *porfiriato*-era bandstand and busts of national heroes scattered around, is the Capilla del Rosario, a 17th-century chapel with a Baroque façade. Nearby is the 16th-century Dominican church of San Agustín, which has a large courtyard. In the same square stands the tree from which 11 patriots, who rebelled against the French occupation under

Carved wooden doorway of the Casa Chata

The garden of the Hacienda de Tlalpan, now a restaurant

the Emperor Maximilian, were hanged in 1866. Maximilian's wife, the Empress Carlota, occupied the Casa de Moneda (on the corner of Juaréz and Moneda), which was later used as a military barracks.

On Avenida San Fernando, the church of Santa Inés has a plaque commemorating the brief detention of independence hero José María Morelos here in 1815.

The former country house of General Antonio López de Santa Anna, the hero of the Alamo, stands at the corner of San Fernando and Madero. He was elected president of Mexico 11 times. On the Calzada de Tlalpan, what was once the old Hacienda de Tlalpan is now an elegant restaurant *(see p330)*, with restful fountains and colorful peacocks in its garden.

Xochimilco ⓫

Prolongación División del Norte. 20 km SE of city center. Ⓜ *Embarcadero.*

Known as "the place of the flower fields" in Nahuatl, the language spoken by the Aztecs, Xochimilco was once a lakeside village connected to Tenochtitlán by a causeway. Today it is the only part of Mexico City still to have the canals and semi-floating flower and vegetable gardens, or *chinampas*, built by the Aztecs. Originally created on a

The yellow façade of the church of San Agustín in Tlalpan

For hotels and restaurants in this region see pp292–4 and pp326–30

The Iglesia de San Bernardino in the main square of Xochimilco

base of aquatic roots that were then covered with soil, the *chinampas* remain an important source of flowers and vegetables to Mexico City even today.

A favorite weekend pastime, popular with tourists as well as *chilangos* (the city's inhabitants), is to rent one of the many flower-decked punts, which have roofs and a table down the middle. A local boatman poles the punt along between banks shaded by willows. Waterborne mariachis will provide entertainment while smaller boats sell typical Mexican snacks. An optional stop provides an opportunity to haggle for rugs or other handicrafts at a local craft market.

On land, Xochimilco has a village-like atmosphere that is far removed from the bustle of the historic center of Mexico City. One of the architectural highlights in the main square is the Iglesia de San Bernardino. A fortified monastery built by the Franciscans in the late 16th century, it has a Classical-style façade with some

hints of early Baroque. The magnificent main altarpiece contains paintings and sculptures of the apostles and other saints. Other altarpieces contain beautiful paintings by colonial-era masters such as Cristóbal de Villalpando and Juan Correa.

Near San Bernardino is the Capilla del Rosario, a pretty chapel built in 1768. It is completely covered in a profusion of high-relief mortar-work and Puebla-style tiles.

A row of colorful boats in Xochimilco

Museo Dolores Olmedo Patiño ⓬

Av México 5843. **Tel** *55 55 12 21.* Ⓜ *La Noria.* ◯ *10am–6pm Tue–Sun.* ▨ *Tue free.* ▰ *reserve in advance.* ▱ ▢ ▤ www.museodolores olmedo.org.mx

This is the largest private collection of works by muralist Diego Rivera. It is housed in a beautiful 17th-century mansion in Xochimilco known as the Finca Noria, which was gifted to the nation in 1994 by the wealthy collector and friend of Rivera, Dolores Olmedo.

As well as 137 works by Rivera, there are also 25 by Frida Kahlo and more than 600 pre-Columbian artifacts. The Rivera collection spans many periods of the artist's life. It includes several self-portraits as well as studies for large works. The excellent portrait, *The Mathematician*, was painted in 1919. Among the best-known of the Kahlo works here are *Self-Portrait with a Monkey*, *The Broken Column*, and *The Deceased Dimas*. There are also some pieces on display by Angelina Beloff, Rivera's first wife. A separate part of the collection is dedicated to Mexican popular culture.

The landscaped grounds of the mansion contain animals and plants native to Mexico, including the Mexican hairless dog, or *xoloitzcuintle*.

SHOPPING IN MEXICO CITY

Handmade wall hanging in the Plaza de San Jacinto

The beauty of shopping in Mexico City is the vast range and accessibility of goods. Strolling around the city, visitors will stumble upon a dizzying number of vibrant street markets, selling anything from quality crafts and fresh flowers to rice-grain sculptures and witchcraft accessories. Those looking for elegant fashions and classy boutiques should head to Avenida Masarik in Polanco, or the touristic outlets of the Zona Rosa. Visitors in search of everyday essentials, as opposed to a hectic shopping experience, will fare better with neighborhood markets and grocery stores, or the ultimate convenience of one of the city's many comprehensive department stores.

A stall in the Plaza de San Jacinto, part of the lively Saturday morning market

CRAFTS AND GIFTS

The most complete selection of Mexican crafts (see pp348–51) can be found at **Fonart**, a state-run chain. Prices here may be above average, but all items are genuine crafts. The staff know the origins of every piece and can arrange international shipping.

A pleasant place to shop for unusual and original handicrafts is the **Bazar del Sábado** (Saturday Market) in the Plaza San Jacinto in San Ángel (see p100). Stalls are open only on Saturdays between 10am and 2pm. The heart of the market is the cluster of stalls around the fountain of an indoor patio belonging to a colonial building. The stalls sell a wide variety of crafts and gift items, including jewelry, clothing, Tiffany lampshades, gilt work, embroidered pillows, rice-grain sculptures, candles, wall hangings, and paper flowers. Shoppers can also enjoy a buffet breakfast to the accompaniment of *marimba* players.

The **Mercado de Londres** (or Mercado de Insurgentes) in the Zona Rosa specializes in silver jewelry, sold by weight, painted papier-mâché trays and picture frames, and also finely embroidered shawls and waistcoats. There is a large selection of crafts from all over the country in the **Mercado de la Ciudadela**. Prices are very reasonable here, although this is often reflected in the fact that many of the articles are not of the finest quality. The **Centro Artesanal de Buenavista**, advertised as Mexico's largest crafts market, is in actual fact a very large and usefully positioned shop selling the usual choice of handicrafts.

ART AND ANTIQUES

Art and antique outlets in Mexico City tend to be concentrated in Polanco, the Zona Rosa, San Ángel, and more recently in Roma as well. In Polanco, **Galería López Quiroga**, **Oscar Román**, and the **Galería Misrachi** specialize in contemporary Mexican art. The antique shops in the Zona Rosa, including **Coloniart**, are concentrated around the **Plaza del Ángel**, where an antique market is also held on Saturday mornings. Some of the best known galleries in Roma include **Galería OMR** and **Casa Lamm**. Downtown, the **Monte de Piedad** (see p62) is a pawnshop that sells second-hand jewelry and is well worth a visit.

BOOKS AND NEWSPAPERS

Local newspapers can be purchased from street vendors, whereas international papers, magazines, guidebooks, and novels are all sold at **Sanborns**, the department store, and in top hotels. Two famous bookstores, **Librería Gandhi** and **El Parnaso**, are found in the south of the city.

SWEETS

Mexicans tend to have a very sweet tooth. The city's many quality candy stores include downtown's **Dulcería de Celaya**. The popular **La Flor de Lis** chain is also well known for its tasty sweets and confectionaries.

The Dulcería de Celaya candy store, which attracts business from all over the city

A stall selling fresh produce in the Mercado de la Merced

CIGARS

For cigar aficionados the best specialty shops are **La Casa del Habano** and **La Casa del Fumador**, which both stock a wide range of national and imported cigars, as well as pipe tobaccos. Genuine *Habanos* (Havanas) can be bought here quite reasonably.

MARKETS

Each neighborhood has its local market, and there are also several larger and more specialized markets. All of these are regular shopping places for Mexico City's residents, and give an insight into their daily life. Beware of pickpockets in all markets.

The **Mercado de Sonora** is a sprawling covered market specializing in seasonal wares, such as Christmas decorations and Easter candy. It also has permanent sections selling herbs, toys, and witchcraft accessories. It makes a heady combination of the kitsch and the occult for the few tourists who come here.

Close by is the huge **Mercado de La Merced** *(see p109)*, one of the largest markets, which operates daily. Of the thousands of stalls, the greatest proportion are devoted to fruit, vegetables, and flowers. The remainder sell a variety of other items.

A modern-looking branch of the Liverpool chain store

DEPARTMENT STORES

The two largest department store chains in Mexico are **El Palacio de Hierro** and **Liverpool**, both of which have branches in most of the city's American-style shopping malls. Here shoppers can find anything and everything they might need. Each branch has large collections of international designer fashions, alongside local designs and the store's own brands. For English-language books, reasonably priced souvenirs, photographic equipment, and toiletries, any branch of **Sanborns** is a good bet. In addition, these stores provide a choice of restaurants. Though influenced by Mexican cuisine, they also serve international "fast food" sure to suit all tastes *(see p318)*.

DIRECTORY

CRAFTS AND GIFTS

Bazar del Sábado
San Jacinto 11,
San Ángel.
Tel 56 16 00 82. **www**.
fondasanangel.com.mx

Centro Artesanal de Buenavista
Aldama 187,
Colonia Guerrero.
Tel 55 26 03 15.

Fonart
Patriotismo 691,
Colonia Mixcoac.
Tel 55 63 40 60.
www.fonart.gob.mx

Mercado de la Ciudadela
Balderas, cnr of Emilio
Dondé. **Map** 3 B2.

Mercado de Londres
Londres 154,
Zona Rosa.
Map 2 E4.
Tel 55 33 25 44.

ART AND ANTIQUES

Casa Lamm
Álvaro Obregón 99A. **Map**
2 F5. *Tel* 55 11 08 99.
www.casalamm.com.mx

Coloniart
Estocolmo 37, Zona Rosa.
Map 2 E3. *Tel* 55 14 47 99.

Galería López Quiroga
Aristóteles 169, Esquino
Oracio, Polanco.
Tel 52 80 17 10. **www**.
lopezquiroga.com

Galería Misrachi
Campos Eliseos 215,
local E Polanco.
Tel 52 81 74 56.
www.misrachi.com.mx

Galería OMR
Plaza Río de Janeiro 54,
Colonia Roma. **Map** 2 F4.
Tel 55 11 11 79.
www.galeriaomr.com

Monte de Piedad
Monte de Piedad 7.
Map 4 E2.
Tel 55 18 20 06.

Oscar Román
Julio Verne 14, Polanco.
Tel 52 81 02 70.

Plaza del Ángel
Londres 161, Zona Rosa.
Map 2 E4. *Tel* 52 08 98 28.

BOOKS AND NEWSPAPERS

Librería Gandhi
Miguel Ángel de Quevedo
134, Chimalistac.
Tel 26 25 06 06.

El Parnaso
Carrillo Puerto 2,
Coyoacán.
Tel 56 58 31 75.

Sanborns
Francisco I. Madero 4. **Map**
4 D2. *Tel* 55 18 01 52.
www.sanborns.com.mx

SWEETS

Dulcería de Celaya
Cinco de Mayo 39. **Map**
4 D2 *Tel* 55 21 17 87.

La Flor de Lis
Huichapan 17, Colonia
Condesa. *Tel* 52 86 22 29.

CIGARS

La Casa del Fumador
Moliere 222, Polanco.
Tel 52 81 16 18.

La Casa del Habano
Av Presidente Masarik 393,
Polanco. **Map** 1 A2.
Tel 52 82 10 46.

MARKETS

Mercado de La Merced
Anillo de Circunvalación &
Callejón de Carretones.

Mercado de Sonora
Av Fray Servando Teresa de
Mier, cnr of Circunvalación.

DEPARTMENT STORES

Liverpool
Venustiano Carranza 92.
Map 4 D2.
Tel 51 33 28 00.

El Palacio de Hierro
Av 20 de Noviembre 3.
Tel 57 28 99 05.

ENTERTAINMENT IN MEXICO CITY

Window detail from Salón México

Mexico City offers a wide variety of entertainment. In the evenings you can choose between salsa music joints or traditional *cantinas*. On a Sunday, you can experience folk ballet at the Palacio de Bellas Artes, watch the *charros* (*see p353*) in their dazzling costumes on horseback, or attend a bullfight in the world's largest bullring. There is also always an excellent range of dance, classical music, and opera. There is a full cultural calendar year round in the city, but the main annual event is the Festival del Centro Histórico, which is usually held before Easter, in March or April.

The Palacio de Bellas Artes, home of the Mexican National Symphony Orchestra

ENTERTAINMENT GUIDES AND TICKETS

For information in English on events, *The News* has a "What's on" section on Fridays and Saturdays, and the local paper *Reforma* has daily listings. The weekly Spanish guides, *Laberinto, Tiempo Libre,* and *Dónde Ir* have complete information including a restaurant guide, sports events, and activities for children.

Tickets for almost all events can be bought through **Ticketmaster**, which charges a commission as well as a delivery charge. Sanborns *(see p115)* have Ticketmaster counters where charges are lower. Most theaters and sports stadiums also sell tickets directly. The **Instituto Nacional de Bellas Artes** (INBA) operates several theaters and auditoriums, and has its own ticket booths and information service.

CLASSICAL MUSIC, DANCE, AND THEATER

The National Opera and the National Symphony Orchestra perform alternate seasons at the **Palacio de Bellas Artes**. The building is also host to a wide range of other music and dance events, including the Amalia Hernández Ballet Folklórico. Large scale classical and contemporary music events are held at the **Auditorio Nacional**. The **Sala Ollin Yoliztli** and the **Sala Nezahualtcóyotl** in the UNAM university complex also play host to a range of events.

At the Consejo Nacional de Artes (CNA), an arts complex, the **Auditorio Blas Galindo** is fast becoming an important concert hall for the city.

Contemporary and classical dance programs are held at the **Teatro de la Danza**. The National Dance School performs at the **Teatro Raúl Flores Canelo** at the CNA.

The **Insurgentes, Hidalgo,** and **Centro Cultural Telmex** theaters feature national and international companies.

CANTINAS

Mexico's answer to the local bar is the *cantina*, which is both a simple lunchtime restaurant and a meeting place in the evenings. *Cantinas* were originally frequented exclusively by men, and some still display the sign outside that bans women, children, and men in uniform. *Cantinas* close around midnight, and on Saturdays and Sundays open only at lunchtime.

El Nivel, near the Zócalo, is the oldest *cantina* in the city and houses an interesting art collection. **La Coyoacana**, in Coyoacán *(see p104)*, is also worth visiting.

BARS, CLUBS, AND ROCK MUSIC

Many bars are reviving the downtown area of Mexico City. The bars around the Juárez and Condesa neighborhoods are popular with the young crowd. Nightclubs range from the trendy to the glamorous. Rock concerts are held at the **Auditorio Nacional** or at various smaller venues around the city.

LATIN AMERICAN MUSIC AND MARIACHIS

One of Mexico's most famous bars for *cumbia*, merengue, *danzón*, and salsa music is **Bar León**, favored by

Dancing to authentic Latin American music in Salón México

lovers of Latin American music who appreciate the loud, authentic sounds. The **Salón Tropicana** has three dance floors and its own bands, as well as visiting performers. **Mama Rumba** is favored by a younger, hipper crowd who come for the potent Caribbean cocktails and Cuban music. **Salón México** is a recreation of the legendary venue of the same name *(see p29)*. Plaza Garibaldi *(see p109)* is a traditional last stop for a night out, where mariachi musicians compete to be

heard above each other. In the bars around the square, such as **Tenampa**, you can listen to the music in comfort.

ENTERTAINMENT FOR CHILDREN

Bosque de Chapultepec *(see pp88–9)* has a number of attractions that will keep children entertained, especially **La Feria** (an amusement park), **"Papalote" Museo del Niño**, **Six Flags**, and the **Zoo**.

SPECTATOR SPORTS

Mexicans are avid sports fans, and soccer is a national passion. Matches can be seen at the **Estadio Azteca**. Baseball, played at the **Foro Sol**, also has a large following, Boxing matches are held at the **Arena Coliseo**. Typical Mexican masked wrestling can be

Footballers in action in Mexico City's Estadio Azteca

Mariachis playing in a café on Plaza Garibaldi

experienced at the **Arena México**. Bullfights take place at the **Plaza Monumental de Toros México** on Sunday afternoons. *Charreadas*, trials of traditional equestrian skills *(see p74)*, are held at the **Rancho del Charro**. For more information on spectator sports, see page 353.

DIRECTORY

TICKET SALES

Instituto Nacional de Bellas Artes
Information
Tel 52 80 87 71.
www.inba.com.mx

Ticketmaster
Tel 53 25 90 00.
www.ticketmaster.com.mx

CLASSICAL MUSIC, DANCE, AND THEATER

Auditorio Blas Galindo
CNA, corner of Calzada de Tlalpan & Río Churubusco.
Tel 12 53 94 00.

Auditorio Nacional
Paseo de la Reforma 50.
Tel 52 80 92 50.

Centro Cultural Telmex
Av Cuauhtémoc 19.
Tel 55 14 23 00.

Palacio de Bellas Artes
Corner of Avenida Juárez and Lázaro Cárdenas.
Tel 52 80 87 71.

Sala Nezahualtcóyotl
Centro Cultural Universitario,
Insurgentes Sur 3000, UNAM. *Tel* 56 22 71 28.

Sala Ollin Yoliztli
Periférico Sur 5141.
Tel 56 06 85 58.

Teatro de la Danza
Campo Marte,
Paseo de la Reforma.
Tel 52 80 87 71.

Teatro Hidalgo
Av Hidalgo 23. **Map** 3 C1.
Tel 53 26 54 45.

Teatro Insurgentes
Av Insurgentes Sur 1587.
Tel 56 11 42 53.

Teatro Raúl Flores Canelo
CNA, corner of Calzada de Tlalpan & Río Churubusco.
Tel 12 53 94 00.

CANTINAS

La Coyoacana
Higuera 14, Coyoacán.
Tel 55 54 62 53.

El Nivel
Corner of Moneda and Seminario. **Map** 4 E2.
Tel 55 22 61 84.

LATIN AMERICAN MUSIC AND MARIACHIS

Bar León
Brasil 5.
Tel 55 10 30 93.

Mama Rumba
Querétaro 230.
Tel 55 64 69 20.

Salón México
Callejón de San Juan de Dios 25.
Tel 55 10 99 15.

Salón Tropicana
Lázaro Cárdenas 43.
Tel 55 29 73 16.

Tenampa
Plaza Garibaldi 12.
Tel 55 26 61 76.

ENTERTAINMENT FOR CHILDREN

Chapultepec Zoo
Bosque de Chapultepec, First Section. *Tel* 55 53 62 63. www.chapultepec.df.gob.mx

La Feria
Bosque de Chapultepec, Second Section. *Tel* 52 30 21 21. www.cie.com.mx

"Papalote" Museo del Niño
Bosque de Chapultepec.
Tel 52 37 17 00.

Six Flags
Carretera Picacho–Ajusco 1500. *Tel* 57 28 72 00.
www.sixflags.com.mx

SPECTATOR SPORTS

Arena Coliseo
Perú 77.
Tel 53 25 90 00.

Arena México
Dr. Lavista 189.
Map 3 A4.
Tel 53 25 90 00.

Estadio Azteca
Calzada de Tlalpan 3465.
Tel 54 87 31 00.

Foro Sol
Magdalena Michuca.
Tel 57 64 84 46.

Plaza Monumental de Toros México
Augusto Rodin 241.
Tel 56 11 44 13.
www.fiestabrava.com.mx

Rancho del Charro
Av Constituyentes 500
Tel 52 77 87 10.

MEXICO CITY STREET FINDER

The map below shows the area covered by the city center street map on the following pages. The map references given in the text for centrally located places of interest, hotels, restaurants, shops, and entertainment venues refer to these maps. Sights in San Ángel and Coyoacán are

Visitor to Mexico City

located on the map on page 97, and more distant attractions in Mexico City can be found on the Farther Afield map on page 107. Opposite is a map showing the main highways used for crossing, or getting around, the vast and potentially confusing area that is greater Mexico City.

KEY

▪ Major sight	🚔 Police station	
▪ Place of interest	✚ Church	
▪ Other building	⊠ Post office	
M Metro station	Pedestrian street	
P Parking		
i Tourist information		
✚ Hospital		

SCALE OF MAPS 1–4

0 meters   300

0 yards   300

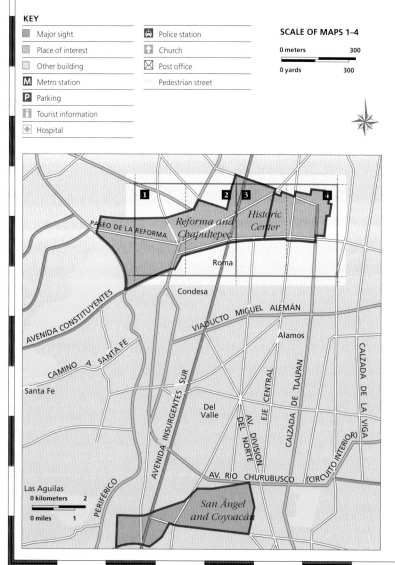

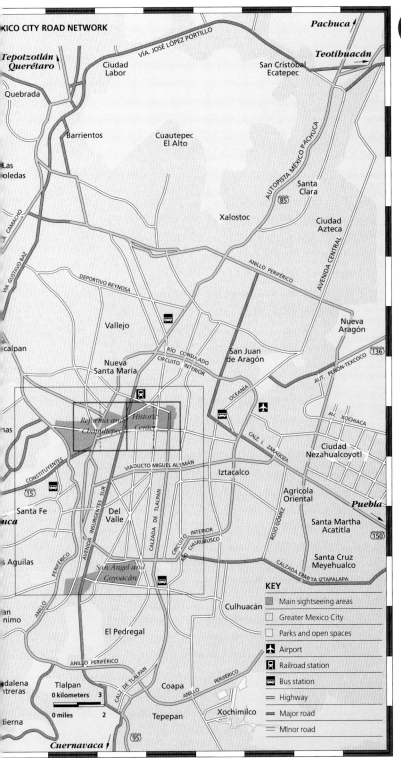

MEXICO CITY ROAD NETWORK

Pachuca

Tepotzotlán
Querétaro

Teotihuacán

Ciudad
Labor

San Cristóbal
Ecatepec

VÍA. JOSÉ LÓPEZ PORTILLO

Quebrada

Barrientos

Cuautepec
El Alto

Las
Arboledas

AUTOPISTA MÉXICO PACHUCA

85

Santa
Clara

VÍA CAMACHO

Ciudad
Azteca

Xalostoc

VÍA GUSTAVO BAZ

AVENIDA CENTRAL

ANILLO PERIFÉRICO

Tlalnepantla

DEPORTIVO REYNOSA

Nueva
Aragón

Vallejo

136

Naucalpan

RÍO CONSULADO

CIRCUITO INTERIOR

San Juan
de Aragón

AUT. PEÑON-TEXCOCO

Nueva
Santa María

OCEANÍA

AV. XOCHIACA

Lomas

*Reforma and
Chapultepec*

*Historic
Center*

CALZ. I. ZARAGOZA

Ciudad
Nezahualcoyotl

VIADUCTO MIGUEL ALEMÁN

Iztacalco

CONSTITUYENTES

Puebla

15

Agrícola
Oriental

Santa Fe

AVENIDA INSURGENTES SUR

CALZADA DE TLALPAN

Del
Valle

CIRCUITO INTERIOR

RÍO CHURUBUSCO

ROJO GÓMEZ

Santa Martha
Acatitla

150

Toluca

Las Águilas

PERIFÉRICO

*San Ángel and
Coyoacán*

Santa Cruz
Meyehualco

CALZADA ERMITA IZTAPALAPA

KEY

ANILLO

San
Jerónimo

Culhuacán

Main sightseeing areas

Greater Mexico City

Parks and open spaces

✈ Airport

🚉 Railroad station

🚌 Bus station

El Pedregal

Magdalena
Contreras

ANILLO PERIFÉRICO

CALZ. DE TLALPAN

Tlalpan

0 kilometers   3

Coapa

PERIFÉRICO

ANILLO

— Highway

— Major road

— Minor road

0 miles   2

Xochimilco

Contierna

Tepepan

95

Cuernavaca

Mexico City Street Finder Index

MEXICO REGION BY REGION

Mexico at a Glance

Mexico is an enormously varied country, and traveling from one part to another can seem like crossing between different worlds. The north is characterized by its deserts, and great mountains and canyons, with the Baja California peninsula as a place apart. The area northwest of the capital has the country's finest colonial architecture. Central and Southern Mexico, and the Gulf Coast region, are most visited for their pre-Columbian ruins.

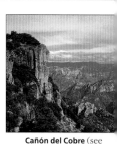

Cañón del Cobre (see pp176–7), *a spectacularly deep and scenic canyon, can be viewed from one of the world's most extraordinary railroads.*

Baja California (see pp162–5) *is popular with visitors from the USA who head especially for the beaches and resorts on its southern tip. In the winter months, whales can be seen off the shores of "Baja."*

NORTHERN MEXICO
(See pp158–79)

THE COLONIAL HEARTLAND
(See pp180–21)

0 kilometers   250

0 miles   250

PACIFIC OCEAN

Guadalajara (see pp188–9) *is dominated by its 16th-century cathedral. It is the largest of the colonial cities to the northwest of Mexico City. Also worth visiting are San Miguel de Allende, Morelia, and Guanajuato.*

◁ **Ocher-colored houses in Campeche, on the Yucatán Peninsula**

El Tajín (see pp242–3) *was home to the Totonac civilization between AD 700 and 900. It is one of the best places in Mexico to see* voladores *dancers perform (see p29).*

Teotihuacán (see pp134–7) *was once the most powerful city of the New World. Its people left behind a fascinating legacy, including the towering Pyramids of the Sun and the Moon.*

Palenque (see pp234–7) *is notable for its fine stucco carvings. Beneath its main temple, the Temple of Inscriptions, is the only known Maya crypt, which was created for Pakal, the ruler of Palenque.*

GULF OF MEXICO

MEXICO CITY

AROUND MEXICO CITY (See pp130–57)

THE GULF COAST (See pp238–55)

SOUTHERN MEXICO (See pp212–37)

THE YUCATÁN PENINSULA (See pp256–87)

Oaxaca (see pp222–5) *is an elegant colonial city with a number of churches and museums, and two lively markets. This relief of the Virgin is found over the main door to the cathedral.*

Chichén Itzá (see pp274–6) *is the best preserved of Mexico's Maya ruins, with temples, an observatory, and the largest ballcourt in Mexico. It flourished from the 11th to the 13th century.*

AROUND MEXICO CITY

GUERRERO (NORTH) · HIDALGO · MEXICO STATE
MORELOS · PUEBLA · TLAXCALA

nowcapped volcanoes, among them Mexico's highest peaks, tower over the country's central plateau – a series of vast plains and broad valleys at altitudes of around 2,000 m (6,550 ft). Centered on the Valley of Mexico, the country's heart for over two millennia, this region has an unparalleled collection of stunning pre-Columbian and colonial monuments, set against dramatic natural backdrops.

These highlands were densely populated even before the arrival of the Spanish in 1519. Great civilizations flourished here and built extensive cities and awesome ceremonial sites such as Tula and Teotihuacán. Spanish missionaries fanned out from here to explore and pacify the vast territories later consolidated as New Spain. They dotted the region with fortress-like convents and opulent churches such as San Francisco Javier in Tepotzotlán. Puebla, the provincial capital east of Mexico City, with its exuberant ecclesiastical and secular architecture, was one of the colony's most important cities. Meanwhile, the discovery of precious metals sparked the development of mining towns, most notably the picturesque Taxco.

Today, busy highways radiate from Mexico City to burgeoning cities in the neighboring states. So far, however, the incursions of modern Mexico into the region have not significantly disturbed the area's natural beauty, protected in part by a series of national parks.

A rich volcanic soil accounts for the region's endless fields of crops – rice and sugar cane at lower altitudes in the south, grain and vegetables elsewhere. The land once belonged to huge estates, run from imposing haciendas. After the Revolution, much of it became communal, and it remains the principal means of subsistence for the region's rural population, many of whom are Nahua and Otomí Indians, the two largest of Mexico's indigenous groups.

The ruins of the great city of Teotihuacán, one of the most fascinating pre-Columbian sites in Mexico

◁ Crafts on display in a market in the colonial town of Taxco

Exploring Around Mexico City

The routes north of Mexico City lead to a colonial treasure trove at the Museo Nacional del Virreinato, and to the pyramids of Tula and Teotihuacán, the latter Mexico's most visited pre-Columbian site. To the east, beyond Popocatépetl and Iztaccíhuatl volcanoes, is the splendid colonial city of Puebla, a good base for visiting isolated Cantona and the ancient murals at Cacaxtla. The western part of the region has cool forests and scenic lakes, while to the south warmer weather attracts visitors to busy Cuernavaca and beautiful Taxco, famed for its silversmiths and Churrigueresque church.

Dome of the Iglesia de la Compañía in Puebla

SIGHTS AT A GLANCE

The Pyramid of the Sun, the largest structure at Teotihuacán

◁ **For additional map symbols** *see back flap*

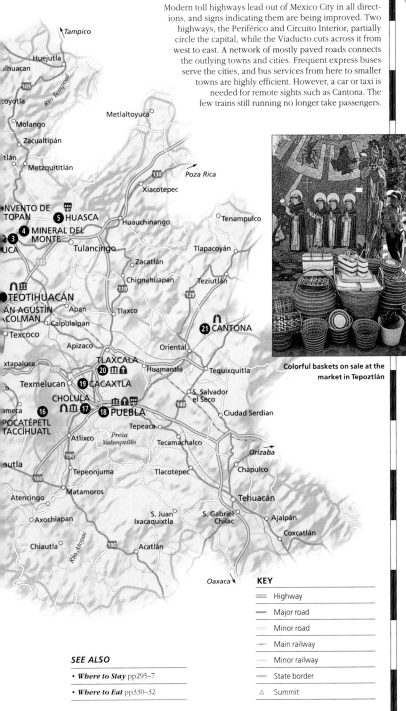

GETTING AROUND

Modern toll highways lead out of Mexico City in all directions, and signs indicating them are being improved. Two highways, the Periférico and Circuito Interior, partially circle the capital, while the Viaducto cuts across it from west to east. A network of mostly paved roads connects the outlying towns and cities. Frequent express buses serve the cities, and bus services from here to smaller towns are highly efficient. However, a car or taxi is needed for remote sights such as Cantona. The few trains still running no longer take passengers.

Colorful baskets on sale at the market in Tepoztlán

SEE ALSO

KEY

═══	Highway
▬▬▬	Major road
∷∷∷	Minor road
⊷⊷	Main railway
——	Minor railway
▬▬	State border
△	Summit

Teotihuacán **①**

Mask on Temple of Quetzalcoatl

Its name meaning "the place where men become gods," Teotihuacán is one of the most impressive cities of the ancient world. Founded before the Christian era, this colossal urban center once housed up to 125,000 people and covered over 20 sq km (8 sq miles). It dominated life in the region for 500 years before being destroyed (possibly by its own people) and abandoned, around AD 650. Later, the site was held sacred by the Aztecs, who believed it had been built by giants. The ceremonial center, with its temples, palaces, and pyramids, bears witness to the city's splendor but has revealed little about its creators and inhabitants. Their origin, way of life, and even demise remain a mystery.

The Temple of Quetzalcoatl with the Pyramid of the Sun behind

Entrance 2

The Superimposed Buildings (Edificios Superpuestos)

Avenue of the Dead
This wide avenue runs the length of the present site but once stretched much farther toward the south. It was named by the Aztecs who mistakenly believed that the buildings lining it were royal tombs.

Palaces of Tetitla, Atetelco, Zacuala, and Yayahuala *(see p137)*

Entrance 1

Mexico City

Restaurant

The Citadel

★ Temple of Quetzalcoatl
Masks of the plumed serpent Quetzalcoatl and a god sometimes identified as rain god Tlaloc decorate this temple. Built around AD 200, it was later covered by a pyramid, which has now been partially removed.

Living quarters for the ruling classes were probably situated here.

| 0 meters | 250 |
| 0 yards | 250 |

★ **Pyramid of the Moon**
Although smaller than the Pyramid of the Sun, this four-tiered structure rises just as high, due to a difference in ground level. It offers the best view of the site.

VISITORS' CHECKLIST

Mexico State. Mex 132D, 47 km (29 miles) NE of Mexico City. **Tel** (594) 956 00 52. from Central Camionera del Norte, Mexico City. 7am–6pm daily (last adm: 5pm). **Museum** 7am–5pm. **www**.inah.gob.mx

★ **Quetzalpapalotl Palace Complex**
This group of buildings has fine carvings and murals (see p136).

Entrance 3

Plaza of the Moon

Entrance 4

Palace of Tepantitla
(see p137)

Entrance 5

Museum *(see p137)*

Jaguar Mural
A fragment of mural on a wall between two staircases depicts a colossal jaguar set against water motifs.

★ **Pyramid of the Sun**
This immense pyramid ranks among the biggest in the world (see p137). *Probably completed during the 2nd century AD, it is made of adobe bricks and earth, covered with gravel and stone. This would have been coated with brightly painted stucco. Chambers and a tunnel have been found beneath the structure.*

STAR FEATURES

★ Temple of Quetzalcoatl

★ Pyramid of the Moon

★ Quetzalpapalotl Palace Complex

★ Pyramid of the Sun

Quetzalpapalotl Palace Complex

This maze of residential and temple structures grew slowly over several centuries. The last part to be built was probably the elegant Palace of Quetzalpapalotl, uncovered in 1962 and reconstructed with mostly original materials. It sits atop the now buried Temple of the Feathered Conches (2nd–3rd century AD). The Jaguar Palace, just to the west, has a large courtyard faced by a portico and a stepped temple base.

The Palace of Quetzalpapalotl *is named for the mythological creatures (bird-butterflies) carved into its courtyard pillars. They have obsidian eyes and are surrounded by water and fire symbols.*

Entrance to lower level

Murals in the Jaguar Palace *show plumed jaguars playing musical instruments made from feathered shells.*

Decorative merlons symbolizing the calendar crown the courtyard.

Exit from lower level

Entrance to Palace of Quetzalpapalotl

Plaza of the Moon

The Temple of the Feathered Conches *is an older structure that archaeologists discovered buried beneath the Palace of Quetzalpapalotl. It sits on a platform adorned with brilliantly colored murals such as this one, which depict green parrot-like birds spewing water from their beaks. Reliefs of feathered conches and four-petaled flowers decorate the temple façade.*

A stone serpent's head *of enormous proportions juts out from the top of a steep staircase and guards the porticoed entrance to the Palace of Quetzalpapalotl.*

Exploring Teotihuacán

In order to appreciate the grandeur and colossal scale of this awesome site, visitors should be prepared for long walks over uneven ground and stiff climbs up steep stairways – all at an altitude of 2,300 m (7,550 ft) and often under a hot tropical sun. Comfortable shoes, a hat, and sunblock are a must, plus basic rain gear in summer.

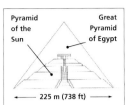

Pyramid of the Sun | Great Pyramid of Egypt

←— 225 m (738 ft) —→

TWO PYRAMIDS

The Pyramid of the Sun stands on a base of very similar dimensions to that of the Great Pyramid of Egypt, but it is only half the height – 65 m (213 ft), as against 144 m (472 ft). It consists of about 2.5 million tonnes of stone and earth, compared with the Great Pyramid's 6.5 million.

Partially restored mural depicting feathered coyotes, at Atetelco

The Museum

The on-site museum is located just south of the Pyramid of the Sun. It displays artifacts found at Teotihuacán, explanatory maps and diagrams, and, beneath the glass floor of its main hall, a scale model of the city. The shady gardens outside are a good place to rest during a tour of the site. They are planted with botanical species native to the area and decorated with original Teotihuacán sculptures.

Outlying Palaces

Several ancient dwelling complexes are situated beyond the fence and road that ring the site. Some 500 m (0.3 miles) east of the Pyramid of the Sun lies the **Palace of Tepantitla**, which contains the most important and colorful murals discovered so far at Teotihuacán. These include representations of elaborately dressed priests, the rain god Tlaloc, and his carefree paradise, Tlalocan, where miniature human figures frolic in an Eden-like setting.

Bird spewing water, in the museum

Just west of the site, and best reached by car, are four other palaces: Tetitla, Atetelco, Zacuala, and Yayahuala. **Tetitla** is a maze-like complex of more than 120 walls, showing remnants of refined frescoes depicting birds, jaguars, priests, and various deities. **Atetelco** is distinguished by a miniature altar in one courtyard and, in another, stunning red murals of jaguars and coyotes with feathered headdresses. **Zacuala** and **Yayahuala** are extensive complexes with sophisticated drainage systems, and vestiges of wall paintings in their many rooms, corridors, courtyards, and porticoes.

THE UNEARTHING OF TEOTIHUACÁN

Bones found on the site

For more than 1,000 years after its decline, the crumbled ruins of Teotihuacán remained hidden below a thick layer of earth and vegetation. Despite being venerated by the Aztecs, the site was never noticed by Cortés and his men when they passed by during their retreat from Tenochtitlán in 1520. The structures visible today, a mere tenth of the city, were excavated at digs that began in 1864 and continue to this day. Early 20th-century reconstructions partially destroyed and distorted some of the principal edifices, but since then more systematic explorations have resulted in the unearthing of the Temple of Quetzalcoatl in the 1920s and the Palace of Quetzalpapalotl 40 years later. Chambers were discovered under the Pyramid of the Sun in 1971, and in 1998 archaeologists found human remains and offerings inside the Pyramid of the Moon.

Bird fresco at Tetitla, excavated in the 1950s

The Plateresque façade of the church of San Agustín Acolman

San Agustín Acolman ❷

Mexico State. Acolman, off Mex 85, 38 km (24 miles) NE of Mexico City. 🚌 Acolman. 🕐 Tue–Sun. 🕏

One of Mexico's oldest monasteries, San Agustín Acolman was founded in 1536 by Augustinian monks sent here to convert the local Indians. It is notable for its atrium, a Christian version of the pre-Columbian ceremonial plaza, where crowds of Indian disciples would gather to hear the new religion preached from a chapel balcony above. The fortress-like building, now housing colonial paintings and sculptures, is typical of New Spain's early monasteries.

The forbidding aspect of the monastery is softened, however, by the adjoining church's beautiful Plateresque façade, which is characterized by classic Italian Renaissance columns, richly decorated door arches, and a choir window replicating the portal below. The sparse interior of the 57-m (187-ft) nave is notable only for its apse, which boasts Gothic fan vaulting and is adorned with rich frescoes.

Detail on façade of San Agustín Acolman

Pachuca ❸

Hidalgo. 🗠 245,000. 🚌 🚹 Av Madero 702, (771) 107 18 10. 🎏 Feria Regional de Pachuca (Oct).

Pachuca, capital of Hidalgo state, lies in the heart of one of Mexico's richest mining areas. The center of town, with its steep, narrow lanes and small squares, retains some buildings from the two mining booms of the 16th and 18th centuries.

Undoubtedly, the most significant colonial complex is the late 16th-century **Ex-Convento de San Francisco** and its adjoining church. The church contains the remains of the 3rd-century martyr St. Columba, whose mummified body was brought here in the 18th century. Part of the massive monastery building houses the **Fototeca Nacional** (National Photographic Archive) and the **Museo de Fotografía**. The latter has exhibits on the history of photography and shows selections from the 1 million photos on file. One section is dedicated to the Casasola Archive, an outstanding chronicle of the Mexican Revolution and post-Revolutionary daily life. It is also worth seeing the photographs and mining equipment at the **Museo de Minería** and the mineral samples at the **Museo de Mineralogía**. The tower in the main plaza, the 40-m

(130-ft) Neo-Classical **Reloj Monumental** (Monumental Clock), has an eight-bell carillon made by the creators of Big Ben in London.

Environs

The hills of **El Chico**, a vast national park north of Pachuca, are very popular with hikers, fishermen, and rock climbers.

🏛 **Fototeca Nacional and Museo de Fotografía**
Casasola. **Tel** (771) 714 36 53. 🕐 Tue–Sun. 🕏 reserve in advance. 🚫

🏛 **Museo de Minería**
Mina 110. **Tel** (771) 715 09 76. 🕐 Mon–Fri. 🕏 🕏 🕏

🏛 **Museo de Mineralogía**
Abasolo 600. **Tel** (771) 717 20 00, ext. 1302. 🕐 Mon–Fri.

Mineral del Monte ❹

Hidalgo. 🗠 11,000. 🚌 🚹 Rubén Licona Ruiz 1, (771) 797 05 10, ext. 1302. 🎏 Día del Rosario (Jan 1).

Also known as Real del Monte, this mining town, at an altitude of 2,700 m (8,800 ft), used to be the richest in the area. Gold and silver were discovered here before the Conquest (see p43), and the Spanish started mining in the mid-1500s. The mines were later abandoned, but reopened in the late 1730s under Pedro Romero de Terreros.

The town's steep streets, stairways, and small squares are lined with low buildings, some dating back to colonial times. The houses with high

The charming colors of houses on the central plaza in Mineral del Monte

Symmetrically patterned fresco at the Convento de Actopan

sloping roofs and chimneys indicate a Cornish influence, the legacy left by the 350 Cornishmen employed by the English company that ran the mines between 1824 and 1848. They are also responsible for *pastes*, a local specialty based on the Cornish pasty, as well as for introducing soccer to Mexico.

Huasca ❺

Hidalgo. 🏠 600. 🚌 to Pachuca. 🛈 Plaza Principal, (771) 792 07 47. 🎉 San Sebastián (Jan 20).

The picturesque village of Huasca is best known for its *haciendas de beneficio*, haciendas where mineral ores were refined. One of the most visited is **San Miguel Regla**, 3 km (2 miles) northeast of town. It is now a hotel *(see p295)* and offers guided tours of its *beneficio* installations. More impressive is **Santa María Regla**, a little farther away, which has vaulted cellars, and patios with stone drag mills and melting ovens. From here visitors can access the spectacular 15-km (9-mile) canyon **Prismas Basálticos**, whose walls are made up of red and ocher basalt hexagons.

Adam and Eve fresco, Convento de Actopan

🏛 **Santa María Regla**
7 km (4.5 miles) NE of Huasca. **Tel** (771) 151 67 08. ◯ daily. 🎥 👍

Convento de Actopan ❻

Hidalgo. Actopan, 36 km (22 miles) NW of Pachuca. 🚌 Actopan. ◯ daily. 🎥 👣 reserve in advance. 👍

This imposing structure, built in the 1550s, is one of Mexico's most remarkable and best preserved 16th-century fortress-monasteries. Even more spectacular than its Plateresque church façade, square Moorish tower, and vaulted open chapel are its frescoes, which are considered the most beautiful and extensive from this era in Mexico.

The finest include the portraits of saints on the main stairs and the depiction of hermits in the De Profundis hall, which is in a style reminiscent of native codices. Perhaps most impressive of all are the naïve scenes of heaven and hell in the open chapel.

Environs
In Ixmiquilpan, 40 km (25 miles) farther north, stands the **Ex-Convento de San Miguel Arcángel**. Now a museum, it displays some fine frescoes that incorporate Indian warriors, Biblical scenes, and pre-Columbian figures.

🏛 **Ex-Convento de San Miguel Arcángel**
Av Angeles, Ixmiquilpan. ◯ daily.

FIESTAS AROUND MEXICO CITY

Chalma Pilgrimages *(Jan 6, Easter week, May 3, Jul 1)*, Chalma *(see p145)*. Hordes of pilgrims, laden with colorful flowers, can be seen making their way to the shrine of El Señor de Chalma – by foot, on their knees, by car, bicycle, or bus. Pentecost celebrations on May 3 include traditional dances by the splendidly attired Concheros dancers.

Chalma pilgrims armed with bunches of flowers

Fiesta de los Tiznados *(Jan 21)*, Tepoztlán *(see p148)*. Revelers smear themselves with ash in remembrance of the ancient Tepoztec king, who fled his enemies disguised as a peasant. **Battle of Puebla** *(May 5)*, Puebla *(see pp150–53)*. The 1862 Mexican victory over the French *(see p52)* is re-enacted, with military parades and fireworks. **Fiesta de la Virgen de la Caridad** *(mid Aug)*, Huamantla *(see p157)*. On the first Sunday of the fiesta the image of the Virgin is carried over 5 km (3 miles) of sawdust carpet, and her church is decorated. The following Sunday, bulls run through the streets as part of the *Huamantlada*. **Reto al Tepozteco** *(Sep 8)*, Tepoztlán *(see p148)*. Following tradition, local villagers race one another up Tepozteco Hill, before consuming copious quantities of *pulque (see p325)*.

Museo Nacional del Virreinato ❼

The country's most complete collection of colonial art and artifacts, one of its finest Baroque churches, and a splendid former Jesuit college built in the 17th and 18th centuries together make up this stunning museum covering Mexico's viceregal era. The church and college buildings, a vast complex with courtyards and gardens in the quaint village of Tepotzotlán, were nearly complete when the Jesuits were expelled from New Spain in 1767. They were extensively restored and opened as a museum in 1964. Exhibits include treasures preserved in situ as well as pieces brought here from other collections around the country.

Gardens
Formerly an orchard, the peaceful gardens have a chapel and an aqueduct.

Claustro de los Naranjos
This courtyard, once a place of meditation for novices, is filled with orange trees.

Ivory Statues
These figures of the Virgin Mary and Christ show the Asian features characteristic of religious carvings created in the Orient. They were probably brought to New Spain from the Philippines.

Stairs to lower level

Stairs to upper level

Claustro de los Aljibes

GALLERY GUIDE
Most of the collection is displayed on the entrance level of the former college building. The upper floor contains exhibits on artisan guilds, convent workshops, and female religious orders, while the lower level (not shown) houses the old kitchen, rare stone sculptures, temporary exhibits, and the museum store.

★ **Capilla Doméstica**
The chapel was for the exclusive use of college residents. Profuse decorations include paintings, statuettes, reliquaries, mirrors, and polychrome plasterwork, all effective means of inspiring religious awe in the students during services.

Iglesia de San Pedro

Atrio de los Olivos

Cristo del Árbol

The so-called "Christ of the Tree" was carved from a single piece of wood and then painted. The anonymous artist was part of a sculptors' guild active in the late 17th century.

Claustro de los Aljibes

Upper level

Portraits of nuns adorned with crowns and flowers are exhibited here.

VISITORS' CHECKLIST

Mexico State. Plaza Hidalgo, Tepotzotlán, 44 km (27 miles) N of Mexico City. *Tel* 58 76 27 71. from Central Camionera del Norte, Mexico City. 9am–6pm Tue–Sun (last adm: 5:45pm). Sun free. in advance.

Relicario de San Pedro y San Pablo

This late 16th-century reliquary of St. Peter and St. Paul is made of embossed gold-plated silver and compares with European examples of the same period. A wealthy miner commissioned it as a gift to the Jesuit order.

Sacristy

At the entrance to the sacristy is this Baroque washbasin of finely worked limestone topped by a polychrome wooden carving. In the sacristy are paintings by Miguel Cabrera (1695–1768).

Entrance to Iglesia de San Francisco Javier

★ Iglesia de San Francisco Javier

The interior of the church (see pp142–3) is awash with ornate detail, such as this painted figure in the Camarín de la Virgen, a side chapel.

Entrance to restaurant

Entrance to museum

STAR FEATURES

★ Capilla Doméstica

★ Iglesia de San Francisco Javier

KEY

☐ Exhibition space

▨ Rooms of special interest

☐ Other accessible areas

Iglesia de San Francisco Javier

Carved angel, Camarín de la Virgen

Constructed in the late 1600s, this majestic Baroque church is famous for its splendid 18th-century additions: the richly decorated Churrigueresque façade and tower, the exuberant gold altars, a trio of unusual chapels on one side, and the Miguel Cabrera murals in the chancel and cross vaults. The façade and interior are both prime examples of Mexican High Baroque. Together they form a harmonious whole equaled only by Santa Prisca in Taxco *(see p147)* and San Cayetano near Guanajuato *(see p205)*.

The altar to St. Stanislaus Kostka honors a Polish Jesuit who served as a model to the novices and students of the institution.

★ Main Altar
The most imposing of the altars in the church is dedicated to St. Francis Xavier, patron saint of the Jesuit college.

Entrance from museum

The altar to the Virgin of Guadalupe centers on a Miguel Cabrera painting of the patron saint of Mexico.

The Casa de Loreto is said to be a replica of the Virgin Mary's Nazareth home, which angels moved to Loreto in Italy when the Muslims invaded the Holy Land. A 17th-century image of the Virgin of Loreto adorns the gold altar in the otherwise sober interior.

Corridor

Corridor

★ Camarín de la Virgen
This profusely decorated octagonal chamber once served as a dressing room for the Virgin of Loreto – the statue's vestments and jewels were changed regularly. The beautiful dome is shaped like a papal tiara.

★ Relicario de San José
Built to house relics revered by the Jesuits, this chapel resembles the inside of a treasure chest.

Dome

The dome rising above the intersection of the Latin Cross nave is best seen from a viewpoint in the museum (see pp140–41).

The altar to St. Ignatius Loyola shows the founder of the Jesuits holding a book displaying the order's crest and motto.

Pulpit

The bell tower has 13 bells hanging on three levels under a tiled dome topped by a filigreed iron cross.

Altar to the Virgen de la Luz

A multitude of cherubs and angels surrounds the central image of the Virgin and Child; one proffers a basket containing souls from purgatory. The pulpit (beside the altar) is from a church in Mexico City.

Façade

The imagery and style of the frontispiece echoes that of the altars inside, while the abundance of finely carved limestone prepares the visitor for the brilliant interior.

Estípite Pilasters

So-called estípite *pilasters form the verticals of the altars. Inspired by the proportions of the human figure, estípites taper off at the base, thus appearing to be upside down. Many are decorated with faces.*

STAR FEATURES

★ Main Altar

★ Camarín de la Virgen

★ Relicario de San José

The towering Atlantes, standing guard on the Pyramid of the Morning Star at Tula

Tula ⑧

Hidalgo. Off Mex 57, 85 km (53 miles) N of Mexico City. 🚌 *Tula de Allende then taxi.* 🚻 *daily.* 📷

The most important Toltec site in Mexico, Tula flourished as a great urban center from AD 900–1200, after the decline of Teotihuacán *(see pp134–7)* and prior to the rise of Tenochtitlán *(see pp41–2)*. At its peak, the city covered up to 16 sq km (6 sq miles) and had an estimated population of 40,000. Then inner strife, invasions, and fire destroyed the Toltec empire and this, its capital. Only remnants of the main palaces, temples, and ballcourts survive on a windswept hill overlooking the small town of Tula de Allende.

The site is most famous for its giant stone sculptures, the Atlantes. At a height of 4.6 m (15 ft), these four warrior figures in battle gear crown the Pyramid of Tlahuizcalpantecuhtli, or the Morning Star. Together with a massive serpent and other pillars, they probably once supported an ornately carved roof. (Note that parts of the sculptures are reproductions.) The base of the temple and the Coatepantli, or Serpent Wall, on its northern flank, are decorated with carved friezes of serpents, eagles, and jaguars, some devouring human hearts.

Certain stylistic elements at Tula – such as the column-filled Palacio Quemado (Burnt Palace), the *chacmool* sculptures, and the huge size of Ballcourt No. 2 – underline the site's similarity to the Maya city of Chichén Itzá *(see pp274–6)*. Legend tells that Toltec king Topiltzín was driven out of Tula and fled to the Yucatán Peninsula where he ushered in a cultural renaissance. Recent theories dispute this, however, suggesting that the similarities are a result of Maya influence on Tula, not vice versa.

Valle de Bravo ⑨

Mexico State. 🏠 21,500. 🚌 🚹 *Antiguo Palacio Municipal, (726) 269 62 00 or 01800 69 69 696 (toll free).* 📷 *Santa Cruz (May 3), San Francisco (Oct 4).*

Set among pine-covered volcanic mountains, this pretty colonial town traces its origins back to the earliest days of Spanish rule. It achieved its current popularity after the construction of an artificial lake in the 1950s. "Valle" offers an equable climate, a wide range of sports (especially hang gliding, horseback riding, and waterskiing), and stunning scenery. The landscape around the town and lake is perfect for hiking, and trails wind past mountain streams, cornfields, and patches of wildflowers.

Easy access from Mexico City and a lively nightlife make the town a favorite weekend destination for the capital's élite, but during the week peace returns to the cobbled streets.

The pastel tones of Templo de la Santa Veracruz in Toluca

Toluca ⑩

Mexico State. 🏠 665,600. 🚶 🚌 🚹 *1st de Mayo corner Robert Bosch, (722) 275 68 91.* 📷 *Virgen del Carmen (Jul 16).*

The capital city of Mexico State is, at 2,680 m (8,790 ft) above sea level, the highest state capital in the country.

Founded by the Spaniards in the late 17th century, Toluca is full of fine buildings. In the city center, near Plaza de los Mártires, are the 18th-century **Templo de la Santa Veracruz** and the 19th-century **Portales**, a series of arched walkways lined with cafés and shops. To the north is the **Museo de Bellas Artes**, which exhibits Mexican art from the last four centuries. Nearby, the **Cosmo Vitral Jardín Botánico** shows botanical specimens in the beautiful old market, its walls and ceiling ablaze with colorful stained glass. Every Friday, Toluca plays host to what is thought to be the country's largest market.

The lake at Valle de Bravo, popular with watersports enthusiasts

To the southeast, the suburb of **Metepec** is famous for its brightly colored, ceramic *árboles de la vida* (trees of life; *see pp348–9)*, loosely based on the story of Adam and Eve; examples can be purchased.

Environs
Just 8 km (5 miles) west of Toluca is the **Centro Cultural Mexiquense**, a large complex of museums devoted to modern art, local history, and regional crafts.

The extinct, snow-capped **Nevado de Toluca** volcano, Mexico's fourth highest mountain at 4,690 m (15,387 ft), is a 45-km (28-mile) drive southwest. A dirt road leads to the top, and hikers can descend into the crater.

The hilltop ceremonial center of **Teotenango** is 25 km (16 miles) south of Toluca. Dating from AD 900, the extensive site features several restored pyramids, plazas, a ballcourt, and a museum.

🏛 **Museo de Bellas Artes**
102 Santos Degollado Poniente.
Tel (722) 215 53 29. ☐ Tue–Sun.
🖼 Wed & Sun free. 🚫

🌿 **Cosmo Vitral Jardín Botánico**
Plaza Garibay. *Tel* (722) 214 67 85.
☐ Tue–Sun. 🖼 📷 ♿

🏛 **Centro Cultural Mexiquense**
Av Morelos Oriente 302. *Tel* (722) 274 14 00. ☐ Tue–Sun. 🖼 Tue free.

View of the town below from the lofty ruins of Malinalco

The stained-glass ceiling of Cosmo Vitral Jardín Botánico in Toluca

Malinalco ⓫

Mexico State. Off Mex 55, 70 km (43 miles) SE of Toluca.
🚌 *Malinalco town*. ☐ *Tue–Sun*.
🖼 www.inah.gob.mx

Hewn from a steep volcanic mountainside, this Aztec ceremonial center sits on a narrow ledge 20-minutes' climb above the town of Malinalco. Begun in 1501, it was still unfinished at the time of the Spanish conquest.

Its main structure, the House of the Eagle, is carved entirely out of the rock. The doorway represents the fanged mouth of a serpent, and the circular chamber inside has integrated sculptures of jaguars and eagles. The building is thought to have been used for initiation ceremonies of high-ranking Aztec knights. Behind it stand the remains of the Temple of the Sun and the Tzinacalli Edifice, where the bodies of knights killed in combat were burned and deified.

Environs
Chalma, a small village in a deep gorge 12 km (7 miles) east of Malinalco, attracts crowds of pilgrims all year *(see p139)*. They venerate an image of Christ that is said to have miraculously replaced a pagan statue in 1533.

Taxco ⓬

See pp146–7.

Xochicalco ⓭

Morelos. Off Mex 95, 40 km (25 miles) SW of Cuernavaca.
🚌 *Alpuyeca then taxi*. ☐ *daily*.
🖼 www.inah.gob.mx

The extensive ruins of Xochicalco, an important city-state in pre-Columbian times, lie on a plateau offering splendid views. The city rose to prominence after the decline of Teotihuacán and flourished from AD 700 to 900, before being eclipsed by the rise of the Toltecs in the region.

About 30 per cent of the site has so far been unearthed, including three ballcourts and the remains of several pyramidal structures. An on-site museum displays artifacts found during archaeological work.

Pyramid of the Plumed Serpent at Xochicalco

The Pyramid of the Plumed Serpent, excavated in 1777, is considered one of the most beautiful monuments in the country. It shows remarkably well-preserved bas-reliefs featuring serpents, figures carved in a distinctly Maya style, and glyphs. One theory suggests that the pyramid commemorates a meeting of astronomers from throughout Mesoamerica.

Another highlight is the Observatory, a large underground cave with a narrow shaft bored 8 m (26 ft) through the rock. Twice a year, on May 14–15 and July 28–29, the sun casts the hexagonal image of the shaft on the chamber floor.

Street-by-Street: Taxco ⑫

Image of the Virgin, Santa Prisca

Set against a spectacular rugged mountainside, 1,800 m (6,000 ft) above sea level, Taxco is one of the least spoiled colonial towns in Mexico. The Spaniards were drawn to the area in 1522 by Aztec tales of rich mineral deposits, and the subsequent silver boom lasted for 100 years. The town's fortunes have been revived twice since, with the discovery of new lodes by José de la Borda in the 18th century, and the arrival of William Spratling in 1932, who established it as a center for silversmiths. There are fine views of the town from the *teleférico* (cable car).

View across the tiled roofs of Taxco

Casa Borda
Overlooking the main square, this house was built by the Borda family in 1759 for the parish priest. Today, it holds exhibitions by local artists.

PLAZUELA DE BERNAL

PLAZA BORD

The Casa de Figueroa was built for the Count of Cadena. It has a dark and interesting history involving subterfuge and murder.

Plaza Borda
This intimate and lively square is lined with charming old buildings. There are numerous restaurants and bars nearby. In addition, the area abounds with silver shops, filled with the high-quality pieces for which Taxco's many silversmiths are famous.

KEY

━ ━ ━ Suggested route

STAR SIGHTS

★ Casa Humboldt

★ Iglesia de Santa Prisca

OJEDA

CUAU

| 0 meters | 25 |
| 0 yards | 25 | Acapulco

★ **Museo de Arte Virreinal Casa Humboldt**
This beautifully maintained building is named after Baron von Humboldt, the German naturalist, who spent a night here in 1803. It contains a well-organized museum.

Cable car
Mexico City

LLE JUAN RUIZ DE ALARCON

DELGADO

CALLE DE LA VERACRUZ

EL ARCO

VISITORS' CHECKLIST

Guerrero. 🚶 48,000. 🚌 Av de los Plateros 310, (762) 622 01 31. 🚏 Av de los Plateros 126, (762) 622 07 98. 🎉 Santa Prisca y San Sebastián (Jan), Feria Nacional de la Plata (Nov/Dec). **Museo de Arte Virreinal Casa Humboldt** *Tel* (762) 622 55 01. ◯ Tue–Sun. **Museo Guillermo Spratling** *Tel* (762) 622 16 60. ◯ Tue–Sun. 🎫 Sun free. 🚫 📷

Museo Guillermo Spratling contains William Spratling's collection of pre-Columbian artifacts and works of art from around the world.

Santa Prisca's octagonal dome is covered with colorful tiles. Rising behind the church's twin towers, it is an unmistakable landmark that can be seen from all over the city.

★ **Iglesia de Santa Prisca**
This magnificent church, with its Churrigueresque façade and ornate sculptures, dominates the Plaza Borda. It was paid for by José (Joseph) de la Borda, who made his fortune by discovering important deposits of silver. No expense was spared in construction, which took seven years (1751–58).

Bar Bertha
claims to be where the Margarita cocktail (*see p325*) was invented.

Local Market
Off the south side of the Plaza Borda is Taxco's bustling market. Stalls laden with fresh produce, basketware, and local crafts crowd the narrow steps.

The imposing façade of the Catedral de la Asunción

Cuernavaca ⑭

Morelos. 🏚 338,000. 🚌 ⓘ Av Morelos Sur 187, (777) 314 38 72. 🎭 Feria de la Flor (Easter), Feria de Tlaltenango (Sep 8). www.morelostravel.com

Cuernavaca, inhabited since 1200 BC, is one of the oldest cities in the country. Originally called Cuauhnáhuac ("Place of the Whispering Trees"), it was renamed Cuernavaca ("Cow's Horn") by the Spanish. Today it is a popular weekend destination for visitors from Mexico City.

The **Palacio de Cortés** was built by the Spanish on the site of the Aztec pyramids they had destroyed. It served as Cortés's residence until his return to Spain in 1540. Known for a series of 1930 Diego Rivera murals depicting Mexico's history, it also contains the Museo Regional Cuauhnáhuac, a fine collection of archaeological and historical artifacts.

The fortress-like **Catedral de la Asunción**, dating from the 1520s, has refurbished murals thought to have been painted by artists brought over from China or the Philippines in the early days of Spanish trade. The **Museo Robert Brady**, situated in a former cloister of the cathedral, holds

the extensive art and craft collection of this American artist.

The well laid-out **Jardín Borda**, created by the former silver magnate José de la Borda (see pp146–7) in the 18th century, became a popular retreat for the Emperor Maximilian and his young wife (see p53).

To the east is the **Taller Siqueiros**, which is dedicated to the work of the great Mexican muralist David Siqueiros. Revolutionary politics shaped his life and work, and fired the revolutionary aesthetic behind his ambitious projects. His studio is now a museum.

Environs

About 25 km (16 miles) northwest of the town is the beautiful **Lagunas de Zempoala Park**, with its six lakes fringed by dense forests. Only 10 km (6 miles) of the 70 km **Cacahuamilpa Caverns** have been explored. Around 20 of the majestic chambers, many more than 40 meters (120 ft) high, are illuminated.

🏛 **Palacio de Cortés**
Av Leyva 100. **Tel** (777) 312 81 71. ◻ Tue–Sun. 🎟 ⓘ reserve in advance. ⓘ

🏛 **Museo Robert Brady**
Netzahualcóyotl 4. **Tel** (777) 318 85 54. ◻ Tue–Sun. 🎟 ⓘ

♣ **Jardín Borda**
Av Morelos 271. **Tel** (777) 318 10 50. ◻ Tue–Sun. 🎟 Sun free. ⓘ ⓘ

🏛 **Taller Siqueiros**
Venus 7, Jardín de Cuernavaca. **Tel** (777) 315 11 15. ◻ Tue–Sun. 🎟

Tepoztlán ⑮

Morelos. 🏚 33,000. 🚌 🎭 Los Tiznados (Jan 20 & 21), Carnival (Feb/Mar), Reto al Tepozteco (Sep 8).

Lying in a lush green valley, Tepoztlán is surrounded by spectacular volcanic rock formations. A tiring but worthwhile climb above the town stands the **Santuario del Cerro Tepozteco**, a shrine dedicated to Tepoztecatl, the ancient god of pulque – an alcoholic beverage made from the agave plant (see p325). The dominant building in the town itself is the massive, fortified 16th-century **Ex-Convento Dominico de la Natividad**, whose austere cloister still has delightful mural fragments in the cloisters, though the building is in a state of disrepair. For lovers of pre-Columbian art, the **Museo Carlos Pellicer** holds a small but interesting collection, the legacy of the Tabascan poet and anthropologist Carlos Pellicer, who lived in Tepoztlán (see p255).

Environs

The town of **Cuautla**, 27 km (17 miles) to the southeast, is the site of the last resting place of Emiliano Zapata, one of the heroes of the Revolution (see p54).

🏛 **Museo Carlos Pellicer**
González. **Tel** (739) 395 10 98. ◻ Tue–Sun. 🎟

Surviving murals in the Ex-Convento Dominico de la Natividad, Tepoztlán

Popocatépetl and Iztaccíhuatl ⓰

Mexico State. Off Mex 115,
14 km (9 miles) E of Amecameca.
***Tel** 52 05 10 36 (updated reports).*
Amecameca then taxi.

The snow-capped volcanoes of Popocatépetl, or "Popo," ("Smoking Mountain") and Iztaccíhuatl ("Sleeping Lady") are the second and third highest peaks in Mexico, standing at 5,465 m (17,930 ft) and 5,230 m (17,160 ft) respectively. On occasion, strong winds manage to blow the smog away, revealing these mountains as two of the country's most awesome sights.

According to legend, the warrior Popocatépetl fell in love with Iztaccíhuatl, an Aztec princess. To win her hand, he defeated a great rival in battle. Wrongly believing him to be dead, the princess herself then died of a broken heart. Legend has it that, in his grief, Popocatépetl turned himself and his princess into these two adjacent mountains. The outline of Iztaccíhuatl bears an uncanny resemblance to that of a sleeping woman.

The **Paso de Cortés**, a saddle between the two peaks accessible by car, is an ideal base for walks on Iztaccíhuatl, but ascents of the peak itself should be left to the experts. Access to Popocatépetl is currently not permitted due to the threat of volcanic activity.

Nuestra Señora de los Remedios, with Popocatépetl behind

The arcade on the western flank of Cholula's *zócalo*

Cholula ⓱

Puebla. 1,350,000. *Portal Guerrero 3, 4 Norte, (222) 261 23 93* Carnival (Feb/Mar), Virgen de los Remedios (1st week of Sep).
www.visitmexico.com

Before subjecting it to one of the bloodiest massacres of the Conquest, Cortés described Cholula as "the most beautiful city outside Spain." In pre-Columbian times it had been a sacred city – a place of pilgrimage – and a large and important commercial center.

The arcade on the west side of Cholula's large *zócalo* (main square) shelters restaurants and cafés. Opposite is the fortified, Franciscan **Convento de San Gabriel**.

The impressive double gateway of San Gabriel, Cholula

Founded in 1529 on the site of a temple to Quetzalcoatl *(see p265)*, the main church has a single nave with rib vaulting and Gothic tracery. Visitors can tour the monastic kitchen, dining rooms, cloisters, and sleeping areas. On the left of the atrium is the **Capilla Real**, built for Indian converts. It acquired its 49 mosque-like domes in the early part of the 18th century.

To the east is the **Zona Arqueológica**, a site which is dominated by the remains of the largest pyramid ever built in Mesoamerica, at 65 m (213 ft) high. Since the 1930s, archaeologists have dug 8 km (5 miles) of tunnels through this Great Pyramid, identifying at least four stages of construction between 200 BC and AD 800. Visitors enter the tunnels on the north side, and emerge several hundred meters later on the east.

Opposite the entrance to the tunnel is a museum with a large cut-away model of the pyramid and artifacts from the site. Digs on the south side have revealed the **Patio de los Altares**, an area of astounding acoustics, used for public ceremonies and probably the sacrifice of children. On top of the pyramid sits the 1874 church of **Nuestra Señora de los Remedios**. The wonderful view from the atrium takes in Puebla *(see pp150–53)*, the volcanoes, and Cholula's many other churches.

Environs

The extraordinary folk-Baroque church of **Santa María Tonantzintla**, 5 km (3 miles) south of Cholula, has an interior that is bursting with colorful saints, fruit, angels, and cherubs. Begun in the 16th century, it took its Indian craftsmen 200 years to complete. The church of **San Francisco Acatepec** *(see p25)*, 1.5 km (1 mile) farther south, has a façade entirely covered in colorful, handmade Talavera tiles *(see p153)*.

🏛 Convento de San Gabriel
Corner of Calle 2 Sur & Av Morelos. ⬡ *daily.* ♿

▲ Zona Arqueólogica
Av Morelos. ⬡ *Tue–Sun.* 📷

Street-by-Street: Puebla ⑱

Mexico's fourth-largest city, Puebla is best known for the beautiful Talavera tiles that adorn its walls, domes, and interiors; for *mole poblano (see p321)*, Mexico's national dish, which originated here; and for being the site of an important battle on May 5, 1862 *(see p52)*. The streets of the compact city center are lined with churches, mansions, and other handsome old buildings and are a delight to stroll around.

Teatro Principal

Templo de San Cristóbal
Built in the 17th century as part of an orphanage, this church is noted for its collection of colonial sculptures.

Calle 6 Oriente is known for its shops selling handmade candies, crystallized fruits, and *rompope* (eggnog, *see p324*).

Museo de la Revolución
The Revolution of 1910 supposedly began in this house, which is now a museum (see p152).

Iglesia de Santa Clara

★ Casa del Alfeñique
This 18th-century house is so named because its delicate white ornamental plasterwork resembles alfeñique, a sugar and almond paste. It houses the state museum (see p152).

Museo de Santa Rosa
Museo de Santa Mónica

VIPS restaurant now occupies this metal-framed building dating from 1910.

Casa de los Muñecos
The façade of this house, built for an 18th-century mayor, is covered with decorative red tiles. Several panels show dancing figures.

City hall

Plaza Principal (zócalo)

STAR SIGHTS

★ Casa del Alfeñique

★ Cathedral

| 0 meters | 100 |
| 0 yards | 100 |

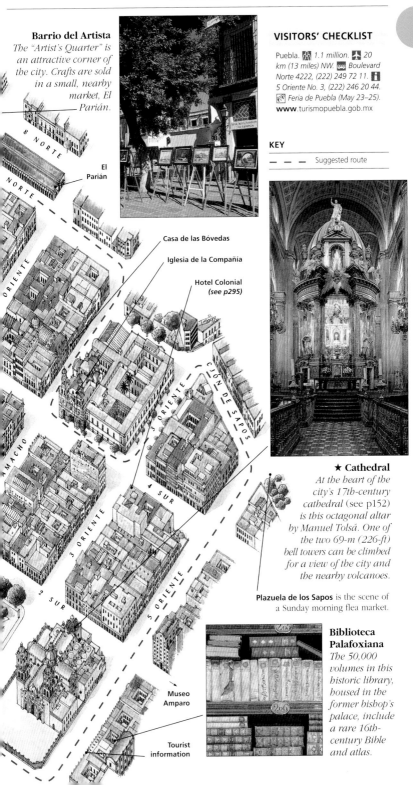

Barrio del Artista
The "Artist's Quarter" is an attractive corner of the city. Crafts are sold in a small, nearby market, El Parián.

8 NORTE

El Parián

NORTE

ORIENTE

Casa de las Bóvedas

Iglesia de la Compañía

Hotel Colonial
(see p295)

CJÓN DE SAPOS

3 ORIENTE

CAMACHO

4 SUR

3 ORIENTE

2 SUR

5 ORIENTE

Museo Amparo

Tourist information

VISITORS' CHECKLIST

Puebla. 1.1 million. 20 km (13 miles) NW. Boulevard Norte 4222, (222) 249 72 11. 5 Oriente No. 3, (222) 246 20 44. Feria de Puebla (May 23–25). **www**.turismopuebla.gob.mx

KEY

– – – – Suggested route

★ Cathedral
At the heart of the city's 17th-century cathedral (see p152) is this octagonal altar by Manuel Tolsá. One of the two 69-m (226-ft) bell towers can be climbed for a view of the city and the nearby volcanoes.

Plazuela de los Sapos is the scene of a Sunday morning flea market.

Biblioteca Palafoxiana
The 50,000 volumes in this historic library, housed in the former bishop's palace, include a rare 16th-century Bible and atlas.

Exploring Puebla

Founded in 1531, Puebla was the first settlement in Mexico to be laid out on a grid pattern by Spanish colonialists, rather than elaborating on an existing settlement. Modern Puebla is a state capital and university city that has preserved its rich heritage of colonial architecture. In recent decades many of its finest buildings have been transformed into museums displaying collections of colonial art and regional crafts, as well as historical and archaeological finds from all over Mexico.

Ornate onyx washbasin situated in the sacristy of the city's cathedral

🔓 Cathedral

Juan de Palafox, Bishop of Puebla, consecrated the city's cathedral (the second largest in Mexico after the one in the capital) in April 1649. It is built in a combination of Renaissance and Baroque styles.

The pillars around the large atrium – the plaza in front of the building – are surmounted by statues of angels, symbols of the town whose full name is Puebla de los Angeles ("People of the Angels").

Inside there are five naves and 14 side chapels. The main altar, known as the *ciprés*, was designed by Manuel Tolsá in 1797. Standing on an octagonal base, it consists of two superimposed "temples" supported by eight pairs of Corinthian columns, crowned by a tiled dome in imitation of that of St. Peter's in Rome. Behind

the *ciprés* is the Altar de los Reyes whose dome was painted in 1688 by Cristóbal de Villalpando.

🏛 Museo de la Revolución Mexicana

6 Oriente No. 206. *Tel (222) 242 10 76.* 🕐 *Tue–Sun.*
🗓 🚫
The event said to have sparked the 1910 Mexican Revolution took place in this house. Aquiles Serdán, his family, and about 17 others who opposed Porfirio Díaz's dictatorship (*see p53*) resisted arrest and were killed by soldiers. The house is now a museum of revolutionary memorabilia.

🏛 Casa del Alfeñique

4 Oriente No. 416. *Tel (222) 232 04 58.* 🕐 *Tue–Sun.* 🗓 *Tue free.* 🚹 🚫
Puebla's state museum now occupies this Baroque mansion. Exhibits include carriages, paintings, costumes, and ornately furnished rooms.

🏛 Museo Amparo

2 Sur No. 708. *Tel (222) 229 38 50.* 🕐 *Wed–Mon.* 🗓 *Mon free.* 🍴 📷 🎥 *for a fee.*
Occupying a restored 18th-century hospital, this museum houses one of the finest collections of pre-Columbian and colonial art in the country.

The first section is devoted to pre-Columbian art. An introductory room includes a timeline comparing Mesoamerican cultures (*see pp44–5*) with contemporary cultures from around the world. A multilingual audiovisual system gives information on the artistic techniques employed, and the significance of the pieces in these rooms. The

first section ends in an area dedicated to the collection's finest pieces, such as a Huasteca necklace of 17 tiny skulls carved out of bone, an Olmec statue known as *The Thinker*, and a Maya altar from Palenque.

Stone statue on display in Museo Ampa[ro]

In the second section, the rooms are filled with colonial pieces, starting with a painting of the Virgin of Guadalupe in a silver frame. Other exhibits here include Manuel Tolsá's model for the altar in the cathedral, and an unusual 18th-century statue of St. Anthony of Padua. A tradition in Puebla is for girls searching for a partner to turn the statue on its head; when they get married, they turn him back on his feet.

🏛 Museo José Luis Bello

Zetina Gonzalez y 5 de Mayo. *Tel (222) 232 47 20.* 🕐 *Tue–Sun.* 🗓 🚹 🚫 *www.*museobello.org
Without ever leaving his beloved city of Puebla, 19th-century industrialist José Luis Bello, owner of cigar and textile factories, managed to assemble this eclectic collection. There are some 2,500 pieces, and the emphasis is very much on variety rather than a particular theme. Exhibits include a collection of locks and keys; Chinese porcelain and ivory; gold and silver pocket watches; European furniture; and 16th- to 18th-century Talavera pottery in colorful, earthy designs.

One of the exquisitely ornate rooms in the Museo Bello

🏺 Taller Uriarte Talavera
4 Poniente No. 911. *Tel (222) 242 54 07.* ☐ *daily.* 🚫 🚫 *Mon–Fri.* 🏠
This Talavera pottery work-shop offers guided tours to visitors. The production process can be seen through from the early purifying of the clay, to the painting, glazing, and final firing of the piece.

⛪ Iglesia de Santo Domingo
Corner of 5 de Mayo and 4 Poniente. *Tel (222) 242 36 43.* ☐ *daily.*
One of the most elaborately decorated chapels in Mexico is contained in this Baroque church. Built in the second half of the 17th century, the **Capilla del Rosario** is a riot of gilt carving. Along the walls, grotesque heads spew golden vines whose tendrils twist and twine to form the frames of six paintings depicting the mysteries of the rosary. The dome is no less ornate with saints, cherubs, dancing angels, and a heavenly choir. The main church has a fine onyx pulpit.

Highly decorated dome of the Capilla del Rosario

🏛 Centro Cultural Ex-Convento de Santa Rosa
14 Poniente No. 305. *Tel (222) 232 77 92.* ☐ *Tue–Sun.* 🗓 *Tue free.* 🚫 🏠
Six blocks north of the city center, in Puebla's market area, is the 17th-century convent of Santa Rosa. The building has served at different times as an Augustinian nunnery, hospital for the mentally ill, and tenement for more than 1,500 people. It was salvaged in 1968 and converted into a museum to display crafts produced in the state of Puebla.

Exhibits here include the huge tree of life *(see pp330–31)* from Izúcar de Matamoros, which represents an Indian interpretation of the story of Adam and Eve. There are also

Kitchen of the former convent of Santa Rosa, now a museum

brightly colored embroideries, carnival masks, and furniture finely inlaid with mother-of-pearl, malachite, and bone.

The highlight of the Santa Rosa museum, however, is the vaulted kitchen, which is entirely covered with tiles. Tradition has it that the famous *mole poblano (see p321)* was invented by the Augustinian nuns in this atmospheric room.

🏛 Museo de Santa Mónica
18 Poniente No. 103. *Tel (222) 232 01 78.* ☐ *Tue–Sun.* 🗓 *Sun free.* 🚫 📷 *for a fee.*
Built around a pretty tile-and-brick cloister, the 17th-century Convento de Santa Mónica was used to hide nuns during the years of clerical persecution after the 1857 Reform Laws. With the help of hidden doors and concealed passages, the

nuns lived here in secret until 1933, when they were finally evicted. The building is now the Museum of Religious Art. As well as paintings, sculptures, and ecclesiastical artifacts, there is a macabre collection of instruments and clothing that were used by the nuns for the purpose of self-mortification.

🌿 Cerro de Guadalupe
2 km (1.5 miles) NE of city center.
This large park, which contains two forts and several museums, marks the site of the historic Battle of Puebla. On May 5, 1862 a small Mexican army under General Ignacio Zaragoza defeated a much larger French army that had invaded Mexico. The victory proved short-lived, but the day has still become one of national celebration.

TALAVERA POTTERY
The colorful, glazed pottery so characteristic of Puebla is a fusion of Arabic, Spanish, Italian, and Chinese influences. The earliest pieces, with cobalt blue designs on a white background are typically Moorish. The technique was brought to Mexico in the 16th century by Dominican monks from Talavera de la Reina, Spain. New colors, such as green, black, and yellow, were introduced from Italy in the 17th century, while pieces imported from China and the Philippines inspired floral and animal designs. It takes six months to produce an authentic piece of Talavera pottery.

Talavera jars for sale in Puebla

Cacaxtla

Tlaxcala. Off Mex 119, 30 km (19 miles) NW of Puebla. *Tel (246) 416 00 00.* 🚌 *from Tlaxcala.* ☐ *daily.* 🎦 ✓
www.inah.gob.mx

Meaning "the place where rain dies in the earth," Cacaxtla was the capital of the Olmeca-Xicalanca, a Gulf Coast group who dominated this area from the 7th–10th centuries AD. Some of Mexico's best preserved murals, probably painted by Maya artists, were discovered here in 1974.

The 22-m (72-ft) *Mural de la Batalla* depicts a violent battle between jaguar and eagle warriors, with no fewer than 48 human figures in vibrant colors. Glyphs *(see pp46–7)* are inserted among the characters.

Two other extraordinary murals are in Edificio A. The *Hombre-jaguar* represents a lord dressed in a jaguar skin standing on a "jaguar-snake." Surrounding him is a border of sea creatures. Also in Edificio A, the *Hombre-ave* is a "bird-man" painted in black with an eagle headdress. He holds a blue serpent staff and stands on a plumed snake. Heads of corn around the edge have small human faces.

Environs

Just 2 km (1 mile) away is another Olmeca-Xicalanca site, **Xochitécatl**, whose platforms and pyramids date from about 1000 BC.

The vivid and well-preserved *Hombre-ave* mural at Cacaxtla

The richly gilded interior of the Basílica de Ocotlán, near Tlaxcala

Tlaxcala ⑳

Tlaxcala. 👥 73,000. 🚌 ℹ️ *Cnr of Av Juárez & Lardizábal, (246) 465 09 60.* 🎭 *Carnival (Feb/Mar), Virgen de Ocotlán (3rd Mon of May).*
www. tlaxcala.gob.mx/turismo

Often seen as a provincial backwater, the city of Tlaxcala is, in fact, one of the country's colonial treasures. Its seclusion is partly due to the historical independence of the local people, the Tlaxcaltecas. During the Conquest they took up arms against their old enemy, the Aztecs, joining Cortés to conquer Tenochtitlán.

The so-called Ciudad Roja (Red City) is dominated by earthy tones of terracotta and ocher. In the center is the spacious tree-filled *zócalo* (main plaza) with its bandstand and fountain, the latter given by King Philip IV of Spain in 1646.

The colorful and richly decorated brick, tile, and stucco façade of the **Parroquia de San José** dominates the northwest corner of the square. At the entrance to this church two fonts have pedestals depicting Camaxtli, the ancient Tlaxcalan god of war and hunting, and the Spanish imperial coat of arms. Beside the altar is a 17th-century painting showing the baptism of a Tlaxcalan chief, watched by Cortés and his mistress, La Malinche.

The 16th-century **Palacio de Gobierno** flanks the north side of the *zócalo*. Exterior details include the French-style stucco added at the start of the 20th century. Inside, murals by artist Desiderio Hernández relate the history of Tlaxcala.

Across Plaza Xicoténcatl to the south, a path leads uphill to the **cathedral**, which has a stunning Moorish-style coffered ceiling and contains the font used to baptize the four local chiefs who allied with Cortés. The **Museo Regional**, in the cloisters next door, has

The ornate bandstand in Tlaxcala's shady and peaceful *zócalo*

◁ **Rich stuccowork in the dome of the *camarín* at Basílica de Ocotlán**

Decoration in Basílica de Ocotlán

a collection of pre-Columbian pieces, including a large stone figure of Camaxtli, the god of war. The two rooms upstairs are dedicated to colonial art.

The **Museo de Artes y Tradiciones Populares** (west of the *zócalo*) is a living museum. Here craftspeople demonstrate their techniques.

Environs

On a hill above the city, the twin-towered **Basílica de Ocotlán** is one of the most lavish Churrigueresque churches in Mexico, comparable with those in Tepotzotlán *(see pp140–3)* and Taxco *(see pp146–7)*. The 18th-century façade combines hexagonal brick and white-stucco decoration. The interior and adjoining *camarín* are an explosion of Baroque giltwork. Pilgrims flock here in May for the procession of the Virgin.

Nearby villages include **Santa Ana Chiauhtempan**, known for its embroidery and weaving, and **Tizatlán**, where a 16th-century chapel with frescoes

stands beside the remains of a pre-Columbian palace.

In **Huamantla**, 45 km (28 miles) east of Tlaxcala, the 16th-century Convento de San Francisco has a polychrome Churrigueresque altarpiece dedicated to the Virgin of Charity. The Virgin is celebrated at a popular fiesta held here in August *(see p31)*.

🏛 Museo Regional
Ex-Convento de San Francisco, off Plaza Xicoténcatl. *Tel* (246) 462 02 62. ◻ *daily.* 💷

🏛 Museo de Artes y Tradiciones Populares
Boulevard Emilio Sánchez Piedras 1. *Tel* (246) 462 23 37. ◻ *Tue–Sun.* 💷 🎫 *reserve in advance.* ♿

Cantona ㉑

Puebla. 30 km (19 miles) NE of Oriental via 4 km (2.5 miles) of unpaved road from Tepeyahualco. 🚌 *tours from Puebla.* ◻ *Tue–Sun.* 💷 www.inah.gob.mx

The remains of what was once a major city occupy a vast area of low hills beside a lava field. Only ten percent of the well-maintained site, which is dotted with yuccas and pine trees, can be visited.

Little is known about the history of Cantona but it was probably inhabited from about AD 700–950. One of the most built-up of all Mesoamerican cities, it may have supported a population of 80,000.

A full visit will take at least two hours. A signposted route from the parking lot sets off on one of the *calzadas,* or cob-

Platforms and a pyramid at Cantona, interspersed with yucca plants

bled streets, which connect the various parts of Cantona. This leads past the ruins of houses and patios before climbing to the **Acrópolis**, the cluster of public buildings at the heart of the city. Soon the route reaches the first of 24 **ballcourts** exca-

vated here – more than at any other site in Mexico. Of these, 12 are unusual in that they form parts of complexes with a pyramid at one end and the playing area at the other.

The path reaches the **Plaza Oriente** and then loops back to **El Palacio** and the **Plaza Central**. The return to the parking lot is along a second *calzada*.

KEY

-- Path
① Calzada 1
② Ballcourt Complex 5
③ Ballcourt Complex 7
④ Plaza Oriente
⑤ El Palacio
⑥ Plaza Central
⑦ Calzada 2

Entrance
🛈 🅿
🚻

ACRÓPOLIS

| 0 meters | 200 |
| 0 yards | 200 |

NORTHERN MEXICO

BAJA CALIFORNIA NORTE · BAJA CALIFORNIA SUR
CHIHUAHUA · COAHUILA · DURANGO · NUEVO LEÓN
SINALOA · SONORA · TAMAULIPAS

With its stark mountains and arid plains, giant cactuses and men on horseback, the North is the Mexico of popular imagination. Sparsely populated and occupying over half the country's landmass, it stretches from the magical beaches of Baja California to the marshes and islands of the Gulf of Mexico.

Two mountain ranges, the eastern and western Sierra Madre, cross this great territory from north to south. Between them lies the vast Chihuahuan Desert, the largest in North America. To the northwest is the Sonoran Desert, which extends down the beautiful 1,300-km (800-mile) long peninsula of Baja California. It is here that the North's best beaches are located.

Although often austere, the mountains conceal beautiful places where cool pine forests, placid lakes, and thunderous waterfalls can be found. The Sierra Tarahumara holds forested ravines, deeper than the Grand Canyon, which are traversed by one of the world's most spectacular railroads.

Though no great pre-Columbian civilization ever developed in this region, the superb pottery and unique architecture of the Paquimé culture and the mysterious cave paintings of Baja California hold their own fascination. Present-day indigenous survivors, like the Tarahumara people of the Sierra Madre Occidental, cling to a traditional way of life quite apart from modern Mexican society.

The region is delimited to the north by the 1,950-mile (3,140-km) border with the United States, which for much of its length follows the Rio Grande (known as the Río Bravo in Mexico). Receiving influences from the cultures on either side of it, the border region is almost a third country, defined by its unique blend of languages, music, and food.

Even as far south as Monterrey, Mexico's industrial heartland, the influence of the gringo is still strongly felt. But here the accumulated wealth and economic power – enshrined in the glass and concrete of bold modern architecture – are purely and soberly Mexican in character.

Local men in the town of Hidalgo del Parral

◁ Desert landscape in flower near Bahía de los Angeles in Baja California

Exploring Northern Mexico

Distances involved when traveling between sights in the region should not be underestimated. Sun worshipers will find some of Mexico's finest beaches on the 800-mile (1,300-km) peninsula of Baja California, which also has spectacular desert scenery and varied wildlife, including the gray whale. On the mainland, Mazatlán is a popular retreat from northern winters. Inland, the vertiginous gorges of the Copper Canyon are great for hiking. Elsewhere, you can walk the streets of western film sets near Durango or take in the culture and nightlife of modern cities such as Tijuana and Monterrey.

Wildflowers and cactuses, common in Northern Mexico

San Diego

1 TIJUANA
Mexicali
2 ENSENADA
La Bufadora
Santo Tomás   El Chinero
Colonet
PN San Pedro Mártir
San Quintín   **3 TRANSPENINSULAR HIGHWAY**
San Fernando
Cataviña
PN del Desierto Central

San Luis
El Golfo de Santa Clara
San Felipe
Puerto Peñasco
El Desemboque

BAJA CALIFORNIA NORTE
Isla Ángel de la Guarda
4 BAHÍA DE LOS ÁNGELES
Rosarito
Isla Cedros   *Bahía Sebastián Vizcaíno*   *PN del Desierto Central*
Isla Natividad
5 GUERRERO NEGRO
Laguna Ojo de Liebre
VIZCAÍNO BIOSPHERE RESERVE
6
Laguna San Ignacio   **7 SAN IGNACIO**   **8 SANTA ROSALÍA**
9 MULEGÉ
Volcán las 3 Vírgenes 1920m

PACIFIC OCEAN

San Juanico
Rosarito
Sierra de la Giganta
10 LORETO
BAJA CALIFORNIA SUR
Villa Insurgentes
Puerto Escondido
Villa Constitución
Punta Coyote
Santa Rita
Isla Espíritu Santo
Isla Cerralvo
LA PAZ 11
Todos Santos
Santiago
CABO SAN LUCAS 13   **12 SAN JOSÉ DEL CABO**

Tucson ↑
Nogales
Caborca
Santa Ana
Las Trincheras
La Libertad
SONORA
Pesqueira
Isla Tiburón
HERMOSILLO 14
Isla Tiburón   Bahía Kino
La Colorada
Ortiz
Guaymas   *Presa Álvar Obregón*
Ciudad Obregón
Navojoa
Etchojoa
22 ÁLAMOS   Choix
El Fuerte
Los Mochis
Guasave
San Juanico

Agua Prieta
Cananea   Janos
Imuris   Fronteras   Nuevo Grande
PAQUIMÉ 15
Moctezuma   Buenaventura
Mazocahui   Zarag
Madera
Sahuaripa
Tónichi
CIUDAD CUAUHTÉMOC
PN Cascadas de Basaseáchic
CREEL 19
CAÑÓN DEL COBRE 21
20 BATOPI
Guadalup y Calv
Guamúchil
Perico
Navolato   Cul
SINALO
El Dorado
La Cru

0 kilometers   200
0 miles   100

Golfo de California

Lovers' Beach at Cabo San Lucas, cut off by rocks and accessible only by boat

SIGHTS AT A GLANCE

GETTING AROUND

The region's road network is generally good, but
distances can be huge and toll roads expensive.
Avoid nighttime driving and beware of deteriorations
in the road surface and *vados* (fords), which – even
when dry – require a slower speed. Buses offer an
alternative to pricey air travel and are usually comfortable. One of the few passenger train
services still running is the spectacular
Chihuahua-al-Pacífico *(see p176)*. Several
car-ferry services link mainland Mexico with
Baja California.

SEE ALSO

• *Where to Stay* pp297–302

• *Where to Eat* pp333–5

A farmer ploughing a field
near the Cañón del Cobre

'buquerque

dad
árez

mada

Sueco

Coyame

Ojinaga

Boquillas

Ciudad Acuña

Picacho del Centinela
2896m

El Sáuz

16

CHIHUAHUA

Llano de los
Caballos
Mesteños

San
Miguel

La Babia

Zaragoza

HIHUAHUA

Delicias

Laguna
El Guaje

Nueva Rosita

Sabinas

Hidalgo

Ciudad Camargo

COAHUILA

Juárez

Nuevo Laredo

Valle de
Zaragoza

Jiménez

Ocampo

Río Salado

Anáhuac

za

18 **HIDALGO
DEL PARRAL**

Cuatro
Ciénegas

Monclova

Sabinas Hidalgo

Mier

↑ San Antonio

Villa
campo

Ceballos

Bolsón de
Mapimí

30

Reynosa

Matamoros

Santa María
del Oro

45

Bermejillo

30

Tlahualillo

San Pedro

**NUEVO
LEÓN**

Cadereyta

Valle
Hermoso

97 **101**

Laguna
Madre

Tepehuanes

Gómez
Palacio

Torreón

Parras

Huachichil

MONTERREY 26

SALTILLO 25

Montemorelos

DURANGO

Cuencame

Linares

San Fernando

Villa
Madero

DURANGO

KEY

Galeana **TAMAULIPAS**

Hidalgo

Jiménez

acio

24

El Salto

Quelite

Mezquital

AZATLÁN

Escuinapa

Guadalajara

Soto la Marina

Ciudad
Victoria

180

Tula

101

85

Aldama

San Luis
Potosí

Ciudad
Mante

Altamira

González

Tampico ↘

KEY	
═══	Highway
───	Major road
┈┈┈	Minor road
┈•┈	Main railway
───	Minor railway
▪▪▪	International border
▫▫▫	State border

The OMNIMAX theater at the Centro Cultural Tijuana

Tijuana ➊

Baja California Norte. 🏛 1,212,000.
✈ 🚌 🛈 Paseo de los Héroes 10289,
(664) 682 33 67. 🎭 Aniversario de
Tijuana (Jul). **www**.discoverbaja.com

Just over the border from San
Diego (California), Tijuana is
the quintessential border city
and claims to be the world's
busiest crossing, with up to
35 million visitors a year.

Towering skyscrapers and
massive shopping malls are a
measure of its modernity. Most
people come here to shop or
party. The best shopping is in
the quiet bazaars on either side
of Avenida Revolución. Painted
pottery, leather boots, silver
jewelry, mezcal, and tequila
are the most popular buys.
Customers are encouraged to
barter with the stallholders. The
vibrant nightlife is also centered on Avenida Revolución,
where there are plenty of
restaurants and cafés.

Tijuana also has a few cultural attractions, the main one
being the futuristic **Centro
Cultural Tijuana** beside the
river. Concerts and art exhibitions are held here, and there
is an OMNIMAX theater that
shows movies about Mexico.

🏛 **Centro Cultural Tijuana**
Cnr of Paseo de los Héroes and Mina.
Tel (664) 687 96 00. ◐ Tue–Sun. ♿
📷 in advance. 🔲 🖥 📹 movies.

THE MEXICO–US BORDER

The US and Mexico are
separated by a land
border that runs for
3,140 km (1,950 miles)
between the Pacific
Ocean and the Gulf of
Mexico. There are 21
crossings between
Tijuana in the west
and Matamoros in the
east. Most US citizens
who cross the border
are on day-trips for a
taste of the exotic, to

Signs and a souvenir stall mark the
Mexico–US border crossing at Tijuana

shop, or to enjoy themselves in a country where their dollar
goes further. For some Mexicans, the border is the gateway
to "El Norte," the promised land of high salaries and
consumer goods. The meeting of the two worlds creates a
vibrant mix of cultures, but it has its down-side – most visible
in the steadily lengthening and constantly patrolled "wall" –
the barrier erected by the US to deter illegal immigrants.

Ensenada ➋

Baja California Norte. 🏛 370,000.
✈ 🚌 🛈 Blvd Lázaro Cárdenas 1477,
(646) 172 30 22. 🎭 Carnival (Feb/
Mar), Vendimia Wine Festival (Aug).
www.descubrebajacalifornia.com

This busy port and cruise-ship
destination is popular with
fishermen, surfers, and
divers. The scenic drive from
Tijuana takes just 90 minutes,
past bays and red bluffs that
hint at the spectacular desert
landscape farther south. A
lookout just before the city
offers a view over the bay.

City sights include the twin-
towered church of **Nuestra
Señora de Guadalupe** and the
giant sculpted heads of three
national heroes – Juárez, Hidalgo,
and Carranza – on the Plaza
Cívica. The **Riviera del Pacífico**,
near the waterfront, was a
hotel in the 1930s but now houses exhibitions. In the lobby is a
remarkable 3-D mural showing
the 18th-century Jesuit missions of the Californias. **Bodegas
de Santo Tomás**, which makes
some of Baja's finest wine
from grapes grown in vineyards south of town, offers
daily tours and wine tasting.

Ensenada's small but lively
"party district" clusters around
the old-fashioned **Hussong's
Cantina** on Avenida López
Mateos. This bar was founded
in the 19th century by the
German Hussong family, still
a powerful force in the city.
Visitors can buy a Hussong's
T-shirt in the Hussong mall.

Environs
The beaches in town are
not recommended, but a few
miles south are the clean and
pleasant **Playa El Faro** and
Playa Estero, both of which
have superb sunsets. Farther
south is **La Bufadora**, where a
cleft in the rock produces a
spout of sea foam, especially
when the waves swell in
windy weather. The best
diving in the area is here.

About 90 km (56 miles)
inland of Ensenada is **Parque
Nacional Constitución de 1857**,
reached by a winding road
among hills made of huge
boulders. Here, surrounded by
pine trees, is tranquil **Laguna
Hanson**, a haven for birds.

The heads of three national heroes on Plaza Cívica in Ensenada

🏛 **Riviera del Pacífico**
Corner of Blvd Costera and Av Riviera. ◯ daily.

🍷 **Bodegas de Santo Tomás**
Av Miramar 666. **Tel** (646) 178 25 09. ◯ Mon–Fri. 🎫 🚫 🍴 🛍

Transpeninsular Highway ❸

Baja California Norte and Sur. Mex 1, Tijuana to Cabo San Lucas.
🚌 serving the whole highway.

The two extremes of Baja California are linked by one highway, the two-lane Mex 1, which runs 1,700 km (1,060 miles) from Tijuana to Cabo San Lucas (see p169). There are few places worth stopping for on the long drive, but the desert landscapes of the north do have an austere beauty. The **Parque Nacional San Pedro Mártir**, reached via a side road 140 km (87 miles) south of Ensenada, includes the 3,095-m (10,154-ft) snowcapped peak, Picacho del Diablo. Farther south, near the truck stop of Cataviña, is the so-called **Rocky Desert**, with its jumble of massive boulders and wide variety of cactus species.

Bahía de los Angeles ❹

Baja California Norte. 🏠 450.

Located on the beautiful bay of the same name, and reached by a paved, if rather rutted, 68-km (42-mile) spur road off Mex 1, Bahía de los Angeles is a peaceful spot even by Baja standards. Popular with sportfishing enthusiasts, it also offers opportunities for diving and kayaking around the numerous islands in the bay. Other attractions include a sea turtle conservation project and trips across a spectacular desert landscape to see Indian rock paintings and the well-preserved San Borja mission. Boats are available to visit various offshore islands.

Desert scenery beside the Transpeninsular Highway south of Cataviña

Guerrero Negro ❺

Baja California Sur. 🏘 *10,000.* 🚶 🚌

Guerrero Negro, "Black Warrior," is named after a whaling ship that ran aground in a lagoon near the town in the middle of the 19th century. The lagoon is the main breeding ground of the California gray whale – which most visitors come here to see. It also provides the raw material for the world's largest sea-salt operation, which environmentalists say may threaten the long-term future of the whales, only recently brought back from the brink of extinction. Seven million tons of salt per year is produced from

Sea salt leaving the evaporation works south of Guerrero Negro

thousands of evaporation ponds south of the town, and barges take the washed salt to the island of Isla Cedros, where it is transferred to ocean-going ships. The island itself remains almost unspoiled and supports unusual plant species and the endangered Cedros mule deer. Isla Cedros can be reached from Guerrero Negro by a light aircraft that makes the crossing twice a week.

Vizcaíno Biosphere Reserve ❻

Baja California Sur. Mex 1, S of Guerrero Negro. 🚌 *Guerrero Negro.*

Covering 25,000 sq km (9,600 sq miles), this preserve is claimed to be the largest protected natural area in Latin America. It stretches from the Península de Vizcaíno across Baja California to the east coast. The whale

Horse and rider, Sierra de San Francisco

sanctuaries of Laguna Ojo de Liebre and Laguna San Ignacio fall within its boundaries, as do the islands of Natividad, Asunción, and San Roque, part of the Sierra de San Francisco, and – in the east – the triple volcano of Las Tres Vírgenes.

Ranging from coastal mangroves and sand dunes to arid upland plateaus and the occasional fresh-water oasis, the preserve's ecosystems harbor a wide variety of species. Apart from the whales, other interesting animals are the endangered bighorn sheep (*borrego cimarrón*), the pronghorn

WHALE-WATCHING IN GUERRERO NEGRO

Two dozen species of cetaceans are found off the coasts of Baja California, from the small, endangered *vaquita*, confined to the northern reaches of the Sea of Cortés, to the world's largest animal, the blue whale. The best place to see these magnificent creatures is at Guerrero Negro, where the most common species, the California gray whale, can be seen in February and March, either from the shore or, better still, from a small boat.

A curious whale approaching two boat-loads of enthusiasts, Guerrero Negro

The California gray whale (*Eschrichtius robustus*), *makes one of the longest migrations of any mammal. After a 9,500-km (6,000-mile) trip from Alaska, it calves in the warm lagoons of Mexico's Pacific coast. Once almost extinct, the species has recovered, and its numbers are now rising.*

How to See the Whales

The whales can be viewed with binoculars from several vantage points on the shore, such as the one reached by a dirt road from Mex 1 approximately 8 km (5 miles) south of Guerrero Negro. A better option is to go on an organized dinghy trip lasting 2–3 hours. Choose a reputable company that will not approach the whales too closely.

One such is Malarrimo, which has an office next to its restaurant (*see p334*) on the same side of the road as Vanessa's Store. An alternative is to strike a deal with a local fisherman to take you out in his boat. Farther south in Baja California you can often see whales at Laguna San Ignacio, Bahía de Magdalena, on the eastern side of the peninsula between Loreto and La Paz, and at Cabo San Lucas.

ANCIENT CAVE PAINTINGS OF BAJA CALIFORNIA

The cave paintings of Baja California have been compared with the aboriginal art of Australia and prehistoric paintings in the caves of France and Spain. When 18th-century Jesuit missionaries asked about the origin of the paintings, the local Cochimí Indians attributed them to a race of giants who had come from the north. It is now thought that ancestors of the Cochimí themselves painted the images. Their exact age is unknown, but some may date from 1200 BC. The complexity of the beliefs suggested by the paintings has led to a reassessment of the supposedly "primitive" hunter-gatherer society encountered by the Spanish on their arrival.

Cave Paintings
The images, usually in black and red, depict human figures with their arms raised, various animals, and abstract designs of unknown significance.

Painting of hunters and prey in a cave near San Ignacio

---

antelope, elephant seals, and several kinds of sea turtle. The Laguna San Ignacio (reached from the town of San Ignacio) holds what is believed to be the densest breeding colony of ospreys in the world. Herons, egrets, brown pelicans, and various other seabirds can also be spotted here.

Much of the interior of the preserve, with its strangely-shaped *cirio* (or "boojum") trees and giant Mexican cereus *(see p171)*, is practically inaccessible, but a passable road leads up the Peninsula de Vizcaíno to Bahía Tortugas.

San Ignacio **❼**

Baja California Sur. 🏠 *750.* 🚌

Standing among thousands of date palms, the church at San Ignacio is one of the most imposing and best-preserved missions in Baja California. Although originally founded by Jesuits in 1728, before their expulsion from Spanish America, the church seen today was actually built in 1786 by Dominicans, with money from the queen of Spain. Its whitewashed Baroque façade, with masonry

details in reddish lava stone, holds four polygonal windows and four niches containing carvings of saints. St. Peter and St. Paul flank the main door, with its intricately carved lintel. The interior has original furniture and altarpieces, as well as a beautiful main altar decorated with 18th-century oil paintings.

In the canyons near San Ignacio are the ancient Indian cave paintings. The **Cueva del Ratón** (Cave of the Mouse) is the easiest to reach, via a turnoff to San Francisco de la Sierra, 45 km (28 miles) north on the Transpeninsular *(see p163)*. However, the most spectacular and best-preserved paintings are to be found in the **Cueva de las Flechas** (Cave of the Arrows) and the **Cueva Pintada** (Painted Cave). You must be accompanied by an approved guide – a visit to the last-named sites in the San Pablo canyon involves a two- or three-day camping trip with mules. A small **museum** in San Ignacio has exhibits on the cave paintings.

🏛 **San Ignacio Museum**
Prof. Gilberto Valdivia Péna.
Tel *(615) 154 02 22.* ◯ *Nov–Apr: daily; May–Oct: Tue–Sat.*

The 18th-century mission church at San Ignacio

The arid landscape of the Sierra de San Francisco, north of San Ignacio ▷

Santa Rosalía **❽**

Baja California Sur. 🚶 10,500. 🚌
🚢 **ℹ** Av Carranza and Plaza Santa
Rosalía, (615) 152 23 11. 🎭 Santa
Rosalía (Sep 4).

This small town was founded
by a French copper-mining
company in the 1880s. The
copper ran out, and the company moved on in the 1950s,
but engines and rolling stock
from the mine railroad, along
with some of the mine installations, can still be seen.

Santa Rosalía has many
two-story timber buildings
with verandas, which give it a
Caribbean look. Another curi-
osity is the **Iglesia de Santa
Bárbara**, a prefabricated church
designed by Gustave Eiffel, of
Eiffel Tower fame, and shipped
here in 1895. The waterfront
walk, the Andador Costero, is
a pleasant place for a stroll.

Overlooking the town is a
small mining museum, the
Museo Histórico Minero.

🏛 **Museo Histórico Minero**
Jean-Michel Cousteau.
⏱ Mon–Sat. 📷

Santa Rosalía's Iglesia de Santa
Bárbara, designed by Gustave Eiffel

Mulegé **❾**

Baja California Sur. 🚶 46,000. 🚌
🎭 Santa Rosalía (Sep 4).

This attractive town has a
lovely church, founded by
Jesuit missionaries. Set on a
bluff, it has superb views of
the Santa Rosalía River below.
Not far away is the **Museo
Mulegé**, which has displays
on the town's history. It is
housed in an old whitewashed
prison building, complete
with tiny, crenellated towers.
Mulegé is popular with scuba
divers, but for some of the
best beaches in Mexico take

A view across to the Bahía Concepción, the bay to the south of Mulegé

the road south out of Mulegé,
past the **Bahía Concepción**.
The color of the water here
changes dramatically from
deep blue to an intense green.

🏛 **Museo Mulegé**
Cananea. ⏱ Mon–Sat. 📷 ♿

Loreto **❿**

Baja California Sur. 🚶 11,800. ✈ 🚌
ℹ Corner of Francisco Madero and
Salvatierra, (613) 13 50 411. 🎭 Virgen
de Loreto (Sep 8), San Javier (Dec 3).

Once the capital of the
Californias (made up of
present-day California and
Baja California), Loreto is now
better known as a magnet for
the sportfishing fraternity. The
heart of the town is the
area around Plaza Cívica
and the superbly restored
**Misión Nuestra Señora
de Loreto**. The mission,
the first in the Californias,
was badly damaged by a
hurricane and earthquake
in the 19th century. The
original stone building
(1699) survives as a side
chapel to the main church.
From here, 18th-century
Jesuit missionaries em-
barked on a campaign to
evangelize (and hence

peacefully subdue) the indigenous population. The **Museo
de las Misiones** in the mission
explains how this was
accomplished and displays
period artifacts, including huge
cooking pots that the priests
used in their attempts – initially
more successful – to influence
the Indians by way of their
stomachs. In the museum
courtyard is a colonial, horse-
driven *trapiche* (sugar mill).

In addition to fishing, there
is good diving, kayaking, and
snorkeling, especially around
the offshore islands of **Isla
del Carmen** and **Coronado**.

🏛 **Museo de las Misiones**
Corner of Loreto and Misioneros.
Tel (613) 135 04 41. ⏱ Tue–Sun.
📷 📷 for a fee.

Fishing boats moored at the small marina
near the center of Loreto

La Paz

Baja California Sur. 197,000. 🛬 🚌 ⛴ ℹ *Carretera Transpeninsular, km 5.5, (612) 124 01 99.* Carnival *(Feb/Mar), Fundación de La Paz (May 2–7).* **www**.bcs.gob.mx

The capital of the state of Baja California Sur, La Paz sits beside the largest bay on the Sea of Cortés, at the foot of a peninsula endowed with some excellent, and often half-deserted, beaches. Its curving, 5-km (3-mile) *malecón* (water-front promenade) is lined with palm trees, hotels, and restaurants and is a lovely place for a stroll. Sit on a bench and enjoy the sunset, or walk along the dilapidated pier. A few blocks farther south is the main square, Plaza Constitución.

La Paz owes its foundation, by the conquistador Hernán Cortés, to the abundance of pearls in nearby waters, and its fortunes have often risen and fallen with those of the pearl industry. It dominated the international market in the 19th century, but in the 1940s a combination of disease and over-exploitation wiped out the oyster beds. Nowadays, in addition to its government offices and port facilities, its economy increasingly relies on tourism and on its status as one of the premier sportfishing destinations in the world.

La Paz's well laid-out **Museo Regional de Antropología** has interesting displays on pre-Columbian rock paintings and other aspects of Baja's indigenous heritage, as well as on its struggle for independence.

The nearby islands are popular with divers for their reefs, caves, and shipwrecks, and many also have fine beaches. **Isla Espíritu Santo** offers fantastic sailing opportunities and the chance to swim with wild sea lions.

🏛 **Museo Regional de Antropología**
Corner of 5 de Mayo and Altamirano. *Tel (612) 125 64 24.* ⭘ *daily.* 🈺

The spectacular rock archway at Lovers' Beach, Cabo San Lucas

San José del Cabo

Baja California Sur. 22,000. 🛬 🚌 ⛴ ℹ *Plaza San José, (624) 142 33 10.* San José *(Mar 13–21).*

Situated at the tip of the Baja peninsula, the pleasant town of San José del Cabo is centered around the shady Plaza Mijares. On weekends there is an arts and crafts market. Farther inland is the old town, while to the south of Plaza Mijares, the streets slope downward to the beachfront boulevard with its modern tourist hotels, resort complexes, and condominiums. On the east side of the town is a palm-fringed estuary, said to be home to over 200 different species of birds, including flocks of migrant ducks, which find refuge here from the northern winter. A few kilometers farther east is

Pelicans at Cabo San Lucas

the village of **Pueblo la Playa**, which has beautiful white-sand beaches, often deserted.

Cabo San Lucas

Baja California Sur. 28,500. 🚌 Día de San Lucas *(Oct 18).* **www**.loscabos.gob.mx

A miniature Acapulco, where it often seems that the official language is English, Cabo San Lucas is famous for its romantic "Lovers' Beach." Accessible only by boat, the beach is set among the jagged rocks known as Los Frailes (The Friars), which seem to form the tip of the peninsula. The beach is framed by a rock archway considered to link the waters of the Pacific with those of the Sea of Cortés.

One of the world's best game-fishing locations, the town has a sizable marina and a waterfront strip crowded with bars, discos, and restaurants. Farther inland, much of the old town remains intact. Beach activities are concentrated on the long **Playa El Médano**, where the swimming is safest and jet-skis can be rented. The diving is excellent around Los Frailes, where there is an immense underwater canyon.

Between Cabo San Lucas and San José del Cabo are several top-class golf courses and some stunning beaches.

A colorful building on one of the streets around Plaza Constitución in La Paz

Ruins of the ancient adobe buildings at Paquimé, northern Mexico's most interesting archaeological site

Hermosillo ⑭

Sonora. 🏔 *609,000.* ✈ 🚌 🛈 *Calle Comonfort, (662) 289 58 00 or 01800 716 25 55 (toll free).* 🎭 *Wine Festival (Jun), San Francisco (Oct 4).* **www**.visitasonora.com

Sonora's busy, thriving capital city – where cattle ranchers rub shoulders with car workers – has a quieter, prettier side too. Centered on the **Plaza Zaragoza**, with its lacy white bandstand, its outstanding feature is the 19th-century **cathedral** with its twin towers and pale yellow dome, each surmounted by a cross. The cathedral's dazzling white façade is a blend of architectural styles, with Neo-Classical predominating. It is remarkably harmonious considering it took over a century to build.

The Neo-Classical **Palacio de Gobierno** contains frescoes painted in the 1980s by three artists whose inspiration ranged from indigenous creation myths to the Mexican Revolution. In

The brilliant white façade of Hermosillo cathedral

a beautifully restored building, that was once the state penitentiary, is the **Museo de Sonora**, with galleries on the geology and ecology of the state and its development from prehistoric times to the present.

🏛 **Palacio de Gobierno**
Doctor Paliza. **Tel** *(662) 213 11 70.* ⏲ *Mon–Sat.* 🎟 *reserve in advance.*

🏛 **Museo de Sonora**
Jesus García Final. **Tel** *(662) 217 00 07.* ⏲ *Tue–Sun.* 🎟 *reserve in advance.* ♿

Paquimé ⑮

Chihuahua. 8 km (5 miles) SW of Casas Grandes. 🚌 *from Chihuahua.* ⏲ *daily.* 📷

The most important archaeological site in northern Mexico, Paquimé is an extraordinary complex of adobe buildings, quite unlike central and southern Mexican sites. Set on a plateau overlooking the Casas Grandes river, it flourished between the 10th and 14th centuries and probably housed over 3,000 people. Its partial destruction by fire in about 1340 and the disappearance of its inhabitants before the arrival of the Spanish have yet to be fully explained.

Walls of packed earth, up to 1.5 m (5 ft) thick, a mazelike construction, and "apartment buildings" as much as five floors high with internal staircases are among the site's characteristic features. The

houses also contain stoves for heating and beds in the form of alcoves. Low doorways in the shape of a thick "T" may have been partly for defence purposes. An impressive network of channels brought spring water from 8 km (5 miles) away for filtration and storage in deep wells. From here it was channeled to domestic and agricultural users, while another system of conduits drained away the waste. The inhabitants of Paquimé, whose language and ethnic origin are unknown, raised macaws for ceremonial purposes. The low, adobe pens with circular entrances, in which the birds were kept, remain intact. Other architectural elements seen here, including ballcourts, suggest cultural influence from Mesoamerican societies farther south.

Unique to Paquimé, however, is a particularly fine type of pottery, distinguished by a high polish and geometric or anthropomorphic designs. The most typical colors are black and reddish brown on a buff background. The style has been revived by local potters, some of whom command high prices for a single piece. More modestly priced examples can be bought in the nearby town of Casas Grandes Viejo. The site museum contains original ceramics as well as a model of the city as it would have looked in its heyday.

Modern Paquimé pot

The Cactuses of Northern Mexico

The landscapes of Northern Mexico are characterized by the extraordinary variety of cactuses that grow there. About 300 species of cactus exist in the Sonoran Desert, the most diverse desert in the world. They are superbly adapted to retain water and withstand fierce climatic extremes. Their fleshy stems, often

Flowers from a pincushion cactus

protected by spines, are filled with water-storing tissue and surrounded by a thick, waxy layer to help retain moisture. Cactuses can remain dormant for long periods and then burst into bloom after a brief downpour. In Mexico, cactuses are used for food and drink, for roof coverings, and to make fish hooks and pot scourers.

Prickly pears (Opuntia species), *the largest cactus group, are also called Indian figs. Many have edible red, green, or purple fruits.*

The desert landscapes *of the North have a certain stark beauty.*

Boojum tree

Prickly pear

Barrel cactus

Agave

The giant Mexican cereus (Pachycereus pringlei) *is a tall, treelike cactus. They are often planted close together in rows to form fences.*

The saguaro (Carnegiea gigantea) *can grow to 16 m (52 ft) tall, taking nearly 150 years to reach its full height. Large specimens can hold several tons of water.*

The boojum tree (Idria columnaris) *is an extraordinary sight. It is seen mainly in the deserts of Baja California.*

Agaves *are used to make tequila (see p325) and henequen (see p273). Some species take up to 50 years to flower.*

SUCCULENTS

Most cactuses store water in fleshy stems, but many other succulents, such as the agaves, store moisture in their leaves. Succulents grow very slowly to reduce their need for water, and many have shallow, but very extensive, root systems.

The barrel cactus (Ferocactus) *derives its name from its rounded shape. Mexico has nine species of barrel cactus.*

Chihuahua ⑯

Chihuahua. 🏛 670,000. ✈ 🚌 🚃
ℹ *Palacio de Gobierno, (614) 429 34
21.* 🎭 *Santa Rita (May 22).* **www.**
chihuahua.gob.mx/turismoweb

The ghosts of two Mexican
heroes, Pancho Villa and Father
Miguel Hidalgo *(see p49)*,
seem to haunt the streets of
Chihuahua. Set among rugged
hills in a semi-desert landscape,
it owes its foundation to the
rich veins of silver discovered
nearby in the colonial period.
The city's **aqueduct**, referred
to by locals as "los arquitos"
(the arches), dates from that
era. Its best-preserved section
is at the intersection of Calle
56 and Calle Allende. Today
Chihuahua relies mostly on
automobile manufacturing
and cattle-ranching.

The Plaza de Armas, the
main square of Chihuahua, is
dominated by the **cathedral**.
This impressive, twin-towered
building in rose-colored stone
dates from the 18th century. Its
1920s altar of Italian marble is
particularly fine. A side chapel
contains a museum of religious
art, open on weekdays.

The **Palacio de Gobierno**
on Plaza Hidalgo (to the
northeast of the main square)
is a late 19th-century building.
Its courtyard features striking
murals by Aarón Piña Mora
that illustrate episodes from
Chihuahuan history. There is
also an eternal flame commemorating Independence hero
Father Hidalgo – it marks the
spot where he was executed
by firing squad in 1811 after
leading a rebellion against the
Spanish crown. Two blocks
away, on Avenida Juárez, the
Palacio Federal preserves
within its walls the remains of
the church tower that served

The Art Nouveau Quinta Carolina, on the outskirts of Chihuahua

as Hidalgo's cell. It contains
a few poignant reminders of
the priest's incarceration and
fate, including a tiny lantern
with which he illuminated the
last few nights of his life.

Undoubtedly the best-known
Chihuahuan resident was
Francisco "Pancho" Villa,
the mustachioed hero
of the 1910–20
revolutionary war
(see p54). The **Museo
Histórico de la
Revolución** features
the bullet-riddled
Dodge at whose
wheel he met his
end in 1923. The
museum is situated
in his former
house, and much of
his furniture and other
household goods are still
here. The galleries behind the
house recount the story of the
Revolution. There is also a
death mask of Villa, taken just
hours after his assassination.

Perhaps the finest house in
the city is the Quinta Gameros,
to the southeast of the Plaza de
Armas, which now houses the
**Centro Cultural Universita-
rio Quinta Gameros**. It is
worth paying the admission
price to this
exquisite Art
Nouveau mansion
just to see the
dining room with
its fantastic wood
carvings. The
rooms upstairs
house permanent
exhibitions, inclu-
ding paintings
and sculptures by
Mexican artist
Luis Aragón.

Statue on the façade of
Chihuahua cathedral

Environs
Around 20 km (12 miles) to
the southeast of Chihuahua
is the picturesque mining
town of **Santa Eulalia**. A
stroll through its cobbled
streets is enjoyable, particularly on a Sunday,
when bands play
in the town plaza.

The **Cumbres de
Majalca National Park**,
situated about 70 km
(43 miles) to the
northwest of
Chihuahua, offers
opportunities for
hiking, rock-
climbing, and
wilderness camping
among forested
canyons and peaks.

🏛 **Museo Histórico de la
Revolución**
Decima 3014. **Tel** *(614) 416 29 58.*
◷ *Tue–Sun.* 🎫 🏛 ♿ *ground floor.*

🏛 **Centro Cultural
Universitario**
Paseo Bolívar 401. **Tel** *(614) 416 66 84.*
◷ *Tue–Sun.* 🎫 📷

Ciudad
Cuauhtémoc ⑰

Chihuahua. 🏛 124,000. 🚌 ℹ *Cnr
of Allende and Agustín Melgar, (625)
58134 88.* 🎭 *San Antonio (Jun).*

The industrious Mennonite
farmers who have made
Cuauhtémoc what it is today
arrived in 1921 at the invitation
of President Obregón. Originally from the Netherlands,
these fundamentalist Christians
had settled in Canada but came
into conflict with the authorities there when they resisted
the draft for World War I.

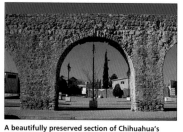
A beautifully preserved section of Chihuahua's
aqueduct, which dates from colonial times

PANCHO VILLA (C.1878–1923)

A member of a bandit group as a young man, Francisco "Pancho" Villa became an influential leader of the Revolution after joining the campaign to depose Porfirio Díaz in 1910 *(see p54)*. His excellent military strategies and charismatic leadership inspired great loyalty in his División del Norte army and made him a folk hero, particularly around Chihuahua where he had his headquarters. In 1920 Álvaro Obregón took power and encouraged Villa to retire to a hacienda in Canutillo (Durango). Three years later, on a trip into Hidalgo del Parral, he was assassinated. About 30,000 people attended his funeral.

The death mask of Pancho Villa

This is the largest Mennonite group in Latin America. Their self-sufficient farms, known as camps, stretch north and south from Cuauhtémoc. Often blond and blue-eyed, the Mennonites stand out from their Mexican neighbors and have remained culturally distinct. Although they have embraced some modern technology, they still have a very traditional way of life. Their pitched-roofed, woodframe houses and barns give this part of Mexico a strangely European aspect.

A Mennonite man in traditional dress

Mennonite men, with their trademark denim overalls, usually speak Spanish, but many of the women speak only the Low German dialect of their ancestors. The easiest way to meet them is to buy some of the excellent cheese, which is their best-known product. The cheese factory at Camp 6½ (all the camps are numbered, not named) is open to visitors, except on Sundays, when everything apart from the churches closes down.

Hidalgo del Parral ⑱

Chihuahua. 🏘 101,000. 🚌
ℹ Mina La Prieta, (627) 525 44 00.
🎺 Francisco Villa (Jul 20).

Most famous as the site of Pancho Villa's murder, Parral (as it is usually known) was founded in 1631. It owes its existence to the gold and silver mines, and at the end of the 19th century it was one of the most opulent cities in Mexico. Its churches are noted for the chunks of ore that went into their construction.

The La Prieta minehead still overlooks the town. Nearby is the **Templo de la Virgen de Fátima**, the church dedicated to the miners' patron saint. Built at the end of the 19th century, it has small pieces of metal from the mines, including silver and gold, set into its walls. In place of traditional pews are stools shaped like claim markers.

Another outstanding building is a 19th-century church, the **Parroquia de San José**. Situated on the town's main square, it has an unusual diamond pattern on its walls.

Farther to the west, at the corner of Calle Primo de Verdad and Riva Palacio, is the splendid **Casa de Alvarado**. It was built at the start of the 20th century for the Alvarado family, whose fortune came from La Palmilla – believed at the time to be the richest silver mine in the Americas. Notice the anguished face over the main door, which is said to be that of an Indian mine worker. Nearby, over one of the bridges that span the Parral River (in winter just a dry arroyo), is

the **Museo Francisco Villa**. It is housed in the building from which Villa's assassins fired the fatal shots, and a bronze starburst on the pavement outside marks the place where he died. The building is now a library, with the Villa museum on the first floor. It includes photos taken after the murder, as well as a model of the scene.

Environs

Parral can be used as a southern gateway to the rugged landscape of the Sierra Tarahumara, which stretches away to the northwest, while 15 minutes' drive east of town are the hot mineral springs of **El Ojo de Talamantes**, in the lush Valle de Allende.

Farther to the east is a stark, inhospitable desert region, the **Bolsón de Mapimí**, which encloses a remote area called the "Zone of Silence." Rumored to be a landing site for UFOs or a kind of Mexican Bermuda Triangle, it gets its name from the popular theory that radio waves cannot enter or leave it. A few kilometers east is the massive **Mapimí Biosphere Reserve**, home to rare desert plants and animals.

🏛 **Museo Francisco Villa**
Corner of Barreda & Juárez. **Tel** (627) 525 32 92. ⬤ Tue–Sun (daily in holidays). 🎫 ♿ ground floor. 📷 reserve in advance. 🚻

The Templo de la Virgen de Fátima, the miners' church in Hidalgo del Parral

The beautiful Lago Arareco, high in the mountains of the Sierra Madre Occidental

Creel ⑲

Chihuahua. 🏔 *4,000*. 🚃 🚌
ℹ *López Mateos, (635) 456 01 26.*
🎭 *Carnival (Feb/Mar).*

Redolent of wood smoke and fresh mountain air, the small logging town of Creel is the main road and rail gateway to the largely unspoiled Sierra Tarahumara and the Copper Canyon *(see pp176–7)*. It is an excellent place to join the spectacular El Chepe railroad *(see p376)*, or to disembark and spend a few days exploring the pine-clad mountains.

Near the railroad station are the town plaza and Creel's main street, Calle López Mateos. Two churches stand on the square along with the Tarahumara Mission shop, which gives informal advice to visitors as well as selling Indian artifacts and books about the surrounding sierra. On the other side of the railroad tracks is the **Casa de las Artesanías**, a government-run museum and craft shop. It tells the story of railway tycoon Enrique Creel (after whom the town is named) and includes exhibits about the numerous Jesuit missions in the area and the culture of the Tarahumara Indians. One glass case contains mummified bodies found in the nearby hills.

The best spot around the town for a gentle stroll or a picnic is at **Lago Arareco**, just 5 km (3 miles) to the south. The U-shaped lake is surrounded by unusual rock formations and a fragrant pine forest. A few kilometers farther along the same road is the start of a 4-km (2.5-mile) trail that winds through a scenic canyon to

Cascada Cusárare, a 30-m (100-ft) waterfall. Other attractions within easy reach of Creel include the hot springs at **Recohuata**, the weird, mushroom-shaped rocks of the **Valle de los Hongos**, and **El Divisadero**, the viewpoint over the breathtaking Copper Canyon. El Chepe trains stop here briefly, but there are also minibus tours to the viewpoint for those who wish to spend longer contemplating the magnificent view. Tours to various sights, including helicopter trips over the canyons, are available in town.

Environs

A three-or four-hour drive northwest of Creel is the dramatic **Cascada de Basaseáchic**. At almost 300 m (1,000 ft) high, this is the third highest waterfall in North America. The towering falls are surrounded by 57 sq km (22 sq miles) of national park, with excellent walking trails and campgrounds. The park also contains several other waterfalls.

🏛 **Casa de las Artesanías**
Av Ferrocarril 178. **Tel** *(635) 456 00 80*. ☐ *daily.* 📷 📄

THE TARAHUMARA INDIANS

A very private people, the Tarahumara Indians moved up into the mountains of the Sierra Madre Occidental about 400 years ago to avoid the Spanish missionaries. Since then, they have kept themselves very much apart from the rest of Mexico, preferring to live in small self-sufficient farming communities. They call themselves the Raramuri (Runners) and are superb long-distance athletes. The traditional tribal sport, *rarajípari (see p22)* involves teams of runners kicking a wooden ball for huge distances across rugged mountain slopes. Participants wear sandals on their feet, and matches can last for several days.

A Tarahumara Indian woman and her children in traditional dress

The Hacienda Batopilas, built by a wealthy silver baron

Batopilas ❷⓿

Chihuahua. 🏘 12,400. 🚌

Barely more than a single street wide, and clinging to the riverbank at the bottom of a 1.5-km (1-mile) deep canyon, Batopilas is one of Mexico's hidden treasures. And it was treasure, in the form of silver, that brought the Spanish, and later the noted US politician Alexander Shepherd, to this remote spot. Not the least remarkable fact about this extraordinary place is that it was built when the only way in and out was by mule train over the mountains. Today, it can still take three hours to traverse the 60 km (37 miles) of dirt road that link Batopilas with the Creel-to-Guachochi highway. As it descends, the road drops over 2,100 m (7,000 ft) down the canyon wall via a hair-raising sequence of bends.

Batopilas was the birthplace of Manuel Gómez Morín, who formed PAN (Partido de Acción Nacional), the main opposition party to the long-running PRI *(see p55)*. There is little more than a plaque and a bust to mark the fact, but monuments to another former resident, Alexander Shepherd, abound. Shepherd, the last governor of Washington DC, created the Batopilas Mining Company in the 1890s. The ruins of his home, the **Hacienda San Miguel**, now overgrown with wild fig and bougainvillea, lie just across the river from the town entrance. Much of the aqueduct he built is still intact, and his hydroelectric plant, which made Batopilas the second electrified town in Mexico, is working again. The **Hacienda Batopilas**, now a hotel, is another noteworthy edifice with fantastic domes and arches.

Environs

Farther down the canyon, remote **Satevó** has a domed church, a testament to the zeal of the Jesuits who brought the Gospel here.

Cañón del Cobre ❷❶

See pp176–7.

Decorative wall tiles in Alamos

Alamos ❷❷

Sonora. 🏘 25,000. 🚌
ℹ️ Guadalupe Victoria 5, (647) 428 04 50. 🎉 Virgen de Concepción (1st Sun of Dec).

A colonial jewel, set on the western edge of the Sierra Madre Occidental, Alamos owed its fame and fortune to the silver discovered here in the 17th century. However, its restoration is largely due to the community of people who have moved here from the US.

On the main plaza is the Baroque **Parroquia de la Purísima Concepción**, built between 1783 and 1804. Its bell tower has china plates, allegedly donated by local women, embedded in its walls. Sadly, most of the plates were broken in the Revolution. Also on the square is the **Palacio Municipal** (1899), which has a square tower and iron balconies. Nearby, the **Museo Costumbrista** charts the local history.

However, it is the restored Sonoran mansions, with their interior patios and large windows with wrought-iron grilles, that give the town its flavor. Tours of some of these homes take place every Saturday.

🏛 **Museo Costumbrista**
Guadalupe Victoria 1. **Tel** (647) 428 00 53. ⏰ Wed–Sun. 🖼️ ♿
🎫 reserve in advance. 📷

The attractive colonial town of Alamos, centered on the Parroquia de la Purísima Concepción church

Cañón del Cobre (Copper Canyon) ㉑

Bigger by far than the Grand Canyon, yet nowhere near as well known, Mexico's Copper Canyon region is one of the great undiscovered wonders of North America. Here, rivers have carved half-a-dozen canyons into the volcanic rock of the Sierra Madre Occidental. Amid the pine forests are spectacular waterfalls, weird rock formations, and tranquil lakes, some of which can be seen from the awe-inspiring railroad that winds across the northern part of the region. Thinly populated, the canyons are home to the Tarahumara Indians *(see p174)* and also contain evocative relics of past mining booms.

The spectacular Cañón del Cobre, over 1.5 km (1 mile) deep and 50 km (31 miles) in length

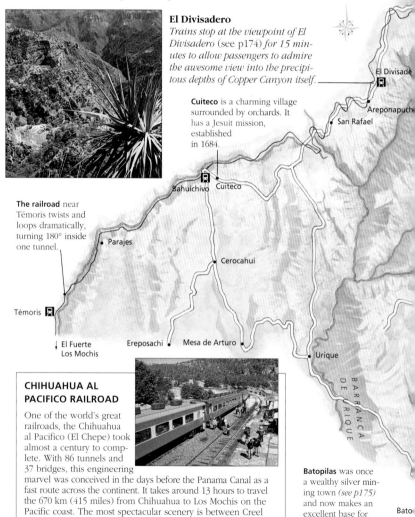

El Divisadero
Trains stop at the viewpoint of El Divisadero (see p174) *for 15 minutes to allow passengers to admire the awesome view into the precipitous depths of Copper Canyon itself.*

Cuiteco is a charming village surrounded by orchards. It has a Jesuit mission, established in 1684.

The railroad near Témoris twists and loops dramatically, turning 180° inside one tunnel.

Pitorr

El Divisade

Areponapuch

San Rafael

Bahuichivo Cuiteco

Parajes

Cerocahui

Témoris

El Fuerte
Los Mochis

Ereposachi Mesa de Arturo

Urique

CHIHUAHUA AL PACIFICO RAILROAD

One of the world's great railroads, the Chihuahua al Pacifico (El Chepe) took almost a century to complete. With 86 tunnels and 37 bridges, this engineering marvel was conceived in the days before the Panama Canal as a fast route across the continent. It takes around 13 hours to travel the 670 km (415 miles) from Chihuahua to Los Mochis on the Pacific coast. The most spectacular scenery is between Creel and El Fuerte, a stretch that drops more than 2,000 m (6,550 ft).

B A R R A N C A   D E   U R I Q U E

Batopilas was once a wealthy silver mining town *(see p175)* and now makes an excellent base for hiking excursions in the canyons.

Bato

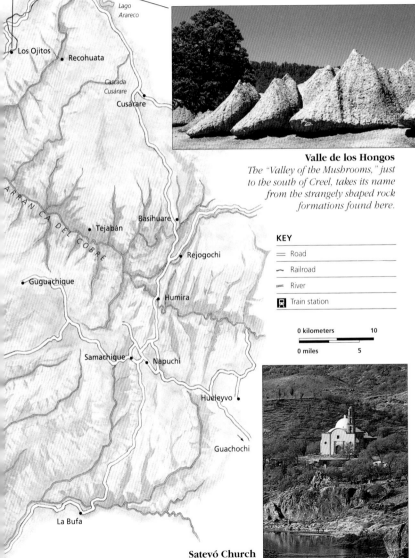

Los Ojitos is the highest point on the line. Nearby is El Lazo (The Bow), a 360° loop of track.

Creel
Winters can be very cold in this logging town of 4,000 inhabitants (see p174). Creel stands at an altitude of over 2,300 m (7,550 ft).

VISITORS' CHECKLIST

Chihuahua. 🚋 *Creel.*
Ferrocarril Mexicano Tel
(614) 439 72 12. There is one westbound and one eastbound train a day. Book in advance (a month before for first class).
www.chepe.com.mx

Valle de los Hongos
The "Valley of the Mushrooms," just to the south of Creel, takes its name from the strangely shaped rock formations found here.

KEY

═══	Road
～	Railroad
═	River
🚉	Train station

0 kilometers ————— 10
0 miles ————— 5

Satevó Church
Known as the "lost cathedral," this remote church was probably built by Jesuit missionaries in the 17th century, long before the first road penetrated the canyon. No record of its construction exists.

atevó

Fishing boats on Mazatlán's peaceful beachfront, the Playa del Norte

Mazatlán ㉓

Sinaloa. ★ 60,000. ✈ ⛴ ☷ ⓘ
Carnaval 1317, (669) 981 88 83. ◎
Carnival (Feb/Mar). www.vivesinaloa.
com or www.gomazatlan.com

Situated just south of the
Tropic of Cancer, Mazatlán is
one of Mexico's most
northerly major resorts. An
agreeable climate and almost
20 km (12 miles) of beaches
make it extremely popular.
Another attraction is the Mazatlán carnival, claimed to be the
third largest in the world, after
those of Rio and New Orleans.

A waterfront boulevard connects the narrow streets and
19th-century architecture of the
old town with the expensive
beach hotels of the touristic
Zona Dorada (Golden Zone).
Of the offshore islands,
Venados, Lobos, and **Pájaros**
all offer an enticing combination of wildlife and uncrowded, sandy beaches, and are
easily and cheaply reached by
small boats. The misleadingly
named **Isla de la Piedra**, however, is not actually an island
but a peninsula across the
estuary. Famous for its sandy
beaches fringed with coconut
palms, it is the site of one of
Mexico's largest tourist devel-
opments, the Estrella de Mar.

Historic Mazatlán is worth
visiting for its beautifully restored, Italianate **Teatro Ángela
Peralta**, named after a famous
Mazatlán-born opera singer,
and its intriguing **cathedral** –
Neo-Gothic on the outside,
exuberantly Baroque on the
inside, and noted for its gilded
altar. Both buildings date from
the late 19th century. However,
Mazatlán's oldest church is the

Iglesia de San José, built in
1842 on the slopes of the
Cerro de la Nevería (Icebox
Hill). The Cerro, which offers
a spectacular view of the city
by day or night, acquired its
name from the 19th-century
practice of storing
imported ice in a
tunnel carved
into the hillside.
The country's big-
gest aquarium, the
Acuario Mazatlán,
has more than
250 species of
fish and other
marine creatures.

Environs
Sinaloa is one of
the few areas where
the pre-Columbian
ball-game known as
hulama is still played *(see
p277).* The town of **El Quelite**,
50 km (31 miles) north of
Mazatlán along Mex 15, holds
matches on Sundays.

⚓ Acuario Mazatlán
Av Deportes 111. **Tel** (669) 981 78
15. ☐ daily. ◎ ☐ ☐ ☐ ☐

**Durango's Baroque cathedral, with
its impressive twin towers**

Durango ㉔

Durango. ★ 491,000. ✈ ☷ ⓘ
Florida 1106, Barrio del Calvario,
(618) 811 21 39. ◎ Feria Nacional
(Jul 8). www.durangoturismo.com

This city's main attraction is its
association with the movie
industry, particularly Westerns.
Many of its restaurants and
shops have cowboy themes.

There are also several
important buildings. On the
north flank of the Plaza de
Armas stands the impressive
cathedral. Begun in 1695, it
has a Baroque façade and a
fine choir with gilded stalls
featuring figures of saints.
A few blocks west of the plaza
is the **Palacio de Gobierno**, the
seat of the state government,
known for its striking set of

**Detail of a mural at
Durango's Palacio
de Gobierno**

20th-century murals
painted by Francisco
Montoya de la Cruz,
Guillermo Bravo,
and Guillermo de
Lourdes. The **Casa
del Conde de Suchil**,
a late 18th-century
mansion east of the
plaza, now houses
shops and a bank.
In the bank, the
original interior
can still be seen.
The exquisite Art
Nouveau **Teatro
Ricardo Castro**,
built in 1900, holds what is
reputedly the country's largest
hand-carved relief made from
a single piece of wood.

Environs
There are a number of
movie locations outside the
city, most notably the **Villa
del Oeste** set. Nearby is the
village of **Chupaderos**, which
was probably Durango's most
used Hollywood location.

For superb views of moun-
tains and canyons, head west
on Mex 40, which reaches
around 2,600 m (8,530 ft)
above sea level. The highlight
is the **Espinazo del Diablo**
(Devil's Backbone), a winding
9-km (6-mile) stretch along a
narrow ridge about 130 km
(81 miles) west of Durango.

🏛 Villa del Oeste
Mex 45, 12 km (7 miles) N of
Durango. ☐ daily. ◎ ☐

Saltillo cathedral's pulpit, with its gold-leaf decoration and saintly figurines

Saltillo ㉕

Coahuila. 🏠 580,000. ✈ 🚌
🛈 Av Universidad 205, (844)
416 48 80. 🎭 Ferias (Jul–Aug).

Dubbed "the city of columns" because of the number of buildings characterized by Neo-Classical colonnades, Saltillo is also famous for what is probably the most beautiful **cathedral** in northeast Mexico. Dominating the old Plaza de Armas, the Churrigueresque façade of this 18th-century building has six columns richly embellished with carved flowers, fruit, and shells.

Inside, visitors can climb the smaller of the two towers, and view the Spanish 16th-century wooden cross in the Capilla del Santo Cristo, which is located in the main body of the church. The cathedral also holds a large collection of colonial oil paintings, but its principal treasure is the remarkable silver front of the side altar dedicated to San José. So fine is the silverwork, in fact, that the piece is often exhibited elsewhere and replaced in the cathedral by a photograph.

On the opposite side of the plaza is the state government headquarters, the **Palacio de Gobierno**, which contains a mural charting the history of Coahuila. The other building of note in the center, which stands out for both its history and for its attractive,

tiled cupola, is the **Templo de San Esteban**. This church served as a hospital for injured Mexican troops during the US invasion of Mexico *(see p52)*.

Saltillo also has a unique museum dedicated to the birds of Mexico. The **Museo de las Aves de México** contains an outstanding collection of stuffed birds, covering over 670 different species. The **Museo del Desierto** aims to promote a greater understanding of the rich biodiversity of desert ecology.

🏛 **Museo de las Aves de México**
Corner of Hidalgo & Bolivar. **Tel** (844) 414 01 67. 🕐 Tue–Sun. 🎟 ♿ 📷

🏛 **Museo del Desierto**
Centro Metropolitano Parque las Mararvillas. **Tel** (844) 986 90 00. 🕐 Tue–Sun. 🎟 ♿

Monterrey ㉖

Nuevo León. 🏠 1.1 million.
✈ 🚌 🛈 Washington 648 Oriente, 01800 832 22 00 (toll free). 🎭 Virgen de Guadalupe (Dec 12). **www**.turismonuevoleon.com

Mexico's third-largest city is a thriving industrial center with some striking 20th-century architecture like the **Planetario Alfa**, which houses science exhibitions and a planetarium, and the **Basílica de la Purísima**, finished in 1946. In the Gran

Plaza the **Museo de Arte Contemporáneo** (MARCO) houses Latin American modern art. A monumental sculpture, the **Faro del Comercio**, towers above Monterrey's cathedral. The city's **Museo de Historia Mexicana de Monterrey** offers five floors of exhibits from the prehistoric era to the present.

Environs
Occupying an area of mountainous semidesert west of Monterrey is the **Parque Nacional las Cumbres de Monterrey**. Two of its most accessible sights are the 25-m (82-ft) Cola de Caballo falls and the spectacular Grutas de García caves.

🏛 **Planetario Alfa**
Ave Gómez Morín 1100. **Tel** (81) 8303 00 03. 🕐 Tue–Sun. 🎟 ♿
📷 📷

🏛 **MARCO**
Cnr Zuazua & Jardón. **Tel** (81) 8262 45 00. 🕐 Tue–Sun. 🎟 Wed free. ♿ 📷 in advance. 📷 📷

🏛 **Museo de Historia Mexicana de Monterrey**
Dr Coss 445 Sur. **Tel** (81) 2033 98 98. 🕐 Tue–Sun.

Monterrey's massive cultural complex, the Planetario Alfa

HOLLYWOOD IN MEXICO

Clear blue skies and magical, semidesert landscapes made Durango for many years a favorite location for the movie industry, especially for Westerns. The stars who have filmed here range from John Wayne and Kirk Douglas to Anthony Quinn and Jack Nicholson. Some of the best-known movies shot near Durango include John Huston's *The Unforgiven* and Sam Peckinpah's *The Wild Bunch* and *Pat Garrett and Billy the Kid*. A few Hollywood locations can be visited, including the Villa del Oeste (officially called Condado Chávez) and Chupaderos.

The dusty village of Chupaderos, one of Durango's Wild West movie locations

THE COLONIAL HEARTLAND

AGUASCALIENTES · COLIMA · GUANAJUATO
JALISCO · MICHOACÁN · NAYARIT · QUERÉTARO
SAN LUIS POTOSÍ · ZACATECAS

*C*harming, well-preserved towns built during colonial times characterize the states to the north of Mexico City, where sun-drenched coastlines and humid jungles adjoin cactus-strewn mesas and snow-capped volcanoes. Indian villages, bustling cities, and beach resorts also form part of this vast and varied territory.

Following the fall of the Aztec empire *(see p43)*, Spanish soldiers marched north to conquer the no-madic Indian tribes of this region. Missionaries also came, to spread the Gospel, and adventurers to seek their fortune, some exploiting the veins of precious metal in the area's arid hills, others its fertile plains.

Soon opulent, Spanish-style cities, brimming with palaces, churches, and convents, were founded in the area. Zacatecas, Guanajuato, and San Luis Potosí boomed as a result of being the principal suppliers of silver and gold to the Spanish royal family. Aguascalientes, San Miguel de Allende, and Querétaro were all important stopovers on the silver route to the capital. The city of Morelia established itself as the cultural and social hub of New Spain's western province, and Guadalajara rose to prominence as the gateway to the Pacific ports of Manzanillo and San Blas.

In the early 19th century, general discontent with Spanish rule began to sim-mer in Querétaro, and nearby colonial strongholds. The plotting, and first armed uprising, by rebels here earned the region the title "the Cradle of Independence." Ferocious battles were fought in the cities of Guanajuato and Morelia, until Mexico declared its independence from Spain in 1821 *(see p49)*.

Today, the Colonial Heartland of Mexico remains a relatively prosperous region, thanks to its rich agricultural lands, thriving industry (which includes the production of tequila), and increasingly popular tourist attractions.

A volcano rises above fertile plains in Nayarit state, where agriculture is the main source of income

◁ The elaborate, polychromatic interior of the Santuario de Nuestra Señora de Guadalupe in Morelia

Exploring the Colonial Heartland

Beaches and colonial cities are the tourist magnets of this region. Big, booming Puerto Vallarta and the smaller, less hectic Manzanillo are resort cities on the long, beautiful Pacific coastline. Inland, Guadalajara is a modern metropolis notable for its majestic colonial core. The old towns of Zacatecas, San Luis Potosí, Aguascalientes, Guanajuato, San Miguel de Allende, and Querétaro were constructed with fortunes amassed from silver. Pátzcuaro and Morelia are colonial jewels in Michoacán. Off the beaten track are Huichol and Cora Indian villages in the Sierra Madre Occidental, the ghost town of Real de Catorce, isolated missions in the untamed Sierra Gorda, and the majestic waterfalls of the lush Huasteca Potosina.

Indian pottery on sale at a market in Pátzcuaro

SEE ALSO

• *Where to Stay* pp302–8

• *Where to Eat* pp335–9

For additional map symbols *see back flap*

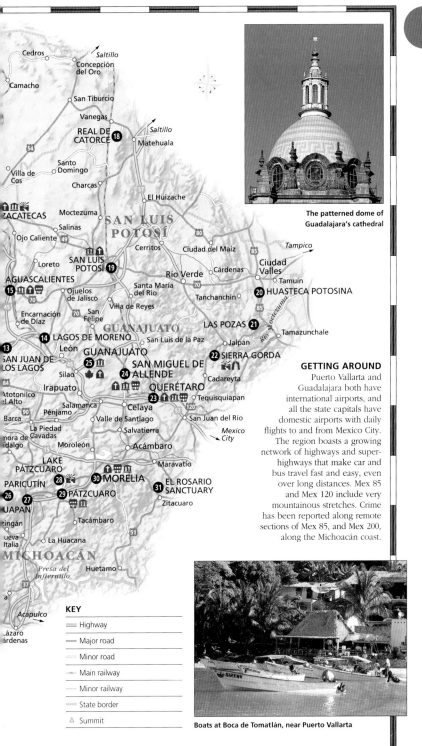

Cedros

Saltillo

Concepción del Oro

Camacho

San Tiburcio

Vanegas

REAL DE CATORCE 18   Saltillo
Matehuala

Santo Domingo

Villa de Cos

Charcas

El Huizache

ZACATECAS   Moctezuma

SAN LUIS POTOSÍ

Salinas

Ojo Caliente 49

Loreto

SAN LUIS POTOSÍ 19

Cerritos   Ciudad del Maíz

AGUASCALIENTES

15

Ojuelos de Jalisco

Río Verde   Cárdenas

Ciudad Valles

Tampico

Santa María del Río

Tamuín

Encarnación de Díaz

Villa de Reyes

Tanchanchín

20 **HUASTECA POTOSINA**

GUANAJUATO

San Felipe

LAS POZAS 21

Tamazunchale

13

14 **LAGOS DE MORENO**   San Luis de la Paz

Jalpan

León

22 **SIERRA GORDA**

SAN JUAN DE LOS LAGOS

GUANAJUATO 25

SAN MIGUEL DE ALLENDE 24

GETTING AROUND

Silao

Cadareyta

Irapuato

QUERÉTARO 23   Tequisquiapan

Atotonilco el Alto

Salamanca   Celaya

Barca   Pénjamo

Valle de Santiago

San Juan del Río

La Piedad   Cavadas

Salvatierra

Mexico City

nora de   idalgo

Moroleón

Acámbaro

LAKE PÁTZCUARO

Maravatío

PARICUTÍN   28   30 **MORELIA**

EL ROSARIO SANCTUARY 31

26   27

29 **PÁTZCUARO**

Zitácuaro

UAPAN

Tacámbaro

zingán

ueva Italia

La Huacana

51

MICHOACÁN

Presa del Infiernillo

Huetamo

37

Acapulco

ázaro árdenas

Puerto Vallarta and Guadalajara both have international airports, and all the state capitals have domestic airports with daily flights to and from Mexico City. The region boasts a growing network of highways and super-highways that make car and bus travel fast and easy, even over long distances. Mex 85 and Mex 120 include very mountainous stretches. Crime has been reported along remote sections of Mex 85, and Mex 200, along the Michoacán coast.

The patterned dome of Guadalajara's cathedral

KEY

━━━	Highway
━━━	Major road
┄┄┄	Minor road
─·─·─	Main railway
┄┄┄┄	Minor railway
▭▭▭	State border
△	Summit

Boats at Boca de Tomatlán, near Puerto Vallarta

Mexcaltitán ❶

Nayarit. 🏃 *1,000.* 🚢 🎉 *Fiesta de San Pedro y San Pablo (Jun 28–9).*

This tiny island, its name meaning "Place of the Moon Temple," is no more than 400 m (1,310 ft) across. It sits in a lagoon in Mexico's largest mangrove swamp area, and in the rains of August and September the streets become canals. According to legend the Aztecs slept here on the way to their promised land.

Although no Aztec artifacts have been found here, the archaeological pieces on display in the **Museo del Orígen**, located in the former town hall, nonetheless emphasize the importance of the island of Mexcaltitán as "The Cradle of Mexicanism".

🏛 **Museo del Orígen**
Plaza Principal. **Tel** *no phone.*
⭕ *Tue–Sun.* 🎫 ♿

San Blas ❷

Nayarit. 🏃 *43,000.* 🚌 ℹ *José María Mercado 29.* 🎉 *Día de San Blas (Feb 2), Carnival (Feb/Mar), Día de la Marina (Jun 1).*

Little remains from San Blas' colonial heyday, when it was a thriving seaport, an important shipbuilding center, and a garrison for the Spanish Armada. The only visible legacies are the ruins of an 18th-century Spanish fort and church, and a large, crumbling 19th-century customs house.

THE HUICHOL INDIANS

There are still some 50,000 Huichol Indians living in Mexico, mostly in villages in the Sierra Madre Occidental mountains. They are known for their secret religious rites. An indispensable ingredient in these ceremonies is the hallucinogenic

peyote cactus, which grows miles away in the state of San Luis Potosí. Every September, Huicholes go to their sacred mountain near Real de Catorce *(see p193)* to gather the plant. Huichol traders are known for their colorful *nierika*

Part of a brilliantly colored yarn painting by the Huichol Indians

yarn paintings and *chaquira* beadwork.

Today San Blas is a sleepy fishing village of palm groves and mangrove-fringed estuaries. It is the state's oldest developed resort, with a few hotels and palm-thatched restaurants catering to the swimmers and surfers attracted by the 19 km (12 miles) of golden beaches around the Bay of Matanchén. Beware of the mosquitoes that descend at sunset.

Environs
For boat trips through the lush jungle estuaries teeming with wildlife, head to the jetties east of town, on the road to Matanchén. The

Boats awaiting intrepid jungle adventurers

most popular destination is **La Tovara**, a freshwater spring and swimming hole adjacent to a crocodile farm.

Tepic ❸

Nayarit. 🏃 *305,000.* ✈ 🚌 ℹ *Cnr of Av México and Calzada del Ejército Nacional, (311) 214 80 71.* 🎉 *Feria Nacional de Tepic (Feb 25– Mar 21).* **www**.visitnayarit.com

A provincial town with an agreeable climate, Tepic was founded in the foothills of an extinct volcano in the 16th century. Not far from the Plaza Principal and the **cathedral** is the **Museo Regional de Nayarit**. Here, finds from shaft-tombs and displays about the Cora and Huichol Indians can be seen. The **Casa de los Cuatro Pueblos** (House of the Four Peoples) is a museum devoted to the Huicholes, Tepehuanos, Mexicaneros, and Coras. These people flock to Tepic on May 3 to visit the grass cross at the **Templo y Ex-Convento de la Cruz de Zacate**.

Environs
In the verdant hills 30 km (19 miles) southeast of Tepic is the picturesque **Santa María del Oro** lake, popular with hikers and birdwatchers.

🏛 **Museo Regional de Nayarit**
Av México 91 Norte. **Tel** *(311) 212 19 00.* ⭕ *Mon–Sat.* 🎫 *in advance.* 🚫

🏛 **Casa de los Cuatro Pueblos**
Hidalgo 60 Oriente. **Tel** *(311) 212 17 05.* ⭕ *Mon–Sat.*

The panoramic view of the serene Bay of Matanchén near San Blas

Puerto Vallarta ❹

Jalisco. 🏛 *184,000.* ✈ 🚌
ℹ *Plaza Marina 144–6, (322) 221 26 76.* 🎭 *Día de Guadalupe (Dec 12).* **www**.visitpuertovallarta.com

Hollywood stars discovered the tropical paradise of Banderas Bay in the 1960s. Since then, Puerto Vallarta has become one of Mexico's top Pacific resorts. Now 1.5 million tourists flock here annually to savor the beautiful beaches, the year-round pleasant climate, and the vibrant nightlife.

The resort stretches for more than 40 km (25 miles) around the bay, but its heart is Puerto Vallarta's old town, **Viejo Vallarta**. This area has managed to conserve some of the quaintness of a Mexican village, with its white-washed, tile-roofed houses and stone-paved streets stretching toward the jungle-clad mountains. The small **Isla Río Cuale**, an island in the river dividing the town, is the location for boutiques, cafés, and a botanical garden.

Head to the *malecón*, the waterfront boardwalk, for water taxis serving other parts of the bay, such as the Zona Hotelera, the main hotel strip which extends to the seaport in the north. Farther north is

Marina Vallarta, Mexico's largest marina, surrounded by luxury hotels, shopping malls, and a golf course. Beside the marina, although in another state (Nayarit) and even another time zone, is **Nuevo Vallarta**. This is the most recent development on the bay, and its miles of beach, river, and estuary frontage reach as far as the town of **Bucerías**. The tourist infrastructure then peters out, leaving a string of small, pristine beaches that stretch to the bay's northernmost point, **Punta Mita**.

The southern, more scenic arc of Banderas Bay begins with **Playa de los Muertos** (Dead Men's Beach), the old town's most popular section of coastline. From here, the road winds past villa-dotted cliffs and sparkling blue coves to **Mismaloya**, before turning inland. Beyond this point, the exotic coves and superb swimming and snorkeling beaches are accessible only by boat.

Environs

To the north of Puerto Vallarta are some of the area's most famous diving sites, including **Las Marietas**, **Corbeteña**, and **El Morro**. Trips to the forests, canyons, and villages of the hinterland are also easily arranged.

FIESTAS IN THE COLONIAL HEARTLAND

Fiesta de Año Nuevo (*Jan 1*), Ihuatzio (Michoacán). Purépecha Indians perform traditional masked dances to music and Pirecua songs. For the dance of "Los Viejitos" (The Old Men), originally dedicated to the elderly pre-Columbian god Huehuetéotl, dancers hobble around wearing masks and woollen shawls.

Masked Indian dancing at the Fiesta de Año Nuevo

Easter Week (*Mar/Apr*), Tzintzuntzan and Tarímbaro (Michoacán). A realistic crucifixion of Christ is re-enacted by a volunteer, who is flogged and carries his own wooden cross. Traditional processions also take place in San Miguel de Allende and Guanajuato.

Feria de San Marcos (*Apr/May*), Aguascalientes. Crowds of up to 100,000 jam the town and fairground around the clock, to see exhibitions, parades, and fireworks, listen to concerts, and cheer at bullfights, cockfights, and *charreadas*, the riding and rodeo shows.

Day of the Dead (*Nov 1–2*), Pátzcuaro and Isla Janitzio (Michoacán; *see p207*). Dead relatives and ancient gods are remembered, and traditional masked dances are performed, including "The Fish," in which fishing nets symbolically haul in a fish-masked dancer.

Sailboats moored in the calm waters of Puerto Vallarta's marina

A sheltered, tranquil bay at the northern end of the Costalegre

Costalegre ❺

Jalisco. 🚌 *Chamela, Barra de Navidad, Cihuatlán.* ℹ️ *Jalisco 67, Barra de Navidad, (315) 355 51 00.* **www**.costalegre.com

Jalisco's beautiful "Happy Coast" stretches for more than 200 km (125 miles), south from Puerto Vallarta *(see p185)* to the border with Colima state. The Mex 200 highway runs parallel with the coastline but mostly inland, taking in lush green mountain ranges and the occasional banana plantation. Most of Costalegre's white-sand beaches are accessible only to hotel guests or from the ocean. The luxury resorts – some with golf courses, polo fields, and airstrips – are shielded by gates and guards and can be reached only by private roads.

Set on a beautiful bay 165 km (102 miles) south of Puerto Vallarta, the resort of **Careyes** was developed in the late 1960s by an Italian entrepreneur. The colorful mix of Mediterranean and Mexican architecture, featuring open living areas and palm-thatched roofs, or *palapas*, has become known as the "Careyes Style." If money is no object, some of the dream houses perched on the soaring cliffs can be rented.

Somewhat more affordable are the lodgings found on the bays of Chamela, Tenacatita, and Cuastecomate. Swimming here is much safer than on the open-ocean beaches, which are subject to both dangerous waves and treacherous currents. The southernmost of the bays on the coast is **Bahía de Navidad**, where the family

resort of **Melaque** and the fishing village of **Barra de Navidad** are found. Most of Barra's small restaurants and modest hotels are squeezed onto a narrow sandbar, which enjoys sunsets over the Pacific Ocean and views of a peaceful lagoon to the east. Small boats from Barra ferry customers to the rustic eateries of **Colimilla**, a lagoon-side hamlet at the foot of a towering wooded peninsula. The peninsula is now dominated by the massive Isla Navidad resort, which has an ecological preserve and a 27-hole golf course with superb views.

Manzanillo ❻

Colima. 🏛️ *124,000.* ✈️ 🚌 ℹ️ *Blvd Miguel de la Madrid 875A, (314) 333 22 77.* 🎉 *Fiestas de Mayo (May 1–10), International Sailfish Fishing Tournament (1st week of Nov).* **www**.visitacolima.com.mx

Mexico's main west coast shipping center, Manzanillo is also Colima state's foremost beach resort and calls itself "The Sailfish Capital of the World." The colorful houses of the old port cling to a hill

overlooking the main harbor, while the newer part of town covers a sandbar separating the lagoon from the ocean. Most of Manzanillo's restaurants and hotels are located along the white sands of **Las Brisas** and **Playa Azul**.

Separating the Bahía de Manzanillo from the Bahía de Santiago is a peninsula, site of **Las Hadas** ("The Fairies"), a luxury Moorish-style hotel with a golf course which opened in the 1970s. Hotels now line most of the Bahía de Santiago, from La Audiencia to Playa Miramar. To see an outstanding collection of pre-Columbian artifacts from the region, head to the **Museo Universitario de Arqueología.**

🏛️ **Museo Universitario de Arqueología**
Glorieta San Pedrito. **Tel** *(314) 332 22 56.* 🕐 *for renovation until Dec 2008.* 🎟️ 📷 *in advance.* ♿

Cuyutlán ❼

Colima. 🏛️ *940.* 🚌 🎉 *Fiesta de la Santa Cruz (May 2–3).*

Cuyutlán is a traditional resort on the central part of Colima's coast. It is characterized by black volcanic sand, pounding surf, and the Mexican tourists that descend on the town on weekends. It is at the tip of the immense Cuyutlán Lagoon, which extends south for 32 km (20 miles) from Manzanillo.

Salt from the area provided an essential ingredient for ore processing in colonial times. The tiny Museo de la Sal gives an insight into the salt economy, its workers, and its harvesting methods. A spectacular springtime phenomenon seen on the

Manzanillo's grand Las Hadas resort

For hotels and restaurants in this region see pp302–8 and pp335–9

Volcán de Fuego, seen from the road heading out of Colima toward Guadalajara

coast here is the ola verde, when glassy green waves up to 10 m (33 ft) in height gleam with phosphorescent marine organisms.

🏛 Museo de la Sal
Juárez. ◯ Peak season: daily; low season: Fri–Sun. ♿

Bandstand in the tropical Jardín de Libertad, Colima

Colima ❽

Colima. 🏘 130,000. ✈ 🚌
ℹ Palacio de Gobierno, (312) 312 83 60. 🎭 San Felipe de Jesús (Feb), Feria de Todos los Santos (Oct 27– Nov 11). **www**.visitacolima.com.mx

The graceful provincial town of Colima, capital of one of Mexico's smallest states, was the first Spanish city on the west coast. It has been rebuilt several times since 1522 because of earthquakes, but the center still boasts Neo-Classical buildings, several museums, and tropical parks, such as the **Jardín de Libertad**.
  La Campana archaeological site on the outskirts of town was an important pre-Columbian settlement between AD 700 and 900, with the earliest remains dating back as far as 1500 BC. Major exploration in the mid-1990s unearthed several monumental plazas and structures. Ceramic vessels and human and animal figu-

rines from early shaft-tombs can be seen in the **Museo de las Culturas de Occidente. The Museo Universitario de Artes Populares** exhibits regional and national folk art, covering both pre-Columbian and more recent periods.

Environs:
The route heading north out of the city offers impressive views of the active **Volcán de Fuego** and the taller, dormant **El Nevado de Colima** behind. The foothills of both provide wonderful hiking opportunities.

🏛 Museo de las Culturas de Occidente
Corner of Galván & Ejército Nacional. **Tel** (312) 312 31 55. ◯ Tue–Sun. 🎟

🏛 Museo Universitario de Artes Populares
Gabino Barreda & Manuel Gallardo. **Tel** (312) 312 68 69. ◯ Tue–Sun. 🎟 Sun free. 🎫 ♿

Tequila ❾

Jalisco. 🏘 35,500. 🚌 ℹ José Cuervo 33. 🎭 Fiesta Septembrina (Sep 16), Feria Nacional del Tequila (Dec 1–12). **www**.tequilajalisco.gob.mx

Everything in Tequila reminds the visitor of Mexico's most famous drink (see p325), especially the heavy scent from more than a dozen distilleries. Plantations of *Agave tequilana weber* surround the town, the cores, or *piñas*, of which have been used to make the precious liquid since the 16th century. The town remains the country's largest producer and now exports to nearly 100 countries. A must is a distillery tour followed by a tasting session. The biggest and oldest factories include La Perseverancia and La Rojeña, where original equipment and a cooking pit can be seen.

Harvesting the *Agave tequilana weber,* in fields near Tequila

Guadalajara  ❿

Until just a few decades ago, the capital of the state of Jalisco was a placid provincial city. Then an industrial boom swiftly transformed Guadalajara into a modern metropolis second only to Mexico City. A broad industrial belt and sprawling suburbs now ring the historic center. However, the traditional flavor of the "Pearl of the West" or "City of Roses" lingers on in the vast series of squares, lined with majestic colonial buildings, that make up the core of the city. Distinctive and once separate communities such as Zapopan, with its sacred basilica, and Tlaquepaque *(see p190)* have their own attractions and are now suburbs of the city.

Guadalajara's imposing cathedral, seen from the Plaza de Armas

⛪ Cathedral Basílica

Construction of this monumental cathedral began shortly after Guadalajara was founded in 1542. However, it was not finished until the early 17th century, and then in a medley of styles. Two earthquakes, in 1750 and 1818, destroyed the original façade and towers. They were replaced in the mid-19th century by the present yellow-tiled twin spires, which soon became the recognized symbol of the city.

More than a dozen mostly Neo-Classical altars grace the otherwise somber interior. Among the 18th- and 19th-century paintings in the sacristy is *The Assumption of the Virgin*, which was painted by the Spanish artist Bartolomé Esteban Murillo.

🏛 Museo Regional de Guadalajara

Corner of Av Hidalgo and Liceo. **Tel** *(33) 3614 99 57.* ⬜ *Tue–Sun.* 📷 ♿ 🛈
A lovely former seminary dating from 1699 is now the home of the Museo Regional de Guadalajara. The ground-floor galleries have displays on palaeontology, prehistory, and archaeology. Among

exhibits here are a complete mammoth skeleton found in the state, and a replica of a shaft tomb discovered in Zapopan. Upstairs are ethnographic displays about Indian tribes, a gallery focusing on local history since the Conquest, and paintings by colonial and contemporary Jalisco artists.

Open, horse-drawn carriages can be hired at the museum entrance for a ride through the city's historic center.

🏛 Palacio de Gobierno

Cnr of Moreno & Av Corona. **Tel** *(33) 3668 18 02.* ⬜ *daily.*
Finished in the Baroque style in 1774, the Palacio de Gobierno is today the seat of the Jalisco state government. Murals by José Clemente Orozco adorn the main staircase, the dome of the former chapel, and the upstairs congress chambers. They celebrate Independence hero Miguel Hidalgo, who proclaimed the abolition of slavery in Mexico here in 1810. The wooden main door is intricately carved with nude female busts. Originally made for the cathedral, the door was deemed inappropriate and later installed here.

The Plaza de Armas, outside the building, has an ornate bandstand where concerts are staged on Thursday and Sunday evenings.

Sculpture on Plaza de Armas

🎭 Teatro Degollado

Plaza de la Liberación.
Tel *(33) 3030 97 71.* ⬜ *daily.*
Eight Corinthian columns topped by a triangular frieze depicting Apollo and the Muses make up the portico of this 1,400-seat Neo-Classical theater. The red-and-gold five-tier interior boasts chandeliers and a dome with a fresco showing scenes from Dante's *Divine Comedy.* The theater has been remodeled several times since its 1866 inauguration.

🏛 Instituto Cultural Cabañas

Cabañas 8. **Tel** *(33) 3668 16 47.* ⬜ *Tue–Sun.* 📷 *Sun free.* ♿ 🛈 📷 🛈 ∅
Founded by Bishop Juan Cruz Ruiz de Cabañas in 1805, this former hospice is the largest colonial edifice in the Americas and one of Mexico's finest Neo-Classical buildings.

The structure, with its large central dome and 22 courtyards, was the work of Manuel Tolsá.

For most of its history, the building served as an orphanage, housing up to 3,000 children at times. In 1979 it was restored and turned into an exhibition center, with permanent and temporary displays, and a school for the performing and fine arts.

Frescoes by José Clemente Orozco, executed in the late 1930s, cover the interior of

Mural of Miguel Hidalgo, painted by José Clemente Orozco, in the Palacio de Gobierno

Frog-shaped fountains in the pedestrianized Plaza Tapatía

the former chapel, with the central *Man in Flames* in the dome. These masterworks take as their themes the Conquest, political terror, and the dehumanization of modern man.

The Plaza Tapatía, fronting the building, marks the end of a nine-block pedestrian zone extending from the cathedral. Nearby is the **Mercado Libertad**, one of Latin America's largest covered markets.

🏛 Churches

There are many fine colonial churches within easy walking distance of the cathedral. The **Templo de San Juan de Dios**, with its vivid gold, white, and blue interior, backs onto a square where mariachi musicians and fans congregate.

To the south is the **Templo de San Felipe Neri**, which has a beautiful Plateresque façade. This church and the **Capilla de Aranzazú**, across the street, used to be part of a Franciscan monastery. The chapel contains three ornate Churrigueresque altars.

The lateral façade of the **Templo de Santa Mónica**, to the northwest, is an excellent example of Baroque styling.

🏛 Basílica de Zapopan

Zapopan, 7 km (4 miles) NW of center. **Tel** (33) 3633 66 14. ◯ daily. ♿

The early 18th-century Basílica de Zapopan is home to one of the most revered religious relics in Mexico, the Virgen de Zapopan. The small cornpaste statue was presented to the Indians of the region by a

VISITORS' CHECKLIST

Jalisco. 🏙 1.6 million. ✈ 17 km (11 miles) S. 🚌 Carretera libre a Zapotlanejo and Carretera Tonalá, (33) 3600 03 91. 🛈 Morelos 102, (33) 3668 16 00. 🎉 Virgen de Zapopan (Oct 12).

Franciscan friar in the 16th century and is believed to bring relief from natural catastrophes. To the right of the basilica's entrance is a small museum displaying Huichol Indian crafts *(see p184)*.

An ornate Baroque side entrance to the Templo de Santa Mónica

GUADALAJARA CITY CENTER

Capilla de Aranzazú ⑨
Cathedral Basílica ①
Instituto Cultural Cabañas ⑤
Mercado Libertad ⑥
Museo Regional de Guadalajara ②
Palacio de Gobierno ③
Teatro Degollado ④
Templo de San Felipe Neri ⑧
Templo de San Juan de Dios ⑦
Templo de Santa Mónica ⑩

0 meters 300
0 yards 300

Key to Symbols see back flap

Tlaquepaque ⓫

Jalisco. 🚌 *Guadalajara.* ℹ️ *Ayuntamiento, (33) 3562 70 50, ext 2319.* 🎉 *Fiestas de Tlaquepaque (Jun).*

Once a separate potters' village and stylish weekend retreat for the residents of Guadalajara *(see pp188–9)*, Tlaquepaque is now effectively a suburb of the city. However, it retains a village atmosphere.

The overwhelming selection of pottery, blown glass, textiles, metal, wood, and papier-mâché items cluttering the crafts shops is the main factor that attracts large numbers of visitors to come here.

There are also many restaurants. A favorite meeting spot off the appealing, flower-filled central square is El Parián. Hailed as the world's biggest cantina, it gathers a total of 47 eating and drinking establishments around its giant courtyard. In the center of the courtyard is a bandstand where mariachi musicians often play.

The best ceramics pieces from Tlaquepaque and the surrounding region can be appreciated at the **Museo Regional de la Cerámica**. Located in a beautiful old mansion, the museum counts a 16th-century kitchen among its most interesting exhibits. Many of the items sold in Tlaquepaque are in fact made in workshops in the neighboring suburb of Tonalá. Like Tlaquepaque, this was once a village outside Guadalajara, and was originally an Indian settlement. Its streets become an open-air craft market on Thursdays and Sundays.

Mariachi statuettes in a shop in Tlaquepaque

🏛 **Museo Regional de la Cerámica**
Independencia 237. **Tel** *(33) 36 35 54 04.* 🕐 *daily.* 📷 🚻

Laguna de Chapala ⓬

Jalisco. 🚌 *Chapala, Ajijic.* ℹ️ *Madero 407 Altos, Chapala, (376) 765 31 41.*

Mexico's largest natural lake, the Laguna de Chapala, supports a popular resort area, the Ribera, along its northwestern shore. However, the lake is

A view of the Laguna de Chapala, Mexico's largest lake

drying up, mainly because of the increasing water needs of the burgeoning population and industry of nearby Guadalajara.

The built-up Ribera has a near-perfect climate, and its proximity to Mexico's second city has for decades resulted in streams of foreign visitors. It stretches for 21 km (13 miles) from the old-fashioned resort of **Chapala**, where writer D.H. Lawrence stayed, to the village of Jocotepec at the western end of the lake. **Ajijic**, an artists' colony with cobblestone streets, crafts shops, galleries, and a 16th-century chapel, is the most picturesque village of the Ribera. Farther west, the spa resort of **San Juan Cosalá** offers the attractions of public swimming pools and a natural geyser.

Boat trips from Chapala head for two islands: the tree-covered **Isla de los Alacranes**, with its fish restaurants; and **Mezcala**, with the ruins of a 19th-century fort where independence fighters held out for four years before surrendering to the Spanish in 1816.

The scenic road along the mostly undeveloped southern shore opens up splendid views of the lake.

San Juan de los Lagos ⓭

Jalisco. 👥 *50,000.* 🚌 ℹ️ *Fray Antonio de Segovia 10, (395) 785 09 79.* 🎉 *La Candelaria (Jan 25–Feb 2), Fiesta de la Primavera (late May).*

The imposing 18th-century cathedral in San Juan de los Lagos is one the most important Catholic sanctuaries in Mexico. An estimated nine million pilgrims travel here every year to venerate the Virgen de San Juan de los Lagos, a small 16th-century corn-paste statue enshrined

A candy stall on Calle de Independencia, Tlaquepaque

For hotels and restaurants in this region see pp302–8 and pp335–9

in an altar originally made for the church of Santa Maria degli Angeli in Rome.

The cathedral, which reaches a height of 68 m (223 ft), has a sumptuous interior. In its vast sacristy is a group of large 17th- and 18th-century paintings, six of which have been attributed to Rubens. Touching votive pictures, expressing gratitude to the Virgin for favors granted, line the walls of a room beside the sacristy.

Many colonial buildings have been lost from the town's narrow streets, but the **Capilla de los Milagros** and **Casa de la Cultura**, both dating from the 17th century, are fine examples that have survived.

A colorful mural depicting life in Mexico, San Juan de los Lagos

Lagos de Moreno ⓮

Jalisco. 130,000. 🚌 Feria de Agosto (late Jul–early Aug).

Tourists rarely stray into this architectural jewel, which boasts many 18th- and 19th-century buildings and is known as the "Athens of Jalisco."

In colonial times, Lagos de Moreno was on the silver road between Zacatecas and Mexico City. The magnificent Baroque **parish church**, the more sober **Templo y Ex-Convento de Capuchinas**, and a bridge with Neo-Classical decoration all date from this era. The town peaked as a prosperous cattle-ranching center in the late 1800s, when it was enhanced by the charming **Teatro Rosas Moreno**. Two stately Neo-Classical residences from the same time are still here and look out onto the central park. These buildings now house the **Palacio Municipal** and the **Hotel de París**.

The arcaded main courtyard of the Palacio de Gobierno, Aguascalientes

Aguascalientes ⓯

Aguascalientes. 640,000. 🚗 🚌 **Palacio de Gobierno** 🚹 Plaza de la Patria, (449) 915 95 04. 🎭 Feria de San Marcos (mid-Apr–mid-May), Las Calaveras (early Nov).

Named after its hot springs, Aguascalientes still attracts visitors to its thermal baths but is today best known for its popular spring fair, the Feria de San Marcos (see p185).

The colonial red and pink **Palacio de Gobierno** has a spectacular maze of arches, pillars, and staircases around its main courtyard. An entertaining series of murals inside were painted by Oswaldo Barra Cunningham, a pupil of Diego Rivera. Across the Plaza de la Patria is the 18th-century **cathedral**, with a gallery of colonial paintings, and the Neo-Classical **Teatro Morelos**.

The **Museo de Arte Contemporáneo** displays prize-winning contemporary works, and the **Museo José**

The 18th-century cathedral on Plaza de la Patria in Aguascalientes

Guadalupe Posada has engravings by Mexico's best known satirical cartoonist. In contrast, **Museo Descubre** is an interactive science museum.

🏛 Museo de Arte Contemporáneo
Morelos and Primo Verdad. **Tel** (449) 918 69 01. ◯ Tue–Sun. 🚫 ♿ ⊘

🏛 Museo José Guadalupe Posada
Díaz de León. **Tel** (449) 915 45 56. ◯ Tue–Sun. 🚫 Sun free. ♿ 🎥 reserve in advance. 🚽

🏛 Museo Descubre
Avenida San Miguel. **Tel** (449) 978 03 38. ◯ daily. 🚫 ♿ 🎥 🖥 🚽

La Quemada ⓰

Zacatecas. Mex 54, 57 km (35 miles) SE of Zacatecas. 🚌 from Zacatecas. ◯ daily. 🚫

The archaeological site at La Quemada stretches over a steep hill rising from a wide, arid valley. From around AD 350, La Quemada was an important religious and political center and the focal point for trade between the area and Teotihuacán (see pp134–7). After AD 700, La Quemada seems to have substituted trade with more bellicose activities. In around 1100, it apparently suffered a violent end, despite an 800-m (2,600-ft) long and 4-m (13-ft) tall defensive wall on its northern slope.

It takes about two hours to explore the site by following the steep, rocky path that leads from the lower Main Causeway and Hall of Columns all the way up to the Citadel.

The Churrigueresque façade of the cathedral in Zacatecas

Zacatecas ⑰

Zacatecas. 🏃 124,000. ✈ ▭
🏠 Av Hidalgo 403, (492) 922 34 26.
🎭 La Morisma (Aug), Feria de
Zacatecas (1st two weeks of Sep).
www.turismozacatecas.gob.mx

Founded in 1546, shortly
after the discovery of metal
deposits in the area, Zacatecas
was soon supplying silver to
the Spanish crown. The city is
remarkable for its Baroque
limestone buildings that fill a
narrow valley between steep,
arid hills. Aristocratic patrons
built many stately mansions,
convents, and churches.

🏠 Cathedral
The profuse decoration on
the three-tiered façade of the
city's cathedral is considered
the prime example of the
Churrigueresque style (see
pp26–7) in Mexico. Apostles,
angels, flowers, and fruit
adorn the pillars, pedestals,
columns, and niches in dizzying excess. This exuberant

exterior contrasts strangely
with an interior whose treasures were lost in the turmoils
of the Reform (see p52) and,
later, the Revolution (see p54).
Most of the building was
constructed between 1730
and 1775, but the northernmost of the two towers was
not completed until 1904.
    The cathedral's two lateral
façades are both compara-
tively sober. A crucified Christ
adorns the one that faces north
toward the Plaza de Armas
and its 18th-century palaces.
On the east side of the plaza is
the most striking of these palaces, the Palacio de Gobierno,
which now contains offices.

🏠 Ex-Templo de San Agustín
Plazuela de Miguel Auza. **Tel** (492)
922 80 63. ☐ Tue–Sun.
This large Augustinian church
and its adjoining convent
were tragically sacked during
the Reform years (see p52).
Their Baroque splendor suffered further when they were
later turned into a hotel and
casino. Presbyterian missionaries from the US purchased
the church in the 1880s and
proceeded to strip it of its
Catholic decoration, tearing
down the tower and ripping
out the main façade. Only
the splendid Plateresque side
entrance was spared. Ornate
blocks from the exterior are
now piled up like giant jigsaw
pieces inside, a stark reminder
of the former grandeur that is
now a blank, white wall.
    These days the church is
used as an exhibition and
convention center, while the
former convent is now the seat
of the Zacatecas bishopric.

🏛 Museo Pedro Coronel
Plaza de Santo Domingo. **Tel** (492)
922 80 21. ☐ Fri–Wed. 🎟
The Zacatecan painter and
sculptor, Pedro Coronel, is
responsible for this
unique art collection
spanning a number of
civilizations and conti-
nents, from Egyptian
mummy cases to
works by Goya and
Hogarth. All this
is housed on the
labyrinthine upper
floors of a former
Jesuit college and
seminary. There is
also a beautiful library
of 25,000 volumes
dating from the 16th
to the 19th century.
Next to the museum
stands the Templo de Santo
Domingo, with its elaborately
gilded Baroque side altars.

Sculptu
Pedro Co

The Palacio de Gobierno, one of the mansions on the Plaza de Armas

🏛 Museo Rafael Coronel

Corner of Abasolo and Matamoros.
Tel *(492) 922 81 16.* ◯ *Thu–Tue.*
📷 ♿ 🖥 🎁

Another Coronel collection,
this one by Pedro's brother
Rafael, is held in the restored
ruins of the Ex-Convento de
San Francisco. An artist and a
lover of folk art, Rafael Coronel
amassed 10,000 ritual and
dance masks from all over the
country. About one-third of
them are exhibited alongside
a mass of other fine examples
of Mexican popular art, pre-
Columbian and colonial
pottery, and architectural
drawings and mural sketches
by Diego Rivera.

**Some of the many masks on display
in the Museo Rafael Coronel**

🏛 Museo Francisco Goitia

Enrique Estrada 102. **Tel** *(492) 922
02 11.* ◯ *Tue–Sun.* 📷

Paintings, silkscreens, and
sculptures by the Coronel
brothers and other Zacatecan
artists are exhibited in a Neo-
Classical villa. Until 1962 the
house was the official residence of state governors. Its
formal gardens overlook the
Parque Enrique Estrada. This
hilly park drops down to the
remains of an 18th-century
aqueduct and the Quinta Real
hotel *(see p308),* which is built
around the city's old bullring.

🎏 Cerro de la Bufa

The hill northeast of the city
center was the scene of a
bloody battle in 1914. A
museum at the summit exhibits
items from the victory won by
Francisco "Pancho" Villa *(see
p173).* There are splendid
views from the cable car, which
stretches 650 m (2,130 ft) from
here to the Cerro del Grillo.

🎏 Cerro del Grillo

This hill's main attraction is
a tour of three of the seven
levels of the legendary Eden

Zacatecas's aqueduct and old bullring, near the Museo Francisco Goitia

silver mine, which includes a
ride in a mine train through
600 m (2,000 ft) of tunnel.

🏛 Museo Regional de Guadalupe

Jardín Juárez Oriente, Guadalupe.
Tel *(492) 923 23 86.* ◯ *daily.* 📷
Sun free. 🎁

Just 10 km (6 miles) east of the
city center lies the town of
Guadalupe, whose imposing
Franciscan church and ex-
seminary house a museum of
colonial religious art second
only in importance to that of
Tepotzotlán *(see pp140–43).*
The treasures include works
by Miguel Cabrera, Rodríguez
Juárez, Cristóbal Villalpando,
and Juan Correa. Beside the
church is the jewel-like Capilla
de Nápoles, built in the 19th
century and considered to be
the paragon of Mexican Neo-
Classical expression.

Environs

About 45 km (28 miles) southwest of Zacatecas lies the
historic town of **Jerez,** with
its uncrowded streets, quiet
squares, and authentic 18th-
and 19th-century buildings.

**View of Zacatecas, from the
summit of the Cerro de la Bufa**

Real de Catorce ⑱

San Luis Potosí. 👥 *1,200.* 🚌
🛈 *Presidencia Municipal, (488) 887
50 71.* 🎉 *Feria de San Francisco de
Asis (Sep/Oct).*

The crumbling structures and
ghost-town atmosphere of
Real de Catorce testify to the
rapidly changing fortunes of
Mexican silver-mining centers.
Hidden high in the mountains
of the Sierra Madre Oriental,
it is accessible only through
a 2.5-km (1.5-mile) tunnel.

In the early 20th century the
town boasted a population of
40,000, served by several newspapers, a theater, a grand hotel,
and an electric tramway. Then,
drastically hit by falling silver
prices, its fortunes slumped
until only a few families
remained. Its eerie, semi-
deserted feel has made
it the chosen set for several
Mexican cowboy films.

Only the Neo-Classical
church, the **Parroquia de la
Purísima Concepción,** with its
reputedly miraculous statue of
St. Francis of Assisi and its large
collection of votive pictures,
was maintained for the sake
of the pilgrims who flood the
town once a year. Opposite
the church is the dilapidated
Casa de Moneda (closed
Mon, Tue), a former silver
warehouse and mint dating
back to the 1860s. The town's
former glory can also be seen
in the shells of ornate mansions, the ruined bullring, and
an octagonal cockfighting ring.

Real de Catorce's fortunes
now look set to rise and at
least one of the surrounding
mines is being tested as a possible new source of precious
metals. Ironically, the arrival of
modern amenities is reducing
the town's touristic appeal.

San Luis Potosí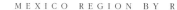

San Luis Potosí. 🚹 670,000. 🚌 ℹ️ *Manuel José Ottón 130, (444) 812 99 39.* 🎪 *San Luis Rey de Francia (Aug 25).* **www**.visitasanluispotosi.com

The mining wealth that the city of San Luis Potosí accumulated in the 1600s is evident in the historic buildings and three main squares at its core. The most central square, the **Plaza de Armas**, is dominated by the cathedral and the stately **Palacio de Gobierno**, which was the seat of Benito Juárez's government when he denied clemency to Emperor Maximilian in 1867 *(see p53)*. Behind it stands the **Real Caja**, or Royal Treasury, whose wide staircase enabled pack animals to reach the storage chambers above.

The second square is the **Plaza de los Fundadores**, the site of a former Jesuit college and two 17th-century churches, the **Iglesia de la Compañía** and the graceful **Capilla de Loreto**. On the eastern side of town is the third main square, the **Plaza del Carmen**, on which stand the church of the same name, the imposing **Teatro de la Paz**, and the Museo de la Máscara.

🏛 Museo Nacional de la Máscara

Villerías 2. *Tel (444) 812 30 25.* 🔲 *daily.* ♿ 📷
The walls of a former mansion, now restored, are adorned with over 1,000 decorative and ritual masks.

The Capilla de Aranzazú in the Ex-Convento de San Francisco

🔒 Templo del Carmen

This Churrigueresque church, built in the mid-1700s, is by far the most spectacular religious structure in the city. The impressive exterior has a three-tiered main façade, an ornate tower, and multi-colored domes. Even more fabulous is the interior, not least for its Baroque side altars and Francisco Eduardo Tresguerras' main altar. The real highlight, however, is the exuberant Altar de los Siete Príncipes, which is not actually an altar but a floor-to-ceiling interior façade enclosing the entrance to a side chapel, the Camarín de la Virgen. Its white-stucco surface is dotted with polychrome statues of angels.

🏛 Ex-Convento de San Francisco

Plaza de Aranzazú. *Tel (444) 814 35 72.* 🔲 *Tue–Sun.* 📷 *Sun free.* 🏠 ♿ *ground floor only.*
The Franciscans, the first religious order to arrive in San Luis Potosí, began work in 1686 on this ambitious convent and church complex, which took over a century to complete. The extensive former convent now contains the Museo Regional Potosino, which has colonial and pre-Columbian exhibits, including displays on the Huastec culture of southeastern San Luis Potosí state.

Upstairs is the splendid Capilla de Aranzazú, the lavish private chapel for the former occupants. A unique Baroque jewel despite the garish colors chosen by its restorers, it has a rare covered atrium and a carved wooden portal.

Behind the convent, on the Plaza de San Francisco, is the Templo de San Francisco. Beyond its classic Baroque façade lies a richly furnished main nave, several side chapels, and an original domed sacristy. The sacristy and the adjoining Sala de Profundis are filled with valuable paintings. Also

Detail of Templo de San Francisco

notable is the church choir, where there are more paintings and the remains of a monumental Baroque organ.

Environs

In the arid hills 27 km (17 miles) to the east lies the ghost town of **Cerro de San Pedro**, whose mines were the source of the city's wealth. To the southeast, around 45 km (28 miles) from San Luis Potosí, is **Santa María del Río**, known for its hand-woven silk and silk-like *rebozos*, or shawls. Traditional dyeing, weaving, and fringe-knotting can be observed in the Escuela del Rebozo. Around **Villa de Reyes**, 57 km (35 miles) south of San Luis Potosí, former haciendas show visitors the architecture of a social system that engendered, and ended with, the Revolution *(see p54)*.

Corner of the late 18th-century Baroque Real Caja

Huasteca Potosina ⑳

San Luis Potosí. ⊞ *Ciudad Valles.*
🈂 *Carretera Tamazuchale.*

The southeastern part of San Luis Potosí state is an area of stunning natural beauty known in pre-Columbian times as Tamoanchán, or "Earthly Paradise." It boasts tropical valleys, lush mountains, clear rivers, and majestic waterfalls. The most spectacular cascade is Tamul, which plunges 105 m (344 ft) into a canyon and is up to 300 m (1,000 ft) wide in the rainy season. It is reached by boat from Tanchanchín, southwest of Ciudad Valles.

Of the area's many archaeological sites, the most notable is **El Consuelo**, near Tamuín to the east. It has remnants of a polychrome altar and stepped ceremonial platforms.

Las Pozas ㉑

San Luis Potosí. Off Mex 120, 3 km (2 miles) NW of Xilitla.
⊞ *Xilitla then taxi.* 🈂

High in the mountains south of Ciudad Valles, near the spectacularly situated town of Xilitla, is this extraordinary, dreamlike jungle estate created by the British artist, eccentric, and millionaire Edward James. He first used the property to grow orchids and then as a private zoo. Later, with the help of local workers, sometimes numbering up to 150 at a time, he set about producing this architectural fantasy, which took over 30 years to complete. Many of the hundreds of

Flowering, a concrete sculpture by Edward James at Las Pozas

Sculpted hands at Las Pozas

Surrealist metal and concrete sculptures are unfinished or already disintegrating. They are scattered amid thick subtropical vegetation, springs, waterfalls, and pools. Slippery paths weave between the massive structures, which include the *Homage to Max Ernst*, *Avenue of the Snakes*, and *Toadstool Platform*.

Sierra Gorda ㉒

Querétaro. ⊞ *Cadereyta, Jalpan.*

One of the largest untamed regions in central Mexico, the semi-arid mountain range of the Sierra Gorda rises northeast of the city of Querétaro *(see pp196–7)* to over 3,000 m (10,000 ft). The lush green of its foothills is interrupted only by the massive monolith **La Peña de Bernal**, which towers 445 m (1,460 ft) above the village of Bernal.

In the mountains beyond **Cadereyta**, with its square of brightly colored churches, are the archaeological sites of **Toluquilla** and **Las Ranas**. These two sites are located on the rugged ridges near San Joaquín, to the east of Mex 120. Both feature fortress-like pre-Columbian ceremonial structures built between the 7th and 11th centuries AD.

Continuing north into the mountains, Mex 120 gets even steeper before descending to **Jalpan**. This town is the site of one of five Franciscan missions founded in the mid-1700s to convert the Indians of these mountains. The missions – the others are in Concá, Tilaco, Tancoyól, and Landa de Matamoros – all have scenic settings, and distinctive façades with strong Indian touches in their profuse mortar decorations.

EDWARD JAMES (1907–84)

The creator of the Las Pozas complex was, according to his friend Salvador Dalí, "crazier than all the Surrealists put together. They pretend, but he is the real thing." Edward Frank Willis James, born into a wealthy English family, was himself a moderately successful poet and artist, but excelled as a patron of the arts. He published books, founded ballet companies, financed large exhibitions, and amassed paintings by Dalí, Picasso, and Magritte, whose social circle he shared. His only marriage, to a Hungarian ballet dancer, ended in a scandalous divorce. In his later years, his private life revolved around the family of his long-time Mexican employee and companion Plutarco Gastelum Esquer, who had helped him create his jungle paradise at Las Pozas. When James died Esquer's children inherited the estate.

Eccentric Edward James relaxing at his Surrealist rain forest home

Querétaro ㉓

The modern suburbs of Querétaro hide its central colonial treasures, which UNESCO added to its protected World Heritage List in 1996. The city's location brought it prosperity in New Spain, but from the early 1800s Querétaro fell into decline, a trend interrupted only in 1848, when invading US troops briefly made it Mexico's capital. It was here that the treaty ceding half of Mexican territory to the United States was signed, and here also that Emperor Maximilian *(see p53)* faced the firing squad.

Neptune, on the Jardín Guerrero fountain

⛲ Plaza de Armas
With its austere colonial fountain, bougainvillea-covered garden, and stately old mansions, this intimate 18th-century square is a corner of Spain transplanted to Mexico. Most of the former residences on the plaza, among them the sumptuous **Casa de Ecala**, now house government offices, including the state congress and court. The only white façade, with plain moldings and sober balconies, is the **Casa de la Corregidora**, which was built in 1700 for Querétaro's royal representatives. Completely restored in 1981, it is now the seat of the state government. A few prison cells have been preserved in its rear courtyard. The bronze statue crowning the square's fountain honors the Marqués de la Villa del Villar, the city's early 18th-century patron.

Façade of a colonial mansion on the Plaza de Armas

🏛 Museo Regional
Corregidora Sur 3. *Tel (442) 212 20 36.* ◯ *Tue–Sun.* 🎫 *Sun free.* ♿ *ground floor only.*
The state's regional museum is housed in the former convent of San Francisco, a building noted for its cloisters, domes, and stone columns. The ethnographic, archaeological, and colonial sections are on the ground floor. The second floor exhibits weapons, furniture, and photographs tracing Querétaro's pivotal role in Mexican history since the fight for independence.
  Both the convent and its adjoining church, the **Templo de San Francisco**, were begun by Franciscan missionaries in 1540, and the complex was finished in a blend of styles in 1727. The church has *trompe l'oeil* murals and the city's tallest tower.

The tower of the convent church of San Francisco, Querétaro's tallest landmark

🔒 Templo de Santa Clara and Templo de Santa Rosa
These two 18th-century churches of former nunneries (at some distance apart) rival one another with the exuberance of their Churrigueresque interiors. Each has profusely carved altarpieces that form a floor-to-ceiling tapestry of foliage, shells, cherubs, and clouds. The naves are closed off by double choirs where the nuns once attended mass behind screens of delicately forged iron and gilded lattice. Both interiors are the work of Francisco Martínez Gudiño. Santa Rosa is also notable for its sacristy with life-size statues of Christ and the twelve apostles. A short walk from Santa Clara is the peaceful Jardín Guerrero, with its Fuente de Neptuno (Neptune Fountain).

🏛 Museo de Arte
Allende Sur 14. *Tel (442) 212 23 57.* ◯ *Tue–Sun.* 🎫 *Tue free.* 🎫 *arrange in advance.* 📷
This vast collection of 17th to 19th-century Mexican paintings is displayed alongside temporary art exhibitions and a smattering of contemporary paintings and photographs. They are housed in the 18th-century Ex-Convento de San Agustín, whose church captures the eye with its finely sculpted Plateresque façade and octagonal blue- and white-tiled dome. The real treasure here, however, is the supremely elegant Baroque main cloister, considered the finest of its kind in the Americas. Its richly carved details include caryatids supporting the arches.

🔒 Convento de la Santa Cruz
Independencia & Felipe Luna. *Tel (442) 212 02 35.* ◯ *Tue–Sun.* 🎫 📷
This plain convent has a long history. It started life in 1531 as a hermitage, on the site of the last battle between the Chichimecs and the Spanish. A 450-year-old stone replica of the cross that miraculously appeared in the sky, inducing the Indians to surrender and embrace Christianity, is mounted over the main altar of the small church. By 1683, the hermitage had become the first missionary college in the

The fortress-like Convento de la Santa Cruz, east of the city center

VISITORS' CHECKLIST

Querétaro. 640,000. Prolongación Luis Vega y Monroy 800, (442) 229 01 81. Luis Pasteur Nte 4, (442) 238 50 67. Fundación de Querétaro (Jul 25), Fiestas de Diciembre (Dec).

Americas, and in 1848 the US invaders made the convent their headquarters. A sparsely furnished cell was Emperor Maximilian's prison before he was led to his death in 1867.

Los Arcos
Financed by the Marqués de la Villa del Villar in the 18th century, this is one of the world's largest aqueducts. It has 74 arches up to 23 m (75 ft) high and is 8 km (5 miles) long.

Cerro de las Campanas
The barren hill where Emperor Maximilian was executed with two of his officers on June 19, 1867, is now a tree-filled municipal park. A broad stairway leads to the Neo-Gothic chapel that was donated by the emperor's family to commemorate the renewal of diplomatic relations between Mexico and the Austro-Hungarian Empire in 1900. Inside, three marble slabs mark the spot where the executions took place. The painting on the altar is a copy of Maximilian's wedding gift from his mother. The cross over the altar is made from wood from the frigate that first brought him to Mexico and later returned his body to Europe. Nearby is a small museum with exhibits on the fall of the Second Mexican Empire. The whole site is dominated by a massive statue on the hilltop of the Mexican hero Benito Juárez, Maximilian's nemesis (*see pp52–3*).

Environs
San Juan del Río, 47 km (29 miles) southeast, is known for its crafts and gemstones. The town's oldest buildings are the hospital and convent of San Juan de Dios, founded in 1661, and the 1690 convent of Santo Domingo.

Just 22 km (14 miles) northeast of San Juan del Río lies the quaint spa town of **Tequisquiapan**. Its cobbled lanes and arcaded main square make it a popular retreat.

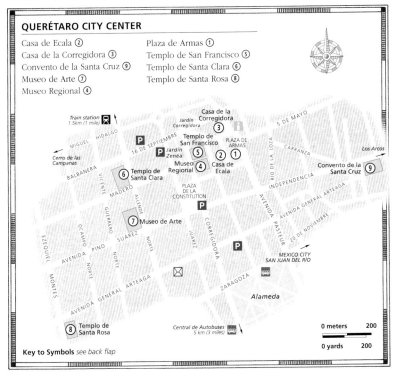

QUERÉTARO CITY CENTER

Casa de Ecala ②
Casa de la Corregidora ③
Convento de la Santa Cruz ⑨
Museo de Arte ⑦
Museo Regional ④

Plaza de Armas ①
Templo de San Francisco ⑤
Templo de Santa Clara ⑥
Templo de Santa Rosa ⑧

Train station
1.5 km (1 mile)

Casa de la Corregidora
Jardín Corregidora ③

Cerro de las Campanas

Templo de San Francisco
Jardín Zenéa ⑤

PLAZA DE ARMAS
② ①

Museo Regional ④ Casa de Ecala

Los Arcos

Convento de la Santa Cruz ⑨

Templo de Santa Clara ⑥

PLAZA DE LA CONSTITUCIÓN

⑦ Museo de Arte

MEXICO CITY
SAN JUAN DEL RÍO

⑧ Templo de Santa Rosa

Central de Autobuses
5 km (3 miles)

Alameda

0 meters 200
0 yards 200

Key to Symbols *see back flap*

Street-by-Street: San Miguel de Allende ⓧ

A delightful colonial town, San Miguel de Allende is filled with opulent mansions and handsome churches, all connected by narrow, cobbled streets. Now a popular tourist destination, it was once an important crossroads for mule trains, which carried silver and gold to the capital and returned with European treasures. The town's active cultural life combines traditional charm with the cosmopolitan air of the large non-Mexican population.

Statue of priest at San Felipe Neri

Templo de la Concepción
A huge dome from 1891 towers over the gilded altar of this church.

Escuela de Bellas Artes
This art school, in a former convent, has an unfinished 1940s mural painted by David Alfaro Siqueiros.

Casa del Mayorazgo de la Canal, the town's most sumptuous mansion, has Neo-Classical and Baroque styling.

Casa Allende, now a historical museum, was the birthplace of Ignacio Allende, a hero of Mexican Independence.

Casa del Inquisidor once housed visiting representatives of the Spanish Inquisition. Built in 1780, the house has fine windows and balconies.

Casa de la Inquisición served as the prison of the Inquisition.

★ **La Parroquia**
Notable for its fantastic Neo-Gothic exterior, this parish church was remodeled by self-taught local architect Zeferino Gutiérrez in the late 19th century.

KEY

 — — — Suggested route

For hotels and restaurants in this region see pp302–8 and pp335–9

★ Santa Casa de Loreto
Along with the Camarín de la Virgen, this is one of two opulent side chapels of the Oratorio de San Felipe Neri. Its multi-tiered lantern illuminates the lavishly decorated octagonal space within.

Iglesia de Santa Ana

★ Oratorio de San Felipe Neri
A series of 33 oil paintings inside this church shows scenes from the life of the Florentine St. Philip Neri. They are attributed to Miguel Cabrera.

Templo de Nuestra Señora de la Salud
This was the chapel for residents of the 18th-century college next door. Its early Churrigueresque entrance beneath a giant shell has strong Indian influences.

Casa de las Postas

Casa del Conde de Casa Loja

Templo de San Francisco
The Neo-Classical tower of this 18th-century church contrasts sharply with its two ornate Churrigueresque façades. The decorated ceiling and high windows relieve the solemnity of the interior.

STAR SIGHTS

★ Santa Casa de Loreto

★ Oratorio de San Felipe Neri

★ La Parroquia

0 meters 75
0 yards 75

Street-by-Street: Guanajuato 🄰

One of Mexico's most beautiful silver cities climbs out of a rugged ravine and up bald hills that once supplied a quarter of New Spain's silver output. Mine owners studded Guanajuato's narrow twisting streets and charming plazas with stately mansions and imposing churches. A later bonanza added splendid late 19th-century touches, and modern engineers burrowed an ingenious tunnel network under the city to help overcome its crazy geography. The unique result is a center devoid of traffic lights and neon signs that was made a UNESCO World Heritage Site in 1988.

A typical city street with overhanging balconies

Casa Diego Rivera
The house where Rivera was born in 1886 is now a museum exhibiting over 100 samples of his work, including sketches of his murals (see p204).

Plaza de los Angeles is a popular spot for students to gather.

Callejón del Beso (Alley of the Kiss) is only 69 cm (2 ft) wide in places. Legend tells of the tragic death of secret lovers who were caught exchanging kisses from opposing balconies.

Casa Rul y Valenciana, a beautiful late 18th-century mansion, is now the courthouse.

Calle Hidalgo
Converted from a riverbed in 1965 to alleviate traffic problems this subterranean street winds under the city center. It is very dangerous and not recommended for visitors.

STAR SIGHTS

★ Templo de la Compañía

★ Jardín de la Unión

★ Teatro Juárez

◁ View of Guanajuato from the Pípila monument south of the city center

★ **Templo de la Compañía**
The Neo-Classical dome of this Jesuit church replaced one that had collapsed in 1808. It is now a city landmark. The façade is an early example of the Churrigueresque style.

Museo del Pueblo houses a collection of regional art in a 17th-century mansion *(see p204)*.

The University was remodeled in Moorish style in 1945. It was originally a Jesuit seminary, founded in 1732.

VISITORS' CHECKLIST

Guanajuato. 141,000. 32 km (20 miles) W. 7 km (4 miles) SW, (473) 733 13 40. Plaza de la Paz 14, (473) 732 15 74 or (800) 714 1086 (in Mexico). San Juan y Presa de la Olla (Jun), Festival Cervantino (Oct).

KEY

– – – Suggested route

LASCURÁIN DE RETANA

PLAZA DE LA PAZ

OBREGÓN

EL TRUCO

AYUNTAMIENTO

ALLENDE

★ **Jardín de la Unión**
Laid out in 1861, this laurel-shaded plaza is the heart of the city and a favorite meeting place. The municipal band plays here several times a week.

Plazuela del Baratillo was once a busy marketplace. The fountain was a gift from Emperor Maximilian.

| 0 meters | 50 |
| 0 yards | 50 |

PLAZUELA DE LA CONSTANCIA

Iglesia de San Diego

Basílica de Nuestra Señora de Guanajuato has an ornate statue of the Virgin Mary *(see p204)*.

★ **Teatro Juárez**
Doric columns, giant statues, and an auditorium hung with velvet set the tone at this lavish theater (see p204).

Exploring Guanajuato

Most of Guanajuato's main sights are located near the center of the city, and one of the pleasures of visiting this colonial gem is strolling around its twisting streets on foot, marveling at the ornate architecture. A range of local buses will take you to sights outside the center, and tours are available from the tourist office.

Madonna statue in the Basílica de Nuestra Señora de Guanajuato

Basílica de Nuestra Señora de Guanajuato

This 17th-century church facing the Plaza de la Paz contains a bejeweled sculpture of the city's patron saint, the Virgin Mary, on a solid-silver pedestal. The statue was given to the city by Charles I and Philip II of Spain in 1557. Reputed to date from the 7th century, it is considered the oldest piece of Christian art in Mexico. The church interior is especially striking in the evening, when it is lit by Venetian chandeliers.

Teatro Juárez

Jardín de la Unión. *Tel* (473) 732 01 83. ◯ *Tue–Sun.* 🔊
Statues of the Muses crown the façade of this Neo-Classical theater. Below them a wide stairway flanked by bronze lions leads up to a stately foyer and Moorish-style auditorium. This is the main venue for the Festival Cervantino, the country's top arts festival (*see p32*).

Museo del Pueblo

Pocitos 7. *Tel* (473) 732 29 90. ◯ *Tue–Sun.* 🔊
The former home of a wealthy mine owner is one of the city's finest buildings. It now exhibits art pieces from pre-Columbian to modern times, concentrating on colonial religious objects.

Casa Diego Rivera

Pocitos 47. *Tel* (473) 732 11 97. ◯ *Tue–Sun.* 🔊 📷 *on second floor.* 📷
The house where Diego Rivera was born is now a museum dedicated to his life and art. His work fills the upstairs rooms, while the ground floor preserves the family living area with its late 19th-century furniture and mementos.

Alhóndiga de Granaditas

Mendizábal 6. *Tel* (473) 732 11 12. ◯ *Tue–Sun.* 🔊 *Sun free.* 📷
This former granary, built at the end of the 18th century, was the site of the first major rebel victory of the War of Independence. In 1810, revolutionaries burned down the gates and killed most of the government troops barricaded inside. Reminders of the battle are the bullet-scarred walls and the hooks dangling from the building's four top corners, where the heads of four rebellion leaders were later hung.

The huge building is now a regional museum covering art, ethnography, and archaeology. The staircase is decorated with murals depicting the city's history by José Chávez Morado.

Imposing façade of the historic Alhóndiga de Granaditas

Museo Iconográfico del Quijote

Manuel Doblado 1. *Tel* (473) 732 67 21. ◯ *Tue–Sun.* 🔊 📷
Hundreds of art pieces relating to Don Quixote, from postage stamps to huge murals, are displayed here. The unusual collection includes works by Dalí, Picasso, and Daumier.

La Valenciana

5 km (3 miles) N of city center. ◯ *daily.* 🔊
Silver and gold mining began here in the mid-1500s and boomed two centuries later after prospectors struck it rich at a new shaft just to the west. The Bocamina de Valencia, the original 1557 entrance shaft, is cut 100 m (330 ft) straight down into the rock. Visitors can climb down to half its depth on steep stairs over which miners once hauled up loads of ore-rich rocks on their backs. A small museum at the entrance tells the mine's history.

Pyramid-style walls of La Valenciana mine, backed by the Templo de San Cayetano

🔒 Templo de San Cayetano

Near La Valenciana mine is the most spectacular of the city's churches. Also known as "La Valenciana," it was built between 1765 and 1788 with funds donated by the Count of Valenciana, owner of the nearby mine. Its three-tiered pink limestone façade abounds with Churrigueresque pilasters. The Baroque interior has three splendid gold and polychrome altars and a pulpit inlaid with tortoiseshell and ivory.

🏛 Museo de las Momias

Explanada del Panteón. *Tel (473) 732 06 39.* ⬭ *daily.* 🎫 ⬤ 📷 🔲
Southwest of the center is this macabre museum, which owes its popularity to the Mexican obsession with death. In cavernous rooms it exhibits over 100 mummies disinterred from a nearby cemetery where they had mummified naturally.

🏛 Museo Ex-Hacienda de San Gabriel de la Barrera

Marfil, 2.5 km (1.5 miles) SW of city. *Tel (473) 732 06 19.* ⬭ *daily.* 🎫 🔲 ⬤
This restored hacienda was built in the late 17th century as an ore-processing center. It is now a museum displaying European furniture from the 17th to the 19th centuries. The grounds have been converted into 16 gardens, each landscaped in a different style.

Environs

In the small town of **Dolores Hidalgo**, 54 km (34 miles) northeast of the city, the battle for independence from Spain began with Father Miguel Hidalgo issuing his famous *Grito*, or "cry" to arms *(see p49)*, from the parish church.

Elegant garden of the Hacienda de San Gabriel de la Barrera

Church half buried by solidified lava from Paricutín volcano

Paricutín ㉖

Michoacán. 38 km (24 miles) NW of Uruapan. 🚌 *Angahuan.*

One of the youngest volcanoes in the world, Paricutín erupted in February 1943. Amid thunderous explosions, its cone grew to more than 330 m (1,100 ft) within one year. Ash and lava flows buried two villages and, while nobody was killed by the eruptions, more than 4,000 people had to flee their homes. The volcano's activity lasted until 1952, leaving behind a barren cone rising 424 m (1,391 ft) from a sea of black frozen lava. The total elevation above sea level is 2,575 m (8,448 ft).

The *mirador* (lookout) at Angahuan offers a dramatic view of the 25 sq-km (10 sq-mile) lava field and Paricutín behind it. The church tower that can be seen above the lava belongs to the buried village of San Juan Parangaricutiro. For a closer look, walk 3 km (2 miles) or hire a guide and a horse to take you down the steep cliff and through the lava rock formations. The stiff 30-minute climb to the crater rim is rewarded with stunning views of the double crater and surrounding lunar landscape.

The town of **Angahuan** itself has preserved its native character despite the influx of visitors to Paricutín. Most of the people speak Purépecha, the Tarascan language, and the women wear colorful traditional clothing.

Uruapan ㉗

Michoacán. 🏠 450,000. ✈ 🚌
ℹ *Juan Ayala 16, (452) 524 71 99.*
🎭 *Coros y Danzas (late Oct).*

Michoacán's second-biggest city, Uruapan is a busy agricultural center. Nestling against the Sierra de Uruapan, it links the cold upland region *(tierra fría)* to the humid lowlands *(tierra caliente)* that stretch toward the Pacific. This subtropical climate supports exuberant vegetation, including vast avocado plantations.

The Spanish monk Juan de San Miguel founded the town in 1533 and divided it into nine neighborhoods *(barrios)*, which still preserve their own traditions. He also built **La Huatapera**, a chapel and hospital that now houses a fine museum of Michoacán crafts.

⛪ La Huatapera

Plaza Morelos. *Tel (452) 524 34 34.* ⬭ *Tue–Sun.*

A Tour Around Lake Pátzcuaro ㉘

The road around this idyllic lake bedded in rolling hills passes colonial and pre-Columbian architectural gems, and towns with rich craft traditions. Pátzcuaro, Tzintzuntzán, and Quiroga are popular destinations, but the western shore and marshlands to the south see fewer visitors. Yet here the winding road offers spectacular vistas of the lake and rare glimpses of Purépechan (Tarascan) Indian village life.

Quiroga ③
A busy market town, Quiroga sells agricultural and handicraft products from all over Michoacán. Lacquerware, such as wooden bowls and trays painted with bright flowers, is a typical local product.

Tzintzuntzán ②
The *yácatas*, multilevel temple bases, near this town reveal its history as the former Tarascan capital. Also noteworthy are the 16th-century Franciscan convent and the crafts market.

Santa Fé de la Laguna ④
Santa Fe has this 17th-century church, as well as roadside stalls selling the local black pottery.

Ihuatzio ①
This peaceful village stands near massive Tarascan ruins, which overlook the lake. A stone coyote sculpture found at the ruins now graces the village church tower.

Erongarícuaro ⑤
This town was a favorite hideaway of French Surrealist André Breton.

Tocuaro ⑥
Famous for its prize-winning wooden masks, Tocuaro has a number of unmarked workshops selling these fantastic creations.

Map labels:
ZAMORA — 15
San Andrés Tziróndaro
Chupícuaro — ④
③ — 15
MORELIA
Lake Pátzcuaro
Oponguio
Isla de Pacanda
② — 120
Pudcaro
⑤
Isla Janitzio
Arocutín — ①
Jarácuaro
San Pedro Pareo
⑥
URUAPAN — 14 — MORELIA
PÁTZCUARO — 120

KEY

▬	Tour route
▬	Highway
⋯	Other roads
☀	Viewpoint

TIPS FOR DRIVERS

Tour length: 89 km (55 miles)
Stopping-off points: Apart from Pátzcuaro, the best places to eat are a rustic restaurant between Erongarícuaro and Arocutín (see p321) and, for picnics, a small swimming beach near Chupícuaro.

0 kilometers — 5
0 miles — 3

View of Isla Janitzio, the most important of the six islands on Lake Pátzcuaro

Pátzcuaro ㉙

Michoacán. 48,000.
Ahumada 9, (434) 342 12 14.
Año Nuevo Purépecha (late Jan),
Day of the Dead (Nov 1–2).

Set amid the pastures
and pine forests on Lake
Pátzcuaro's southern shore,
this historic town was once
an important religious and
political center of the Tarascan
people. Its colonial splendor
owes much to Michoacán's
first bishop, Vasco de Quiroga,
who temporarily turned it
into the civic, religious, and
cultural seat of the state.

The **Basílica de Nuestra
Señora de la Salud**, an ambitious Vasco de Quiroga project,
was to boast five naves and
accommodate tens of thou-
sands of people. However,
only one nave was completed.
Fires and earthquakes ravaged
the building over the centuries,
and the church was finally
finished in a jumble of styles
in 1833. Devout Indians flock
here to visit the bishop's tomb.

Just to the south is the **Museo
de Artes Populares**, a craft
museum installed in the 16th-
century Colegio de San Nicolás.
The museum's collection includes a cabin-like *troje*, with
typical Purépecha furnishings,
that sits on a former
pyramid platform.

The town's other
architectural high-
lights include the
Baroque **Templo
del Sagrario** and
an 18th-century
Dominican nunnery.
The latter is now the
**Casa de los Once
Patios**, a crafts cen-
ter with workshops and stores.
Its most attractive section is a
small arcaded cloister where
a nun and her servants lived.

Huge ash trees shade the
quiet, elegant **Plaza Vasco de
Quiroga** with its large fountain and statue of the town's
benefactor. Many of the colonial mansions that face the
square have been converted
into shops, restaurants, and

The tranquil courtyard
of the Museo de
Artes Populares

hotels, but the real commercial
hub of the town is the nearby
Plaza Gertrudis Bocanegra.
Named after a local Independence heroine, it gives access
to the covered market. On
Fridays, the streets toward the
Neo-Classical
**Santuario de
Guadalupe** church
(1833) fill with
stalls, and pottery is
sold in the Plazuela
de San Francisco.

Environs
Tours to the islands
on Lake Pátzcuaro
leave docks north
of town. **Janitzio**, with its
monument to Morelos *(see
p49)*, is the most popular.

**Museo de Artes
Populares**
Corner of Enseñanza and
Alcantarilla. **Tel** (434) 342 10 29.
Tue–Sun. in advance.

Casa de los Once Patios
Madrigal de las Altas Torres.
daily.

DAY OF THE DEAD

Although Mexicans all over the country
commune with the dead on the night of
November 1 *(see pp34–5)*, the ceremonies on
the island of Janitzio and in the villages around
Lake Pátzcuaro are particulary impressive. This
is largely because of their deep indigenous roots
and unique settings. Throughout the night boats
decorated with candles and flowers and laden
with chanting people travel between Pátzcuaro
docks and the island. The air is filled with wafts
of incense and the ringing of bells. In the bustling
cemeteries, each grave is covered with private
tokens – special foods, photographs, and toys –
intended to summon back the dead in celebration.

Wooden
skeleton

The 17th-century Templo del
Sagrario in Pátzcuaro

For hotels and restaurants in this region see pp302–8 and pp335–9

Street-by-Street: Morelia ③

Capital of the state of Michoacán, Morelia was founded in the mid-1500s under the name of Valladolid on fertile territory once ruled by Tarascan kings. The first settlers were Spanish nobility and religious orders, who laid out a city of magnificent palaces, convents, and churches, along flagstone avenues and around plazas. The historic center has retained its Spanish character over the centuries; even new buildings sport colonial façades in pink limestone. The city's name was changed in 1828 to honor José María Morelos *(see p49)*, the native son instrumental in leading Mexico toward Independence.

★ **Conservatorio de las Rosas**
The peaceful courtyard of this former Dominican nunnery is enhanced by the sounds of practicing music students
(see p210).

Teatro Ocampo

Templo de las Rosas *(see p210)*

★ **Palacio Clavijero**
Government offices now surround the courtyard of this former Jesuit college (see p210). The austere Baroque building was named after a historian who taught here in the 1700s.

ZARAGOZA

SANTIAGO TAPIA

PRIETO

MELCHOR OCAMPO

NIGROMANTE

FRANCISCO I MADERO

GALEA

Templo de la Compañía de Jesús
This church was built in the 17th century for the adjoining Palacio Clavijero. Since 1930 it has been home to the Public Library.

Colegio de San Nicolás is the alma mater of several illustrious Mexicans. It has been an educational institution since the 16th century.

Centro Cultural

Palacio Municipal

STAR SIGHTS

- ★ Conservatorio de las Rosas
- ★ Palacio Clavijero
- ★ Cathedral

0 meters	50
0 yards	50

Plaza de Armas
was laid out as
the center of
town in the
16th century.
The bandstand
dates from
1887.

VISITORS' CHECKLIST

Michoacán. 🏛 620,000.
✈ 27 km (17 miles) NE. 🚌
Libramiento Norte, (443) 334 10
71. ℹ Av Tatabasco 80, (443)
317 80 32. 🎉 Aniversario de la
Fundación de Morelia (May 18).
www.michoacan-travel.com

Palacio de Gobierno
*This former seminary (see
p210) has been the seat of
the state government
since 1867. Bright
murals decorate
the upper level.*

KEY

– – – Suggested route

**Aqueduct
Nuestra Señora
de Guadalupe**

**Casa Natal
de Morelos**
is where the
Independence
hero José
María Morelos
was born
in 1765.

★ Cathedral
*Built in a mixture of styles
between 1660 and 1774, the
cathedral (see p210) has two towers
that soar to a height of more than
60 m (200 ft). Its monumental
4,600-pipe German organ
is the main star of the
annual International
Organ Festival.*

**Museo Regional
Michoacano**
*One of Mexico's old-
est museums spans
pre-Columbian
to modern eras
(see p210). This
figure dates from
the Classic Period.*

**Palacio
de Justicia**

Iglesia de San Agustín
*Part of a 16th-century
Augustinian ex-convent, this
church has a sober Plateresque
façade. It is seen here through the
arches of the courtyard in front of it.*

Exploring Morelia

Starting from Avenida Francisco I. Madero or the Plaza de Armas, almost all of Morelia's important sights are within short walking distance. The colonial-style streets and captivating Spanish architecture make this a pleasant city to stroll around. A short bus or taxi ride will take you east of the center, to the impressive aqueduct that runs alongside the city park.

🔒 Cathedral
This majestic structure in pink trachyte stone was begun in 1660 but not completed until a century later. The resulting blend of styles – Neo-Classical, Herreresque, and Baroque – can be seen in the twin towers that dominate the surrounding historic city center. Among the remnants of past splendor are the silver baptismal font in a side chapel and the 16th-century corn-paste statue of the Señor de la Sacristía. The statue's gold crown was a gift from Philip II of Spain.

🔱 Palacio de Gobierno
Avenida Francisco I. Madero 63. **Tel** *(443) 313 07 07.* ⭕ *daily.*
This colonial edifice opened in 1770 as the Tridentine Seminary, which was attended by several key figures of the Independence *(see p49)* and Reform *(see pp52–3)* movements. It later became the seat of state government. In the 1950s, Alfredo Zalce adorned the staircase and first floor with murals on local themes.

Ornately carved stonework on Morelia's cathedral

🔒 Templo y Conservatorio de las Rosas
Dominican nuns arrived here in 1590, but most of their original buildings were replaced in the 17th and early 18th centuries with the convent and church that now face the Jardín de las Rosas. The Baroque façade of the church has twin portals, a typical feature of nunneries. Other notable features are the unusual gargoyles in the form of crocodiles, and the three gold altars inside. The convent itself was later converted into an orphanage and has housed a music school since 1904.

🔱 Palacio Clavijero
Nigromante 79. **Tel** *(443) 312 80 81.* ⭕ *daily.*
The grand proportions and Baroque styling of the former Colegio de San Francisco Javier, a 17th-century Jesuit college, are best appreciated from its vast main courtyard. Elegant arcades on

the ground floor contrast with a closed upper cloister where 28 windows with sober moldings replace the arches below. Geometrical patterns in the stone pavement imitate the layout of gardens that once surrounded the octagonal central fountain. The building now houses government offices, including the state tourist information bureau.

🏛 Museo Regional Michoacano
Allende 305. **Tel** *(443) 312 04 07.* ⭕ *Tue–Sun.* 📷 🎫 *in advance.* 🔒
For more than a century, the Regional Museum has collected objects relating to the state's ecology and history from pre-Columbian to modern times.
  About one fifth of its treasures are on public display in the Baroque mansion where Emperor Maximilian *(see p53)* lodged during his visits. Highlights include Indian codices, a rare 16th-century Bible written in three languages, and a celebrated early 18th-century painting entitled *Traslado de las Monjas (The Moving of the Nuns).* One of the few realistic portrayals of Mexican colonial society, it depicts the 1738 procession of nuns from one convent to another. They are escorted by dignitaries and observed by elegantly dressed ladies, dancing Indians, and black musicians.

🔱 Casa de Artesanías
Fray Juan de San Miguel 129. **Tel** *(443) 312 08 48.* ⭕ *daily.* ♿ 🔒
The 16th-century Convento de San Buenaventura was restored in the 1970s and is now a showcase for Michoacán's rich craft tradition. The rooms around the arched courtyard contain a selection of items for sale, including pottery, textiles, and lacquerware. In the upstairs rooms visitors can observe artisans at work.

🔱 Aqueduct and Calzada Fray Antonio de San Miguel
Avenida Acueducto.
Water once flowed along this 18th-century aqueduct from a well 8 km (5 miles) away to the city's 30 public fountains and 150 private outlets. The final 1.5-km (1-mile) stretch consists of 253 arches, some

Alfredo Zalce's mural above the grand staircase of the Palacio de Gobierno

The vividly decorated dome of Santuario de Nuestra Señora de Guadalupe

of which reach a height of 10 m (33 ft). It is especially stunning when lit up at night.

The aqueduct was built by Bishop Fray Antonio de San Miguel, who also created the *calzada* (avenue) that bears his name. This pedestrian esplanade leads from the city end of the aqueduct to the Guadalupe Sanctuary. With its ash trees, Baroque benches, and 18th-century mansions, it recalls a long-gone era.

Las Tarascas fountain, where the aqueduct meets the *calzada*

🏠 Santuario de Nuestra Señora de Guadalupe

This 18th-century church at the far end of Calzada Fray Antonio de San Miguel has a sober Baroque façade but a remarkable interior. Molded clay rosettes and other floral motifs in bright colors and gold cover the walls, ceiling, and dome. These decorations were added in the early 1900s and combine Baroque, Art Nouveau, and folk-art styles.

Environs

North of Morelia are two wonderfully preserved 16th-century Augustinian monasteries that can be explored on a leisurely day trip. The first is in **Cuitzeo**, a fishing village 34 km (21 miles) from Morelia at the end of a causeway across a vast, shallow lake. The second is in **Yuriria**, an additional 32 km (20 miles) to the north. Both have Indian-influenced Plateresque façades, Gothic vaulting, and elegant cloisters. Fortress-like Yuriria was described by a chronicler in the 1620s as "the most superb building imaginable."

El Rosario Monarch Butterfly Sanctuary ㉛

Michoacán. Off Mex 15, 13 km (8 miles) E of Ocampo. *Tel* (715) 153 50 55. 🚌 Ocampo. ⬤ Nov–Mar: daily. 🔲 🔲

Santuario El Rosario is one of two sanctuaries open to the public in the Monarch Butterfly Biosphere Reserve in the mountains west of Mexico City. The 160-sq-km (60-sq-mile) preserve is the winter home of an estimated 100 million monarch butterflies, which migrate here each year from northern US and Canada. The mystery of where monarchs overwinter was solved by Canadian zoologist Fred Urquhart, who found the isolated roosts in the 1970s.

The best time to visit is late February when rising temperatures encourage the insects to search for flowers or begin their journey back north. The hiking route is well marked.

Environs

The nearby **Sierra Chincua Monarch Butterfly Sanctuary** sees fewer visitors than El Rosario, but is easier to reach and offers horses for its more rustic trails. Guides will accompany visitors on request.

🐾 Sierra Chincua Monarch Butterfly Sanctuary
Llano de las Papas, 9 km (6 miles) NE of Angangueo. ⬤ Nov–Mar: daily. 🔲

MIGRATION OF THE MONARCH BUTTERFLY

The annual migration of the monarch butterfly (*Danaus plexippus linneo*) begins in the northern parts of North America in early autumn. It is then that a special generation hatches, with a life cycle of up to nine months, four times that of spring and summer butterflies. These autumn-born individuals fly south in groups of several hundred to escape the winter. They cover up to 300 km (190 miles) a day and within a month reach the *oyamel* fir forests

Monarch butterfly

of central Mexico where they spend the winter. In spring they mate and head north again. En route, the females lay about 500 eggs each. Their offspring take up the baton and continue north to arrive in early June. None of the original migrants will survive to return to Mexico the following year.

SOUTHERN MEXICO

CHIAPAS · GUERRERO (SOUTH) · OAXACA

*W*ith attractions ranging from the world-class beach resort of Acapulco to magnificent colonial cities and monumental pre-Columbian sites, Mexico's southern states could be a microcosm of the whole country. The region is also home to many of the country's indigenous communities, whose language, customs, and costume animate rural villages and city markets.

Southern Mexico's mild climate and fertile soils attracted some of the earliest recorded settlements in Mesoamerica, with the Oaxaca Valley first inhabited in the 7th century BC. Three centuries later, the Zapotecs built their capital at Monte Albán, which dominated the valley for hundreds of years, before giving way to other, smaller cities. Meanwhile, in the east, the Maya were reaching their cultural peak and building the magnificent city of Palenque.

The Spanish Conquest in the 16th century had a massive, and often destructive, impact but resulted in a unique fusion of pre-Columbian and colonial cultures. This is seen in the lives of the local Indians, whose dress, cuisine, fiestas, crafts, and markets rank among the best in the country. Only their languages remained immune, and Spanish is still a minority tongue outside the major towns. This integration has not been achieved without difficulties, however. Long-standing grievances have resulted in rising levels of crime and the emergence of the Zapatista revolutionaries in Chiapas, certain areas of which cannot now be visited.

Geographically, the South is dominated by the mountains of the Sierra Madre del Sur, which make travel difficult but provide spectacular scenery. The Pacific coast is mostly unspoiled. Its sandy beaches are lined with palm trees and pounded constantly by surf.

Peaceful and colorful Plaza Santo Domingo in the attractive colonial city of Oaxaca

◁ A villager beside the vividly painted church in San Juan Chamula, near San Cristóbal de las Casas

Exploring Southern Mexico

The beach resorts of Mexico's southern Pacific coast include the world-famous Acapulco; the up-and-coming Ixtapa and Zihuatanejo, Puerto Escondido and Huatulco; and the lesser known and more intimate Puerto Angel and Zipolite. The open, un-protected nature of the coast, however, means that the water is usually rough, and strong undertows make swimming unsafe except in sheltered bays.

The interiors of Chiapas and Oaxaca are, by contrast, best known for their colonial towns – such as Oaxaca and San Cristóbal de las Casas – but above all for their pre-Columbian sites. The hilltop Monte Albán and the jungle-shrouded Palenque are both easy to get to and worthy of a long visit. Lesser known but attractive sites include Yagul and Mitla, and the less easily accessible Bonampak (with its splendid murals) and Yaxchilán.

Tzotzil women and children in a village in Chiapas

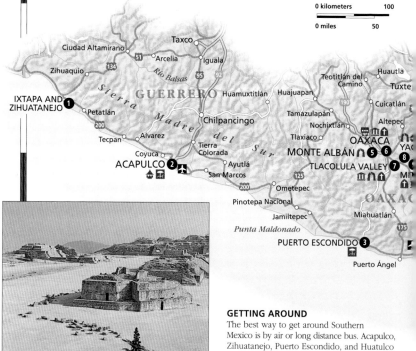

0 kilometers   100

0 miles   50

View of Monte Albán from the south platform

GETTING AROUND

The best way to get around Southern Mexico is by air or long distance bus. Acapulco, Zihuatanejo, Puerto Escondido, and Huatulco have international airports. There are domestic airports at Oaxaca and Tuxtla Gutiérrez. Bus services linking all the major towns and cities are reliable and frequent. For shorter journeys, minibuses *(colectivos)* are a cheap, though often uncomfortable, option. Mountainous terrain, the scarcity of gas stations, and the poor quality of the roads make driving an ordeal. Those who choose to drive are advised to do so only during the day. Access to some parts of Chiapas is restricted because of the Zapatista problem *(see p230)*.

Detail of the façade of the Basílica de la Soledad, Oaxaca

SIGHTS AT A GLANCE

Acapulco pp218–9 ②
Agua Azul ⑬
Bonampak ⑮
Cañón del Sumidero ⑪
Huatulco ④
Ixtapa and Zihuatanejo ①
Mitla ⑨
Monte Albán pp220–21 ⑤
Oaxaca pp222–5 ⑥
Palenque pp234–7 ⑭
Puerto Escondido ③
San Cristóbal de las Casas ⑫
Tuxtla Gutiérrez ⑩
Yagul ⑧
Yaxchilán ⑯

Tours
Tlacolula Valley ⑦

SEE ALSO

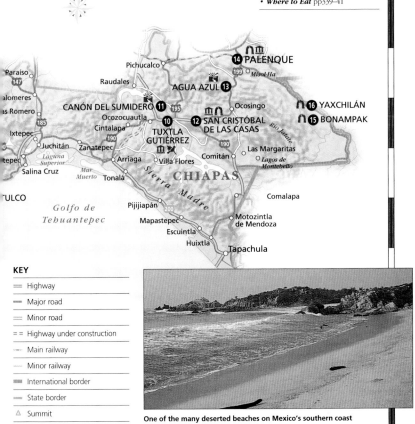

One of the many deserted beaches on Mexico's southern coast

(map labels)

Paraíso
147
alomeres
as Romero
185
Ixtepec
Juchitán
teped
Salina Cruz
ULCO

Pichucalco
Raudales

CANÓN DEL SUMIDERO ⑪
Ocozocuautla
⑩
Cintalapa
190
TUXTLA
GUTIÉRREZ
Zanatepec
Arriaga
Villa Flores
Tonalá

AGUA AZUL ⑬

195
⑫ SAN CRISTÓBAL
DE LAS CASAS
190

Ocosingo

Comitán

⑭ PALENQUE
199 Misol-Ha

⑯ YAXCHILÁN
⑮ BONAMPAK

Río Jataté

Las Margaritas
Lagos de
Montebello

PALENQUE

CHIAPAS

Laguna
Superior
Mar
Muerto

Sierra Madre

Golfo de
Tehuantepec

Pijijiapán
200
Mapastepec
Escuintla
Huixtla
Tapachula

Comalapa

Motozintla
de Mendoza

KEY

═══ Highway

─── Major road

─── Minor road

= = Highway under construction

-·- Main railway

─── Minor railway

▬▬▬ International border

─── State border

△ Summit

Ixtapa and Zihuatanejo ❶

Guerrero. 🏘 *1,200.* ✈ *at Zihuatenejo.* 🚌 ℹ *Ayuntamiento (755) 55 44 83 50.*

Ixtapa and Zihuatanejo are actually two resorts in one. Ixtapa, 10 km (6 miles) to the northwest of its smaller neighbor, is a glitzy modern resort, full of luxury high-rise hotels. It is set along an attractive gently curving 4-km (2.5-mile) beach, Playa Palmar, which backs onto a very broad, palm-lined avenue packed with restaurants, shops, and nightclubs.

Zihuatanejo, in contrast, is low-rise and intimate, and still has the feel of a close fishing community. Set in a scenic, sheltered bay, fishermen come here to sell their daily catch.

Both Ixtapa and Zihuatanejo offer world-class deep-sea fishing, and some of the best scuba diving on Mexico's Pacific coast. They are also a good starting point from which to explore the spectacular, deserted beaches along the surrounding coast.

The magnificent beach at Zihuatanejo

Acapulco ❷

See pp218–19.

Puerto Escondido ❸

Oaxaca. 🏘 *15,000.* ✈ 🚌 ℹ *Blvd Benito Juárez, (954) 582 01 75.* 🎉 *Surfing festival (end of Nov).* **www**.oaxaca.com

Puerto Escondido, literally the "undiscovered port," lived up to its name until discovered by hippies in the 1970s

The Beaches of Oaxaca

Although blessed with some of the country's best beaches and lagoons, the coast of Oaxaca was untouched by tourism until the 1970s. Since then, limited development has taken place, but with 480 km (300 miles) of coast and only a couple of significant resorts, the area still retains a sense of undisturbed charm. The coast has some remarkable flora and fauna, especially in the freshwater lagoons west of Puerto Escondido. The ocean along this stretch of coast is inviting, but swimming is dangerous as the undertow can be very strong. Crime is also a problem in the region, particularly on the beaches and roads after dark.

Laguna Manialtepec, *"the place of spring-fed waters," is a natural lagoon. Encircled by mangroves, it is home to a wide range of plant, animal, and bird life. It also has some beautiful beaches, accessible by boat.*

ACAPULCO

San Pedro Tututepec

San Gabriel Mixtepec

San Pedro Mixtepec

Río Grande

Charco Redondo

Laguna Manialtepec

Puerto Escondido

The Parque Nacional Lagunas de Chacahua is an ecological preserve with deserted beaches and a few small fishing communities. A crocodile sanctuary can also be visited on a tour from Puerto Escondido.

Puerto Escondido *strikes a happy medium between the simplicity of the smaller resorts on Oaxaca's coast and the expensive luxury of Huatulco. It is especially popular with surfers.*

KEY

▬▬ Major road

═══ Minor road

〰 River

and has since become a significant tourist destination. Although showing some signs of the strain of development, it retains much of the fishing village character that originally made it popular.

Playa Marinero, the main beach, is popular with locals and tourists alike. Shaded by palm trees, it faces a small cove dotted with fishing boats and fed by an endless supply of gentle surf. Playa Zicatela is a larger beach to the west and is very popular with surfers, especially in the late summer months when the waves are at their highest.

At the end of November, the town comes alive for an international surfing festival. A popular local fiesta with music and dancing takes place at the same time. Puerto Escondido is also a good base for trips to the nearby freshwater lagoons, such as Laguna Manialtepec.

Huatulco ❹

Oaxaca. 25,000.

🛈 Blvd Benito Juarez, Bahia de Tangolunda, (958) 581 01 76. www.oaxaca.com

Following the success of Cancún *(see p279)*, the Mexican government looked for an equivalent on the Pacific coast. The result was Huatulco, until then virtually unknown except to the local Zapotec people. Based around nine bays and 35 km (22 miles) of beaches, the resort sprang up in the 1980s, and now includes a small international airport, a golf course, and a marina. Beautiful, largely unspoiled, and relatively undiscovered.

Boats moored in the Santa Cruz marina in Huatulco

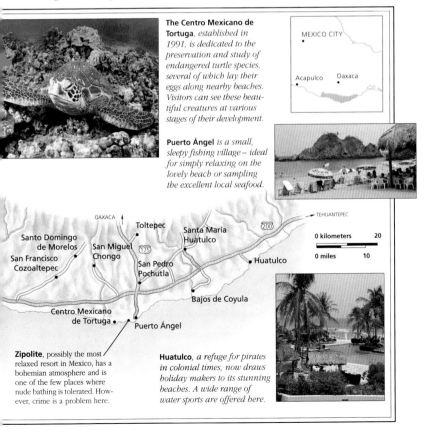

The Centro Mexicano de Tortuga, *established in 1991, is dedicated to the preservation and study of endangered turtle species, several of which lay their eggs along nearby beaches. Visitors can see these beautiful creatures at various stages of their development.*

Puerto Ángel *is a small, sleepy fishing village – ideal for simply relaxing on the lovely beach or sampling the excellent local seafood.*

MEXICO CITY

Acapulco   Oaxaca

OAXACA

Toltepec
Santa María Huatulco
Santo Domingo de Morelos
San Miguel Chongo
San Francisco Cozoaltepec
175
San Pedro Pochutla
Huatulco
Bajos de Coyula
Centro Mexicano de Tortuga
Puerto Ángel

TEHUANTEPEC
200

0 kilometers   20
0 miles   10

Zipolite, possibly the most relaxed resort in Mexico, has a bohemian atmosphere and is one of the few places where nude bathing is tolerated. However, crime is a problem here.

Huatulco, *a refuge for pirates in colonial times, now draws holiday makers to its stunning beaches. A wide range of water sports are offered here.*

Acapulco ❷

Fringing one of the most beautiful bays on Mexico's Pacific coast, Acalpulco is the country's most famous resort. The Spaniards founded the city in the 16th century, and for the next 300 years it served as the country's main gateway to the Far East. Continued prosperity was guaranteed in the 1940s when the then president, Miguel Alemán, selected Acapulco as Mexico's first tourist resort. Hollywood celebrities such as John Wayne, Errol Flynn, and Elizabeth Taylor arrived shortly afterward, and the high-rise hotels soon followed.

View across Acapulco Bay from the southeast headland

MAP OF ACAPULCO BAY

Exploring Acapulco

Acapulco can be divided into two distinct sections. To the west is the older, historic downtown area, or **Centro**; to the east is the "strip," which runs along the 11-km (7-mile) coastal road known as **La Costera Miguel Alemán**. This is lined with hotels, shops, restaurants, and nightclubs. The Centro is home to the

Señor Frog's, a popular restaurant overlooking the bay

1930s, Moorish-style **cathedral**, which overlooks the main square, as well as the bullring, the docks, and **La Quebrada**, where the world-renowned cliff divers perform their daily routine. Two blocks east of La Quebrada is a house where artist Diego Rivera spent time toward the end of his life. His colorful mosaics adorn the house.

The city boasts magnificent beaches and a worldwide reputation for the high life. It is also a working port and does not escape the environmental implications which that involves. The quality of the bay's water, for example, is not always perfect and drops noticeably in the rainy season (June–October) when litter is washed down from the hills.

Mosaic of Quetzalcoatl by Rivera, on a house near La Quebrada

♣ Fuerte de San Diego

Costera Miguel Alemán. **Tel** (744) 482 38 28. ☐ Tue–Sun. 🎟 Sun free. 📷
Today, one of the few reminders of the city's history is the star-shaped Fuerte de San Diego, an early 17th-century fort that now houses the Museo de Acapulco. The museum details the city's history from pre-Columbian times to Independence, with special emphasis on its importance as a commercial center.

For hotels and restaurants in this region see pp308–11 and pp339–41

Brightly colored hotels overlooking Playa Icacos

The Beaches

The city's main bay – 7 km (4 miles) wide – is broken up into a number of separate beaches. **Playa Caletilla** and **Playa Caleta** are situated on the peninsula south of the Centro. Smaller and more intimate than the other beaches, they are popular with local families who enjoy the calm, clean waters. Boats can be taken from here for the ten-minute trip to **Isla la Roqueta**, a small offshore island with thatched-roof restaurants, a small zoo, and several beaches.

Playa Honda, Playa Larga, and **Playa Manzanillo**, on the northern side of the same peninsula and just south of the main square, were popular

in the 1930s and 40s, but now serve mainly as departure points for charter fishing trips. **Playa Hornos** and **Playa Hornitos** occupy a central position on the bay. They have a family atmosphere but can get busy on the weekends. They also have the advantage of several beachside restaurants and nearby Papagayo Park, which has boating, rides, and other children's activities.

Farther to the east is **Playa Condesa**, the best known and most crowded of all the beaches. It is considered by those in the know to be the resort's "hot-spot" and is a favorite with younger visitors. On the eastern side of the bay, **Playa Icacos** runs from the Presidente Hotel to the naval base and is often less crowded than the other beaches.

Environs

Pie de la Cuesta, just 25 minutes' drive west of the city, is an attractive, broad, palm-fringed beach, but swimming here can be dangerous because of the powerful currents. The nearby **Laguna de Coyuca** is a large freshwater lake that featured in the early *Tarzan* films, as well as *The African Queen and Rambo II*. Fishermen and water-skiers share the lagoon with a wide variety of birds and wildlife. The sunsets here are superb.

VISITORS' CHECKLIST

Guerrero. 🏠 721,000. ✈ 30 km (19 miles) SE. 🚌 Ejido 47, (744) 469 20 30. 🛈 Costera Miguel Alemán 4455, (744) 484 44 16. 🎭 Festival Acapulco (late May), Virgen de Guadalupe (Dec 6–12). www.guerrero.gob.mx

Puerto Marqués is a large bay to the east of the city, with a few luxury hotels, food stands on the beach, and safe swimming. Farther to the east is **Playa Revolcadero**, unsafe for swimming due to the strong undertow, but relatively free of crowds and perfect for sunset-watching, surfing, and riding horses (rentals available).

LA QUEBRADA CLIFF DIVERS

The death-defying cliff divers of La Quebrada provide Acapulco's most famous and spectacular attraction. The performance starts with the young men climbing a 38-m (125-ft) cliff on the side of a narrow inlet. On reaching the top, they offer a prayer at a small altar before launching themselves into the shallow waters below. Each dive must coincide with an incoming wave if the diver is to avoid being dashed on the sharp rocks below. The five daily shows, one at 12:45pm and the rest in the evening, can be seen from a viewing platform or from Hotel El Mirador (see p308). The last two shows are performed holding flaming torches.

The palm-lined Laguna de Coyuca, west of the city

Monte Albán ⑤

A skull found on the site

Spectacularly situated on a mountain 400 m (1,315 ft) above the Oaxaca Valley, Monte Albán is the greatest of the Zapotec cities. In a triumph of engineering, the mountain top was leveled to allow for the creation of the ceremonial site. Its long history began with the Olmecs *(see p254)* around 500 BC. The city came to dominate the cultural, religious, and economic life of the region. Falling under the influence of Teotihuacán *(see p134–7)* during the height of its power, Monte Albán declined in later years and by AD 800 was largely abandoned. It was subsequently adopted by the Mixtecs, primarily as the site for some magnificent gold-laden burials.

★ **Los Danzantes**
This gallery of carvings shows humans in strange, tortured positions. Once identified as dancers, they are now thought to be prisoners of war.

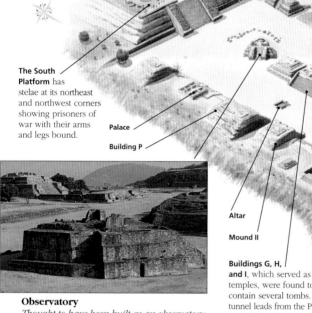

Mound III

Mound M

The South Platform has stelae at its northeast and northwest corners showing prisoners of war with their arms and legs bound.

Palace

Building P

GRAN PLAZA

Altar

Mound II

Buildings G, H, and I, which served as temples, were found to contain several tombs. A tunnel leads from the Palace to Building H, possibly so that dignitaries could appear here as if by magic.

Stela

Observatory
Thought to have been built as an observatory, or to celebrate victory in battle, this structure has glyphs carved on its walls. These may be the names of conquered tribes.

Ballcourt
A typical ballcourt, this I-shaped structure was used for playing the ceremonial ballgame (see p277). There would originally have been a stone ring at the top of each sloping side to act as a "goal."

The enormous Gran Plaza, aligned on a north-south axis

VISITORS' CHECKLIST

Oaxaca. Off Mex 190, 8 km (5 miles) W of Oaxaca. **Tel** (951) 516 12 15. 🚌 from Oaxaca. 🕐 8am–6pm daily. 📷 ♿ 🎫 🍴 🏪
www.inah.gob.mx

System IV is almost identical to Mound M. Both are well-preserved pyramids that would once have been surmounted by one-room wooden temples.

The Sunken Patio has an altar at its center.

Building B

★ Tomb 104

Above the entrance to Tomb 104 is this ceramic urn in the form of a figure seated on a jaguar throne. An image of Cocijo, the Zapotec rain god, is in the center of the headdress. When the tomb was opened in 1937 a vaulted burial chamber containing a single skeleton, surrounded by urns, perfuming pots, and other offerings, was discovered.

Tomb 103

STAR SIGHTS

★ Los Danzantes

★ Tomb 104

| 0 meters | | 75 |
| 0 yards | | 75 |

Museum, Tomb 7 & entrance

North Platform

A broad staircase leads up to the North Platform, the largest structure at Monte Albán. At the top of the steps are two rows of broken columns that would once have supported a flat roof.

Oaxaca ❻

Figure on family tree in Iglesia de Santo Domingo

Set in a fertile valley 1,500 m (4,900 ft) up in the mountains of the Sierra Madre del Sur, the city of Oaxaca (pronounced "Wa-harker") is one of the best preserved and most charming of all Mexico's colonial cities. Laid out in 1529, in an area once dominated by the Mixtec and Zapotec cultures, the Spanish settlement quickly became the most important town in the south. Now a major commercial and industrial center, it still manages to retain a certain provincial feel. This is due, in part, to the cultural presence of a large indigenous population.

The main façade of the cathedral, with the Alameda de Léon in front

Central Oaxaca

The **Plaza de Armas**, or *zócalo*, is the geographical and social center of the city. Closed to traffic, it bustles instead with vendors, students, tourists, and colorfully dressed villagers from outside the city. It is a great place to relax and watch the world go by, especially from the many cafés situated around its perimeter. Just northwest of the *zócalo* is the **Alameda de León**, a lovely square with market stalls that specialize in arts and crafts.

🏛 Cathedral

The cathedral is on the north side of the *zócalo* but faces the Alameda de León. It was originally constructed in 1553, but a series of earthquakes meant that it had to be rebuilt in 1730, which explains its solid walls and asymmetrical towers. The attractive Baroque façade includes a fine relief of the Assumption of the Virgin Mary above the main door. Inside, the main feature is the splendid bronze altar, which was crafted in Italy.

🏛 Museo de Arte Contemporáneo

Alcalá 202. **Tel** (951) 514 28 18.
◯ *Wed–Mon.* 📷 *Sun free.* 🅿
www.museomaco.com

The city's contemporary art museum is housed in a carefully refurbished 16th-century building, called the Casa de Cortés (House of Cortés) after the conquistador who is reputed to have commissioned it. The museum displays works of note by local and international modern artists, including Francisco Toledo and Rodolfo Morales. It is also a popular venue for temporary exhibitions and other cultural events.

🏛 Iglesia de Santo Domingo

Of the many churches in the city, this is the one most likely to take your breath away. Begun in 1572, it was completed over 200 years later at a total cost of over 12 million pesos in gold. Its misleadingly simple façade hides an interior that dazzles with gilded plaster and colored stucco,

Gold ornament in the Centro Cultural Santo Domingo

BENITO JUÁREZ (1806–72)

A portrait of reformer Benito Juárez by the artist Ángel Bracho

Benito Juárez, one of Mexico's greatest liberal reformers, was born just north of Oaxaca. Of Zapotec Indian parentage, he was orphaned at the age of three, but was educated by priests and went on to become a champion of agricultural reform and Indian rights. He was made president in 1858 and, after defeating the French, personally oversaw the execution of Emperor Maximilian in 1867 *(see p53)*. He continued to pursue reform until his death.

Main altar in the Iglesia de Santo Domingo

varying sizes. Another highlight is the unusual family tree of St. Dominic, painted on the low ceiling above the main entrance.

🏛 Centro Cultural Santo Domingo

Corner of Alcalá & Gurrión. **Tel** (951) 51 62 991. ☐ Tue–Sun. 🖾 🛈
Housed in a former monastery attached to the Iglesia de Santo Domingo, the Centro Cultural Santo Domingo has a museum, a botanical garden, a university library, and a bookstore. The museum is dedicated to pre-Columbian artifacts from the ancient cities of Oaxaca state. On display here are some of the remarkable treasures found at Monte Albán *(see pp220–21)*, in particular the extraordinary cache of Mixtec art and jewelry discovered in Tomb 7. This hoard includes beautifully

in a sublime combination of Gothic, Romanesque, Baroque, and Moorish styles. On the south side is the gilt-covered Capilla del Rosario, where there are numerous paintings of saints and Madonnas in

VISITORS' CHECKLIST

Oaxaca. 🏘 257,000.
✈ 8 km (5 miles) S.
🚌 Calz Niños Héroes 1036, (951) 515 12 14. 🛈 Av Independencia 607, (951) 516 01 23.
🎭 Guelaguetza (end Jul); Noche de Rábanos (Dec 23).
http://oaxaca-travel.com

crafted pieces in alabaster, obsidian, jade, and other precious materials, but is most famous for the objects in gold, regarded as the finest of their kind in the Americas.

🏛 Casa de Juárez

García Vigil 609. **Tel** (951) 516 18 60. ☐ Tue–Sun. 🖾
The house where Benito Juárez lived between 1818 and 1828 now contains a museum devoted to his life and times. Situated around a shady patio, the rooms have been kept almost exactly as they were when Juárez lived here, and provide fascinating insights into the lives of the middle classes in 19th-century Mexico.

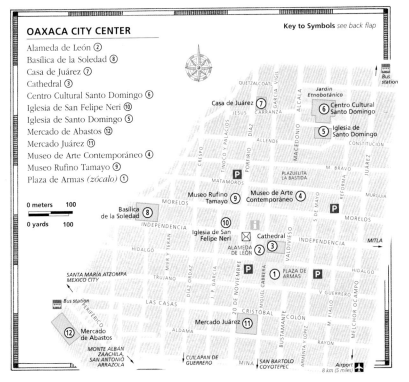

OAXACA CITY CENTER

Alameda de León ②
Basílica de la Soledad ⑧
Casa de Juárez ⑦
Cathedral ③
Centro Cultural Santo Domingo ⑥
Iglesia de San Felipe Neri ⑩
Iglesia de Santo Domingo ⑤
Mercado de Abastos ⑫
Mercado Juárez ⑪
Museo de Arte Contemporáneo ④
Museo Rufino Tamayo ⑨
Plaza de Armas (*zócalo*) ①

Key to Symbols *see back flap*

0 meters   100
0 yards   100

Exploring Oaxaca

Oaxaca has its fair share of interesting museums and colonial churches, all within walking distance of the center. However, its real charm lies in the rich blend of cultures on the streets themselves. Zapotec Indians, Mixtecs, and many other groups gather in force on Saturdays – the main trading day at the Mercado de Abastos, the country's biggest Indian market – to sell their traditional crafts. Techniques used to fashion textiles, ceramics, wood, and metal are passed down within families, and can be seen at workshops in villages around the city.

Preclassic female figure from Veracruz, in Museo Rufino Tamayo

The impressive façade and dome of the Basílica de la Soledad

🔒 Basílica de la Soledad
The Basílica de la Soledad is particularly noted for its 24-m (79-ft) high Baroque façade, which resembles a folding altarpiece, and for its heavily gilded interior. It was built between 1682 and 1690 to house the image of the Virgin of Solitude, Oaxaca's patron saint. This figure can be seen inside, encrusted with 600 diamonds and topped with a 2-kg (4-lb) gold crown. There is a small religious museum attached to the church.

🏛 Museo Rufino Tamayo
Av Morelos 503. *Tel* (951) 516 47 50. ◻ Wed–Mon. 🈶 🎫 reserve in advance. 📷
This beautifully presented museum, housed in a charming 17th-century building, contains a collection of pre-Columbian art once owned by the artist Rufino Tamayo (see p87). It was partly Tamayo's intention in collecting the pieces to stop them from falling into the

hands of illicit artifact traders. He then left them to his native state to make his fellow Mexicans aware of their rich heritage. The fascinating displays are arranged according to aesthetic themes.

🔒 Iglesia de San Felipe Neri
This church also has a façade shaped like an altarpiece, but its highlight is the gilt altarpiece itself, in the Churrigueresque style (see p27). Benito Juárez, Mexico's most celebrated president, was married here.

🏪 Mercado Juárez
Corner of 20 de Noviembre & Las Casas. ◻ daily. ♿
Mercado Juárez was once the city's main market and is still a great place to pick up crafts made in surrounding villages. Traditional clothing, leather goods, and the famous Oaxaca pottery are all sold here.

🏪 Mercado de Abastos
Corner of Periférico and Las Casas. ◻ daily. ♿
Most of the serious trading happens at this huge market, southwest of the center. Crafts such as ceramics, jewelry, and

---

OAXACA'S BLACK AND GREEN POTTERY

Distinctive black or dark green ceramics are seen all around Oaxaca. The black style, from San Bartolo Coyotepec, was popularized by Doña Rosa Real, who mastered and demonstrated the ancient art until her death in 1980. The green pottery, made in Santa María Atzompa, is beautifully decorated. It is best to buy both in the villages themselves.

Potter hard at work at the famous Doña Rosa Pottery in San Bartolo Coyotepec

Green-glazed pot with raised design from Santa María Atzompa

For hotels and restaurants in this region see pp308–11 and pp339–41

The Virgin of Solitude, draped in a cloak of black velvet, in the Basílica de la Soledad

painted wooden animals are sold here, but the real attraction is the chance to take in the noise, heat, smells, and color of one of the most vibrant markets in the country. The buyers and sellers chatter not in Spanish but mostly in the local Zapotec and Mixtec tongues, as they haggle at stalls laid out with the utmost care and attention. The liveliest day is Saturday.

Painted wooden carving

Environs

The village of **Santa María Atzompa**, 8 km (5 miles) northwest of the city, is home to hundreds of artisans dedicated

to making green-glazed pottery. **San Antonio Arrazola,** close to Monte Albán (see pp220–21), produces carved wooden figures of animals painted in vivid, multicolored designs.

The former convent at **Cuilapan de Guerrero**, 10 km (6 miles) southwest of the city on Mex 131, was established on the site of a Zapotec pyramid in 1550. It was abandoned two centuries later, but today still retains some impressive architectural features and murals. The roofless chapel has a Renaissance façade, an elegant columned nave, and thick earthquake-proof walls. Vicente Guerrero, hero of the War of Independence (see p49), was imprisoned here before being executed on Valentine's Day 1831. A monument to his memory stands at the convent. **Zaachila**, 16 km (10 miles) southwest of Oaxaca on the same road, is the site of the last Zapotec capital. A pyramid and two impressive tombs are open to the public. **San Bartolo Coyotepec**, 10 km (6 miles) south of the city, is where the gleaming black pottery (barro negro brillante), so common in souvenir shops, is made.

FIESTAS OF SOUTHERN MEXICO

Dancers performing at the Guelaguetza in Oaxaca

Guelaguetza (last two Mondays of Jul), Oaxaca. Dancers from all over the state re-enact Zapotec and Mixtec ceremonies, wearing traditional outfits and feathered headdresses.
Easter Week (Mar/Apr), San Juan Chamula and Zinacantán (Chiapas). Catholic ceremonies combine with pagan rituals in colorful festivals rated among the best in Mexico.
Feria de San Cristóbal (Jul 25), San Cristóbal de las Casas. A torch-lit procession in honor of the town's patron saint finishes at the church of San Cristóbal, which opens its doors to the public only on this day.
Noche de los Rábanos (Dec 23), Oaxaca. On the Night of the Radishes locals compete to carve the vegetables into people, animals, and plants.

The chapel of the former convent at Cuilapan de Guerrero, with the main church in the background

A Tour of the Tlacolula Valley ❼

The area around Oaxaca, and in particular the Tlacolula Valley, has been an important cultural and historical center since the 7th century BC. Over 2,500 years of civilization have filled the 50-km (31-mile) valley with diverse attractions reflecting its Olmec, Zapotec, Mixtec, Aztec, and Spanish heritage.

Teotitlán del Valle ④
The oldest town in the Tlacolula Valley, Teotitlán is known for its Zapotec rugs, made with natural dyes. It also has a small museum and some Zapotec ruins.

Santa María del Tule ①
Reputed to be over 2,000 years old, the Arbol del Tule in the churchyard here is one of the world's largest trees.

San Jerónimo Tlacochahuaya ②
The 16th-century church in this village was constructed as part of a Dominican monastery. It was decorated by Zapotec artisans and has an ornate bellows organ.

Dainzú ③
Once a Zapotec city, Dainzú has a tiered pyramid, a ballcourt, several tombs, and a unique collection of carved stone reliefs depicting ballgame players. Parts of the site date from 350 BC.

KEY

▬▬	Tour route
▬▬	Highway
····	Other roads
✣	Viewpoint

Yagul ❽

Oaxaca. Mex 190, 36 km (22 miles) SE of Oaxaca. 🚌 from Oaxaca. ⬜ daily. 📷 www.inah.gob.mx

The city of Yagul was first inhabited by the Zapotecs in about 500 BC. However, it gained real religious and political influence in the region only after the decline of Monte Albán *(see pp220–21)*, at the end of the 8th century AD, and most of the buildings at the site date from this period. Yagul was subsequently taken over by the Mixtecs and was finally abandoned after the arrival of the Spanish.

Dramatically set on and around a rocky outcrop, the city had a good defensive position. It is divided into two main areas. The lower level, called the **Acropolis**, includes a large ballcourt, more than 30 tombs, and a labyrinthine complex of buildings known as the Palace of the Six Patios. On the summit of the outcrop is the **Fortress**, surrounded by a strong defensive wall and offering superb views.

Zapotec ruins on the lower level of the city of Yagul

Mitla ❾

Oaxaca. Off Mex 190, 44 km (27 miles) SE of Oaxaca. *Tel (951) 568 03 16.* 🚌 from Oaxaca. ⬜ daily. 📷 www.inah.gob.mx

An important Zapotec city-state after the decline of Monte Albán *(see pp220–21)*, Mitla was home to approximately 10,000 people at its height. The city was later occupied by the Mixtecs, who had a significant influence on the architecture and decoration of its buildings. Many of Mitla's temples were destroyed by the Spanish when they invaded, and the stonework was used to build the Iglesia de San Pablo, the Catholic church that dominates the site.

Five main groups of buildings remain, two of which are readily accessible. The **Grupo de las Columnas**, in the east of the site, is a former palace. It consists of three large rooms set around tombs and a courtyard. The palace walls are decorated with the distinctive

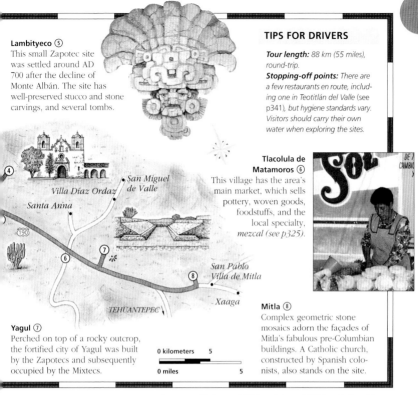

Lambityeco ⑤
This small Zapotec site was settled around AD 700 after the decline of Monte Albán. The site has well-preserved stucco and stone carvings, and several tombs.

TIPS FOR DRIVERS
Tour length: 88 km (55 miles), round-trip.
Stopping-off points: There are a few restaurants en route, including one in Teotitlán del Valle (see p341), but hygiene standards vary. Visitors should carry their own water when exploring the sites.

Tlacolula de Matamoros ⑥
This village has the area's main market, which sells pottery, woven goods, foodstuffs, and the local specialty, *mezcal (see p325)*.

Yagul ⑦
Perched on top of a rocky outcrop, the fortified city of Yagul was built by the Zapotecs and subsequently occupied by the Mixtecs.

0 kilometers 5

0 miles 5

Mitla ⑧
Complex geometric stone mosaics adorn the façades of Mitla's fabulous pre-Columbian buildings. A Catholic church, constructed by Spanish colonists, also stands on the site.

Map labels: San Miguel de Valle, Villa Díaz Ordaz, Santa Anna, 190, San Pablo Villa de Mitla, Xaaga, TEHUANTEPEC

Mitla's Catholic church, surrounded by pre-Columbian buildings decorated with distinctive geometric mosaics

geometric mosaics that characterize Mitla's buildings. Each frieze is made up of up to 100,000 separate pieces of cut stone. One of the rooms, the Salón de las Columnas, houses six monolithic pillars that once supported the roof. To the north is the **Grupo de la Iglesia**, centered around the colonial Catholic church. The pre-Columbian buildings that survived its construction are of similar design to those in the Grupo de las Columnas, but on a smaller scale. They still retain traces of paintwork.

Housed in a typical Oaxacan building, the **Museo de la Filatelia** allows a closer look at all things postal, from stamps to post-office furniture.

🏛 **Museo de la Filatelia**
Reforma No. 504, Col. Centro.
Tel (951) 514 23 75. ☐ Tue–Sun.

The twelve apostles on the bell tower of the cathedral in Tuxla Gutiérrez's main square

Tuxtla Gutiérrez ⑩

Chiapas. 🏛 434,000. 🚌 🚉 ❓
Boulevard Belisario Domínguez 950,
(961) 617 05 50, 01800 280 3500.
🎭 San Sebastián (Jan 15–23),
San Marcos (Apr 20–25).
www.visitmexico.com

The capital of the state of Chiapas, Tuxtla Gutiérrez is a modern, working city, and a major gateway for visitors.

Plaza Cívica, the main square, bustles with life and is regularly used for music and street theater performances. On its south side is the **cathedral**, built at the end of the 16th century and refurbished in a more modern style in the 1980s. Twelve carved wooden figures of the apostles appear from the bell tower as the bells chime out the hour.

To the west, and just south of Avenida Central, is the impressive, if somewhat dilapidated, **Monumento a la Bandera** (Monument to the Flag), which celebrates the union of Chiapas and Mexico. Farther west on the same street is the Hotel Bonampak *(see p311)*, which has reproductions of the Maya murals at Bonampak *(see p232)* in its lobby. The **Museo Regional**, northeast of the center, provides information on the geography and history of Chiapas. Nearby, the **Jardín Botánico** contains a range of plants native to the state, including beautiful orchids.

On the outskirts of town, in the foothills of the Sierra Madre de Chiapas, is the excellent **Zoológico Miguel Alvarez del Toro**, opened to help prevent the extinction of the state's indigenous animals. A 1-km (0.5-mile) walk leads through a lush jungle environment in which over 150 species live in their natural habitats.

A street performer in Plaza Cívica

🏛 **Museo Regional**
Calzada de los Hombres Ilustres.
Tel (961) 613 44 79. ◯ Tue–Sun.
📷 🎥 in advance. ❌ ◻

🐾 **Zoológico Miguel Alvarez del Toro**
Corner of Calzada Cerro Hueco & Libramiento Sur. **Tel** (961) 614 47 00. ◯ Tue–Sun. 📷 Tue free. ◻ ◻

Part of a mural in support of the Zapatista rebels of Chiapas

THE ZAPATISTA UPRISING

On January 1, 1994, the EZLN (Ejército Zapatista de Liberación Nacional), led by the masked "Subcomandante Marcos," seized the town of San Cristóbal de las Casas. Their aims – taken from those of Emiliano Zapata *(see p54)* – were a redistribution of power and the state's resources, from the wealthy few to the poor majority. The "Zapatistas," as they became known, were forced out of the town by the army and fled into the jungle. Although a ceasefire was agreed in 1995, the land the Zapatistas occupy is still heavily patrolled by government forces. So far, in spite of talks, the two sides have been unable to reconcile their differences.

The dramatic Cañón del Sumidero, almost 1 km (half a mile) deep

Cañón del Sumidero ⑪

Chiapas. 🚌 Tuxtlagutierrez. ◯ daily. 📷 🎥 by boat from Chiapa de Corzo or Cahuaré, (961) 616 15 72.

The breathtaking Sumidero Canyon forms the heart of a beautiful national park. Legend has it that in the mid-16th century several hundred Indians chose to hurl themselves down its precipitous sides after a defiant last stand, rather than submit to the invading Spanish forces.

Nearly a kilometer (half a mile) deep, and around 14 km (9 miles) in length, the canyon was carved by the Grijalva river over the course of millions of years. This important river stretches from Guatemala to the Gulf of Mexico.

Excellent views of the sheer-sided canyon are available from a series of five lookout points along its western rim. Alternatively, visitors can enjoy a two-hour boat trip along the river. Boats leave from two embarkation points, one at Cahuaré (on the west bank of the Grijalva, on Mex 190), and the other at the docks in Chiapa de Corzo. The trip passes caves and waterfalls. It also provides an opportunity to see a variety of unusual plants, and many animals and birds, including monkeys, crocodiles, iguanas, herons, and kingfishers.

◁ The flamboyant façade of the cathedral in San Cristóbal de las Casas

San Cristóbal de las Casas ⑫

Chiapas. 132,000. *plaza 31 de Marzo, (967) 678 06 60. Primavera y Paz (1 week before Easter), San Cristóbal (Jul 25).*

Founded by the Spaniards in 1528 and marked by centuries of geographical isolation, San Cristóbal is still imbued with an atmosphere of sleepy colonial charm. However, it has a long and troubled history of conflict between the descendants of the Spanish and the local Indians. It was here that the Zapatista uprising began in 1994, and there is still a strong military presence in the town.

Situated at 2,300 m (7,550 ft) above sea level in the Chiapan highlands, San Cristóbal has a refreshingly cool climate. The town's main square, Plaza 31 de Marzo, is dominated by the **Palacio Municipal** and the **cathedral**. The latter was started in the 16th century, but construction and alterations continued until the beginning of the 19th century. Its lavish interior contains an elaborate gold-encrusted pulpit and several notable altarpieces.

Part of an elaborately gilded altarpiece in the Templo de Santo Domingo

A few blocks to the north is the 16th-century Dominican **Templo de Santo Domingo**, the most impressive church in the city. It has an intricate pink façade, a gilded Baroque interior with several magnificent altarpieces, and a pulpit carved from a single piece of oak. Farther north, on General Utrilla, is the main market, where Indians from the surrounding hills come to trade.

The **Na Bolom** museum and research center, on the east side of the town, is devoted to studying and protecting the indigenous Lacandón Indians and their rainforest home. It was founded by a European couple in the 1950s, and is credited with having helped to stop the tribe from dying out.

The **Iglesia de San Cristóbal** to the west, and the **Iglesia de Guadalupe** to the east, offer excellent views over the city from their hilltop positions.

Environs:

There are several Indian villages 10 km (6 miles) or so from San Cristóbal, including **San Juan Chamula**, which has a beautiful church. A trip here provides an insight into the mix of Christian and pre-Columbian traditions of the Tzotzil-speaking inhabitants. The village's fiestas and markets are among the best in Mexico. Visitors are warned not to take photos, especially in religious buildings, as this may cause serious offense.

Some 84 km (52 miles) to the southeast of San Cristóbal is the charming border town of **Comitán de Domínguez**, a good base for exploring the ruins of **Chinkultic**, including several pyramids, a ball court, and a number of stelae. The **Lagos de Montebello** nearby is a chain of lakes, with lovely green and blue water.

🏛 **Na Bolom**
Av Vicente Guerrero 33. **Tel** (967) 678 14 18. daily (tours Tue–Sun at 11:30am, 4:30pm). www.nabolom.org

Chinkultic
Off Mex 190, 41 km (25 miles) SE of Comitán de Domínguez. Tue–Sun. www.inah.gob.mx

Crowds in front of the church in San Juan Chamula

For hotels and restaurants in this region see pp308–11 and pp339–41

Agua Azul

Chiapas. Off Mex 199, 125 km (78 miles) NE of San Cristóbal de las Casas. 🚌 from Palenque or San Cristóbal de las Casas. 🚾

A good stopping-off point en route from San Cristóbal de las Casas to Palenque, the Parque Nacional Agua Azul has some of the most beautiful waterfalls in Mexico. There are over 500 cascades in all, ranging from 3 to 30 m (10–100 ft) in height, together with a series of aquamarine-colored rock pools. It is possible to swim in some of these, which brings welcome relief from the heat and humidity of the lowlands, but do not swim where there are signs warning of dangerous currents. The falls are best visited outside of the rainy season (Jun–Sep), during which the waters become murky.

Environs
Some 22 km (14 miles) before the road from Agua Azul reaches Palenque is the spectacular, 30-m (100-ft) high waterfall at **Misol-Ha**. Set within the lush surroundings of a tropical rainforest, this is another good place at which to stop for a swim.

Palenque 🄮

See pp234–7.

One of the spectacularly beautiful waterfalls at Agua Azul

Bonampak 🄯

Chiapas. 153 km (95 miles) SE of Palenque. ✈ from Palenque. 🚌 tours from Palenque. 🔘 daily. 🚾 www.inah.gob.mx

Discovered in the 1940s, the Maya site of Bonampak is of ancient origin but reached its apogee under Yahaw Chan Muwan (776–90). The subject of three fine stelae at the site, Yahaw Chan Muwan commissioned Bonampak's remarkable Temple of the Paintings. The walls and vaulted ceilings of the three chambers of this temple are covered with vividly colored murals. These give rich insights into the courtly life of the nobility of Bonampak and the pageantry surrounding Maya warfare. Murals in the two outer rooms (Rooms 1

and 3) show noblemen in fine clothes and elaborate head-dresses. Below them are musicians and dancers, and on the ceiling animals and figures representing constellations of the Maya cosmos.

The two main paintings in the middle room (Room 2) depict a battle, in which Maya warriors are shown defeating their enemy.

As an alternative to making the trip to the site itself, reproductions of the murals can be seen in a hotel in Tuxtla Gutiérrez (see p230).

Yaxchilán 🄰

Chiapas. 130 km (80 miles) SE of Palenque. ✈ from Palenque. 🚌 tours from Palenque. 🔘 daily. 🚾 www.inah.gob.mx

The city of Yaxchilán, located 20 m (66 ft) above the Usumacinta River in the heart of the Lacandón rainforest, is one of the most dramatic of all Maya sites. It can only be reached by air or by taking first a bus and then a boat along the river.

Built between AD 350 and 800, it rose to prominence during the 8th century under the command of its most famous kings, "Shield Jaguar," and his son "Bird Jaguar." Yaxchilán is rich in glyphs, stelae, carved lintels, stucco roof combs, and temples. One of the best preserved buildings is Temple 33.

Yaxchilán is in the homeland of the Lacandón Indians (see p231), Mexico's last pagan native people, who live outside Hispanicized society.

Temple 33 at Yaxchilán, with its prominent roof comb

The Art of the Maya

Of all Mesoamerican civilizations, the Maya produced the most enduring works of art, in the greatest quantity. Maya art is distinguished by its naturalistic approach which makes it more accessible to the modern eye than the art of other ancient Mexican cultures. The Maya used a variety of materials to decorate their buildings and to make sacred and functional objects: stone, wood, ceramics, stucco, shell, jade, and bone. Particularly striking are the Maya's portraits of themselves – as seen especially in the wall paintings of Bonampak and the carved bas-reliefs of Palenque – which give us an understanding of their way of life, methods of warfare, costumes, customs, and beliefs.

Feather plume

Ear flare

Jade bracelet

Glyphs (see pp46–7), *often recording royal biographies and events, were carved in stone or modeled in stucco.*

Stelae, *upright stone slabs placed at ritual sites, usually chronicle the lives of rulers and their victories in war. This one is from Yaxchilán.*

Ceramics *were used to make delicate sculptures. This figurine, probably of a ruler, was found in a Maya tomb on the island of Jaina off the coast near Campeche (see p260).*

Bas-reliefs *show the Maya's skill in representing themselves, as seen in this detail from the Tablet of the Slaves in Palenque museum (see p237).*

Vases, *such as this example depicting a supernatural jaguar, were painted with a mineral slip before firing.*

The murals of Bonampak *depict scenes of Classic Maya life in vivid colors with an evocative sense of realism. This detail from the battle scene in Room 2 shows a warrior dressed in a jaguar skin seizing an enemy by the hair. Other remarkable frescoes believed to be by Maya artists can be seen at Cacaxtla (see p156).*

Palenque ⑭

Detail of glyphs from the Palace courtyard

Palenque is everything that an archaeological site should be: mysterious, solemn, well preserved, and imposing in its beautiful jungle setting. The Maya first settled here as early as 100 BC, and the city reached its apogee between AD 600 and 800, when it served as a regional capital. It fell into a precipitous decline in the early 10th century and was abandoned to the ever-encroaching jungle. Excavations have uncovered ruins emblazoned with fine sculpture and splendid stuccowork.

The Temple of the Foliated Cross is named after a panel showing a cruciform corn plant.

The Temple of the Cross has a striking roof comb, and carvings inside.

Temple XIV
Although badly damaged, this temple has been largely reconstructed. It contains some well-preserved glyphs and carvings, among them this portrait of the ruler Ken Balam II, who is wearing a feathered headdress.

Central Palenque
The site's most important buildings, shown in the illustration, are known as the Principal Group.

Path to Groups B and C, waterfalls, and museum (see p237)

Ballcourt

STAR FEATURES

★ Temple of the Inscriptions

★ The Palace

North Group
This consists of five temples on a single platform. At the base of the platform is this carving of the god Tlaloc.

The Temple of the Count was for two years in the 1830s the home of an eccentric European nobleman.

Temple of the Sun
One of the best-preserved buildings on the site, this temple on a four-level pyramid is crowned with a prominent roof comb – a massive carved stone slab. Inside are glyphs and stucco friezes, one of which shows the sun.

VISITORS' CHECKLIST

Chiapas. 8 km (5 miles) SW of Palenque town. from Palenque town. 8am–4:45pm daily. Museum 9am–4:45pm Tue–Sun. www.inah.gob.mx

Water channel

Path to Temple of the Jaguar (see p237)

★ Temple of the Inscriptions
This pyramid contains the tomb of Pakal, ruler of Palenque (see p236).

Temple XIII

Temple of the Dying Moon

0 meters   50

0 yards   50

Entrance

Tomb of Alberto Ruz Lhuillier (see p236)

★ The Palace
Standing on a raised platform, the Palace is a complex of courtyards, corridors, and rooms. It is distinguished by a four-tier tower that probably served as an observatory or lookout post (see p237).

Temple X

Palace carvings
This stone slab carved with a figure is one of nine that can be seen in the courtyard of the palace.

The Temple of the Inscriptions

The tallest and most imposing building at Palenque is shown here as a reconstruction, complete with its roof comb. It was constructed during the 68-year reign of Pakal (AD615–83) and subsequently contained his funerary crypt, a fact that was revealed only by the dramatic discovery of his tomb by Alberto Ruz Lhuillier in 1952. Many of the artifacts and pieces of jewelry found in the tomb are now on display in the Museo Nacional de Antropología in Mexico City *(see pp90–95).*

The steep climb of the main stair-case at the front of the pyramid

The entrance to the tomb *is by way of two flights of steep stone steps that descend 25 m (82 ft). When the staircase was discovered in 1949 it was filled with rubble, which took three years to remove before the tomb could be explored.*

The roof comb would have been carved with deities and animal motifs.

The temple that surmounts the pyramid is divided into two halls.

Two shafts above the landing let in light and air from outside the pyramid.

RECONSTRUCTION OF THE TEMPLE OF THE INSCRIPTIONS

In the time of the Classic Maya the temple would have been covered with plaster and painted a vivid red. The detailed carvings on the temple and the roof comb were picked out in other bright colors.

The inscriptions, *which give the temple its name, can be seen on the temple walls. There are 617 carved glyphs in total, arranged on three stone slabs. To date, they have been only partially deciphered.*

The Tomb of Pakal *is a chamber measuring 9 m by 4 m (30 ft by 13 ft), with a vaulted ceiling almost 7 m (23 ft) high. Nine stucco figures, representing dynastic precursors, adorn the walls. The heavy stone lid of the sarcophagus is decorated with a symbolic scene of Pakal's resurrection from the jaws of the underworld. The tomb is currently closed to the public.*

Exploring Palenque

The most interesting and best preserved buildings are in the Principal Group (shown on the previous pages). A few lesser-known temples can be reached by easy paths through the jungle. Another path leads from the Principal Group past a series of waterfalls to the site museum.

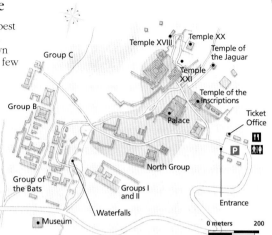

KEY

▨ Principal Group (see pp234–5)

Labels on map: Temple XVIII, Temple XX, Temple of the Jaguar, Group C, Temple XXI, Group B, Temple of the Inscriptions, Palace, Ticket Office, Group of the Bats, North Group, Groups I and II, Entrance, Museum, Waterfalls

0 meters 200
0 yards 200

The Palace

Set on a platform some 100 m by 80 m (328 ft by 262 ft) and 10 m (33 ft) high, the palace complex is the product of many kings. The earliest buildings date to the time of Pakal, but the basal platform conceals earlier phases, some preserved as underground galleries. The palace was the home of the royal family and their immediate entourage. Carvings and stucco decorations can be seen in parts of the building. Particularly interesting are the sculptures of captives in the courtyard (see p235), where visitors could be suitably impressed by the might of the Palenque kings. The Oval Tablet depicts the accession of Pakal, who receives the

Oval Tablet in the Palace

emblems of office from his mother, a short-reigning queen.

Temple of the Jaguar

A short path behind the Temple of the Inscriptions leads to this ruined structure. Its name derives from the image of a king seated on a jaguar throne inside, now destroyed. Unexcavated and overgrown, it gives an idea of what the site must have been like when it was first explored in the late 18th century.

Outlying Temples

Two clearly marked paths that set off from in front of the Temple of the Sun lead to Temples XVIII and XXI, and other isolated buildings that are nearby but hidden by trees.

Temple of the Jaguar, one of many buildings in the jungle

More buildings can be reached by the path from the site to the museum, which passes through Group B and the Group of the Bats. Branches off this path lead to Group C, Group I, and Group II. There are hundreds of similar but less accessible structures at Palenque that are hidden by the surrounding jungle.

The Museum

This modern building on the road between Palenque town and the archaeological site provides an overview of the development of the Maya city. Many artifacts found on the site are on display, including the so-called Tablet of the Slaves (see p233).

The Palace, dominating the center of Palenque

THE GULF COAST

TABASCO · VERACRUZ

*T*he lush, tropical plains fringing the Gulf of Mexico were once home to three major pre-Columbian cultures – the enigmatic Olmecs, the "mother culture" of ancient Mexican civilization; the Totonacs of Central Veracruz; and the Huastecs. Centuries later, this coast was once again at the fulcrum of Mexican history, when the first Spaniards set out on their historic conquest of the Aztec empire.

This green and fertile region stretches from Tampico and the Huasteca region in the north, to the steamy, low-lying jungle of the Istmo de Tehuantepec – Mexico's narrow "waist" – in the south. Much of Mexico's sugar cane, tropical fruits, cocoa, and coffee are produced on this coastal plain. Inland temperatures drop as the land rises toward the great heights of the Sierra Madre Oriental and the snow-capped Pico de Orizaba, Mexico's highest mountain at 5,747 m (18,856 ft).

The Olmec civilization arose in the southern part of this area in about 1000 BC. Later, the Maya people used the wide, meandering rivers that crisscross Tabasco as their trading routes.

Meanwhile, in the north of the region, other indigenous races built great cities, most notably at El Tajín. In 1519, the Spanish conquistador Hernán Cortés disembarked on the coast of Veracruz. He burnt his boats, before going into alliance with the Totonac Indians and setting off to conquer the Aztecs. Throughout the next three centuries, the port of Veracruz shipped endless quantities of gold and silver back to Europe. At the same time, colonial towns like Tlacotalpan grew and prospered. In recent decades, parts of Tabasco and the southern area of Veracruz have been transformed by another economic boom, this time stemming from the exploitation of oil.

A farmer with his crop of sugar cane, one of many plants grown in the humid Gulf Coast region

◁ Palm trees providing welcome shade in the Plaza de Armas, the main square of El Puerto de Veracruz

Exploring the Gulf Coast

The humid Gulf Coast region has a rich hoard of pre-Columbian treasures. Artifacts from various cultures are preserved in Xalapa, in one of Mexico's best museums; in Villahermosa, meanwhile, an outdoor archaeological park exhibits the monumental art of the Olmec civilization. The ruined city of El Tajín, sacred to the god of thunder, should also not be missed. Other sights in the region include the vibrant port of Veracruz and the charming colonial towns of Tlacotalpan and Coatepec.

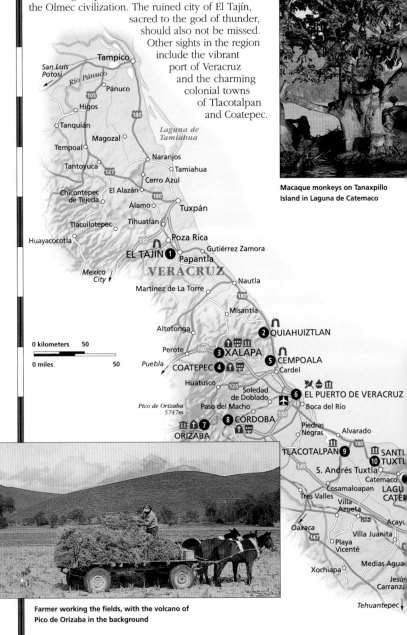

Macaque monkeys on Tanaxpillo Island in Laguna de Catemaco

Tampico
San Luis Potosi
Río Pánuco
105
Pánuco
Higos
180
Tanquián
Magozal
Laguna de Tamiahua
Tempoal
Naranjos
Tantoyuca
127
Tamiahua
Cerro Azul
Chicontepec de Tejeda
El Alazán
180
Álamo
Tuxpán
Tlacuilotepec
Tihuatlán
Huayacocotla
132
Poza Rica
Mexico City
EL TAJIN ❶
Gutiérrez Zamora
Papantla
VERACRUZ
Nautla
Martínez de La Torre
180
Misantla
Altotonga
QUIAHUIZTLAN ❷
0 kilometers 50
Perote
140
XALAPA ❸
0 miles 50
Puebla
COATEPEC ❹
CEMPOALA ❺
Cardel
Huatusco
125
Soledad de Doblado
EL PUERTO DE VERACRUZ ❻
Pico de Orizaba 5747m
Paso del Macho
Boca del Río
CÓRDOBA ❽
150
ORIZABA ❼
Piedras Negras
Alvarado
TLACOTALPAN ❾
180
SANTI TUXTL
TUXTLA ❿
145
S. Andrés Tuxtla
Catemaco
Cosamaloapan
LAGU
Tres Valles
CATE
Villa Azueta
Isla
Acay
Oaxaca
Villa Juanita
147
Playa Vicente
Medías Agua
Xochiapa
Jesú Carranza
Tehuantepec

Farmer working the fields, with the volcano of Pico de Orizaba in the background

For additional map symbols see back flap

SIGHTS AT A GLANCE

Cempoala ❺
Coatepec ❹
Comalcalco ⑫
Córdoba ❽
Laguna de Catemaco ⑪
Orizaba ❼
El Puerto de Veracruz ❻
Quiahuiztlan ❷
Santiago Tuxtla ❿
El Tajín pp242–3 ❶
Tlacotalpan ❾
Villahermosa ⑬
Xalapa pp246–9 ❸

KEY

═══	Highway
▬▬	Major road
═══	Minor road
∙∙∙∙	Main railway
‒‒‒	Minor railway
▬▬	International border
═══	State border
△	Summit

SEE ALSO

• *Where to Stay* pp311–13

• *Where to Eat* pp341–2

Fishing boats in the harbor of Veracruz

GETTING AROUND

The region has two large airports, at Veracruz and Villahermosa, with Veracruz offering more international destinations. The main towns in the area are linked by highways and regular bus services. However, the northern region is less visited and less well served – the easiest way to get to El Tajín is to fly to the domestic airport at Poza Rica. In the south, Villahermosa is a transportation hub offering road connections with the Yucatán Peninsula *(see pp256–87)* and convenient access to Palenque *(see pp234–7)*.

Brightly painted arches
in the unspoiled town
of Tlacotalpan

*GULF OF
MEXICO*

El Tajín ●

Developed from an earlier settlement, the city of El Tajín was a political and religious center for the Totonac civilization. Many of its buildings date from the early Postclassic period, between AD 900 and 1150. Decorated with relief panels and sculptures, they would have been painted in strong colors such as red, blue, and black. The excavated nucleus of this spectacular ancient city covers about 1 sq km (0.4 sq miles), but the entire urban area once spread over 10 sq km (4 sq miles) and had a population of 25,000.

★ Pyramid of the Niches
Originally crowned by a temple, this pyramid has 365 niches, representing the days of the year. Each niche may have held an offering.

Building 12

Building 10

★ Southern Ballcourt
Six relief panels on the side walls of this ballcourt illustrate rituals of the game (see p277), including the sacrifice of one or more players.

Entrance, visitors' center, museum, and *voladores*

★ Statue of Dios Tajín
This small statue probably represents Tajín, god of thunder and lightning, an important deity to the people of El Tajín.

Plaza del Arroyo
The four pyramids that surround this massive square stand at the cardinal points. They are some of the oldest structures in the city.

Los Voladores

This ancient ritual (see p29) of the Totonac people from the Papantla region takes place daily near the site entrance. The voladores *(fliers) launch themselves from the top of a pole and slowly descend as the ropes around the pole unwind.*

VISITORS' CHECKLIST

Veracruz. Off Mex 180, 12 km (7 miles) SE of Poza Rica. 🚌 from Papantla or Poza Rica. ◯ 9am–5pm daily. 🌐 🎟 in advance. 🍴 🏠 www.inah.gob.mx

El Tajín Chico

Northern Ballcourt

Gran Xicalcoliuhqui

Seen from above, this structure to the north forms an interlocking fretwork. It is thought to be associated with Quetzalcoatl (see p265).

Plaza Oriente and Gran Xicalcoliuhqui ➤

Ballcourt 13/14

0 meters 50

0 yards 50

STAR SIGHTS

★ Pyramid of the Niches

★ Southern Ballcourt

★ Statue of Dios Tajín

PLAN OF SITE

The Building of the Columns, on the highest part of the site, was the home of the ruler known as 13 Rabbit.

El Tajín Chico, the middle level of the site, was the residential area for the elite ruling class.

The buildings in the lower part of the site were used for cere-monial or religious purposes only.

Entrance, museum, and *voladores*

Pyramid of the Niches

PLAZA DEL ARROYO

PLAZA ORIENTE

Gran Xicalcoliuhqui

PLAZA DE HURACÁN

0 meters 100

0 yards 100

KEY

▢ Illustrated area

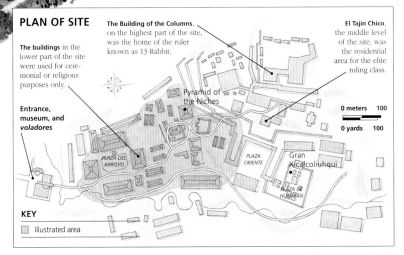

The steep ascent of the Pyramid of the Niches, which offers stunning views ▷

Small stone tombs in the Totonac cemetery at Quiahuiztlan

Quiahuiztlan ❷

Veracruz Mex 180, 24 km (15 miles) N of Cempoala. 🚍 to Cerro de los Metates then 2-km (1-mile) walk. ⬜ daily. 🖥 www.inah.gob.mx

Once inhabited by 15,000 people, the Totonac city of Quiahuiztlan was a hilltop stronghold. It was constructed in the late Classic period, when raids by warlike nomads from the north forced sites like El Tajín to be abandoned. Despite originally being ringed by defensive walls, it was twice conquered, first by the Toltecs in the 9th century and then by the Aztecs in the 13th century.

Today the only part of the terraced site that can be visited is the cemetery. Here some 100 tiny tombs were discovered, each resembling a pre-Columbian temple. Many had human bones and skulls in burial chambers in their bases. Small holes in the backs of the tombs may have been for relatives to communicate with the dead.

Across the main road (Mex 180) from Quiahuiztlan is Villa Rica de la Vera Cruz, the first Spanish settlement in Mexico, and now a fishing village.

Xalapa ❸

Veracruz. 🚶 413,000. 🚍 🛈 Torre Animas 5, (228) 812 75 85. 🎭 Feria de las Flores (Apr).

The capital of Veracruz state, Xalapa (or Jalapa) is known for its university and cultural life, and has the second most important anthropology museum (see pp248–9) in Mexico. The city enjoys a beautiful setting: on a clear day there are splendid views of the 4,250-m (13,940-ft) Cofre de Perote peak from Parque Juárez, the main plaza. To one side of this square is the Neo-Classical **Palacio de Gobierno**, which has a mural by Mario Orozco Rivera (1930–98) on its stairs. Opposite the Palacio is the 18th-century **cathedral**. Uphill from the city center, brightly colored houses with sloping tiled roofs and wrought-iron balconies line the pretty, cobbled streets around the market.

Environs

The **Hacienda Lencero**, originally a 16th-century inn, was bought by the controversial General Santa Anna (see p52) in the 19th century. It is now a museum of furniture, utensils, and ornaments from that era.

The remote **Filobobos** consists of two archaeological sites 4 km (2.5 miles) apart, which date from AD 700–1200. Access to the site nearest to the road, El Cuajilote, is by an organized rafting trip along the River Bobos, or via an 8-km (5-mile) scenic walk. It is worth the effort of getting there, however, because the Filobobos ruins are truly spectacular.

🏛 **Palacio de Gobierno**
Av Enriques. **Tel** (228) 841 74 00. ⬜ Mon–Fri. ⬆

🏛 **Hacienda Lencero**
10 km (6 miles) E of Xalapa. **Tel** (228) 820 02 70. ⬜ Tue–Sun. 🖼 🎥 📷

🏛 **Filobobos**
Off minor road from Tlapacoyan to Plan de Arroyos, 110 km (68 miles) NW of Xalapa. ⬜ Tue–Sun. 🖼

A charming cobbled street with colorful houses, near the market in Xalapa

For hotels and restaurants in this region see pp311–13 and pp341–2

Las Chimeneas, named after the hollow columns that line its upper tier

Coatepec 4

Veracruz. 🏠 *80,000.* 🚌 👤 *Miguel Rebolledo 1, (228) 816 09 64.* 📷 *San Jerónimo (Sep 29–30), Feria del Café (Apr 30–May 1).*

A lovely town, Coatepec is famous for its coffee, fruit liqueurs, orchids, and seafood restaurants. The town's elegant houses, with tiled roofs and ornate balconies and grilles, were built with the proceeds of the early 20th-century coffee boom. A converted hacienda in the center of the town is now one of Mexico's most charming hotels, the Posada Coatepec *(see p312).* Near the Posada is the attractive Basílica Menor de Nuestra Señora de Guadalupe.

Environs

The area around Coatepec has a humid, semitropical climate with exuberant vegetation – in some places balls of grass even grow on telephone wires

The Basílica Menor de Nuestra Señora de Guadalupe in Coatepec

where birds have left traces of soil. The quiet colonial town of **Xico**, 9 km (6 miles) south of Coatepec, is worth a visit, especially on a Sunday (market day). From Xico, a path leads through coffee and banana plantations to the 40-m (131-ft) high **Texolo Waterfall**.

Cempoala 5

Veracruz. Mex 180, 44 km (27 miles) N of Veracruz. 🚌 *from Veracruz.* ⭕ *daily.* 🖥 www.inah.gob.mx

Shortly after their arrival in Mexico in 1519 *(see p43),* Cortés and his men sheltered in the Totonac city that stood on the site of modern-day Cempoala (or Zempoala). Like many other cities at the time, it was subjugated by the Aztecs, and the city's governor collaborated with Cortés in return for protection.

The walled archaeological site, which contains the ruins of the Totonac city, adjoins Cempoala town. Around a central plaza, buildings faced with smooth, rounded river stones show strong Aztec influences. Straight ahead from the entrance is the **Templo Mayor**, a 13-tier pyramid topped by a sanctuary, which was originally thatched with palm leaves. Nearby, in **Las Chimeneas** (The Chimneys), so-called because of its hollow columns, archaeologists found a *chacmool*-like figure *(see p44),* suggesting the Maya were associated with the site. The east-facing **Gran Pirámide** was a temple dedicated to the sun.

FIESTAS OF THE GULF COAST

Carnival *(Feb/Mar).* Celebrated in most parts of the Gulf Coast, but particularly in Veracruz, Villahermosa, and Tenosique (Tabasco), Carnival starts with the burning of a huge figure, representing "bad temper," who usually resembles an unpopular politician. There are also floats, parades, and dancing. Tenosique's Carnival is famous for its flour war, the Guerra de Pocho y Blanquitos.

Carnival in Veracruz

Candelaria *(week leading up to Feb 2).* Celebrated throughout Mexico, the Christian festival of Candelaria (Candlemas) is particularly vibrant in the towns of Tlacotalpan and Catemaco. The festival traditionally features numerous street stalls, as well as dancing and music. In Tlacotalpan the local Virgin is taken on a river procession involving hundreds of boats.

Corpus Christi *(May/Jun).* The religious festival of Corpus Christi is especially associated with Papantla. Here the renowned *voladores (see p243)* perform their spectacular ancient rite of twirling upside down from a towering pole, with the intention of invoking fertility and honoring the sun.

Feria de Santiago Tuxtla *(Jul 25),* Santiago Tuxtla. In this saint's day celebration, gigantic *mojiganga* dolls are taken around the town. *Danzas de los liseres* (jaguar-mask dances) also take place.

Museo de Antropología de Xalapa

Huastec toy dog on wheels

Second only in importance to the anthropology museum in Mexico City, this outstanding collection is displayed in spacious marble halls and open-air patios. It consists of sculptures and artifacts from the Gulf Coast's major pre-Columbian civilizations, found at various sites within the region. The first halls are dedicated to the Olmec civilization (*see p254*). Central Veracruz and the Totonacs follow, and the final room exhibits the highly stylized sculptures of the Huastec culture.

The Olmec Patio, dominated by El Rey

GALLERY GUIDE

The exhibits are displayed in a descending series of halls and patios with steps and wheelchair ramps linking each level. Beginning at the main entrance, the items are arranged chronologically. The gardens contain flora representative of different areas of Veracruz state.

Olmec Funerary Urn

When it was discovered in Catemaco, this huge terracotta urn held the remains of a small child, along with ritual offerings.

El Señor de Las Limas

Found in Las Limas, this greenstone figure (900–400 BC) is thought to be an accession monument. It depicts a lordly figure holding the Werejaguar baby, an important Olmec symbol of divine power.

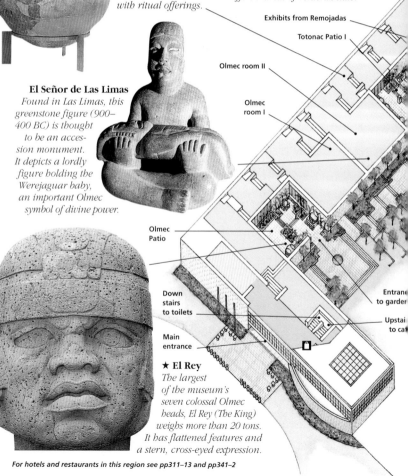

Exhibits from Remojadas

Totonac Patio I

Olmec room II

Olmec room I

Olmec Patio

Down stairs to toilets

Main entrance

Entrance to gardens

Upstairs to café

★ El Rey

The largest of the museum's seven colossal Olmec heads, El Rey (The King) weighs more than 20 tons. It has flattened features and a stern, cross-eyed expression.

Mictlantecuhtli

Representing Mictlantecuhtli, the god of death, this extraordinary skeletal figure (AD 600–900) is made from terracotta and painted with tar.

odel
El
jin

Totonac Patio II

Rear entrance

Huastec room

VISITORS' CHECKLIST

Av Xalapa, Xalapa. **Tel** (228) 815 09 20. 🚌 Avila Camacho, Centro and Tesoreria. ☐ 9am–5pm Tue–Sun. 📷 ♿ 📷 11:30am (reserve in advance). ☐ 📷

KEY

☐	Permanent collection
☐	Temporary exhibitions
☐	Non-exhibition space

★ Tlaloc

This expressive terracotta figure (AD 600–900) from El Zapotal (see p250) may represent Tlaloc, the rain god of the central highlands, or a warrior or ballplayer.

Exhibits from El Zapotal

Los Gemelos, "the twins," (AD 600–900) is one of the main exhibits here.

Exhibits from El Tajin

Cihuateotl

This life-size figure (AD 600–900) depicts Cihuateotl, a woman deified after dying in childbirth. Her closed eyes and open mouth evoke the screaming faces of women sacrificed in her honor.

Smiling Figure from Veracruz

Characteristic of Central Veracruz culture, smiling figurines such as this one (AD 600–900) may have played a significant part in festive rituals.

Xipe-Totec

The scaly skin of this terracotta figure (AD 1200–1521) represents the flayed skins of human sacrifices worn by priests during rites to honor Xipe-Totec, the god of spring.

STAR EXHIBITS

★ El Rey

★ Tlaloc

El Puerto de Veracruz ❻

Veracruz. 🏙 *512,000.* ✈ ⛴
ℹ *Palacio Municipal, (229) 200
20 17.* 🎭 *Carnival (Feb/Mar).*
www.veracruz-puerto.gob.mx

Veracruz is, more than anything else, a place of fun.
The life of the city revolves
around the Plaza de Armas
and the *malecón* (waterfront
promenade), an enjoyable
place to stroll and watch the
ships come and go. The tree-
lined Plaza de Armas is
flanked by the elegant 17th-
century **Palacio Municipal** and
the **cathedral**. The dome of
the cathedral is covered with
Puebla tiles *(see p153)* and
crowned with a lantern and a
small cross. Opposite the
cathedral, the **Portales** (arcades)
are filled with hotels and cafés.
Musicians play here all day and
most of the night, and most
evenings there is dancing to
watch, whether it is a frenetic
zapateo or a poised, serene
danzón. The entertainment
reaches a peak during the city's
famous carnival *(see p247)*.

Situated on the *malecón*
is the **Gran Café de la
Parroquia** *(see p342)*. This
lively, convivial café, opened
in 1808 and is an institution.
Farther south is the **Acuario
de Veracruz**, said to be the
largest and best aquarium in
Latin America. Boat trips from
the *malecón* run past the Isla
de los Sacrificios and around
the harbor to the fortress of
San Juan de Ulúa. Fortified in
1692, it was home to the last
Spanish garrison to accept
Mexican Independence *(see
p49)* and has since seen several foreign invasions, the last
by the US in 1914. It also
became the country's most
notorious prison during the

Palacio Municipal, with the busy harbor in the background

porfiriato (see p53). The tiny
Isla de los Sacrificios was the
first place the conquistadors
landed *(see p43)*, and is
named after the remains of
human sacrifices
they found.

The best of
several museums
in Veracruz, the
**Museo Histórico
Naval** is housed
in the ex-Naval
Academy in the
city center. It tells
the maritime his-
tory of the port.
Exhibits include
over 300 types of
knots, and some
intricate models of ships.

In 1880, the fortified wall
around Veracruz was torn
down leaving only one of
the nine original bastions,
the **Baluarte de
Santiago**. This
small fort, built in
1635, now houses
a good collection
of pre-Columbian
gold jewelry.

Sailors aboard a ship
in Veracruz harbor

Environs

South of the town
are the hotel-filled
satellite suburbs of
Playa de Oro and

Mocambo. The beaches here
are cleaner and less crowded
than in Veracruz, but not very
appealing. **Boca del Río**, farther
along the coast, is famous for
its seafood.

In the 1970s,
excavations at **El
Zapotal**, 75 km (47
miles) south, un-
covered hundreds
of clay sculptures –
offerings to the god
of the underworld,
Mictlantecuhtli *(see
p265)*. Most are in
Xalapa's Museo de
Antropología *(see
pp248–9)*, but the
central figure of
Mictlantecuhtli, made of un-
fired clay, is still at El Zapotal.

🍴 **Acuario de Veracruz**
Blvd Manuel Avila Camacho **Tel**
(229) 932 79 84. ⭘ *daily.* 📷 ♿
www.acuariodeveracruz.com

⚓ **San Juan de Ulúa**
Calle Pedro Sainz de Baranda.
Tel (229) 938 51 51. ⭘ *Jul–Aug:
daily; Sep–Jun: Tue–Sun.* 📷 ♿
ground floor only. 📷

🏛 **Museo Histórico Naval**
Calle Arista 418. **Tel** (229) 931 40
78. ⭘ *Tue–Sun.* 📷 📷

⚓ **Baluarte de Santiago**
Calle Francisco Canal. **Tel** (229)
931 10 59. ⭘ *Tue–Sun.* 📷

The 17th-century fortress, San Juan de Ulúa

For hotels and restaurants in this region see pp311–13 and pp341–2

One of the cafés serving rich local coffee in Córdoba's Portal de Zevallos

Orizaba ➐

Veracruz. 🏠 *117,000.* 🚌 🛈 *El Palacio de Hierro, (272) 728 91 36.* 🎭 *San Miguel (Sep 29).*
www.orizaba.gob.mx

Home to an Aztec garrison, and then to Spanish soldiers, Orizaba held a strategic position on the trading route between Veracruz and Mexico City in the 15th and 16th centuries. Dominated by the Cerro del Borrego hill, Orizaba today is an industrial city, but it still has some colonial character.

On the corner of the main plaza, Parque Apolinar Castillo, is the 17th-century church **Iglesia de San Miguel**. The **Ex-Palacio Municipal**, also on the plaza, is an ornate Art-Nouveau construction. Built in Belgium in the late 19th century, it was brought over in pieces and reassembled here.

The Neo-Classical **Palacio Municipal**, on Calle Colón, was the base for a workers' education center after the Revolution. It boasts a 1926 mural, *Reconstrucción*, by

José Clemente Orozco. Orizaba's **Museo de Arte del Estado** has a fine collection of paintings housed in 10 beautifully restored rooms.

Environs
Pico de Orizaba, Mexico's highest mountain, lies 23 km (14 miles) northwest of Orizaba. A volcano that last erupted in 1546, it is 5,747 m (18,856 ft) high. The Aztecs gave it the name Citlaltépetl, "star mountain," for the way moonlight reflects off its snowy summit.

At the other extreme, the **Sierra de Zongolica**, south of Orizaba, has some of the world's deepest caves.

🏛 **Museo de Arte del Estado**
Corner of 4 Oriente & 23 Sur.
Tel *(272) 724 32 00.* 🔲 *Tue–Sun.*
🎫 *Sun free.* 🎭 *Tue & Thu 10am & 5pm.*

Córdoba ➑

Veracruz. 🏠 *186,000.* 🚌 🛈 *Palacio Municipal, (271) 717 17 00, ext. 1778.* 🎭 *Expo Feria (May).*
www.cordoba.gob.mx

Córdoba is a busy, modern town, although traces of its colonial heritage are still to be found around the central Plaza de Armas. Viceroy Diego Fernández de Córdoba ordered the town's construction in 1618 to protect traders on the route between Veracruz and Mexico City from holdups by slaves.

Historically, Córdoba's most significant building is the 18th-century **Portal de Zevallos**, an arcade on the north side of the Plaza de Armas. The Treaties of Córdoba, endorsing Mexican Independence, were signed here in 1829. Also on the plaza are the Neo-Classical **Palacio Municipal** and the **Catedral de la Inmaculada Concepción**, which houses a lifelike image of the town's patron saint, the Virgen de la Soledad (Virgin of Solitude).

The Virgen de la Soledad, Córdoba's patron saint

Environs
West of Córdoba is the **Barranca de Metlac**, a spectacular gorge spanned by four bridges. One of these, a 19th-century railroad bridge, features in several paintings by artist José María Velasco.

Mexico's highest mountain, Pico de Orizaba, towering above the Gulf Coast

Colorful colonnade-fronted houses in the charming town of Tlacotalpan

Tlacotalpan ❾

Veracruz. 👥 14,000. ⬜ ℹ️ Palacio Municipal, Plaza Zaragoza, (288) 884 21 51. 🎭 Candelaria (Feb 2), San Miguelito (Sep 29).
www.tlacotalpan.gob.mx

Exploring this delightful town is like turning the clock back 100 years. Its quiet streets are lined with striking houses fronted by colonnades and painted in a flamboyant range of colors. As the Mexican writer Elena Poniatowska puts it, "when we want to smile, we think of Tlacotalpan."

The town is situated on the banks of the Río Papaloapan ("River of Butterflies"), which is over 300 m (984 ft) wide. Most of the elegant houses, with their Mozarabic-style portals, date from the second half of the 18th century, when large sugar and cotton plantations were established here. Important shipyards were also moved here from Cuba as a direct result of an English blockade of Havana, another Spanish possession, in 1762. During this era, Tlacotalpan was the principal town in southern Veracruz and an important international port, often more in touch with Europe and Cuba than with the rest of Mexico. However, the building of railroad lines left Tlacotalpan without a commercial role. Paradoxically, the same isolation that caused its decline has helped preserve this picturesque town.

The **Museo Jarocho Salvador Ferrando** is named after a local artist, and houses many of his portraits and landscapes, painted in the

19th century. Locally made furniture and crafts from the same period are also on display in the museum.

🏛 **Museo Jarocho Salvador Ferrando**
Manuel María Alegre 6. ◻ daily.

Santiago Tuxtla ❿

Veracruz. 👥 55,000. ⬜ 🎭 San Juan (Jun 24), Santiago (Jul 22–7).
www.santiagotuxtla.gob.mx

The town of Santiago Tuxtla is a gateway to the world of the ancient Olmecs (see p254), who lived more than 3,000 years ago. A colossal stone head, typical of the Olmec culture, stands in the middle of the town's main square. The largest of the giant heads found so far, it is 3.4 m (11.2 ft) high and weighs around 50 tons. It is the only one of the heads yet discovered to have closed eyes and lacks the realism of the others.

The **Museo Tuxteco**, on one side of the plaza, has an interesting collection of pieces from nearby sites. They include a head called "El Negro," the legendary powers of which were formerly tapped by local witch doctors. Other exhibits include examples of the Olmec practices of skull deformation and tooth sculpting (probably expressions of beauty and class), another colossal head (this one from San Lorenzo Tenochtitlán), and ceremonial and domestic objects made out of jade and stone.

One pre-Columbian custom that lives on in Santiago Tuxtla is the *danza de los liseres*, in which the dancers don the mask of a jaguar deity. It is performed during summer fiestas.

Environs
A 20-km (12-mile) drive through lush, tropical vegetation, along a potholed road, leads to **Tres Zapotes**. This archaeological site was the center of Olmec culture around 400 BC, after La Venta

Giant Olmec head in the main square of Santiago Tuxtla

THE WITCH DOCTORS OF VERACRUZ

Witch doctors still practice in the state of Veracruz, around San Andrés Tuxtla and Catemaco. Using an assortment of medicinal plants, potions, charms, effigies of saints and devils,

dolls with pins stuck in them, and either black or white magic, they will undertake to cure their clients of diseases, help them find a better job, or resolve their marital problems. The practice is hereditary and can be traced back to a distant pre-Columbian past.

A witch doctor with the tools of his trade

Salto de Eyipantla waterfall, near San Andrés Tuxtla

of **Tanaxpillo**, which is home to a colony of macaque monkeys. Two ecological parks on the north shore of the lake are accessible by boat or car. The more interesting of these, **Nanciyaga**, is a large swath of tropical rainforest. Visitors to the park can take part in pre-Columbian rituals, such as the *temazcal* (steam bath), or swim in spring-fed pools.

The town of Catemaco itself is dominated by the **Iglesia del Carmen**, a brightly painted church with twin bell towers. The statue of the Virgen del Carmen inside is dripping with jewelry and trinkets left by the many pilgrims who come here.

Environs

Ten of the 17 great Olmec heads so far discovered were found at **San Lorenzo Tenochtitlán**, 37 km (23 miles) southeast of Acayucan. This great Olmec ceremonial center flourished from 1200 BC to 900 BC, when it was destroyed. Most of the objects found here have been removed from the site. However, some of the pieces are on show in three small museums at **Potrero, El Azuzul**, and **Tenochtitlán**. Exhibits at El Azuzul include the sculpture known as *Los Divinos Gemelos* (The Divine Twins).

One of the Divine Twins from San Lorenzo

🌿 **Nanciyaga**
7 km (4.5 miles) NE of Catemaco. **Tel** (294) 943 01 99. ⬜ daily; Oct: Thu–Tue. ▨ ▢ ▯

(see p254) had been abandoned. The site itself is now just a series of mounds, but several of the finds are displayed in the museum in Tres Zapotes village nearby.

San Andrés Tuxtla, 14 km (9 miles) east of Santiago Tuxtla, is a sprawling commercial town famous for its cigars. There are fields of tobacco everywhere, and the roadside is lined with stalls selling the finished products.

A 3-km (2-mile) walk from San Andrés Tuxtla along a dirt track leads to the **Laguna Encantada** (Enchanted Lake), so-named because its water level mysteriously rises in the dry season and falls when it rains. Easier to reach, via a paved road that runs through mountains and fields of sugar cane, papaya, tobacco, and bananas, is the **Salto de Eyipantla**, a 50-m (164-ft) high waterfall. Local children act as guides, accompanying visitors down the 244 steps to the bottom of the falls.

🏛 **Museo Tuxteco**
Parque Juárez. **Tel** (294) 947 10 76. ⬜ Tue–Sun. ▨ ▮

Laguna de Catemaco ⓫

Veracruz. 🚌 ⓘ *Palacio Municipal, Av Carranza, Catemaco, (294) 943 02 58.* 🎉 *Carmen (Jul 16).* **www**.catemaco.info

This picturesque lake lies in the crater of an extinct volcano. Its hot, humid climate suits many birds, including parrots and toucans, and its waters also contain a few crocodiles. Boat trips round the lake leave from the wharf in the town of Catemaco and circle the island

Boat trip around the islands of Laguna de Catemaco

Comalcalco ⑫

Tabasco. Off Mex 187, 58 km
(36 miles) NW of Villahermosa.
🚌 from Comalcalco town,
Villahermosa, or Cardenas. ⏲ Tue–
Sun. 📷 www.inah.gob.mx

In the lush, green, cocoa-
producing area northwest of
Villahermosa are the Maya
ruins of Comalcalco. Dating
mainly from the late Classic
period of Maya civilization
(AD 700–900), the architecture
differs quite markedly from
that found at Palenque *(see
pp234–7)*, which was occupied
around the same time. Unlike
Palenque, Comalcalco has
structures built from bricks,
held together with oyster-shell
mortar. The bricks were sometimes incised with figures and
glyphs when wet. Comalcalco's
main structures are two pyramids, the Gran Acrópolis and
the Acrópolis Este, and the
North Plaza. Originally many
of the site's structures would
have been covered in high-
relief stucco carvings. Of those
that survive today, the most
distinctive is a mask of the
god El Señor del Sol, near the
base of the Gran Acrópolis.

Mask of El Señor del Sol at the base of the Gran Acrópolis in Comalcalco

Villahermosa ⑬

Tabasco. 🚹 558,000. ✈ 🚌
ℹ Avenida Juan Estrada, (993) 310
97 00. 🚣 Río Usumacinta Nautical
Marathon (Mar/Apr), Tabasco State
Fair (Apr/May). www.villahermosa.
gob.mx

Now the capital of the state
of Tabasco, Villahermosa
was founded in the late 16th
century by a community forced
to move inland by repeated
pirate attacks. Situated on the
banks of the Grijalva River,

Villahermosa today is a
friendly, bustling city. It has
two excellent museums, the
Parque-Museo de La Venta
and the **Museo Regional de
Antropología Carlos Pellicer**.
The latter contains fascinating
exhibits from the Olmec, Maya,
and other Mesoamerican
cultures, including pottery, clay
figurines, and jade carvings.

Environs
Yum-Ká, an ecological park a
short drive east of Villahermosa,
is named after a mythical Maya
dwarf who protects the
jungle. Animals, including the
endangered ocelot, manatee,
and howler monkey, are
found in its 100 hectares (247
acres) of natural habitats.
    La Venta, 117 km (73 miles)
to the west of Villahermosa, is
the site of the most important
Olmec settlement. Its principal
sculptures are now in the
Parque-Museo de La Venta.

🏛 **Museo Regional de
Antropología Carlos Pellicer**
Av Carlos Pellicer Cámara 511. **Tel**
(993) 312 63 44. ⏲ Tue–Sun. 📷 ♿

🦌 **Yum-Ká**
16 km (10 miles) E of Villahermosa.
Tel (993) 356 01 15. ⏲ daily. 📷
🎫 🅿 🍴 ♿ www.yumka.org

THE OLMECS

Mexico's first notable culture, the Olmec, was established
on the hot, humid Gulf Coast by 1200 BC. Often called the
cultura madre (mother culture) because of their influence
on later civilizations, the Olmecs are
something of a mystery. Their main
sites, at San Lorenzo and La Venta,
wielded political, economic, and
religious authority over big
regions and large numbers
of people. The earliest, San
Lorenzo *(see p253)*, was sys-
tematically destroyed in about
900 BC, although why and by
whom is a mystery. About
the same time La Venta, farther east, reached the peak
of its influence, becoming an
important religious and political
center and establishing far-flung
trade routes. Around the beginning of the first millennium AD

Colossal Olmec head

Olmec civilization gradually faded into
obscurity. Today the most impressive
reminders of the ancient culture are the colossal carved stone
heads, of which the first to be discovered in modern times
was found at Tres Zapotes *(see p252)*. They were fashioned
from massive basalt blocks weighing up to 20 tons, which
the Olmecs moved large distances, probably using river rafts.

An ocelot, one of the endangered
species in Yum-Ká ecological park

Parque-Museo de La Venta

For nearly 600 years, from 1000 to 400 BC, the settlement at La Venta was the center of Olmec culture. In the 1950s its treasures were threatened by oil exploration nearby. Tabascan anthropologist Carlos Pellicer organized their rescue and had them installed on the shores of the Laguna de las Ilusiones in Villahermosa. To further protect the Olmec heads, altars, stelae, and mosaics, many pieces will be moved inside a museum (construction begins 2010) and be replaced by replicas along the winding jungle paths. Part of the park is a wildlife area, with some animals housed in the archaeological section.

VISITORS' CHECKLIST

Blvd Adolfo Ruíz Cortínes, Villahermosa. **Tel** *(993) 314 16 52.*
🚌 *from Central Camionera or
Mercado.* 🕐 *8am–4pm Tue–Sun.*
♿ 🅿 📷 🎦 www.inah.gob.mx

KEY

① La Abuela (The Grandmother)
② Jaula de Jaguar (Jaguar's Cage)
③ Personajes con Niños (People with Children)
④ Jaguar Humanizado (Human Jaguar)
⑤ Gran Altar (Great Altar)
⑥ Mosaico del Jaguar (Jaguar Mosaic)
⑦ El Rey (The King)
⑧ Cabeza Colosal 1 (Giant Head 1)
⑨ La Diosa Joven (The Young Goddess)

La Abuela ①
This kneeling old woman holds a vessel as if in offering.

Gran Altar ⑤
The figure under this monument holds a rope binding the two men, probably captives, carved on its sides.

AIRPORT →

Wildlife Park

Entrance (from wildlife park)

BOULEVARD ADOLFO RUÍZ CORTÍNES

PASEO TABASCO AND CITY CENTER

Craft shop

Jaguar enclosure

Parque Tomás Garrido Canabal

| 0 meters | 40 |
| 0 yards | 40 |

Exit

LAGUNA DE LAS ILUSIONES

Crocodile enclosure

Personajes con Niños ③
Seated in front of this altar, or throne, is an adult figure holding an infant in his arms.

El Rey ⑦
Wearing a tall head-dress and carrying a staff across his chest that signifies his power, the figure on this stela was clearly important. He is surrounded by six smaller figures, similarly attired and carrying staves.

THE YUCATAN PENINSULA

CAMPECHE · QUINTANA ROO · YUCATAN

*T*he stunning ruins of the Yucatán's famous Maya cities and ceremonial sites are reason enough to visit. But the fine white-sand beaches of the Caribbean – often refered to as the "Mayan Riviera" – make the peninsula even more irresistible. Small wonder that for many visitors to Mexico this region is their first or only experience of the country, providing enough to see and do to fill a long vacation.

When the Spanish first arrived on the Yucatán Peninsula in 1517 they found one of the most remarkable civilizations in the Americas. But the Spanish soldiers, and Franciscan friars who came with them, had scant regard for the Maya's high level of social organization, great knowledge of astronomy, or sophisticated writing system. They swiftly defeated the Maya, colonized their lands, and destroyed most of their historical records. As undisputed rulers of the Yucatán, the Spanish founded Mérida, Campeche, and other colonial cities as bastions in their fight for control of the Caribbean against English, French, and Dutch pirates. In 1847, after Mexico had achieved independence, civil war erupted on the peninsula between settlers of European origin and the much-exploited descendants of the ancient Maya. This conflict, known as the Caste War, ended in defeat for the Maya, followed by bloody reprisals. The production of henequen and sisal (for rope and fabric making) led to a period of prosperity in the Yucatán in the late 19th and early 20th centuries. Today, oil is the peninsula's main industry, followed by tourism, which centers on the mushrooming resort of Cancún. Away from the coasts, traditional life continues much as it has done for years, in villages where the indigenous Maya live in palm-roofed huts, and preserve their own language, customs, and culture.

Brightly painted colonnade in Izamal, a colonial town in the north of the peninsula

◁ Carvings of the god Chac on the corner of a building at the ancient Maya city of Uxmal

Exploring the Yucatán Peninsula

Some of the finest archaeological sites in the Americas are situated on the Yucatán Peninsula. They include the sensational Chichén Itzá and Uxmal, as well as many lesser-known sites such as Cobá, Edzná, Tulum, and Ekbalam. The interior of the peninsula is jungle, some of which is conserved in its natural state, while the Mayan Riviera, on the east coast, has some of Mexico's best beaches. Many people come to the Yucatán to visit the offshore islands of Cozumel and Isla Mujeres and dive or snorkel over the superb coral formations of the Great Mesoamerican Reef, the world's second longest barrier reef. Attractive Spanish colonial architecture can be seen in Campeche, Mérida, Valladolid, and Izamal, and in the Franciscan churches of several towns south of Mérida.

The Ex-Templo de San José in the center of Campeche

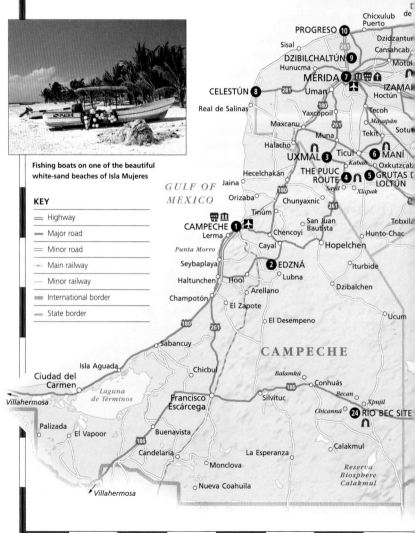

Fishing boats on one of the beautiful white-sand beaches of Isla Mujeres

KEY

===	Highway
—	Major road
===	Minor road
---	Main railway
—	Minor railway
■■■	International border
—	State border

GULF OF MEXICO

PROGRESO ❿
Chicxulub
Puerto
Sisal
DZIDZILCHALTÚN ❾
Hunucma
CELESTÚN ❽
Real de Salinas
MÉRIDA ❼
Umán
IZAMAL
Hoctún
Yaxcopoil
Tecoh
Maxcanú
Mayapán
Muna
Tekit
Sotu
Halachó
UXMAL ❸
Ticul
MANÍ ❻
Hecelchakán
THE PUUC
ROUTE ❹
Kabah
Oxkutzcab
GRUTAS DE
LOLTÚN ❺
Jaina
Sayil
Xlapak
Orizaba
Chunyaxnic
Tinúm
Tobxila
CAMPECHE ❶
San Juan
Bautista
Lerma
Chencoyi
Hunto-Chac
Cayal
Hopelchen
Punta Morro
Seybaplaya
EDZNÁ ❷
Iturbide
Haltunchen
Hool
Lubna
Dzibalchen
Champotón
Arellano
El Zapote
El Desempeno
Ucum
Sabancuy

CAMPECHE

Isla Aguada
Chicbul
Balamkú
Conhuás
Ciudad del
Carmen
Laguna
de Términos
Silvituc
Becan
Xpujil
Villahermosa
Francisco
Escárcega
Chicanná
RÍO BEC SITE ❷❹
Palizada
El Vapoor
Buenavista
Calakmul
Candelaria
La Esperanza
Monclova
Reserva
Biosphere
Calakmul
Villahermosa
Nueva Coahuila

SIGHTS AT A GLANCE

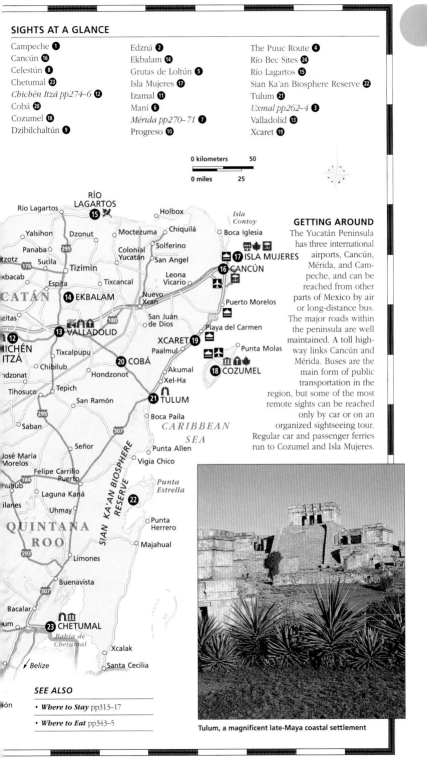

0 kilometers 50

0 miles 25

GETTING AROUND

The Yucatán Peninsula has three international airports, Cancún, Mérida, and Campeche, and can be reached from other parts of Mexico by air or long-distance bus. The major roads within the peninsula are well maintained. A toll highway links Cancún and Mérida. Buses are the main form of public transportation in the region, but some of the most remote sights can be reached only by car or on an organized sightseeing tour. Regular car and passenger ferries run to Cozumel and Isla Mujeres.

SEE ALSO

Tulum, a magnificent late-Maya coastal settlement

Vivid exteriors of colonial houses in Campeche city center

Campeche ❶

Campeche. 🏛 239,000. ✈ 🚌
ℹ Av Ruiz Cortines, (800) 226 73
24. 🎭 Carnival (Feb/Mar), Cristo
Negro de San Román (Sep 15–30).
www.campeche.travel

The Spanish settlement of Campeche was built on the site of a former Maya fishing village in about 1540. In colonial times it was the most important port on the Yucatán Peninsula, exporting timber and roots used to make dyes in European textile production.

Campeche's prosperity made it a frequent target for attacks by English, French, and Dutch pirates, who harassed ships in the area, and looted and destroyed the city several times. The worst attack, in 1663, resulted in the massacre of many of the city's inhabitants. As a consequence, thick walls were built around the town. These were strengthened by eight baluartes (bastions), seven of which have been put to other uses and can be visited. The largest of them, in the middle of the stretch of wall facing the sea, is the **Baluarte de la Soledad**. It is now a museum displaying an important collection of Maya stelae (see p233), many of which were found at the Maya burial ground on the island of Jaina, 40 km (25 miles) to the north of Campeche. The **Baluarte de Santiago**, at the northwestern corner of the walls, has been transformed into a walled botanical garden containing over 200 species of subtropical plants. On the landward side of the walls, the **Baluarte de San Pedro** sells a small selection of regional handicrafts.

Two gateways in the walls – the **Sea Gate** and the **Land Gate** – give access to the old

Jade mask,
in Fuerte de
San Miguel

part of the city. Between them runs Calle 59, on which stand several restored, single-story colonial houses, painted in bright blues, pinks, and ochers. One of the finest buildings is the **Casa de Teniente del Rey** (King's Lieutenant's House), the former residence of the Spanish king's military representative in the Yucatán. Transformed into offices, the house has a splendid courtyard, which can be visited.

The focal point of the old part of Campeche is the main square, the **Parque Principal**, which has elegant arcades and an elaborate, modern bandstand. Tours of the city in open-sided trams start from here. In the northern corner of the square is the **cathedral**, one of the first churches built on the Yucatán mainland, although much of the present building was constructed later, in the Baroque style. Behind it, on Calle 10, is the **Mansión Carvajal**, now divided into government offices. This building is a good example of 19th-century Spanish-Moorish architecture. Another attractive building in the city center is the **Ex-Templo de San José**, a former Jesuit church, now used as a cultural center, which has an elaborate façade of blue and yellow tiles.

Campeche's defenses were completed by two forts on hills outside the city, both of which are now museums. Situated to the north is the

Tiled doorway of the Ex-Templo de San José, now a cultural center

---

PANAMA HATS

The town of Becal, between Campeche and Mérida, is renowned for its production of Panama hats. Known locally as jipis, they received their common name when they became popular with workers building the Panama canal. The palm leaves used to make the hats are split and braided in caves, where the heat and humidity make the fibers more flexible. The finest hats (finos) have a smooth and silky feel and can be rolled up so tightly that they are able to pass through a man's wedding ring, and then regain their former shape.

Monument to the Panama hat in the main square of Becal

The Edificio de los Cinco Pisos (Building of the Five Levels) at Edzná

Fuerte de San José, with exhibits on colonial military history. To the south of the city is the **Fuerte de San Miguel**, begun in 1771 and protected by a moat crossed by a drawbridge. Exhibits inside this fort include distinctive jade masks from Calakmul (see p287), and ceramic figurines from the island of Jaina.

On the way to the Fuerte de San Miguel is the **Iglesia de San Román**, the city's most popular shrine. It is famous for its large black ebony statue of Christ, which is believed to possess miraculous powers.

🏛 **Baluarte de la Soledad**
Calle 8 Circuito Baluartes (seaward side). ☐ Tue–Sun. 🖼

⚰ **Casa de Teniente del Rey**
Calle 59 No. 38, corner of Calle 14.
Tel (981) 816 91 11. ☐ Mon–Fri.

🏛 **Fuerte de San José**
Av Morazan. ☐ Tue–Sun. 🖼

🏛 **Fuerte de San Miguel**
Av Escénica. ☐ Tue–Sun. 🖼

Edzná ❷

Campeche. Mex 180 and 186,
60 km (37 miles) SE of Campeche.
🚌 from Campeche. ☐ daily.
🖼 📷 www.inah.gob.mx

A sophisticated and extensive canal system radiates out from the center of this Maya settlement to the agricultural areas beyond. The canals were primarily used for the transportation of goods, but quite possibly also served a defensive purpose. Edzná may have been founded in around 600 BC, and in its heyday between AD 600 and 900, it is thought to have had a population of 25,000. The main structure is the Gran Acrópolis, which is dominated by the Edificio de los Cinco Pisos (Building of the Five Levels). Another building of interest is the Templo de los Mascarones (Temple of the Masks), named after its distinctive stucco mask.

Stucco mask on the Templo de los Mascarones, Edzná

FIESTAS OF THE YUCATÁN

Equinoxes (Mar 21 and Sep 21), Chichén Itzá. An optical illusion created by the ancient Maya can be seen when the sun casts a shadow on the north side of El Castillo (see p276), making a "snake" move down the steps behind each of the two stone serpent heads at the base.

The stepped El Castillo pyramid, at Chichén Itzá

Carnival (Feb/Mar). Celebrated in most parts of the Yucatán, but particularly in Campeche. In many villages, a papier-mâché figure of "Juan Carnaval" is paraded through the streets, put in a coffin, and symbolically burned to conclude the festivities.

Cristo de las Ampollas (Sep 27), Mérida. Festivities and processions in honor of "Christ of the Blisters," a wooden statue made in Ichmul and later moved to Mérida cathedral (see p270). The statue is said to have blistered and blackened, but not burned, in a fire at Ichmul's parish church.

Fuerte de San Miguel, once an integral part of Campeche's defenses against naval attack

Uxmal ⓫

The late-Classic Maya site of Uxmal ("thrice built") is one of the most complex and harmonious expressions of Puuc architecture *(see p268)*. The city's history is uncertain, but most of the buildings date from the 7th–10th centuries AD, when Uxmal dominated the region. The real function of many of the structures is unknown, and they retain the fanciful names given to them by the Spanish. Unlike most Yucatán sites, Uxmal has no cenotes *(see p275)*, and water was collected in manmade cisterns *(chultunes)*, one of which can be seen near the entrance. The scarcity of water may explain the number of depictions of the rain god Chac on the buildings.

Mask at entrance to the site

View of the Nunnery Quadrangle and Magician's Pyramid from the south

Cemetery Group

Dovecote
Named after its unusual roof comb, this ruined palace faces a rectangular garden and is one of Uxmal's most evocative and peaceful spots.

Great Pyramid
A stairway climbs the 30-m (100-ft) pyramid to a temple decorated with Chac masks and macaws, the latter associated with fire, suggesting it was a temple to the sun.

South Temple

STAR FEATURES

★ Governor's Palace

★ Nunnery Quadrangle

★ Magician's Pyramid

★ Governor's Palace
Regarded as the masterpiece of Puuc architecture, the 9th–10th-century palace is actually three buildings linked by Maya arches. The distinctive hooked noses of the Chac masks stand out against the mosaic frieze that runs the length of the structure.

★ **Nunnery Quadrangle**
This impressive structure was given its unlikely name because the Spanish thought that the 74 small rooms set around a central courtyard looked like the cells of a nunnery. The stone latticework, ornate masks of Chac, and carved serpents on the walls are remarkable examples of closely fitting mosaic.

VISITORS' CHECKLIST

Yucatán. Mex 261, 78 km (48 miles) S of Mérida. ▆ tours from Mérida. ◯ 8am–5pm daily. ▨ ▨ ▨ ▨
www.inah.gob.mx

Entrance to site

★ **Magician's Pyramid**
The spectacular pyramid (seen here through an arch in front) is, at 35 m (115 ft), the tallest structure at Uxmal. Begun in the sixth century AD, it was added to over the next 400 years (see p264).

Ballcourt

Jaguar Throne
This throne is carved as a two-headed jaguar, an animal associated with chiefs and kings.

Pyramid of the Old Woman

0 meters	100
0 yards	100

House of the Turtles
The upper level of this elegant rectangular building is simply decorated with columns and, above them, a frieze of small turtles in procession around the building. Their presence suggests that it might have been dedicated to a water god.

The Magician's Pyramid

Tall, steep, and set on an unusual oval base, the Magician's Pyramid is the most striking of Uxmal's monuments. Legend tells that it was built in one night by a dwarf with supernatural powers – the magician – but, in fact, it shows five phases of construction from the 6th–10th centuries AD. At each phase a new temple was built, either on top of or obscuring the previous one. There are thus five temples on the pyramid. Unfortunately, visitors are no longer allowed to climb to the summit, to prevent further erosion.

View of the pyramid showing the west staircase and façades of Temples I and IV

The façade of Temple IV *is actually an expressive Chac mask with large rectangular eyes and a curling moustache. Its wide-open, toothed mouth forms the entrance. Temple III is behind Temple IV.*

Temple V is part of the final phase of construction – which took place around AD 1000 – and appears to be a small-scale reproduction of the nearby Governor's Palace *(see p262)*. It obscures the original roof comb on top of Temples II and III.

The east staircase provides access to Temple II, which is just a dark room today.

Entrance to Temple IV

Chac masks on façade of Temple I

Entrance to Temple I (now blocked)

Temple I was built in the sixth century AD, according to the results of radiocarbon dating, and is now covered by the pyramid. Partially collapsed, it is filled with rubble and cannot be visited.

RECONSTRUCTION OF THE MAGICIAN'S PYRAMID

This shows how the pyramid looked around AD 1000. The surface was probably painted red, with details in blue, yellow, and black. The colors and plaster have now eroded to reveal the limestone beneath.

The west staircase, *at the front of the pyramid, is flanked by representations of Chac, the rain god. The staircase is extremely steep and ascends the pyramid at an angle of 60°, meaning that the climb to the summit was very difficult.*

The Gods of Ancient Mexico

A vast array of gods and goddesses were worshiped by the civilizations of ancient Mesoamerica *(see pp 44–5)*. Some of them related to celestial bodies, such as the stars, sun, and moon. Some had calendrical significance. Others held sway over creation, death, and the different aspects of daily life. Frequently

Xilonen, an Aztec goddess

gods were passed from one civilization to another, usually changing their names in the process. These deities were feared as much as revered. If they had created the world, and ran it, they could just as easily destroy it. It was therefore essential to appease them as much as possible, often through human sacrifice.

RAIN GODS

Abundant rainfall was vital to farming communities, and rain and lightning gods were venerated in all the civilizations of ancient Mexico.

Tlaloc *was the central Mexican god of rain and lightning. He can be recognized by his goggle-like eyes and jaguar teeth, as in this sculpture from Teotihuacán (see pp134–7).*

QUETZALCOATL

The most famous Mexican god was Quetzalcoatl (called Kukulcan by the Maya). A plumed or feathered serpent, he was a combination of quetzal bird and rattlesnake. The first carvings of him were made by the Olmecs. Subsequent representations of Quetzalcoatl/Kukulcan can be seen at many ancient sites; this bas-relief is on the Pyramid of the Plumed Serpent at Xochicalco *(see p145).*

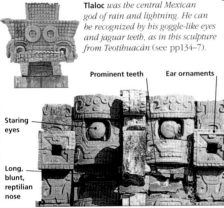

Prominent teeth   **Ear ornaments**

Staring eyes

Long, blunt, reptilian nose

Chac, *the Maya god of rain and lightning, was often represented on buildings. The mask seen here is from a palace at Kabah in the Yucatán (see p268).*

CREATOR GODS

Mesoamerican societies had differing accounts of creation. According to one myth from central Mexico, Tonacatecuhtli resided in the 13th, or uppermost, heaven with Tonacacihuatl, his consort. From here they sent down souls of children to be born on earth.

Tonacatecuhtli

THE SUN GOD

This deity was associated with the jaguar in ancient Mexico, an animal that evoked the vigor and power of the rising sun. The Classic and Postclassic Maya venerated Kinich Ahau, the "great sun" or "sun-eyed" lord, seen here as a huge mask at Kohunlich *(see p287).*

Kinich Ahau

GODS OF THE UNDERWORLD

Only those who suffered violent death went directly to one of the heavens. All other mortal souls were condemned to descend the nine levels of the underworld. In Aztec mythology, the soul had to pass through a series of hazards before reaching the deepest of these levels, the dreaded Mictlan, ruled over by Mictlantecuhtli and his consort Mictecacihuatl. The Aztecs depicted their god of death as a frightening skeletal figure, such as this one unearthed at the Templo Mayor in Mexico City *(see pp68–70).*

Mictlantecuhtli, Aztec god of death

Kabah's palace, the Codz Poop, ornamented with hundreds of Chac masks

The Puuc Route ❹

Yucatán. Starts from Mex 261, 20 km (12 miles) SE of Uxmal.
🚌 *tours from Mérida.* **All sites**
🕐 *daily.* 🌐 **www**.inah.gob.mx

Forming a low ridge across the western part of the Yucatán, about 100 km (62 miles) south of Mérida, the Puuc hills provide a welcome relief from the flat monotony of the rest of the peninsula.

Despite a lack of water, they offered a strong defensive position for the ancient Maya people, as well as good soil for cultivating maize, squash, and other vegetables. Several Maya settlements have been discovered in the region. All are believed to have reached their peaks from about AD 600 to AD 900 and they share the striking style of architecture and ornamentation that has become known as the Puuc style. This style is characterized by a façade which has plain walls at the base and detailed stone mosaic masks (often depicting gods) on its upper sections.

Some settlements are linked to each other and to the contemporary site of Uxmal (*see pp262–4*) by *sacbeob*, or "white roads," which were mainly used for ceremonial purposes.

The Puuc Route runs through four Maya sites, starting with **Kabah**. The main building here is the Codz Poop. The façade of this palace is decorated with more than 250 masks representing the rain god Chac (*see p265*), with his distinctive hooked nose. Kabah was the closest settlement to the important Maya city of Uxmal. A single, undecorated arch straddles the entrance road.

Of all the Puuc sites, **Sayil**, around 10 km (6 miles) south of Kabah, is the one that provides most evidence of how the Maya in this area lived. Around the edge of the site, many of the ordinary dwellings have been excavated, as have the homes of the settlement's ruling elite, located in the central area. It is hard to envisage today, but the excavations suggest that Sayil was once populated by more than 8,000 people, with a similar number living in small, outlying communities surrounding the city. The huge three-tiered palace of Sayil's rulers is a splendid example of the rich Puuc style.

Sayil has no accessible supply of surface water, but several *chultunes*, large man-made cisterns for storing water, have been found at the site.

About 8 km (5 miles) east of Sayil is **Xlapak**. The best-preserved building here is the palace, which has masks of Chac, the rain god, above its entrances. Details such as a frieze of columns stand out on other buildings, but much of this site has yet to be cleared.

The last settlement on the Puuc Route is **Labná**, 5 km (3 miles) to the northeast of Xlapak. Among several spectacular structures here, the Arch is the best known. Originally part of a building between two courtyards, it is adorned

A snake with a human head in its jaws carved on the corner of Labná palace

The magnificent three-tiered palace in Sayil, with its frieze of small columns

◁ Detail of Chac masks adorning the façade of the Codz Poop palace in Kabah

El Mirador (The Observatory) in Labná, crowned by a 4-m (13-ft) crest

with several Chac masks and two representations of thatched Maya huts. Nearby is a structure with a high crest above its façade. Known as El Mirador (The Observatory), it may have been a temple.

At the other end of the site is the main two-story palace, which has a frieze of masks and latticework. On one corner of the palace is a powerful carving of a serpent's head with a human head in its jaws.

Another impressive structure is the Temple of Columns, which has a frieze around it, decorated with small columns.

Grutas de Loltún ❺

Yucatán. Off Mex 180, 20 km (12 miles) SW of Maní. *tours from Mérida.* ◯ *daily.* 🎫 🎦

Visitors are taken on a tour that travels more than 1 km (half a mile) through the Grutas de Loltún, the longest cave system in the Yucatán. The earliest remains discovered here are bison, mammoth, and other animal bones, suggesting that Loltún was inhabited soon after the last Ice Age. The caves contain fascinating wall paintings from various periods of occupation. These include stylized humans and animals, and the superb Warrior of Loltún. However, the caves' most striking features are the stalagmites and stalactites that give them the name Loltún, meaning "stone flowers."

Maní ❻

Yucatán. 🏠 4,800. 🚌 🎨 *Fiesta tradicional (Aug 20).*

From the fourth decade of the 16th century, Catholic priests, and in particular Franciscan friars, came from Spain to convert the Maya population of the Yucatán Peninsula. They constructed a network of huge, fortress-like churches and monasteries, often on the sites of earlier Maya temples. The most imposing of these is the **Iglesia de San Miguel Arcángel**, which dominates the town of Maní. It has a vast atrium, an open chapel, and a monastery with 114 cells. It was constructed by

Part of the beautiful altarpiece in Maní's Franciscan church

Iglesia de la Candelaria, Tecoh's Franciscan church

around 6,000 slaves on ground that was already holy to the Maya – a Maya cenote (natural well) is visible under the front of the church.

Environs

Other Franciscan churches can be found in the towns all around Maní. Built in 1693–9, the church in Oxkutzcab, 10km (6 miles) to the south, has a lovely Baroque altarpiece. The Iglesia de San Pedro Apóstol in Teabo, east of Maní, was begun in 1694, and traces of Franciscan murals can still be seen in its powder-blue interior. The road north out of Teabo leads through Tekit, which also has a Franciscan church, to Tecoh. The church here houses a huge red and blue wooden altarpiece and a beautiful wooden cross with the last hours of Christ's life painted on it.

Between Tekit and Tecoh is **Mayapán**, which became the Maya capital in the north of the peninsula after the fall of Chichén Itzá. Abandoned in the mid-15th century, Mayapán's most remarkable surviving feature is the pyramid of Kukulcan, which is built on nine levels and topped with a temple.

🏛 **Mayapán**
60 km (37 miles) N of Maní. ◯ *daily.* 🎫

Mérida

The conquistador Francisco de Montejo the Younger founded this city in 1542 on the ruins of a large Maya settlement. He named it Mérida because it reminded him of the ruined Roman city of the same name in Spain. An important city during Spanish colonial rule, Mérida rose to prominence again at the turn of the 20th century when it enjoyed an economic boom, based on sales of locally grown sisal for rope-making. In the early 1900s, Mérida was said to have more millionaires per head of population than anywhere else in the world. This prosperity is reflected in its grand mansions, squares, parks, and statues. Modern Mérida is an important manufacturing city, and also a university, business, and cultural center.

The lofty interior of the grand Catedral de San Ildefonso

The Palacio Municipal on the Plaza Mayor

Exploring Mérida

Mérida is built on a grid system based around the main square, the Plaza Mayor (also known as the Plaza Grande or Plaza de la Independencia). In the evenings, and on Sundays, dancing and concerts take place outside the city hall, the **Palacio Municipal**. This building is in a mix of styles and has a notable 1920s clock tower.

The **Casa de Montejo** *(see p24)*, on the south side of the plaza, was built between 1543 and 1549 as the palace of the first Spanish governors. Now a bank, it still has its original portico, with the Montejo family coat of arms.

East of the Plaza Mayor lies Mérida's historic post office, now the **Museo de la Ciudad** with exhibits on the city's colonial past as well as contemporary artworks. Opposite the city hall is the **cathedral**, the oldest in the Americas. It was begun in the early 1560s, and finished in 1598. Three arched doors in the imposing façade lead to a soaring interior with a barreled roof and crisscross arches. There is a huge wooden sculpture of Christ behind the main

altar. Another wooden statue, *Cristo de las Ampollas* (Christ of the Blisters, *(see p261)*, stands in a small chapel on the right. It is a copy of a statue that was brought to Mérida after miraculously surviving a fire. The original, which was later destroyed, is said to have developed blisters, as skin would, instead of burning.

The 19th-century **Palacio de Gobierno** houses the Yucatán state authorities. It is remarkable for the numerous large murals adorning its courtyard, stairs, and first-floor lobby. They were painted in the 1970s by Fernando Castro Pacheco, a local artist, and show his vision of Yucatán history from the time of the first Maya to the 19th century.

Just off Calle 60, one of the city's major roads, is **Parque** Cepeda Peraza, a small but bustling square. Visitors can watch the many musicians and street merchants, or relax in one of the open-air cafés. The imposing Jesuit church, the **Templo de la Tercera Orden** (Temple of the Third Order), on the north side of the square, dates from the 17th century. It has a huge entrance and two narrow bell towers. Inside, the gold altar and friezes of biblical scenes are the only decoration.

Mérida prides itself on being the cultural capital of the Yucatán Peninsula, and the **Teatro José Peón Contreras** is one of its main showcases. Built at the turn of the 20th century, it is an extravagant Neo-Classical creation in beige and white, with elaborate chandeliers in its massive foyer.

The small **Iglesia de Santa Lucía**, one of the earliest and most harmonious of the city's churches, is where the local Maya Indians were encouraged to come and worship.

A mural by Fernando Castro Pacheco, in the Palacio de Gobierno

The Arco de San Juan, one of eight city entrances built by the Spanish

Across the street, the Parque Santa Lucía is used for dancing and cultural events, and has a flea market on Sundays. Bronze busts placed on tall, white columns lining one corner of the park honor *Yucateco* musicians and songwriters. Farther south, on Calle 64, the **Arco de San Juan** stands west of the Plaza Mayor, arguably the finest of eight arches. Farther north, the

Paseo Montejo stretches for several kilometers. It is lined with the elegant town mansions of rich henequen or sisal plantation owners and the private banks that prospered in the late 19th century. Many of the houses were built by Italian architects and are a medley of Neo-Classical elements. One of the finest, the Palacio Cantón, houses the excellent **Museo Regional de Antropología**. Its pre-Columbian exhibits include a jaguar throne from Uxmal *(see pp262–4)*, a *chacmool* from Chichén Itzá *(see pp274–6)*, and fine examples of Mayan funerary offerings. At the northern end of the Paseo Montejo is the **Monumento a la Patria** (Monument to the Fatherland), an elaborate 20th-century work by Colombian sculptor Rómulo Rozo. The striking monument shows historical figures and

Detail, Monumento a la Patria

animal sculptures, and encloses an eternal flame, a symbol of Mexico's independence.

Environs
Situated a short drive southwest of Mérida, **Hacienda Yaxcopoil**, a mansion surrounded by a henequen plantation, is now a museum providing a view into life on a hacienda *(see pp50–51)*.

VISITORS' CHECKLIST

Yucatán. 🏠 781,000. ✈ 5 km (3 miles) S. 🚌 Calle 70 No. 555, (999) 920 44 44. 🛈 Centro de Convenciones, Calle 60 Norte, (999) 930 37 60. 🎉 Cristo de las Ampollas (Sep 27). **www.**mayayucatan.com.mx

🏛 **Museo Regional de Antropología Palacio Cantón**
Paseo Montejo 485. **Tel** (999) 923 05 57. ◯ Tue–Sun. 🎫 🖼 in advance.

🏨 **Hacienda Yaxcopoil**
Yaxcopoil, 35 km (22 miles) SW of Mérida. **Tel** (999) 900 11 93. ◯ daily. 🎫 🖼 📷
www.yaxcopoil.com

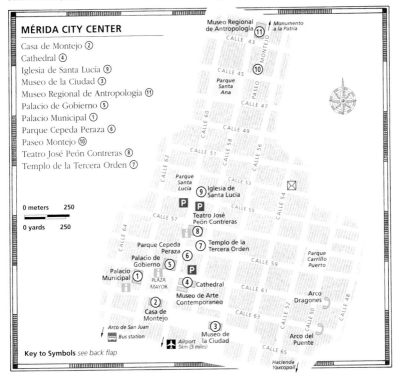

MÉRIDA CITY CENTER

Casa de Montejo ②
Cathedral ④
Iglesia de Santa Lucía ⑨
Museo de la Ciudad ③
Museo Regional de Antropología ⑪
Palacio de Gobierno ⑤
Palacio Municipal ①
Parque Cepeda Peraza ⑥
Paseo Montejo ⑩
Teatro José Peón Contreras ⑧
Templo de la Tercera Orden ⑦

0 meters   250
0 yards   250

Key to Symbols see back flap

Celestún

Yucatán. 🏘 6,000. 🚌

The small fishing village of Celestún is situated on a spit of land almost entirely separated from the mainland. Several kilometers of palm-fringed beaches line the coast to the west of the village, but it is the flamingos on the estuary to the east that attract most of the visitors. Boats can be hired to get closer to the birds, which include pelicans and various waders, as well as flamingos. However, strict environmental laws now prohibit anyone from disturbing the birds, so it is a good idea to bring a pair of field glasses with you so that you can see their natural behavior up close.

Pink flamingos in the estuary

Other excursions on small launches are available, depending on weather conditions, including visits to the *bosque petrificado*, a forest of petrified wood. This surreal, desolate place, on the Isla de Pájaros to the south of Celestún, was created by prolonged salinization.

Dzibilchaltún ⑨

Yucatán. Off Mex 261, 15 km (9 miles) N of Mérida. 🚌 from Mérida. ◯ daily. 🎫 📷 www.inah.gob.mx

Literally the "place with writing on flat stones," Dzibilchaltún was one of the most important centers in pre-Columbian Yucatán, and one of the earliest to be built. However, it was explored only in the 1940s, making it one of the latest to be rediscovered.

The site is arranged concentrically. A *sacbe*, or "white road," leads from the central plaza to the impressive Temple of the Seven Dolls. This building is named after the tiny clay dolls found buried in front of its altar. Several of the dolls have deformities, and are thought to be associated with rituals. Replicas are displayed in the ultra-modern and well laid-out museum. Other notable exhibits include the stelae and sculptures in the gardens leading up to the museum, ceramic figures, wooden altarpieces from the colonial era, and an attractive display on the pirates who plagued the seas around the Yucatán coast in the 16th and 17th centuries. Interactive screens and audio-visual commentaries provide information about the ancient Maya world view, the Maya today, and the history of the henequen industry.

The remains of a Franciscan chapel built of Maya masonry, probably at the end of the 16th century, are also worth seeing. This open chapel, where the monks preached to the local Indians, is still standing.

Dzibilchaltún's cenote, a natural turquoise pool more than 40 m (130 ft) deep, is a refreshing place for a swim after visiting the other sights. Many artifacts have been recovered from its depths.

The Temple of the Seven Dolls in Dzibilchaltún

The cenote at Dzibilchaltún, a good place for a refreshing swim

Progreso ⑩

Yucatán. 🏘 49,500. 🚌 ℹ Between Calles 25 and 27, (969) 935 01 04.

Situated on the north Yucatán coast, Progreso was once an important port. With the construction of the railroad linking the port to Mérida in the 1880s, it experienced a boom that is hard to imagine now as one approaches the relaxed, low-lying town past mangrove swamps.

Progreso has probably the longest stone pier in the world, often bustling with people. Near its landward end is an attractive 19th-century lighthouse. On the town front, by the narrow sandy beach, are many good seafood restaurants. Several cruise liners stop in Progreso, and there are a number of ocean-front resorts, making the town popular with people from the north looking for a warmer winter.

Progreso's stone pier, thought to be the longest in the world

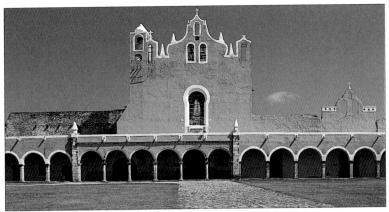

Izamal's imposing Convento de San Antonio de Padua, built by Franciscan monks from Spain

Izamal ⓫

Yucatán. 🏛 24,400. 🚌 🎭 Cristo de Sitilpeth (Oct 18), Virgen de la Inmaculada (Dec 7–8). **www**. mayayucatan.com.mx

Once as important a site as Chichén Itzá, Izamal is believed to have been founded around AD 300. The original village grew into an influential city-state and, by AD 800, it was governing the surrounding region. Modern Izamal is a fascinating combination of Maya remains and Spanish colonial buildings. There are around 20 Classic Maya structures still standing. Chief among these is the pyramid K'inich K'ak' Mo', named after the ruler "Great-Sun Fire Macaw." It is one of the largest pyramids in the Yucatán.

The importance of Izamal had declined by the time the Spanish arrived in the mid-16th century, but it retained enough religious influence for the Franciscan monks to construct the spectacular Convento de San Antonio de Padua here. They demolished a Maya temple and built the church on its massive platform base, giving it an elevated position. The huge atrium is surrounded by open cloisters, and contains some early Franciscan frescoes.

The church acquired even more importance when Bishop Diego de Landa installed in it a statue of the Virgen de la Inmaculada, which he had brought from Guatemala. This was immediately attributed

with miraculous powers by the local Maya population, and in 1949 the Virgin was adopted as the patron saint of the Yucatán. A small museum in the church commemorates Pope John Paul II's visit to Izamal in 1993, the International Year of Indigenous People, when he pledged the Catholic Church's support for the Maya Indians. Adjacent to the church are two pretty arcaded squares. Here, and in the surrounding streets of low Spanish colonial houses, most of the buildings' façades are painted a glowing ocher color. This led to Izamal being nicknamed La Ciudad Amarilla, literally "The Yellow City."

The massive Maya pyramid, K'inich K'ak' Mo', in Izamal

HAMMOCKS

Brightly colored hammocks are a common sight in the markets of Campeche, Mérida and Izamal. Probably introduced to Mexico by Spanish colonists from the Caribbean, they are now used for sleeping by many Mexicans in the Yucatán region. The hammocks are traditionally made from twine produced from henequen, a type of fibrous agave plant that can be seen growing all over the Yucatán Peninsula (though modern hammocks tend to be made from cotton or silk). The leaves are cut from the spiky plants, shredded into long fibers, and then dried. The fibers can be dyed and braided, or woven into twine or rope. Other products made from henequen include mats and bags.

Traditional hammocks for sale in Mérida

Chichén Itzá ⑫

Carved figure, Temple of the Warriors

The best preserved Maya site on the peninsula, Chichén Itzá confounds historians. The date of first settlement in the southern part of the site is not certain, but the northern section was built during a renaissance in the 11th century AD. Similarities with Tula *(see p144)*, and myths that tell how exiled Toltec god-king Quetzalcoatl (Kukulcan) settled at Chichén Itzá, suggest that the renaissance was due to a Toltec invasion. However, other theories hold that Tula was influenced by the Maya, not vice versa. In its heyday as a commercial, religious, and military center, which lasted until about the 13th century, Chichén Itzá supported over 35,000 people. In 2007 it was voted one of the New Seven Wonders of the World.

★ **Ballcourt**
At 168 m (550 ft) in length, this is the largest ballcourt in Mesoamerica. Still in place are the two engraved rings that the ball had to pass through (see p277).

Pisté and Mérida

Main entrance

Tomb of the High Priest

★ **Observatory**
Also called El Caracol (The Snail) for its spiral staircase, this building was an astronomical observatory (see p47). The various slits in the walls correspond to the positions of certain celestial bodies on key dates in the Maya calendar.

Nunnery
So named because its small rooms reminded the Spaniards of nuns' cells, this large structure, built in three stages, was probably a palace. The façade of the east annex (seen here) has particularly beautiful stone fretwork and carvings.

Chichén Viejo

The Church, or Iglesia, is decorated with fretwork, masks of the rain god Chac, and the *bacabs* – four animals who, in Maya myth, held up the sky.

0 meters 150
0 yards 150

The Tzompantli is a low platform whose perimeter is carved with grinning skulls. Archaeologists believe that it was used to display the heads of victims of human sacrifice, practiced during Chichén Itzá's late period.

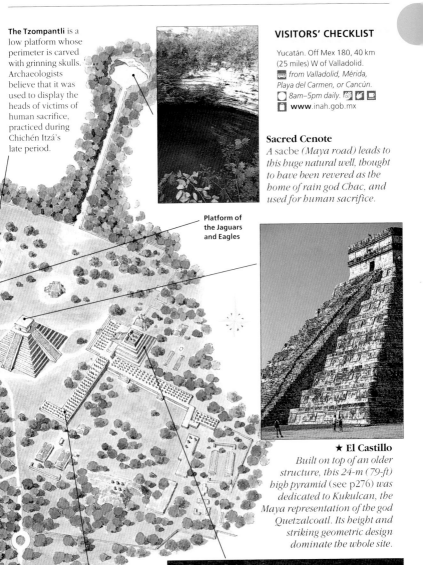

Platform of the Jaguars and Eagles

VISITORS' CHECKLIST

Yucatán. Off Mex 180, 40 km (25 miles) W of Valladolid. from Valladolid, Mérida, Playa del Carmen, or Cancún. 8am–5pm daily. www.inah.gob.mx

Sacred Cenote

A sacbe (Maya road) leads to this huge natural well, thought to have been revered as the home of rain god Chac, and used for human sacrifice.

★ El Castillo

Built on top of an older structure, this 24-m (79-ft) high pyramid (see p276) was dedicated to Kukulcan, the Maya representation of the god Quetzalcoatl. Its height and striking geometric design dominate the whole site.

The Group of a Thousand Columns, made up of carved stone colonnades on two sides of a huge plaza, may have been used as a market.

Entrance

Valladolid and Cancún

STAR FEATURES

★ Ballcourt

★ Observatory

★ El Castillo

Temple of the Warriors

Set on a small pyramid, this temple is decorated with sculptures of the rain god Chac and the plumed serpent Kukulcan. A chacmool (see p44), and two columns carved to represent snakes, guard the entrance.

El Castillo

The most awe-inspiring structure at Chichén Itzá is the pyramid known as El Castillo (The Castle), built around AD 800. It has a perfect astronomical design: four staircases face the cardinal points, various features correspond to aspects of the Maya calendar (see pp46–7), and, twice yearly at sunrise, a fascinating optical illusion occurs on the north staircase (see p261). Continuing excavations on the eastern side allow visitors to watch the painstaking process of archaeology as it reveals that the pyramid was built on the remains of a much older settlement.

View of El Castillo from beside the Platform of the Jaguars and Eagles

RECONSTRUCTION OF EL CASTILLO

This shows how the pyramid would have looked on completion. It was originally covered in plaster and painted a vivid red.

Temple entrance, divided by snake-shaped columns

Temple of Kukulcán

The 52 panels on each of the pyramid's faces represent the number of years in the Maya sacred cycle.

The nine stepped levels on each side of the pyramid are divided by the staircase into 18 terraces, which symbolize the 18 months of the Maya calendar.

The temple at the top of the inner pyramid contains a chacmool (see p44), a beautiful, bright-red throne carved as a jaguar and encrusted with jade.

North staircase

Entrance to inner pyramid

Inner pyramid

Two serpents' heads at the foot of the north staircase are thought to represent the god Kukulcan, the Maya Quetzalcóatl. At the two yearly equinoxes, the play of light and shadow on the staircase makes them appear to crawl up the pyramid.

The west staircase, like the other three, is made up of 91 steps. So the four staircases, together with the temple platform at the top, make a total of 365 steps, the number of days in the year. Since the site was designated as one of the new seven wonders of the world, climbing the staircases is no longer permitted.

The Ballgame

More than a sport or a form of entertainment, the ballgame that was played throughout Mesoamerica had some kind of ritual significance. Two teams would compete against each other to manipulate a large rubber ball through a stone ring set high on the wall at the side of the court. It is thought that the losers of the game were subsequently put to death. Ballcourts have been found at all the main pre-Columbian sites, the largest being at Chichén Itzá. The cities of Cantona (see p157) and El Tajín (see pp242–3) each had a great number of ballcourts. A version of the game, called *hulama*, is still played today by Indians in the state of Sinaloa (see p178).

Maya figurine of a ball player

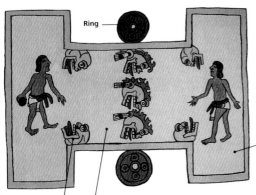

Ring

THE BALLCOURT
Although there were probably several versions of the game, it was always played on an I-shaped court, as seen in this Aztec codex illustration. Ballcourts varied in size, but early examples were usually aligned north-south, and later ones east-west.

Outer court

Stone markers are thought to have been part of the normal system of scoring.

The aisle or central court had steeply sloping sides.

A heavy rubber ball, about as big as a man's head but shown here in exaggerated size, was used to play the game.

The ballgame player *wore substantial body protection, as seen in this decoration on a Maya vessel. The ball had to be kept off the ground using only knees, elbows, or hips, never the hands or feet.*

Arm protector

The ballcourt ring *was a tiny "goal" that the ball had to pass through. This was just one way of scoring and would have been a rare event, as it clearly took a prodigious feat to achieve.*

Padded hip protector

THE FATE OF THE LOSERS

The losers were often sacrificed after the game, but this was considered an honorable way to die. This carved panel, one of six that decorate the South Ballcourt at El Tajín, shows two victors killing one of the losing team with an obsidian knife, while a third player looks on from the right. A savage looking death god descends from the skyband at the top of the panel to receive the human offering.

Valladolid ⑬

Yucatán. 🏘 69,000. ▨ ℹ *Palacio Municipal, Calle 40 No. 200, (985) 856 25 51.* 🎭 *Candelaria (Feb 2).* **www**.valladolid.com.mx

Lying almost exactly halfway between Mérida and Cancún, Valladolid is the third-largest city on the Yucatán Peninsula. It was founded by the Spanish on an earlier Maya settlement known as Zaci, and quickly became an important religious center. In 1552 the Franciscans built the Yucatán's first ecclesiastical buildings here, the **Iglesia de San Bernardino de Siena** and the adjoining **Ex-Convento de Sisal**. These have been restored, revealing original frescoes behind two side altars in the church. Also restored are the small Spanish colonial houses on Calle 41-A, the street from the town center to the church.

The *zócalo* (main square) is the focal point, and often the liveliest part, of this quiet and attractive city. Maya women sell *huipiles* (embroidered dresses) around its perimeter, and in the northeast corner small, inexpensive restaurants serve tasty local dishes and fruit juices late into the night. Overlooking the square is the **cathedral**, with its elegant

Statue on the main square in Valladolid

façade, and the colonial hotel **El Mesón del Marqués** *(see p317).* Also on the square is the **Palacio Municipal** (City Hall). In the first-floor hallway are painted panels showing the history of the town from Maya times, and portraits of military leaders from Valladolid who helped initiate the Revolution *(see p54).*

A little farther out from the main square, the churches of **Santa Ana** (four blocks east) and **Santa Lucía** (six blocks north), are fine examples of stark Franciscan architecture. These churches were originally used by Maya converts, and are still the most popular in the town.

Environs
West of town is the **Cenote de Dzitnup**, a natural well, apparently unearthed by a pig in the 1950s. Visitors can climb down the steep steps to the underground pool, where a hole in the roof and electric lighting illuminate the dramatic setting. You can also swim here among the fish in the blue water.

West, near Chichén Itzá, are the **Grutas de Balamkanché**,

The intricately painted high altar of the Iglesia de San Bernardino de Siena, Valladolid

Hanging stalactites and clear, turquoise water in the Cenote de Dzitnup

huge caves discovered in 1959. Maya artifacts found here suggest that this was a place of worship as early as 300 BC, dedicated to the rain god Chac. Guides point out some of the Maya objects still in situ, which include miniature corn-grinding stones, and decorated incense burners. There is a small museum on site.

🏛 **Cenote de Dzitnup**
7 km (4 miles) W of Valladolid. ◯ *daily.* 🎟

🏛 **Grutas de Balamkanché**
Off Mex 180, 35 km (22 miles) W of Valladolid. ◯ *daily.* 🎟

Ekbalam ⑭

Yucatán. Off Mex 295, 25 km (16 miles) N of Valladolid. ▨ *Temozón then taxi.* ◯ *daily.* 🎟

Ongoing excavation work has revealed Ekbalam ("Black Jaguar") as an important Maya city and religious center. It dates predominantly from AD 700–1000, is relatively compact, and has an unusual double perimeter wall for fortification. The main entrance is through a fine Maya arch, but the real highlight is the Tower – a 30-m- (98-ft-) high tiered pyramid that visitors can climb. On each of the pyramid's tiers, pits sunken into the structure are thought to be *chultunes* (Maya cisterns). From gaps in the surrounding walls at the cardinal points, Maya processional roads, or *sacbeob (see p285),* radiate out to a distance of over 1.5 km (1 mile).

Río Lagartos ⓯

Yucatán. Mex 295, 104 km (65 miles)
N of Valladolid. *from Valladolid
and Mérida.* daily.

The nature preserve of Río
Lagartos, occupying brackish
lagoons on the north coast of
the peninsula, is a bird-
watcher's paradise. It is home
to over 260 species, including
the huge colonies of pink
flamingos that breed here in
the summer. Between April
and June, the flamingos' nests
are protected, but at other
times of the year, boat trips to
see the elegant birds can be
arranged in Río Lagartos village. Occasionally, snakes
and turtles can also be seen.

Thatched shelters on Playa Marlín in Cancún

The safe waters of Playa Langosta, Cancún

Cancún ⓰

Quintana Roo. 573,000.
Av Yaxilan s/n, 17M
Lote 6, (998) 881 90 00.
www.caribemex.com

Before 1970, Cancún was
little more than a sandy
island and a fishing village of
barely 100 inhabitants. The
government decided to turn it
into a new resort, and in the
late 1960s building began in

earnest. Since then the population has soared to hundreds
of thousands, and over 12
million (mainly non-Mexican)
visitors flock here every year
to enjoy the white-sand
beaches and
perfect weather.
There are, in
fact, two Cancúns.
The downtown
area, on the main-
land, has very few
hotels and no
beaches, while the
Cancún that most
visitors see has
plenty of both.
The latter, known as **Isla
Cancún** or the *zona hotelera*
(hotel zone), is a narrow, 23-
km (14-mile) L-shaped island
connected to the mainland by
two bridges.
Although many of the hotels
appear to command private
stretches of sand, all beaches
in Mexico are public and can
be enjoyed by anybody. The
ones in front of the Hyatt
Cancún and Sheraton hotels
are particularly beautiful.

If the resort beach scene and
constant presence of hotel
staff do not appeal, however,
head for the equally attractive
"public" beaches. **Playa Linda**,
Playa Langosta, and **Playa
Tortugas**,on the northern arm
of the island, offer relaxed
swimming in the calm Bahía
Mujeres, while bigger waves
and fine views can be found
at **Playa Chac-Mool**, **Playa
Marlín**, and **Playa Ballenas**,
which face the open sea on the
eastern side. The protected
Laguna Nichupté, between
Isla Cancún and the mainland,
is perfect for watersports.
Toward the southern end of
the island is the small Maya
site of **El Rey** (The King),
occupied from AD 1200 until
the Conquest. Here, a low
pyramid and two plazas provide a quiet, cultural retreat
from the beachfront action.
Some ferries for Isla Mujeres
(see p281) leave from a dock
near Playa Linda, but the
majority depart from Puerto
Juárez or Punta Sam, both
just to the north of Cancún.

The pyramid and other ruins of El Rey, echoed by one of Cancún's many hotels in the background

The Mayan Riviera

The development of Cancún (see p279), and other smaller resorts, has brought profound changes to the Yucatán's east coast. Now known as the Mayan Riviera, it is a major tourist destination, and it is easy to see why. As well as idyllic sandy beaches and warm waters, the coast has the second longest coral reef in the world, providing ideal conditions for snorkeling and diving.

A dolphin, one of the animals that visitors can see at Xcaret (see p284)

Playa del Carmen is the second biggest resort on the coast after Cancún. The town has a relaxed atmosphere and Quinta Avenida, the main street, is lined with small shops, coffee bars, and traditional restaurants. Ferries to Cozumel leave from a pier close to the lively central square.

Akumal is an uncrowded resort based around what was once a coconut plantation. Its beautiful beach is a breeding ground for green turtles, and migrating whale sharks can sometimes be spotted swimming past in December and January. Since the 1990s, the sheltered bay has increasingly attracted windsurfers, divers, and snorkelers.

VALLADO

0 kilometers   20

0 miles   10

VALLADO

Xcaret (see p284) is a combination of zoo, beach resort, archaeological area, and theme park.

Xel-Ha nature preserve is a series of interconnecting lagoons set among spectacular rocks and caves. A huge variety of tropical fish swims in its beautifully clear waters. For years it was government-run and rather neglected, but it is now franchised to the same company that operates Xcaret. It has taken on a new lease of life, offering superb snorkeling and diving.

Playa c Carme

Pamul

LAGUNA EL CONTINENTE

Puerto Aventuras is a purpose-built resort with a range of facilities, including an 18-hole golf course and a marina. It is popular for reef diving.

Akumal

307

Xel-Ha

COBÁ

Tulum Pueblo

Tulum

CHETUMAL

Tulum Playa

Tulum Playa, the most easy-going resort along the coast, is essentially a rapidly growing strip of beach huts and a handful of restaurants, bordering a magnificent sandy beach. Nearby is the late-Maya site of Tulum (see pp284–5).

Puerto Morelos *is the least developed place on the riviera, a small, laid-back resort built around a fishing village. There is excellent snorkeling and diving on the reef just offshore.*

Isla Mujeres, situated close to the coral reef, is popular with divers.

LAGUNA CHACMOCHUK

Punta Sam

Puerto Juárez

dalgo

CANCÚN

LAGUNA NICHUPTÉ

ISLA CANCÚN

Cancún is huge, attracting more visitors than any other resort in Mexico.

307

Puerto Morelos

CARIBBEAN SEA

Punta Bete

Punta Molas

San Miguel de Cozumel

COZUMEL

Cozumel *(see p282)* is one of the world's top diving sites.

Punta Celarain

Key to Symbols *see back flap*

A flotilla of small tour boats moored in the harbor on Isla Mujeres

Isla Mujeres ⑰

Quintana Roo. 🚢 *passenger ferry from Puerto Juárez, car ferry from Punta Sam.* 🚹 *Avenida Rueda Medina 130, (998) 877 03 07.* www.isla-mujeres.com.mx

This small island is just 1 km (half a mile) wide by 8 km (5 miles) long. Its name, meaning "The Island of Women," probably derives from Maya female statuettes found here and destroyed by the Spanish. It has developed considerably since first becoming popular in the 1960s, but there are few high-rise buildings, and its small town is still quiet, especially in the evening when the day trippers from Cancún have left.

The best way to explore the island is on a bike or scooter. Its middle part is taken up by a brackish lagoon and an airstrip for small planes from the mainland. Also in the center is the ruined **Mundaca Hacienda**, said to have been built by the pirate Fermín Mundaca to impress an island beauty.

Playa Los Cocos, located just to the north of the island's only town, has clean white sand and warm shallow water.

At Isla Mujeres' rather rugged southern tip are the **Garrafón National Park**, and **Playa de Garrafón**. The exciting diving afforded by the coral reef just offshore

A lifeguard's lookout on Playa Los Cocos

here is one of the main reasons for visiting the island. The snorkeling is also spectacular, but the beach gets very crowded in the middle of the day. Nearby are the ruins of what is said to be an old Maya lighthouse.

Environs
A popular day trip from Isla Mujeres is to **Isla Contoy**, a tiny island 30 km (19 miles) away, off the northern tip of the Yucatán Peninsula. It is located at the northernmost part of the barrier reef, where the waters of the Caribbean Sea and Gulf of Mexico meet. The mingling currents create ideal conditions for plankton – food for the many fish, which in turn support an abundant bird life. Over 90 species of birds, including large flocks of egrets, pelicans, frigate birds, and flamingos, nest on the island, which is now a protected nature preserve.

An intricate bas-relief carving on the entrance arch of the Mundaca Hacienda

Cozumel ⑱

Quintana Roo. ✈ 🚢 car ferry from Puerto Morelos and Calica, passenger ferry from Playa del Carmen. ℹ Calle 15 Sur and 20 Av, (987) 869 02 12. **www**.cozumel.gob.mx/turismo

Situated off the east coast of the Yucatán Peninsula, Cozumel is Mexico's largest island, 14 km (9 miles) wide by 50 km (31 miles) long.

The Maya called the island Cuzamil, the "place of the swallows." It was an important center for the cult of Ixchel, goddess of fertility, pregnancy, and childbirth, and traces of Maya occupation can be found in several parts of the island. The ruins of two of the main settlements are at **El Cedral** and **San Gervasio**. Both are overgrown, but visiting them provides an opportunity to see some of Cozumel's varied birdlife in the jungle habitat that characterizes the interior of the island. San Gervasio, the larger site, has several restored buildings. **El Caracol** in the south of the island, is an

Moored boats at the pier in San Miguel de Cozumel

A pelican, one of many birds seen on Cozumel

isolated Maya shrine that is thought to have been used as a landmark for navigation. The Spaniards also came to Cozumel. The first Mass in Mexico was said here in 1518, and Hernán Cortés, warmly received by the local inhabitants, planned his conquest of mainland Mexico from the island. Today, Cozumel is a tourist resort, and one of the world's foremost diving locations. Ferries from the mainland arrive at the pier in **San Miguel de Cozumel**, the island's only town. Near the dock are many tourist shops and restaurants, but a few blocks away,

the town is quieter with a more traditional feel. The pretty **Iglesia de San Miguel Arcángel**, the town's only church, stands on the main square. Three blocks north of this square is the **Museo de la Isla**.

Cozumel is ringed by stunning beaches, many of which are accessible only in a four-wheel drive vehicle. Those on the eastern, windward side are beautiful, but the sea here is dangerous, with heavy waves and a strong undertow. Safe swimming beaches are on Cozumel's sheltered western side. The best diving sites are here too, particularly around the **Colombia**, **Palancar**, **San Francisco**, and **Santa Rosa** reefs. Also on the west coast is **Chankanaab Park**, with hundreds of varieties of tropical plants.

🏛 Museo de la Isla
Cnr of Av Rafael Melgar & Calle 6 Norte. **Tel** (987) 872 14 34. ⬜ daily. 🎫 ▢ ▢ ▢

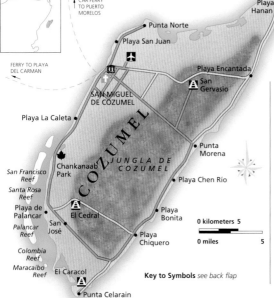

FERRY TO PLAYA
DEL CARMEN

CAR FERRY
TO PUERTO
MORELOS

Punta Molas
Playa Hanan
Punta Norte
Playa San Juan
Playa Encantada
San Gervasio
SAN MIGUEL DE COZUMEL
Playa La Caleta
JUNGLA DE COZUMEL
COZUMEL
Punta Morena
San Francisco Reef
Chankanaab Park
Santa Rosa Reef
Playa Chen Río
Playa de Palancar
El Cedral
Playa Bonita
Palancar Reef
San José
Colombia Reef
Playa Chiquero
Maracaibo Reef
El Caracol
Punta Celarain

0 kilometers 5
0 miles 5

Key to Symbols see back flap

The Iglesia de San Miguel Arcángel in Cozumel's only town

Diving in the Mexican Caribbean

The great Mesoamerican Reef System stretches for more than 1,000 km (620 miles) down the eastern coast of Yucatán to Belize, Guatemala, and Honduras. Home to an amazing variety of sea creatures, the crystal waters along the Yucatán coast are ideal for snorkeling and skindiving. There are diving sites

Snorkeling in the clear tropical waters around Cozumel

on the reefs to suit every ability, from beginner to professional, the best known places being off the island of Cozumel. Equipment can be bought or rented from the many diving schools found on the coast. These also offer diving training, and lead groups of more experienced divers to explore the reef.

Blue chromis are a common midwater sight in Cozumel.

Blue-striped grunts, often seen in schools, shelter on the reef by day and feed by night.

A tiger grouper can change color to blend in with a coral reef or a rocky bottom.

Flamingo tongue
Unlike most snails, this mollusk species extends its mantle over its shell as camouflage. It feeds and reproduces on soft corals.

Sea rods, a soft coral, have skeletal spicules, or spikes, in their skin instead of internal skeletons.

Sea fans, which are often brilliantly colored, are a very delicate and brittle type of coral.

Fire coral is named after its stinging, poisonous cells.

Tube sponges can grow up to 2 m (7 ft) high. Their size depends on age, food supply, and environmental conditions.

Massive corals are the main basis of a reef. They grow only 3 mm (1/10 inch) a year, but can reach over 10 m (33 ft) in diameter.

YUCATÁN CORAL GARDEN
The dramatic underwater landscape boasts abundant and colorful coral gardens, whose nooks and crannies teem with marine creatures in search of food and shelter.

Splendid toadfish
Active only at night, the pointed barbels and striped head of the splendid toadfish may give away its daytime hideaway.

Hawksbill turtle
These increasingly rare turtles nest along Cozumel's eastern coast. An endangered species, they are protected by law.

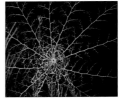

Basket star
Capable of reaching a diameter of up to 1 m (3 ft), basket stars can sometimes be seen when feeding at night.

For hotels and restaurants in this region see pp313–17 and pp343–5

Xcaret ⑲

Quintana Roo. Mex 307, 7 km (4 miles) S of Playa del Carmen. **Tel** (998) 883 31 43. 🚌 from Cancún and Playa del Carmen. ⬭ daily. 📷 🔲 🔲 www.xcaret.com

This large, well-planned "eco-archaeological" theme park is a combination of zoo, activity center, and beach resort. It is built around the ruins of Polé, an important Postclassic Maya coastal settlement. A highlight for many visitors is a chance to float down the clear waters of the two naturally illuminated subterranean rivers that cross the park. Another popular activity is to swim with dolphins in a saltwater pool. The park's animal collection includes bats, butterflies, and turtles, as well as pumas and jaguars, kept on two Big Cat Islands. Other attractions are a re-created Maya village and a sound-and-light show about the Maya.

Puma, on Xcaret's Jaguar Island

Beaches fringing a lagoon in Xcaret theme park

Cobá ⑳

Quintana Roo. 47 km (29 miles) NW of Tulum. 🚌 from Valladolid and Cancún. ⬭ summer: 8am–7pm daily; winter: 7am–6pm daily. 📷 www.inahqr.gob.mx

Built around a group of lakes, Cobá is one of the most inter-esting archaeological sites in the Yucatán Peninsula. The

Tulum ㉑

Spectacularly positioned on a cliff overlooking the Caribbean, Tulum is a late-Maya site that was at its height from around AD 1200 until the arrival of the Spanish. The name, which means "enclosure" or "wall," is probably modern. It is thought that the site was originally called Zama, or "dawn," reflecting its location on the east coast, and the west-east alignment of its buildings. Its inhabitants traded with Cozumel, Isla Mujeres, Guatemala, and central Mexico.

The House of the Cenote *is so named because it stands above a cenote, a subterranean well.*

A perimeter wall runs along three sides of the site. It is 5 m (16 ft) thick and pierced by five gates.

House of the Northeast

House of the Halach Uinic, or Overlord

House of Columns or Grand Palace

The Temple of the Frescoes *was used as an observatory for tracking the movements of the sun. Its interior walls are richly adorned with paintings in which supernatural serpents are a common motif.*

House of Chultún

Entrance

For hotels and restaurants in this region see pp313–17 and pp343–5

city flourished from about AD 300 to AD 1000, and stood at the center of a network of *sacbeob* (meaning "white roads"): straight processional routes paved with limestone that connected Maya buildings or settlements to each other. More of these roads have been found here than anywhere else.

Up to 40,000 people are thought to have lived at this enormous site, thanks to the local abundance of water. However, only a small proportion of its area has been excavated so far. Much of it is still shrouded in jungle.

There are three principal clusters of buildings to visit. Be prepared for long walks between them, or rent a bike. Close to the entrance of the site is the **Cobá Group**. The main building in this group is a pyramid known as La Iglesia

The ballcourt, part of the extensive ruins of Cobá

(the Church), because local people regard it as a shrine. Nearby is a ballcourt *(see p277)*. A trail beginning on the other side of Lago Macanxoc leads to the **Macanxoc Group**, where a collection of stelae carved by the Maya as historical records can be seen.

About 1.5 km (1 mile) to the north is the **Nohoch Mul Group**. Standing at 42 m (138 ft), Nohoch Mul is the highest pyramid in the Yucatán. It's a hard climb to the temple at the top, but once reached, there is an incomparable view of the lakes and jungle below.

The Temple of the Descending God *has a carving over its door showing a swooping or falling figure. Similar carvings, of what is thought to be a deity associated with the setting sun, can be seen on El Castillo and in several other buildings on the site.*

Temple of the Wind

The temple that crowns El Castillo has three niches above the doorway. A beautiful sculpture of the descending god remains in the central niche.

Temple of the Initial Series

To Temple of the Sea

Ceremonial platform

El Castillo *(The Castle) is the largest and most prominent building on the site, and as such would have served as a landmark for seafarers. Its wide external staircase leads up to a late-Postclassic temple.*

VISITORS' CHECKLIST

Quintana Roo. Mex 307, 128 km (80 miles) S of Cancún. 🚌 *from Cancún.* ☐ *summer: 8am–7pm daily; winter: 7am–6pm daily.* 📷

El Castillo, on its spectacular clifftop vantage point

Sian Ka'an Biosphere Reserve ㉒

Quintana Roo. 🚌 *tours from Tulum.*
📷 *Cesiak, Carretera 307, 68 Tulum,
(984) 871 24 99.*
www.cesiak.org

Comprising over 4,500 sq km (1,700 sq miles) of low jungle and marshlands, and 110 km (69 miles) of coral reef, Sian Ka'an has a range of natural habitats that makes it one of the most important conservation areas in Mexico. It is run by a government agency and is not primarily geared toward tourism.

The rare Jabirú stork, Sian Ka'an

Indeed, the poor roads within the preserve deter all but the most intrepid. However, the Amigos de Sian Ka'an (Friends of Sian Ka'an) run night tours for visitors, which focus on the crocodiles that inhabit the mangrove swamps. Lucky visitors may also see the flocks of local and migrating birds in the marshlands around Boca Paila, in the northern part of the preserve, including the rare Jabirú stork, or the elusive turtles and manatees that live in the waters off the coast.

Punta Allen, south of Boca Paila but still within the preserve, is a small fishing village. Lobsters, the main source of income here, are still caught using old Maya methods.

The Maya site of Kohunlich, near Chetumal

Chetumal ㉓

Quintana Roo. 🏠 *135,500.* ✈ 🚌
ℹ *Calzada del Centenario 622,
(983) 835 08 60.* **www**.qroo.gob.mx

Founded on the estuary of the Río Hondo in 1898, Chetumal is now the capital of Quintana Roo state. It is situated near the frontier with Belize, and is a typical border town. There is a large naval base and a duty-free zone, with stores selling cut-rate luxury items from all over the world. Visitors from Belize and Guatemala come here for shopping, giving the city an exciting atmosphere. Most of the original wooden and tin-roofed buildings were destroyed in a hurricane in the 1950s, and the

**State emblem of
Quintana Roo**

town has been rebuilt around wide avenues, some of which still end in undergrowth. Chetumal's spacious **Museo de la Cultura Maya** explores the Maya world, including astronomy, daily life, and Maya codices. Many of the exhibits are replicas, but there are good explanatory panels and interactive screens.

Environs
Situated 40 km (25 miles) northwest of Chetumal, is the village of **Bacalar**. There is a natural pool here, over 60 m (200 ft) deep. Named **Cenote Azul** for its vivid blue color, it is perfect for a swim. Nearby **Laguna de Siete Colores**, overlooked by the Spanish fort in Bacalar, is also popular. West along Mex 186, farmed fields

A pleasure boat plying the clear, blue waters of the Laguna de Siete Colores, near Chetumal

For hotels and restaurants in this region see pp313–17 and pp343–5

give way to jungle, the setting for the Maya site of **Kohunlich** and its Temple of Masks. Dedicated to the Maya sun god, the steps of this 6th-century pyramid are flanked with masks facing the setting sun. About 29 km (18 miles) north of Kohunlich lie the attractive, if rather unremarkable, ruins of **Dzibanché**.

🏛 **Museo de la Cultura Maya**
Cnr of Av Héroes and Cristobal Colón. **Tel** (983) 832 68 38.
◯ *Tue–Sat.* 🖼 🅰 ⛔
🅰 **Kohunlich & Dzibanché**
◯ *daily.* 🖼 www.inah.gob.mx

Río Bec Sites ㉔

Campeche. Mex 186, 120 km (75 miles) W of Chetumal. 🚌 *Xpujil.* **All sites** ◯ *daily.* 🖼 www.inah.gob.mx

A group of stylistically similar Maya sites, situated in the lowlands west of Chetumal, are known collectively as the Río Bec sites. Many are hidden by jungle, but three of them, Xpujil, Becán, and Chicanná, are near enough to the main road (Mex 186) to be accessible to the casual visitor. These three can be visited on a day-trip from Chetumal, or en route to the city from Villahermosa *(see p254)* or Palenque *(see pp234–7)*.

The area may have been occupied from at least 550 BC, but the Río Bec style, which the sites share, was dominant between AD 600 and 900. The style is characterized by elongated platforms and buildings, flanked by slender towers with rounded corners. These towers are "fake" temple-pyramids – the steps are too steep to be used, and the structures seem to have no inner chamber and no special function apart from decoration. Representations of Itzamná, the creation god responsible for life and death, are the main ornamentation.

Coming from Chetumal, the first site is **Xpujil**, just across the border in the state of Campeche, and clearly visible from the road. Here, 17 building groups surround a central square, but the most remarkable structure is the main temple, whose three towers rise over 15 m (50 ft) from a

Structure X at Becán, its decorative stonework just visible at the top

low platform. These pointed towers, which are a classic example of Río Bec architecture, soar enigmatically above the surrounding jungle.

Just 6 km (4 miles) farther west, a track north of the main road leads to **Becán**. The site dates from around 550 BC, and is thought to have been the principal Maya center in the Río Bec region. The substantial number of nonlocal artifacts found during excavations suggests it was an important trading center linking the two sides of the peninsula. Unusually, the main buildings here were surrounded by a trench or moat (now dry) that is up to 5 m (16 ft) deep and 16 m (52 ft) wide, and about 2 km (1 mile) in circumference.

Various Río Bec towers can be seen here, but Becán is also noted for the unusual rooms found inside Structure VIII. These chambers had no means of light or ventilation and may have been used for religious rituals that required darkness and isolation.

Chicanná, 3 km (2 miles) farther west, and south of the main road, has the most extraordinary architecture of the three sites. Its name means "house of the serpent's mouth," which refers to Structure II, whose façade is a snake's head formed by an intricate mosaic of stone. This striking zoomorphic shape represents the god Itzamná, while the snake's mouth forms the doorway. Structure XX, set apart from the main plaza, is a two-level building that echoes the design of Structure II. Its sides are decorated with masks of Chac, the rain god *(see p265)*.

Environs
Near the village of Conhuás, 60 km (37 miles) west of Xpujil, a minor road branches to the south and, after another 60 km, reaches **Calakmul**, one of the most important Maya cities in the Classic period. The 50-m (165-ft) high pyramid here is the largest in Mexico. Around a hundred stelae remain on site, but the jade masks found in the tombs are now on display in Campeche *(see p260)*.

Just west of Conhuás is the site of **Balamkú**, discovered by chance in 1990. Its most striking feature is a 17-m (55-ft) long stucco frieze on the building known as the House of the Four Kings. The frieze is thought to represent the relationship between Maya royalty and the cosmos.

The three Río Bec towers rising above the principal temple at Xpujil

TRAVELERS' NEEDS

WHERE TO STAY

The constant increase in numbers of visitors to Mexico has been matched by a growth in the variety of accommodations available. Apart from hotels, there are guest houses, apartments, hostels, campgrounds, and even hammocks for rent. The hotels themselves range from budget motels to world-class luxury resorts in extraordinary settings. Room prices vary greatly, depending on region of the country,

Maids in a hotel in Querétaro

location of the hotel, season, prestige, and services provided. Visitors should be aware that inexpensive establishments may not conform to the standards they might expect in the US or Europe. The hotel listings *(see pp292–317)* describe some of the best hotels around Mexico in every style and price category, from modern chain hotels to small, typical, family-run lodgings and stunningly converted colonial haciendas.

The small luxury Hotel Xcanatun in Mérida on the Yucatán Peninsula

HOTEL GRADING

Room prices are regulated by the state, and hotels are classified into categories ranging from one to five star, plus a special category and a Grand Tourism category. Private bathrooms with showers, linen change, and daily room cleaning are provided in all hotels from one star upward. At the other extreme, Grand Tourism hotels are very luxurious and usually offer a gym, a nightclub, and a gourmet restaurant. Special category hotels are ones that have been designated historic monuments. They are not classified by their facilities, nor given a star rating.

CHAIN HOTELS

Mexico has a number of hotel chains, with varying services and prices. **Fiesta Americana** and **Presidente Intercontinental** are two local

chains that offer reliable service, while **Camino Real** and **Quinta Real** have luxurious rooms. International chains, such as **Sheraton**, **Westin**, and **Marriott**, are also represented, and two good mid-range options are **Calinda** and **Howard Johnson**.

HISTORIC BUILDINGS

Mexico has plenty of old convents, mansions, and haciendas *(see pp50–51)* that have been converted into extraordinary hotels. Many have been declared national monuments and feature original furniture and decor. Those housed in haciendas often have spacious gardens and modern amenities. However, some hotels in convents and mansions are not permitted to alter their structure in order to provide modern facilities.

BUDGET ACCOMMODATIONS

There are many inexpensive hotels in towns and villages across Mexico, but ask to have a look before you commit to staying anywhere as the standards can vary hugely. The so-called *casas de huéspedes*, family-run guest houses, are one of the best forms of budget accommodations.

Camping is also very popular. Beaches in Mexico are public property; in some places it is acceptable to camp on them. There are also numerous campgrounds scattered around the country, particularly in Baja California, on the Pacific coast, and on the Yucatán Peninsula. In the south, *cabañas* (beachside cabins) and hammocks, which can be rented and hung almost anywhere, offer a lowcost way to spend the night.

Reservoir at the Hacienda San Miguel Regla, near Huasca *(see p295)*

◁ Ornate interior of La Casa de la Marquesa in Querétaro *(see p305)*

Tranquil garden at Cuernavaca's Las Mañanitas hotel *(see p295)*

BOOKING AND PAYING

It is advisable to book rooms in advance if you are traveling during high season. This includes July and August, and the days around Christmas, Easter, and other public holidays *(see p31)*. Mexico has a number of hotel booking services, among them **Utell International** and **Corresponsales de Hoteles**, which provide lists of available quality lodgings all around the country.

Otherwise, it is safest to book through a travel agent or by telephone or fax because the postal service can be unreliable. If a deposit is required you can pay by credit card and ask for a confirmation. In some hotels you may be asked to sign a blank credit card slip

on arrival. Travelers' checks are accepted in most hotels, and many will change or accept foreign currency, but not always at the best rate. Some budget hotels are cash only.

Most hotels have set prices that may vary according to season, facilities, and type of room. Hotels that depend on business travelers often have reduced rates for long stays and weekends. The normal 15% IVA tax is supplemented with a 2% lodging tax. These are not always included in the advertised rate. It is customary to tip bellhops and chambermaids US$1–2. Checkout time is normally around noon.

EFFICIENCY APARTMENTS

Budget-priced, comfortable apartments which all have well-equipped kitchens are available for rent all over the country. Some rental agencies, such as **Condo**

Corner and **Olinalá**, have properties in a range of locations. Others which concentrate on one resort include **Cozumel Vacation Rentals, Se Renta Luxury Villas** (Acapulco), and **Finca Sol** (Puerto Vallarta). At the beach resorts there are also luxury houses and apartment hotels with hotel-standard services. The rates charged inevitably vary according to location and season.

YOUTH HOSTELS

Most of the country's youth hostels are attached to sports centers and have clean, single-sex dormitories. A number of private hostels also exist. **Mundo Joven** and **ASATEJ** are the representatives of Youth Hosteling International in Mexico and will make reservations for hostels all over the country.

Villas with *palapa* (palm-thatched) roofs near Careyes *(see p186)*

DIRECTORY

Choosing a Hotel

The hotels in this guide have been included because of the excellence of their service and facilities, in a range of price categories and a good variety of locations. Many hotels will charge higher rates at Christmas, New Year, and Easter, and lower rates in off seasons (January to March, May to June, and September to November).

PRICE CATEGORIES
The following price ranges are for a standard double room and taxes per night during the high season. Breakfast is not included, unless specified.

$ under $50
$$ $50–$100
$$$ $100–$150
$$$$ $150–$200
$$$$$ over $200

MEXICO CITY

HISTORIC CENTER Hotel Flemming
$
Revillagigedo No. 35, Col. Centro **Tel** *55 10 45 30* **Fax** *55 12 02 84* **Rooms** *80*   **Map** *2 B2*

A marble-floored, modern lobby welcomes visitors to the hotel. The carpeted rooms are well lit and comfortable, with a long desk, coordinated furnishings, and travertine marble bathrooms. Cheery restaurant off the lobby. Good location at the corner of Artículo 123, only three blocks from the Alameda. **www.hotelfleming.com.mx**

HISTORIC CENTER Hotel Isabel
$
Isabel la Católica 63, Col. Centro **Tel** *55 18 12 13* **Fax** *55 21 12 33* **Rooms** *72*   **Map** *2 D3*

A portrait of Spain's Queen Isabel hangs over the refurbished lobby, lending an elegant air to this older downtown budget hotel, a favorite with professors, students, and price-conscious travelers. Eight rooms have shared bath; all are decently, if not fashionably, furnished. Good restaurant and bar. Close to historic sites. **www.hotel-isabel.com.mx**

HISTORIC CENTER Hotel Lepanto
$
Guerrero 90, Col. Buenavista **Tel** *57 03 39 65* **Fax** *55 35 00 70* **Rooms** *100*

The Lepanto's gleaming, marble-floored, spotless lobby bodes well for the quality of the hotel. Modern furnishings in the guest rooms with matching drapes and bedspreads, and marble bathrooms. Separate lobby bar. Five blocks north of the Alameda between Violeta and P. Moreno. **www.hotellepanto.com**

HISTORIC CENTER Gran Hotel Ciudad de México
$$
Av 16 de Septiembre 82, Col. Centro **Tel** *55 10 83 77 00* **Fax** *55 10 83 77 00* **Rooms** *75*   **Map** *4 D2*

A turn-of-the-19th-century hotel, this is known to be the first place in the city where Art Nouveau decoration was used. The restaurant offers Mexican food, and there's also a buffet with international specialties and splendid views from its outside terrace. Just a few steps from Zócalo. **www.granhotelciudaddemexico.com**

HISTORIC CENTER Hotel Catedral
$$
Donceles 95, Col. Centro **Tel** *55 18 52 32* **Fax** *55 12 43 44* **Rooms** *116*   **Map** *2 E1*

Thoroughly modern, this six-story hotel is ideally located near the Museo Templo Mayor and the Zócalo. It has a fine restaurant, nicely furnished rooms, room service, TV, and telephone. Rooms at the rear have a fine view of the Catedral Metropolitana. There are many used book stores along this street. **www.hotelcatedral.com.mx**

HISTORIC CENTER Hotel Gillow
$$
Isabel La Católica 17, Col. Centro **Tel** *55 18 14 40* **Fax** *55 12 20 78* **Rooms** *103*   **Map** *2 E2*

The small lobby of this popular hotel gleams with marble, polished brass, and wood. Rooms are comfortable, furnished in browns and gold, with ample space for luggage. Good restaurant. Excellent historic center location two blocks from the Zócalo at 5 de Mayo. Reserve ahead. **www.hotelgillow.com**

HISTORIC CENTER Hotel Metropol
$$
Luis Moya 39, Col. Centro **Tel** *55 21 49 01* **Fax** *55 12 12 73* **Rooms** *165*   **Map** *2 C2*

The lobby welcomes with the sophistication of a well-run hotel. The stylishly decorated rooms are color-coordinated in grays and pale blue. Bathrooms have purified water from a special tap. Inexpensive buffet breakfast. A convenient two blocks south of the Alameda between Independencia and Artículo 123. **www.hotelmetropol.com.mx**

HISTORIC CENTER Holiday Inn Zócalo
$$$
Avenida 5 de Mayo Nº 61, Col. Centro **Tel** *51 30 51 30* **Fax** *55 21 21 22* **Rooms** *105*   **Map** *2 E2*

This six-story hotel offers all the modern amenities including stylish rooms with dataport connections. The historic site once held Moctezuma's palace, then a residence for the conqueror, Hernán Cortés, and later for the governing viceroys. The roof-top restaurant has views of the Zócalo. **www.hotelescortes.com**

HISTORIC CENTER Best Western Majestic
$$$$
Francisco I. Madero 73, Col. Centro **Tel** *55 21 86 00* **Fax** *55 12 62 62* **Rooms** *84*   **Map** *2 E2*

The lobby, with exquisite use of Talavera tiles, is more impressive than the rooms. Though beautifully cared for and coordinated, the rooms are old-fashioned. Some have windows opening to an interior atrium. Others face Madero and the Zócalo – and experience the rousing 6am flag raising. Rooftop restaurant/bar. **www.hotelmajestic.com.mx**

Key to Symbols *see back cover flap*

REFORMA & CHAPULTEPEC La Casa de la Condesa $$

Plaza Luis Cabrera 16, Col. Roma Sur **Tel** *55 74 31 86* **Fax** *55 74 31 86* **Rooms** *32* **Map** *1 F5*

The five-story Condesa, in a residential area opposite the lovely Plaza Luis Cabrera, offers colorfully furnished rooms. All but six have small kitchens so are ideal for a long-term stay. Some rooms have balconies facing the plaza. Computer dataport in each room. No air conditioning. **www.extendedstaymexico.com**

REFORMA & CHAPULTEPEC Casa González $$

Río Sena 69, Col. Cuauhtémoc **Tel** *55 14 33 02* **Fax** *55 11 07 02* **Rooms** *32* **Map** *1 E3*

The side-by-side residences that make up the Casa Gonzalez offer a homey atmosphere in a residential, garden setting. Each room is unique – simply furnished, with tiled floors and private bathroom. Meals can be arranged in the little dining room. The hotel is within walking distance of the Zona Rosa.

REFORMA & CHAPULTEPEC Hotel Park Villa $$

Gómez Pedraza 68, Col. San Miguel Chapultepec **Tel** *55 15 52 45* **Fax** *55 15 52 45* **Rooms** *43* **Map** *1 F2*

The garden setting of this hotel creates a country feel in the midst of the city. The one-story rooms are all different. The standard, double, and junior suite rooms do not have air conditioning. Lovely garden restaurant open for all meals. Just a block from the Constituyentes side of Chapultepec Park. **www.hotelparkvilla.com.mx**

REFORMA & CHAPULTEPEC María Cristina $$

Río Lerma 31, Col. Cuauhtémoc **Tel** *55 66 96 88* **Fax** *55 66 91 94* **Rooms** *150* **Map** *1 E2*

The Maria Cristina, a nice four-story hotel in a neighborhood setting, has a little garden restaurant and small gift shop. The comfortable rooms have matched furnishings. Only deluxe rooms have air conditioning, but the windows open and fans are available for those rooms without. Reserve ahead. **www.hotelmariacristina.com.mx**

REFORMA & CHAPULTEPEC Polanco $$$

Edgar Allan Poe 8, Col. Polanco **Tel** *52 80 80 82* **Fax** *52 80 80 82* **Rooms** *71* **Map** *1 E3*

In the cosmopolitan Polanco area, this moderately priced hotel offers five floors of rooms, and a fine little restaurant with Italian specialties. Rooms are small, carpeted, and modestly furnished. Internet available. Room service. The lack of air conditioning is no problem when it is cool. Fans are available on request. **www.hotelpolanco.com**

REFORMA & CHAPULTEPEC Sevilla Palace $$$

Paseo de la Reforma 105, Col. Revolución **Tel** *57 05 28 00* **Fax** *57 03 15 21* **Rooms** *413* **Map** *2 A2*

With a soaring lobby, sitting areas, bars, and restaurants, this bustling hotel offers quality and top location. Rooms are large and nicely decorated. The whole city is on view from glass-walled, 23rd-floor bar El Chicote, open 7pm– 12:30am with live entertainment. **www.sevillapalace.com.mx**

REFORMA & CHAPULTEPEC La Casona $$$

Durango 280, Col. Roma **Tel** *52 86 30 01* **Fax** *52 11 08 71* **Rooms** *29* **Map** *1 D5*

A stunningly elegant hotel in a building registered with the National Institute of Fine Arts. Rooms are all different, with gorgeous furnishings and antique accents. Breakfast is included, and set inside a small wall opening in each room. Antique musical instruments decorate public areas. Lovely little restaurant and small bar. **www.hotellacasona.com.mx**

REFORMA & CHAPULTEPEC Galería Plaza $$$$

Hamburgo 195, Col. Juárez **Tel** *52 30 17 17* **Rooms** *434* **Map** *1 D3*

This well-located modern hotel, a block from Reforma and the Independence Monument, greets visitors with a wall of windows fronting the cosmopolitan lobby and bar. Rooms, all with blond wood and attractive textiles, offer two-line phones and dataport. There are two rooms for disabled visitors. **www.galeriaplaza.com.mx**

REFORMA & CHAPULTEPEC Gran Melia México Reforma $$$$

Reforma 1, Col. Tabacalera **Tel** *51 28 50 00* **Fax** *51 28 50 27* **Rooms** *489* **Map** *2 B1*

One of the elegant hotels along Reforma, this offers all the services and amenities of a top hotel, including spa services. The tastefully furnished rooms have high-speed internet access. There is a fine lobby bar, as well as two restaurants. Six long blocks from the Alameda and close to the Monumento a la Revolución. **www.solmelia.com**

REFORMA & CHAPULTEPEC Camino Real $$$$$

Calz Mariano Escobedo 700, Col. Polanco **Tel** *52 63 88 88* **Fax** *52 50 69 35* **Rooms** *714* **Map** *1 B3*

Opened in 1968 as one of the most sophisticated hotels in the city, Camino Real still maintains that rank. Spacious public areas hold renowned works of art plus seven restaurants-bars, two swimming pools, and four tennis courts. The large rooms, all tastefully decorated, have Internet connection. **www.caminoreal.com/mexico_i/main.php**

REFORMA & CHAPULTEPEC Casa Vieja $$$$$

Eugenio Sue 45, Col. Polanco **Tel** *52 82 00 67* **Fax** *52 82 00 61* **Rooms** *10* **Map** *1 E3*

Created from a former two-story home, this all-suite, one-of-a-kind inn showcases the best of Mexico's rich colors, textiles, and furnishings. Each individually created suite comes with kitchen, sauna, hydromassage tub, large-screen TV, fax, and Internet access. Small rooftop restaurant. Continental breakfast included. **www.casavieja.com**

REFORMA & CHAPULTEPEC Condesa df $$$$$

Avenida Veracruz 102, Col. Condesa **Tel** *52 41 26 00* **Fax** *52 41 26 40* **Rooms** *40* **Map** *1 B5*

Among the capital's hip minimalist hotels, this was created from a multi-story 1928 apartment building. Rooms, all themed in white, have stone floors, terrace, flatscreen TV, two-line cordless telephone, DVD player, and iPod. Rooftop sushi bar – near the Parque España in the Condesa area. **www.condesadf.com** or **www.designhotels.com**

REFORMA & CHAPULTEPEC Four Seasons

Paseo de la Reforma 500, Col. Juárez **Tel** *52 30 18 18* **Fax** *52 30 18 08* **Rooms** *240* **Map** *1 C4*

One of the most serene settings for an inner city hotel, the Four Seasons is centered around a large interior garden. The spacious guestrooms, all elegantly furnished, offer Internet access. Full spa with all services. Rooms available for visitors with disabilities. Specialist-led art, architecture, and archeological tours. PlayStation for kids. **www.fourseasons.com**

REFORMA & CHAPULTEPEC Hotel Geneve

Londres 130, Col. Juárez **Tel** *50 80 08 00* **Fax** *50 80 08 31* **Rooms** *261* **Map** *1 E3*

A popular hotel in the Zona Rosa, the Geneve was built in 1907. Thoroughly up-to-date, it offers attractive rooms and a range of amenities, including in-room computer connection. The stained-glass Salon Jardín, beyond the lobby, is a national treasure. A branch of Sanborns is the off-lobby restaurant. **www.hotelgeneve.com.mx**

REFORMA & CHAPULTEPEC Habita

Avenida Presidente Masaryk 201, Col. Polanco **Tel** *52 82 31 00* **Fax** *52 82 31 01* **Rooms** *36*

Modern and so minimalist it is almost retro 1950s. Rooms, all carpeted and with primarily white furnishings, offer platform beds, natural wood bedside table, Eames chairs, flatscreen cable TV, and Internet access. The rooftop tapas bar, "Area", attracts a youthful cosmopolitan crowd. Spa and lap pool. **www.hotelhabita.com**

REFORMA & CHAPULTEPEC Hotel Nikko

Campos Eliseos 204, Col. Polanco **Tel** *52 80 11 11* **Fax** *52 80 91 91* **Rooms** *754* **Map** *1 E3*

The 38-story Japanese-owned Nikko was the first of the status hotels in Polanco, with its attractive Asian overtones, lovely public spaces, spacious rooms, and restaurants. Three tennis courts and a rooftop golf range provide an edge. Two of four restaurants offer Japanese food. High-speed Internet. **www.hotelnikkomexico.com.mx/nikko**

REFORMA & CHAPULTEPEC Hotel W

Campos Eliseos 252, Col. Polanco **Tel** *91 38 18 00* **Fax** *91 38 18 99* **Rooms** *237*

Located in the trendy Polanco neighborhood, this is W's first hotel in Latin America. It mingles modern design with a zealous commitment to comfort. The excellent restaurant, Solea, serves fine seafood with Mexican and Asian influences. There is also a bar and a lounge, as well as a pampering spa. **www.whotels.com**

REFORMA & CHAPULTEPEC JW Marriott

Andrés Bello 69, Col. Polanco **Tel** *59 99 00 00* **Fax** *59 99 00 01* **Rooms** *312* **Map** *1 E3*

This cosmopolitan hotel, with its rose brick and soaring wall of glass, rises 26 stories along Polanco's fashionable hotel row. Large rooms with two-line phone and wireless Internet access. Heated outdoor pool. Full service spa. Two restaurants, one bar, and a gym. **www.marriott.com/property/propertypage/MEXJW**

REFORMA & CHAPULTEPEC María Isabel Sheraton

Avenida Juárez 70, Col. Centro **Tel** *51 30 52 52* **Fax** *51 30 52 55* **Rooms** *457* **Map** *1 D3*

One of the original top hotels in the capital, the 27-story Sheraton still offers all the status draws: central location, fashionable rooms in many price ranges, including the deluxe Tower Suites, good restaurants, lobby bar, stores, and traveler services, such as high speed Internet access. Located at the Diana Circle. **www.sheraton.com.mx**

REFORMA & CHAPULTEPEC Marquis Reforma

Paseo de la Reforma 465, Col. Cuauhtémoc **Tel** *52 29 12 00* **Fax** *52 29 12 12* **Rooms** *209* **Map** *1 C4*

The striking pink stone Art Deco façade stands out on Reforma. Inside, it is all glamour, spaciousness, and service. The rooms, luxuriously furnished in mahogany, come in many configurations, with several choices of pillows, Internet access, and cable TV. Non-smoking rooms available. Full spa. Two restaurants. **www.marquisreforma.com**

REFORMA & CHAPULTEPEC Presidente Inter-Continental

Campos Eliseos 218, Col. Polanco **Tel** *53 27 77 00* **Fax** *53 27 77 30* **Rooms** *659* **Map** *1 E3*

A sophisticated Polanco hotel for 20 years, this offers 42 stories of spacious, nicely decorated rooms with Internet connection. Its six restaurants include Au Pied de Cochon, a popular French venue. Balmoral is an English tea room which also serves meals. Lobby bar with vast tequila selection. **www.intercontinental.com**

FARTHER AFIELD Hotel Aeropuerto

Boulevard Aeropuerto 380, Col. Peñón de los Baños **Tel** *57 85 58 88* **Fax** *57 84 13 29* **Rooms** *52*

A no-frills budget choice opposite the airport. The dimly lit lobby features a clerk enclosed behind glass. The rooms are furnished with all the basics, including TV and bathroom. The hotel is accessible either by taxi or via the pedestrian bridge at the National Arrivals end of the airport. No shuttle service.

FARTHER AFIELD Hotel Riazor

Viaducto Miguel Aleman 297 **Tel** *57 64 90 98* **Fax** *56 54 38 40* **Rooms** *139*

A mile and a half from the airport, the Riazor offers hospitable lodging at bargain prices. The carpeted rooms are nicely furnished. All the services of the better hotels nearer the airport, including sauna, business center, Internet, and cable TV. Round-trip airport shuttle from 5am to midnight at National Arrivals Gate 3. **www.hotelriazor.com.mx**

FARTHER AFIELD Hotel Hilton

International Mexico City Airport, Col. Peñón de los Baños **Tel** *51 33 05 05* **Fax** *51 33 05 00* **Rooms** *129*

The Hilton is accessible from the third level inside the airport terminal at the International Arrival area F1. Elevator also at ground level. The nicely furnished rooms are soundproofed against airport noise and offer cable TV, video games, and dataport. Rooms for disabled guests available. Restaurant open all hours. Bar. **www.hilton.com**

AROUND MEXICO CITY

CHOLULA Club Med Villas Arqueológicas
 $$

2 Poniente 601, Zona Arqueológica **Tel** *(222) 273 79 00* **Fax** *(222) 47 15 08* **Rooms** *44*

With a glorious view of the Tepananca pyramid from the front, and centered around a lovely pool and garden area, this Villa offers peace and tranquility. Rooms have single beds in wall niches. Though within site of the ruins in Cholula, the entrance to them is on the far side of the pyramid from the hotel. **www.villasarquelogicas.com.mx**

CHOLULA La Quinta Luna
$$$$

Calle 3 Sur 702, Centro **Tel** *(222) 247 89 15* **Fax** *(222) 247 8916* **Rooms** *7*

In a beautifully restored elegant colonial mansion dating from the 1700s, this luxury inn is only three blocks from Cholula's main square. The handsomely decorated guest rooms face the inner courtyard. Guests can dine in the former chapel. Extensive library. Beauty and health services by appointment. Parking. **www.laquintaluna.com**

COCOYOC Hacienda Cocoyoc
 $$$

México 95, 32 km (20 miles) E of Cuernavaca **Tel** *(735) 356 22 11* **Fax** *(735) 356 12 12* **Rooms** *286*

Hacienda Cocoyoc, on historic land once belonging to Moctezuma's daughter, is a resort vacation destination. Rooms, all nicely furnished and comfortable, are spread out over 22 garden-filled acres. Three swimming pools and nine-hole golf course on-site. Children's activities on weekends and school vacations. **www.cocoyoc.com.mx**

CUERNAVACA Posada María Cristina
$$$

Benito Juárez 300, Centro **Tel** *(777) 318 69 84* **Fax** *(777) 318 69 84* **Rooms** *20*

A garden oasis on land formerly holding the 16th-century gardens and stables of the Palace of Cortés. The one-story lineup of rooms is connected by a stepped, gently sloping walkway. All are accented with handsome Mexican tiles and colonial-style touches, and light-filled windows. Lovely pool area. Fine restaurant, El Tequila. **www.maria-cristina.com**

CUERNAVACA Hostería las Quintas
$$$$

Boulevard Diaz Ordaz 9, Col. Canta Ranas **Tel** *(777) 362 39 49* **Fax** *(777) 362 39 40* **Rooms** *93*

In a Cuernavaca neighborhood, this hotel features several sections of rooms set among beautifully landscaped gardens. Each section has a feel and décor of its own, all stylishly furnished. Many have balconies or private patios. Superior restaurant. Full service spa with attentive staff. **www.hosterialasquintas.com**

CUERNAVACA Hacienda de Cortés
$$$$$

Plaza Kennedy 90, Atlacomulco **Tel** *(777) 315 88 44* **Fax** *(777) 315 00 35* **Rooms** *23*

In Atlacomulco, a southern suburb of Cuernavaca, what is today a lovely secluded, garden-centered inn was once a sugar hacienda belonging to Hernán Cortes. Brick pathways meander to the spacious one-story rooms. The former sugar grinding room is the hotel's beautiful restaurant. Lovely pool. **www.hotelhaciendadecortes.com**

CUERNAVACA Las Mañanitas
$$$$$

Ricardo Linares 107 **Tel** *(777) 362 00 00* **Fax** *(777) 318 36 72* **Rooms** *32*

One of the most prestigious inns in Cuernavaca, guests choose from five categories of rooms and three sections, all impeccably furnished in a beautiful garden setting. Garden Section rooms are the most luxurious and secluded, most with patios. Breakfast for hotel guests at Las Mañanitas garden restaurant. **www.lasmananitas.com.mx**

HUASCA Hacienda San Miguel Regla
$$$

Huasca de Ocampo **Tel** *(771) 792 01 02* **Fax** *(771) 792 00 54* **Rooms** *142*

This hacienda, in a country setting, was built in the 17th century by silver miner Pedro Romero de Terreros – Count of San Miguel Regla. Plain rooms, with stone floors and fireplaces, are spread over the grounds. All meals included. Organized activities include boating, horseback riding, and hiking to local haciendas. **www.sanmiguelregla.com**

PACHUCA Fiesta Inn
 $$$

Carretera México-Pachuca Km 85.5 Col. Venta Prieta **Tel** *(771) 717 07 00* **Fax** *(771) 717 07 00* **Rooms** *114*

On the highway to Mexico City, and next to the Club de Golf Campestre, this hotel was built for the business traveler but is also ideal for travelers passing through. Rooms are large and nicely furnished in yellow tones with sitting areas and desk. Each has in-room Internet access and coffee pot. Restaurant downstairs. Lobby bar. **www.fiestainn.com**

PUEBLA Hotel Royalty
 $

Portal Hidalgo 8 **Tel** *(222) 242 47 40* **Fax** *(222) 242 47 43* **Rooms** *45*

With a prime location facing the central plaza and cathedral, the four-story Hotel Royalty has been refurbished. The rooms vary in size, but most are small. The hotel's streetside restaurant is perfect for people watching with a drink or a meal. The hotel is within walking distance to Puebla's museums and restaurants. **www.hotelr.com**

PUEBLA Hotel Puebla Plaza
$

5 Poniente 111, Centro Histórico **Tel** *(222) 246 31 75* **Fax** *(222) 242 57 92* **Rooms** *31*

With its handsome blue façade and wrought-iron balconies facing the street, the Puebla Plaza fills a much-needed slot for reasonably priced and comfortable downtown lodging. The three stories of carpeted rooms are small, with natural-finish pine furniture, cable TV, and telephone. Situated near the cathedral. **www.hotelpueblaplaza.com.mx**

PUEBLA Hotel Colonial

Calle 4 Sur 105 **Tel** *(222) 246 46 12* **Fax** *(222) 246 08 18* **Rooms** *67*

This popular hotel began as a Jesuit monestary in the 17th century. With colonial arches, Puebla Talavera tiles, yellow walls, and wrought-iron touches, it is very appealing. Rooms have hardwood floors, and attractive but spare furnishings. The popular first-floor restaurant serves *mole de Puebla* daily. Wireless Internet access. **www.colonial.com.mx**

PUEBLA Posada San Pedro
$$

Avenida 2 Oriente 202 **Tel** *(222) 246 50 77* **Fax** *(222) 246 53 76* **Rooms** *80*

A family friendly hotel, in a 17th-century building, the heated pool is in the first-floor atrium, and there are a few kid-friendly activity options. Rooms, all with hardwood floors, and tiled baths are large and have tall ceilings. Small lobby bar. Two blocks from the main plaza. Free parking. **www.hotelposadasanpedro.com.mx**

PUEBLA Camino Real
$$$

7 Poniente 105, Centro Historico **Tel** *(222) 229 09 09* **Fax** *(222) 232 92 51* **Rooms** *84*

Built as the Convento de la Limpia Concepción in the 15th century, and occupied until 1861, this luxury hotel is both an architectural and an artistic gem. The spacious rooms all have antiques and luxurious bed coverings. Most have remnants of original frescos. Lobby bar with live music at weekends. **www.caminoreal.com/puebla**

PUEBLA Mesón Sacristía

Calle 6 Sur 304, Callejon de los Sapos **Tel** *(222) 242 35 54* **Rooms** *8*

Created from a 18th-century mansion, the rooms, all on the second floor, overlook the patio holding the restaurant-bar area. All are large and stylishly furnished, with antiques that are for sale. Ask for a room facing the street; music may drift up from the bar (but it stops around 11pm). **www.mexicoboutiquehotels.com/mesonsacristia**

PUEBLA Holiday Inn Centro Histórico
 $$$$

Avenida 2 Oriente 211 **Tel** *(222) 223 66 00* **Fax** *(222) 242 11 76* **Rooms** *80*

Formerly the Hotel Palacio San Leonardo, in a 120-year-old building, the lobby features Asian carpets, antiques, and a beautiful stained-glass ceiling. The rooms, though small, are brightly decorated. The rooftop pool area offers panoramic city views. Lobby bar. High-speed Internet access. **www.holidayinn.com/pueblacentro**

TAXCO Los Arcos

Juan Ruiz de Alarcón 4 **Tel** *(762) 622 18 36* **Fax** *(762) 622 79 82* **Rooms** *21*

The beautiful central patio, surrounded by arches, is probably all that is left of the 17th-century monastery that once stood here. Rooms are scattered over several levels and a labyrinth of stairways. All have *saltillo* tile floors and colonial-style furniture. Two blocks from the Zócalo but away from the traffic noise. **www.hotellosarcos.net**

TAXCO Posada Emilia Castillo
$

Juan Ruiz de Alarcón 7 **Tel** *(762) 622 13 96* **Fax** *(762) 622 13 96* **Rooms** *15*

This small hotel is so nicely furnished with exquisite carved wood, lots of plants, and colorful touches that it is a delight to stay here. Opposite the Hotel Los Arcos, it shares that same, relatively quiet zone but it is only two blocks to the Zócalo. Staff are very helpful. Named after one of Taxco's best silversmiths. **www.hotelemiliacastillo.com**

TAXCO Santa Prisca

Cenaobscuras 1 **Tel** *(762) 622 00 80* **Fax** *(762) 622 29 38* **Rooms** *31*

Centrally located on the Plaza San Juan, the Santa Prisca is one of the most charming old hotels in Taxco, centered around a patio. The immaculately kept rooms are small, but comfortable, with matching wooden furniture from a bygone era. Excellent restaurant. Top-floor library with views. **htl_staprisca@yahoo.com**

TAXCO Hotel Victoria
$$

Carlos J. Nibbi 5 **Tel** *(762) 622 02 10 or 01800 008 2920 (toll free)* **Fax** *(762) 622 00 10* **Rooms** *63*

Staying here is a romantic step back in time. The beautifully preserved wooden furniture is original from the 1930s, when this hotel was the fashionable place to stay. The preserved old-time feel and the magnificent views from most rooms are part of the charm of staying at this hotel on a hill overlooking Taxco. Free parking. **www.victoriataxco.com**

TAXCO Loma Linda
 $$

Avenida de los Plateros No. 52 **Tel** *(762) 622 02 06* **Rooms** *72*

A good choice for those driving, since it is on the highway entering Taxco from Cuernavaca, but not outside of town. Motel-like, parking is free in front of each room. The comfortable rooms have tile floors and carved natural pine colonial-style furniture. Balcony or patio. Children's play area. **www.hotellomalinda.com**

TAXCO Best Western Taxco
 $$$

Carlos J. Nibbi 2/Plazuela de San Juan **Tel** *(762) 627 61 94* **Fax** *(762) 622 08 60* **Rooms** *23*

One of several Best Western hotels in Mexico, this establishment features a typically colonial exterior and modern decor throughout. It offers comfortable accommodation near several of the main attractions in town. Parking is available. **www.bestwesterntaxco.com**

TAXCO Posada de la Misión
 $$$$

Cerro de la Misión No.32 **Tel** *(762) 622 00 63* **Fax** *(762) 622 21 98* **Rooms** *118*

Built in 1940, this inn has been modernized while retaining its popular restaurant and the famous poolside mural by Juan O'Gorman. Rooms in two sections – the old section has comfortable, small, and plainly furnished rooms; the new multi-story section offers large rooms with more luxury details. **www.posadamision.com**

Key to Price Guide *see p292* **Key to Symbols** *see back cover flap*

TEOTIHUACÁN Villas Arqueológicas $$

Periférico Sur N/N, Zona Arqueológico **Tel** *(583) 69 020* **Fax** *(222) 247 1508* **Rooms** *43*

Near the main entrance to the Teotihuacan ruins, this Villa is centered around a lovely pool and garden area. It offers a refreshing place to land before or after a day at the ruins. The comfortably furnished rooms have single beds in wall niches. **www.villasarquelogicas.com.mx**

TEPOZTLÁN Posada el Tepozteco $$$$$

Paraíso 3, Barrio San Miguel **Tel** *(739) 395 00 10* **Fax** *(739) 395 03 23* **Rooms** *22*

This four-story inn offers large rooms with tile floors, Mexican loomed rugs, and wrought-iron Mexican furniture. All except standard rooms have balconies with grand views. This posada is close to Tepoztlán's main plaza, market, and restaurants. Has its own restaurant with sophisticated menu. **www.posadadeltepozteco.com**

TEQUESQUITENGO Hacienda Vista Hermosa $$$$

KM 7 Carretera Alpuyeca-Tequesquitengo, Puente de Ixtla **Tel** *(734) 345 53 62* **Rooms** *105*

This countryside hacienda, owned by the son of Hernán Cortés, dates from 1615. It exudes history at every turn, with centuries-old rock walls, turrets, wrought-iron balconies, and a swimming pool watered by the remains of an aqueduct. Huge rooms with antiques. Restaurant in the former cane grinding room. **www.haciendavistahermosa.com.mx**

TLAXCALA Hotel Alifer $

Morelos No. 11 **Tel** *(246) 462 56 78* **Fax** *(246) 466 00 22* **Rooms** *40*

The Hotel Alifer is a good budget choice close to the main plaza and within walking distance of restaurants and museums. The two stories of rooms are clean, with carpeted floor, tile bathrooms, comfortable beds, and good lighting. The restaurant is only passable – better ones can be found nearby. Parking is free. **www.hotelalifer.com.mx**

TLAXCALA Posada San Francisco $$

Plaza de la Constitución 17 **Tel** *(246) 462 60 22* **Fax** *(246) 466 00 22* **Rooms** *68*

Fashioned from an early 1900s building, the best city-center hotel is ideally positioned across from the main plaza. On two stories, the rooms are all different and nicely furnished. All include heat, TV, and telephone. Small café on the first floor and fine dining on the second floor. Two tennis courts. Valet parking. **www.posadasanfrancisco.com**

TOLUCA Hotel Colonial $

Avenida Hidalgo Oriente 103 **Tel** *(722) 215 97 00* **Fax** *(722) 214 70 66* **Rooms** *33*

This decades-old standby in downtown Toluca is charming with its old-fashioned but well-kept furnishings. Rooms are moderately sized with tall ceilings, hardwood or carpeted floors, and armoires. Rooms on the front, with doors opening to little balconies, will be noisy. Close to all the museums and downtown restaurants.

TULA Hotel Sharon $

Callejón de la Cruz 1, Boulevard Tula-Iturbe No. 1 **Tel** *(773) 732 09 76* **Rooms** *120*

Located on Tula's main square, the seven-story Sharon is the most imposing building and the nicest hotel. Rooms are all well furnished, with TV, telephone, and tiled bathrooms. The restaurant, open for all meals, will pack a sack lunch. From here the archeological site is approximately a 15- to 20-minute walk. **www.hotelsharon.com.mx**

VALLE DE BRAVO Hotel Los Arcos $$

Bocanegra 310, Centro **Tel** *(726) 262 00 42* **Rooms** *24*

Only four blocks from the main square and close to the market, restaurants, and stores. The two buildings of two- and three-story rooms, in an L shape, face the pool and have mountain views. Rooms, most with fireplaces, are nicely furnished and come with one or two double beds and cable TV. Some rooms have balconies.

VALLE DE BRAVO Avándaro Golf & Spa Resort $$$$

Vega del Río, Fracc. Avándaro **Tel** *(726) 266 03 70* **Fax** *(726) 266 01 22* **Rooms** *74*

Set in a beautiful forested area four miles from Valle de Bravo, this 296-acre resort offers a beautiful 18-hole golf course and a top quality destination spa. Two choices of rooms types – cabaña and villas. The latter are luxurious. All have fireplaces. Seven tennis courts. Miniature golf. Free parking. **www.hotelavandaro.com.mx**

NORTHERN MEXICO

ALAMOS Hacienda de los Santos $$$$$

Molina 8 **Tel** *(647) 428 02 22* **Fax** *(647) 428 03 67* **Rooms** *27*

Three colonial-era mansions create this luxurious inn in the remote village of Alamos. Two blocks from the plaza, the inn and all rooms exude the sumptuous luxury of today, with the refined antiques, art, and architecture of centuries ago. Fireplace and TV with DVD/VCR in all rooms. Full spa on site. Breakfast included. **www.haciendadelossantos.com**

BAHÍA DE LOS ANGELES Villa Vitta $$

Bahía de los Angeles **Tel** *(664) 686 11 52 in Tijuana* **Fax** *(664) 682 80 20 in Tijuana* **Rooms** *40*

In a place with few amenities, it is a comfort to find the Villa Vitta. Its main draw is facilitating fishing excursions. To accommodate all guests they have both a hotel and an RV site with hookups. Rooms are very nice with tile floors, matching furnishings, and murals of Baja scenes on the walls. **www.villavitta.com**

BATOPILAS Hotel Juanita   ⑤

Colonia Centro   **Tel** *(649) 456 90 43*   **Rooms** *10*

These are basic but very comfortable rooms near the main plaza. Very reasonably priced for the location, and impeccably clean. There's a lovely interior courtyard and gardens overlooking the river, with bougainvillea everywhere. Charming and low key, there are just ten rooms, all with private baths.

BATOPILAS Hacienda Riverside Lodge   🍽   ⑤⑤⑤

Batopilas   **Tel** *(635) 456 00 36 (Creel)*   **Rooms** *15*

This mansion in the heart of Batopilas is over 100 years old. Comfortably furnished rooms are filled with antiques, with tile or hardwood floors and private bathrooms. Restaurants nearby. Guided hikes available. Advance reservations required, as well as a two-night minimum stay. **www.sierratrail.com**

CABO SAN LUCAS Casa Rafael   🍽🛏📋   ⑤⑤

Calle Medano at Camino el Pescador   **Tel** *(624) 143 07 39*   **Fax** *(624) 143 16 79*   **Rooms** *10*

The landscaped turquoise house on the hill is a boutique hotel and fine-dining restaurant. The 10 rooms are all different, have tile floors, and a French frilly style with ruffled bedspreads and white furniture. Nice sun deck and swimming pool. Excursions and wedding packages available. **www.allaboutcabo.com/casarafaels.htm**

CABO SAN LUCAS Club Cabo Inn   🅿🛏📋🏊   ⑤⑤

Km. 3, Old road to San José del Cabo   **Tel** *(624) 143 33 48*   **Fax** *(624) 143 33 48*   **Rooms** *10*

A ten-room inn with camping sites 2 miles from central Cabo San Lucas. The comfortably outfitted rooms all have king-or queen-size beds, equipped kitchens, and patios. Five minute walk to the beach. Barbeque pits and fish cleaning area. Internet access available. Free parking. **www.clubcabo.com**

CABO SAN LUCAS Siesta Suites   🅿🍽📋   ⑤⑤

Calle Emiliano Zapata betw. Guerrero & Hidalgo   **Tel** *(624) 143 27 73*   **Fax** *(624) 143 27 73*   **Rooms** *20*

Painted an attractive shade of yellow and built around a beautiful little pool, this is a four-story gem of comfort and hospitality Fifteen 'rooms' are suites with separate bedroom and full kitchens. Five are standard rooms with refrigerator. All are colorfully decorated. Pool area pleasantly furnished. **www.cabosiestasuites.com**

CABO SAN LUCAS The Bungalows   🏊📋   ⑤⑤⑤

Boulevard Miguel Angel Herrera   **Tel** *(624) 143 50 35*   **Rooms** *16*

This hospitable inn offers a combination of three-stories of one-bedroom suites, and two-bedroom garden and patio bungalows. The spotlessly clean, cheerful rooms are tastefully outfitted in Mexican-style wood and leather, with kitchen and living area. All centered around a lovely palm lined pool. Gourmet breakfast daily. **www.cabobungalows.com**

CABO SAN LUCAS Casa del Mar Beach, Golf & Spa Resort   🍽🏊🍽📋   ⑤⑤⑤⑤⑤

Carretera Transpeninsular km 19.5   **Tel** *(624) 14 5 77 11*   **Fax** *(624) 14 5 77 00*   **Rooms** *31*

The luxury, two-story Casa del Mar nestles within lushly landscaped palm-dotted grounds. The elegantly outfitted rooms have marble floors, light-toned wicker and rush furniture, and a Jacuzzi bath. Full or partial ocean views and balcony or terrace. Full spa. Close to Cabo Real Golf Course. **www.casadelmarloscabosmexico.com**

CABO SAN LUCAS One & Only Palmilla   🍽🏊🍽📋   ⑤⑤⑤⑤⑤

Corredor Turístico km 7.5   **Tel** *(624) 146 70 00*   **Fax** *(624) 144 51 00*   **Rooms** *172*

One of the most prestigious and exquisite resorts in Mexico, set amid abundant tropical gardens against a backdrop of the Sea of Cortez. The comfortable guestrooms are all luxuriously decorated. All have flat-screen TV with DVD/CD player and voice and data lines. Full service spa. 27-hole golf course adjacent. **www.oneandonlyresorts.com**

CABO SAN LUCAS Pueblo Bonito Rosé   🍽🏊📋   ⑤⑤⑤⑤⑤

Playa El Médano   **Tel** *(624) 142 98 98*   **Fax** *(624) 143 5972*   **Rooms** *260*

A luxury, all-suite hotel built around a large, gorgeous palm-lined pool facing the beach. The beautifully furnished suites have tile floors, sitting area, terrace or balcony, fully equipped kitchens, TV and telephone. Full service spa on the property. Two restaurants. **www.pueblobonito.com**

CABO SAN LUCAS Sheraton Hacienda del Mar   ⑤⑤⑤⑤⑤

Corredor Turístico km 10   **Tel** *(624) 145 80 00*   **Fax** *(624) 145 80 02*   **Rooms** *270*

Looking like a perfect Mexican village, immaculately painted and landscaped. Rooms, in a horseshoe around a large pool facing the beach, are exquisitely decorated in cream and terra-cotta. All rooms have Jacuzzis and Internet access. Reserve for the kid's club. Full service spa. 7 miles to Cabo San Lucas. **www.sheratonloscabos.com/index.php**

CABO SAN LUCAS Solmar Suites   ⑤⑤⑤⑤⑤

Avenida Solmar 1   **Tel** *(624) 146 77 00*   **Fax** *(624) 143 04 10*   **Rooms** *190*

This all-suite hotel is perched on a secluded beach where the Sea of Cortéz meets the Pacific Ocean. The suites, with views, all have tile floors and stylishly coordinated furnishings. Many have kitchenettes. One tennis court. Three pools. Private fishing fleet. Nearby restaurants and one mile to Cabo. **www.solmar.com/suites**

CABO SAN LUCAS Las Ventanas al Paraíso   🍽🏊🍽📋   ⑤⑤⑤⑤⑤

Corredor Turístico km 19.5   **Tel** *(624) 144 28 00*   **Fax** *(624) 144 28 01*   **Rooms** *71*

Opened 1997, this all-suite hotel exudes elegance. The exterior is Mediterranean, and the rooms offer impeccably selected Mexican furnishings. All rooms have terraces, TV, dual-line phone, CD player, VCR and DVD. Two tennis courts and three golf courses at hand. Full service spa. Private yacht excursions organized. **www.lasventanas.com**

Key to Price Guide *see p292*   **Key to Symbols** *see back cover flap*

CHIHUAHUA Quality Inn San Francisco

Calle Victoria 409 **Tel** *(614) 439 90 00* **Fax** *(614) 415 35 38* **Rooms** *131*

Ideally situated downtown to facilitate both business travelers and tourists. Guestrooms are carpeted and stylishly outfitted with light-hued wood furniture, including a writing desk and small sitting area. Rooms are equipped with Internet access and voice mail. Heated in winter. **www.qualityinnchihuahua.com**

CIUDAD CUAUHTEMOC Tarahumara Inn

Allende 373 **Tel** *(625) 581 19 19* **Fax** *(625) 581 19 19* **Rooms** *61*

The modern, colonial-style two-story, motel-like Tarahumara Inn, stands out with its sienna colored walls. Those driving can park at the guestroom door. The carpeted rooms are themed around southwest colors and come in many bed configurations. Most have a small writing table and chairs. **www.tarahumarainn.com**

CREEL Motel Cascada Inn

Adolfo López Mateos No. 49 **Tel** *(635) 456 02 53* **Fax** *(635) 456 01 51* **Rooms** *33*

A fine addition to Creel's hotel lineup. Motel-like, with two stories of rooms, and parking in front, Cascada Inn is also one of the best. Rooms are plainly but comfortably furnished. The restaurant, with cloth-clad tables, serves all meals. The heated pool is inside a nice enclosure. Cybercafe on site. **www.motelcascadainn.com**

CREEL Parador de la Montaña

Avenida López Mateos s/n **Tel** *(635) 456 00 23* **Fax** *(635) 456 00 85* **Rooms** *50*

Once the only nice hotel in Creel, the Parador has been serving canyon guests for decades. Rooms are comfortable, with one or two double beds, tile floors, rustic furniture, TV, and nice tiled bathrooms. The hotel also organizes horseback riding tours. Hotel parking available. **www.hotelparadorcreel.com**

CREEL Copper Canyon Sierra Lodges

Creel **Fax** *(635) 456 00 36 (Creel)* **Rooms** *18*

A few miles outside Creel, deep into a Copper Canyon world, the lineup of immaculately kept log cabins with inter-connected porch is a welcome sight. Each comfortably furnished cabin has a log fire, kerosene lamp, and private bath. Meals (included) are taken in the cozy dining room. No electricity or telephone. Guided hiking. **www.sierratrail.com**

DURANGO Gobernador

20 de Noviembre Oriente 257 **Tel** *(618) 813 19 19* **Fax** *(618) 811 14 22* **Rooms** *99*

A half mile from Durango's central square, this is one of the city's best places to stay. The carpeted rooms, all furnished in colonial style, feature TV, telephone, and tiled bathrooms. The elegant restaurant is one of the best in the downtown area. It is possible to make hunting and sightseeing arrangements here. **www.hotelgobernador.com.mx**

EL DIVISADERO Divisadero-Barrancas

Mirador 4516, Residencial Campestre **Tel** *(614) 415 11 99* **Fax** *(614) 415 65 75* **Rooms** *52*

The original hotel in the canyon still has the most convenient and spectacular views. It is just a few steps from the train stop. The log exterior rooms are all nicely decorated, each with its own fireplace. Some have balconies over-looking the canyon. The good restaurant also has canyon views. Popular with group tours. **www.hoteldivisadero.com**

EL DIVISADERO Mansión Tarahumara

El Divisadero **Tel** *(635) 578 30 30* **Fax** *(614) 416 54 44* **Rooms** *59*

This hospitable inn offers rock-walled cabins, with nice pine furniture, gas heaters, and fireplaces. From every vantage point are lovely views. The restaurant, in a castle, has a huge picture window with forest and train views. Wonderful food. Evening guitarist. Pool, sauna, table game area. Hikes. Meals included. **www.mansiontarahumara.com.mx**

ENSENADA Baja Inn Hotel Cortés

Avenida López Mateos 1089 **Tel** *(646) 178 23 07* **Fax** *(646) 178 39 04* **Rooms** *82*

Comfortable hotel with a pale peach colonial-style façade embellished with ornate wrought-iron window grills. Two stories of rooms facing a nice little pool. Courtesy coffee and newspaper in the lobby. In the heart of Ensenada's shopping district and a block and a half from the boardwalk and pier. Free secure parking. **www.bajainn.com**

ENSENADA Estero Beach Hotel

Playa del Estero, Ejido Citapultepec **Tel** *(646) 176 62 25* **Fax** *(646) 176 69 25* **Rooms** *105*

A comfortable beachfront hotel on its own estuary. Landscaped grounds with lovely palms dot the grounds and freeform pool. Most of the tastefully furnished rooms have balcony or terrace, with water views. Three tennis courts. Great sunset viewing from this location. **www.hotelesterobeach.com**

GUERRERO NEGRO Malarrimo

Emiliano Zapata S/N **Tel** *(615) 157 02 50* **Fax** *(615) 157 01 00* **Rooms** *18*

At the entrance to Guerrero Negro, this cluster of plain cabañas is readily visible. Rooms are clean and comfortable and have TV and coffeemakers. RV spaces available. This is the place to arrange whale watching trips, fishing, and cave excursions, and more. Excellent seafood restaurant and bar. Lots of helpful information. **www.malarrimo.com**

HERMOSILLO Araiza Hermosillo

Boulevard Franco E. Kino 353, Col. Lomas Piti **Tel** *(662) 210 27 17* **Fax** *(662) 210 45 41* **Rooms** *156*

A lovely four-story, nicely landscaped hotel aimed at the business traveler, but perfect too for vacationers. Rooms are furnished with lovely mahogany furniture and handsome bedspreads. Several rooms with disabled access. Wireless Internet access. The lively cafeteria-style restaurant is open long hours. **www.araizahoteles.com**

HIDALGO DE PARRAL Hotel Acosta

Augustín Barbachano 3 **Tel** *(627) 522 02 21* **Fax** *(627) 522 06 57* **Rooms** *26*

Near the Plaza de Armas (the central plaza), the three-story Acosta is a family-owned and operated budget-priced hotel. Rooms are clean and comfortable, all with bath and hot water and one or two beds. The rooftop terrace offers a panoramic view of the whole town and is special at sunset.

LA PAZ La Concha Beach Resort

Kilometro 5, Carretera a Pichilingue **Tel** *(612) 121 63 44* **Fax** *(612) 121 62 29* **Rooms** *113*

Secluded on its own beach, near the marina and on the edge of La Paz proper. A lovely palm shaded pool anchors the property, edged with tropical plants. Decorated in cool tropical colors, the rooms, all with ocean view, have mahagony-toned furniture, balcony, and refrigerator. Fully equipped water sports facility. **www.laconcha.com**

LA PAZ La Perla

Álvaro Obregón 1570 **Tel** *(612) 122 07 77* **Fax** *(612) 125 53 63* **Rooms** *109*

In the heart of La Paz, fronting the bay, La Perla's location is ideal. Within its yellow-gold walls and semi colonial-style architecture are comfortable rooms. Each has off-white tile floors, finished natural pine furniture, pretty seashell themed bedspreads, and a mini refrigerator. Heated pool. **www.hotelperlabaja.com**

LA PAZ Los Arcos

Avenida Álvaro Obregón 498 **Tel** *(612) 122 27 44* **Rooms** *130*

Tropical plants, bougainvillea, and towering Indian Laurel trees form a tranquil oasis. Three stories of spacious rooms, with white wicker furniture and floral bedspreads, all have sitting areas and balcony. At the back is a charming group of thatched-roof bungalows with private garden and pool. **www.losarcos.com**

LORETO Oasis Loreto

Corner López Mateos and Baja California **Tel** *(613) 135 01 12* **Fax** *(613) 135 07 95* **Rooms** *40*

A tropical oasis on the beach with meandering walkways lined with palms and tropical vegetation. The clean, comfortable, and spacious rooms are simply furnished and have either a patio or private balcony. Heated pool. Fishing and nature excursions arranged. 18-hole golf nearby. Meal plans available. **www.hoteloasis.com**

LORETO Posada de las Flores

Salvatierra corner of Madero **Tel** *(613) 135 11 62* **Fax** *(613) 135 10 19* **Rooms** *15*

This refined boutique hotel faces Loreto's main square. Exquisitely adorned in antiques, carefully chosen Mexican tiles, beautiful fabrics and textiles, this is a top hotel. Wakeup comes with coffee and pastries. Full breakfast included. Rooftop terrace restaurant with ocean view. Free shuttle to golf and tennis. **www.posadadelasflores.com**

MAZATLÁN Hotel Playa Mazatlán

Avenida Playa Gaviotas 202 **Tel** *(669) 989 05 55* **Fax** *(669) 914 03 66* **Rooms** *418*

Mazatlán's first beachfront hotel opened in 1955 and remains highly rated. Beautiful mature landscaping with palms and gardens. Rooms, all with handsome tile floors, are spacious, nicely furnished, and have balconies. Wheelchair accessible rooms. Popular *Fiesta Mexicana* buffet with entertainment by the beach. **www.playamazatlan.com.mx**

MAZATLÁN Costa de Oro Beach Hotel

Avenida Camarón Sabalo 710 **Tel** *(669) 913 53 44* **Fax** *(669) 914 42 09* **Rooms** *290*

A full-service resort, with four sections of rooms from lowrise to multi-story, on a wide swath of beach and a prime location in the Zona Dorada. Cool white tile floors are used in all rooms against white walls and pastel floral bedspreads. Some of the suites have full kitchens; all have cable tv. Three tennis courts. **www.costaoro.com**

MAZATLÁN Pueblo Bonito

Avenida Camarón Sabalo 2121 **Tel** *(669) 989 8900* **Fax** *(669) 914 1723* **Rooms** *249*

A beautiful all-suite resort with a wide beach on Playa Sabalo, and a backdrop of lush, mature gardens. Refined, stylish, and comfortable, all the well-arranged and immaculate suites have a kitchen or kitchenette, comfortable sitting areas, and balconies. Good for nearby shopping and dining. **www.pueblobonito-mazatlan.com**

MONTERREY Crowne Plaza

Avenida Constitución Oriente 300 **Tel** *(818) 319 60 00* **Fax** *(818) 344 30 07* **Rooms** *413*

An attractive, modern, 18-story hotel, with soaring lobby, several restaurants, and all the amenities for business and vacationing travelers. The stylishly furnished and carpeted rooms all have dual-line phone, TV, Internet connection, and coffeemaker. Children's activities during Sunday brunch. Heated indoor pool. **www.ichotelsgroup.com**

MONTERREY Gran Hotel Ancira

Hidalgo and Escobedo **Tel** *(818) 150 70 00* **Fax** *(818) 345 11 21* **Rooms** *267*

This luxury hotel has a magnificent French inspired façade. Built in the early 1900s in the heart of downtown Monterrey, it was completely renovated in 2009. From the elegant lobby bar to the refined rooms, it remains a top hotel. Rooms offer sitting area, dual-line phones, and Internet access. **www.hotel-ancira.com**

MULEGE Las Casitas

Madero 50 **Tel** *(615) 152 30 23* **Rooms** *5*

The hotel portion of Las Casitas is found behind the popular restaurant by the same name. The clean guestrooms are simply but colorfully furnished and include pleasant Mexican touches. All have tile floors and bathrooms, plus wireless Internet. Noise from the restaurant may drift over, but it is not obtrusive. **www.santarosaliacasitas.com**

MULEGE Serenidad

El Cacheno **Tel** *(615) 153 05 30* **Fax** *(615) 153 03 11* **Rooms** *50*

Located 2 miles south of Mulege, the cluster of accommodations includes rooms, cottages, new villas, and RV hookups. The standard rooms are decorated in Mexican style and are comfortable. Villas are more luxurious. Wheelchair access. Famous for its lively Friday night pig roast. **www.hotelserenidad.com**

NUEVO CASAS GRANDES Hotel Piñón

Benito Juárez 605 **Tel** *(636) 694 06 55* **Fax** *(636) 694 17 05* **Rooms** *55*

Offering reliable comfort, the Piñon is centrally located near the cathedral, and is also only six miles from the ruins of Paquimé. Rooms are pleasantly comfortable with matching furniture, TV, and telephone. There's an interesting display of artifacts from Paquimé in the lobby. Free parking. **www.chihuahua-online.com/hotelpinon**

SALTILLO Camino Real

Boulevard Los Fundadores 2000 **Tel** *(844) 438 00 00* **Fax** *(844) 438 00 07* **Rooms** *164*

This modern Real is set on 12 garden-filled acres on the outskirts of the city. Each tastefully arranged room is spacious, and has Internet connection. There are two tennis courts lit for night play and a putting green. Fully equipped children's playground. Ten minutes to central Saltillo. **www.caminoreal.com/saltillo**

SAN IGNACIO La Pinta

San Ignacio **Tel** *(615) 154 03 00* **Rooms** *28*

Like San Ignacio itself, La Pinta is shrouded in palm trees. The white, one-story, colonial-style hotel with its palm backdrop is a haven in the desert. Rooms, linked by a covered tiled walkway, are all pleasantly furnished and embellished with hand stenciling. All have heaters. **www.lapintahotels.com/SanIgnacio**

SAN JOSÉ DEL CABO El Delfín Blanco

Calle Delfines, Pueblo la Playa **Tel** *(624) 142 12 12* **Fax** *(624) 142 11 99* **Rooms** *17*

In a cool, shaded setting near the plaza, this two-story budget-priced inn offers charm and comfort. Outside, colorful hammocks hang here and there. There is a well-equipped communal kitchen. Around the pool and gardens are comfortable tables and chairs. Large, tile-floored rooms are simply furnished. **www.eldelfinblanco.net**

SAN JOSÉ DEL CABO El Encanto Inn

Calle Morelos 133 **Tel** *(624) 142 03 88* **Fax** *(624) 142 46 20* **Rooms** *28*

In the heart of the village, within walking distance to shopping and restaurants is this lovely yellow colonial-style inn. Set amidst gardens and dripping with purple bougainvillea, guest rooms are in the garden or pool section. All are tastefully furnished in Mexican style with rugs, local textiles, and hand-stenciled wall designs. **www.elencantoinn.com**

SAN JOSÉ DEL CABO La Playita

Pueblo la Playa **Tel** *(624) 142 41 66* **Fax** *(624) 142 41 66* **Rooms** *24*

Two miles from San José, Pueblo La Playa holds this tidy little white stucco hotel and its two stories of rooms. Guest-quarters, all of which face the small pool, are nicely furnished, clean, and comfortable with cable TV and bathroom. Local fishermen are for hire and a local restaurant will prepare your catch. **laplayitahotel@prodigy.net.mx**

SAN JOSÉ DEL CABO Tropicana Inn

Boulevard Mijares 30 **Tel** *(624) 142 09 07* **Rooms** *40*

Set around the lovely pool behind the Tropicana Inn restaurant, this is a very comfortable hotel. The three stories of rooms are comfortably furnished and have small refrigerator, cable TV, and coffee maker. Suites are more elegant, including a complete authentic carved log *troje* (cabin) from Michoacan. **www.tropicanainn.com.mx**

SAN JOSÉ DEL CABO Casa Natalia

Boulevard Mijares No. 4 **Tel** *(624) 142 51 00* **Fax** *(624) 142 51 10* **Rooms** *16*

This is a visually appealing, three-story boutique hotel. Many details enhance the look, from carved wood supports and locally hand-crafted furniture to colorful fabrics and folk art. Individually decorated rooms have large checkered floors and a retro look embellished with bright colors. Breakfast included. **www.casanatalia.com**

SAN JOSÉ DEL CABO Hotel Riu Palace

Camino Viejo a San José **Tel** *(624) 146 71 60* **Fax** *(624) 146 71 61* **Rooms** *642*

The size of this all-inclusive luxury hotel means that intimacy is not its strongest point, but the staggering number of activities, amenities, and features make it a very popular choice, especially for families and small groups. It's located right on the beach. **www.riu.com**

SAN JOSÉ DEL CABO Westin Resort & Spa

Carretera Transpeninsular km 22.5 **Tel** *(624) 142 90 00* **Fax** *(624) 142 9050* **Rooms** *243*

This huge curved resort set against the aquamarine Sea of Cortez has a beautiful location. This is a full-service facility suitable for families, singles, or couples. Enormous public spaces and wide beach. Large, tastefully furnished, marble-floored rooms with balconies. Full spa on site. **www.westin.com**

SANTA ROSALÍA El Morro

Highway 1, km 1.5 **Tel** *(615) 152 04 14* **Fax** *(615) 152 0414* **Rooms** *40*

A mile south of Santa Rosalia, El Morro sits on a cliff with stunning views of the Sea of Cortez. The one-story rooms are simply furnished and have two double beds and sliding doors to the patio. All are linked by a covered walkway lined with tropical vegetation. Some have ocean views.

SANTA ROSALIA Hotel Francés

Calle Jean Michel Cousteau **Tel** *(615) 152 20 52* **Fax** *(615) 152 2052* **Rooms** *17*

This fancy 1886 hotel was built during Santa Rosalia's mining heyday in elegant French-colonial style, and is now a national monument. Though faded from its glory days, there are enough antique furnishings, a wide wraparound porch, large rooms, hardwood floors, and tall ceilings to still experience the long-ago elegance. Pool and patio.

TIJUANA El Conquistador

Boulevard Agua Caliente 1777 **Tel** *(664) 681 79 55* **Fax** *(664) 686 22 51* **Rooms** *105*

Opposite the Tijuana Country Club, the motel-like Conquistador's white façade is set back from the street. A drive-under overhang creates privacy. The two stories of rooms are carpeted, have floral bedspreads, white French provincial-style furniture, ample bedside lighting, and small table and chairs. **www.hotelconquistador-tij.com**

THE COLONIAL HEARTLAND

AGUASCALIENTES Calinda Hotel Francia

Avenida Francisco I. Madero 113 **Tel** *(449) 918 73 00* **Fax** *(449) 915 73 17* **Rooms** *74*

The six-story Francia, built in 1917, remains the choice for those nostalgic for another era. Located on Aguascaliente's main square, opposite the cathedral, the hotel has large, nicely furnished rooms with satellite TV, dual-line telephone, dataport, and coffeemaker. The restaurant is Sanbornes.

AGUASCALIENTES Quinta Real

Avenida Aguascalientes Sur 601 **Tel** *(449) 978 58 18* **Fax** *(449) 978 56 16* **Rooms** *85*

An elegant colonial-style hotel in a resort once best known for its thermal waters. This Quinta Real is an all-suite hotel with many configurations of suites. All elegant, all spacious. Rooms are equipped with three-line telephone, Internet connection, satellite TV, sumptuous bathrooms, and a pillow menu. **www.quintareal.com.mx**

AJIJIC Posada las Calandrias

Carretera Chapala-Jocotepec 8 Poniente **Tel** *(376) 766 10 52* **Rooms** *33*

Awash in colorful bougainvillea, this tidy, family-owned and operated little motel is set back from the highway on the outskirts of Ajijic. An ideal location for those driving and for anyone considering a long-term stay. The large clean rooms, all with tile floors, have kitchenettes and a nice dining area. Parking in the courtyard.

AJIJIC Los Artistas B&B

Constitución 105 **Tel** *(376) 766 10 27* **Fax** *(376) 766 17 62* **Rooms** *6*

This hospitable B & B is set in lovely landscaped grounds and has a beautiful swimming pool. Spacious rooms are decorated in colorful Mexican style. A large glass-walled living room/dining room/ library is a great place to relax, with its couches and magazines. Lavish breakfast with fruit, juice, and pastries. **www.losartistas.com**

AJIJIC La Nueva Posada

Donato Guerra 9 **Tel** *(376) 766 13 44* **Fax** *(376) 766 14 44* **Rooms** *19*

A hotel in 18th-century colonial style, La Nueva Posada has lovely arches, baronial staircase, and tall beamed ceilings. Rooms are decorated in Mexican style, with Internet access and lake views. Some have disabled access. Garden villas with kitchenettes available. Rooftop terrace. Breakfast included. **www.mexconnect.com/MEX/rest/nuevaposada**

ANGANGUEO Don Bruno

Morelos 92 **Tel** *(715) 156 00 26* **Fax** *(715) 156 00 26* **Rooms** *30*

Don Bruno, near the center of this colonial-era town, is popular with travelers focused on birding and monarch butterflies. The large rooms, with pine furniture and tile floors, are simple but comfortable. Eleven of the rooms have fireplaces, which are welcome in this cold climate. Free parking.

CAREYES El Careyes Beach Resort

KM 53.5 Carretera, Barra de Navidad **Tel** *(315) 351 00 00* **Fax** *(315) 351 0100* **Rooms** *51*

Sophisticated, secluded beachfront inn built in a horseshoe shape around palm trees and a pool. The rooms are all exquisitely furnished and comfortable, with colorful Mexican touches and tile floors. Some with balcony, Jacuzzi, and plunge pool. Full Spa. Polo, horseback riding, tennis. Excursions available. **www.elcareyesresort.com**

CAREYES El Tamarindo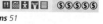

Kilometro 7.5 Carretera Barra de Navidad **Tel** *(315) 351 50 32* **Fax** *(315) 351 50 70* **Rooms** *29*

Luxury secluded villas in a magnificent forest-beach setting on Tenacatita Bay. Exquisite individual *casitas* (little houses) feature colorful textiles and teak floors, patio, Jacuzzi, and plunge pool. Challenging 18-hole golf course by Robert Trent Jones and David Fleming. Nature preserve with turtles and birds. **www.eltamarindoresort.com**

COLIMA América

Morelos 162 **Tel** *(312) 312 95 96* **Fax** *(312) 314 44 25* **Rooms** *125*

This modern, bustling hotel catches a lot of business and tourist traffic because of good service and its prime location in the heart of the city. Rooms are modern, carpeted, have TV, telephone, and coffeemaker. It is a convenient block and half from the central plaza, and within walking distance of several museums. **www.hotelamerica.com.mx**

COLIMA Los Candiles

Boulevard Camino Real 399 **Tel** *(312) 312 32 12* **Fax** *(312) 313 17 07* **Rooms** *75*

Located away from town center and near the University of Colima, this modern hotel-motel has an impressive exterior and modern lobby. Rooms are carpeted, nicely coordinated with carved wood furniture, and have cable TV and tile bathrooms. Helpful staff to assist with directions, museum times, and nearby shopping. **www.hotelloscandiles.com**

GUADALAJARA Hotel San Francisco Plaza

Degollado 627 **Tel** *(333) 613 32 56* **Rooms** *76*

An exceedingly pleasant hotel, close to everything, yet slightly apart from city noise. The two-story pastel-colored hotel looks like a colonial-era gem, but it is not. The spotless rooms, all built around four interior patios, have high ceilings, and dark wood furniture. Wonderful restaurant off the lobby. **www.sanfranciscohotel.com.mx**

GUADALAJARA La Rotonda

Liceo 130 **Tel** *(333) 614 10 17* **Rooms** *35*

Just a block and a half from the Cathedral, this former convent makes a fine little hotel. Rooms, all on two stories, have high ceilings, TV, tidy bathrooms, and an eclectic mix of furniture with a few Mexican touches. The restaurant receives neither great praise nor condemnation. It is, however, handy.

GUADALAJARA Holiday Inn Centro

Juárez 211 **Tel** *(333) 560 12 00* **Rooms** *90*

Only a couple of blocks to the Centro Historico, this is a well-situated hotel. The handsome lobby is furnished with nice sitting areas. Fashionable stores line the corridor. The carpeted rooms are well furnished and nicely coordinated bathrooms. Each one has Internet access and coffeemaker. Free limited parking. **www.holidaycentrogdl.com**

GUADALAJARA Quinta Real

Avenida México 2727, Fracc. Vallarta Norte **Tel** *(333) 669 06 00* **Fax** *(333) 669 06 00* **Rooms** *76*

Opened in 1986, this is one of the most fashionable hotels in Guadalajara, and the best place to meet, greet, and stay. The several stories of rooms are centered on manicured gardens. Rooms are spacious and beautifully furnished but vary widely in details. All have Internet access. **www.quintareal.com.mx**

GUADALAJARA Río Caliente Spa

Primavera Forest, La Primavera **Tel** *(333) 615 95 43* **Fax** *(333) 615 06 01* **Rooms** *48*

This relaxing, natural hot spring, vegetarian spa is 27 miles west of Guadalajara, surrounded by forest. Select quarters in a *casita* by the pool or in the older section around the patio. All appealingly furnished in Mexican style. No phones or TV in rooms. Daily hikes and spa services available. **www.riocaliente.com**

GUADALAJARA Villa Ganz

López Cotilla 1739, La Fayette **Tel** *(333) 120 14 16* **Rooms** *10*

Near the American Consulate, this is an elegant and stylish boutique hotel. Rooms are large and beautifully decorated in European style. Beautiful small garden and terrace dining. Breakfast included; other meals on request. Internet, cable TV, honor bar, and parking. Massage available. Airport transportation arranged. **www.villaganz.com**

GUANAJUATO Hotel Embajadoras

Parque Embajadoras **Tel** *(473) 731 01 05* **Fax** *(473) 731 00 63* **Rooms** *25*

Away from the central city bustle, this appealing hotel is set on a red tile courtyard attractively decorated with plants and shade trees – a pleasant place to sit and relax. The one-story of rooms are simply but comfortable furnished. A charming restaurant serves all meals. **www.mexonline.com/embajadoras.htm**

GUANAJUATO La Casa de los Espíritus Alegres

La Exhacienda la Trinidad 1 **Tel** *(473) 733 10 13* **Fax** *(473) 733 10 13* **Rooms** *8*

A joyful, artfully arranged, comfortable inn set inside the walls of a 16th-century hacienda on the edge of Guanajuato. Each room is imaginatively arranged with a spirited collection of textiles, folk art, and a skeleton or two. The dining table is set spectacularly at breakfast (included). Cozy living room. **www.casaspirit.com**

GUANAJUATO Hostería del Frayle

Sopeña 3 **Tel** *(473) 732 11 79* **Fax** *(473) 732 11 79* **Rooms** *37*

This posada has rooms created from a tall 17th-century building once used to separate ore. Just off the main plaza, the location is ideal, though noisy. The rooms, all with original, tall, beamed ceilings have hardwood floors, and rustic furnishings. Can be a little drafty in winter. **www.hosteriadelfrayle.com**

GUANAJUATO Posada Santa Fe

Jardín Unión 12 **Tel** *(473) 732 00 84* **Fax** *(473) 732 46 53* **Rooms** *47*

On Guanajuato's main plaza, and built in 1892, Posada Santa Fe has been updated, but still retains a comforting feel of yesteryear. From the grand staircase embellished with Mexican tiles to the rooms, it bespeaks another era. Rooms have lovely hand-stenciled wainscoting and colonial-style furniture. **www.posada-santafe.com**

GUANAJUATO Camino Real

Plaza Aldama 92 **Tel** *(473) 732 22 22* **Fax** *(473) 732 31 14* **Rooms** *105*

Away from the town center, this handsomely kept hotel was created from a colonial-era silver-processing hacienda. Vestiges of that era can be seen in the conference rooms and a few guestrooms in the main section. The ample rooms, in a garden setting, exude the charm of Mexico with carved pine furniture. **www.caminoreal.com**

GUANAJUATO Quinta Las Acacias

Paseo de la Presa 168 **Tel** *(473) 731 15 17* **Rooms** *17*

An elegant 19th-century former mansion, Las Acacias reflects a time when Mexico coveted all things French. Antiques are used throughout the handsome rooms, each designed around a historic or regional theme. Breakfast is included. Near the dam *(presa)* and opposite Florencio Antillon park. **www.quintalasacacias.com**

HUASTECA POTOSINA Posada el Castillo
$$

105 Calle Ocampo, Xilitla **Tel** *(489) 365 00 38* **Fax** *(489) 365 00 55* **Rooms** *8*

The house where Edward James once lived now welcomes guests. Architecturally eclectic with Mexican, English, and Moorish styles. Each of the eight bedrooms is comfortable and individual. Three have cathedral-like Moorish windows. Meals can be arranged. Naturalist-led hikes available. Prime birding nearby.

MORELIA Best Western Hotel Casino
$$$

Portal Hidalgo 229 **Tel** *(443) 313 13 28* **Fax** *(443) 312 12 52* **Rooms** *43*

Occupying a large expanse over the Portales facing Morelia's Plaza de Armas and Cathedral, this three-story hotel has been housing travelers for decades. Rooms offer nicely coordinated furnishings and coffeemaker. Some rooms across the front have small balconies. Attractive restaurant. Free parking. **www.hotelcasino.com.mx**

MORELIA Hotel de la Soledad
$$$

Zaragoza 90 **Tel** *(443) 312 18 88* **Fax** *(443) 312 21 11* **Rooms** *57*

Step inside this large colonial-era home and back to its early 1700s origin with multiple patios, graceful arches, tall beamed ceilings, and thick walls. Rooms feature period details and are carpeted and comfortable with an air of yesteryear. Lovely restaurant-bar on the first patio. Half block to the main square. **www.hsoledad.com**

MORELIA Los Juaninos
$$$$

Morelos Sur 39 **Tel** *(443) 312 00 36* **Rooms** *30*

Gorgeous colonial-era structure, large rooms, baronial halls, patios, and elegant stonework. Today, art and antiques embellish spaces once used as a hospital by the order of Los Juaninos. The individually decorated rooms, with original features, are stunning. Restaurant with city views. **www.hoteljuaninos.com.mx**

MORELIA Virrey de Mendoza
$$$$

Avenida Madero Poniente 310 **Tel** *(443) 312 00 45* **Fax** *(443) 312 67 19* **Rooms** *55*

A beautiful hotel on three stories in a colonial-era building. Great views of the plaza and cathedral. Antiques and comfortable couches embellish the lobby. Rooms are similarly furnished with antiques, comfortable beds and hardwood floors, plus Internet connection. Pleasant lobby bar and good restaurant. **www.hotelvirrey.com**

MORELIA Villa Montaña Spa
$$$$$

Patzimba 201, Col.Vista Bella **Tel** *(443) 314 02 31* **Fax** *(443) 315 14 23* **Rooms** *36*

On a hill overlooking all of Morelia, and on four acres, this is a spectacular location for a small luxury hotel. The spacious *casitas* are exquisitely outfitted with carefully selected antiques, luxury textiles, fireplaces, and TV. Wonderful restaurant and cocktail hour on the terrace. Full service spa and tennis court. **www.villamontana.com.mx**

PARICUTIN Centro Turístico de Angahuan
$$

Camino al Paricutin **Tel** *(452) 523 39 34* **Fax** *(452) 523 39 34* **Rooms** *9*

At the edge of Angahuan, where the dirt road leads to Paricutin, you'll find these rustic cabins. Most sleep up to 24 people in bunk beds, but there may be other choices for smaller groups or couples. Sparsely furnished, with fireplace and bathroom. Sheets provided, but bring towels, and a thermal blanket in winter. Small restaurant may be open.

PÁTZCUARO Posada de la Salud
$

Serrato 9 **Tel** *(434) 342 00 58* **Rooms** *15*

This little hotel fits the bill nicely for pleasant, well-kept rooms at budget prices. The two stories of rooms are built facing a planter-decorated patio. Each comfortable room is sparsely furnished with pine furniture. Two have a fireplace. It faces one side of the basilica and is three blocks from the Plaza Grande.

PÁTZCUARO La Casa Encantada Bed & Breakfast
$$$

Dr. Coss 15 **Tel** *(434) 342 34 92* **Rooms** *11*

This exquisite 1784 home-turned-inn exudes both old and new Mexico. The suites, located around two plant-lined patios, feature colorful Mexican textiles, *equipale* tables, and tiled floors; each has either fireplace or gas heater, plus heated mattress pad. Living room with piano. Breakfast included. **www.lacasaencantada.com/suites.php**

PÁTZCUARO Posada de la Basílica
$$$

Arciga 6 **Tel** *(434) 342 11 08* **Fax** *(434) 342 06 59* **Rooms** *12*

An 18th-century home-turned-charming-inn centered around a patio. Rooms offer comfortable beds, armoires, small bathrooms, and hardwoods floors. Some with fireplace. The rooms facing the basilica have balconies. Lovely restaurant. **www.posadalabasilica.com**

PÁTZCUARO Hacienda Mariposas Resort & Spa
$$$$

Carretera Pátzcuaro-Sta.Clara Km 3 **Tel** *(434) 342 47 28* **Rooms** *5*

On 25 acres surrounded by forest, orchards, and gardens, this eco-centered hotel offers a special respite. Rooms, in a one-story lineup with covered walkway, are comfortably furnished. Tile floors, spacious bathrooms, and either fireplace or heater. Breakfast included. Horseback riding and special interest tours available. **www.haciendamariposas.com**

PÁTZCUARO Mansión Iturbe Bed & Breakfast 11 $$$$

Portal Morelos 59 **Tel** *(434) 342 03 68* **Fax** *(434) 342 36 27* **Rooms** *12*

This beautiful mansion-turned-hotel is owned and managed by descendents of the original 17th-century owners. The large rooms, all on the second floor, have hardwood floors. Some have small balconies overlooking the Plaza Grande. Lovely first-floor patio and superior restaurant. Rooftop terrace. Full breakfast. **www.mansioniturbe.com**

PÁTZCUARO Mansión de los Sueños 11 $$$$$

Ibarra 15 **Tel** *(434) 342 57 08* **Fax** *(434) 342 57 18* **Rooms** *12*

This beautifully conceived two-story inn, recently created from a 17th-century home, is focused around two original interior patios. Each luxuriously furnished room features antiques and a fireplace. Covered walkways link the rooms. Outdoor Jacuzzi, small beauty salon, and two small restaurants within the manicured grounds. **www.prismas.com.mx**

PUERTO VALLARTA Los Cuatros Vientos  $$

Matamoros 520 **Tel** *(322) 222 01 61* **Fax** *(523) 222 28 31* **Rooms** *13*

One of the most charming little hotels in Mexico. In the heart of Puerto Vallarta, on three levels around a small patio and pool. The immaculate rooms have colorful Mexican folk art details. Sitting areas overlook the town. Rooftop bar with great sunset views. Chez Elena is an evening-only restaurant. Breakfast included. **www.cuatrovientos.com**

PUERTO VALLARTA Molino de Agua  $$$

Vallarta 130 **Tel** *(322) 223 10 12* **Rooms** *60*

A tropical oasis in the heart of the old town, with rubber trees and palms meandering along walkways to the beach. Rooms are divided between bungalows with private patios and a three-story section on the beach. All have tile floors and comfortable wooden furnishings. **www.molinodeagua.com**

PUERTO VALLARTA Playa Los Arcos $$$

Olas Altas 380 **Tel** *(322) 222 05 83* **Fax** *(322) 226 71 04* **Rooms** *175*

A longtime favorite on Playa Los Muertos, this small hotel, with a soaring lobby, occupies prime beach property. Its four stories frame the pool, leading to the beach and the hotel's lineup of blue lounge chairs. Rooms from economy to suites have white tile floors, pastel walls, and white bedspreads with matching drapes. **www.playalosarcos.com**

PUERTO VALLARTA Hacienda San Angel $$$$$

Miramar 336, Centro **Tel** *(322) 222 26 92* **Rooms** *16*

Three hillside homes were combined to create this sophisticated boutique hotel overlooking the cathedral and bay. Each elegantly decorated suite comes with cable TV and DVD player. Facilities include several pools, Jacuzzi, rooftop sunning area, movie library, and Internet access. Continental breakfast included. **www.haciendasanangel.com**

PUERTO VALLARTA Sheraton Buganvilias $$$$$

Boulevard Medina Ascencio 999 **Tel** *(322) 226 04 04* **Fax** *(322) 222 05 00* **Rooms** *477*

A large remodeled resort hotel studded with gardens and palms. Built around a large swimming pool on a prime beachfront location. Rooms are standard resort chic and priced according to view and size. It is ideally located – close to old Vallarta, shopping, and restaurants. Fantastic *mariachi* brunch buffet on Sunday. **www.sheraton.com**

PUERTO VALLARTA Velas Vallarta Grand Suite Resort 11 $$$$$

Paseo de la Marina 485 **Tel** *(322) 221 00 91* **Fax** *(322) 221 07 55* **Rooms** *339*

A handsome 10-acre, beachfront, all-suite hotel built in a horseshoe shape. Impeccably kept, with beautiful marble floors, pastel walls, Huichol art, and Mexican textiles. Studios have a kitchenette. Other suites have state-of-the-art Mexican kitchens. Four tennis courts and a walk to 18-hole golf course. **www.velasvallarta.com**

PUERTO VALLARTA Westin Resort $$$$$

Paseo de la Marina Sur 205 **Tel** *(322) 226 11 00* **Fax** *(322) 221 11 21* **Rooms** *280*

A large, sophisticated full-service resort that appeals to singles, couples, and families. With its spacious soaring open-air lobby, fashionable lineup of shops, restaurants, pools, full spa, and kid's club, it has a lot going for it. Guest quarters are large and beautifully furnished. Disabled-accessible facilities. **www.westinpv.com**

QUERÉTARO Mesón de Santa Rosa 11 $$$

Pasteur Sur 17 **Tel** *(442) 224 26 23* **Rooms** *21*

Facing the historic Plaza de Armas, and opposite the famed Corregidora's house, this attractive hotel began life as an overnight stable for mule trains and their drivers. It now offers upscale quarters for well-heeled travelers. The presidential suite, over the front portal, faces the Plaza de Armas. **www.mesonsantarosa.com**

QUERÉTARO La Casa de la Marquesa 11 $$$$

Madero 41, Col. Centro **Tel** *(442) 212 00 92* **Fax** *(442) 212 00 98* **Rooms** *25*

A stunning three-story, private residence built in 1756 in Querétaro's historic center, this opened as a luxury all-suite hotel in 1995. It is testament to the opulence of the period, with dramatic Moorish arches, lavish tile and stonework, exquisite carved doors, and antiques. Rooms feature exquisite antiques and fabrics. **www.lacasadelamarquesa.com**

REAL DE CATORCE Mesón de la Abundancia 11 $$

Lanzagorta 11 **Tel** *(488) 887 50 44* **Fax** *(488) 887 50 45* **Rooms** *11*

An pleasantly rustic, hospitable 18th-century home-turned-hotel. Up the stairs to two stories of large rooms around an open patio. Each room has a private bathroom, hardwood floors, rustic wooden furniture, and Mexican folk art. Some have small balconies. Cozy restaurant. **www.mesonabundancia.com**

SAN BLAS Garza Canela $$

Paredes 105 Sur **Tel** *(323) 285 01 12* **Rooms** *50*

This sanctuary of hospitality is memorable by the warm welcome, quality of service, and comfortable accommodations. The immaculate rooms are nicely separated and framed by patches of garden and leafy plants. Handsome restaurant and large plant-lined pool. Many tour services arranged. **www.garzacanela.com/home.htm**

SAN JUAN DEL RÍO Fiesta Americana Hacienda Galindo $$$

Carretera a Amealco km 5.5, Querétaro **Tel** *(427) 271 82 00* **Fax** *(427) 271 82 22* **Rooms** *168*

Among Mexico's hacienda hotels, this is one of the most visually stunning with its enchilada red façade and architectural details. Dating from the 16th century, today it is an elegant hotel with much of the original hacienda intact. Rooms are off the main lobby. Upper-floor rooms with balconies face the pool. **www.fiestamericana.com**

SAN LUIS POTOSÍ Hotel Panorama $$

Avenida Venustiano Carranza 315 **Tel** *(444) 812 17 77* **Fax** *(444) 812 45 91* **Rooms** *126*

Ideally located in the heart of the city facing the main plaza and within walking distance of most museums and restaurants. Rooms are comfortable, supremely clean, and carpeted. Beds are in great shape, but the furnishings could use an update. Noted for its service and friendly staff. Guarded parking in back. **www.hotelpanorama.com.mx**

SAN LUIS POTOSÍ Westin Hotel $$$$$

Avenida Real de Lomas 1000 **Tel** *(444) 825 0125* **Fax** *(444) 825 02 00* **Rooms** *123*

An upscale hotel, in an upscale San Luis Potosí neighborhood. All the amenities of a top hotel. Rooms in three stories are beautifully decorated, carpeted, spacious, and have a sitting area and high ceilings. Special events are held in the central courtyard-garden; note that rooms facing that area may be noisier. **www.westin.com**

SAN MIGUEL DE ALLENDE Parador San Sebastián $

Mesones 7 **Tel** *(415) 152 70 84* **Rooms** *27*

Once a genteel colonial-era mansion with multiple patios, today its two stories of rooms offer guests budget-priced quarters. The plant-decorated patio-lobby welcomes with umbrella-clad tables. The large, comfortable guestrooms have hardwood floors and simple furnishings. Some have fireplaces. Apartments have kitchens. Two blocks from the Jardín.

SAN MIGUEL DE ALLENDE Rancho El Atascadero $

Prolongación Santo Domingo s/n **Tel** *(415) 152 02 06* **Rooms** *51*

This hacienda-style property on the outskirts of town is one of the oldest hotels in San Miguel and has been wonderfully restored. It has a nice pool, Jacuzzi, tennis, and racquetball courts but also provides an oasis of peace and quiet for those who prefer it. **www.hotelatascadero.com**

SAN MIGUEL DE ALLENDE Mansión del Bosque $$

Calle de Aldama No. 65 **Tel** *(415) 152 02 77* **Fax** *(415) 152 02 77* **Rooms** *24*

The charming Mansion del Bosque offers the warmth of home among its winding, garden-filled patios and walkways. Charming restaurant and cozy library. Comfortable rooms are handsomely outfitted with carefully selected crafts, textiles, and furniture. Breakfast and dinner included. **www.infosma.com/mansion**

SAN MIGUEL DE ALLENDE Pensión Casa Carmen $$

Correo 31 **Tel** *(415) 152 08 44* **Fax** *(415) 152 08 44* **Rooms** *11*

Enter where carriages once passed, into the plant-filled patio at this old home-turned-inn, which has catered to guests for decades. Rooms, all cozy and simply furnished, center on patios, with added rooms on the rooftop. Home-cooked breakfast and lunch. Lovely dining room. Gas heaters.

SAN MIGUEL DE ALLENDE Quinta Loreto $$

Calle de Loreto 15 **Tel** *(415) 152 00 42* **Fax** *(415) 152 36 16* **Rooms** *40*

Long a budget traveler's choice, the motel-like Quinta Loreto offers respite with its colorful walls, little gardens, sitting areas, and cheerful restaurant. Rooms have tile floors, basic but comfortable furniture, and heaters. Economical breakfast and lunch. Near the craft market. **www.quintaloreto.com.mx**

SAN MIGUEL DE ALLENDE La Casa de Liza en el Parque B&B $$$

Bajada del Chorro No. 7 **Tel** *(415) 152 03 52* **Fax** *(415) 152 73 22* **Rooms** *9*

Built within a 17th-century private estate, staying at La Casa de Liza is the equivalent of occupying rooms in *Architectural Digest*. Each of the six exquisite *casitas* is totally different and contains dramatic architectural touches and furnishings using local and international art and antiques. Gourmet breakfast. **www.casaliza.com**

SAN MIGUEL DE ALLENDE Posada Carmina $$$

Cuna de Allende 7 **Tel** *(415) 152 04 58* **Fax** *(415) 152 10 36* **Rooms** *24*

A sunny plant-filled patio and restaurant welcomes guests to this large colonial-era home. Rooms in the two stories are huge and handsomely outfitted, each with tile floors, and all different in arrangement and style. Some have Mexican touches, others a French flair. Next to the Paroquia church. Breakfast included. **www.posadacarmina.com**

SAN MIGUEL DE ALLENDE Villa Mirasol $$$

Pila Seca 35 **Tel** *(415) 152 66 85* **Fax** *(415) 152 15 64* **Rooms** *12*

One of the loveliest boutique hotels in San Miguel within a multi-patio mansion. Immaculate rooms are sunny, with tile floors and soothing pastel walls. Most exude a sophisticated French Riviera charm with Mexican accents. All have patios or sitting areas. Continental breakfast. Lovely living room. Afternoon tea. **www.villamirasolhotel.com**

Key to Price Guide *see p292* **Key to Symbols** *see back cover flap*

SAN MIGUEL DE ALLENDE Casa Luna

$$$$

Pila Seca 11 **Tel** *(415) 152 11 17* **Fax** *(415) 152 11 17* **Rooms** *24*

The luxury Casa Luna is two houses, a block and a half apart. Both are 12-room colonial-era homes converted to unique guest quarters. Each room is embellished with a world of textiles and furnishings from many cultures. No two are alike. All with fireplaces and most have patios. Full breakfast. Cooking classes on request. **www.casaluna.com**

SAN MIGUEL DE ALLENDE Casa Quetzal

$$$$

Hospicio 34 **Tel** *(415) 152 05 01* **Fax** *(415) 152 67 48* **Rooms** *11*

The luxury Casa Quetzal, three blocks from the Jardín, consists of two beautifully furnished rooms and five large themed suites. Each of the suites has its own dining room, kitchenette, cable TV, telephone, and gas fireplace. Breakfast included. Dinner can be arranged. Airport pickup, private car tours, and wireless Internet available. **www.casaquetzalhotel.com**

SAN MIGUEL DE ALLENDE La Morada

$$$$

Correo 10, Centro **Tel** *(415) 152 16 47* **Fax** *(415) 152 00 17* **Rooms** *15*

Located half a block from San Miguel de Allende's main square, La Morada is a superior boutique hotel. Most of the rooms have sitting rooms, fireplaces, and Jacuzzis. One of the suites has a rooftop terrace with twin Jacuzzi and a solarium with spectacular views. The colonial-style decor is offset by modern touches. **www.lamoradahotel.com**

SAN MIGUEL DE ALLENDE Casa de Sierra Nevada

$$$$$

Hospicio 35 **Tel** *(415) 152 70 40* **Rooms** *33*

A collection of colonial-era homes refined as a luxury hotel, each room in each casa is different. There are sumptuous furnishings, antiques, and many elegant Mexican details. Most have fireplaces. Some have views of the city; others are grouped around a beautiful, large patio-centered mansion facing Parque Juárez. **www.casadesierranevada.com**

SIERRA GORDA Misión Concá

$$

Carretera Jalpan-Río Verde 57, km 32, Arroyo Seco, Querétaro **Tel** *(487) 877 42 51* **Rooms** *48*

This small hotel has a few original hacienda rooms besides more modern, motel-like rooms. The one-story original sugar hacienda section is more charming, with tile floors and thick walls. The gorgeous Junipero Sierra Misión Concá is across the road. Delicious river crayfish in season. **www.hotelesmision.com**

TLAQUEPAQUE Quinta Don José B & B Hotel

$$$

Calle Reforma 139 **Tel & Fax** *(333) 635 75 22* **Rooms** *18*

Only two blocks from Tlaquepaque's main square, the Don José offers a lot of comfort and service for the price. Rooms are spacious and nicely furnished. Several have kitchens and some are by the pool. Full breakfast included. Free airport or bus station pick-up. WiFi and free Internet desk. Massage available. **www.quintadonjose.com**

TLAQUEPAQUE Villa del Ensueño B & B

$$$

Florida 305 **Tel** *(333) 635 87 92* **Fax** *(333) 659 61 52* **Rooms** *20*

This lovely bed and breakfast, in a residential neighborhood and former home, is built around patios, gardens, and a pool. The welcoming and comfortable rooms, all of which are different in size, have tile floors and colorful, tasteful Mexican decoration. WiFi and dataport. Easy walk to shopping and dining. **www.villadelensueno.com**

URUAPAN Villa de las Flores

$

Emilio Carranza 15 **Tel** *(452) 524 28 00* **Rooms** *28*

This old-time charmer is a block off the main plaza, but decades back in time. The spotless rooms, all built around two large plant-filled patios, contain impeccably kept furniture from the 1940s. All have tile floors and bathrooms and two singles or one double bed. Electrical outlets are in short supply, however.

URUAPAN Mansión del Cupatitzio

$$$$

Corner of Rodilla del Diablo & Parque Nacional **Tel** *(452) 523 21 00* **Fax** *(452) 5 24 67 72* **Rooms** *57*

With decades of service, this is a central Mexico resort with two-and three-stories of rooms built around patios, gardens, and a pool. It overlooks the Parque Nacional with access to the park from the hotel. Comfortable, Individually arranged rooms feature stylishly coordinated furnishings. Five long blocks to the central plaza. **www.mansiondelcupatitzio.com**

ZACATECAS Best Western Argento Inn

$$

Avenida Hidalgo 407 **Tel** *(492) 925 17 18* **Fax** *(492) 925 17 22* **Rooms** *42*

The Argento has an excellent downtown location with superb views of Zacatecas. Housed in a former royal mint, there is a modern interior behind the colonial façade. Bi-lingual staff, and wireless Internet access available. A very good choice within this price range. Breakfast included. **www.argento-inn.com**

ZACATECAS Mesón de Jobito

$$$

Jardín Juárez 143 **Tel** *(492) 924 17 22* **Fax** *(492) 924 35 00* **Rooms** *53*

Opposite a small park on a narrow street near the central plaza, the Jobito was created from a 100-year-old building that was once occupied by slum apartments. Stone walkways decorated with plants connect the two stories of tastefully furnished rooms. Many room sizes and configurations. **www.mesondejobito.com**

ZACATECAS Emporio Zacatecas

$$$$

Avenida Hidalgo 703 **Tel** *(492) 922 61 83* **Fax** *(492) 922 62 45* **Rooms** *113*

In the heart of the city, opposite the main plaza and the cathedral, the façade of this four-story hotel dates from colonial times. But the interior, opened as a hotel in 1989, is thoroughly modern. The nicely arranged rooms are carpeted; two are wheelchair accessible. Live entertainment at weekends. **www.hotelesemporio.com**

ZACATECAS Quinta Real Zacatecas

Avenida Ignacio Rayón 434, Col. Centro **Tel** *(492) 922 91 04* **Fax** *(492) 922 84 40* **Rooms** *49*

This architecturally stunning luxury hotel was developed on the site of a bullring, and still retains most of its original look. From the lobby and many rooms, the view is of the interior ring and its verdant grassy circle. Each exquisite and spacious room offers thick bedspreads and drapes, sitting area, and desk. Internet available. **www.quintareal.com**

ZITÁCUARO Rancho San Cayetano

Highway 51 to Huetamo km. 2.3 (1.5 miles) **Tel** *(715) 153 1926* **Fax** *(715) 153 78 79* **Rooms** *12*

In the countryside, this haven of tranquility is surrounded by manicured gardens. Rooms are set back from the pool, and are dressed with Mexican footloomed rugs and folk art. Covered walkways in front of the rooms are perfect for a lounge chair and reading. Guest living room and library. **www.ranchosancayetano.com**

SOUTHERN MEXICO

ACAPULCO Hotel Misión

Felipe Valle 12 **Tel** *(744) 482 36 43* **Fax** *(744) 482 20 76* **Rooms** *29*

Tucked within the warren of streets in central Old Acapulco stands this one-story, 100-year-old budget charmer under the shade of a gigantic mango tree. Meals are served on the shaded red brick patio. The simple, clean, and pleasant rooms have tile floors, bed, basic furnishings and private bathroom. Alas, no hot water.

ACAPULCO El Mirador

Quebrada 74 **Tel** *(744) 483 12 21* **Fax** *(744) 483 88 00* **Rooms** *133*

Once a prime vacationing spot, when the cliff divers were a prime Acapulco top draw. Now a nice hotel, with great bay views, cliff divers daily, and close to Old Acapulco restaurants and beaches. The rooms have been fashionably remodeled and all have balconies and kitchenettes. **www.hotelelmiradoracapulco.com.mx**

ACAPULCO Hotel Los Flamingos

Avenida López Mateos, Fracc. Las Playas **Tel** *(744) 482 06 90* **Fax** *(744) 483 98 06* **Rooms** *36*

It is not hard to imagine droves of Hollywood stars visiting this cliffside hotel in the 1930s–50s, especially when you see the pictures in the lobby. The charm is intact, and the rooms are still alluring. Clean and simply furnished, most have either balcony or patio with magnificent bay views. Few have air-conditioning. **www.hotellosflamingos.com**

ACAPULCO Hotel Malibú

Avenida Costera Miguel Alemán 20 **Tel** *(744) 484 10 70* **Fax** *(744) 484 09 94* **Rooms** *80*

This waterfront hotel located on the main avenue of buzzing Acapulco is housed in two circular buildings. The octagonal rooms are equipped with refrigerators, and they all have balconies. The hotel prides itself on its family-friendly atmosphere. **www.acapulcomalibu.com**

ACAPULCO Hyatt Regency

Costera Miguel Alemán 1 **Tel** *(744) 469 12 34* **Fax** *(744) 484 30 87* **Rooms** *640*

With a large stretch of beach, a mature tropical landscaping, and resort service, there is a lot of comfort in this older hotel. The enormous rooms all have balconies. July and August there is Camp Hyatt to entertain the kids. Kosher cuisine in high season and on site synagogue all year. Dedicated spa facility. **www.grandhotelacapulco.com**

ACAPULCO Hotel El Cano

Costera Alemán 75 **Tel** *(744) 435 15 00* **Fax** *(744) 484 22 30* **Rooms** *180*

Ideally located, the stylish 11-story El Cano faces the bay, occupying a broad section of beach. A wonderful design combination of retro '50s and modern is a feast for the senses, awash in breezes, white tile and cerulean and navy blue décor. The light-filled rooms have been given the same treatment. Free parking. **www.hotel-elcano.com**

ACAPULCO Las Brisas

Carretera Escénica 5255 **Tel** *(744) 469 69 00* **Fax** *(744) 466 53 22* **Rooms** *263*

The hot-pink façade is a trademark of this luxury hotel. It has a fabulous bay view and refined amenities. Spacious guest quarters are set within 40 acres of flower-bedecked hillside, with marble floors and private patios. Private or shared pools. Continental breakfast delivered. Beach Club. Five tennis courts. **www.brisas.com.mx**

ACAPULCO Quinta Real

Paseo de la Quinta 6, Fracc. Real Diamante **Tel** *(744) 469 15 00* **Fax** *(744) 469 15 16* **Rooms** *74*

Opened in 1998, the five-story, cliffside Quinta Real is on the prestigious Punta Diamante where the bay views are stupendous. Luxurious in every way, this all-suite hotel is decorated in soothing beige, cream, and white with a sea motif running throughout. Marble floors and baths. **www.quintareal.com**

ACAPULCO Villa Vera Hotel & Racquet Club

Lomas del Mar 35, Fracc. Club Deportivo, Costera **Tel** *(744) 484 03 34* **Fax** *(744) 484 74 79* **Rooms** *59*

Once the exclusive haunt of celebrities and the outlandishly rich, the Villa Vera still has a classy appeal but, alas, also a timeshare connection. On 15 landscaped acres it offers a combination of tastefully furnished villas, *casitas*, and a hotel-like building. Four tennis courts. Spa facilities available. **www.villavera.com**

HUATULCO Meigas Binniguenda $$

Boulevard Santa Cruz 201, Santa Cruz **Tel** *(958) 587 00 77* **Fax** *(958) 587 02 84* **Rooms** *165*

Opened in the early 1980s, as Huatulco's first hotel, guests will still enjoy the beautiful colonial style, mature tropical gardens, charm, and quality of Meigas Binniguenda. Rooms, all with cool tile floors and double doors opening to tiny balconies, are nicely furnished. Close to the main square in Santa Cruz. **www.meicerhotels.com.mx**

HUATULCO Camino Real Zaashila $$$$$

Boulevard. Benito Juárez 5, Tangolunda **Tel** *(958) 583 03 00* **Fax** *(958) 581 04 68* **Rooms** *148*

This is among the most beautiful of the Tangolunda Bay hotels, with stark white façade, Mediterranean architecture, and exuberant tropical vegetation. Rooms meander to a wide stretch of beach. Each one has an ocean view. Some have balconies and private pools. All are spacious and elegantly appointed. One tennis court. **www.caminoreal.com**

HUATULCO Quinta Real $$$$$

Paseo Benito Juárez L-2, Tangolunda **Tel** *(958) 581 04 28* **Fax** *(958) 581 04 29* **Rooms** *28*

Facing Tangolunda Bay, this all-suite boutique hotel with its distinctive Moorish architecture offers luxury accommodation and service. The suites are simply yet elegantly outfitted with lavish use of hardwood and marble furnishings. Each has a balcony, cable TV, and telephone. Situated next to an 18-hole golf course. **www.quintareal.com**

IXTAPA Barcelo Ixtapa $$$$

Boulevard Ixtapa **Tel** *(755) 555 20 00* **Fax** *(755) 555 20 32* **Rooms** *397*

Graciously arranged with large public areas and a broad expanse of beach, Barcelo is an all-inclusive hotel. The rooms are stylish, with quality natural wood furniture. All rooms have TV, telephone, Internet access, coffeemaker, and most have ocean views. Rooms with disabled access available. **www.barceloixtapa.com**

IXTAPA Las Brisas Ixtapa $$$$$

Boulevard Ixtapa, Playa Vistahermosa **Tel** *(755) 553 21 21* **Fax** *(755) 553 10 38* **Rooms** *416*

Designed by Ricardo Legoretta, with expansive use of space, this is a large luxury hotel without the feeling of being overcrowded. Guestrooms have minimalist beauty with assiduous use of Mexican color and style, large private terraces, and ocean views. Plenty of choice in pools, restaurants, and tennis. **www.brisas.com.mx**

OAXACA Golondrinas $

Tinoco y Palacios 411 **Tel** *(951) 514 32 98* **Fax** *(951) 514 21 26* **Rooms** *26*

Beyond the bright blue wall are walkways lush with tropical vegetation. Discover the one-story of rooms tucked away among the foliage and whimsical plant-laden Oaxaca pottery. There are little places to sit, and a magical garden patio for breakfast. All simply furnished, comfortable, with touches of Mexico. **lasgolon@prodigy.net.mx**

OAXACA Hotel Azucenas $

Calle Prof. M. Aranda 203 **Tel** *(951) 514 79 18* **Fax** *(951) 514 79 18* **Rooms** *10*

Opened in 2000, the Azucenas combines family hospitality and historic charm. The building is turn-of-the-20th-century colonial style, with a handsome central patio surrounded by rooms. Small, attractive rooms with dark wood matching furniture and Mexican touches. Rooftop garden terrace. Breakfast included. **www.hotelazucenas.com**

OAXACA Hotel Maela $

Constitución 206 **Tel** *(951) 516 60 22* **Fax** *(951) 516 60 22* **Rooms** *26*

A block from the Santo Domingo church, and six from the Zócalo, the Maela fills a growing gap for economical lodging that is close to everything. On two stories, around a small colorful interior courtyard, each room has nice tile floors, matching bedspreads and furniture. Internet access available. Free parking. **www.mexonline.com/maela.htm**

OAXACA Hotel Principal $

5 de Mayo 208 **Tel** *(951) 516 25 35* **Fax** *(951) 516 25 35* **Rooms** *14*

The Principal retains the charm of a colonial-era, patio-centered home. Housed on two floors, the rooms have tall beamed ceilings, old furniture, and offer simple comfort. Do note, however, that rooms at the front with balconies, are noisy. The hotel is family-managed and owned. Just three blocks from the Zócalo. **hotelprincipal@gmail.com**

OAXACA Casa del Sotano $$

Tinoco y Palacios 414 **Tel** *(951) 516 24 94* **Fax** *(951) 501 18 27* **Rooms** *23*

With a striking ochre façade, this colonial structure seamlessly incorporates a comfortable modern section to provide a comfortable two-story inn, art gallery, and terrace restaurant. The small, stylish rooms have tile floors, handsome wood and iron furniture, and Mexican touches. Lower floor rooms can be dark. **www.hoteldelsotano.net**

OAXACA Hotel Casa Cué $$

Aldama 103, Centro Histórico **Tel** *(951) 516 77 86* **Fax** *(951) 516 13 36* **Rooms** *23*

The Casa Cue is a modest, three-story, modern hotel opposite the market and two blocks from the Zócalo. Rooms are clean, neat, and comfortable with matching furnishings, TV, and private bathroom. Double thick windows reduce noise. Rooftop terrace with city views. **www.mexonline.com/casacue.htm**

OAXACA Hotel de la Parra $$$

Guerrero 117, Centro **Tel** *(951) 514 19 00* **Fax** *(951) 516 15 58* **Rooms** *14*

This boutique hotel gets stars for its location and the quality of the rooms for the price. Rooms, all with tile floors and marble bathrooms, have refined furnishings with dark wood furniture. There is a small garden pool. Within walking distance of all the main tourist attractions. **www.hoteldelaparra.com**

OAXACA Camino Real

Calle 5 de Mayo 300 **Tel** *(951) 516 06 11* **Fax** *(951) 516 07 32* **Rooms** *91*

This city center convent-turned-elegant-hotel was built in 1576 around five patios. Behind thick walls, the guest rooms are tastefully furnished with colorful fabrics loomed in Oaxaca. Most rooms have garden view. Buffet breakfast included. Poolside cocktails and appetizers in the afternoons. **www.caminoreal.com/oaxaca**

OAXACA Hacienda los Laureles

Hidalgo 21 **Tel** *(951) 501 53 00* **Fax** *(951) 501 53 01* **Rooms** *23*

Located in a quiet residential area north of the city center, this luxury getaway was once a hacienda. Built around beautiful gardens and a pool, and shaded by towering Indian Laurel trees, the guest quarters are tastefully decorated. Beautiful garden restaurant with excellent food. Spa facilities. **www.hotelhaciendaloslaureles.com**

PALENQUE Hotel Misión Palenque

Periferico Oriente s/n **Tel** *(916) 345 02 41* **Fax** *(916) 345 03 00* **Rooms** *210*

Just a 15-minute drive from Palenque's archaeological site, this appealing modern hotel has a tropical decor and is surrounded by lush jungle. An impressive range of facilities includes wireless Internet access, tennis courts, and complimentary bicycle rental. **www.hotelesmision.com.mx**

PALENQUE Maya Tulipanes

Calle Cañada 6, La Cañada **Tel** *(916) 345 02 01* **Fax** *(916) 345 10 04* **Rooms** *72*

This lovely hotel is situated in the preserved wooded area known as La Cañada. Rooms in the older section are smaller, but all have tiled floors and attractive furniture. Many Maya-inspired architectural details have been incorporated into the buildings. **www.mayatulipanes.com**

PALENQUE Chan-Kah Ruinas Resort

Carretera las Ruinas km 3 **Tel** *(916) 345 11 34* **Fax** *(916) 345 08 20* **Rooms** *72*

The charm of this hotel is its setting within 50 acres of jungle. Many of the guestrooms are in individual stone cottages set within this tropical forest. Others are linked by pathways through the lush gardens. All are large, nicely furnished, and comfortable, and have small patios. It is about two miles to the ruins. **www.chan-kah.com.mx**

PUERTO ANGEL Hotel Puesta del Sol

Barrio del Sol **Tel** *(958) 584 33 15* **Fax** *(958) 584 30 96* **Rooms** *14*

This charming hotel is located between two main beaches – neither is farther than a pleasant three-minute walk. With carved archways, a small library for guests, and a porch with hammocks for afternoon siestas, it provides an ideal budget accommodation option. Tours to local sights can be arranged at reception. **www.puertoangel.net**

PUERTO ANGEL La Buena Vista

Domicilio Conocido s/n **Tel** *(958) 584 31 04* **Rooms** *28*

Built on a hillside, with many stairs, this is one of those charming Mexico finds. Each spotless room features the essence of Mexico, from foot-loomed bedspreads and rugs, to colorful decorative touches. All pleasing to the eye and comfortable, but not fancy. Many have private balconies and views. All have patios. **www.labuenavista.com**

PUERTO ESCONDIDO Flor de María

1ra. Entrada a Playa Marinero s/n **Tel** *(954) 582 05 36* **Fax** *(954) 582 26 17* **Rooms** *24*

This hotel's popular appeal is its comfortable rooms around a central courtyard and laid-back style. Each of the tiled rooms has two double beds and features a colorful mixture of Mexican textiles and pottery. Library and Internet access. The restaurant is open for lunch and dinner. Near the beach. **www.mexonline.com/flordemaria.htm**

PUERTO ESCONDIDO Santa Fé

Calle de Morro s/n **Tel** *(954) 582 01 70* **Fax** *(954) 582 02 60* **Rooms** *61*

The Santa Fé, with its colonial hacienda-style architecture and verdant tropical vegetation, offers welcome comforts. The large rooms, built around two pool-centered courtyards, have tile floors, dark wood furniture, and colorful use of Mexican style in bedspreads and pottery. All have balconies or patio. **www.hotelsantafe.com.mx**

SAN CRISTÓBAL DE LAS CASAS Don Quijote

Cristóbal Colón 7 **Tel** *(967) 678 09 20* **Fax** *(96) 778 03 46* **Rooms** *25*

The three-story Don Quijote offers simple comfort at a reasonable price. Each carpeted room is nicely furnished with matching furniture, handsome bedspreads, two double beds, good reading lights, and bathroom. Located at the corner of Real de Guadalupe and only two blocks to the central square. **www.hoteldonquijote.com.mx**

SAN CRISTÓBAL DE LAS CASAS Palacio de Moctezuma

Juárez 16 **Tel** *(967) 678 03 52* **Fax** *(967) 678 15 36* **Rooms** *46*

Created from a patio-centered colonial home, the first impression is of yesteryear. A flower-decorated central well fronts the cozy restaurant. Farther back, three stories of rooms have been added, ranging from small to large, with beamed ceilings and matching furnishings. **www.hotelpalaciodemoctezuma.com**

SAN CRISTÓBAL DE LAS CASAS Casa Mexicana

28 de Agosto 1 **Tel** *(967) 678 06 98* **Rooms** *55*

Centrally located, near the Santo Domingo church and central plaza, this colonial mansion originally belonged to a wealthy family. Today its plant-filled patios and public spaces hold Mexican art. Guest rooms are all spacious, carpeted, and nicely furnished. Sauna and massage available. **www.hotelcasamexicana.com**

SAN CRISTÓBAL DE LAS CASAS Casa Vieja

 $$

María Adelina Flores 27 **Tel** *(967) 678 03 85* **Fax** *(967) 678 63 86* **Rooms** *40*

This lovely hotel, formed from a 1740 residence, has an attractive central garden fronted by an appealing restaurant on an open portico. Sun-filled rooms open off of several passages and stairways. All are beautifully decorated. Casa Vieja is located three blocks north of the central plaza. **www.casavieja.com.mx**

SAN CRISTÓBAL DE LAS CASAS Hotel Rincón del Arco

$$

Ejército Nacional 66 **Tel** *(967) 678 13 13* **Fax** *(967) 678 15 68* **Rooms** *50*

From a gracious home built in 1891, this family-owned hotel has blossomed into an exceedingly comfortable hotel. Rooms in the original structure have tall ceilings, hardwood floors, and the atmosphere of late 19th-century Mexico. Those in the newer colonial style section are handsomely outfitted. All with fireplaces. **www.rincondelarco.com**

SAN CRISTÓBAL DE LAS CASAS Na-Bolom

$$

Vicente Guerrero 33 **Tel** *(967) 678 14 18* **Rooms** *15*

Founded in 1951, in a multi-patio colonial home, today it is part hotel, part museum, and part cultural center. Staying here is a special experience, as is the dining. Guest rooms are charmingly themed and decorated around an indigenous Chiapan village. All have fireplace, small in-room library, and writing table. **www.nabolom.org**

TUXTLA GUTIERREZ Camino Real

$$

Boulevard Belisario Dominguez 1195 **Tel** *(961) 617 77 99* **Rooms** *194*

This contemporary, modern hotel is located in the commercial zone. Guests have access to gardens and a terrace with a spectacular view of the city. The restaurant is within the same five-story complex, and there is also an atrium with a waterfall and two pools. **www.caminoreal.com/tuxtla/**

ZIHUATANEJO Hotel Susy

$

Juan Alvarez 3 **Tel** *(755) 554 23 39 or 01800 702 8579 (toll free)* **Rooms** *18*

Enter the cheerful shaded and plant-filled patio where caged birds chatter. Rooms face this charming scene are on two levels. Though small and simply furnished with tile floors, comfortable bed, and small table and chairs, each is clean and has screened windows. Good location in the village center at the corner of Guerrero.

ZIHUATANEJO Hotel Sotavento

$$$

Play La Ropa **Tel** *(755) 554 20 32* **Fax** *(755) 554 29 75* **Rooms** *91*

The Sotovento Cliffside perch rises above the beautiful white-sand Playa la Ropa. Though it has a 1960s feel, with well-kept but dated furnishings, it also has large rooms on several levels. Second-floor rooms are more directly connected to the lobby, with spacious terraces. **www.beachresortsotavento.com**

ZIHUATANEJO La Casa Que Canta

$$$$$

Camino Escénico a Playa La Ropa **Tel** *(755) 555 70 00* **Fax** *(755) 554 79 00* **Rooms** *25*

On a cliff facing the bay, its sinuous gold-colored, molded adobe walls create a striking contrast against the sky and ocean. Beginning in the lobby, the choice of refined furniture and folk art create a delight at every turn. Rooms, all spacious and casually elegant, have marvelous terraces with bay views. Spa services. **www.lacasaquecanta.com**

ZIHUATANEJO The Tides

$$$$$

Playa la Ropa **Tel** *(755) 55 55 500* **Fax** *(755) 55 42 758* **Rooms** *70*

The luxurious, intimate Tides, with its beach-front location, is a destination in itself. Tropical plants line walkways linking the several categories of rooms. Each one is individually decorated, with elegant touches – beamed ceilings, separate living room, some with private infinity pool. Spa. Two tennis courts. **www.tideszihuatanejo.com**

THE GULF COAST

CATEMACO Posada Koniapan

$$

Avenida Revolución y Paseo del Malecón s/n **Tel** *(294) 943 00 63* **Fax** *(294) 943 09 39* **Rooms** *22*

The rooms at this small hotel are linked by a walkway, and line up in a row facing the lake. Each one is spacious and comfortable, with wood furniture and either one or two double beds. Hammocks strung up in the gardens are a nice touch. Breakfast included. Restaurants and the market close by. **www.hotelposadakoniapan.com.mx**

CATEMACO La Finca

$$$

Catemaco **Tel** *(800) 523 46 22* **Fax** *(294) 947 97 20* **Rooms** *57*

La Finca is the area's most popular resort hotel, partly due to its prime location on Lake Catemaco. The rooms, set amidst landscaped grounds, are all spacious and nicely furnished, and include a patio and large tile bathrooms. Many have lake views. Water sports and tours arranged. Located outside of Catemaco proper. **www.lafinca.com.mx**

CHACALACAS Chachalacas

$$

Playa Chachalacas **Tel** *(296) 962 52 40* **Rooms** *96*

Just 5 miles (8 km) from the ruins of Cempoala is this welcoming beach resort on a portion of Veracruz's Emerald Coast. The hotel is a favorite with vacationing Mexican families. The comfortable rooms are a nice size, with tile floors and views of the water. It is next to an ecological reserve noted for mangroves. **www.hotelchachalacas.com**

COATEPEC Posada Coatepec
 $$

Hidalgo 9 & Aldama **Tel** *(228) 816 05 44 or 01800 712 6256 (toll free)* **Rooms** *23*

Mention Coatepec, and someone will suggest a stay at this stylish little hotel. Opened in 1987 in a charming restored home, there is a beautiful colonial fountain at the entrance, a restaurant, and spacious guest rooms, handsomely furnished with Mexican accents. Rooms with disabled access are available. **www.posadacoatepec.com.mx**

CORDOBA Villa Florida
 $$

Avenida 1 3002 **Tel** *(271) 716 33 33* **Fax** *(271) 716 33 36* **Rooms** *81*

The modern three-story Villa Florida is a comfortable landscaped resort-like hotel. It features two wings of rooms all facing an attractive pool. The rooms are carpeted, and stylishly furnished with mahogany furniture, comfortable beds, and large tile bathrooms. **www.villaflorida.com.mx**

ORIZABA Fiesta Cascada
$$

Autopista Puebla–Cordoba, km 275 **Tel** *(272) 724 15 96* **Fax** *(272) 724 55 99* **Rooms** *70*

Outside of Orizaba proper and on the highway to Veracruz, the Cascada is next to the golf course. This beautiful little colonial-style hotel is set on five acres of land. Two stories of rooms face a central garden and pool. The rooms are all rather uniform, with one or two double beds. There is a tennis court. **www.hotelcascada.com.mx**

PAPANTLA Provincia Express
 $

Enriquez 103 **Tel** *(784) 942 16 45* **Fax** *(784) 842 42 13* **Rooms** *20*

The top lodging choice in Papantla, the Provincia is midway down Papantla's hill and across from the main plaza. The pleasant rooms, all rather large, have tile floors and private baths. Those in back are newer and quieter. Front rooms have balconies with a view of the Zócalo. Conveniently close to restaurants, market, and the bus station.

PAPANTLA Hotel Tajín
 $

José de Jesús Nuñez y Dguez 104 **Tel** *(784) 842 01 21* **Fax** *(784) 842 10 62* **Rooms** *73*

On top of the hill in Papantla, the Hotel El Tajín is as prominent as the church beside it. The modern hotel is undergoing renovation, making it a second choice to the Provincia Express (below). Rooms are ample in size, all with pastel colored walls, tile floors, private baths, and mismatched furnishings. **www.hoteltajin.com.mx**

SANTIAGO TUXTLA Gran Santiago Plaza
  $$

Corner of Comonfort & 5 de Mayo **Tel** *(294) 947 03 00* **Rooms** *53*

This hotel's prime location, on the beautiful central plaza, is opposite the Regional Museum, and within close view of the enormous stone Olmec head from Tres Zapotes. Rooms are modern, clean, comfortable, and nicely furnished. The excellent restaurant is a local favorite, offering well-prepared regional specialties.

TLACOTALPAN Doña Lala
 $$

Venustiano Carranza 11 **Tel** *(288) 884 25 80* **Fax** *(288) 884 24 55* **Rooms** *40*

Built in 1932, the Doña Lala is a national monument building. It's exterior, with frilly wrought-iron and pastel walls, looks like it was lifted out of New Orleans. Each of the large guest rooms has a high ceiling, tile floor, and floral bed covering. Suites have antiques. Doña Lala restaurant is one of the best hotels in the city. **www.hoteldonalala.com**

VERACRUZ Calinda Veracruz
 $$

Independencia esq. Lerdo **Tel** *(800) 292 33 00* **Fax** *(229) 989 38 22* **Rooms** *116*

Facing the Plaza de Armas, Calinda Veracruz is the newest and most modern hotel on the square. Rooms are tastefully coordinated, with tile floors, coffee maker, dual line phones, and dataport. Most have a balcony. On the seventh floor is a solarium with pool, and spectacular views of the city. **www.hotelveracruz.com.mx**

VERACRUZ Colonial
$$

Miguel Lerdo 117 **Tel** *(800) 614 90 90* **Fax** *(229) 932 24 65* **Rooms** *179*

Facing the Plaza de Armas, the location of the Colonial is prime for all the action that takes place here night and day. Newer rooms are in the back, and interior rooms are quieter. Your choice of room determines whether you will see and hear the action, or be somewhat shielded from it. There is secure parking behind the hotel. **www.hcolonial.com.mx**

VERACRUZ Hotel Emporio
 $$$

Paseo del Malecón 244 **Tel** *(229) 932 22 22* **Fax** *(229) 931 2261* **Rooms** *203*

With a fantastic view of Veracruz's immaculate harbor and docked ships, the nine-story Emporio offers a prime Malecón location, ideal for watching carnival parades. It is also next door to the city's most famous coffee parlor. Rooms, most of which have port views (if not a balcony), are stylishly attired. **www.hotelesemporio.com**

VERACRUZ Mocambo
   $$$

Calzada Adolfo Ruiz Cortines 4000 **Tel** *(800) 290 01 00* **Fax** *(229) 922 02 12* **Rooms** *101*

The graceful, sprawling Mocambo, with breezy, view-filled arches, was the first resort hotel in Veracruz. Opened in 1932, it retains that old-time charm. Rooms, though sparsely and simply furnished, are comfortable, with ocean views. Some have balconies. Spa, tennis court, and kids' activites during major vacations. **www.hotelmocambo.com.mx**

VILLAHERMOSA Best Western Maya Tabasco
$$

Avenida Ruiz Cortinez 907 **Tel** *(993) 358 11 11* **Fax** *(993) 312 11 33* **Rooms** *151*

Conveniently located beside the expressway, a mile from La Venta Museum, and a straight shot to downtown. The rooms have been renovated and are comfortable and nicely furnished. All are large with ample closet and luggage space and come with TV, dataport, and coffeemaker. **www.bestwestern.com/reservations/mx/main.asp**

VILLAHERMOSA Hotel Quality Inn Cencali
$$$

Juárez 105, Col. Lindavista **Tel** *(993) 313 66 11* **Fax** *(993) 315 19 99* **Rooms** *160*

The popular and bustling Cencali caters to both business and vacation travelers. The attractively furnished rooms have Internet access, and a coffeemaker. It is conveniently located next to the Olmec La Venta Museum. There is a free shuttle to and from the airport. **www.cencali.com.mx**

XALAPA Hotel del Museo
$

Ruiz Cortines 802 **Tel** *(228) 840 32 99* **Fax** *(228) 840 32 99* **Rooms** *32*

The Hotel del Museo's salmon-colored façade is easily seen from the street. This clean budget hotel is on four stories and within two blocks of the Museo Antropología. Although tiny, the rooms are comfortable with tile floors; the bathrooms are equally small. There is a little hotel restaurant on the first floor.

XALAPA Posada del Caféto
$

Canovas 8 and 12 **Tel** *(228) 812 04 03* **Fax** *(228) 817 00 23* **Rooms** *32*

Such a charming, impeccably kept little hotel facing a verdant and luscious tropical garden set with tables and chairs. With three stories of light-filled rooms, each one is cheerfully decorated with lovely hand-stenciled wall designs and colorful bedspreads. All have tile floors and dark wood furniture. Breakfast included. **www.pradodelrio.com**

XALAPA Mesón del Alférez
$$

Sebastián Camacho 2 **Tel** *(228) 818 01 13* **Fax** *(228) 818 01 13* **Rooms** *17*

The stately Alférez, a remodeled 1808 home-turned-hotel, offers a delightful escape. This was the home of the last Spanish Viceroy Representative. Opened as a hotel in 1993, rooms are grouped in two stories around a small central courtyard. Each one has antiques and decorative hand-stenciled walls. Internet access. **www.pradodelrio.com**

THE YUCATÁN PENINSULA

AKUMAL Hotel Club Akumal Caribe
$$$

Mex 307, 104 km (65 miles) S of Cancún **Tel** *(984) 206 35 00* **Fax** *(984) 875 90 15* **Rooms** *89*

Relaxing resort hotel right on the beach in Akumal's lovely Half Moon Bay. It offers a big range of accommodations – hotel rooms around a pool, garden bungalows, self-contained condos – and personal service. Great for diving and snorkeling, it also has an excellent Kids' Club. **www.hotelakumalcaribe.com**

BACALAR Casita Carolina
$

Avenida Costera 17 **Tel** *(984) 206 35 00* **Fax** *(983) 834 23 34* **Rooms** *7*

Guests get an especially warm welcome at this lakeside guest house in Bacalar. The rooms have plenty of character: each one is different, but they are all very comfortable. Kayaking, cycling, and diving are all available to guests. **www.casitacarolina.com**

BACALAR Villas Ecotucan
$$

Mex 307, 5km N of Bacalar **Tel** *(983) 834 2516* **Rooms** *7*

Especially tranquil, this little "ecohotel" is set amid bird-filled forest beside the exquisite Bacalar lake. The seven cabins are low-impact but pretty and comfortable, with solar power and bathrooms. The friendly Canadian-Mexican owners also offer kayaks, bikes, and other activities, and fresh breakfasts are included. **www.villasecotucan.info**

CAMPECHE Hotel Francis Drake
$$

Calle 12 no. 207, between Calles 63 & 65 **Tel** *(981) 811 75 35* **Fax** *(981) 811 56 28* **Rooms** *24*

Ideally located in the heart of Campeche's old city, this good value mid-range hotel occupies a converted old house. The traditionally styled rooms are very comfortable, with excellent bathrooms, TVs, air-conditioning, and other services, and there is a little restaurant and off-street parking. **www.hotelfrancisdrake.com**

CAMPECHE Hacienda Puerta Campeche
$$$$$

Calle 59 no. 71, between Calles 16 & 18 **Tel** *(981) 816 75 08* **Fax** *(999) 923 79 63* **Rooms** *15*

This luxurious hotel emulates the style of the same group's country haciendas, but in a more intimate colonial town mansion beneath Campeche's old Spanish city walls. The stylish rooms have every comfort, and the seductive pool, gardens, and restaurant are just as striking. **www.haciendasmexico.com**

CANCÚN Hotel Kin Mayab
$

Avda. Tulum 75, near corner of Avenida Uxmal **Tel** *(998) 884 29 99* **Fax** *(998) 884 31 62* **Rooms** *43*

Another hotel near the bus station that is popular with travelers spending just one or two nights in Cancún. Rooms are simple but pretty and colorful, with TV, decent bathrooms, and other comforts. The hotel also has frequent low-price offers. **www.hotelkinmayab.com**

CANCÚN Hotel Plaza Caribe
$$

Avenida Tulum, corner of Avenida Uxmal **Tel** *(998) 884 13 77* **Fax** *(998) 884 63 52* **Rooms** *134*

This popular hotel sits opposite the bus station in downtown Cancún, so is very convenient for anyone arriving in or leaving the city. The area is busy, but inside the hotel the restaurant, patios, and pool are remarkably calm and pretty. Rooms are very comfortable, and it's excellent value. **www.hotelplazacaribe.com**

CANCÚN Hotel Xbalamqué

$$ $$

Avenida Yaxchilán 31 **Tel** *(998) 887 38 28* **Fax** *(998) 892 46 46* **Rooms** *92*

An unusual hotel on a lively street in Cancún city, lined with enjoyable restaurants that are favorites with locals. The hotel's atmosphere is mellow, and as well as bright, modern rooms it contains a small spa – with low prices – and a health food café. Despite the location, it is not noisy. **www.xbalamque.com**

CANCÚN Suites El Patioz

$$ $$

Avda. Bonampak 51, corner of Calle Cereza **Tel** *(998) 884 35 00* **Fax** *(998) 884 35 40* **Rooms** *15*

This little guest house away from the center of Cancún city offers an unusual level of comfort, with spacious, cosy rooms with air-conditioning and a pretty patio where simple breakfasts (included) are served. Owners and staff are especially charming and helpful. This is one of Cancún's best budget options. **www.cancuninn.com**

CANCÚN Gran Meliá Cancún

$$$

Boulevard Kukulcán Km16.5 **Tel** *(998) 881 11 00* **Fax** *(998) 881 17 40* **Rooms** *676*

This giant resort complex has rooms in three huge pyramids – recalling those of the ancient Maya – linked by exuberant gardens. Guests are given a raft of options: two pools, stores, 10 restaurants offering a global range of cuisines, a 9-hole golf course, watersports, and more. **www.solmelia.com**

CANCÚN NH Krystal Cancún

$$$

Boulevard Kukulcán Km9 **Tel** *(998) 848 98 00* **Fax** *(998) 848 98 13* **Rooms** *453*

More modest and relaxed in style than the biggest resort hotels, the Krystal has an especially attractive terrace and pool area above the beach, and a superior Mexican restaurant, La Hacienda del Mortero. Service is excellent. **www.nh-hotels.com**

CANCÚN Hilton Cancún Golf & Beach Resort

$$$$

Boulevard Kukulcán Km17 **Tel** *(998) 881 80 00* **Fax** *(998) 881 80 93* **Rooms** *426*

The Hilton offers every kind of service, but has especially good sports facilities, including a jogging track and a full 18-hole golf course. The style is less sumptuous than in some resort hotels, but the rooms are fresh and modern, most with fabulous ocean views. **www.hiltoncancun.com**

CANCÚN The Ritz-Carlton

$$$$$

Retorno del Rey 36, Blvd Kukulcán Km14 **Tel** *(998) 881 08 08* **Fax** *(998) 881 80 82* **Rooms** *365*

One of the most opulent of the resort hotels along Cancún beach. Guests can choose between two pools, a spa offering conventional and Mayan treatments, and six restaurants, from poolside-casual to very elegant. This luxurious hotel also has two lounges and a culinary center with cooking classes. **www.ritzcarlton.com**

CHETUMAL Hotel Caribe Princess

$$

Avenida Obregón 168 **Tel** *(800) 282 05 95* **Fax** *(983) 832 05 20* **Rooms** *54*

A likeable good-value hotel in the middle of Chetumal, open several years but regularly refurbished, most recently with a luminously bright lobby. Rooms are airy, spacious, and well-kept, all with good bathrooms, TV, and air-conditioning – a great relief in the heat of Chetumal. **www.caribeprincesschetumal.com**

CHETUMAL Holiday Inn Chetumal-Puerta Maya

$$

Avenida Héroes 171 **Tel** *(983) 835 04 00* **Fax** *(983) 835 04 29* **Rooms** *85*

Modern and providing all the facilities associated with the Holiday Inn chain, this hotel lacks local character but stands out in an area with relatively few upper-scale hotels. Staff are charming, and the excellent restaurant has fine local cuisine. Various tours to archaeological sites are available. **www.holiday-inn.com/chetumalmex**

CHICHÉN ITZÁ Hotel Dolores Alba

$$

Mex 180 Km122, 3km E of Chichén Itzá **Tel** *(985) 858 15 55* **Fax** *(985) 858 15 55* **Rooms** *40*

By the Highway a little east of Chichén Itzá, Hotel Dolores Alba is by far the best of the mid/budget-range hotels near the ruins. There are two pools and an enjoyable restaurant, and rooms are air-conditioned, bright, and pretty. Free transport is provided to the ruins. **www.doloresalba.com**

CHICHÉN ITZÁ Villas Arqueológicas

$$

Mex 180, E of the Archaeological Site **Tel** *(985) 856 60 00* **Fax** *(985) 856 60 08* **Rooms** *45*

One of three very attractive, near-identical hotels beside the major Mayan ruins of Chichén Itzá, Cobá, and Uxmal. Rooms are in cabins around a delightful garden, together with a great restaurant and pool. Prices are lower than at similar-standard hotels, so they're exceptional value. **www.villasarquelogicas.com.mx**

COBA Villas Arqueológicas

$$$

Near entrance to Archaeological Site, Cobá village **Tel** *(985) 858 15 27* **Fax** *(985) 858 15 26* **Rooms** *43*

Another of the "villa hotels" beside the Yucatán's biggest Mayan sites. As at Chichén Itzá and Uxmal, rooms are decorated with traditional textiles, and set around an exuberant tropical garden centered on the restaurant and pool, both wonderful for relaxation after you've explored the ruins of Cobá. **www.villasarquelogicas.com.mx**

COZUMEL Tamarindo Bed & Breakfast

$

Calle 4 Norte no. 421, between Avda. 20 & 25 **Tel** *(987) 872 36 14* **Fax** *(987) 872 36 14* **Rooms** *8*

This very pretty guest house is as charming as its Mexican-French owners, and offers exceptional value. Each room is individually decorated, fresh breakfasts are included, and there's an open kitchen and a garden. They also have a Caribbean bungalow with two air-conditioned rooms located one block from the ocean. **www.tamarindcozumel.com**

Key to Price Guide *see p292* **Key to Symbols** *see back cover flap*

COZUMEL Hotel Flamingo — $$$

Calle 6 Norte, off Avenida Rafael E Melgar **Tel** *(987) 872 12 64* **Rooms** *17*

Excellent diving facilities and dive packages are a specialty of this San Miguel hotel, but it is also a very enjoyable, fine value general hotel, with attractive, refurbished rooms and suites that offer plenty of extras. There is an imaginative restaurant, Aqua, and a rooftop bar that is wonderful at sunset. **www.hotelflamingo.com**

COZUMEL Baldwin's Guest House — $$$

Avda 55 Sur, betw. Calle A. Rosado Salas & Calle 1 Sur **Tel** *(987) 872 11 48* **Fax** *(987) 872 11 48* **Rooms** *5*

In a quiet part of San Miguel, this little guest house has four ultra-comfortable rooms and a family-sized bungalow with its own kitchen, all within a lush walled garden with a pool. Generous breakfasts are included, and the American owners' special hospitality has won them many return guests. **www.moosepages.com**

COZUMEL Casa Mexicana — $$$

Avda Rafael E Melgar 457, betw. Calles 5 & 7 Sur **Tel** *(987) 872 90 90* **Fax** *(987) 872 90 73* **Rooms** *88*

A distinctly stylish hotel built on the waterfront in San Miguel town. The strikingly chic, amply-equipped rooms combine Mexican traditional touches with clean modern lines and colors, making the most of the Caribbean sunlight and superb sunsets. Restaurant and pool are just as impressive. **www.casamexicanacozumel.com**

COZUMEL Meliá Cozumel — $$$$

Carretera Costera Norte Km5.8 **Tel** *(987) 872 98 70* **Fax** *(987) 872 15 99* **Rooms** *148*

A family resort hotel with lots to do: diving, snorkeling, or other watersports, a Flintstones-themed fun park for small children, and varied day- and night-time entertainment programs. Plus, Cozumel's best golf course is just opposite. There are five restaurants, and rooms are fresh and pretty. **www.solmelia.com**

COZUMEL Playa Azul Golf & Beach Hotel — $$$$

Carretera a San Juan Km4 **Tel** *(987) 869 51 60* **Fax** *(987) 869 51 73* **Rooms** *51*

With a pretty cove to itself, this modestly-sized beach hotel is family-run, and so has a more individual feel than the bigger resort hotels. It still offers plenty to do, and diving, fishing, and golf are specialties. There are two restaurants and two bars, and a lovely beachside pool. **www.playa-azul.com**

ISLA MUJERES Hotel Vistalmar — $

Avenida Rueda Medina, corner Avda. Matamoros **Tel** *(998) 877 02 09* **Fax** *(998) 877 00 96* **Rooms** *58*

One of the most pleasant of Isla's budget hotels, on the waterfront and painted in yellow and orange. There is a terrace restaurant, and the plain rooms (some without air-conditioning) are well kept. Some have balconies with great sea views, for no extra charge.

ISLA MUJERES Villa Kiin — $$

Calle Zazil-Ha 129 **Tel** *(998) 877 00 45* **Fax** *(998) 877 00 45* **Rooms** *23*

An eccentric, friendly hotel in a lovely setting, on the sheltered Playa Secreto beach, ideal for children. Each room is different in size and facilities: some are quite simple and without air-conditioning, others are large and very comfortable, but all are prettily decorated. Prices vary as well. **www.villakiin.com**

ISLA MUJERES Cabañas María del Mar — $$$

Avenida Carlos Lazo 1 **Tel** *(998) 877 01 79* **Fax** *(998) 877 02 13* **Rooms** *73*

In a prime location right on Isla's best beach, this long-popular hotel has rooms with all modern comforts in *cabaña*-style beach bungalows around a garden and in a larger block farther back. There is a laidback beach bar, and the atmosphere is mellow; massages and health treatments are specialties. **www.cabanasdelmar.com**

ISLA MUJERES Hotel Secreto — $$$$$

Punta Norte **Tel** *(998) 877 10 39* **Fax** *(998) 877 10 48* **Rooms** *9*

Isla's most chic address, this award-winning boutique hotel has a secluded, intimate feel, and faces the rocky east side of the island rather than the main beaches. Rooms, pool, and terrace are strikingly contemporary; service is excellent, and there's a "SpaZenter" for more luxurious pampering. Breakfast included. **www.hotelsecreto.com**

IZAMAL Macanché — $$

Calle 22 no. 302, between Calles 33 & 35 **Tel** *(988) 954 02 87* **Rooms** *16*

A very tranquil place to stay with pretty rooms in 13 very spacious bungalows, each one different and some with kitchens, around a lush garden with a rock swimming pool. Breakfast is included, and other meals can be provided on request. The friendly owners also host yoga retreats. **www.macanche.com**

MAHAHUAL Balamkú Inn on the Beach — $$

Carretera Mahahual-Xcalak Km 5.7 **Tel** *(983) 839 53 32* **Fax** *(983) 839 53 32* **Rooms** *6*

An ideal place to get away from it all, with plenty of beach to itself on the still little-developed coast near Mahahual. The attractive, comfortable palm-roofed cabins have solar power and low-impact bathrooms. Refreshing breakfasts and kayak use are included, and there is excellent diving and fishing nearby. **www.balamku.com**

MÉRIDA Hotel Dolores Alba — $

Calle 63 no. 464, between Calles 52 & 54 **Tel** *(999) 928 56 50* **Fax** *(999) 928 31 63* **Rooms** *70*

Long one of Mérida's most popular hotels, the Dolores Alba is located four blocks from the main square, with rooms both around a giant old patio and in an annexe around the pool, with less character but newer amenities. All are excellent value. **www.doloresalba.com**

MÉRIDA Casa Esperanza $$

Calle 54 no. 4786, between Calles 55 & 57 **Tel** *(999) 155 60 49 (cell)* **Fax** *(999) 923 47 11* **Rooms** *3*

This grand old traditional Mérida house, with huge patios hidden from the street, has been wonderfully restored by its Canadian-Mexican owners. The rooms are beautiful, with every comfort and decorated with Mexican craftwork, and there is a pretty pool. Enormously welcoming, and breakfasts (included) are superb. **www.casaesperanza.com**

MÉRIDA Hotel Medio Mundo $$

Calle 55 no. 533, between Calles 64 & 66 **Tel** *(999) 924 54 72* **Fax** *(999) 924 54 72* **Rooms** *12*

Another small hotel that makes the most of the colonial patio architecture of old Mérida, with fresh tropical colors throughout and spacious, attractive rooms with modern amenities. The owners provide a warm, individual welcome, and there's a pretty pool, beside which fresh, fruit-packed breakfasts are served. **www.hotelmediomundo.com**

MÉRIDA Hotel del Peregrino $$

Calle 51 no. 488, between Calles 54 & 56 **Tel** *(999) 924 54 91* **Fax** *(999) 924 54 91* **Rooms** *13*

A good value hotel lcated in a colonial house, with airy, light, and comfortable double and family rooms. There's a rooftop bar and many other extras. Continental breakfast is included. Bookable day trips to Progreso, Uxmal, and Chichén Itzá. **www.hoteldelperegrino.com**

MÉRIDA Casa del Balam $$$

Calle 60 no. 488, corner of Calle 57 **Tel** *(999) 924 50 11* **Fax** *(999) 924 50 11* **Rooms** *51*

One of Mérida's most respected hotels, right beside all the action on Calle 60. Rooms are in the 19th-century main building or a newer annexe, connected by a charming patio; all combine some original features with modern comforts. Service is very attentive, and many tours are available for guests. **www.hotelcasadelbalam.com**

MÉRIDA Hotel Marionetas $$$

Calle 49 no. 516, between Calles 62 & 64 **Tel** *(999) 928 33 77* **Fax** *(999) 923 33 77* **Rooms** *9*

A charming, popular small hotel in an old Mérida house. The rooms, around a garden patio with pool, are imaginatively decorated with bright colors and tiles, and excellent bathrooms. The owners, international travelers, take great care of their guests, and varied breakfasts, served on the patio, are a specialty. **www.hotelmarionetas.com**

MÉRIDA Hacienda Xcanatún $$$$$

Xcanatún, 12km N of Mérida **Tel** *(999) 941 02 13* **Fax** *(999) 941 02 13* **Rooms** *18*

A seductively opulent hotel in an 18th-century hacienda, with gardens, in the middle of a village just north of Mérida. Rooms are all suites, with terraces and particularly luxurious bathrooms, and there are two pools, a spa, and a fine restaurant, La Casa de Piedra, with sophisticated fusion cuisine. **www.xcanatun.com**

PLAYA DEL CARMEN Casa de las Flores $$

Avenida 20, between Calles 4 & 6 **Tel** *(984) 873 28 98* **Fax** *(984) 873 25 34* **Rooms** *29*

A pleasant small hotel in a quiet part of Playa, and so much more tranquil than the places nearer the beach. The well-equipped rooms are prettily decorated in traditional Mexican style, and there's a nice pool at the patio. The owners are charming, and it is very good value. **www.hotelcasadelasflores.com**

PLAYA DEL CARMEN Posada Freud $$

Avenida 5, between Calles 8 & 10 **Tel** *(984) 873 06 01* **Fax** *(984) 873 06 01* **Rooms** *13*

An individual hotel right on Playa's Quinta Avenida, with plenty of character and a friendly, relaxed atmosphere. The brightly colored rooms are comfortably equipped, and there's a spacious suite on the ground floor. Despite the busy location, inside the hotel it can be surprisingly quiet. **www.posadafreud.com**

PLAYA DEL CARMEN Blue Parrot $$$

Avenida 1, by Calle 12 **Tel** *(984) 206 33 50* **Fax** *(984) 873 00 83* **Rooms** *80*

Once a cluster of basic cabañas, the Blue Parrot now offers very stylish, contemporary beach accommodations in Suites Property, elegant studios complete with kitchens, or the slightly cheaper (but still chic) 5th Avenue Hotel. In the center of Playa nightlife – the Blue Parrot also has the town's most popular bar. **www.blueparrot.com**

PLAYA DEL CARMEN La Tortuga Hotel & Spa $$$

Avenida 10, by Calle 14 **Tel** *(984) 873 14 84* **Fax** *(984) 873 07 98* **Rooms** *51*

La Tortuga is a *palapa*-style Caribbean hideaway with all modern amenities, located in the heart of the city. Every room is different, and all enclose a large inner courtyard with pool, outdoor bar, and covered patio areas. One of Playa del Carmen's defining hotels. **www.hotellatortuga.com**

PLAYA DEL CARMEN Shangri-La Caribe $$$$

Calle 38 Norte, by the beach **Tel** *(984) 803 28 04* **Fax** *(984) 873 05 00* **Rooms** *70*

This "hotel-village" offers the most seductively comfortable version of the palm-roofed beach hut: spacious, beautifully decorated and with all modern amenities. Some face the beach and some the garden, and they vary in size and price: penthouse cabins are superb. There is a fabulous pool, and a dive shop. **www.shangrilacaribe.net**

PUERTO MORELOS Rancho Sak-Ol/Libertad $$

Beach road, south of the town plaza **Tel** *(998) 871 01 81* **Fax** *(998) 871 01 81* **Rooms** *14*

A very relaxing beach retreat, with palm-roofed *palapa* rooms that ideally combine rustic simplicity and comfort. All have balconies or terraces with hammocks, but the upper cabins catch more of the breeze. Breakfast is included, and there is an open kitchen. Bikes and snorkels available for rent. **www.ranchosakol.com**

Key to Price Guide *see p292* **Key to Symbols** *see back cover flap*

PUNTA ALLEN Cuzán Guest House

Punta Allen village, 50km S of Tulum **Tel** *(983) 834 03 58* **Fax** *(983) 834 02 92* **Rooms** *8*

Few visitors get to Punta Allen because of the grueling dirt road from Tulum, so it feels very remote. The Cuzán's specialty is fishing, but bird-watching and other wildlife tours, snorkeling, and kayaking are all available. Rooms are rustic, and the restaurant often has excellent fresh fish. **www.flyfishmx.com**

PUNTA BETE Tides Riviera Maya

Riviera Maya Playa Xcalacoco, Fracc 7 **Tel** *(984) 877 30 00* **Fax** *(310) 752 09 60* **Rooms** *30*

Perhaps the most luxurious hotel on the Riviera Maya, this spectacularly designed modern beach retreat and spa has 29 villas, each with its own small pool and dining room, where gourmet meals from the elegant restaurant can be served for intimate dining. Five-day packages can make it a little less expensive. **www.tidesrivieramaya.com**

RÍO BEC Río Bec Dreams

Mex 186, Km142, near Chicanná ruins **Tel** *(983) 124 05 01* **Rooms** *6*

A hotel-restaurant created in a clearing in the jungle by a Canadian couple, who are huge Mayan enthusiasts and provide all sorts of information on visiting the local ruins. They have generously-sized cabins with bathrooms or cheaper "jungalows" with shared showers. The bar-restaurant is highly enjoyable. **www.riobecdreams.com**

RÍO BEC Chicanná Ecovillage Resort

Mex 186, Km144, near Chicanná ruins **Tel** *(981) 811 91 90* **Fax** *(981) 811 11 19* **Rooms** *42*

The most amply-equipped hotel for hundreds of kilometers, with comfortable modern rooms in palm-roofed villas, a pleasant restaurant, and a pool that is great for cooling off after visiting the Río Bec archaeological sites. No tours are provided, so guests must arrange their own, or have their own transport. **www.chicannaecovillageresort.com**

RÍO LAGARTOS Hotel San Felipe

Calle 9, between Calles 14 & 16, San Felipe **Tel** *(986) 862 20 27* **Fax** *(986) 862 20 36* **Rooms** *30*

This is the best of the few hotels around Río Lagartos, in San Felipe, west of the town. Its rooms are simple but well-kept, and the best have balconies from which to watch the sunsets. The restaurant has enjoyable local food, and the owners are expert fishing guides.

TULUM Cabañas Copal-Azulik-Zahra

Beach road, Km5 **Tel** *18888 989 922* **Rooms** *84*

Three adjacent cabaña-hotels on Tulum beach, with the same owners and very mellow atmosphere. Azulik has villas, made only of natural materials; Copal has cabins of different sizes, and Zahra is geared toward families. They share two restaurants, and the Maya Spa, with Mayan and conventional treatments. **www.ecotulum.com**

TULUM Dos Ceibas

Beach road, Km10 **Tel** *(984) 877 60 24* **Fax** *(984) 877 60 24* **Rooms** *8*

Another of the seductive *cabaña*-hotels along Tulum beach, with delightful, bright, and comfortable cabins in a garden running down to the shore. The restaurant is equally pretty, and snorkeling, massage, and yoga are among the activities on offer. Electricity, from solar power, runs from sunset until 7am. **www.dosceibas.com**

TULUM Piedra Escondida

Beach road, Km3.5 **Tel** *(984) 130 99 32* **Fax** *(984) 871 20 92* **Rooms** *8*

Set on a lovely sheltered beach, this very enjoyable hotel has brightly decorated rooms in palm-roofed villas, each room with its own terrace or balcony and ocean view. The restaurant, also on the beach, serves Mexican and Italian food. There are very good rates in off-seasons. **www.piedraescondida.com**

UXMAL Flycatcher Inn

Off Mex 261 in Santa Elena, 13km E of Uxmal **Tel** *(997) 107 41 26* **Rooms** *7*

This bed-and-breakfast in the village of Santa Elena, between Uxmal and Kabah, is the home of an American woman and her Mayan husband, and their local knowledge can make any visit a special experience. The rooms are spacious and pretty, with good modern facilities and distinctive décor. Breakfast included. **www.flycatcherinn.com**

UXMAL Hacienda Temozón

8km E of Mex 261, 44km N of Uxmal **Tel** *(999) 923 80 89* **Fax** *(999) 923 79 63* **Rooms** *28*

A spectacular hotel in a converted 17th-century colonial hacienda, between Mérida and Uxmal. The rooms all have high ceilings, huge bathrooms, and many other luxuries, and the gardens, restaurant, and pool are equally ravishing. The same company has converted other haciendas in Yucatán and Campeche. **www.haciendasmexico.com**

VALLADOLID Ecotel Quinta Regia

Calle 40 no. 160-A, between Calles 27 & 29 **Tel** *(985) 856 34 72* **Fax** *(985) 856 34 72* **Rooms** *112*

This hotel is modern but was built in neo-colonial style, with attractive rooms that combine contemporary amenities with colorful semi-traditional décor. The "eco" part of its name refers to the huge gardens, which grow all the fruit used in the hotel, and there is a pretty restaurant and pool. **www.ecotelquintaregia.com.mx**

VALLADOLID El Mesón del Marqués

Calle 39 no. 203, between Calles 40 & 42 **Tel** *(985) 856 20 73* **Fax** *(985) 856 22 80* **Rooms** *90*

A venerable hotel in a gracious old house on Valladolid's main plaza. The restaurant occupies the lovely main patio, and the pool is in another garden patio farther back. The rooms, some with original features, are cozy and comfortable, and the hotel has a distinctive charm. **www.mesondelmarques.com**

WHERE TO EAT

Mexican cuisine is considered by many to be one of the world's richest and most creative. Chiefly a mix of Spanish and pre-Columbian elements, it has been influenced more recently by other European and Asian flavors. Dishes originating from all corners of the country are served in a wide variety of restaurants. Visitors will find authentic Mexican cuisine different from the "Tex-Mex" Mexican food they may be used to at

Waitress with bread and pastries

home. For one thing, it is not necessarily as spicy. However, those who prefer it still milder can order their meals without chili (*sin chile*). In the big cities there are a good number of French and Italian restaurants, as well as other international options, such as Japanese sushi, Argentinian steaks, and Chinese chop suey. Vegetarian restaurants are rare, but many ordinary Mexican dishes, especially *antojitos (see p322)*, are meat-free.

Outdoor café at Parque Cepeda Peraza in Mérida (see p270)

TYPICAL RESTAURANTS AND BARS

The cheapest places to eat good Mexican food are the small, family-run *fondas* where fixed-price menus (*menú del día* or *comida corrida*) are served at lunch time. These are generally four-course meals followed by coffee or tea.

The most common restaurants are the popular *taquerías*, small places serving tacos at a few tables around a cooking area, where the tortilla-makers can often be seen in action.

Cantinas *(see p116)* are rowdy establishments where heavy drinking is common,

and women will not generally feel very comfortable. They can be differentiated from other, more elegant bars, by their Wild West-style swing doors.

The big cities also have a good selection of cafés, which generally serve light snacks rather than three course meals.

CHAIN RESTAURANTS

All the principal US fast-food chains are conspicuous in Mexico, including McDonald's, Burger King, KFC, and Pizza Hut. These days, however, there are also a number of good homegrown chains. One of the most famous is VIPS, which offers great breakfasts and international dishes like steaks and burgers. These are true fast-food restaurants – customers are not encouraged to linger. Carlos and Charlie's and Señor Frog's serve similar food to VIPS, but have a more relaxed, party atmosphere.

Those who fancy some shopping with their meal should try one of the many branches of Sanborn's where CDs, books, magazines, and videos are sold alongside the restaurant. The specialties here are the *enchiladas (see p322)*.

Other chains are more typically Mexican. Taco Inn serves tasty and original tacos, as well as a good range of vegetarian options. El Fogoncito sells *tacos al carbon (see p323)*. Potzolcalli specializes in *pozole (see p322)* and *tostadas (see p323)*, while Pollos Río offers a selection of grilled chicken dishes.

One of the Sanborn's chain, in the Casa de los Azulejos (see p326)

FOOD HYGIENE

In well-visited areas of Mexico, health standards are reasonably good, but it is still worth taking precautions. Outside of cities, drink only purified water, canned or bottled carbonated drinks, beer, wine, spirits, or hot drinks made from boiled water. Bottled water is available in restaurants, hotels, drugstores, and supermarkets. In restaurants and bars, order drinks without ice (*sin hielo*). Diners should avoid salads and uncooked vegetables in

A rustic roadside café near Laguna de Chapala (see p190)

Interior of the charming Café Tacuba (see p326), in the historic heart of Mexico City

all but the best restaurants and remember to peel all fruit. Steer clear of unpasteurized milk and undercooked shellfish, meat, or fish. Open-air markets and street food stalls should be treated with caution.

EATING HOURS

The streets are always full of food vendors because Mexicans will eat at any time of day. They often have two breakfasts (*desayunos*). The first, eaten at home, is a light meal of fruit or pastries with milky coffee. A more substantial breakfast, or *almuerzo*, may follow between 10 and 11am and is usually available in restaurants until lunchtime. It may consist of spicy eggs with tortillas, or even a steak.

From about 1:30pm restaurants are ready to provide lunch (*comida*), traditionally the main meal of the day. Mexicans take two or three hours for lunch, so restaurants are busy until 4 or 5pm.

Between 6 and 8pm is the *merienda*, a time for snacks, or *antojitos* (see p322), and coffee, tea, or alcoholic drinks. A normal Mexican dinner (*cena*) at home is a light meal served between 8 and 10pm. However, restaurants will also serve more substantial dinners.

Although many restaurants are open all year round, some close for various public holidays (see p31).

ENTERTAINMENT

Mexicans like their meals accompanied by music, and many restaurants have live acts performing at least once a week. The music ranges from classical piano to local styles such as festive *mariachi* (see p28), with dancers in colorful costumes, *jarocho* songs from Veracruz, and Mexican-style country music known as *música ranchera*.

PRICES AND PAYING

Fixed-price menus such as *comida corrida* normally offer better value than the à la carte equivalent. Prices shown on menus do not include the mandatory 15 percent tax (IVA), but this will automatically be added to your bill. Service charge is not included, and the level of tip is left to diners' discretion. It is usual to tip around 10 percent if you have had good service. You are not obliged to leave anything if the service has been poor.

Credit cards can be used in many restaurants in the larger cities, but in smaller places cash will definitely be necessary. If in doubt, check before ordering. VISA is the most widely accepted card, followed by MasterCard and American Express; few places take Diners Club. Travelers' checks are usually accepted but often at a poor rate of exchange.

WHEELCHAIR ACCESS

Some restaurants in Mexico make special provision for wheelchair users. The staff in most establishments will do their best to be helpful, and restaurants usually have a lavatory that can accommodate a wheelchair.

Tortilla-maker at a traditional restaurant in Oaxaca (see pp222–5)

CHILDREN

Mexicans as a rule love children and most restaurants welcome them, especially family-run places. Few provide high chairs, however, and there is often little room for maneuvering strollers. Child portions are not usually available, but you can always ask for a spare plate and share a dish between two.

SMOKING

Throughout Mexico smoking is prohibited in indoor public places such as hotels, restaurants, and airports, but is permitted in outdoor dining areas, and some areas with special ventilation systems. Fines are steep so always check before lighting up.

Diners at a thatch-roofed beachside restaurant in Puerto Ángel (see p217)

The Flavors of Mexico

In Mexico, each region's cuisine is distinctive, influenced by the soil, climate, and local produce. The Mexican diet is based on beans, corn, and chilies, and visitors are always amazed at the wide variety of dishes created from such simple foods. Tortillas (the soft, flat pancakes made from wheat or corn) may be tiny or huge, salsas mild to fiery, and beans, which might be red, pinkish-brown, or inky black, may be simply boiled, mashed ("refried"), or stewed with beer and spices. You can taste the rich heritage of the Aztecs, Maya, Olmecs, Mixtecs, and Zapatecs on your plate, along with that of Spanish and other settlers.

Cilantro
(coriander)

Browsing the fruit stall at a
Mexican street market

NORTHERN MEXICO

Baja (lower) California is a peninsula surrounded by sparkling sea, and well-known for its delicious fish tacos. It is also Mexico's vineyard.

El Norte (Chihuahua, Sonora, and Nuevo Leon) is a parched land of cowboys and cattle-raising. As a result, the most common meat is beef, usually cooked over an open fire or salted and dried. The cattle are also a source of dairy produce, and many dishes feature cheese. Beans are served spicy or cooked in beer, and tortillas are made from wheat instead of corn.

On the Pacific coast (from Mazatlan to Puerta Vallarta and Acapulco) shrimp, octopus, clams, oysters, squid, and crayfish are supremely good, and are served as *ceviche, antojitos,* or *tamales,* or grilled over an open fire.

CENTRAL MEXICO

The verdant, lush Central Plains (Aguascalientes, Jalisco, Guanajato, Michoacán, Zacatecas, San Louis Potosi, and Hidalgo) are the source of a wealth of *antojitos (see p322),* best enjoyed with a crisp, cool beer, or shots of tequila. *Pozole,* a stew of pork and hominy (a type of corn) is practically a cult, so beloved is it by the people of Jalisco.

Watermelon　　Guavas　　　　　　　　　Papayas　　　　Mangoes
　　　　　　　　　　　　　　　　　　　　　　　Tomatillos

Selection of luscious, ripe Mexican fruits

MEXICAN DISHES AND SPECIALTIES

At nearly every meal, a plate of beans, rice, or tortillas will appear on the table. Tortillas are not only the bread of Mexico but also its knife and fork, the soft corn pancakes being torn to pieces and used to wrap up delicious morsels and transport them to the mouth. Salsa will always be on offer, freshly made and full of flavor, often with a hot kick to it. It can be a mixture of any number of ingredients, depending on the region you are in: tomatoes or tomatillos *(see p323),* onions, chilies, garlic, avocado, citrus fruits, and cilantro (coriander) are all common. And, if that's not spice enough for you, a few bottles of Mexico's myriad hot sauces are usually to hand as well.

Red, black, and
garbanzo beans

Huevos rancheros *Strips of mixed peppers are sautéed, then eggs are broken into the pan and lightly cooked.*

Stallholder's basket of mixed chili peppers

The Yucatán peninsula (Merida, Cancun, and Cozumel) is the land of the Mayas, once cut off from the rest of Mexico by dense jungle. As well as fresh fish and seafood, try a bowl of *sopa de limon*, chicken soup with tiny yellow limes and crisp tortillas. The Yucatán offers myriad tortilla, bean, and egg dishes, often with pumpkin-seed sauces. Game is traditional, though pork and chicken are more common today. They are rubbed in spice pastes, then wrapped in leaves and baked. Spice pastes are the main flavorings of Yucatecan cuisine – you'll see them piled high in every market.

Mexico City is a place of many cultures, where Italian or French food, sushi, gaucho steaks, dim sum, and *cocina nuevo Mexicana* (new Mexican cuisine) can all be enjoyed. To the southeast lies Puebla, whose convents created the famous *mole poblano*, a thick sauce of puréed chilies, seeds, fruits, nuts, spices, and chocolate.

SOUTHERN MEXICO

The Gulf coastline is rich with shrimp, red snapper, sea bass, crab, octopus, and crayfish. Veracruz is famous for its distinctive garnish of tomatoes, olives, capers, and long peppers.

The Isthmus (Tabasco, Chiapas, and Oaxaca) is a land of fertile soil, home of the Olmecs, Mixtecs and Zapatecs. In Oaxaca you'll find hand-pounded chocolate, a rainbow of *moles*, and a range of white cheeses as well as delicacies such as fried grasshopper (eaten like popcorn) and crisp-dried maguet worms, ground with chilies as a seasoning.

Ocean-fresh fish, straight from the Gulf of Mexico

STREET FOOD

Any number of delicious foods are sold in the street. For a sweet start to the day, find a stall selling *churros* or *buñuelos* (crisp fried pastries) along with coffee or hot chocolate in which to dip them. Walk down any street and inhale the aroma of bar-becuing meat, then try some folded into a fresh tortilla. For a vitamin-rich and invigorating snack, buy a slab of fresh pineapple, a whole peeled orange, or a wedge of *jícama (see p.323)* rubbed with fresh lime and sprinkled liberally with hot chili powder. And if you see a sign for *tortas* you must try one – it's a meal-in-a-roll, filled with meat, refried beans, avocado, salsa, and pickled onion.

Carne asada *Spiced steak is barbecued with scallions, chilies, and peppers, and served with tortillas.*

Ceviche *Raw fish is diced and marinated in lemon juice, then mixed with chili, tomato, onion, and cilantro.*

Tamales *Corn husks are lined with corn dough and filled with shredded meat, then steamed.*

Antojitos

Mexican appetizers are called *antojitos* and are similar to
Spanish *tapas*. The name derives from the word *antojo* –
"a craving" or "a whim" – and *antojitos* are literally
"what you fancy." An *antojito* can be anything from
decorative fruit to a substantial savory dish. These tasty
little snacks are enjoyed everywhere in Mexico – in homes,
bars, restaurants, markets, parks, and streets – at any time,
day or night. An *antojito* can be ordered as an aperitif
with drinks (when it is called a *botana*) or, in a
restaurant, served as a first course.

Guacamole

Tostadas *is a dish of crisp-fried tortillas
topped with refried beans, chicken,
salad, guacamole, and sour cream.*

Tortas compuestas, *tasty sandwiches
made with small French-style loaves
called* bolillos *or* terelas, *come with a
choice of fillings.*

Salsa *can be
served with*
antojitos *as a
fresh and
spicy dip.*

Flautas *are tortillas
filled with chicken
or cheese, deep-fried
and served with
guacamole
or salsa.*

Tacos al carbon *are
small tortillas folded
over barbecued meat,
salsa, and guacamole.*

Enchiladas, *fried, filled,
rolled tortillas with a sauce,
can have a variety of fillings, such
as cheese and onion or chicken.*

Sopes *are miniature fried
corn-dough bowls filled
with beans and sauce
and topped with
salad or cheese.*

**Street food stallholder preparing a
variety of fresh *antojitos***

POPULAR ANTOJITOS

If you were asked to describe the food of Mexico,
the chances are that you would name dishes that
are, in fact, *antojitos* – tacos, tostadas, enchiladas,
quesadillas – things that you might find on a
combination plate in a Mexican restaurant abroad.
The most commonly available *antojitos* are dishes
of tortillas and *masa* (corn flour), prepared in a
variety of shapes and guises and topped or filled
with the wide array of ingredients. Quesadillas
(fried or grilled corn or wheat tortillas filled with
melted cheese) are a delicious *antojito*. In addition
to the cheese, they might contain *rajas* (sautéed
mild chilies) or *carnitas* (long-simmered small
pieces of pork). Tacos are popular *antojitos*, with
a huge range of possible fillings, such as shrimp
or fish with avocado, lobster with beans, stewed
meat or simmered beans, or even strange
ingredients such as the ants' eggs of Oaxaca.

Reading the Menu

General vocabulary likely to be useful when eating out is given in the Phrase Book on pages 405-8. The list below gives the main items and ingredients you will probably see on a Mexican menu, in alphabetical order. Not all regional variations of dishes are listed here. Some dishes commonly thought to be Mexican – burritos, fajitas, taco shells, and nachos – were actually invented in the United States. In Mexico, the main meal of the day is quite formal, starting with a soup or rice dish, followed by meat or fish, and ending with flan or a fruit dessert.

Chilies

achiote red paste made from annatto seeds.

adobo light version of *mole*.

albóndigas meatballs.

annatto small, dark red seed used by the Maya Indians to color and flavor food.

ate thick fruit jelly, typically made of quince or guava, often served with cheese.

atún tuna fish. Note that *tuna* is a fruit.

barbacoa lamb cooked in a pit.

buñuelos dessert of crispy, fried wheat pancakes.

cajeta de Celaya fudge sauce made with goat's milk.

caldo largo soup made with fish and seafood.

carne a la Tampiqueña thin strips of beef, grilled.

carnitas marinated fried pork.

cecina semi-dried, salted meat in thin slices.

chalupas boat-shaped, fried corn tortillas garnished with sauce, lettuce, and onions.

chicharrón pork scratchings.

chiles rellenos chilies stuffed with cheese or ground meat, battered, fried, and covered in tomato sauce.

chongos milky dessert of curds in syrup and cinnamon.

Dishes on a street food stall in the market at Oaxaca (see p222-5)

Street market in San Cristóbal de las Casas (see p231)

chorizo spicy pork sausage.

churros sugary, deep-fried batter sticks.

cochinita pibil Maya dish of suckling pig cooked in a pit.

cuitlacoche (or *huitlacoche*) fungus growing on corncobs; it is considered a delicacy.

dulce de calabaza stewed pumpkin in cinnamon syrup.

enchiladas suizas corn tortillas filled with chicken, covered in sauce, melted cheese and cream.

energético breakfast fruit salad with muesli and yogurt.

entomatada soft tortilla in a tomato sauce.

epazote aromatic herb used to flavor many dishes.

flor de calabaza pumpkin flower.

frijoles beans. Often eaten refried (see p320) or freshly cooked as *frijoles de olla*.

gorditas thick tortillas stuffed with cheese.

horno, al baked.

huevos a la mexicana scrambled eggs with tomatoes, chilies, and onions.

huevos motuleños tortilla topped with ham, fried eggs, and a sauce made with cheese, peas, and tomato.

huevos revueltos scrambled eggs.

jícama vegetable similar to a turnip; salted and sprinkled with lime and chili powder.

machaca sundried shredded beef from Nuevo León.

mole means "sauce" in Nahuatl. All *moles* are made in a similar way using chilies, nuts, and spices. Green, red and yellow *moles* are usually served with pork or chicken.

moros con cristianos rice dish made with black beans, garnished with fried plantain.

nopal the fleshy leaf of the prickly pear (paddle cactus).

panucho a Yucatecan dish of layered tortillas stuffed with beans.

pescado al mojo de ajo fish filet in a white, garlic sauce.

pipián pumpkin-seed sauce.

plátano macho frito fried plantain. Goes well with rice.

pollo verde almendrado chicken in green tomatillo and almond sauce.

pozole pork and corn soup.

puntas de filete quartered beef filet ends.

queso fresco a white cheese that is crumbled over some cooked dishes.

rajas chili strips and onion slices in tomato sauce.

sopa soup. Varieties include *de aguacate* (avocado), *de fideo* (chicken broth with noodles), and *de lima* (chicken stock flavored with lemon).

tacos al carbón soft corn tortillas wrapped around cooked meats.

tomatillo a berry related to the Cape gooseberry *(Physalis)*, which is used for flavoring sauces.

Veracruzana, a la fish cooked with tomatoes and onions.

What to Drink in Mexico

Mexico offers a wide variety of drinks, both alcoholic and nonalcoholic, but choose carefully if you don't want health problems. Outside of cities, don't drink tap water – buy bottled water from a supermarket or reputable shop. It is wise to avoid fruit juices, milkshakes, and other drinks sold at market and street stalls or in bars of dubious cleanliness. Soft drinks in bottles, cartons, and cans are all safe.

Los Danzantes bar in Mexico City *(see p329)*

BEER

Beer *(cerveza)* was introduced to Mexico by German immigrant miners. Much of the beer drunk is lager *(cerveza rubia)*, but there are also several good dark beers *(cerveza oscura)* available. Popular brands are Corona, Negra Modelo, and XX Dos Equis. *Michelada* is a refreshing drink made with beer and lime juice, and served with salt on the rim of the glass.

Light and dark Mexican beers

WINES

Although Mexico is the oldest wine producer in the Americas, Mexicans are not big wine drinkers. The main vineyards are in the Valle de Guadalupe near Ensenada *(see p162)*, where the pioneer Bodega Santo Tomás is based, as is Monte Xanic. Other Baja California producers include Pinson and Cetto. Wine is made in Querétaro (by Cavas de San Juan, Freixenet, and Domecq), in Zacatecas (by Pinson), and in Coahuila (by Casa Madero). Imported wine is available too.

White wine by Domecq

OTHER ALCOHOLIC DRINKS

Many other drinks are served in Mexican bars and restaurants, especially *kahlúa*, (a coffee liqueur flavored with vanilla), *ron* (rum), and *rompope*, an eggnog made in Puebla, often offered to children or the elderly. *Aguardiente* is a fiery spirit, not for the faint hearted. Standard international cocktails include piña colada, a refreshing blend of pineapple juice, rum, and coconut, and daiquiri, made with rum, lime juice, and sugar.

Kahlúa   **Rompope**

COLD DRINKS AND FRUIT JUICES

There are plenty of soft drinks available, but in a bar always make sure you drink from a bottle that has been opened in front of you.Water can be ordered still *(sin gas)* or fizzy *(con gas)*. Canned fizzy drinks are called *refrescos*. All the international varieties are available. A selection of freshly prepared fruit juices is also available, but try to choose those made with fruits that need to be peeled. Made like lemonade, *naranjada* is a refreshing orange juice drink. *Agua de Jamaica* is made from a hibiscus flower steeped in hot water and served chilled.

Agua de Jamaica   **Orange juice**

HOT DRINKS

Coffee is generally medium-strength filter coffee *(café americano)* which can be served with milk. For a strong, authentic Mexican coffee order *café de olla*, sweetened and flavored with cinnamon. Black coffee is *café negro, tinto,* or *solo*. Tea is not widely drunk but herb teas, such as camomile *(manzanilla)*, mint *(hierbabuena)*, and lemon grass *(té limón)*, are available. *Atole* is a nutritious drink of corn meal and milk, flavored with chocolate or fruits. Hot chocolate *(chocolate caliente)*, made with vanilla or cinnamon, is also popular.

Atole   **Café de olla**   **Hot chocolate**

Tequila and Mezcal

Tequila and Mezcal are both internationally known Mexican aperitifs, distilled from the sap of different species of the agave plant. Tequila is to mezcal as Cognac is to brandy – a refined, connoisseur's drink. Both are made from similar ingredients by a similar process, but tequila can be produced only in a strictly defined region that centers on the town of

Statue in Tequila

Tequila near Guadalajara *(see p187)*. Both drinks are distantly derived from pulque, a low-alcohol, fermented beverage made from another species of agave, which was drunk by the people of ancient Mexico. If you stay any length of time in Mexico you will almost certainly be offered at least one glass of mezcal or tequila.

Pulque *was first made as early as 200 BC. It was used by priests as a way of inducing a religious trance and given to sacrificial victims to ease their passage into the next world. Pulque, which is never bottled, is an acquired taste.*

BUYING TEQUILA AND MEZCAL

The best tequila is made from 100 percent blue agave: this is stated on the label to prove that sugar has not been added. Tequila comes in three varieties. *Blanco* (white) is unaged, clear, and colorless. *Reposado* and *añejo* are tequilas which have been aged in oak barrels (for up to a year and three years respectively), turning them an amber color. *Mezcal con gusano* is made near Oaxaca. A caterpillar is placed in the bottle to prove that the mezcal is high enough in alcohol to preserve it.

Mezcal con gusano   **Tequila reposado**

HOW TEQUILA IS MADE

Tequila is made by fermenting the sap of the agave and distilling the resultant mixture twice before bottling.

Stage one *The agave* (Agave tequilana weber) *is harvested after 8–10 years, before it flowers. The leaves are removed, leaving a compact heart or piña (literally "pineapple").*

Stage two *The* piñas *are steamed in an oven and crushed to release their sap, the raw material for tequila.*

Stage three *Yeast is added to the sap. After a period of fermentation the liquid is distilled twice to purify it. The tequila is then either bottled or aged in oak vats.*

HOW TO DRINK TEQUILA

Tequila is usually served with lime and salt or as a *vampiro* with a tomato and orange chaser called a *sangrita*. Tequila blanco is often mixed with other drinks to make cocktails like tequila sunrise (with grenadine and orange juice), and margarita, made with lime juice and triple sec and served with salt around the rim of the glass.

Tequila with lime and salt

Choosing a Restaurant

The restaurants in this guide have been selected for their atmosphere and the excellence of their food. In some parts of Mexico, however, there may be few restaurants worth a visit in their own right. In such cases we suggest somewhere to eat which at least offers good value. For details on Mexican cuisine see *pp320–23*.

PRICE CATEGORIES
The following price ranges are for a three-course meal for one, with a glass of house wine, including tax and service.

Ⓢ Under $15
ⓈⓈ $15–$25
ⓈⓈⓈ $25–$35
ⓈⓈⓈⓈ $35–$45
ⓈⓈⓈⓈⓈ Over $45

MEXICO CITY

HISTORIC CENTER Café El Popular
Ⓢ
Avenida de 5 de Mayo 52 **Tel** *55 18 60 81*
Map *4 E2*

An inviting window of fresh baked goods, a bustling crowd of patrons, and reasonable prices are clues to why El Popular is so named. Though small, it is cozy, with dining on two levels, both with views. Regional specialties include a variety of *tamales* from Oaxaca. Breakfast, lunch, and dinner daily.

HISTORIC CENTER Café Trevi
Ⓢ
Colón 1, Col. Centro **Tel** *55 12 30 20*
Map *3 B1*

Large picture windows face the Alameda where the Trevi has been serving pasta specialties, the best pizza in the area, and breakfast to downtowners for decades. Inside, the large dining room is plain chrome and Formica. Spaghetti is served many ways, including with garlic and seafood. Breakfast, lunch, and dinner daily.

HISTORIC CENTER Churrería El Moro
Ⓢ
Lázaro Cárdenas 42 **Tel** *55 12 08 96*
Map *3 C5*

With its beautifully tiled walls and columns, this restaurant two blocks from the Palacio de Bellas Artes is an institution. The specialty *churros* are made with dough in a large vat with oil and sugar. Four different types of hot chocolate are also offered, alongside milkshakes. Breakfast, lunch, and dinner daily.

HISTORIC CENTER Café Tacuba
ⓈⓈ
Tacuba 28, Col. Centro **Tel** *55 21 20 48*
Map *4 D1*

The front window filled with scrumptious baked goods, and interior walls with paintings of colonial-era nuns have been Café Tacuba's calling card since 1912. Regional food from all over Mexico is another attraction. Try the *tamales* or *tinga* – (chicken, tomatoes, and jalapeno peppers rolled in corn tortillas and fried). Breakfast, lunch, and dinner.

HISTORIC CENTER El Cardenal
ⓈⓈ
Palma 23, Col. Centro **Tel** *55 21 88 15*
Map *4 E2*

El Cardenal's stately appearance, with cloth covered tables and refined atmosphere, is foil for reasonable prices, and pre-Hispanic food specialties, as well as just plain good home cooking. Try the delicious *escamole* (ant eggs) or *robalo* (sea bass) in *epazote* (a pungent herb) sauce. Breakfast and lunch daily.

HISTORIC CENTER Casa de los Azulejos – Sanborns
ⓈⓈ
Francisco Madero 4, Col Centro **Tel** *55 12 13 31*
Map *4 D2*

The exterior of this 16th-century edifice, covered in blue and white tiles (*azulejos*) from Puebla, was the home of the Count of Orizaba. The most famous Sanborns restaurant in Mexico is the supreme downtown meeting place with an international menu. Try the *Huevos divorciados* ("divorced eggs") for breakfast. Breakfast, lunch, and dinner daily.

HISTORIC CENTER Fonda Don Chon
ⓈⓈ
Calle Regina 160, Col. Centro **Tel** *55 42 08 73*
Map *4 E3*

The most famous restaurant in the city for pre-Hispanic food, the emphasis is on the food, not the mismatched furniture. Here, savor ant eggs in mushroom sauce, armadillo stew, *tepezquintle* (a type of rodent) roast, and perhaps wild boar in a mango sauce or batter-fried century plant blossoms. Lunch Mon–Sat.

HISTORIC CENTER Hosteriá Santo Domingo
ⓈⓈ
Belisario Dominguez 72, Col. Centro **Tel** *55 10 14 34*
Map *4 E1*

Famed for its longevity – 140 years and counting – and its year-round specialty of *chiles en nogada* (stuffed peppers in almond sauce), it is also one of the most lively, colorful, and popular downtown restaurants. The best of Mexico's regional specialties are served, including *mole poblano* (Puebla-style *mole*). Breakfast, lunch, and dinner daily.

HISTORIC CENTER La Terraza
ⓈⓈ
Francisco Madero 73-7, Col. Centro **Tel** *55 21 86 00*
Map *4 E2*

Since 1937, the top-floor restaurant of the Hotel Majestic has offered the most popular dining spot with a view of the Zócalo. International menu with an emphasis on Mexican specialties. Try the *chilaquiles* – a baked mixture of tortillas, white cheese, cream, and eggs or chicken. Breakfast, lunch, and dinner daily.

Key to Symbols *see back cover flap*

HISTORIC CENTER Bar La Ópera
$$$

*Avenida 5 de Mayo 10, Col. Centro **Tel** 55 12 89 59* **Map** 4 D1

The most opulent remainder of the city's turn-of-the-20th century *cantinas*, Bar La Ópera is a supreme visual and cultural treat for visitors. Baby eels *(anguilas)* with crackers are tasty for a starter, fish Veracruz-style for the main course, and something from the pastry cart for dessert. Lunch and dinner daily (no dinner Sun).

HISTORIC CENTER Casa de la Sirena
 $$$

*República de Guatemala 32, Col. Centro **Tel** 57 04 33 45* **Map** 4 F1

Up a flight of stairs, the main dining floor and patio showcase a stunning rear view of Mexico's Catedral Metropolitana. Housed in a 16th-century building, nouvelle Mexican cuisine is the specialty. The chicken in mango sauce, and *mole poblano* are worthy choices. Well-stocked bar. Lunch and dinner Mon–Sat.

HISTORIC CENTER Casino Español
$$$

*Isabel la Católica 29, Col. Centro **Tel** 55 21 88 94* **Map** 4 D5

Housed in a turn-of-the-20th-century mansion, the Casino Español has dished out large portions of Spanish favorites to loyal patrons for decades. The seafood-filled *paella* is a popular specialty. The large menu offers the opportunity to taste several specialties. Lunch until early evening daily.

HISTORIC CENTER Centro Castellano
 $$$

*Uruguay 16, Col. Centro **Tel** 55 18 29 37* **Map** 4 D2

Housed in a restored old house close to the Zócalo, this rustic restaurant serves authentic Spanish food, specializing in seafood. A main course favorite is *huachinango a las brasas* (red snapper); for dessert, try the delicious *leche frita*. Spanish wine list. Good service. Lunch and dinner daily.

HISTORIC CENTER Danubio
$$$

*Uruguay 3, Col. Centro **Tel** 55 12 09 12* **Map** 4 D2

Danubio's sustained popularity since 1936 is testament to a world of well-prepared fish and seafood recipes. Legions of waiters ferry platters of stuffed red snapper, smoked Norwegian salmon, and the specialty *langostinos* (crayfish) in *mojo de ajo* (garlic), and much more. Lunch and dinner daily.

HISTORIC CENTER Los Girasoles
$$$

*Xicotencatl 1, Col. Centro **Tel** 55 10 32 81* **Map** 4 D1

One of the few Centro Historico street-level restaurants offering both interior dining (cozy country French décor) or outside (with a view of the Museo Nacional de Arte). The menu ranges from pre-Hispanic specialties through nouvelle Mexican. Lunch and dinner daily.

REFORMA & CHAPULTEPEC La Tecla
$

*Molière 56, Col. Polanco **Tel** 52 82 00 10*

This restaurant serves innovative Mexican cooking in a contemporary setting. The dishes include pumpkin flowers stuffed with goat's cheese, beef consommé flavored with smoked oysters, and grilled prawns on a bed of rice and cactus. Lunch daily.

REFORMA & CHAPULTEPEC Los Almendros
$$

*Campos Eliseos 164, Col. Polanco **Tel** 55 31 66 46* **Map** 1 A3

Yucatecan food springs to life in this upscale branch of the Yucatecan-based chain. From the *pollo* and *cochinita pibils* (slow-roasted pork) using the deliciously fragrant *achiote* paste, to the *salbutes* – a fried *masa* appetizer, and *sopa de lima* (lime soup), it is all authentic, even when there's a nouvelle twist. Breakfast, lunch, and dinner daily.

REFORMA & CHAPULTEPEC Fonda Mexicana
$$

*Homero 1910, Col. Polanco **Tel** 55 57 61 44* **Map** 2 A2

A dressy clientele out for a special meal gathers at one of the city's best restaurants, serving specialties from Puebla. The pleasing *arrachera a la parrilla*, is unique. The authentic *mole poblano* doesn't get much better than here. Reservations recommended. Breakfast and lunch daily; dinner Mon–Sat.

REFORMA & CHAPULTEPEC Fonda del Recuerdo
$$

*Bahia de las Palmas 37, Col. Verónica Anzures **Tel** 91 12 74 76* **Map** 1 C2

Rousing, vivacious musicians accompany diners here who choose from all the best fish and seafood *platillos* the country offers. Toss in a few non-fish specialties such as *carne Tampiqueña* (a hearty beef specialty), and there is something for all. Breakfast, lunch & dinner daily.

REFORMA & CHAPULTEPEC Mazurka
$$$

*Nueva York 150, Col. Nápoles **Tel** 55 43 45 09*

The city's oldest Polish restaurant offers baked duck stuffed with fruit and cheese crepes as its two best known dishes. But the keilbassa sausage with potatoes and cabbage and the lamb in cream sauce have a loyal following. Large bar. Diners are offered a complimentary vodka on arrival. Lunch and dinner daily (no dinner Mon & Sun).

REFORMA & CHAPULTEPEC Bellinghausen
 $$$

*Londres 95, Col. Juárez **Tel** 52 07 49 78* **Map** 2 E3

Swarms of smart waiters serve platters of meat and seafood daily either in the stately dining room or outside on the patio. The house specialty is *filete chemita* (grilled beef steak), but if you've never had a perfectly prepared leg of goat, this would be the place to try. Ice cream is made on the premises. Lunch and early dinner daily.

REFORMA & CHAPULTEPEC La Bottiglia $$$

Edgar Allan Poe 8, Col. Polanco **Tel** *52 80 06 09* **Map** 1 B3

Invitingly intimate with gleaming wood and glass all around, closely placed cloth-covered tables, and candles in Chianti bottles, La Bottiglia offers solid innovations in Italian food. Trout in basil sauce delights the tastebuds along with the seafood linguine. Extensive wine list includes Italian labels. Lunch and dinner daily (no dinner Sun).

REFORMA & CHAPULTEPEC Casa Portuguesa $$$

Emilio Castelar 121, Col. Polanco **Tel** *52 81 00 75*

Located opposite Parque Polanco, this restaurant offers delicious Portuguese specialties, including many fish dishes. In particular, try one of the six different codfish specials, all accompanied by an excellent glass of port. The decor is modern, with white walls and big windows. Lunch and dinner daily (no dinner Sun).

REFORMA & CHAPULTEPEC Chalet Suizo $$$

Niza 37, Col. Juárez **Tel** *55 11 75 29* **Map** 2 E3

From the Swiss Chalet architecture to the menu, this is pure Swiss with German twists. The menu changes daily but may include veal with morel mushrooms, German pot roast, and, of course, *sauerbraten*. Fondue, either sweet or savory, is paired with pots of smooth, warm cheese. Rainbow trout leads the daily specials. Lunch and dinner daily.

REFORMA & CHAPULTEPEC Fonda del Refugio $$$

Liverpool 166, Col. Juárez **Tel** *52 07 27 32* **Map** 2 E4

With gleaming white walls, copper pots, and folk art, this decades old, small restaurant showcases Mexico's regional food. Mainstays include *chiles rellenos* (stuffed chilis). Daily specials include the *mole verde de pepita* (green *mole*). An ample *aguas frescas* (fresh fruit-flavored drinks) menu. Lunch and dinner daily.

REFORMA & CHAPULTEPEC Matisse $$$

Amsterdam 260, Col. Condesa **Tel** *52 64 58 53*

A delightful and cozy neighborhood restaurant in a restored 1930s house, filled with period furniture. The European menu includes delicious fresh juices, eggs served Matisse style, and a breakfast omelet with salmon and cheese. Try the home-made pastries. Live jazz Friday and Saturday evening. Breakfast, lunch, and dinner daily.

REFORMA & CHAPULTEPEC Nautilus $$$

Masaryk 360–4. Col. Polanco **Tel** *52 80 22 83* **Map** 1 A2

Welcoming, and casually trendy with cloth-covered tables, Nautilus gets better with the years. The extensive menu includes three kinds of *chilaquiles* at breakfast, delicious fish and seafood *taco* starters, and main courses of meat, fish, and seafood using recipes from many cultures. Breakfast Sat & Sun, lunch and dinner daily.

REFORMA & CHAPULTEPEC Non Solo Pasta $$$

Julio Verne 89, Col. Polanco **Tel** *52 80 97 06*

Pleasing prices and authentic Italian food keeps this small, trendy Polanco restaurant in business. It not only serves pasta, as the name informs; there is *vitello tonnato* (veal in a delicate mayonnaise sauce). For pasta, a good choice is the house specialty – *tagliatelle amatriciano* (with a pancetta-laced sauce). Full bar. Lunch and dinner daily.

REFORMA & CHAPULTEPEC Otro Lugar de la Mancha $$$

Esopo 11, Chapultepec los Morales **Tel** *52 80 48 26*

Situated in front of the Conservatorio Nacional de Música, Otro Lugar de la Mancha takes its inspiration from the novel *Don Quixote* and even has a bookstore attached. It is not unusual to see people devouring books along with their meals. The restaurant has a wooden decor and a pretty floral garden. Breakfast, lunch, and dinner daily.

REFORMA & CHAPULTEPEC Thai Garden $$$

Calderón de la Barca 72, Col. Polanco **Tel** *52 81 38 50*

You do not have to go all the way to Asia to enjoy the real flavor of Thai food. In the heart of the commercial district of Polanco, this elegant restaurant with Thai decoration serves authentic Thai food – spring rolls, chicken curry, lamb with hot peppers, and fine herbs and vegetables. Lunch daily, dinner Mon–Sat.

REFORMA & CHAPULTEPEC Mandarin House $$$$

Cofre de Perote 205B, Lomas de Chapultepec **Tel** *55 20 98 70*

One of the most renowned gourmet Chinese restaurants in Mexico, near the bridge between Tecamachalco and Palmas, Mandarin House specializes in Peking duck and "shrimp 44" with Oriental sauce. Good service. Contemporary, almost minimalist décor. Lunch and dinner daily (no dinner Sun).

REFORMA & CHAPULTEPEC Au Pied de Cochon $$$$

Campos Elisios 218 **Tel** *53 27 77 56* **Map** 1 A3

This is one of the finest restaurants in Mexico, and has a great atmosphere. The seafood is very good, and French specialties include pork shank with green cabbage in butter. The classic *coq au vin* is served with braised vegetables. Lunch and dinner daily.

REFORMA & CHAPULTEPEC Specia $$$$

Amsterdam 241, Col. Hipódromo Condesa **Tel** *55 64 13 67*

Dine with a view of this trendy area through large picture windows. Eastern European specialties focus on dishes from Poland and Hungary, as well as from Italy. Try the stuffed cabbage or baked lamb. Deliciously flavored noodles and potatoes. Lunch and dinner daily (no dinner Sun).

Key to Price Guide *see p326* **Key to Symbols** *see back cover flap*

REFORMA & CHAPULTEPEC Le Cirque $$$$$

Calz Mariano Escobedo 700 **Tel** *52 63 88 88* **Map** *1 B3*

The menu here offers an abundance of French and Italian dishes, as well as a variety of more locally sourced seasonal dishes. The wine cellar has over 600 wines from all around the world. The colorful, contemporary design evokes the gaiety of the circus. Lunch and dinner daily.

REFORMA & CHAPULTEPEC Hacienda de los Morales $$$$$

Vazquez de Melia 525, Col. del Bosque **Tel** *52 83 30 29*

Housed in a spacious 16th-century hacienda, the international menu includes many Mexican specialties and some nouvelle Mexican dishes. On Wednesday and Sunday the specialty is pit-baked lamb wrapped in maguey leaves Texcoco-style. There is a vast tequila selection. Lunch and dinner daily.

REFORMA & CHAPULTEPEC Izote $$$$$

Presidente Mazaryk 513, Col. Polanco **Tel** *52 80 16 71* **Map** *1 A3*

Patricia Quintana, owner, chef, and cookbook author, is queen of the kitchen here. She serves Mexico's best with a nouvelle twist unlike any other. The lobster *enchiladas* with a pumpkinseed sauce, and the shrimp in tamarind *mole*, are two examples of her much touted fare. Reservations recommended. Lunch and dinner daily (no dinner Sun).

REFORMA & CHAPULTEPEC Les Moustaches $$$$$

Rio Sena 88, Col. Cuauhtémoc **Tel** *55 33 33 90* **Map** *2 D2*

With delectable French cuisine and an excellent wine list, this is considered to be one of the best restaurants in Mexico. Housed in a turn-of-the-20th century mansion, it exudes subdued elegance with candle-lit tables. The cream of onion soup is wonderful as is the fish Veronique. Jacket and tie. Lunch daily, dinner Wed–Sun.

REFORMA & CHAPULTEPEC Restaurante Lago de Chapultepec $$$$$

Lago Mayor, 2a Sección **Tel** *55 15 95 85*

The tiered dining room overlooks the lake, creating one of the city's most sophisticated dining venues. Restaurante Lago de Chapultepec has a Mexican menu, and offers dishes such as *pámpano* (a type of fish) stuffed with seafood and covered in a *poblano* pepper sauce. Prime rib and steak specialties. Jacket and tie. Reservations recommended.

REFORMA & CHAPULTEPEC Rincón Argentino $$$$$

Presidente Masaryk 177, Col. Polanco **Tel** *52 54 87 75* **Map** *1 A3*

This little corner of Argentina offers the best of that country's famed meat specialties. From the authentic *chimicurri* sauce to the steaks, chicken, and sausage, the huge portions are straight from the Argentine grill. *Empanadas* make a terrific starter. Arrive early or late at lunchtime for more chance of getting a table. Lunch and dinner daily.

REFORMA & CHAPULTEPEC Tezka $$$$$

Amberes 78, Col. Juárez **Tel** *52 28 99 18* **Map** *2 E3*

Located on the second floor of the Royal Zona Rosa Hotel, Tezka's Basque cuisine is delightfully innovative with nouvelle twists. Notable are the sea bass in a delicious pistachio sauce, and the shrimp and asparagus soup. James Beard featured cuisine. Reservations recommended. Lunch and dinner Mon–Sat (no lunch Sat).

FARTHER AFIELD Cantina La Coyoacana $$$

Higuera 14, Col. Coyoacan **Tel** *56 58 53 37*

This charming cantina attracts many customers. Partly it is the fabulous bar, and partly the full assortment of Mexican specialties that go well with libation. *Barbacoa* (earth-cooked lamb) and *tlacoyos* are a specialty of the house. Lunch and dinner daily.

FARTHER AFIELD Casa Merlos $$$

Victoriano Zepeda 80, Col. Observatorio **Tel** *52 77 43 60*

In a neighborhood south of Chapultepec Park, a block off Observatorio, this haven of Puebla food welcomes with a façade of Puebla tiles. *Moles* in every color – green, white, yellow, brown, red, and black – are a big draw, along with other Puebla favorites including *tinga* and *molotes*. The menu changes by season. Lunch Thu–Sun.

FARTHER AFIELD Los Danzantes $$$

Plaza Jardin Centenario 12, Col. Coyocan **Tel** *56 58 64 51*

A glass of mezcal upon arrival sets the tone for the Oaxacan-Mexican fusion specialties offered in a colonial-style edifice. The shrimp in coconut and sweet sour sauce primes tastebuds. The *huitlacoche* ravioli is a true innovation that shows the sophistication of the contemporary menu. Breakfast Sat–Sun; lunch and dinner daily.

FARTHER AFIELD Fonda San Angel $$$

Plaza San Jacinto 3, Col. San Angel **Tel** *55 50 16 41*

Almost beside the famed Bazar del Sábado, and in an old mansion, Fonda San Angel is busy on market day, but is also a haven of good food. The pork in a plum-orange sauce hits the mark. Delicious cheese soup flavored with *poblano* peppers. Breakfast Mon–Fri; lunch and dinner daily (no dinner Sun).

FARTHER AFIELD Antigua Hacienda Tlalpan $$$$

Calzada de Tlalpan 4619, Col. Tlalpan **Tel** *56 55 73 15*

Though in the far south of the city, it is worth the effort to stroll and dine in the gardens and rooms of this former hacienda. The sophisticated international menu includes Mexican specialties such as *carne asada tlalpeña* (marinated grilled beef) and *huachinango* (red snapper) in a shrimp and chili sauce are special. Lunch and dinner daily.

FARTHER AFIELD El Convento
Fernández Leal 96, Col. Coyoacan **Tel** *55 54 40 65*

In a former convent building which has been beautifully restored, this restaurant offers an exquisite menu which includes contemporary Mexican dishes of some accomplishment. One of the specialties is *pollo relleno de frutas secas* – chicken stuffed with sun-dried fruit. Lunch Mon–Wed & Sun, dinner Mon–Sat.

FARTHER AFIELD San Angel Inn
Diego Rivera 50, Col. San Angel **Tel** *56 16 22 22*

Generations of diners have been served in the gracious rooms and gardens of this 17th-century former hacienda. The international menu offers *chateaubriand* and *osso bucco*, and Mexican specialties, including crepes *huitlacoche*. One of the capital's most popular restaurants. Jacket and tie. Reservations recommended. Lunch and dinner daily.

AROUND MEXICO CITY

CHOLULA Los Jarrones
Portal Guerrero 7 **Tel** *(222) 247 10 98*

Among the many restaurants under the *portales* facing the main square, the clean and inviting Los Jarrones offers a quality respite after sightseeing. The menu includes traditional Mexican fare plus a variety of soup, sandwiches, and pastries. Strolling musicians play for donations. Breakfast, lunch, and dinner daily.

CUERNAVACA Los Arcos
Jardin de los Heroes 4 **Tel** *(777) 312 15 10*

Opposite the Plaza de Armas in the heart of Cuernavaca, for decades this plain-but-popular sidewalk restaurant has been a prime location for people watching while dining. Any of the *enchiladas*, sandwiches, or soup would make a good choice. Breakfast, lunch, and dinner daily.

CUERNAVACA El Tequila
Juárez 20, Col. Centro, Hotel Posada María Cristina **Tel** *(777) 318 57 67*

With its enclosed patios with cloth-covered tables and walls of windows overlooking the gardens, El Tequila is one of the most welcoming and peaceful restaurants in the city. It also has a comfortable living room for drinks or dessert. Try the Sunday brunch buffet. Breakfast, lunch, and dinner daily.

CUERNAVACA La India Bonita
Dwight Morrow 15, Col. Centro **Tel** *(777) 318 69 67*

Some of the city's best regional food appears here in the former home of U.S. Ambassador Dwight Morrow. The *cecina de Yecapixtla* (thin salted meat with cream) is outstanding and comes with refried beans, nopal cactus, fresh cheese, and fresh tortillas. Breakfast, lunch, and dinner daily (no dinner Sun).

CUERNAVACA Gaia
Blvd Benito Juárez 102, Col. Centro **Tel** *(777) 310 00 31*

Situated in the very heart of Cuernavaca, with good views of the cathedral, this modern restaurant serves exceptional Italian and international cuisine. Specialties include salmon Gaia with apricot and chipotle sauce, and marinated tuna with a sesame crust. Lunch daily, dinner Mon–Sat.

CUERNAVACA Las Mañanitas
Ricardo Linares 107, Col. Centro **Tel** *(777) 314 14 66*

Once the standard setter for fine dining in Cuernavaca, in a garden setting with strolling peacocks. The international menu also boasts Mexican specialties. *Chiles en nogada* (chilies in walnut sauce) are served while shrimp in tamarind sauce is a popular dish. Reservations recommended. Jacket and tie for dinner. Breakfast, lunch, and dinner daily.

CUERNAVACA El Madrigal
Sonora 115, Col. Vista Hermosa **Tel** *(777) 316 78 25*

El Madrigal offers style, class, and a garden setting. Sophisticated blend of Mexican and international specialties, such as filet mignon. *Arroz con leche brûlé* is a take on traditional rice pudding. Reservations recommended. Lunch and dinner Tue–Sun.

METEPEC Shefali
Zaragoza 116, Espíritu Santo **Tel** *(722) 232 56 16*

With Mexican décor, this popular spot is a good place to take a break, whether to enjoy a hot cup of tea, or to indulge with delicious waffles. This restaurant also has a good selection of vegetarian dishes. Breakfast, lunch and dinner daily.

PACHUCA Don Horacio
Avenida Hidalgo 24, Col. Centro Pachuquilla **Tel** *(771) 716 05 25*

Since 1927, this temple of pre-Hispanic food has been earning awards for the authenticity of its food. This is the place to try *pulque* (fermented maguey juice), delicious *mixiotes* (steamed lamb in a maguey leaf pouch) and other delicacies not easily found elsewhere. Breakfast, lunch, and dinner daily.

Key to Price Guide *see p326* **Key to Symbols** *see back cover flap*

PACHUCA Alex Steak
 $$$

Glorieta Revolución 102 **Tel** *(771) 713 00 56*

An award-winning restaurant famed for the excellence of its steaks, this busy place also offers a full lineup of seafood. To sample both, select the *Mar y Tierra*, a combo of lobster (or other seafood or fish) and a steak of your choice. Portions are huge. Lunch and dinner daily.

PUEBLA Fonda de Santa Clara
$

Avenida 3 Poniente 920 **Tel** *(222) 242 26 59*

Some of Puebla's most traditional food has been prepared here for decades. Try the *tinga* (pork or chicken in a tomato and chili sauce), the *mole poblano* (since this is the city where it originated), or the steamed *mixiotes* (lamb or beef in a maguey-leaf wrapper). Breakfast, lunch, and dinner daily.

PUEBLA Tortas Meche
$

Portal Juárez 111 **Tel** *(222) 232 11 95*

Facing the main plaza, Tortas Meche offers plain, comforting food, good coffee, and hot chocolate, without the frills, pomp, or prices of other places. The *consomeche* (chicken soup) is one of the favorites here. Try *torta de jamon*, which is also popular. Breakfast, lunch, and dinner daily.

PUEBLA La Vaca Negra
$

Avenida Reforma 106 **Tel** *(222) 246 20 51*

Located in a colonial-style building in the main town square, this typical Mexican restaurant offers local specialties, such as *mole poblano* and *chalupas*, as well as all-time favourites such as hamburgers and giant hot dogs. Breakfast, lunch, and dinner daily.

PUEBLA Bola Roja
$$

5 Poniente 2522-A, Col. La Paz **Tel** *(222) 230 16 07*

Although perhaps the best of Puebla's restaurants serving regional cuisine, it is also the least known to outsiders since it is off the beaten path. The *escamoles* (ant eggs) are prepared in a butter and wine sauce. The fresh *mixiotes* are steamed in a perfect chili sauce. Lunch and dinner daily.

PUEBLA Mesón de Sacristía
$$

Calle 6 Sur 304 **Tel** *(222) 232 45 13*

Located in the covered patio of the stylish small hotel by the same name, the kitchen of the Mesón de Sacristía specializes in the local food of Puebla. Especially recommended are the delicious *mole poblano*, *enchiladas*, and *chalupas*. Lunch and dinner daily.

PUEBLA El Mural
$$$

16 de Septiembre 506, Col. Centro **Tel** *(222) 242 66 96*

El Mural offers a range of delicious food from Spain. Among their specialties is the hearty seafood and rice dish of *paella*. But downtowners often opt for one of the tasty regional specialties, such as *mole poblano*. Lunch and dinner daily.

TAXCO El Adobe
$

Plazuela San Juan 13 **Tel** *(762) 622 14 16*

With a good location in the heart of Taxco, this charming place serves inexpensive and tasty Mexican food such as steak with guacamole, and chicken with onion, potatoes, and guacamole. Weekends are especially lively here, when live music is played. Brunch served on Sundays. Breakfast, lunch, and dinner daily.

TAXCO La Hacienda
$

Plaza Borda 4 **Tel** *(762) 622 11 66*

Located inside the Hotel Agua Escondida, with colonial furniture and Mexican décor, La Hacienda's menu includes handmade tortillas and traditional Mexican dishes, such as *cecina* steak with rice, beans, and *guacamole*. Try the Sunday buffet. Breakfast, lunch, and dinner daily.

TAXCO Restaurant Ethel
$

Plazuela San Juan 14 **Tel** *(762) 622 07 88*

Facing the circular Plazuela San Juan, the menu here is standard Mexican with some regional specialties such as *cecina* and *pozole*. But the multi-course *comida corrida* is a solid choice with soup, main course of perhaps chicken or pork chops, rice, and finally dessert. Whatever is on offer will be tasty. Breakfast, lunch, and dinner daily.

TAXCO Del Angel Inn
$$

Celso Muñoz 4 **Tel** *(762) 622 55 25*

With the cathedral dome as backdrop, and surrounded by colonial-era buildings, this open-air, rooftop restaurant offers the best views in the central village. The international menu offers steak, pasta, and shrimp, as well as tortilla soup. Full wine list. Breakfast, lunch, and dinner daily.

TAXCO Sotavento Restaurant Bar
$$

Benito Juarez 12, Col. Centro **Tel** *(762) 627 12 17*

Relaxing and inviting for leisurely dining, the Sotovento occupies a beautiful old home with tables set out on the gracious front porch and on the plant-filled back patio. Select from international and Mexican dishes such as tortilla soup, and the *filete Butler* prepared in a wine and mushroom sauce. Full bar. Lunch and dinner Tue–Sun.

TEOTIHUACAN Villas Arqueológicas
Periférico Sur s/n Zona Arqueológica **Tel** 58 36 90 20

This tranquil location, a five-minute walk from the front entrance to the ruins, is a relaxing place to revive after climbing the ruins. Select from among the regional specialties of lamb *mixiotes*, or red snapper Veracruz-style (steamed with tomatoes, onions, olives, and capers). Full bar. Breakfast, lunch, and dinner daily.

TEPOZTLÁN Los Colorines
Avenida del Tepozteco 13, Col. La Santísima **Tel** (739) 395 01 98

Gaily decorated with festive banners and colorful walls, the primarily Mexican menu offers unusual delights. There is a dish made from the red *colorin* flower that lends its name to the restaurant, batter-fried *huazontles* (like broccoli), and a wide assortment of bean soups. Breakfast, lunch, and dinner (no dinner Sun).

TEPOZOTLÁN Los Virreyes
Plaza Vierreinal 32 **Tel** 5 876 02 35

One of several small restaurants on the shaded plaza opposite the museum. This one stands out for the good food and efficient service. The soup and sandwich menu may suffice, but the *cabrito* (young goat) is the main attraction, served with fresh lime, beans, and rice. Breakfast and lunch daily, dinner Fri–Sun.

TEPOZTLÁN El Ciruelo
Zaragoza 17 **Tel** (739) 395 12 03

With stylish and comfortable patio dining, this is one of the most casually sophisticated dining venues in the village. Savor the innovative gourmet delicacies along with the vista of the nearby Cerro Tepozteco. The breast of chicken in plum *mole* sauce tops the specialty list. Bread and tortillas are made on the premises. Lunch daily, dinner Fri–Sun.

TLAXCALA La Arboleda
Lira y Ortega 33 **Tel** (246) 462 14 77

Located near Plaza de la Constitución, this restaurant offers excellent home-made Mexican food at bargain prices. The dining area is decorated with masks and crafts from various Mexican states. Try *pollo tocatlán* (chicken in a spicy green sauce, with cheese), the house specialty. Breakfast, lunch, and dinner Mon–Fri.

TLAXCALA Café Avenida
Plaza de la Constitución 16 **Tel** (246) 466 36 69

Start the day here with the special egg dishes. *Huevos Tarascos* arrive bathed in a green sauce with speckles of ham. *Huevos poblanos* come in a tomato sauce with corn and cream. Veracruz eggs rest on a corn tortilla covered in a bean sauce mixed with sausage and cream. Breakfast, lunch, and dinner daily.

TLAXCALA Los Portales
Plaza de la Constitución 8 **Tel** (246) 462 54 19

Under the Colonial-era *portales* facing Tlaxcala's main square, amid the bustle of shops and restaurants, this is a fine place for ice cream, coffee, sandwiches, and full meals. The house specialty is the bean-based Tlaxcalteca soup embellished with crisp strips of tortilla, white cheese, and avocado. Breakfast, lunch, and dinner daily.

TLAXCALA Las Cazuelas
km 20, carretera San Martín Tlaxcala **Tel** (246) 462 30 88

This award-winning countryside restaurant, close to Tlaxcala, emphasizes Tlaxcaltecan specialties. Offers some of the best yet least known of Mexico's food. Try the soup, Tocatlán chicken steamed in maguey leaves, or chicken in amaranth sauce with a nutritious pre-Hispanic grain. Breakfast, lunch, and early dinner Tue–Sun.

TOLUCA Restaurant Biarritz
Nigromante 200, Col. Centro **Tel** (722) 213 46 24

With a red awning over the door, opposite the Plaza Gonzalez Arratia, Biarritz offers traditional food including many varieties of taco. The specialty, *molcajete Biarritz*, comes in an earthen bowl, loaded with warm cheese, beef, and peppers. Breakfast, lunch, and dinner daily.

TULA Pizza In Out
Melchor Ocampo 20 **Tel** (773) 732 26 26

With red- and white-checked cloths and plenty of seating, Pizza In Out is inviting enough to stay. (But they are prepared to box your food up, too.) Popular choices include pizza with pineapple, hot peppers, *chorizo* (spicy sausage), and hamburger. Spaghetti Bolognese and lasagna are also available. Lunch and dinner daily.

VALLE DE BRAVO La Michoacana
Calle de la Cruz 100, Col. Cento **Tel** (726) 262 16 25

Huge windows overlook the village, lake, and mountains surrounding Valle de Bravo. Diners drink in the view while sampling food from the international menu with many Mexican and pre-Hispanic offerings. *Cecina* (thin salted beef) served with rich Mexican cream, and beans is a regional specialty. Breakfast, lunch, and dinner daily.

VALLE DE BRAVO Da Ciro
Vergel 201 **Tel** (726) 262 01 22

Tempting aromas of wood-oven baked pizza and other Italian specialties lead to this weekend-only restaurant. Dining is casual either on the plant-filled patio or the cozy interior. Specialties include Hawaiian pizza, spaghetti Bolognese, and fish with pasta. Great garlic bread. Carry out available. Lunch Fri–Sun; dinner Fri–Sat.

NORTHERN MEXICO

CABO SAN LUCAS La Dolce
 $$

Hidalgo and Zapata **Tel** *(624) 142 66 21*

La Dolce serves authentic wood oven pizzas and signature pasta specialties. Pizza Gregorio finds arugula (rocket) among the chicken, mushroom, and pinenut toppings. The home-made pasta includes zucchini tortellini in a light gorgonzola sauce, with onions and parmesan. Dinner daily.

CABO SAN LUCAS The Office on the Beach
$$$

Paseo Pescador at Médano Beach **Tel** *(624)143 34 64*

The perfect beachfront restaurant – sand floors, seafood, sandwiches, cerveza, and fun. The shrimp fajitas sizzle, while tacos come loaded with choices of fish, shrimp, beef, and chicken. Juicy hamburgers arrive with large old-fashioned fries. Happy hour 3–5pm, serving great margaritas. Full bar. Breakfast, lunch, and dinner daily.

CABO SAN LUCAS Panchos
$$$$

Corner of Hidalgo & Zapata **Tel** *(624) 143 09 73*

Pancho Villa should be proud: the tequila bar is almost unrivaled in Mexico, and the enormous platters of Mexican and seafood specialties keep everyone satisfied. Fish in mango sauce and grilled shrimp served in several different ways are the house specialties. Oaxaca *tamales* are a menu staple. Breakfast, lunch, and dinner daily.

CABO SAN LUCAS Casa Rafael's
$$$$$

Calle Medano at Camino el Pescador **Tel** *(624) 143 07 39*

Refined dining atmosphere and service. The fresh seafood bisque primes the appetite for other specialties, including Cornish hen in a smooth champagne sauce and the signature dish, a duo of Lobster medallions with Oriental black bean sauce and filet mignon with morel mushrooms. Reservations recommended. Dinner daily.

CABO SAN LUCAS Don Emiliano
$$$$$

Boulevard Mijares 27, Col. Centro, San José **Tel** *(624) 142 02 66*

One of the best restaurants in the state, Don Emiliano offers fine Mexican cuisine and an excellent Mexican wine list. The menu is sophisticated, specializing in shrimp. Located in the historic center of San José del Cabo, the décor here is contemporary Mexican, complemented with plants and art works. Excellent service. Dinner daily.

CABO SAN LUCAS Mi Casa
 $$$$$

Town Square **Tel** *(624) 143 19 33*

The vivid cobalt blue exterior and colorful décor suggest *fiesta* in Mexico. The menu, a combination of traditional and nouvelle Mexican specialties, also features plenty of fresh seafood. *Tikin-xik*, a Yucatecan fish specialty, is smothered in authentic and fragrant *achiote* paste and baked in a banana leaf. Lunch and dinner daily (no dinner Sun).

CABO SAN LUCAS Mi Casa de Mariscos
$$$$$

Camino Viejo a San José, corner Paseo a la Marina **Tel** *(624) 143 68 98*

Gaily decorated and festive, the draw is expertly conceived fish and seafood. The Caesar salad is studded with shrimp. The Veracruz-inspired, paella-like *arroz a la tumbada* holds fresh fish, octopus, crab, and clams. Among the few non-seafood specialties is *cochinita pibil* (pork in achiote sauce) from Yucatán. Lunch and dinner daily.

CABO SAN LUCAS Peacocks
$$$$$

Paseo del Pescador **Tel** *(624) 143 18 58*

Outdoors on a plant-filled tropical patio, the candlelit, linen-covered tables create a fine dining experience. The international menu features pecan-crusted baked brie as an appetizer. The delicious seafood-loaded fettuccini Alfredo is on the specialty list. Domestic and imported wines. Dinner daily.

CHIHUAHUA Degá
 $$

Calle Victoria 409, Hotel San Francisco **Tel** *(614) 416 77 70*

This popular downtown restaurant offers reliably swift service and excellent food. The *plato Mexicana* showcases a *tamal* and stuffed chili. The extensive breakfast menu includes several international and Mexican specialties, as well as omelets prepared to your liking. Buffet Sunday. Breakfast, lunch, and dinner daily.

CIUDAD CUAUHTEMOC Tarahumara Inn
$$$

Avenida Allende 373, Hotel Tarahumara Inn **Tel** *(625) 581 19 19*

A popular inn with a good restaurant. The *filete Barba* aims at the varied clientele with grilled beef accompanied by *rajas* (grilled chili and onion slices) to please the locals, and a side of nachos to please the tourists. The kitchen opens early and closes late. Breakfast, lunch, and dinner daily.

CREEL La Cabaña
 $

López Mateos 36 **Tel** *(635) 456 00 68*

The cabin architecture and Tarahumara decoration befits Creel's logging center status in the heart of Tarahumara country. Service can be erratic, but the food is good. Fried chicken, steaks, and pork may be on the menu all with rice or potatoes, and beans. There is a large selection of tacos on offer. Breakfast, lunch, and dinner daily.

CREEL Parador de la Montaña
Avenida López Mateos and Chapultepec 44 **Tel** *(635) 456 00 75*

This Parador achieves the requirement for restaurant fame in Creel: regular hours, edible food, and a well-stocked bar. The steaks, pork chops, and chicken, all served with fries, are filling and tasty, not gourmet. Breakfast is basic eggs, toast, bacon, and pancakes. Breakfast, lunch, and dinner daily.

DURANGO La Fogata
Cuauhtémoc 200 **Tel** *(618) 817 03 47*

For nearly 30 years this spiffy, pine-walled, thatched-roofed restaurant has earned fame for the superb quality of meat prepared many ways. Beef is king, of course, in Durango's ranch country, but there are *cabrito* (young goat), ribs, and chicken as well. Finish off with *cajeta* (carmelized milk) ice cream. Lunch and dinner daily.

ENSENADA El Charro
López Mateos 454 **Tel** *(646) 178 21 14*

Chickens roasting in the front window entice diners who cannot resist the heavenly aroma. One of the best dishes on the menu is *pollo al pastor*, a take-off on the lamb and pork dish so wonderfully flavored with *achiote* paste (made from annatto seeds), onions, and herbs, and dripping with fresh pineapple. Breakfast, lunch, and dinner daily.

ENSENADA Las Cazuelas
Agustine Sangines 6 **Tel** *(646) 176 10 44*

Clay-pot casserole cooking reaches new heights at this award-winning restaurant with beautiful stained-glass windows. At breakfast, classic *chilaquiles* are front and center, either with chicken or eggs. The specialty, though, is the shrimp *cazuela*. Breakfast, lunch, and dinner daily.

GUERRERO NEGRO Malarrimo
Emiliano Zapata s/n **Tel** *(615) 157 11 93*

Malarrimo is the quintessential favorite hangout decorated with nautical remains and offering great meals. The food receives applause from the giant scallops to the fresh fish, lobster, and shrimp. Lobster omelets at breakfast are delicious. Well stocked bar. Breakfast, lunch, and dinner daily.

HERMOSILLO Viva Sonora
San Pedro el Sauceto, km 15 **Tel** *(662) 237 02 00*

Nine miles outside the city, the country setting and delicious food are worth the drive. In cattle country beef dishes are the specialty. *Cocido*, a hearty beef stew is more like a soup. Mixed grills might include a combo of *carne asada* (grilled beef) and *costillas* (pork ribs) with sides of beans, flour tortillas, and special tamal or quesadilla. Lunch daily.

HIDALGO DE PARRAL Turista
Plazuela Independencia 12 **Tel** *(627) 523 40 24*

It is worth overlooking the shabby exterior of this restaurant and hotel of the same name. The good, inexpensive food has been satisfying downtowners for decades. The tasty and filling *alambre* kabob (marinated in spices) is the specialty and comes with delicious *charro* beans. Breakfast, lunch, and dinner daily (no dinner Sun).

LORETO Café Olé
Madero e Hidalgo 14, Centro **Tel** *(613) 135 04 96*

In the heart of Loreto, this little streetside café is a great place to start the day. Enjoy one of the delicious egg breakfasts under the *palapa* (palm frond) roof. The lunch and dinner offerings are traditional Mexican dishes. There is also a good selection at the bar. Breakfast daily; lunch and dinner Mon–Sat.

MAZATLÁN Pura Vida
Bugambilia 100 **Tel** *(669) 916 58 15*

Vegetarian central in Mazatlán, with soy burgers and fruit plates. Also chicken and fish sandwiches, soup, and whole wheat pancakes. Since Mazatlán is ringed by fruit plantations, fresh fruit appears in more than 100 drinks blended with water or yogurt in combination with flavors from tamarind to coconut. Breakfast, lunch, and dinner daily.

MAZATLÁN Jungle Juice
Las Garzas 101 **Tel** *(669) 913 33 15*

The breezy bar is upstairs and the comfortable open-air patio dining fills the downstairs. Despite the name, there is far more than juice on offer here. Savor the specialties from the grill – meats and seafood, especially lobster. Vegetarians will find much to enjoy from salads and fruit to soup and sandwiches. Breakfast, lunch, and dinner daily.

MAZATLÁN El Shrimp Bucket
Avenida Olas Altas 1126, Hotel Fiesta **Tel** *(669) 982 80 19*

Popular night and day. Like its counterpart in Cabo San Lucas, shrimp comes many ways. Plus the food bucket here includes steaks and Mexican plates. Breakfast is almost as popular as any other meal with the full range of pancakes, waffles, and eggs. Breakfast, lunch, and dinner daily.

MAZATLÁN Señor Pepper
Avenida Camarón Sábalo Norte s/n **Tel** *(669) 914 01 01*

On the romantic and upscale side of Mazatlán dining, with cloths, crystal and candlelit tables, the specialty is mesquite-grilled Sonoran beef. But shrimp and lobster make it to the grill as well. Portions are huge. Great salads. Full bar open later than the restaurant. Dinner daily.

Key to Price Guide *see p326* **Key to Symbols** *see back cover flap*

MULEGE Los Equipales $$

Calle Moctezuma **Tel** *(615) 153 03 30*

Catch the breeze on this second-floor restaurant where the covered terrace overlooks the street. The leather *equipal* tables and chairs, for which the restaurant is named, are set with colorful cloths, Mexican pottery, and candles at night. Sonoran beef and Sea of Cortez seafood are the specialties. Bar. Breakfast, lunch, and dinner daily.

NUEVO CASAS GRANDES Hacienda $

Avenida Benito Juarez 2603, Motel Hacienda **Tel** *(636) 694 10 48*

The restaurant of the Motel Hacienda, one of the most popular inns in town, feeds a world of travelers Mexican and international specialties. Standards are soup, sandwiches, and platter meals such as pork chops, grilled chicken, and *enchiladas*. Box lunches available. Breakfast, lunch, and dinner daily.

SALTILLO El Tapanco $$$

Allende Sur 225, Centro **Tel** *(844) 414 43 39*

A top dining address in Saltillo, El Tapanco is located in an 18th-century mansion with an open patio. International menu with Mexican leading the way. Among the specialties is *mole poblano* – a grilled chicken breast covered in a *poblano* pepper sauce. Lunch and dinner daily (no dinner Sun).

SAN JOSÉ DEL CABO Damiana $$$

Boulevard Mijares 8 **Tel** *(624) 142 04 99*

An intimate dining spot in an 18th-century home. Cozy bar indoors, and shaded dining on the patio. Famed for their tortilla soup and the "Imperial Shrimp Steak" – a large shrimp made into a filet and grilled. Special coffee menu. Extensive bar list. Reservations recommended Nov–May. Brunch, lunch, and dinner daily.

SAN JOSÉ DEL CABO Mi Cocina $$$

Boulevard Mijares 4 **Tel** *(624) 142 51 00*

Part of Casa Natalie, a small boutique inn, this restaurant is another stylish and intimate setting for fine outdoor dining. The "nouvelle Mexican-Euro" offerings present delicious fusion dishes such as beef medallions paired with Roquefort cheese in a *chipotle* chili sauce. Full service bar. Breakfast, lunch, and dinner daily.

SAN JOSÉ DEL CABO Tropicana $$$

Boulevard Mijares 30 **Tel** *(624) 142 15 80*

San José's Mecca for convivial dining and entertainment provides good service and a patio dining setting. An excellent place to unwind. International menu with something for everyone. Shrimp fajita and steaks are the house specialties. Superior bar. Breakfast, lunch, and dinner daily.

SANTA ROSALIA El Muelle $

Corner Constitución and the plaza **Tel** *(615) 152 09 31*

Facing the main plaza, this modern restaurant features seating both inside and on a palm-studded patio. El Muelle is something of an oasis catering to all tastebuds. The specialties are grilled seafood and meat, with large portions the norm. The hamburgers and pizzas here get rave reviews. Bar. Breakfast, lunch, and dinner daily.

TIJUANA Cien Años $$$

José María Velasco 1407, Rio Tijuana **Tel** *(664) 634 30 39*

Classy, sophisticated dining from the linen-covered tables to the food. Nouvelle Mexican tops the menu that includes a fair number of pre-Hispanic ingredients. Among the specialties are crepes *huitlacoche*, chicken in *mole* sauce, and shrimp in lobster sauce. Huge tequila selection and full bar. Lunch and dinner daily (closes early Sun).

THE COLONIAL HEARTLAND

AGUASCALIENTES La Bamba $$

Héroe de Nacozari Sur, 1315 in Hotel Hacienda de la Noria **Tel** *(449) 918 43 43*

The fashionable restaurant of the upscale hotel Hacienda La Noria attracts locals and tourists alike with its Mexican specialties and gracious service. Standouts include *enchiladas* in a red sauce, and pork loin in a fragrant, mild chili sauce. The hearty *sopa campesina* hold large chunks of meat and vegetables. Full bar. Breakfast, lunch, and dinner daily.

AJIJIC Manix $

Ocampo 57 **Tel** *(376) 766 00 61*

Great food and a quiet, refined atmosphere of dark wood and bright accents. The menu offers international food as well as Mexican dishes, with a range of pasta, soup, and meat dishes. Usually there is a choice of three *comidas* each with soup or salad, main course, and dessert – all delicious. Lunch and dinner Mon–Sat.

AJIJIC La Rusa $$$

Donato Guerra 9 in La Nueva Posada **Tel** *(376) 766 14 44*

Clearly the place to meet and greet in Ajijic. The lake view and patio setting create the perfect place for a leisurely meal. The large lunch menu offers a selection of soup, pasta, green salads, and sandwiches. The much expanded evening menu includes grilled specialties, fish, and pasta. Breakfast, lunch, and dinner daily.

ANGANGUEO Hotel Don Bruno

Morelos 92 **Tel** *(715) 156 00 26*

Restaurants come and go in Angangueo, but this one is always welcoming to hotel guests and locals alike. Though the food is basic at all meals, it is tasty enough to look forward to the next meal. Service is good and the bar has most of the basics. A warm, cozy place to be on nippy days. Breakfast, lunch, and dinner daily.

COLIMA Los Naranjos

Gabino Barrera 34, Col. Centro **Tel** *(312) 312 00 29*

Off Colima's central plaza, Los Naranjos is one of those cozy restaurants that has been feeding loyal locals for more than 50 years. Regional and international recipes. *Pollo los Naranjos* (chicken in an orange sauce) is a house special, and the *pollo casserola*, in a clay pot, is baked in a white sauce. Breakfast, lunch, and dinner daily.

GUADALAJARA La Chata

Avenida Corona 126, Col. Centro **Tel** *(33) 3613 05 88*

Perennially popular since 1942, La Chata is all about Jalisco food. The sampler platters are centered around meat or *enchiladas*, and there are also three kinds of *pozole blanco* (a white broth) – with chicken, pork, or two kinds of meat. The breakfast menu is as compelling as the other meals. Breakfast, lunch, and dinner daily.

GUADALAJARA Los Itacates

110 Avenida Chapultepec Norte **Tel** *(33) 3825 11 06*

Renowned for the huge taco selection plus *chiles rellenos* and specialties of the area. Los Itacates translates roughly as "packed food," the sort a hostess sends home with guests. But the restaurant is such a stay and eat place that it is sometimes hard to find a seat – a testament to the quality of the food. Breakfast and lunch daily; dinner Wed–Sat.

GUADALAJARA La Fonda de San Miguel

Donato Guerra 25, Centro Histórico **Tel** *(33) 3613 08 09*

Dine in the atmospheric central patio of this 17th-century Carmelite convent. The best of downtown dining offers both a festive atmosphere and fine food from regional Mexico. The *moles* and *pozole* are definitely worth tasting here. Breakfast, lunch to 6pm; Sun–Tues. Breakfast, lunch, dinner Wed–Sat.

GUADALAJARA La Trattoria

Avenida Niños Héroes 3051, Col. Jardines del Bosque **Tel** *(33) 3122 18 17*

A wall of windows under a broad awning welcomes from the street. Inside it is casual and sleek with natural wood and crisp linen-covered tables. Partake of some of the city's best Italian food, featuring homemade bread and pasta and a fabulous salad bar. Fully stocked bar. Italian wine. Lunch and dinner daily.

GUANAJUATO Truco 7

Truco 7 **Tel** *(473) 732 83 74*

Cozy, bohemian, casual, arty, and with an eclectic décor, Truco 7 is housed in a centuries-old house on a street of the same name. The restaurant has a full menu of well-prepared Mexican specialties, including *mole poblano*, terrific soups, homemade bread, and a memorable *comida corrida*. Fresh fruit drinks. Breakfast, lunch, and dinner daily.

GUANAJUATO El Gallo Pitagórico

Constancia 10 A **Tel** *(473) 732 94 89*

Recognizable by its bright blue façade, this house-turned-restaurant sits on the hill above the Santa Fe church. At the top of a long flight of stairs you have a superior view of almost the whole city. Italian specialties include minestrone, lasagna, and steaks. Lunch and dinner daily.

GUANAJUATO Casa del Conde de Valencia

Valencia km 5 **Tel** *(473) 732 25 50*

Dine in the plant-filled courtyard of the former hacienda of the Count of Valenciana (Valenciana is the name of the opulent church across the street and local silver mine). This is one of the more gracious upscale dining experiences in Guanajuato. The food is Mexican traditional with nouvelle twists. Lunch daily.

GUANAJUATO Quinta Las Acacias

Paseo de la Presa 168, Hotel Quinta Las Acacias **Tel** *(473) 731 15 17*

Without exception, the food, service, ambience, and view make this a place for a special meal. The menu is international, but includes Mexican overtones. Excellent meat and fish dishes, as well as desserts. Try the *poblana* soup with zucchini flower, chili, corn, and mushrooms, finished with cream. Delicious. Breakfast, lunch, and dinner Mon–Sat.

GUANAJUATO Hotel Posada Santa Fe

Jardín Unión 12 **Tel** *(473) 732 00 84*

Clearly this is the prime location, day or night, in Guanajuato, with classy outdoor seating facing the Jardín Unión (the main plaza) and beautiful indoor seating where there is less bustle. Some of the specialties include *pozole* with all the condiments, beef brochettes, and chicken *mole*. Full bar. Breakfast, lunch, and dinner daily.

GUANAJUATO Chez Nicole

La Hacienda de Marfil. Arcos de Guadalupe 3, Col.Marfil **Tel** *(473) 733 11 48*

Enjoy French and nouvelle Mexican cuisine inside the remains of an old hacienda. Service is gracious and sophisticated with cloth-covered tables set out on covered patios. Tequila-laced fondue, steaks, and crepes with several fillings are among the specialties. Full bar. Lunch Tue–Sun.

MORELIA Fonda las Mercedes $$

León Guzmán 47 **Tel** *(443) 312 61 13*

Stylish mansion setting with plants, exposed brick walls, art, and stone pillars. The food at this top dining spot is international. Pasta, steak, and seafood lead the menu. Terrific soups. Crepes come with many fillings. Complimentary starter. Homemade bread. Full bar and wine list. Lunch and dinner daily (no dinner Sun).

MORELIA Las Trojes $$$

Juan Sebastian Bach 51 **Tel** *(443) 314 73 44*

In a traditional Purépechan carved log house, decades of patrons have experienced the Mexican and Michoacán specialties of the house. There is the bean-based Tarasca soup for starters and the *filet poblano* – steak folded around strips of pepper with a cheese sauce. Lunch and dinner daily (no dinner Sun).

MORELIA Villa Montaña $$$

Patzimba 201 **Tel** *(443) 314 02 31*

On a hill overlooking Morelia, there is no better spot than this stylish international restaurant. Breakfast features a regional buffet including *uchepos* and *corundas* (two different Michoacán *tamales*). Evening meals start with cocktails on the terrace. Dinner reservations. Jacket and tie required at dinner. Breakfast, lunch, and dinner daily.

MORELIA Los Mirasoles $$$$

Avenida Madero Poniente 549, Col. Centro **Tel** *(443) 313 25 87*

A private home has been converted into a cozy, sophisticated, art-filled restaurant. Bathed in soft golden light, the colorful, beautifully decorated tables create a fine dining atmosphere. Argentinian-style grilled meat heads the innovative menu. Salmon steak comes atop a bed of fettuccine in a wine cheese sauce. Full bar. Lunch and dinner daily.

PÁTZCUARO Los Escudos $

Portal Hidalgo 73, Centro Hotel Los Escudos **Tel** *(434) 342 68 24*

One of the central gathering places in Pátzcuaro day and night is in the front section of the Hotel Los Escudos. Michoacán specialties are the main attraction, including Tarascan soup. Assorted coffee and a full bar. The service here is efficient. Breakfast, lunch, and dinner daily.

PÁTZCUARO El Viejo Gaucho $$

Iturbe 10, Centro **Tel** *(434) 342 36 28*

This back section of the Hotel Iturbe is the casual, evening-only, gathering place for food and entertainment, and one of the few places to eat after 9:30pm. The menu provides a fine mix of appetizers, salads, hamburgers, *empanadas*, pizzas, pastas, and its specialty – steak with delicious Argentine-style *chimichurri* sauce. Dinner Tue–Sat.

PÁTZCUARO Doña Paca $$$

Portal Morelos 59 **Tel** *(434) 342 36 28*

Pátzcuaro's most inviting, cozy place to dine on the first floor of a historic family-owned mansion facing the Plaza Grande. The menu is a delightful mix of Mexican and Michoacán specialtes. Trout served with a smooth creamy herb sauce is a house innovation. Great coffee and hot chocolate. Breakfast, lunch, and dinner daily (no dinner Sun).

PÁTZCUARO Hostería de San Felipe $$$

Avenida Lázaro Cárdenas 321, Col. Centro **Tel** *(434) 342 12 98*

This is one of the oldest restaurants in the city, its history closely bound up with that of the grand Michoacán families. It is famous for its *botanas* (appetizers). The main items on its menu are also based on traditional Purépecha cooking – a good Tarascan soup, white fish with garlic, and marinated spare ribs. Breakfast, lunch, and dinner daily.

PÁTZCUARO El Primer Piso $$$

Vasco de Quiroga 29 **Tel** *(434) 342 01 22*

Despite its name, El Primer Piso is on the second floor of a charming old mansion, with wooden floors and small balconies overlooking the Plaza Grande. The menu is Mexican with a twist – *pechuga en nogada* (breast of chicken in a creamy almond sauce) is one of the specialties. Good coffee. Fine desserts. Lunch and dinner Wed–Mon.

PUERTO VALLARTA Le Petite France $$$

Boulevard Francisco Medina Ascencio Km. 2.5, Hotel Zone, **Tel** *(322) 293 09 00*

Traditional French cuisine with an occasional fusion surprise. Linens, crystal, and fine service set the upscale tone. Try the ribeye in a fragrant bordelaise sauce, or for fusion cuisine, there is tempura soft-shell crab with shrimp dumplings and stir-fried vegetables in ginger soy syrup. Dinner reservations recommended. Breakfast, lunch, and dinner daily.

PUERTO VALLARTA Los Pibes $$$

Basilio Badillo 261 **Tel** *(322) 223 15 57*

Tops for Argentinian grilled meat. At Los Pibes you select your cut of fresh meat from a platter tableside – brochettes, platter-size steak, sausage, and more, with a selection of sides – baked potato, pasta, salad. Terrific *empanadas*. Large servings. Gracious décor and service. Argentinian and Chilean wine. Lunch and dinner Wed–Mon.

PUERTO VALLARTA Café Maximilian $$$$

Olas Altas 380– B **Tel** *(322) 223 07 60*

A taste of Europe/Austria/Mexico in Puerto Vallarta in a bistro atmosphere. With a nod to Mexico there is braised baby lamb strips with rosemary and *chili poblano*. From Austria comes *rahmschnitzel* (sautéed pork loin escalope with homemade noodles and a cream mushroom sauce.) Full bar. Reservations recommended. Dinner Mon–Sat.

PUERTO VALLARTA Le Bistro Jazz Café

$$$$

Río Cuale 16-A **Tel** *(322) 222 02 83*

Since 1979, a swanky, classy-but-casual dining experience beside the Río Cuale. Steak, chicken, seafood, pastas, and crepes are prepared with taste-filled flair. Shrimp Portuguese, a chef's special, is grilled shrimp stuffed with jack cheese in an orange vinaigrette. Reservations recommended in high season. Breakfast, lunch, and dinner Mon–Sat.

PUERTO VALLARTA Trio

$$$$

Guerrero 264, Centro **Tel** *(322) 222 21 96*

One of Mexico's top restaurants featuring a sophisticated menu that changes daily. Appetizers may include garbanzo hummus with tender octopus sautéed with garlic and *guajillo* pepper, while main courses could be papardelle with garlic shrimp, basil, and sun-dried tomato. Reservations recommended. Lunch daily (Dec–Mar only); dinner year-round.

PUERTO VALLARTA Café des Artistes

 $$$$$

Guadalupe Sánchez 740 **Tel** *(322) 222 32 28*

Sophisticated menu and several dining venues with linen, crystal, candles, and art. Innovative French food nods to Mexico's ingredients. For a starter there is king crab timbal with *chilpotle chili* vinaigrette, and for main try the lamb medallion with wild mushroom and garlic sauce. Reservations recommended. Lunch and dinner daily.

PUERTO VALLARTA Mark's

$$$$$

Lázaro Cárdenas 56, Bucerias **Tel** *(329) 298 03 03*

Memorable, casually sophisticated patio dining in Bucerias. Innovative and delicious recipes include mahi mahi in a crust of crushed herbs with lobster-mashed potatoes, and filet mignon paired with gorgonzola ravioli. Pizza, pasta, salads. Save room for the terrific desserts. Lunch and dinner daily.

PUERTO VALLARTA Porto Bello

$$$$$

Marina Sol, Local 7 **Tel** *(322) 221 00 03*

Refined dining, either inside or outside and with linen tablecloths and excellent service, this little slice of Italy fronts the boat-filled marina. Among the specialties are fish, shrimp, and clams in a saffron sauce, and veal scaloppini covered in a savory white wine cream sauce. Assorted desserts. Full bar. Lunch and dinner daily.

QUERÉTARO La Mariposa

 $

Angela Peralta 7 **Tel** *(442) 212 11 66*

Plainly furnished but with light-filled windows, this bustling neighborhood restaurant has been serving locals and tourists for decades. The specialties of salads, sandwiches, *enchiladas*, and tacos are the prelude to dessert. The adjacent bakery makes everything on the premises, including ice cream and yogurt. Breakfast, lunch, and dinner daily.

QUERÉTARO Restaurant Padeca

$$$

Pasteur Sur 17, Hotel Mesón Santa Rosa **Tel** *(442) 224 26 23*

Some of the best, most atmospheric dining in the historic center can be found in this 18th-century restored mansion facing the Plaza de Armas. Elegant dining room and more casual patio. Both serve Mexican specialties such as *pollo* in lime, green *enchiladas*, and other well-prepared international dishes. Full bar. Breakfast, lunch, and dinner daily.

REAL DE CATORCE El Mesón de la Abundancia

$

Lanzagorta 11 **Tel** *(488) 887 50 44*

For a remote village, some good food occasionally comes out of this cozy hotel restaurant. The building is a 19th-century multi-story former home. The menu varies according to what ingredients are available, but usually includes Italian, Swiss, or Mexican dishes. The bar is limited. Breakfast, lunch, and dinner daily.

SAN BLAS El Delfin

$$

Paredes 106 Sur, Hotel Garza Canela **Tel** *(323) 285 01 12*

This cheerful dining room, with plenty of light and leafy plants, is a welcome sight for the hungry. Though there are other dishes on the menu (pasta, chicken, pork), seafood dominates with sophisticated preparations from various cultures. Homemade soup and desserts. Delightful breakfast menu. Breakfast, lunch, and dinner daily.

SAN LUIS POTOSÍ Fonda de Orizatlán

 $$$$$

Pascual M. Hernández 240 **Tel** *(444) 814 67 86*

Decorated with photos from San Luis' past, the food is Huastecan (both a nearby region and culture.) *Tamales* are the specialty, including the delicious *zacahuil*, a huge fragrant pork tamal that is pit-baked – a specialty that is seldom featured outside the region. Breakfast, lunch, and dinner daily (no dinner Sun).

SAN MIGUEL DE ALLENDE Mama Mia

 $$

Umaran 8 **Tel** *(415) 152 20 63*

A central gathering place, with a large open dining patio, Mama Mia features Italian, Mexican, and American food and live entertainment almost daily. The substantial breakfast menu is popular. There are also pizzas, pasta, steak, and seafood. Many coffee-based drinks. Extensive bar list. Breakfast, lunch, and dinner daily.

SAN MIGUEL DE ALLENDE Mesón de San José

 $$

Mesones 38 **Tel** *(415) 152 38 48*

One of the most relaxing, casual, and beautiful settings in San Miguel in a tree-shaded courtyard surrounded by little boutiques. The contemporary food is international, with pasta served many different ways, chicken curry, *achiote*-flavored *tacos*, delicious salads, and desserts. Good service. Breakfast, lunch, and dinner daily.

Key to Price Guide *see p326* **Key to Symbols** *see back cover flap*

SAN MIGUEL DE ALLENDE El Pegaso
 $$

*Corregidora 6 **Tel** (415) 152 1351*

With three cozy dining rooms, windows on the street, a trendy casual ambience, and good food, El Pegaso is very popular. Wonderful breakfast menu includes especially tasty eggs Benedict. Lighter fare is also available – soup, salads, sandwiches – along with more substantial specialty dishes from Mexico and Asia. Breakfast, lunch, and dinner daily.

SAN MIGUEL DE ALLENDE El Correo
 $$$

*Correo 23 **Tel** (415) 152 49 51*

Small and friendly in another of San Miguel's centuries-old buildings. Tortilla soup is the house specialty, but the menu offers top Mexican regional food that includes *corundas*, a *tamal* found mainly in Michoacán, and *sopes* – a ubiquitous masa appetizer found mainly in central Mexico. Breakfast, lunch, and dinner daily.

SAN MIGUEL DE ALLENDE La Bugambilia
 $$$$$

*Hidalgo 42 **Tel** (415) 152 01 27*

Welcoming and with good food created in a large gracious patio-centered historic home, this is a place for leisurely dining. Specialties are based on the best of Mexico and include *chiles en nogada*, *mole* served several ways, and *sopa Azteca* (a vegetable soup). Full bar. Breakfast, lunch, and dinner daily.

TLAQUEPAQUE El Abajeño
 $$

*Juárez 231, Tlaquepaque **Tel** (333) 635 90 97*

A festive restaurant with colorfully covered tables and lanterns strung in the trees, situated on a large shaded, plant-filled patio where musicians stroll. The menu consists of regional and traditional Mexican food, including hearty *birria* (beef, goat, or lamb in a delicious broth). Also grilled steaks, lamb, and seafood. Lunch and dinner daily.

URUAPAN La Mansión Cupatitzio
 $$

*Corner of Rodilla del Diablo & Parque Nacional **Tel** (452) 523 21 00*

Light-filled and gracious, this hotel restaurant overlooking the Parque Nacional is one of Uruapan's central attractions. Choose a spot inside in the large refined dining room, or outside by the pool. Known for Mexican and regional dishes. *Trucha Tarasca*, a trout specialty, is covered in an almond sauce. Breakfast, lunch, and dinner daily.

ZACATECAS La Cantera Musical Restaurant Bar
$$

*Tacuba 2 – El Mercado **Tel** (492) 922 88 28*

Below the beautifully restored old market place in central Zacatecas, La Cantera offers regional food along with traditional Mexican fare. The house specialties are *asado de boda* and *carne adobada* – beef cooked in a rich sauce and served with beans and guacamole. Handmade tortillas. Breakfast, lunch, and dinner daily.

ZACATECAS Parrilla Zacatecana
$$

*López Mateos 401 bis **Tel** (492) 922 08 38*

Located downtown, close to the cathedral, this typical Mexican restaurant offers traditional specialties such as *carne tampiqueña* (steak with green chile and cheese) and *arrachera* (steak in a garlic and lemon marinade). The dining room is decorated in rustic Mexican style. Lunch and dinner Tue–Sun.

ZITÁCUARO San Cayetano
$$$

*Mexico 51, km 70.5 Carretera a Toluca **Tel** (715) 153 19 26*

The verdant grounds and gardens, in a quiet country setting, are perfect for relaxed dining either inside the glass-walled dining room, or on the open patio. The food is French and Mexican with a daily changing menu. Vegetables and herbs are grown on the grounds. Breakfast, lunch, and dinner daily (at set hours).

SOUTHERN MEXICO

ACAPULCO El Amigo Miguel – 1
 $$

*Juárez 31 **Tel** (744) 483 69 81*

Join the locals at this favorite casual and simple old Acapulco restaurant. Totally fresh fish and seafood menu. Try the delectible *camarones borrachos* (drunken shrimp), served with garlicky rice, the *filete Miguel* (fish stuffed with seafood), or the large seafood cocktails. Lunch (starts at 10am) and dinner daily.

ACAPULCO Bambuco
 $$$

*Costera Alemán 75, Hotel El Cano **Tel** (744) 435 15 00*

This delightful terrace restaurant of the El Cano Hotel is at beach level with all the ocean views and vistas. The international menu holds many beach staples with sandwiches, salads, pasta, seafood, and fish. All expertly prepared. Tender fried *calamari* is a specialty appetizer. Breakfast, lunch, and dinner daily.

ACAPULCO Pámpano
$$$$$

*Carretera Escénica, Fracc. Guitarrón **Tel** (744) 446 56 36*

One of city's most elegant restaurants with gorgeous bay views. The sophisticated international menu with Mexican overtones may include such delicacies as Tamarind shrimp with mash potato or tuna *piloncillo* – marinaded tuna over sweet potato purée with cilantro-ginger *pico de gallo*. Reservations recommended. Dinner Wed–Mon.

ACAPULCO El Olvido

 $$$$$

Glorieta Diana traffic circle, Plaza Marbella **Tel** *(744) 481 02 03*

Gorgeous terrace dining at the far end of a shopping mall. The glittering vistas of the bay are as beautiful as the food presentation. The ingredients may be Mexican, but the preparation is international – quail with honey and chilies, for example. Many specialty house drinks worth trying. Reservations recommended. Dinner daily.

ACAPULCO Su Casa/La Margarita

 $$$$$

Avenida Anahuac 110 **Tel** *(744) 484 43 50*

With a hot pink façade on a cliffside overlooking Acapulco and the bay, this open patio restaurant is one of the best casually classy and relaxing in the city. Innovative menu changes frequently. Beef and seafood are specialties here. *Filete al Madrazo* is marinated in fruit juice and flambéd. Great margaritas. Useful street-level elevator. Dinner daily.

HUATULCO El Sabor de Oaxaca

$$

Guamuchil 206, Hotel Las Palmas **Tel** *(958) 587 00 60*

Just off the main plaza, and with an open front to the street, this is tasting central for the food of Oaxaca. *Moles* in several distinct colors and flavors, delicious Oaxacan tamales, plus soup, appetizers, and grilled meat showcasing the region. The *platillo Oaxaca* provides a taste of what is special. Bar. Breakfast, lunch, and dinner daily.

IXTAPA Beccofino

 $$$$

Marina Ixtapa **Tel** *(755) 553 17 70*

Outdoors on the marina, settle in for some of the best Italian food anywhere. The owner brings family recipes and plenty of skill from San Remo, Italy. Wide selection of pasta, much of it including seafood. The mixed seafood grill is a combo of shrimp, lobster, and fish. Impressive wine list. Lunch and dinner daily.

IXTAPA Villa de la Selva

 $$$$$

Paseo de la Roca **Tel** *(755) 553 03 62*

The most romantic setting in Ixtapa offers dining on several levels facing the ocean. The food is international and both beautifully presented and served. Steak, seafood, and poultry are specialties. Red snapper and shrimp are paired to create a delicious dish known as *filet Villa de la Selva*. Splendid desserts. Dinner daily.

OAXACA Doña Elpidia

 $

Miguel Cabrera 413 **Tel** *(951) 516 42 92*

Off the beaten path and behind walls, Doña Elpidia is in a patio home surrounded by gardens. Patrons enjoy a relaxing fixed-price, multi-course lunch. The exact content of the meal changes daily but has the same lineup of appetizer, soup, main course usually served with rice, and dessert. Breakfast and lunch daily.

OAXACA La Casa de la Abuela

 $$

Avenida Hidalgo 616 **Tel** *(951) 516 35 44*

With a prime location overlooking both the Alameda and *zócalo*, Oaxaca's central plazas, the well-prepared specialties are all from Oaxaca. Among them is *tasajo*, a thin piece of salted beef paired with a rich cream. The sampler appetizer plate is one way to get a taste of many regional dishes. Lunch and dinner daily.

OAXACA El Naranjo

 $$

Valerio Trujano 203 **Tel** *(951) 514 18 78*

In a colonial-era house, with covered patio dining, this is one of the best restaurants for exploring Oaxacan food and a few other regions as well. Appetizers include *pasilla chiles* stuffed with Oaxaca string cheese flavored with *epazote* (a herb). Cooking classes are also offered. Lunch and dinner daily.

OAXACA Los Pacos Santo Domingo

$$

Abasolo 121, Centro **Tel** *(951) 516 17 04*

With several small, cozy rooms, this is one of the most relaxing establishments offering tasty Oaxacan specialties. A sampler plate of Oaxacan *mole* is a great way to plunge into the interesting flavors that distinguish each one. The appetizer sampler includes *memela* – a *masa* tidbit with meat and bean topping. Lunch and dinner daily.

OAXACA El Asador Vasco

$$$

Portal de Flores 10 A **Tel** *(951) 514 47 55*

For decades this restaurant, overlooking the *zócalo*, has been a popular favorite. Many of the specialties are from Oaxaca, including the rich Oaxacan *mole*, but there are international favorites featuring beef, fish, and seafood as well. Arrive early for an outside seat with a view of the *zócalo*. Lunch and dinner daily.

PALENQUE Maya

 $

Corner of Independencia & Hidalgo **Tel** *(916) 345 00 42*

Since 1958, Maya has been one of the most dependably good places to eat in Palenque, facing the main plaza. The menu holds regional specialties and international basics, such as soup, sandwiches, and chicken prepared several different ways. The sea bass in garlic is delicious as are the local *tamales*. Breakfast, lunch, and dinner daily.

PALENQUE La Selva

 $$

Carretera Palenque-Ruinas km 0.5 **Tel** *(916) 345 03 63*

At night the linen-draped tables flicker with candlelight, at this long-established and superior restaurant. Steaks, fish, and regional *enchiladas* are specialties. *Filete jacaranda* is a filet of beef with ham and cheese flambéed in brandy. *Pigua*, a freshwater lobster, is the restaurant's most famous specialty. Lunch and dinner daily; Sunday buffet.

Key to Price Guide *see p326* **Key to Symbols** *see back cover flap*

PUERTO ANGEL Villa Florencia

Avenida Virgilio Uribe **Tel** *(958) 584 30 44*

Casual and open-air, Villa Florencia is on Puerto Angel's main drag and with water views from the dining terrace. Italian food is the specialty. A full range of seafood and pasta is offered, including seafood linguini and seafood pasta salad. Short wine list. Great coffee. Breakfast, lunch, and dinner daily.

PUERTO ESCONDIDO Restaurant Santa Fe

Calle de Morro s/n, Hotel Santa Fe **Tel** *(954) 582 01 70*

Beachside and with an ocean view, this open-walled, thatched roof restaurant, beside the hotel of the same name, has a seafood-centered menu as well as sandwiches and salads. The delicious crispy fried tortillas, heaped with well chosen ingredients, require two hands. Full bar. Satisfying margaritas. Breakfast, lunch, and dinner daily.

SAN CRISTÓBAL DE LAS CASAS Madre Tierra

Avenida Insurgentes 19 **Tel** *(967) 678 42 97*

In a one-story former home with wood floors and the judicious use of ethnic textiles, this is one of the best and most comfortable places to relax and eat. Aromas of curry and oregano indicate curried chicken or lasagna are on the menu. Wonderful *comida corrida* daily. Whole-wheat baked goods and tortillas. Breakfast, lunch, and dinner daily.

SAN CRISTÓBAL DE LAS CASAS Tuluc

Avenida Insurgentes 5 **Tel** *(967) 678 20 90*

Another of San Cristobal's favorite dining spots, hospitable Tuluc features Guatemalan textiles and good home cooking. *Filete Tuluc* – steak stuffed with spinach and cheese – is a specialty here. The enticing breakfast menu includes the filling Chiapan *tamales*. Special three-course *comida corrida* daily. Breakfast, lunch, and dinner daily.

SAN CRISTÓBAL DE LAS CASAS El Fogón de Jovel

Avenida 16 de Septiembre 11 **Tel** *(967) 678 11 53*

A top choice for experiencing both Chiapan food and culture. In a Colonial-era home decorated with textiles, waiters in regional dress serve the state's specialties. Full descriptions help diners decide among the bread soup, *chiles relleno*, *chancletas*, and more. The *tamal* plate is a sampler of three of Chiapa's huge, delicious *tamales*. Lunch and dinner daily.

TEOTITLAN DEL VALLE Tlamanalli

Avenida Juárez 39 **Tel** *(951) 524 40 06*

One of the first restaurants in the area to truly celebrate the cuisine of Oaxaca. A meal might include the huge platter-size tortilla filled with beans, meat, and vegetables, or *mole negro de Oaxaca*, or any number of regional specialties. A big attraction is *tamales*, *mole amarillo* and *mole zapoteco*. Lunch Fri–Sun.

TUXTLA GUTIÉRREZ Las Pichanchas

Avenida Central Oriente 837 **Tel** *(961) 612 53 51*

It's a treat to eat at this fine cathedral of Chiapan food in a colorfully decorated enclosed patio. The *platón de botana*, a sampler appetizer platter, includes a variety of local sausages with condiments to go with them. Great place to order one of the Chiapan *tamales*. Refreshing fresh fruit water drinks. Full bar. Lunch and dinner daily.

TUXTLA GUTIÉRREZ Azulejos

Boulevard Belisario Dominguez 1195 **Tel** *(961) 617 77 77*

Azulejos serves daily buffet breakfasts and select international cuisine, as well as a variety of desserts. At lunch you can have *parillada* (mixed grill), choosing from a selection of fish, chicken, or beef. Also serves a traditional Sunday brunch. Breakfast, lunch, and dinner daily.

ZIHUATANEJO Nueva Zelandia

Cuauhtémoc 19 **Tel** *(755) 554 23 40*

Comfort food is served at this small, pleasant, open-air restaurant where there's counter service or table dining. The specialties are *enchiladas* and *tortas* (sandwiches) – created using special bread, often cream, and usually sliced avocados. At breakfast the fluffy pancakes take top billing. Fresh fruit drinks. Breakfast, lunch, and dinner daily.

ZIHUATANEJO Sirena Gorda

Paseo del Pescador 90 **Tel** *(755) 554 26 87*

Ever popular, the Fat Mermaid (as the name translates) offers casual, pleasant, and shaded dining. Bountiful breakfast menu with fresh yogurt and fruit. Seafood tacos are the specialty – with many variations. The hamburgers are juicy and authentic. The daily fish specials are a good buy. Breakfast, lunch, and dinner Thu–Tue.

THE GULF COAST

CATEMACO Hotel Catemaco

Venustiano Carranza 8 **Tel** *(294) 943 02 03*

This central village hotel hosts the busiest restaurant, especially in the evening. It specializes in steak, but offers fish as well. Regional specialties include *pellizcada* (a thick, salted, regional tortilla) and black beans with fried bananas. Bar. Good breakfast menu. Breakfast, lunch, and dinner daily.

COATEPEC Casa Bonilla
Juárez 20 **Tel** *(228) 816 03 74*

In a colonial setting, this seafood restaurant offers an extensive menu focused on fish and seafood. Try the sea bass wrapped in the fragrant *acuyo (hoja santa)* leaf, or different preparations of shrimp. Casa Bonilla's house specialty is langostinos – and they are delicious. Breakfast and lunch daily.

CORDOBA Doña Lala
Calle 7 325 **Tel** *(271) 712 71 11*

Located near the Palacio Municipal, in a colonial-style building, Doña Lala offers inexpensive regional Mexican food. The house specialties are *huevos motuleños* (eggs on tortillas with black beans and cheese) and *carne arrachera* (steak with a garlic and lemon marinade). Breakfast and lunch daily.

ORIZABA Romanchú
7 Poniente 208 **Tel** *(272) 725 25 85*

In a new Colonial-style building three blocks from the central plaza, this stylish restaurant feeds well-heeled patrons grilled meat and seafood. The house specialty, *langostinos Romanchú*, are prepared prepared in garlic and served with a tangy garlic-flavored rice, salad, and freshly made bread or tortillas. Bar. Breakfast, lunch, and dinner daily.

PAPÁNTLA Sorrento
Enriquez 105 B **Tel** *(784) 842 00 67*

In a village with few dining options, Sorrento is the most visible. With an open wall and plain tables and chairs, it offers a place to perch, eat, and people watch. The Mexican and Veracruz specialties include Papantla-style *molotes* – a football shaped *masa* appetizer. *Comida corrida* daily. Breakfast, lunch, and dinner daily.

PAPÁNTLA Totonaco
José de Nuñez 104 **Tel** *(784) 842 01 21*

Located inside the Hotel Tajín, this restaurant makes a good place to sample some tasty Veracruz-style dishes. Totonaco is located in the downtown Papantla area, some 15 minutes from El Tajin archaeological site. Breakfast, lunch, and dinner daily.

SANTIAGO TUXTLA Los Faisanes El Vigia
Corner of Comonfort & 5 de Mayo, Gran Hotel Plaza Santiago **Tel** *(294) 947 04 00*

This popular hotel-restaurant offers a good assortment of Mexican and Veracruz specialties. Among the latter are *pellizcadas* – the thick, corn tortilla of this part of Veracruz, traditionally served with black beans and fried plantains. Mojarra, the local white fish, is another specialty. Breakfast, lunch, and dinner daily.

TLACOTALPAN Doña Lala
Carranza 11, Hotel Posada Doña Lala **Tel** *(288) 884 25 80*

Recommended in Saveur, and by cookbook author and chef Zarela, a native Veracruzana, this is the restaurant of the 19th-century Posada Doña Lala. The emphasis is on seafood and regional specialties – barbecued meat is wrapped in the fragrant *acuyo* leaf, and rice is mixed with seafood. Breakfast, lunch, and dinner daily.

VERACRUZ Gran Café de la Parroquia
Insurgentes Veracruzanos 340 **Tel** *(229) 932 18 55*

The glass wall front of the city's most famous coffee house looks out on the massive port of Veracruz. Of course you can eat here, and people do, all day. But this coffeehouse is most famed for hosting coffee-drinking Mexican presidents and other dignitaries. Their packaged blend is for sale. Breakfast, lunch, and dinner daily.

VERACRUZ Villa Rica Mocambo
Calzada Mocambo 527, Boca del Río **Tel** *(229) 922 21 13*

In a relaxing, plant-filled setting under a thatched roof and near the Hotel Mocambo, this restaurant serves some of the city's best seafood. The "shrimp steak," a novelty on this coast, is whole shrimp pounded to steak size and cooked in a fragrant orange sauce. *Caracol al ajillo* is sea snail in garlic sauce. Lunch and dinner daily.

VILLAHERMOSA Los Tulipanes
Conjunto Cicom 1511 **Tel** *(993) 312 92 17*

This popular restaurant, by the Museo Carlos Pellicer, overlooks the Río Grijalva. The food is international and also known for a wide assortment of regional dishes such as *posta de robalo al mango* – sea bass in a rich mango sauce. Fish *empanadas* are also a specialty. Lunch and dinner daily; breakfast Tue–Sun.

XALAPA Churrería de Mis Recuerdos
Clavijero 17, Centro **Tel** *(228) 165 03 03*

Popular and casually trendy with modern décor and Mexican favorites such as tacos, *enchiladas*, and *tamales*. Their *tamales* with pineapple and coconut were a James Beard Foundation featured food. *Churros* are sugary, tube-shaped fritters served with hot chocolate and *atole* – a corn-based drink. Breakfast, lunch, and dinner daily.

XALAPA La Casona del Beaterio
Zaragoza 20, Centro **Tel** *(228) 818 21 19*

Old photos of Xalapa decorate the walls and multiple patio and interior rooms provide table choices. La Cason del Beaterio is a top relaxing dining spot in the city. The menu features mainstays of spaghetti and crepes, as well as innovative dishes using Mexican ingredients. Filling daily *comida corrida*. Breakfast, lunch, and dinner daily.

Key to Price Guide *see p326* **Key to Symbols** *see back cover flap*

THE YUCATÁN PENINSULA

AKUMAL La Buena Vida  $$$$

Media Luna Bay **Tel** *(984) 875 90 61*

A big, lively and popular restaurant on the exquisite crescent beach of Half Moon Bay, with a fun bar and tables shaded by palm *palapas*. The menu has something for everyone, from burgers and salads to Yucatecan and Caribbean dishes, and excellent seafood. Lunch and dinner daily.

CAMPECHE Marganzo $

Calle 8 no.267 **Tel** *(981) 816 38 99*

A charming restaurant in a fine old colonial building, just off the main square in the heart of old Campeche. Decorated in bright tropical colors, it is a more casual place in which to try local specialties like *pan de cazón* (shark/dogfish in tomato and baked between tortillas). Breakfast, lunch, and dinner daily.

CAMPECHE La Pigua $$$

Malecon Miguel Alemán 179-A **Tel** *(981) 811 33 65*

This pretty restaurant is considered a showcase for Campeche's distinctive cuisine, with delicious versions of dishes like *arroz con pulpo* (octopus and rice salad) or *camarón al coco* (shrimp in coconut). Discreet, relaxed and very comfortable. Lunch daily (noon–5:30pm), dinner daily.

CANCÚN 100% Natural $

Avenida Sunyaxchén 62 **Tel** *(998) 884 01 02*

One of a chain of bright healthfood café-restaurants that can offer a welcome change from heavier local food – some meats, plenty of vegetarian options, a big choice of imaginative salads and fabulously refreshing fruit juice combinations. There are branches in Cancún hotel zone, Playa del Carmen, and Mérida. Breakfast, lunch, and dinner daily.

CANCÚN La Parrilla $$

Avenida Yaxchilán 51 **Tel** *(998) 193 39 73*

Since 1975 La Parrilla has been a Cancún favorite, with a good family atmosphere, Mexican cuisine, and *mariachi* music. The menu includes appetizers, salads, soups, tacos, fondues, fine cuts of meat, and traditional Mayan and Caribbean cuisine. Lunch and dinner daily.

CANCÚN La Dolce Vita $$$$

Boulevard Kukulcán Km14.6 **Tel** *(998) 885 01 61*

Excellent Italian food that imaginatively combines classic dishes and homemade pasta with local Caribbean seafood, spices, and other ingredients. Diners can choose between an air-conditioned dining room and a broad, stylish terrace beside Cancún lagoon. The wine selection is also excellent. Lunch and dinner daily.

CANCÚN La Habichuela $$$$$

Calle Margaritas 25 **Tel** *(998) 884 31 58*

One of downtown Cancún's longest-running restaurants, open since 1977, La Habichuela has some of the city's best Mexican and Yucatecan food, with richly flavored dishes like shrimp in tamarind sauce. Service is charming, and another highlight is the lush, romantic garden, with tables beneath the stars. Lunch and dinner daily.

CANCÚN La Joya $$$$$

Fiesta Americana Grand Coral Beach Hotel, Boulevard Kukulcán Km9.5 **Tel** *(998) 881 32 00*

One of Cancún's most elegant places to dine, La Joya in the Grand Coral Beach hotel has refined Mexican and international cuisine, making subtle use of local ingredients. The setting, on three levels and with stained-glass windows and a fountain, is suitably sumptuous. Dinner Tue–Sun.

CHETUMAL Sergio's Pizzas $$

Avenida Alvaro Obregón 182 **Tel** *(983) 832 29 91*

This charming, very comfortable restaurant is a local institution in Chetumal. Pizza is on the menu, but it is less memorable than Sergio's excellent versions of local specialties like conch or red snapper with tropical fruit seasonings, or the delicious traditional breakfasts. Breakfast, lunch, and dinner daily.

CHICHÉN ITZÁ Las Mestizas $

Calle 15, 15A Pisté village

The long main street of Pisté, the village next to Chichén Itzá, is lined with small restaurants. Las Mestizas is one of the best, a broad, well-shaded terrace with charming waitresses in traditional embroidered *huipiles* and delicious local dishes like *sopa de lima* (chicken, lime, and *tortilla* soup). Breakfast, lunch, and dinner Tue–Sun.

CHICHÉN ITZÁ Villas Arqueológicas $$$

Mex 180, E of the Archaeological Site **Tel** *(985) 856 60 00*

All of the three villa hotels at the major Mayan sites of Chichén Itzá, Cobá and Uxmal have equally pretty restaurants (open to non-residents), in bougainvillea-filled gardens beside swimming pools. The menu features a mix of French and Mexican dishes. Breakfast, lunch, and dinner daily.

COZUMEL Casa Denis $$

Calle 1 Sur no.132, between Avenidas 5 & 10 **Tel** *(987) 872 00 67*

One of Cozumel's oldest restaurants, in a picturesque Caribbean-style wooden house right on San Miguel's main square, with terrace tables ideal for people watching. The food, a mix of Yucatecan favorites like *pollo pibil* and some international dishes, is consistently enjoyable, and good value. Breakfast, lunch, and dinner daily.

COZUMEL La Choza $$

Av 10 no.236 at Calle 3 sur and A. Rosado Salas **Tel** *(987) 872 09 58*

A big, popular restaurant in the middle of San Miguel, remodeled in the hacienda style, with an extensive choice of enjoyable, typically Mexican dishes like *arracherasteaks*, great *guacamole*, and *huevos a la mexicana* (scrambled egg with peppers) for breakfast. Breakfast, lunch, and dinner daily.

COZUMEL La Veranda $$$

Calle 4 Norte, between 5a Ave and 10a Ave **Tel** *(987) 872 41 32*

Set in a lovely tropical garden around a Caribbean-style house with a big, shady veranda, this restaurant feels far away from the hustle and bustle of the streets. Try the tasty shrimp Caribbean, mango fish, and the delicious dessert of the day. Dinner Tue–Sun.

COZUMEL Pepe's Grill $$$$

Avenida Rafael E Melgar, corner of Calle A. Rosado Salas **Tel** *(987) 872 02 13*

Grills are naturally the specialty here, whether of steaks or fresh fish, lobster, and other seafood. Many dishes are flambéd at your table, like snapper with coconut and pineapple. The spacious room is on a second floor above the waterfront, with beautiful views of the sunsets. Dinner daily.

ISLA MUJERES Manolo's $

Avenida Matamoros, between Avenidas Juárez and Rueda Medina

An attractively simple and tranquil little restaurant in a garden patio on a quiet street in Isla town. Manolos's is run by a charming family, who prepare delicious Yucatecan dishes and freshly grilled seafood and fish like *huachinango al mojo de ajo* (red snapper cooked in garlic). Superb value. Dinner daily.

ISLA MUJERES Pizza Rolandi's $$

Avenida Hidalgo 110, between Avenidas Madero & Abasolo **Tel** *(998) 877 04 30*

A favourite of many Isla Mujeres visitors, with a bright dining space opening onto one of Isla town's main streets. Pizzas – cooked in a wood-burning oven – pastas and other Italian dishes dominate the menu, sometimes making original use of local ingredients, as in the specialty lobster calzone. Breakfast, lunch, and dinner daily.

ISLA MUJERES Sombrero de Gomar $$

Avenida Hidalgo, corner of Avenida Madero **Tel** *(998) 877 06 27*

This big, long-established restaurant is hard to miss, on a second-floor balcony with colorful paintwork and *palapa* roof above one of Isla town's main crossroads. Relaxed and very friendly, it has appetizing *enchiladas de pollo* and many other classic Mexican dishes at low prices. Breakfast, lunch, and dinner daily.

IZAMAL Kinich $

Calle 27 no.299. Between Calles 28 & 30 **Tel** *(988) 954 04 89*

Very near Izamal's K'inich K'ak Mo pyramid, this delightfully pretty restaurant in a garden is one of the Yucatán's best for traditional local dishes such as *pavo en relleno negro* (turkey in black chilli sauce). It is only open in the evenings on the nights of Izamal's Sound-and-Light show. Breakfast, lunch, and dinner daily.

MÉRIDA Los Almendros $$

Calle 50-A no.493, on Parque de la Mejorada **Tel** *(999) 928 54 59*

A well-known showcase for Yucatecan country cuisine, particularly specialties like *poc-chuc* (pork marinated in bitter oranges and garlic). Service, by waitresses in traditional dresses, is charming, and music and folk dancing accompany the meal. Standards can vary, but on a good day it is very enjoyable. Lunch and dinner daily.

MERIDA Amaro's $$

Calle 59 no.507, between Calles 60 & 62 **Tel** *(999) 928 24 51*

Occupying the lovely patio of a historic Mérida house, dominated by a magnificent giant orchid tree, Amaro's is unusual in offering a large number of vegetarian choices. They are based on traditional Yucatecan dishes, and often use a local spinach-like vegetable, *chaya*. Open to the stars, this is a very relaxing place. Lunch and dinner daily.

MÉRIDA Hacienda Teya $$

Off Mex 180, 12.5 km E of Mérida **Tel** *(999) 988 08 00*

Dating from 1683, this grand colonial hacienda has been made into a restaurant, open only for lunch, with refined Yucatecan cuisine. Delicious appetizers and dishes like *cochinita pibil* (pork marinated in bitter oranges and *achiote* spices) are served in a spacious dining room or on the terrace, beside a magnificent garden. Lunch daily (noon–6pm).

MÉRIDA Villa María $$$

Calle 59 no.533, corner of Calle 68 **Tel** *(999) 923 33 57*

This sophisticated restaurant occupies the exquisite patio of a grand old Mérida house, which is also now a luxurious hotel. The chef is Austrian, and produces a refined, Mediterranean-oriented mix of international cuisine, making interesting use of local ingredients. Lunch and dinner daily.

Key to Price Guide *see p326* **Key to Symbols** *see back cover flap*

MÉRIDA Pancho's

$$$$

Calle 59 no.509, between Calles 60 & 62 **Tel** *(999) 923 09 42*

An entertaining restaurant with Mexican bandit-theme décor and waiters in cartridge belts and big sombreros, and a lively bar and patio dance floor with live salsa bands. To eat there are tasty *enchiladas*, *quesadillas*, and other Mexican snacks, and well-prepared steaks, seafood, and other larger dishes. Dinner daily.

PLAYA DEL CARMEN Media Luna

 $

Avenida 5, between Calles 12 & 14 **Tel** *(984) 873 05 26*

With a trendily decorated little terrace on the Quinta Avenida, this mellow café offers an eclectic mix of salads, pastas, noodles, and tasty dishes that combine Mexican, Mediterranean, and Oriental styles and local tropical ingredients. Great for a light lunch, with lots of choice for vegetarians. Breakfast, lunch, and dinner daily.

PLAYA DEL CARMEN Glass Bar

$$$

Calle 10 between Av 1 and 5 **Tel** *(984) 803 16 76*

A sleek and stylish modern restaurant on the busiest corner of Playa's Quinta Avenida, well placed for watching the crowds go by. The refined menu is mainly modern Italian, but also features a mix of Italian and fashionably global dishes. Plus, there is one of the Riviera's best wine lists. Breakfast, lunch, and dinner daily.

PROGRESO Flamingo's

$

Malecón, corner of Calle 72 **Tel** *(969) 935 21 22*

This is one of the most enjoyable of the several big terrace restaurants along Progreso's seafront. Flamingo's specializes in fresh fish – diners can choose between giant grilled fish platters or lighter but still excellent seafood *ceviches* made with vividly fresh limes and coriander. Staff are very welcoming. Breakfast, lunch, and dinner daily.

PUERTO MORELOS Los Pelícanos

Town plaza, by the beach **Tel** *(998) 871 00 14*

A long-established feature of Puerto Morelos – rebuilt after the 2005 hurricane – this big, *palapa*-roofed restaurant sits right beside the beach. Its wide terrace is an excellent place from which to watch the waves and the seabirds, over a plate of grilled sea bass or a *ceviche* of octopus or conch. Breakfast, lunch, and dinner daily.

PUERTO MORELOS John Gray's Kitchen

 $$$

Avenida Niños Héroes, just off the plaza **Tel** *(998) 871 06 65*

Acclaimed American chef John Gray has chosen to set up his main restaurant here, in tranquil Puerto Morelos. The dining room and garden are compact, elegant, and comfortable, and his adventurous, very sophisticated cooking, making full use of local ingredients, is memorable. The menu changes daily. Dinner Mon–Sat.

TULUM Cetli

$$

Calle Polar Oriente **Tel** *(984) 108 06 81*

With excellent views of the lagoon and the sea, Cetli is very unobtrusive, but the chef-owner, from Mexico City, prepares delicious original variations on traditional Mexican dishes. The *chiles en nogada*, with fragrant spices and walnut sauce, are outstanding. Dinner Thu–Tue.

TULUM Don Cafeto Centro

Avenida Tulum, three blocks N of town hall **Tel** *(984) 871 22 07*

A big terrace restaurant on the main street of Tulum village, with plenty of tables from which to take in the atmosphere. This is a reliable spot at all times of day, whether for traditional breakfasts, *tostadas*, and other snacks, or larger dishes like grilled fish *a la veracruzana*. Breakfast, lunch, and dinner daily.

TULUM Mezzanine

$$$

Carretera Boca Paila, Km1.5 **Tel** *(984) 131 15 96*

Part of an unusual, ambitiously chic boutique-style hotel on Tulum beach, with trendily contemporary design in strong colors. The menu of the sleek terrace restaurant is equally international, with Thai and other light, Asian-influenced dishes. There is a bar and pool in similar style, and DJs perform every Friday night. Breakfast, lunch, and dinner daily.

UXMAL Villas Arqueológicas

Off entrance road to Uxmal archaeological site **Tel** *(997) 974 60 20*

The villa hotel at Uxmal, like its sister-hotels at Chichén Itzá and Cobá, has a delightfully relaxing restaurant (open to non-residents), next to an especially pretty pool. There are French and international dishes on the menu, but local favorites like *pollo pibil* are also excellent. Breakfast, lunch, and dinner daily.

UXMAL Hacienda San Pedro Ochil

$$

Off Mex 261, 38km N of Uxmal **Tel** *(999) 924 74 65*

This 17th-century hacienda has been converted into a restaurant, gift shop, and museum. Workshops line the entrance, where local artisans make traditional hammocks, stone carvings, and jewelery. Diners enjoy refined versions of Yucatecan dishes, such as *pollo pibil* and *panuchos*. Breakfast, lunch, and dinner daily.

VALLADOLID El Mesón del Marqués

$

Calle 39 no.203, between Calles 40 & 42 **Tel** *(985) 856 20 73*

One of the Yucatán's prettiest restaurants, in the patio of Valladolid's most distinguished traditional hotel, with a fountain, palms and vividly colored flowers. Service is charming, and it is a fine place to try the town's own specialties like *lomitos de valladolid* (diced pork with chili, garlic, and tomatoes). Breakfast, lunch, and dinner daily.

SHOPPING IN MEXICO

For many people, shopping is one of the highlights of a trip to Mexico. Some enjoy the upscale boutiques or jewelry stores in big-city malls or beach resorts. (For shopping in Mexico City, see pp114–5.) Others prefer the excitement of a colorful, bustling street market piled high with unfamiliar fruits and vegetables, or of finding an isolated roadside stall selling beautiful earthenware pots or bright, handwoven rugs.

Basket seller taking his wares to market

Bartering is not appropriate everywhere. At craft stalls in tourist resorts, a certain amount of haggling is usually acceptable and even expected, but in most shops, prices are fixed. You can ask *¿Cuánto es lo menos?* (What is your best price?) but when buying from craftsmen, bear in mind that their profit is usually already pitifully low. Larger stores will ship your purchases home for you; it is illegal to export archaeological artifacts.

Roadside stall selling colorful souvenirs including rugs and bags

OPENING HOURS

Shops generally open from 9am through 7 or 8pm, Monday through Saturday. Bakeries and corner shops may open earlier, at 8am, and some stay open until 10pm. Boutiques and craft shops usually open at 10am. Sunday shopping is possible at supermarkets and in tourist areas.

Large American-style shopping malls have sprouted all over Mexico's cities in recent years. They open on Sundays, but some close on Mondays.

Outside Mexico City, most shops close for lunch between 2 and 4pm. Department stores and supermarkets everywhere stay open over lunchtime. Street markets usually pack up at about 2 or 3pm.

PAYING

Cash and major credit cards (VISA, MasterCard, and, to a lesser extent, American Express and Diners Club) are acceptable forms of payment in most Mexican shops. Prices generally include 15 percent

IVA (sales tax, or VAT). Credit card payments are usually subject to a small surcharge. All but the most touristy markets accept only cash.

GENERAL STORES

Glitzy department stores, modern malls, and expensive, trendy boutiques are the norm in certain parts of the capital and in a handful of cities and resorts around the country. In most big cities, there is at least one Sanborns *(see p114)*, which has a good

The bustling market in Tepoztlán, a lively jumble of people and products

selection of books, magazines, maps, gifts, chocolates, and toiletries. For everyday shopping, supermarkets like Superama or Comercial Mexicana are huge and well stocked with many familiar brand names.

Away from modern shopping centers, ordinary life in Mexico still revolves around the market and traditional shops in the surrounding streets: the *panadería* (bakery), *abarrotes* (grocery store), and *ferretería* (hardware store).

SPECIALTY SHOPS

León, Guadalajara, and Monterrey are all known for their fine-quality leatherware. Shoes, with designs ranging from trendy to classical, are particularly good value, and are sold in shops and markets all over the country. Belts and bags are also an excellent buy. The sturdy, rubber-soled *huarache* sandals are best bought in Guadalajara's *(see pp188–9)* San Juan de Dios market. In Jalisco, craftsmen also make *equipales*, the typically Mexican, rustic leather and wood armchairs.

Mexico is the world leader in silver production, and prices are well below those of Europe or the US. Silversmiths in Taxco *(see pp146–7)*, Guanajuato *(see pp202–4)*, and Zacatecas *(see pp192–3)* create modern designs, as well as those inspired by pre-Columbian jewelry. A 925 stamp will ensure that the silver is good quality. Alpaca, which is on sale all over Mexico, is a nickel alloy and contains no silver at all. Opals, jadeite, lapis lazuli, obsidian, onyx, and many other semi-precious stones, are relatively inexpensive to purchase.

CLOTHING

Casual clothing is available in all major tourist resorts and big cities. Imported designer labels, such as Gucci and Hermès, can be found in a few select boutiques and department stores. Less expensive clothes are on sale in smaller shops and markets everywhere. Any designer clothes and accessories that are for sale on cheap market stalls are almost certain to be fakes.

Villages in the south and southeast of Mexico are the best places to buy traditional, hand-embroidered Indian costumes. The more commercial designs – often using synthetic fabrics – are sold in craft shops everywhere.

Hats and scarves on a souvenir stall in a street market

REGIONAL PRODUCTS

The variety of crafts available in Mexico is vast *(see pp348–9)*. Every region has its specialties, and it is more interesting – and usually cheaper – to buy *artesanías* in the region where they are made. For an overview of what is available, most regional capitals have a Casa de las Artesanías, which houses exhibitions and

Typical tourist shops in the resort of Playa del Carmen

sales of local craftwork. The most outstanding *artesanías* are found in those areas which have a significant Indian population, such as the states of Oaxaca, Puebla, Chiapas, Guerrero, Michoacán, and Nayarit.

FOOD AND DRINK

Fresh and dried chilies, spices, and pastes for preparing *mole* and other Mexican dishes are best bought from market stalls. Although not quite as good, *mole* is also found in jars or packages at supermarkets. Similarly, there are several varieties of chili bottled and in cans, which are more easily packed.

The best *añejo* tequilas *(see p325)* are made in Jalisco, and good brands, like Herradura or Centenario, can be bought at supermarkets and *vinaterías* (liquor stores) all over Mexico. Avoid non-labeled tequila, which may be contaminated with methanol. Mezcal, less widely sold, is best bought in its native Oaxaca.

Handmade sweets and candies are a specialty of central Mexico's colonial towns. Sweet-toothed visitors will want to try *cajeta* from Celaya, *chongos* from Zamora, *camote* from Puebla, and *cocada envinada* from Guadalajara. These, and more, can be found in Mexico City's Dulcería de Celaya *(see p114)*.

MARKETS

Every town in Mexico has at least one market. There is often a permanent indoor market, as well as a once-weekly street market, or *tianguis*, which is usually held in or around the main square. In large cities, each neighborhood has its *mercado sobre ruedas* (street market) on a different day of the week. These markets are a colorful array of fresh fruit, vegetables, fish and meat, and piles of herbs, spices, and chilies. Clothes, trinkets, and household items are also for sale. Prices are generally cheaper here than in supermarkets.

Markets are transformed at fiesta time. At Easter in Mexico City, there is an abundance of red papier mâché *diablos* (devils). Just before the Days of the Dead *(see pp34–5)*, stalls overflow with sugar skulls and dancing skeletons. And at Christmas, the usual decorations rub shoulders with typically Mexican nativity figures.

Vivid array of chilies, legumes (pulses), and spices for sale in a Mexican market

Folk Art of Mexico

Crafts in Mexico are an essential part of daily and ceremonial life, with techniques passed down from generation to generation. Contemporary folk art results from the fusion of Old and New World traits. After the Conquest, the impact of Spanish technology was widely felt. While some native arts such as feather working were lost, others were gained. Mission schools taught European skills, and Spanish methods for treating leather were introduced, together with treadle-loom weaving and the glazing of ceramics. Today, traditional methods and designs co-exist with recent innovations, producing a wide range of high-quality crafts for sale *(see pp350–51)*.

Ceremonial beaded gourd

Spanish galleons, displaying the sign of the cross, brought Christianity to Mexico.

Religious festivals marked out the pre-Columbian year. Despite efforts by Spanish missionaries to ban the dance of the *voladores*, it is still performed today *(see p29)*.

The art of pottery goes back thousands of years in Mexico, and in other parts of the New World. Many ancient techniques are still in use today.

Pot making *still utilises traditional methods. Tzeltal women, for instance, work without a wheel in Amatenango del Valle, Chiapas. Tubes of clay are coiled and pressed down with the fingers. The surfaces are burnished and decorated before being fired.*

This weaver *is using a backstrap loom. Textile skills in Tzotzil and other indigenous communities, are used primarily to make clothing. As in pre-Conquest times, weavers rely on techniques such as brocading to pattern cloth on the loom.*

Corn (or maize) originated in the Americas, and formed part of the staple diet of Mesoamerican civilizations *(see p45)*. Then, as now, it was ground on a *metate* (grinding stone).

Silversmiths have practiced *their art for many centuries in Mexico. After the Conquest, some processes like "lost wax casting" disappeared, but modern jewelers retain enormous skill. The above pieces were sand-cast.*

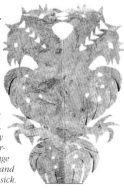

Bark paper (amate) *is still made in the Otomí village of San Pablito (Puebla), using an ancient, pre-Columbian method. Popular with collectors, the cut-out figures represent supernatural forces. They are used by Otomí shamans during rituals to encourage the growth of crops and to cure the sick.*

THE MEETING OF TWO WORLDS

Metepec, outside Toluca, is famous for its exuberant pottery. Brightly painted "Trees of Life" are inspired by history, nature, and the Bible. The one pictured here, by Tiburcio Soteno, shows Spanish conquistadors discovering Aztec civilization in 1519.

Markets *have always been good sources of local craft items. The vendors, who are often the makers, may travel long distances to sell their wares.*

The Aztec calendar alluded to on the Sun Stone *(see p95)* combined a solar calendar of 365 days and a sacred calendar of 260 days, leading to cycles of 52 years *(see p47)*.

Human sacrifices took place in Aztec temples. The victims, regarded as the gods' messengers, had their hearts cut out on the sacrificial stone.

Tenochtitlán *(see p94)* was founded when the Aztecs entered the Valley of Mexico and saw the promised sign of an eagle on a prickly pear *(see p43)*.

This papier-mâché dragon (alebrije) *is by Felipe Linares. European paper, introduced after the Conquest, is used in Mexico City and Celaya (west of Querétaro) to make fantastical papier-mâché figures of all shapes and kinds.*

Glazed ceramics *are decorative as well as functional. The pottery must be fired twice, and enclosed kilns have generally replaced pre-Columbian firing methods. The glaze is often transparent, but yellow, black, and green are used too.*

Embroidery *was practiced in Mexico before the Conquest, but was given new impetus under Spanish rule. The blouse, here embroidered with flowers, was a garment introduced from Spain.*

Tinsmiths *are particularly prominent in Oaxaca City. The craftsmen use shears to cut through thin and flexible sheets of tin. Lanterns and decorative figures can be plain, or painted with bright, industrial colors.*

Buying Mexican Crafts

Mexican folk art has a unique vitality. Good craft items are sold in street markets, as well as in shops and galleries. Work can also be bought directly from the makers. Craftspeople of various trades can be found in many villages and small towns by making inquiries on arrival. Although it is advisable to negotiate a fair price when buying crafts, purchasers should take into consideration the rising cost of materials, as well as the skill and time invested by the maker. Many folk artists now sign their work, aware that it is highly valued by an increasing number of museums and private collectors.

Tin-glazed earthenware dish
from Guanajuato

CERAMICS

Mexican ceramists practice a vast range of ancient and modern techniques. In Oaxaca, traditional firing methods produce pottery with a black, metallic lustre. Green glazes are popular in Michoacán. Puebla City is famous for its tin-glazed earthenware, and brightly-painted toys are produced in many places.

Painted pottery mermaid

Pottery bandstand

Ceramic
Adam and Eve

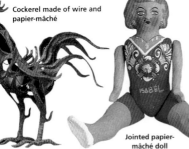

Cockerel made of wire and
papier-mâché

Jointed papier-
mâché doll

PAPIER-MACHE

Papier-mâché is used to create decorative figures and toys for seasonal festivities. Masks are made all year round, skeletons and skulls for the Days of the Dead *(see pp34–5)*.

Human and animal masks for children

WOODEN TOYS AND CARVINGS

Inexpensive wooden toys are made in several states, including Michoacán, Guerrero, and Guanajuato. In the villages of Oaxaca, carved, painted figures and dance masks can fetch high prices.

Wooden tiger with sequin eyes

Fragile items
When transporting craft objects, any hollows should be padded out, and projecting features wrapped in paper.

Toy truck and passengers

Lacquer-coated wooden lizard from Guerrero

TEXTILES

In some states, traditional garments such as sashes, shawls, wrap-around skirts, and *huipiles* (tunics) are woven on a backstrap loom from hand-spun wool or cotton. Treadle-loomed blankets and rugs are made in Oaxaca. Embroidered blouses can be found in many regions. The Huichol specialize in netted beadwork.

Woven cloth, patterned on the loom

Otomí cloth with embroidery

Caring for textiles
Textiles should always be washed by hand in cold water. Even under these conditions, colors may run, so it is advisable to test-wash a small corner first.

Huichol netted beadwork bag

Nahua embroidered blouse

METALWORK AND JEWELRY

Copper is worked only in Michoacán. It is hammered while red hot to form jugs, platters, and candlesticks. Taxco is world famous for its silverwork. In the Yucatán, gold- and silversmiths specialize in delicate earrings and necklaces.

Bull

Cockerel

Tin decorations
In Oaxaca City, the tinsmiths work from sheets of tin. The shapes are cut out and painted with translucent colors to form lamps, boxes, and shimmering figures. In central regions of Mexico, elegant candlesticks and Baroque mirror-frames are made from unpainted tin.

Silver earrings from Puebla

Mexican bird

Armadillo

Oaxacan woman

OTHER CRAFTS

In Mexico, there is hardly a substance that is not made to serve a functional, decorative, or ceremonial purpose. Fine and unusual work is done using sugar, bone, horn, vanilla, and gum. Pictures are often painted on tree-bark paper.

Lacquered gourd

Basketry
Beautiful yet sturdy, baskets are made in several regions of Mexico, including Oaxaca and Guerrero. Makers use palm, willow, cane, wheat-straw, and agave fibers.

Lacquered box

Lacquer work
Gourds and wooden items such as trays and boxes are given a hard, glossy coat. Archaeological remnants show that lacquer working dates from pre-Columbian times.

ENTERTAINMENT IN MEXICO

One of Mexico's most fascinating features is its home-grown tradition in music, dance, and popular arts. The country has produced a huge range of uniquely Mexican musical styles, and equally distinctive, colorful dances. Cities and resorts offer buzzing nightlife, from salsa venues to trendy clubs. Mexico City and other big cities host quality classical music and theater. Sport is also hugely popular in Mexico – every Mexican soccer league game is shown live, and baseball is broadcast live on the radio. For a uniquely Mexican sporting event, nothing beats the exciting displays of horsemanship at a *charrería*. For annual events throughout Mexico, see pages 30-35.

Mexican soccer players

Folk dancers performing to *jarana* music in the Yucatán

TRADITIONAL MUSIC AND DANCE

Virtually every part of Mexico has its own style of music and dance. The most famous, *mariachi* music, originated in Jalisco state but can now be found all over the country. *Mariachis* are part of Mexico's wandering minstrel tradition, and can be heard in the street, or going from table to table in restaurants.

In many regions, though, the violins and trumpets of *mariachis* are less prominent than local styles and instruments: Caribbean *danzón* in Veracruz, *marimbas* in Chiapas, and the *jarana* music and dancers of the Yucatán.

The best occasions to experience other kinds of music and dance are local *fiestas*. Many cities, such as Mérida, also host smaller festivals with displays of local music and dance every week. In other towns, there are regular displays by folklore groups, and permanent theatrical shows. Some spectacular festivals celebrate a particular region's traditional dances, the most dazzling being Oaxaca's *La Guelaguetza*, every July *(see p31)*.

POP, ROCK, LATIN DANCE, AND CLUBS

Mexico also has a vibrant modern music scene, and artists such as Julieta Venegas and Paulina Rubio increasingly cross over to non-Latin audiences. Many performers mix Mexican styles with hip-hop, rock, and other international influences. Other stars from around the Hispanic world, as well as US and international artists, are also popular. Mexico City and other large cities have a big choice of live music venues. Concerts also feature in major *fiestas*, such as Carnival in Veracruz, or *Feria de Tabasco* in Villahermosa in April-May.

Salsa, merengue, and other Latin dances are hugely popular, and every city and resort has a choice of Latin dance clubs, often with live bands. Clubs with international dance music are just as common, and vary from basic to dazzlingly chic and glamorous. Giant mega-clubs, with several different spaces and the latest technology, are the specialties of resorts like Cancún. For more intimate nightlife head for smaller resorts, like Puerto Escondido or Playa del Carmen.

CLASSICAL MUSIC, DANCE, AND THEATER

Mexico City has, by far, the largest classical music program, with three resident orchestras and regular visits by international orchestras, opera companies, and soloists. Guadalajara also has its own symphony orchestra, and Mérida has the Orquesta Sinfónica de Yucatán.

Classical ballet and contemporary dance can be seen in Mexico City at the Palacio de Bellas Artes *(see p80)* and

Julieta Venegas performing her own brand of accordion-based rock

Teatro de la Danza *(see p116).* For Spanish-speakers there is a varied mix of live theater, especially in Mexico City and Guadalajara. Cultural festivals worth seeking out include the International Chamber Music Festival in San Miguel de Allende (Aug), Guadalajara's October Festival, Zacatecas' Culture Festival (Semana Santa), and the Festival Internacional Cervantino in Guanajuato (Sep–Oct), with an international mix of music and theater.

Charro riders in high-speed action in a *lienzo charro (charreria* ring)

MOVIES

Mexicans are eager movie-goers, and the country has a long movie-making tradition, producing a large number of films. In the 1930s and 1940s it produced hundreds of movies before falling into decline. The industry has since been revived with the emergence of actors such as Salma Hayek and Gael García Bernal, and movies like *Amores Perros* that have won international acclaim.

Cities offer a choice of modern, air-conditioned multiplex movie theaters. In multiplexes, Hollywood movies are often shown in English with Spanish subtitles on at least one screen.

The masked wrestlers of *lucha libre* – a popular sport in Mexico

SPECTATOR SPORTS

Sports attract the biggest audiences of all in Mexico. Soccer (football) inspires the most passion – above all in central Mexico – with several teams in Mexico City, and one in each of the other major cities. TV provides constant coverage, but the best place to see a big game is Mexico City's vast Estadio Azteca *(see p117)* . Baseball is also popular, especially along the Pacific coast, the Gulf Coast, and on the Yucatán Peninsula, with two competitive professional leagues.

Two other sports are peculiarly Mexican. Mexico has produced many boxing champions, and there are matches every weekend in the capital and other cities. Even more popular is wrestling *(lucha libre).* Mexican wrestlers are popular idols. They often fight in masks and outrageous costumes and develop superhero-like personalities.

Ticket for a bullfight in Mexico City

BULLFIGHTING

Spanish-style bullfights are held every Sunday at Mexico City's Plaza Mexico *(see p110)* – the largest bullring in the world – during the November–April season. This is the closed season for bullfighting in Spain, so many top Spanish *toreros* spend their winters in Mexico. Many other cities, and resorts like Cancún, also have bullrings with regular *corridas* throughout the year.

Smaller-scale bullfights are also part of many small town and village *fiestas.* These bullfights are much less formal, more raucous events, and often fairly chaotic as well – frequently though, the bull is not killed.

CHARRERÍAS

A uniquely Mexican event, a *charrería* is a rodeo in which cowboys *(charros)* in the traditional big *sombrero,* embroidered jacket, and trousers (and cowgirls – *charras,* riding side-saddle and wearing elaborate layered skirts) perform spectacular tests of horsemanship. There are *charrería* rings *(lienzos charros),* in every city, but the best are in the northern and western states – especially Jalisco, also home to *mariachi* music, which always accompanies a *charrería.* The annual Día del Charro (September 14) is the occasion for *charrería* displays throughout the country.

ENTERTAINMENT FOR CHILDREN

To entertain young visitors, there is the huge Six Flags Mexico theme park, just outside Mexico City. Closer to the center, Chapultepec Park houses an amusement park and zoo *(see p88).* Resorts like Cancún and Acapulco have a choice of water parks, and on the Riviera Maya "eco-parks" like Xcaret *(see p284)* provide a child-friendly introduction to a tropical environment.

Young visitors are fascinated by the colors of local *fiestas,* which always include different events for children, and temporary funfairs.

OUTDOOR ACTIVITIES & SPECIALIST HOLIDAYS

Mexico's enormously varied landscapes provide ideal settings for all kinds of activities. Along the coasts are long surf beaches, some of the world's richest sportfishing grounds, and coral reefs that are perfect for diving and snorkeling. Inland are fast-flowing rivers in spectacular gorges, and unforgettable forests,

Fisherman with rainbow trout

deserts, and mountains to explore by hiking, climbing, or on horseback. Other possibilities include discovering the country's wealth of wildlife, its special cuisines, or fascinating historic culture. Local tourist offices can provide the latest information on the ever-increasing number of activities available.

DIVING AND SNORKELING

The Great Maya Reef off Yucatán's Caribbean coast form one of the world's largest coral reef systems. Despite the growth in visitor numbers, huge areas are still vividly alive, with brilliantly colorful fish and coral gardens. There are reefs of every grade of diving difficulty, from novice dives to awesome wall dives. There are scuba diving centers all along the Riviera Maya, but for beginners and less experienced divers the best locations are Isla Mujeres, Puerto Morelos, Playa del Carmen, or Cozumel.

Snorkeling is an easier alternative, and some dive operators also offer snorkel tours. Off Cozumel, where reefs come close inshore, you can often see as much with a snorkel as with scuba tanks.

The waters of the Pacific coast are not as clear as those of the Caribbean, but there is still fine diving around Puerto Escondido, Ixtapa, and

Zihuatanejo. The best Pacific diving and snorkeling is in the Sea of Cortéz, between Baja California and the mainland.

Thanks to the Yucatán's unique geology, riddled with limestone caverns, underground rivers, and open sinkholes called cenotes, this is also one of the world's foremost areas for cave diving. Operators in Akumal and Tulum such as **Aquatech** and **Cenote Dive Center** specialize in cave dives, and **Hidden Worlds** in Tulum gives a great first taste of swimming in caves. You must have open-water diving certification to cave dive, but without this you can still snorkel in the upper levels of cenotes.

SURFING

The Pacific coast is lined with surfing beaches. Baja California has beaches almost along the whole of its length, and near its southern tip many companies like **Baja Wild** offer boat trips to remote surf

beaches and islands. On the mainland, surfing centers include Mazatlán, Manzanillo, Troncones, Ixtapa and Zihuatanejo in Guerrero, and, the most popular, Puerto Escondido. Most surfers find their own way, but many agencies offer surf camps, courses, and trips to special locations.

FISHING

Yucatán's Caribbean coast has fine deep-sea fishing for marlin, bonito, tuna, and more. Cozumel, Puerto Morelos, and Puerto Aventuras are all good fishing centers. **Captain Rick's Sportfishing** in Puerto Aventuras offers combined fishing and snorkeling trips.

Inshore fishing is just as popular: Ascension Bay, south of Tulum, has some of the richest fly-fishing grounds in the world, especially for bonefish, and there are fishing lodges scattered along the dirt road down to Punta Allen. **Cuzan Guest House** makes a good base and offers fly, offshore, and spin fishing trips.

On the Pacific, Mazatlán is the deep-sea fishing mecca, especially for marlin and billfish. **Pro Team Sportfishing** in Mazatlán has well-organized billfishing trips. Prices include preparation of your catch. Freshwater fisheries are less developed, but there is good fishing for bass on Lago El Salto, inland from Mazatlán.

All fishing centers have agencies with boats for rent, and many US-based companies arrange fishing packages.

Snorkeling in Chankanaab National Park Island, Cozumel

A golf course in the grounds of a Cancún hotel resort

Many dive shops, adventure tour agencies, and hotels also offer fishing trips, and in small towns these can be arranged informally with local fishermen. Licenses are required for deep-sea fishing; your boat agency will arrange this.

OTHER WATER SPORTS

Sailing through the Sea of Cortéz off Baja California is a wonderful experience, with many rocky coves and islands to explore. There are excellent marinas at La Paz, San Carlos, Mazatlán, Puerto Vallarta, and Zihuatanejo, while on the Caribbean, Puerto Aventuras, and Cozumel are also sailing centers. The **Sonoran Sport Center** in San Carlos has a sailing school, while **The Moorings Boat Charters** offers the choice of crewed charters or boats to hire, supplied with a specially devised itinerary for your trip.

Windsurf boards can be rented in most resorts, but Mexico's windsurfing magnet is Los Barriles, in Baja California. In the bigger resorts you can also find Jet Skis, water skis, and banana boats (inflatables pulled along by a speedboat).

For more tranquil exploration, in Baja California, sea kayaking is one way of getting close to sea lions and whales. Around the southern Riviera Maya, many hotels offer kayaks for trips through the mangroves toward Ascension Bay, or around the

exquisite lake at Bacalar. Recently there has been a huge expansion in freshwater kayaking and whitewater rafting on Mexico's many spectacular rivers. Popular routes include the Río Filolobos in Veracruz, the Amacuzac in Morelos, and the Huasteca Potosina region of San Luís Potosí. **Agua Azul** takes trips through the rivers of Oaxaca. In Chiapas, **Explora** organizes trips of several days rafting down La Venta gorge or kayaking through the Lacandón rain forest.

White-water rafting

GOLF

The number of golf courses in Mexico has grown fast, and there are now courses near all the main cities and resorts, especially Cabo San Lucás, Mazatlán, and Cancún. The **Cabo del Sol Golf Courses** in

Cabo San Lucas has two large courses, and the **Cozumel Country Club** offers package deals with participating hotels. Some hotels have courses attached, and there's a growing number of golf resorts. Most are open to non-residents for an extra fee. For more on golfing in Mexico, check **www.golfinmexico.net**

HIKING, CLIMBING, AND ADVENTURE SPORTS

Mexico's rugged mountain ranges provide spectacular opportunities for outdoor sports. The awe-inspiring Copper Canyon of Chihuahua *(see pp176–7)* is the most popular area, with trekking and bike trails of every grade of difficulty, and dramatic gorges for more challenging activities like canyoneering and abseiling. Many US-based agencies like **Native Trails** organize canyon treks, and local agencies, like **Expediciones Umarike** and the **Cooperativa de los Guías**, provide equipment and Tarahumara Indian guides. Elsewhere, a popular trip from Mexico City is the climb up the massive 5,230-m (17,150-ft) volcano of Iztaccihuátl. You can also hike into tropical forest environments, like Los Tuxtlas in Veracruz or the Sierra Gorda mountains near Querétaro.

Many Mexican agencies offer adventure trips, such as **Tour by Mexico**. For Spanish speakers, information on adventure trips can be found on **www.ecoadventure mexico.com**

Taking a hike in Copper Canyon (Cañon del Cobre), Northern Mexico

HORSEBACK RIDING

Mexico has an ingrained horse culture, and there are plenty of opportunities to explore spectacular scenery on horseback. The best places are Copper Canyon, around Laguna de Chapala, Real de Catorce, and San Miguel de Allende and – along trails that lead to the migration-refuges of monarch butterflies – above Valle de Bravo. **El Caballo Rojo** in Laguna de Chapala has tours for riders of all abilities. In San Cristóbal, Chiapas, agencies offer horseback tours up to nearby Mayan villages.

Around coastal resorts, there are often horses to hire along beaches, and many hotels and eco-parks like **Xcaret** have horses to ride on well-organized trails.

AIR SPORTS

The most exciting way to see Mexico's resorts must be to skydive onto their beaches. **SkyDive Cuautla** is based at Cuautla, outside Mexico City, but also has operations at Puerto Vallarta, Ixtapa, and Puerto Escondido. On the Riviera Maya, **SkyDive Playa** offers jumps over Playa del Carmen. Parasailing rides are available at most big resorts, but note that these operators are virtually unregulated, so check safety provisions carefully before trying any ride.

Globo Aventura and **Fly Volare** offer hot-air balloon tours of the Valley of Mexico and the Teotihuacán pyramids.

WHALE AND SHARK WATCHING

The waters around Baja California contain one of the world's largest concentrations of whales and dolphins, from smaller species in the Sea of Cortez to giant whales that migrate along the Pacific coast from December to March. Guerrero Negro on the west coast is the best place to see larger whales, but whales can be found all around the peninsula, and all Baja-based dive shops and adventure sports agencies offer whale-watching trips. Whales and dolphins can also be seen off Puerto Vallarta, in the same season. **Discover Pacific Tours** based in Puerto Vallarta runs organizes enjoyable whale and dolphin spotting boat trips.

A much rarer phenomenon is the gathering of whale sharks, the world's largest fish, between July and September off Cabo Catoche, north of Cancún. Trips to see and swim with these huge – but entirely harmless – creatures are run by operators on Holbox island, such as the **Hotel Faro Viejo**.

CYCLING

Bicycles are a universal means of transport in Mexico, and bikes can be rented in most resorts. For mountain biking, the most popular location is Copper Canyon, where local companies like **Expediciones Umarike** rent bikes and provide information, but there are countless other possibilities. **Mountain Bike Mexico** and Canada-based **Bike Mexico** provide excellent guided bike tours.

WILDLIFE AND NATURE

Mexico has a wealth of wildlife in many different habitats – desert, mountain, rain forest, and the dry Yucatán woods. In the north, **Solipaso**, based near Copper Canyon, offers a range of excursions. Among the unmissable sights of central Mexico are the valleys that shelter millions of migratory monarch butterflies between November and March. Agencies in Morelia, Mexico City, and abroad run tours.

Farther south, trips are possible into the rain forests of Chiapas and Campeche, with the possibility of seeing jaguars, monkeys, and blue macaws. The Yucatán peninsula is exceptionally rich in birdlife, and Yucatán state hosts a bird festival, the Toh Festival, each November or December to coincide with the arrival of winter migrants from North America (www.yucatanbirds.com). The Yucatán's most famous birds are its flamingo colonies at Celestún and Río Lagartos, which are easy to reach.

Longer guided trips around the region are available from specialists like **Ecoturismo Yucatán** or **Ecocolors**. Another destination not to be missed is Sian Ka'an reserve, home to forest animals and millions of birds. Tulum-based **CESiak** runs excellent one-day tours. For dedicated wildlife enthusiasts there are more gruelling options, such as the 10-day treks offered by the **Mesoamerican Tourism Alliance** into the vast El Triunfo reserve of southern Chiapas, the refuge of Mexico's rarest birds such as the Quetzal.

SPECIALIST HOLIDAYS

One of the most rewarding ways to travel is to pursue a personal interest or a new skill, in ways that also give you extra insights into Mexico's culture. Food is one such field, and residential cooking courses – in English – are ever more popular. **Cook with Us**, **Alma de mi Tierra**, and **Los Dos** are among the schools that give an enjoyable introduction to Mexico's culinary heritage.

Elsewhere, you can try photography workshops at **Aper Tours** in San Cristóbal de Las Casas, and there are several art workshops, especially in Baja California and San Miguel de Allende. If you want to know more about Mexico's past and cultural traditions than conventional tours may tell you, several agencies offer tours with archaeologists and experts as guides, such as US-based **Far Horizons** or **Mexican Art Tours**.

Learning Spanish is another way of getting closer to Mexican life, and there are many schools that offer residential courses. Two good-value schools are **Becari** in Oaxaca and **Instituto Jovel** in San Cristóbal.

For more information on Spanish-language schools, workshops, and tours, you can browse the Internet for Mexico travel websites.

For an overview of spas and health retreats in Mexico, see pp358–9.

DIRECTORY

DIVING AND SNORKELING

Aquatech-Villas de Rosa
Aventuras Akumal, Akumal, Quintana Roo. **Tel** (984) 875 9020. www.cenotes.com

Cenote Dive Center
Av. Tulum, Tulum, Quintana Roo. **Tel** (984) 871 2232. www.cenotedive.com

Hidden Worlds
Mex 307, north of Tulum, Quintana Roo. **Tel** (984) 877 8535. www.hiddenworlds.com

SURFING

Baja Wild
San José del Cabo, Baja California Sur. **Tel** (624) 172 6300. www.bajawild.com

FISHING

Captain Rick's Sportfishing
Puerto Aventuras, Quintana Roo. **Tel** (984) 873 5195. www.fishyucatan.com

Cuzan Guest House
Punta Allen, Quintana Roo. **Tel** (983) 834 0358. www.flyfishmx.com

Pro Team Sportfishing
Sabalo Country Club, Mazatlán, Sinaloa. **Tel** (669) 913 2606. www.probillfish.com

OTHER WATERSPORTS

Agua Azul
Esquina Guamachil & Carrizal, La Crucecita, Oaxaca. **Tel** (958) 589 1718. www.aguaazul.com

Explora
Calle 1 de Marzo 30, San Cristóbal de Las Casas, Chiapas. **Tel** (967) 678 4295. www.ecochiapas.com

The Moorings Boat Charters
Tel 1 888 952 8420 (US). **Tel** 01227 776677 (UK). www.moorings.com

Sonoran Sport Center
San Carlos, Sonora. **Tel** (622) 226 0929. www.sonoransportcenter.com

GOLF

Cabo del Sol Golf Courses
Cabo San Lucas, Baja California Sur. **Tel** (624) 145 8200. www.cabodelsol.com

Cozumel Country Club
Carretera Costera Norte, Cozumel, Quintana Roo. **Tel** (987) 872 9570. www.cozumelcountryclub.com.mx

CLIMBING, HIKING, & ADVENTURE SPORTS

La Cooperativa de los Guías
PO Box 203, Bozeman, MT 59771, USA. **Tel** (406) 587 3585 (US). www.coppercanyonguide.com

Expediciones Umarike
Creel, Chihuahua. **Tel** (635) 406 5464. www.umarike.com.mx

Native Trails
613 Querétaro Drive, El Paso, TX 79912, USA. **Tel** (915) 833 3107 (US). www.nativetrails.com

Tour by Mexico
Plaza el Pueblito, Cuernavaca, Morelos. **Tel** (777) 318 6541. www.tourbymexico.com

HORSEBACK RIDING

El Caballo Rojo
Ajijic, Laguna de Chapala, Jalisco. **Tel** (333) 459 9300.

Xcaret
Quintana Roo. Mex 307, 4 miles (7km) S of Playa del Carmen **Tel** (998) 883 3143. www.xcaret.com

AIR SPORTS

Fly Volare
www.flyvolare.com.mx

Globo Aventura
www.globoaventura.com

SkyDive Cuautla
Tel (55) 5517 8529. www.skydivecsc.com/skydiving-mexico

SkyDive Playa
Plaza Marina, Playa del Carmen, Quintana Roo. **Tel** (984) 873 0192. www.skydive.com.mx

WHALE AND SHARK WATCHING

Discover Pacific Tours
Puerto Vallarta, Jalisco. **Tel** (322) 224 9027. www.discoverpacifictours.com

Hotel Faro Viejo
Holbox, Quintana Roo. **Tel** (984) 875 2217. www.faroviejoholbox.com.mx

CYCLING

Bike Mexico
344 Wycliffe Ave, Woodbridge, Ontario L4L 3N8, Canada. **Tel** (416) 848 0265 (Can). www.bikemexico.com

Mountain Bike Mexico
Tel (55) 5846 0793. www.mtbmexico.com

WILDLIFE AND NATURE

CESiak – Centro Ecológico Sian Ka'an
Carretera 307, Tulum, Quintana Roo. **Tel** (984) 871 2499. www.cesiak.org

Ecocolors
Calle Camarón 32, SM27, Cancún, Quintana Roo. **Tel** (998) 884 3667. www.ecotravelmexico.com

Ecoturismo Yucatán
Calle 3 no. 235, Mérida, Yucatán. **Tel** (999) 920 27 72. www.ecoyuc.com

Mesoamerican Ecotourism Alliance
4076 Crystal Court, Boulder, CO 80304, USA. **Tel** 1 800 682 0584. www.travelwithmea.com

Solipaso
Calle Obregón 3, Alamos, Sonora. **Tel** (647) 428 0466. www.solipaso.com

SPECIALIST HOLIDAYS

Alma de mi Tierra
Calle Pino Suárez 508, Oaxaca. **Tel** (951) 515 5645. www.almademitierra.net

Aper Tours Photography Workshop
Calle Tonalá 27, San Cristóbal de Las Casas, Chiapas. **Tel** (967) 678 5727. www.apertours.com

Becari Language School
Calle M. Bravo 210, Plaza San Cristóbal, Oaxaca. **Tel** (951) 514 6076. www.becari.com.mx

Cook with Us
Todos Santos, Baja California Sur. **Tel** 01 877 935 2665. www.cookwithus.com

Far Horizons
PO Box 2546, San Anselmo, CA 94979, USA. **Tel** 1 800 552 4575. www.farhorizon.com

Instituto Jovel Language School
Francisco I. Madero 45, San Cristóbal de Las Casas, Chiapas. **Tel** (967) 678 4069. www.institutojovel.com

Los Dos Cookery School
Calle 68 no.517, between 65 and 67, Mérida, Yucatán. **Tel** (999) 928 1116. www.los-dos.com

Mexican Art Tours
1233 E Baker Drive, Tempe, AZ 85282, USA. **Tel** (480) 730 1764. www.mexicanarttours.com

SPA BREAKS IN MEXICO

Mexico's seductive climate, brilliant light and color, and laid-back atmosphere have made it an ever-more popular destination for spa breaks, whether for a few days of pampering and deep relaxation or more spiritually-oriented programs. Spas are enormously varied. Many are attached to hotels, but there are also "destination spas" where the spa experience is an essential reason to visit, and "day spas"

Infinity pool at El Santuario spa retreat

where you can drop in for your choice of treatments. Most spas offer similar basic treatments – a wide range of massages, aromatherapy, reflexology, facials, body wraps, and more – but some focus more on beauty treatments or fitness, while others highlight yoga and holistic therapies. Many spas offer ancient local treatments such as the *temazcal* (traditional sweat bath), or Mayan healing and massage techniques.

HOTEL AND RESORT SPAS

The largest concentration of spas is in hotels and resort complexes, especially in and around the main beach resort areas like Baja California, Puerto Vallarta, Acapulco, and Yucatán's Riviera Maya. The use of the spa is generally an optional extra, charged for separately on the final bill.

Most high-end hotels and large resort complexes have some kind of spa, but they vary widely, ranging from just a few massage and beauty rooms to magnificent facilities with every kind of treatment. Major luxury hotels, such as the **Four Seasons** at Punta Mita, north of Puerto Vallarta, offer some of the finest spas. In Cancún, the **Ritz-Carlton**'s is perhaps the most sumptuous.

For a far more intimate experience, there are spas in stylish, seductive smaller resorts like the chic **The Tides** on the Riviera Maya, as well

as in exquisite beach retreats on their own isolated coves, like **El Careyes** near Puerto Vallarta. Here, restoring body and mind in an utterly tranquil tropical setting is an essential part of the luxury experience, and honeymoons are a specialty.

Less isolated but beautifully relaxing are the **Cabañas Copal, Azulik,** and **Zahra** hotels in their own patch of jungle on Tulum beach in the Riviera Maya. They share the Mayan Spa, offering massage and other therapies by the beach.

Away from the coasts, there are delightful spas combined with hacienda-style buildings and lush gardens in some hotels around Mexico's colonial cities, such as **Hostería Las Quintas** in Cuernavaca. One of the most sumptuous spas in the country is in **El Santuario**, a spectacular resort hotel with a fabulous view over the lake at Valle de Bravo, west of Mexico City.

DESTINATION SPAS

Spa treatments are the central purpose of a stay at a "destination spa." Most guests stay on packages that include their treatments and activities, accommodations, and meals. Some of these spas are as enticingly opulent as any small luxury hotel, and nearly all are in spectacular mountain or beach locations.

Several spas are in the hills around Cuernavaca, in Morelos state south of Mexico City, an area celebrated since Aztec times for its natural springs and fine mountain air. They include some of Mexico's most luxurious spa retreats, such as the **Hostal de la Luz** and **Misión del Sol**, which combine indulgent health and beauty treatments using natural materials with a range of therapies and practices from India, Japan, ancient Mexico and other countries. Other spas combine yoga and wellness programs with an energetic range of activities such as horseback riding or mountain biking. Two such spas are **Rancho La Puerta**, just south of the US border in Baja California, and **Río Caliente**, in a magnificent location amid forests and next to hot springs in Jalisco state.

Tulum on the Riviera Maya has both the **Amansala** "bikini boot-camp" – an imaginative mix of fashionable beauty care, fitness training, and Mayan health treatments geared to women – and the **Maya Tulum**, with a program based on

A treatment room at the Maroma Resort and Spa, Riviera Maya, Mexico

yoga and Indian beliefs. On the Pacific coast, in a wonderful location, **Mar de Jade** is a remarkable center that offers a huge choice of activities from yoga and intensive spa health programs to water sports, gardening, dance, and Spanish classes, as well as workshops in cooking, arts, and music, in a relaxed, eco-friendly setting. There are also special programs for families and teens.

DAY SPAS

In all the main resorts there are small "day spas" where visitors can come for treatments. Many hotel spas are also open to non-guests on a pay-per-session basis. Day spas concentrate on massage, health, and beauty treatments, but two that also give casual visitors the opportunity to experience traditional pre-Hispanic *temazcal* baths and other treatments are the **Maya Spa**, in between the Copal, Azulik, and Zahra hotels in Tulum, and **Terra Noble**, in Puerto Vallarta.

SMALL-GROUP RETREATS

Many groups (mostly US-based) organize small-group retreats around Mexico, lasting one to two weeks, with a wide range of emphases, from writing to intensive dance therapy in a variety of venues, from beachside cabaña hotels to remote mountain haciendas. Two popular permanent retreat centers are **El Santuario** in Baja California and **Present Moment** in Guerrero.

NATURAL SPRINGS

Several natural hot springs can be discovered around Mexico. Guadalupe Canyon, a short distance from the US border near Mexicali in Baja California, is famous for its hot pools. In central Mexico, as well as the hot springs at Río Caliente in Jalisco, are some scarcely developed springs in a beautiful mountain location at Los

A relaxing massage treatment

Azufres in Michoacán, with a charming, rustic cabaña hotel, **Balnearios Eréndira**.

SPAS WITH MEDICAL FACILITIES

Some spas cater for guests with specific medical problems. **Sanoviv**, in Baja California, is a fully equipped clinic with a complete range of modern technology and a center for complementary medicine.

DIRECTORY

SURVIVAL
GUIDE

PRACTICAL INFORMATION

Mexico is acquiring a modern tourist infrastructure and is a relatively easy country to travel around, although tourist facilities in more remote areas may be limited. There are national tourist offices in all large cities and major resorts. In smaller towns, visitors can obtain information on hotels, restaurants, attractions, and activities in

MÉXICO

Mexican Ministry of Tourism logo

the area from the *palacio municipal* (town hall). Be prepared to slow down your pace of life in Mexico: everything tends to take a little longer. This may be desirable when embarking on a relaxing beach holiday, but it can become frustrating if you are up against bureaucracy. It helps to be patient and develop a philosophical outlook on life.

WHEN TO GO

The best time to visit inland sites is from February to June, before the rainy season begins (*see pp36–7*). In Chiapas, Tabasco, and Veracruz, the rains are diluvial, but in most areas the rains are only a refreshing daily downpour.

November is ideal for the beach: the climate is fresh, and prices are lower than the mid-December high season. Mexicans also visit the coast during July, August, and on *puentes (see pp30–33)*. On the Caribbean coast, September and October may bring hurricanes. The smog in Mexico City is worst in winter, from December to February.

VISAS AND PASSPORTS

Citizens of North America, Australasia, Great Britain, Israel and Western European countries do not require visas

to enter Mexico as tourists, but if going more than 30 km (19 miles) past the border or staying longer than 72 hours, they must obtain a *Forma Migratoria de Turista* (FMT). This carries a non-immigrant fee of around US$22, usually included in airfares, and permits visits of up to 180 days (on request). The law requires you to carry your FMT at all times.

To obtain the FMT visitors need a passport valid for six months from the date of travel, proof of funds and an onward ticket. Technically, US and Canadian citizens only require certain official photo ID to enter Mexico, but a passport is recommended. Anybody intending to cross into the US, including returning US

citizens, must have a valid passport. Visa and passport requirements are prone to change – check before travel.

CUSTOMS INFORMATION

Customs searches are conducted randomly at push-button traffic lights found after passport control at all ports of entry. A green light means you can pass, a red light means you must surrender your luggage.

Visitors over 18 have a duty-free allowance of 3 bottles of wine, beer, or spirits, and 400 cigarettes or 50 cigars. All visitors are allowed two video cameras and two still cameras, one laptop, one portable music player and two mobile phones. If carrying prescription drugs, check the law before travel.

Anyone driving beyond the 30-km (19-mile) border zone will need a vehicle permit (*permiso de importación temporal de vehículos*) from customs, or the Registro Federal de Vehículos (*see p379*).

Archaeological artifacts may not be taken out of Mexico; the penalties for doing so are harsh. Good, certified reproductions are acceptable.

Mexican customs alcohol allowance

TOURIST INFORMATION

SECTUR (Secretaría de Turismo) offices are generally well stocked with maps, brochures and English-

Mexico City on a rare smog-free day, from the Torre Latinoamericana

◁ A carnival parade in Huejotzingo, near Puebla

Sign for a tourist office

speaking staff, but quality varies and some are not geared towards public visits at all, particularly those in rural areas. Most towns have at least two types of office with some degree of overlap. The municipal tourist office, usually located in the *palacio municipal* (town hall), offers information on local sights; the state tourist office can inform on wider attractions. You also may find small kiosks that hand out maps and flyers – Mexico City has them at all the major sights, as well as an English-speaking tourist helpline. Beware of time-share vendors or other commercial outfits posing as tourist information centers as they may try to sell you unwanted services.

SOCIAL CUSTOMS

Courtesy is appreciated in Mexico. On greeting, it is usual to shake hands or kiss on one cheek. When addressing people, use their relevant title *(señor, señora, señorita)*, or professional title according to their university degree, such as *Licenciado (Lic.)* for arts or law graduates.

Attire is casual, except when visiting churches. Observe signs that forbid photography. Some indigenous people also do not like to be photographed, so ask first to avoid any confrontation.

Mexican *machismo* is world famous but generally harmless, although lone women should avoid isolated areas *(see p364)*.

LANGUAGE

The official language of Mexico is Spanish, spoken by almost everyone. In the big tourist towns many locals will speak some English, but for anyone traveling off the

beaten track, a smattering of Spanish is a great advantage.

There are some 62 indigenous groups in Mexico and each has its own language. In remote villages some people may speak little Spanish, although there are usually a few bilingual locals.

ADMISSION PRICES

Most of Mexico's museums and archaeological sites are governed by the state-run INAH (Instituto Nacional de Antropología e Historia) and art galleries are under the care of the INBA (Instituto Nacional de Bellas Artes). Entrance fees rarely exceed US$5, although you may be charged extra for using a camera. Many museums and archaeological sites are technically free on Sunday, but in practice this may be reserved for Mexican nationals only. Children, seniors and students can often expect a discount.

ISIC student card

OPENING HOURS

Opening hours vary between resorts, cities and rural villages. City banking hours are generally 9am to 4pm, Monday to Friday; some open 9am to 1pm on Saturday. Most offices, including tourist offices, follow these hours, but some may work as late as 8pm with a lunch break between 2–4pm. In cities, stores are generally open 10am to 8pm, every day. In towns and villages they often open Monday to Saturday with an afternoon siesta. Many (but not all) museums open Tuesday to Sunday, 9am to 5pm. Major archaeological sites are open seven days a week. Nearly all businesses close on Christmas, Easter and public holidays.

ACCESSIBILITY TO PUBLIC CONVENIENCES

Public toilets are few and far between in Mexico, and those that do exist are often badly equipped and unhygienic. It is advisable to carry some toilet paper, as this is often lacking. Soap or disinfectant hand wipes are a good idea too. In larger cities it is best to make for a Sanborns *(see p114)*, or another large department store, restaurant, or supermarket, as they provide better facilities. Some enterprising people in Mexico City allow the public to use their toilets for a small fee; you will see signs around the Historic Center *(see pp61–81)*.

TAXES AND TIPPING

In Mexico, tips are generally unofficial, but appreciated. In restaurants, tip between 10 and 15 percent of the total bill. Taxi drivers do not expect to be tipped unless they have carried your luggage. Porters, however, especially those at airports or large hotels, expect a gratuity. It is usual to give small change to people who help you, such as chambermaids or gas station attendants, as tips are an essential part of their income. Parking attendants and children who help in supermarkets survive on tips.

Prices usually include 15 percent sales tax, or VAT, *(Impuesto al Valor Agregado, or IVA)*. If a price is given as *más IVA* (plus sales tax) it means that 15 percent will be added to the bill.

Chichén Itzá, open seven days a week

TRAVELERS WITH SPECIAL NEEDS

Most airports, upscale hotels, and good restaurants, particularly those in well-developed resort towns, usually have wheelchair access and adapted toilets, but always check in advance. Sidewalks can be difficult to negotiate and in bad repair, especially in the countryside, while long-distance buses are generally poorly equipped; consider traveling by air. Elsewhere, disabled facilities are scant but the situation is improving in big cities. Most Mexicans, ever helpful by nature, will be glad to assist if they can.

TRAVELING WITH CHILDREN

Facilities for children are most prevalent in and around major resorts, where you'll find theme parks with water slides, aquariums, and roller-coasters. Elsewhere, youngsters can try their hand at snorkeling, white-water rafting, rock-climbing, kayaking, horse-riding, and surfing. Most mid-range and high-end hotels will arrange a cot or baby-sitter and make recommendations for family activities. The best resort complexes have family-sized apartments, playgrounds, and pools.

Mexicans are very family orientated, so expect lots of warm attention when traveling with young ones. Children are welcome at nearly all restaurants but not all offer high chairs and child menus. Major car rental agencies should be able to install a child safety seat.

SENIOR TRAVELERS

Many foreign retirees have settled in Mexico – retirement communities are concentrated in San Miguel de Allende, Guanajuato, and around Lake Chapala, where you'll find no shortage of amenities. Elsewhere, major resorts offer the best services and comfort.

Getting around is not always straightforward in Mexico so it's worth using tour operators who specialize in senior activities. Elders are widely respected in Mexico, though foreigners are sometimes targeted by unscrupulous types. Expect reasonable discounts on admission costs, bus fares and, occasionally, hotel fees. Many travel agents also offer deals for senior clients.

Seniors taking in the view at Copper Canyon

GAY AND LESBIAN TRAVELERS

Homosexuality is generally tolerated in Mexico, but public affection is frowned upon. Discrimination on the basis of sexual orientation has been officially outlawed but there is still widespread prejudice and some straight males may feel unnerved by unconventional sexual behaviour. Gay scenes can be found in Puerto Vallarta, Guadalajara, Cancún, Mazatlán, Acapulco,

Monterrey, Oaxaca, Veracruz, and especially in Mexico City's Zona Rosa village. Most big cities have gay-friendly bars and clubs, but few exclusively gay establishments.

WOMEN TRAVELERS

Women are loved and respected in Mexico, but are not regarded as equals. Any woman who travels alone may get a stream of uninvited compliments. If the attention becomes too persistent, a firm *Déjeme en paz* ("Leave me be") should work. Mexican machismo can also sometimes be a help, since men will often come to your aid.

Women should avoid going to isolated beaches or rural areas, or wandering through lonely streets at night. Nude or topless bathing is not generally acceptable.

TRAVELING ON A BUDGET

Economical hotels can be found across the country, and are often more cost effective than youth hostels. Bear in mind that the cheapest lodgings may lack windows, bathroom, television, or any charm whatsoever. Couples and groups can make good savings on accommodation, and in very warm areas a hammock may often suffice for the night.

Lunch-time rather than dinner is best for economical meals, with set menus, often described as *comida corrida*, served for just a few dollars. The cheapest restaurants tend to be clustered around the markets, where you'll also find economical street food, but beware of bad hygiene (*see p366*). Head to a bakery for breakfast.

On the coast, prices may triple during high season, but good rates can often be negotiated at quieter periods. Outside the resorts, southern Mexico tends to be the cheapest region to travel. Allow US$50-60 per day for a comfortably modest trip; US$30 per day for a challenging one. Long-distance first-class bus travel will knock a big hole in your budget.

Children and families enjoying an outdoor concert

Relaxing in a beach hammock at Quintana Roo

WHAT TO TAKE AND WHAT TO WEAR

If you intend to do a lot of traveling, it's worth investing in a good backpack. Pack hiking boots if you intend to do any serious walking or, at the very least, comfortable trainers. In the wet season (*see pp.36-7*) take a lightweight, waterproof jacket, or a compact umbrella – also mandatory when visiting the rainforest. Light clothing is sufficient on the coast but a sweater is useful in the mountains, where evenings can be chilly.

It's wise to pack a small medical kit, and insect repellent is essential. Bring sufficient amounts of any prescribed medication with you. The sun is fierce in Mexico, so pack sunscreen with a protection factor of at least 25+, as well as a sunhat.

TIME

Most of the country is six hours behind Greenwich Mean Time (GMT). Quintana Roo is five hours behind; Baja California Sur, Nayarit, Sinaloa, Sonora, and Chihuahua seven hours; and Baja California Norte eight hours behind.

ELECTRICITY

Electrical current is the same in Mexico as in the US and Canada. Three-prong, polarized, and European two-pin plugs will need adaptors.

CONVERSION CHART

US to metric
1 inch = 2.54 centimeters
1 foot = 30 centimeters
1 mile = 1.6 kilometers
1 ounce = 28 grams
1 pound = 454 grams
1 pint = 0.6 liter
1 gallon = 3.79 liters

Metric to US
1 millimeter = 0.04 inch
1 centimeter = 0.4 inch
1 meter = 3 feet 3 inches
1 kilometer = 0.6 mile
1 gram = 0.04 ounce
1 kilogram = 2.2 pounds
1 liter = 2.1 pints

RESPONSIBLE TRAVEL

Mexico has been slow to embrace ecotourism and many hotels and tour companies continue to act irresponsibly, damaging wild habitats and coral reefs. You can do your part by choosing local over corporate interests and using ethically minded companies such as members of **Tour Operators Initiative**, who are committed to responsible tourist development.

In 2008 the Mexican Tourism Secretariat allocated 500 million pesos (about US$37 million) to the development of ecotourism in Mexico. Meanwhile, dozens of government bodies and NGOs are involved in green tourism – although there is often poor communication between them.

The **Mesoamerican Reef Tourism Initiative (MARTI)** works to cut energy and waste in Caribbean resorts, as well as campaigning for sustainability and green legislation. Baja California has made great strides as a major eco- and adventure-tourism destination. Over 200 islands and islets now protected, as well as breeding areas for migratory gray whales.

DIRECTORY

EMBASSIES

Australia
Rubén Darío 55,
Polanco, DF 11580.
Tel 11 01 22 00.

Canada
Schiller 529,
Polanco, DF 11580.
Tel 57 24 79 00.

United Kingdom
Río Lerma 71,
Cuauhtémoc,
DF 06500.
Tel 52 42 85 00.

USA
Reforma 305,
Cuauhtémoc,
DF 06500.
Tel 50 80 20 00.
For all other embassies, consult:
www.sre.gob.mx/
acreditadas/

National Migration Institute of Mexico

Avenida Ejército Nacional 862, Col. Los Morales Sección Palmas, Del. Miguel Hidalgo, C.P. 11540, México D.F
www.inm.gob.mx

SECTUR OFFICES

Mexico
Avenida Presidente Masaryk 172, Col Chapultepec Morales 11587, México DF.
Viaducto Miguel Alemán 105, Col Escandón, DF 11580.
Tel 078; (55) 30 02 63 00; 01800 987 8224 (toll free).
www.sectur.gob.mx;
www.visitmexico.com

Canada
2 Bloor St West,
Suite 502,
Toronto, ONT, M4W 3E2.
Tel (416) 925 0704.

United Kingdom
Wakefield House, 41 Trinity Square, London EC3N 4DJ.
Tel (020) 7488 9392.

USA
New York:
400 Madison Avenue,
Suite 11,
NY 10017.
Tel (212) 308 2110.
Houston:
4507 San Jacinto,
Suite 308,
TX 77004.
Tel (713) 772 2581.
Los Angeles:
1880 Century Park, Suite 511, CA 90067.
Tel (310) 282 9112.

GREEN ORGANIZATIONS

Ecocolors
Camaron 32, SM 27,
Cancún, Quintana Roo
Tel (998) 884-9580, 884-3667.
www.ecotravelmexico.
com

Mesoamerican Reef Tourism Initiative (MARTI)
Tel (703) 341 27 03.
www.rivieramaya.org.mx/
marti

Tour Operators Initiative
c/o World Tourism Organization (UNWTO), Capitán Haya 42, 28020 Madrid, Spain.
Tel (34) 91 567 81 00.
www.toinitiative.org

Personal Security and Health

Sunhat

Crime is on the increase in Mexico, but the overwhelming majority of foreign visitors have a trouble-free experience. Threats to security are greatest in the capital, along the US border, and in built-up tourist areas, where you should follow big city rules and stay alert. Nasty tropical diseases are also present in Mexico, but these are rare and can be avoided by obtaining appropriate medicines and vaccinations prior to departure. Always check the latest information regarding more serious diseases, such as dengue fever or swine flu, before travel. Common ailments like mosquito bites, and upset stomachs can be prevented with sensible precautions. The sun's rays are very strong in Mexico, so pack a high protection sunscreen, as well as a sunhat.

POLICE

It is best to avoid the police in Mexico; they are rarely helpful and can make difficult situations worse. Reporting a crime is often a slow, bureaucratic affair – consider contacting your embassy or **SECTUR** first. In the event of your arrest, always contact your embassy.

Police corruption is rife and many consider bribes or *mordidas* (literally "little bites") a supplement to their low income. Drivers should expect to be approached and "fined" at some stage; try explaining that you are a tourist or otherwise negotiate the fee downward.

The traffic police *(Policía de Tránsito)* are nicknamed *tamarindos*

Insect repellent and a mosquito coil for protection against bites

(tamarinds) in Mexico City for their dark brown uniforms. The auxiliary police *(Policía Auxiliar)*, dressed in dark blue, provide backup to the traffic police and work as security guards. Bank and industry police *(Policía Bancaria e Industrial)* also wear blue uniforms. Plain-clothed *Policía Judicial Federal* (PJF) have a sinister reputation and are best avoided. Outside the cities, the federal traffic police *(Policía Federal de Caminos)* patrol the highways in black and white cars. A few states have approachable tourist police *(Policía Turística)*.

LOST AND STOLEN PROPERTY

Only report lost or stolen property to the police if you need to file an official report *(levantar un acta)* for insurance purposes. Do this at the nearest police station *(delegación)* within 24 hours. Lost passports and traveler's checks should be reported to your embassy and the issuing bank.

WHAT TO BE AWARE OF

Petty theft is the greatest security threat to tourists. Beware pickpockets, leave valuables in a hotel safe (never on the beach), and keep cash in a concealed money belt. Also, avoid driving at night. Park in hotel parking lots, and never leave possessions visible inside the car. Steer clear of isolated routes or beaches, and in the rare event of a mugging, always hand over your cash.

Stomach upsets, known locally as "Montezuma's revenge", are a common affliction. Outside resorts, drink purified or bottle water only and take care with salads, unpeeled fruits, ice and uncooked food,

especially raw fish. Choose restaurants that look clean and be wary of unhygienic street food stalls.

Mosquitoes are rife in low-lying regions and have a ferocious appetite for tourists. DEET is the strongest insect repellent, but sensitive skin may prefer organic alternatives. Take care in the heat. Dehydration can lead to the potentially fatal condition of sun stroke, so always carry bottled water, sunscreen, and a hat when visiting archaeological sites, the beach or any exposed places. Snakes, such as the deadly fer-de-lance, can be a danger in the jungle. Watch where you step and wear long trousers and boots. If undertaking a lengthy trek, ensure your guide is packing antivenin. Mexico City's high altitude and air pollution can aggravate respiratory problems like asthma; seek medical advice before traveling.

IN AN EMERGENCY

In case of emergency, the Red Cross has an ambulance service in most major cities and tourist centers. If you are in a remote area, it may be quicker to take a taxi to the nearest hospital. If you are not covered by medical insurance, go to the emergency room *(Emergencias)* of any state hospital.

SECTUR, the Mexican Ministry of Tourism, has a 24-hour telephone hotline. Although this is primarily for immediate assistance, it can also provide general, non-emergency health guidance.

Police car used by traffic police

Mexican ambulance

HOSPITALS AND PHARMACIES

There are three types of hospital in Mexico. Social Security (IMSS) hospitals are restricted to Mexican residents, and ISSSTE hospitals and clinics are for civil servants and university workers only. Everyone else, including visitors, must either pay for private treatment or rely on the local, and generally overcrowded, Centro de Salud (Civil Hospital) run by the state, or the Cruz Roja (Red Cross). Hotels have lists of English-speaking doctors.

Sign for a Cruz Roja hospital

Prices of all drugs are high, except for social security patients who receive basic drugs free of charge. Packets of oral rehydration salts are provided free at health centers for people suffering from diarrhea. Many tablets are sold individually, with generic names the cheapest. However, beware of fake or unlicensed medicines.

MINOR HAZARDS

Coral cuts and jellyfish stings should be bathed in vinegar, then dabbed with antiseptic ointment. If the wound becomes infected, seek the advice of a doctor. The majority of visitors to Mexico are unlikely to come across any dangerous creatures, and it is rare for tourists to become seriously ill as a result of an insect bite. However, scorpions are common. Black or dark brown ones are quite harmless, but the light yellow ones, found in hot, dry places, will need an antidote (free from any Centro de Salud). Tarantulas look more intimidating than they are; far worse is the *capulina*, or black widow spider, found in western Mexico. Always check shoes and shake out clothing before putting them on, especially in more rural areas. Beware ticks when hiking in the jungle. If bitten, carefully extract them using tweezers.

TRAVEL AND HEALTH INSURANCE

Travel insurance is essential in Mexico. Check the policy's small print and ensure you are covered for emergency flights, ambulance use, mugging, and any specialist activities you may require, such as trekking or diving. Private doctors and hospitals will require on the spot payment in cash, so retain all receipts for the purposes of your claim.

To speed claims for theft or loss, always retain receipts of valuables, and photograph the items before departure. Some general US health insurance policies extend to Mexico; check prior to travel.

VACCINATIONS

No specific vaccinations are required to enter Mexico, but you will need evidence of a Yellow Fever vaccination if coming from South America or other infected areas. All travelers are advised to seek immunization against hepatitis A, typhoid, tetanus, diphtheria, and for some, hepatitis B and rabies. Malaria is present in some rural parts of Mexico, so ask your doctor about anti-malarial medicines.

SERIOUS DISEASES

Standard food and water precautions are the best forms of protection against cholera. Common parasitic infections include tapeworm as well as giardiasis, which is acquired by drinking contaminated water. It can cause chronic diarrhea, abdominal cramps, fatigue, nausea, loss of appetite, and weight loss. Treatment with the drug metronidazole is usually very successful.

Dengue fever is a viral illness spread by mosquitoes. The best protection is to use plenty of insect repellent, cover up well when outside, and sleep under mosquito nets. The onset of dengue is sudden, with fever, headache, joint pains, nausea, vomiting,

and a rash. Outbreaks of swine flu (H1N1) in 2009 caused concern. The World Health Organization (WHO) provides up-to-date information on serious diseases.

NATURAL DISASTERS

In the event of an earthquake, move away from electricity poles, wires, or any high structure. Do not attempt to use elevators. If a hurricane hits, stay in your hotel, shut all windows, and stand as far away from them as you can. In all cases, follow the instructions given by staff.

Access to the area around Popocatépetl volcano *(see p149)* and Colima's Volcán de Fuego *(see p187)* is restricted because of seismic activity. If you plan to hike in the vicinity, check posted warnings and contact your embassy or **SECTUR** *(Secretaría de Turismo)* for the latest information.

Popocatépetl volcano

DIRECTORY

EMERGENCY NUMBERS

Ambulance
Tel 065.

Fire Department and Earthquake Advice
Tel 56 83 11 42.

Police
Tel 060; 5242 51 00.

Stolen Property
Tel 061.

Tourist Security/SECTUR helpline
Tel 078; (55) 30 02 63 00; 01800 987 8224 (toll free).

HOSPITALS

ABC (American British Cowdray) Hospital (Mexico City)
Tel 52 30 80 00.

Banking and Currency

The unit of currency in Mexico is the peso, but US dollars are widely accepted in resorts and border towns. In order to support the local economy, visitors are advised to use pesos as their main currency. Most large hotels, shops and restaurants accept major credit cards, and US dollars are readily exchanged in all banks. There are no restrictions on the import or export of peso notes and coins.

Example of a standard cash dispensing machine

BANKS AND BUREAUX DE CHANGE

The three largest banks in Mexico are **BBVA Bancomer**, **HSBC**, and **Banamex**, but there is a growing number of foreign banks which also operate branches in Mexico. Opening hours are normally from 9am to 4pm, weekdays only, although in the capital and other large cities, HSBC stays open until 7pm, and is open on Saturdays until 1pm. Ask at your hotel for opening times of the nearest branches. It is important to remember that many branches do not change foreign currency or traveler's checks after 2pm, so aim to go in the morning. Bureaux de change *(casas de cambio)* are open longer hours than banks, and offer a quicker service and better

Changing money at a *casa de cambio*

exchange rates, particularly compared to hotels and shops. The main international airports have at least one *casa de cambio* – useful for changing a small amount for taxis or buses. Non-dollar currencies can sometimes be tricky to change.

ATMS

Cash dispensing machines *(cajero automático)* are widespread in Mexico and you should be able to draw cash in all but the most obscure places. Visa, MasterCard, Plus, Cirrus debit and credit cards are all valid. Exchange rates on foreign ATMs are based on the equitable inter-bank lending rate. However, you will be charged a small transaction fee at the point of withdrawal, as well as by your own bank – rates vary with accounts, so check before departure. To protect against fraud, some banks require notification that you will be traveling, otherwise you will find your card temporarily frozen. As a precaution against theft, draw money from machines only during business hours, and in populated areas like main streets, or shopping malls.

Look out for any strange attachments to the machine that may be used to record card details. Technical hitches are rare, but keep an emergency supply of cash or traveler's checks, just in case.

TRAVELER'S CHECKS

Traveler's checks drawn in US dollars are the safest way of carrying money. They can be changed at *casas de cambio*, and at most banks. When cashing the checks you will be asked to show your

passport or another form of identification. Fees are not charged, but the exchange rate is likely to be lower for checks than for cash. Keep the receipt and a record of the serial numbers separate from the checks, in case they are lost or stolen.

WIRING MONEY

Money can be wired safely and easily provided you are in possession of a passport or other official photo ID. Western Union "Dinero en Minutos" is the main service, available in most cities and resorts. Senders can arrange their transaction online or at a Western Union office and must designate an appropriate collection point. Recipients will be required to show ID and fees will be levied for the service. For US citizens, post offices also operate money transfers to Bancomer banks.

DIRECTORY

BANKS

Banamex
Isabela Católica 44,
Mexico City.
Tel 52 25 30 00.

BBVA Bancomer
Bolivar 38,
Mexico City.
Tel 56 21 34 34.

HSBC
Paseo de la Reforma 347,
Mexico City.
Tel 57 21 22 22.

LOST CARDS AND TRAVELER'S CHECKS

American Express
Call hotline in country of origin.
Or:
Tel 52 07 7049 (Mexico City office).

MasterCard
Tel 001 800 307 7309 (toll free).

VISA
Tel 001 800 84 72 911 (toll free).

WIRING MONEY

Western Union.
Tel 1800 325 6000 (US only).
www.westernunion.com

CURRENCY

The Mexican peso is divided into 100 centavos. The symbol for the peso is $, and is easily confused with that of the US dollar. To solve this problem, prices are often printed with the letters MN after them, meaning *moneda nacional* (national currency). Some border towns and resorts will accept the US dollar, although using the peso will help to support the local economy.

Always carry small amounts of cash around in both coins and small denomination bills, for tips and minor purchases. Beware that shops, taxis, and buses are often unable to give change for larger denomination notes.

Coins

Peso coins come in denominations of $1, $2, $5, and $10. There is also a limited-edition $20 coin. All peso coins are colored silver and gold, and increase in size according to their value. Centavo coins are in denominations of 5¢, 10¢, 20¢, and 50¢.

Bank Notes

Mexican bank notes are issued in six denominations: $20, $50, $100, $200, $500, and $1,000. It can be hard to get change for larger denominations.

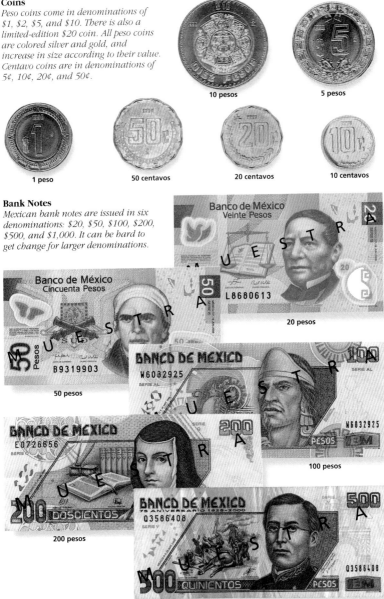

10 pesos

5 pesos

1 peso

50 centavos

20 centavos

10 centavos

20 pesos

50 pesos

100 pesos

200 pesos

500 pesos

Communications and Media

Logo of the Mexican telephone company TELMEX

The telephone is the most popular means of communication in Mexico, largely because the postal service is so slow and unreliable – letters can take weeks, even months to reach their destination. Public telephones are easy to find and, in most cases, take phonecards. If mailing a letter, mail boxes are mostly yellow, although in Mexico City and tourist resorts mail boxes marked *Buzón Expreso* are bright red. Internet cafés are widespread and cheap, while many mid-range and upscale hotels are now equipped with Wi-Fi. For entertainment, Mexico has 11 television channels and two national radio stations. English-language visitors can catch up on events by reading *The News*.

INTERNATIONAL AND LOCAL TELEPHONE CALLS

Local telephone calls are cheap and many hotels will let you make them for free. Conversely, international calls from hotels are nearly always expensive, so instead use a *caseta de teléfono* (calling shop) or a long-distance phonecard, available at kiosks and grocery shops. You could also consider getting a Skype account, which allows international and video calls to other Skype users for free. Many Internet cafés have this facility, otherwise a reasonably modern Wi-Fi-enabled laptop should suffice. Collect calls can be made nationally and internationally, though these are expensive for the recipient.

Full numbers in Mexico are 10 digits long and comprise a 7-digit local number and 3-digit area code. If calling locally, simply enter the 7-digit number. If calling long-distance within Mexico, you will first need to enter 01, followed by the 3-digit area code, then the main 7-digit number. Exceptions are Mexico City, Monterrey, and Guadalajara. These cities have 2-digit area codes and 8-digit local numbers. To make an international call from Mexico, dial 00, then the country code, the area code, and the local number. To call a Mexican landline from another country, dial your international access code, then 52, then the 10-digit number.

CELL PHONES

If you want to use your cell phone in Mexico, you will need a "roaming"-enabled quad-band handset – consult your service provider for tariffs. Calls can be expensive for both caller and recipient, so consider purchasing a Mexican SIM card or phone once you've arrived.

Cell phone numbers have 10 digits, composed of an area code and main number. If calling a cell from a landline, add a prefix of 044 for local calls or 045 for long-distance calls. If calling from a cell phone, simply enter the whole 10-digit number.

PUBLIC TELEPHONES

Local calls are inexpensive and can be made from call boxes in the street, and from coin-operated phones in stores or restaurants.

The blue LADATEL telephones, run by Teléfonos de México (TELMEX), take LADATEL phonecards, which are available in denominations of 30, 50 or 100 pesos from most newsstands and stores. Long-distance calls are cheapest at weekends, and after 8pm on weekdays. A 50-peso LADATEL phonecard will get you a 5-minute transatlantic call, but not much more. Instead, use a long-distance phonecard. If no LADATEL phone is available, most towns and some villages have a *caseta*

de larga distancia. These telephone booths charge higher rates than public phones but are cheaper than phoning from a hotel.

Blue LADATEL telephone

INTERNET AND EMAIL

Internet connections in Mexico tend be quite fast until you get into the countryside, when they can then become incredibly slow. Prodigy Internet, owned by TELMEX and Telnor, is the main provider of broadband and Wi-Fi (also known as Prodigy Infinitum in the case of broadband). A sticker bearing the black and white Wi-Fi ZONE logo indicates availability of a wireless connection, although it's

DIALING CODES

- Operator / directory service: 040
- Collect call / reverse charges: 020 (domestic) or 090 (international)
- Long-distance: 01 – area code – number
- Landline to cell phone (local): 044 – area code – number
- Landline to cell (long-distance): 045 – area code – number
- International: 00 – country code – area code – number
- Country codes: Australia 61; Ireland 353; New Zealand 64; South Africa 27; UK 44; USA and Canada 1.

always worth asking at the hotel if you don't see one of these.

Internet cafés are widely available across nearly all Mexican towns, cities, and villages. Rates tend to be very reasonable and the better equipped places have CD burners and memory card readers, should you need to make CDs of your photos. Some are also equipped with Skype facilities. Wi-Fi is also becoming available in good hotels, restaurants, and coffee-shops, allowing you to use your own laptop to access the Internet.

ZONE

Logo for a Wi-Fi ZONE

POSTAL SERVICES

Sending (and receiving) parcels by regular mail service in Mexico is not recommended. Registering both letters and parcels improves the odds against pilfering. Conventional mail times from Mexico to Europe are 1 to 2 weeks; from Mexico to Canada/USA, 4 days to 2 weeks. Mark all air mail *Vía Aérea*. However, the safest way to send anything abroad is through one of the international courier services such as DHL.

The main post offices (*oficinas de correos*) open from 8am to 8pm on weekdays, and from 8am to 3pm on Saturdays. Smaller post offices usually have shorter opening hours. Stamps for postcards can usually be purchased from the larger hotels.

A mail holding service is available at most main post offices. *Poste restante* letters should be addressed to the *Lista de Correos*, followed by the name of the town and state. You will need to show ID when collecting letters.

American Express also provides a free holding service for their customers. You can have your mail sent directly to one of their offices, from where you can then collect it.

MEXICAN ADDRESSES

Mexican addresses list the house number after the name of the street. Sometimes the street number is followed by a hyphen and then the number or letter of the apartment. The next line of the address may indicate the name of the *Fraccionamiento (Fracc.)* if the house is in a private community. The *colonia (col.)* refers to the area within the city. Include the *Código Postal* (zip code) if you can.

NEWSPAPERS AND MAGAZINES

The News, published in the capital, covers mostly Mexican and US news, and has listings pages for cultural activities in Mexico City. (For Spanish-speaking visitors, the listings in *Tiempo Libre*, published on Thursdays by *La Jornada* newspaper, and *¿dónde?* are more complete.)

Mail box

Outside Mexico City, English-language newspapers are published in areas with English-speaking communities, such as Guadalajara and San Miguel de Allende.

Sanborns *(see p114)* is a good place to pick up English-language publications, while online discussion groups are an alternative way to keep up with the latest

happenings in Mexico. *The International Herald Tribune* and *New York Times* are usually on newsstands the day after publication. News magazines such as *Time* and *Newsweek* are also available.

The widely read national broadsheet newspapers are *Reforma, El Universal, La Jornada,* and *Excelsior.* The tabloids, such as *La Prensa*, have a far larger readership.

TELEVISION AND RADIO

Not all of Mexico's 11 television channels can be seen across the whole country, and some regions broadcast local programs at certain times of the day. Channels 11, 22, and 40 broadcast programs of cultural and scientific interest.

The largest television companies are Televisa and TV Azteca; Cablevisión and Sky are the two principal cable television companies.

Foreign programs are generally dubbed into Spanish, but movies are occasionally shown in their original language with Spanish subtitles. Most hotels provide cable television, with programs in both Spanish and English. Satellite TV is often available at the more upscale hotels throughout the country.

Almost every city in Mexico has a local radio station, and some, particularly in the more touristy areas, play English-language songs and also have daily slots for English programs. In northern areas it is possible to pick up US radio stations.

English-language and local newspapers for sale in Querétaro

TRAVEL INFORMATION

Mexico is a huge country, and although internal travel is not always as fast as visitors might hope, the transport system is increasingly easy to use. There are airports within reach of all the major cities. Flights from the USA and around the world arrive at more than a dozen international airports, and domestic flights offer an alternative to land travel. Privatization of the railroad system has

Sign to the airport

eliminated passenger services, except for the Tequila Express and the "El Chepe" route. However, there is an extensive bus network reaching even tiny villages. Driving offers most flexibility in terms of speed and accessibility, but it can be hair-raising, with road conditions not always good. Ferries connect the mainland with Baja California and the Caribbean islands of Cozumel and Isla Mujeres.

GREEN TRAVEL

Mexico's extensive bus system provides a viable low-carbon alternative to internal flights, but may not be feasible for traveling long distances if you have only limited time. If you intend to focus your trip in southern Mexico, consider flying into Cancún so you do not have to travel to and from the capital. Alternatively, if you wish to follow the classic route from Oaxaca to Quintana Roo, fly into Mexico City and out of Cancún.

You can do your part to improve air quality in the capital by using the metro system instead of buses, taxis, and *peseros (see p380).* An exception is the Metrobus, which runs on clean diesel and traverses the length of Insurgentes. Mexico City has launched a campaign to promote cycling in the capital as part of a wider plan to clean up the city's air and water, but considering how busy the roads are, you will need nerves of steel for that *(see p381).*

Arriving by Air

There are 60 airports in Mexico. Of these, 15 operate international flights for tourists. Another 30 are classified as "international," but are either towns on the US border or operate only one or two flights to foreign destinations. The other 15 airports are for domestic flights only *(see p375).*

Mexicana airplane waiting to depart

AIRPORTS

Mexico City's Aeropuerto Benito Juárez is the key arrival point for international flights into Mexico, closely followed by Cancún, with scheduled flights to the capital from over 20 US cities. Additionally, travelers can fly direct from numerous cities in the USA to Acapulco, Cozumel, Guadalajara, Guaymas, Huatulco, Loreto, La Paz, Manzanillo, Mazatlán, Puerto Vallarta, San José del Cabo,

Veracruz, and Zihuatanejo. Flying times from New York and Los Angeles to Mexico City are approximately five and three-and-a-half hours respectively. **Air Canada** flies daily from Toronto to Mexico City in around five hours.

From Europe, some international airlines still fly via the USA, although **Aeroméxico**, **British Airways**, **Iberia**, **Air France**, **North West/KLM**, and **Lufthansa** operate direct flights, cutting travel time considerably.

AIRPORT	![info] INFORMATION	DISTANCE TO TOWN OR RESORT	AVERAGE TIME BY ROAD FROM AIRPORT
Mexico City	24 82 24 24	Zócalo 15 km (9 miles)	45 minutes
Acapulco	(744) 435 20 60	Downtown 30 km (19 miles)	30 minutes
Cancún	(998) 848 72 00	Cancún City 20 km (12 miles)	30 minutes
Cozumel	(987) 872 04 85	Cozumel town 6 km (4 miles)	5 minutes
Guadalajara	(33) 3688 51 20	Downtown 16 km (10 miles)	20 minutes
La Paz	(612) 124 63 36	Downtown 14 km (9 miles)	10 minutes
Puerto Vallarta	(322) 221 12 98	Calle Madero 7 km (4 miles)	10 minutes
Tijuana	(664) 607 82 00	Downtown 7 km (4 miles)	15 minutes
Veracruz	(229) 934 90 08	Downtown 18 km (11 miles)	15 minutes

British Airways (BA) operates four direct flights from London to Mexico City each week, with a flying time of 12 hours. There is also a weekly BA scheduled flight to Cancún. Air France and Aeroméxico fly direct from Paris; Northwest/KLM from Amsterdam; Lufthansa from Frankfurt; and Iberia and Aeroméxico from Madrid (a flight time of just over 11 hours). Some chartered flights travel direct from Europe to the major beach resorts. Visitors transferring in Mexico City must claim their baggage before boarding their onward domestic flight.

Modern interior of Mexico City's international airport

There are no direct flights from New Zealand or Australia, but you can transfer in LA or San Francisco to a connecting flight. The total flying time from Sydney to Mexico City, via LA, is 16.5 hours.

Central and South American airlines **Taca** and **Copa** run flights into Mexico City. **Mexicana** and **Aeroméxico** also offer connections between Central and South American cities and Mexico City.

TICKETS AND FARES

Air fares vary greatly, depending on travel agencies and seasons. Christmas, summer, and to a lesser extent, Easter, tend to be the most expensive times. Fixed-date returns are always cheaper than open returns and international air tickets are comparatively expensive to buy in Mexico.

Inside Cancún airport

Inclusive packages for major resorts are available at travel agencies worldwide. These are increasingly popular and tend to be cheaper than independent travel. There are also companies, both in Mexico and abroad, that focus in regions of particular interest, such as the ruins of Yucatán, or specialist activities like mountain climbing, horse riding, scuba diving, white-water rafting, and bird-watching.

Infants under two often travel free on domestic flights, provided they do not have a seat of their own. Children over two, but under 12, pay roughly two thirds of the full fare, and are entitled to a seat and standard baggage allowance. Certain airlines also offer discounts for students and senior citizens (ID required).

Both Aeroméxico and Mexicana offer the Mexipass, which offers reduced air fares for any foreign visitor who intends to make several domestic flights. The pass must be purchased before traveling to Mexico, and is issued in conjunction with an international airline ticket. The cost is calculated according to ten designated zones and passengers must purchase a minimum of two coupons, to be used within 90 days. Conditions of travel vary so check with your agent before traveling.

TO AND FROM THE AIRPORT

From Mexico City's international airport, tickets for set-price taxis can be bought from kiosks by the exit. Avoid taxi touts. Direct metro links also connect with the city center. There are bus connections to nearby cities including Toluca and Cuernavaca. From Cancún, a shuttle bus runs to the downtown area every 10–15 minutes.

DIRECTORY

AEROMEXICO
Tel 51 33 40 00.
Tel 01 800 02 14 000 (toll free).
www.aeromexico.com

MEXICANA
Tel 53 48 09 90.
Tel 01 800 50 22 000 (toll free).
www.mexicana.com

OTHER AIRLINES

Air Canada
Tel 91 38 02 80.
www.aircanada.com

Air France
Tel 21 22 82 00.
www.airfrance.com

British Airways
Tel 001 866 835 4133.
www.britishairways.com

Iberia
Tel 11 01 15 15.
www.iberia.com

Lufthansa
Tel 52 30 00 00.
www.lufthansa.com

Northwest/KLM
Tel 52 79 53 90.
www.klm.com

CENTRAL AND SOUTH AMERICAN AIRLINES

Copa
Tel 52 41 20 00.
www.copaair.com

Taca
Tel 52 11 66 40.
www.grupotaca.com

ARRIVING FROM THE UNITED STATES

Visitors crossing from the US are free to enter Mexico's border zone (including the Baja California peninsula and the Sonora Free Trade Zone) without passing through immigration control. However, if you wish to travel beyond the free zone, you must obtain an FMT tourist card *(Forma Migratoria de Turista)* or visa *(see p362).*

Several international bus companies, including **Greyhound**, offer connections from major US border towns into Mexico. Alternatively, many visitors choose to cross the border on foot and pick up one of the cheaper Mexican buses on the other side. At present, there are no international rail crossings. Cruise-ships offer connections by sea, docking at locations in Baja California, the Yucatán Peninsula and all along the Pacific Coast. Ships usually stay a couple of days in port and passengers tend to disembark for short periods of time only.

Vehicle entry into Mexico is strictly regulated, and drivers bringing their cars across the border from the US need to obtain a temporary import permit *(a permiso de importación temporal),* as well as separate car insurance *(see pp378–9).*

The border crossing between Mexico and the USA, which is strictly controlled at all times

ARRIVING FROM CENTRAL AMERICA

The official immigration procedure is the same as when entering from the USA, although it is invariably less efficient and occasionally subject to dubious "fees". Visitors traveling south of the border must hand in their tourist card; on returning to Mexico, a new FMT will be issued. Direct bus services run between Guatemala City and Mexico City (stopping in Chiapas en-route); Belize City and Chetumal; and Flores and Chetumal. Otherwise, you can simply cross the border on foot and catch a frequent shuttle to the nearest local transport hub. There are no ferry or rail connections with Central America, although some adventurous souls may want to cross the Mexico–Guatemala border by *lancha* (high-speed motorboat) on the Usumacinta river.

BORDER CROSSINGS

Exactly where you cross the US–Mexico border will depend much on your intended destination. If heading to Baja California, San Diego–Tijuana is the most popular crossing, which can be very crowded if heading into the US; get there early or expect to queue for up to 3 hours. Alternatively, try one of the quieter crossings, such as Tecate or Calexico–Mexicali. Nogales is the main crossing for those heading to the Pacific northwest, but if heading to the Copper Canyon or colonial heartland, cross at El Paso–Ciudad Juárez. Laredo–Nuevo Laredo – and a string of quiet crossings east on the Río Grande – offer access to the northeast and gulf coast.

Crossings in and out of Central America can be hectic; take care with money changers particularly. Chetumal is the main crossing into Belize with buses running direct to Belize City a few times daily. There are also buses to Flores, Guatemala from here. There are three conventional crossings into Guatemala. Ciudad Cuatémoc–La Mesilla connects with San Cristóbal de las Casas in Chiapas. El

Aerial view of the runway at Cozumel airport, served by both international and domestic flights

Small, domestic planes at Palenque Airport

Carmen–Talismán and Ciudad Hidalgo–Tecún Umán provide access to Tapachula in Chiapas. In Guatemala, all crossings offer highway access to the capital. The Río Usumacinta crossing is an interesting adventure involving a 30 minute motorboat ride. In Mexico, head to Corozal in eastern Chiapas and visit immigration, then take a *lancha* to Bethel, which connects with Flores.

DOMESTIC AIR TRAVEL

In a country the size of Mexico, internal flights can be a convenient alternative to long bus journeys. Standard fares for domestic flights are usually at least double the equivalent trip by bus, but special deals are often available, so it is worth shopping around. The domestic network is extensive, but not all routes are direct.

In order to get these special deals, reservations should be made as far in advance as possible, especially at the peak seasons of Christmas and Easter, and during the summer. Tickets can be reserved by telephone or in person at the airline reservation and ticket office, through a travel agent, or sometimes, on-line. A small airport departure tax, payable either in US dollars or pesos, is levied on all flights in Mexico. This may be included in the price of your ticket.

The baggage allowance for domestic flights is usually 25 kilos (55 lbs). Be sure to arrive for check in at least two hours before

takeoff for domestic flights, and up to three hours before takeoff for all international flights.

Most internal flights are operated by the two largest airlines, **Aeroméxico** and **Mexicana**. Between them, they reach most national, as well as many international (*see p372*), destinations. From Mexico City airport, there are frequent daily flights to all the regional capitals. They also serve the main tourist centers, including Acapulco, Cancún, and Zihuatanejo.

Mexico has a number of other regional, often low-cost, airlines. Mexicana's subsidiaries include the no-frills Click Mexicana and **Mexicanalink**, serving a range of cities including Ciudad Juárez, Los Cabos, Monterrey, Mérida, Cancún, Oaxaca, Puerto Escondido, Saltillo, Colima, and Cozumel. **Aeroméxico Connect** (formerly Aerolitoral), is a subsidiary of Aeroméxico and flies various routes in northern Mexico, as well as to Tucson, Arizona. **Aviacsa** serves the southeast, in addition to Mexico City, Guadalajara, Monterrey, and Tijuana. It also operates flights to Las Vegas and Houston in the US. **Aeromar** operates in central Mexico

and has its own terminal at Aeropuerto Benito Juárez in Mexico City. **Volaris** is based in Toluca and flies to Ciudad Juárez, Los Cabos, Monterrey, Villahermosa, Mérida, Cancún, and Guadalajara, among others. **Alma**, **Interjet** and **VivaAerobus** are other popular low-cost carriers that serve airports including Guadalajara, Los Cabos, Ciudad Juárez, Cancún, Monterrey, Tampico, and Puerto Vallarta.

DIRECTORY

INTERNATIONAL COACHES

Greyhound
Tel 01 800 231 2222.
www.greyhound.com.mx

DOMESTIC AIRLINES

Aeromar
Tel 51 33 11 11 (Mexico City).
Tel 01 800 237 66 27.
www.aeromar.com.mx

Aeromexico Connect
Tel 01 800 02 14 000 (toll free).
www.aeromexico.com

Aviacsa
Tel 54 82 82 80.
www.aviacsa.com.mx

Interjet
Tel 01800 011 2345.
www.interjet.com.mx

Mexicana
Tel 22 82 62 62.
www.mexicana.com

Mexicanalink
Tel 1800 380 8781 (US reservations).
www.mexicana.com

VivaAerobus
Tel (81) 82 150 150.
www.vivaaerobus.com

Volaris
Tel 01800 122 8000.
www.volaris.com.mx

Passenger planes on the runway at Puerto Vallarta

Traveling Around

Since privatization of the country's extensive rail network and the shut-down of passenger train services, buses are the best and most economical form of public transportation. Although second-class buses can provide a bone-rattling experience, the luxury services are extremely comfortable. Tickets are significantly cheaper than domestic air travel (see p375), but expect slower journeys.

A long-distance luxury bus for direct intercity services

TRAINS

Although most of Mexico's original train lines still exist, passenger services have dwindled as a result of privatization, coupled with road improvements. Two notable tourist services are the Expreso Maya, which runs through Yucatán, Campeche, and Chiapas; and the **Tequila Express** in Jalisco, which offers a fun day trip to a tequila-producing hacienda. The Chihuahua-al-Pacífico Railroad, which runs through the Cañón del Cobre region (see pp176–7), is the only bona fide public passenger train remaining. Its first-class service departs at 6am daily from Los Mochis on the Pacific coast, and from Chihuahua in the north. The second-class service is scheduled to depart an hour later. Considered one of the world's great railroad journeys, it covers 670 km (415 miles) over 13 hours, traversing some of Mexico's most spectacular landscapes.

The colorful Chihuahua al Pacifico Railroad first-class passenger train

TRAIN TICKETS

First-class tickets for the Chihuahua al Pacifico train (nicknamed "El Chepe") are available up to a week in advance from Los Mochis and Chihuahua stations. Second-class tickets are available 24 hours in advance. Same-day tickets can also be purchased from Los Mochis, Chihuahua, and Creel stations; get there early to avoid queues or disappointment. Advance reservation is really only necessary during high season and public holidays. Purchase options through travel agents are limited, but you could try **Viajes Flamingo** in Los Mochis. Otherwise, purchase your ticket on the train. The cost of accomplishing the journey in staggered sections is exactly equal to completing it in one go, meaning it's quite feasible to stop off for excursions. While second-class tickets are roughly half the price of first class, you are still advised to travel first class for the best comfort and views. For Tequila Express and Expreso Maya tickets, contact the operators directly. Children under 12 pay a reduced adult fare, and children under 5 travel free.

BUSES AND COACHES

Mexico's numerous private bus companies can make a typical bus terminal – known as the *Central Camionera* or *Terminal de Autobuses* – busy and initially confusing. These are usually located on the outskirts of town, sometimes with separate buildings for first- and second-class services. Mexico City has four bus terminals serving places to north, south, east, and west.

There are three types of intercity bus (*camión*), offering luxury, first-class, or second-class services. For long-distance travel, luxury or first-class is recommended. These services are more reliable, more comfortable, safer, and less likely to break down. Top-of-the-range luxury (*de lujo*) buses offer direct intercity services, with air-conditioning, fully reclining seats, hostesses, refreshments, video screens, and on-board toilets, although fares are between 30 and 50 percent more than first-class tickets. First-class (*primera*) buses are air-conditioned, with semi-reclining seats, video, and a toilet. On shorter trips, less reliable second-class buses may be the only option. Services marked *directo* or *sin escalas* (nonstop) are faster than those that make stops.

BUS TICKETS

Generally, you should expect to pay US$3–5 per hour of first-class travel. For long-distance journeys of over four hours it is advisable to book in advance, especially at Christmas or Easter. At other times, just turning up at the station should be sufficient.

One of Mexico City's main bus terminals

Timetables, fares, and routes are posted at the terminals, but information and advance bookings are also sometimes available from travel agents. Many large companies have their own booking offices in town centers and some have websites to check timetables and book on-line. If traveling in the south of the country, the **Ticketbus** website is very useful and will let you book your journey with a range of companies. **Bamba Experience** offers a backpacker multi-pass that lets you hop on and off at major destinations. Tickets are usually refundable if canceled at least three hours before departure. Some buses give student discounts to travelers who can show an International Student Identification Card (ISIC).

LOCAL BUSES

The local bus, also known as a *camión*, is the cheapest and easiest way to get around the provincial towns of Mexico. Apart from taxis, they are also the principal means of getting between the bus station and downtown area. Fares rarely exceed US$0.30; buy your

ticket on the bus, then pull the chord or shout "*Baja*" when you want to get off. Supplementing this service are *colectivos* – vans or minibuses that follow fixed routes but charge a flat rate, regardless of distance. They can often be cramped and uncomfortable, but offer an

Boarding an island passenger ferry destined for Playa del Carmen

authentic opportunity to rub shoulders with the locals. They often stop on request rather than at designated points, so just tell the driver when you want to get off. Central plazas and market places are usually the main hubs of local transport.

FERRIES

Passenger and car ferries leaving from Santa Rosalía and La Paz connect the Baja California peninsula to Guaymas, Topolobampo, and Mazatlán on the Pacific mainland. Two standards of cabin are offered – a *turista*, with bunkbeds and a wash-basin, or a more expensive

especial, which has an entire suite of rooms. Schedules often change at random and should always be confirmed in advance. The Santa Rosalía–Guaymas ferry may sometimes operate sporadically in low season.

On the Caribbean coast, ferries leave from Puerto Morelos (car ferry) and Playa del Carmen (passenger only) to the island of Cozumel *(see p282)*. Ferries from Puerto Juárez (passenger only) and Punta Sam (car ferry), both north of Cancún, travel to Isla Mujeres *(see p281)*. Another, more expensive ferry leaves for Isla Mujeres from Playa Linda, in Cancún, four times every day.

DIRECTORY

BUS TERMINALS IN MEXICO CITY

Norte
Eje Central Lázaro Cárdenas 4907.
Ⓜ Autobuses del Norte.
Tel 55 87 15 52.
www.ticketbus.com.mx
Destinations:
Acapulco, Huatulco, Colima, Cuernavaca, Chihuahua, Durango, Guadalajara, Guanajuato, Hermosillo, Ixtapa and Zihuatanejo, León, Mazatlán, Mexicali, Monterrey, Morelia, Pátzcuaro, Poza Rica, Puerto Escondido, Puerto Vallarta, Querétaro, Saltillo, San Luis Potosí, San Miguel de Allende, Taxco, Tepic, Tijuana, Uruapan, Zacatecas.

Oriente TAPO
Calz Ignacio Zaragoza 200.
Ⓜ San Lázaro.
Tel 51 33 24 44.
Destinations:
Campeche, Cancún, Chiapas, Mérida, Oaxaca, Puebla, Tlaxcala, Veracruz, Xalapa.

Poniente
Sur 122, corner of Río Tacubaya.
Ⓜ Observatorio.
Tel 52 71 45 19.
Destinations:
Aguascalientes, Colima, Guanajuato, León, Manzanillo, Morelia, Puerto Vallarta, Querétaro, San Juan de los Lagos, San Luis Potosí, San Miguel de Allende, Toluca, Uruapan.

Sur
Av Taxqueña 1320.

Ⓜ Taxqueña.
Tel 56 89 97 45.
Destinations: *Acapulco, Cuernavaca, Ixtapa and Zihuatanejo, Oaxaca, Puebla, Taxco, Tepoztlán.*

BUS TICKETS

Ticketbus
Tel 01800 702 8000.
www.ticketbus.com.mx

Bamba Experience
Tel 01800 462 2622.
www.bambaexperience.com

TRAIN SERVICES

Ferrocarril Mexicano Railroad
Corner of Mendez & 24, Chihuahua.
Tel (614) 439 72 12.
Prolongación Bienestar, Los Mochis.
Tel (668) 824 11 67.

www.chepe.com.mx

Tequila Express
Vallarta Av 4095, Jalisco.
Tel 01800 503 9720 (toll free).
www.tequilaexpress.com.mx/ingles

Viajes Flamingo
Hotel Santa Anita, Avenida Leyva esq. Hidalgo, Los Mochis
Tel (668) 812 1613.
www.mexicoscoppercanyon.com

FERRY SERVICES

Baja Ferries
Tel 01800 337 74 37.
www.bajaferries.com

Santa Rosalía Ferries
Tel (615) 152 12 46.

Driving in Mexico

Traveling around by car at your own pace is the most practical and flexible way to explore Mexico (the only exception being Mexico City). Driving is generally safe, but motorists need to take some precautions. Robberies do occur, and it is advisable not to drive at night and to avoid overnight street parking. In Mexico city, drive with the doors locked and the windows rolled up. Try to plan your trip in advance, take a good road map, and know where your stops are likely to be. Hitchhiking is not recommended.

Street signs

Lonely highway in Northern Mexico

RULES OF THE ROAD

Mexicans drive on the right-hand side of the road, and distances are measured in kilometers rather than miles. Most traffic regulations and warnings are represented by internationally recognized symbols and signs, but some signs are unique to Mexico.

Parking, which can often be a problem in the big cities, is permitted where you see a sign with a black E (for *estacionamiento*) in a red circle. The same E with a diagonal line through it means no parking. A white E on a blue background indicates a parking lot. The wearing of seat belts is compulsory. Normal speed limits are 40 km/h (25 mph) in built-up areas, 70 km/h (45 mph) in rural areas and 110 km/h (68 mph) on freeways. Traffic must come to a complete stop at *Alto* (halt) signs.

Slow down when approaching villages, where there are often speed bumps *(topes)*. Beware that these can be very high, and are not always marked.

Take extreme care at rail crossings, both in cities and in the open country, as there is often no system to warn that a train is coming, and accidents can occur. Avoid driving at night when there is increased risk of robbery, and animals roam freely. Potholes are often unmarked, and it is hard to spot obstacles on the road.

WHAT YOU NEED

Regulations for bringing cars into Mexico are very strict. Obtain a *permiso de importación temporal* (temporary import permit) from Banjercito banks at border crossings, various Mexican consulates in the United States, or online from the Banjercito website. Expect to be charged a fee from US$30–50, for the six-month, multiple-entry permit, depending on point of issue.

Several other original documents are also needed, and these should all be photocopied once or twice. These include an authorized immigration form (FMT) or visa; a valid driver's license (US, Canadian, British, Australian, and New Zealand licenses are all valid); a passport (or other compliant document for North American residents); vehicle registration papers; and a credit card (Visa, MasterCard, or American Express) in the same name as the car registration papers. Those without a credit card must pay a bond, or make a substantial cash deposit.

Rented vehicles require a contract from the rental firm and their written permission to take it over the border. If driving a company car, you'll need proof of employment and proof of the company's ownership of the vehicle.

If you wish to cross the border several times, you may do so for the period specified on your FMT. Ask officials for a *tarjetón de internación*, which you can exchange for a *comprobante de retorno* when you leave, and again for a *tarjetón* when you return. Don't forget to cancel your import permit when you leave Mexico for the final time. This can be done as you enter the border zone. Failure to do this can result in fines to your credit card.

Note that US car insurance does not cover driving south of the border, so separate coverage must be arranged. Insurance is sold in most cities and towns on both sides of the border.

Rows of rush hour traffic in Mexico City

MEXICAN ROAD SIGNS

End of surfaced road

Public convenience

Medical assistance

Car parking available

ROAD CLASSIFICATION

There are three main kinds of highway in Mexico: four-lane *super carreteras*, ordinary *cuota* (toll) roads, and *libre* (free) roads.

The cost of the tolls on the *super carreteras* is much higher than the ordinary *cuota* roads. As a result, there is less traffic, no trucks, and few buses. Beware that there aren't many service stations on the *super carreteras*.

Cuota highways range from fast, four-lane roads, to those that are little better than *libre* (free) roads. Tolls are charged according to distance and the number of axles on the vehicle. If there is a choice of toll payment booth, opt for the lane marked *autos*. On *cuotas*, drivers are insured against accident or breakdown.

Two-lane *libre* (free) roads are often very busy with local traffic, trucks and buses, and are not ideal for long-distance or inter-city travel. For shorter trips, however, they can provide a scenic alternative to the main roads.

lleno por favor (fill the tank please), or specify an amount.

ACCIDENTS AND BREAKDOWN

In the event of an accident, stay with your vehicle. Inform the insurance companies immediately, and file a claim before leaving the country. If anyone has been hurt, you may be detained by the police until fault can be established. If nobody is hurt, it is best to resolve the situation without involving the police (*see p366*).

The *Angeles Verdes* (Green Angels) are a fleet of pickup trucks which patrol major tourist routes, helping motorists in difficulties. The service is provided free of charge by Mexico's Ministry of Tourism (SECTUR). The mechanics speak English and can administer first aid. They only charge for spare parts or fuel, although tips are appreciated.

Traveling by moped

CAR, BICYCLE, AND MOTORBIKE RENTAL

Car rental is expensive in Mexico. International car rental companies, such as Hertz and Budget, have offices in main airports, and large towns, but local companies may offer the cheapest deals. When pre-booking, make sure the price incorporates the 15 percent tax, and full insurance. It is important that the insurance includes theft and collision damage waiver. Some policies provide only nominal coverage, and additional insurance cover may be necessary. To rent a car in Mexico you must be 21 or over (25 for some agencies) and have held a valid driver's license for at least one year. Rental must be paid for with a major credit card. Companies often require customers to sign a blank credit card slip, which is then torn up when the car is returned intact.

Bicycles, mopeds, and motorbikes can be rented in resorts. Before setting out, make sure that the vehicle is in good condition and that your insurance cover is adequate. Also check that your personal travel insurance covers motorbike accidents.

HITCH-HIKING

For safety reasons, hitch-hiking is not recommended. Robberies and worse have occurred near the US border, and banditry exists in some regions, such as Sinaloa. Many Mexican landscapes are harsh and remote with sparse passing traffic. The north and Baja California are particularly unforgiving.

However, in some isolated areas hitching is the only way to get around and tends to be quite common among locals over short distances. A small fee may be expected in such cases where individual drivers serve as the local transportation. Truck drivers may also demand a fee.

![One of the many PEMEX gas stations found across the country]

One of the many PEMEX gas stations found across the country

FUEL AND GAS STATIONS

PEMEX franchises all gas stations in Mexico, so fuel is the same price throughout the country, bar the US border where it is cheaper. Priced by the liter, *Gasolina* is unleaded. It is graded either *Magna Sin* (standard) or *Premium*.

Gas stations are plentiful in towns but are less common in rural areas. In some regions it is possible to drive for 100 km (62 miles) without seeing a gas station. Gas stations are usually open 7am–10pm and are not self-service. The attendant asks *¿cuánto?* (how much?), to which you reply

MAPS

A selection of reliable city, regional, and national road maps are published by PEMEX (Petróleos Mexicanos, the state gasoline monopoly), and by the publishing company Guía Roji. These maps can be bought at bookstores, supermarkets, branches of Sanborn's (*see p114*), newsstands, and some gas stations. SECTUR offices can provide free maps. The American Automobile Association (AAA) also publishes a map of Mexico, which is available to AAA members.

Getting Around Mexico City

An old-fashioned trolleybus

Traffic congestion in Mexico City is appalling, and driving is not practical. Walking is the easiest way to negotiate certain areas in the center or south of the city, but elsewhere distances are so vast that some form of transport is necessary. Trolleybuses still run on a few routes, but more regular services are provided by an extensive bus and subway system. In the south, an electric train connects the subway at Taxqueña to Embarcadero in Xochimilco. Taxis are inexpensive, and *peseros* (collective taxis) are cheaper. Traffic is worst during rush hours (6:30–9am and 4–7pm).

Crowd in front of the Basílica de Guadalupe *(see p108)*

WALKING

Walking is a great way to explore the historic center, as well as areas like San Ángel, Coyoacán, and the Zona Rosa. Allow time to adjust to the altitude and pollution *(see pp366–7)* before long walks.

Those on foot generally take second place to vehicles. Do not assume that a car will automatically stop at a pedestrian crossing, and be prepared for uneven road surfaces and sidewalks. Look both ways when crossing one-way streets, as on some, buses are allowed to travel in both directions. Keep to busy, well-lit streets at night and avoid underpasses. Carry valuables in a money belt and keep your camera in front of you, instead of to the side.

BUSES AND PESEROS

Buses are cheap but crowded, especially at rush hour. They run from 5am to midnight, and fares are paid to the driver on entering the bus. Route maps are available at tourist offices. Routes are identified by destination; a west–east route links Chapultepec Park with the Zócalo, along Reforma and past the Alameda. North–south, buses run along Avenida Insurgentes. *Peseros* (sedans, vans, or minibuses) use the same routes and charge a flat rate. On Ave Insurgentes, between Indios Verdes and San Ángel, there are also extra-large metrobuses, which run relatively quick services to the southern districts. Buy a swipe card before boarding and "top up" as needed. Turibús (www.turibus.com.mx) runs hop-on, hop-off buses that pass most of the city's notable sites.

TAXIS

Mexican taxis are good value, and it is possible to hire one by the hour for sightseeing. Due to incidences of robbery and assault on passengers, it is unsafe to flag down a taxi in the street. Fortunately, there are plenty of *sitios* (radio taxis) available. These white-and-beige cars are a much safer option. As a precaution, ask the telephone dispatcher for the driver's name and the cab's license plate number. Green-and-white VW street taxis are being phased out in favor of more environmentally-friendly vehicles. Hiring one of these cars is not advisable.

From the airport, it is essential to take a pre-paid, official taxi *(see pp372–3)*. Tariffs for any taxi go up by 10 percent after 10pm. *Turismo* sedans, with hooded meters and English-speaking drivers, tend to park outside big hotels. They are more expensive for short trips but can be hired by the hour. Check with the hotel that the driver is genuine.

DRIVING

Driving in Mexico City can be a nerve-racking experience and is best avoided if possible. If you do decide to drive, keep calm and take nothing for granted. A green traffic light does not necessarily mean the road is clear. Check in your mirror before stopping at an amber light, as the driver of the car behind may not think you are going to stop. Car theft is rife, so remove or hide all possessions and be sure your hotel has safe night-parking. Signs on the city's freeways are erratic at best. If it is hard to get on them, it is harder to know where to exit. There are two main ring roads: an inner one, *El Circuito Interior*, and an outer one, the *Anillo Periférico*. A third freeway, *Viaducto Miguel Alemán*, cuts across from west to east *(see map on p119)*. Invest in a good map, such as the *Guía Roji* guide. To reduce pollution, some cars are banned in the city between 5am and 10pm, one day a week. The day depends on the last digit of the number plate: 5 and 6 on Mondays; 7 and 8 on Tuesdays; 3 and 4 on Wednesdays; 1 and 2 on Thursdays; 9 and 0 on Fridays. New models, with Mexico City number plates and the required paperwork and stickers, are exempt.

CYCLING

A network of dedicated bike lanes is being developed, but cycling in Mexico City is still not recommended due to volume of traffic and poor quality roads. Chapultepec Park is one exception. You can hire bicycles from outside the Museo de Antropología. Ask at the tourist office for good routes around the city, including the one that follows the old Cuernavaca railroad.

THE METRO

The subway system in Mexico City is one of the cheapest, cleanest, and busiest in the world. Lines are represented by numbers and colors; stations are identified by their name and a pictographic representation. There is usually a metro map on the wall at each station and inside the trains themselves, but none on the platforms.

Tickets *(boletos)* are sold at metro stations, singly or in strips of five. Bulk-buying saves standing in line but is no cheaper. Tickets must be validated in the machine at the entrance to the platforms. Each flat-rate ticket is valid for one trip, including transfers to other metro lines.

At peak times, the metro can be unbearably crowded. People with large or bulky luggage may not be allowed on the metro at busy times.

Sign outside Copilco station

Mexico City Metro symbol

There are special carriages designated for women and children only during the rush hours.

Some of the central subway stations are worth visiting in their own right, even if you do not plan to use the metro to travel. The Zócalo station has interesting models of the city center, before and after the Spanish conquest. Inside Pino Suárez station there is a small Aztec pyramid, discovered during construction of the subway. Replicas of archaeological pieces are displayed at Bellas Artes station; and contemporary art exhibitions are often organized at Copilco station.

USEFUL MEXICO CITY METRO ROUTES

Most visitors will only use sections of lines 1, 2, and 3. The electric train from Taxqueña is shown as a dotted line. Line 12 is under construction and is due to open in 2012.

Politécnico — 5
Indios Verdes — 3
El Rosario — 6 7
Deportivo 18 de Marzo
La Villa-Basílica
4 6 Martín Carrera
Instituto del Petróleo
Autobuses del Norte
Potrero
Misterios
Cuatro Caminos — 2
Tacuba
Buenavista — B
Tlatelolco
La Raza
Ciudad Azteca — B
San Joaquín
Colegio Militar
Guerrero
8 Garibaldi/Lagunilla
Consulado
Polanco
Revolución
Bellas Artes
Allende
Morelos
Oceanía
Auditorio
Hidalgo
Juárez
San Juan de Letrán
Zócalo
Candelaria
Merced
San Lázaro
Terminal Aérea
Pantitlán — 1 5 9 A
Balderas
Salto de Agua
Isabel la Católica
Pino Suárez
Ciudad Deportiva
Constituyentes
Cuauhtémoc
Insurgentes
Sevilla
Niños Héroes
Doctores
San Antonio Abad
Velódromo
Canal de San Juan
Tepalcates
Observatorio — 1
Chapultepec
Patriotismo
Centro Médico
Jamaica
La Paz — A
9 Tacubaya
Chilpancingo
Etiopía/Plaza de la Transparencia
Chabacano
Xola
Santa Anita — 4
Mixcoac — 12
San Antonio
Zapata
Coyuya
Constitución de 1917
Coyoacán
Viveros/Derechos Humanos
Ermita
Atlalilco
8
Miguel Ángel de Quevedo
General Anaya
Nezahualpilli
La Noria
Embarcadero
12 Tiáhuac
Barranca del Muerto — 7
Universidad — 3
Tasqueña — 2
Registro Federal
Xochimilco

General Index

Acknowledgments

Dorling Kindersley would like to thank the following people whose contributions and assistance have made the preparation of this book possible.

Contributors and Consultants
Antonio Benavides has worked as an archaeologist in the Yucatán Peninsula since 1974. He has written several books on the Maya and the colonial history of the Yucatán.
Nick Caistor is a specialist on Latin American literature, is a writer, translator, and broadcaster. He works for the BBC World Service.
Maria Doulton is a freelance writer who has been involved with Mexico for many years.
Petra Fischer is a writer and television producer working in Mexico. German born, she has spent much of her life in Mexico.
Eduardo Gleason, a former tour guide, is a writer and researcher based in Mexico City.
Phil Gunson is a journalist and naturalist. He is the former Latin America correspondent for *The Guardian* newspaper.
Alan Knight is Professor of Latin American history at St Anthony's College, Oxford.
Felicity Laughton, a freelance writer, has lived and worked in Mexico for many years.
Simon Martin is an epigrapher at the Institute of Archaeology, University College London, and specializes in ancient Maya inscriptions.
Richard Nichols is half-Mexican and has had a life-long connection with Mexico. He is a former businessman turned writer.
Chloë Sayer has written numerous books about Mexico, worked on television documentaries about the country, and made ethnographic collections in Mexico for the British Museum.

Additional Contributors
Marita Adair, Andrew Downie, David Maitland, Nick Ryder, Rosa Rodríguez.

Proofreader
Stewart J Wild.

Indexer
Hilary Bird.

Editorial and Design Assistance
Richard Arghiris, Tessa Bindloss, Sam Borland, Stephanie Driver, Ellen and James Fields, Joy Fitzsimmons, Eva Gleason, Geoffrey Groesbeck, Emily Hatchwell, Carolyn Hewitson, Claire Jones, Elly King, Priya Kukadia, Maite Lantaron, Francesca Machiavelli, Sue Metcalfe-Megginson, Rebecca Milner, Sonal Modha, Helen Partington, Naomi Peck, Rada Radojicic, Zoë Ross, Sands Publishing Solutions, Helen Townsend.

Maps
Michael Bassett, Sharon O'Reilly, Richard Toomey (ERA-Maptec Ltd) (BIMSA Cartosistemas, S.A. de C.V.).

Photographers
Demetrio Carrasco, Linda Whitwam, Peter Wilson, Francesca Yorke.

Additional Photography
Paul Franklin, Eva Gleason, Ian O'Leary, Rough Guides/Sarah Cummins, Clive Streeter.

Illustrators
Gary Cross, Richard Draper, Isidoro González-Adalid Cabezas (Acanto Arquitectura y Urbanismo S.L.), Paul Guest, Stephen Guapay, Claire Littlejohn, John Woodcock

Additional Illustrations
José Luis de Andrés de Colsa, Javier Gómez Morata (Acanto Arquitectura y Urbanismo S.L.).

For Dorling Kindersley
Fay Franklin, Louise Bostock Lang, Annette Jacobs, Vivien Crump, Gillian Allan, Douglas Amrine, Marie Ingledew, David Proffit

Special Assistance
Arq. Humberto Aguirre; Emilia Almazán; Margarita Arriaga; Juan Francisco Becerra Ferreiro; Patricia Becerra Ramírez (Posada Coatepec); Sergio Berrera; Lic. Marco Beteta; Giorgio Brignone; Rosa Bugdud; Fernando Bustamante (Antropólogo); Libby Cabeldu; Canning House (London); Lic. Laura Castro; Santiago Chávez; Josefina Cipriano; Ana Compean; María Eugenia Cruz Terrazas (INEGI); Greg Custer; Jane Custer; Mary Lou Dabdoub; Avery Danziger; Lenore Danziger; Areli Díaz (Instituto Nacional de Antropología, Mexico); Lucía Díaz Cholico; Fernando Díaz de León; Lic. Roberto Durón Carrillo; Peter McGregor Eadie; Ana María Espinoza; Ludwig Estrada; José Falguera; Lic. Lincoln Fontanills (Secretaría de Turismo, Mexico); Elena Nichols Gantous; Robert Graham; Ma. del Carmen Guerrero Esquivel; Lic. José Luis Hernández (Secretaría de Turismo del Estado de Puebla); Ing. Guillermo Hidalgo Trujillo; Ariane Homayunfar; Jorge Huft; Instituto Nacional Indigenista (Nayarit); Carlos Jiménez; Lourdes Jiménez Coronel; Ursula Jones; Eric Jordan; La Mexicana Quality Foods Ltd; Marcela Leos (Mexican Embassy to the UK); Kevin Leuzinger (Cozumel Fan Club); Sol Levin Rojo (Instituto Nacional de Antropología, Mexico); Oscar López; Carlos Lozano de la Torre; Alan Luce; Arq. Alfredo Lugo; Berta Maldonado; Gabriel Martínez; Manuel Mata; Cathy Matos (Mexican Tours); Fabián Medina; Enrique Mendoza; Meteorological Office; Mexico Ministry of Tourism, London; Ivalu Mireles Esparza; Silvia Niembro (Antropóloga, Museo de Antropología de Xalapa); María Novaro; Diego de la O Peralta; Magdalena Ordóz Estrada; Dolores Ortuño Araiza; Margarita Pedraza; Ma. Irma del Peral; Ma. del Pilar Córdoba; Margaret Popper; Petra Puente;

Bertha Alicia Ramírez; José Rangel Navarro;
Jesus Rodríguez Morales; Anita Romero de
Andrade; Celia Romero Piñón; Elena de la
Rosa; Idalia Rubio; Paulina Rubio; Carlos
Salgado; Alejandro Sánchez Galván; Alejandro
Santes García (Antropólogo); Marta Santos;
David Saucedo; Gloria Soledad González;
Lisette Span; Pablo Span; Turismo del Estado
de Aguascalientes (Dirección); Turismo del
Estado de Colima (Secretaría); Turismo del
Estado de Guanajuato (Secretaría); Turismo
del Estado de Hidalgo (Dirección General);
Turismo del Estado de Jalisco (Secretaría);
Turismo del Estado de Michoacan (Secretaría);
Turismo del Estado de Nayarit (Secretaría);
Turismo del Estado de Querétaro (Secretaría);
Turismo del Estado de San Luis Postosí
(Dirección General); Turismo del Estado de
Veracruz-Llave (Dirección); Turismo del
Estado de Zacatecas (Dirección); Juan Carlos
Valencia; Gilberto Miguel Vázquez; Josefina
Vázquez; Luis Antonio Villa; Jesús Villafaña;
Helen Westwood; John Wiseman.

Special Photography
© INAH, Cambridge Museum of Archaeology
and Anthropology, Philip Dowell, Neil Mersh,
Stephen Whitehorne, Jerry Young, Michel Zabé.

Mexico's Cultural Heritage
All archaeological and historical sites form
part of the Cultural Heritage of Mexico, which
is protected by the Instituto Nacional de
Antropología e Historia (INAH), Mexico. The
reproduction, by whatever means, of any
images in this book which form part of the
Cultural Heritage of Mexico, is subject to the
Mexican federal laws pertaining to monuments
and artistic, historical, and archaeological sites,
and the Mexican federal law of copyright.
Reproduction of these images must be
previously approved by INAH.

Photography Permissions
The Publisher would like to thank all the
cathedrals, churches, museums, restaurants,
hotels, shops, galleries, and others sights,
too numerous to thank individually, for
their co-operation and contribution to
this publication.

Picture Credits
Key: t=top; tl=top left; tlc=top left centre;
tc=top centre; trc=top right centre; tr=top right;
cla=centre left above; ca=centre above;
cra=centre right above; cl=centre left;
c=centre; cr=centre right; clb=centre left
below; cb=centre below; crb=centre right
below; bl=bottom left; b=bottom; br=bottom
right; bcl=bottom centre left; bc=bottom
centre; bcr=bottom centre right; (d)=detail.
Every effort has been made to trace the
copyright holders. Dorling Kindersley

apologizes for any unintentional omissions
and would be pleased, in such cases, to add
an acknowledgment in future editions.
Some of the following photographs form part
of the Cultural Heritage of Mexico, which is
protected by the Instituto Nacional de
Antropología e Historia, Mexico.

Works of art have been reproduced with the
permission of the following copyright holders:
Palacio del Gobierno *Miguel Hidalgo* José
Clemente Orozco © DACS, 2006 188b; Ex-
Aduana de Santo Domingo (west wall)
Patriots and Parricides David Alfaro Siqueiros
(1945) © Instituto Nacional de Bellas Artes
(INBA) – Sala de Arte Público Siqueiros 72b.

The publisher would like to thank the following individuals, companies, and picture
libraries for their kind permission to reproduce
their photographs in this publication:

PABLO DE AGUINACO, Mexico: 17b, 23c, 31c,
31b, 32c, 34b, 34–35, 35t, 139c, 165ca, 225b;
A.P. Giberstein 165ca, 247c; Carlos Puga
170cb, 179cb, 227b, 355c; AKG PHOTO,
London: 48t; Erich Lessing 53t; ALAMY IMAGES:
Sue Clark 321tl; Creatas/Dynamic Graphics
Group 354tc; David Sanger Photography 10cr;
Danita Delimont/Cindy Miller Hopkins 364c;
Danita Delimont 11c, 352cl, 354bl; Diana Bier
Puebla Carnival 366crb; Tony Gale 372ca;
Geogphotos 320cla; Steve Hamblin 371br;
Frans Lemmens 365tl; Lightworks Media 67c,
78br; CJ Middendorf 363tl; John Mitchell 368bl;
PCL 10bl; Moreleaze Tropicana 366br;
Travelwide 373cb; Sergey Torockov 375br;
Ollie Weait 370cra; Janusz Wrobel 355br; ARDEA
LONDON LTD: Piers Cavendish 19br; Wardene
Weisser 19br; THE ART ARCHIVE: Archaeological
and ethnological Museum Guatamala
City/Dagli Orti 8–9. BANCO NACIONAL DE MEXICO
SA: Fomento Cultural 43t; JOHN BRUNTON: 28t,
29cla, 218b, 219b, 255bl.

MICHAEL CALDERWOOD: 14, 216tl; DEMETRIO
CARRASCO: 366bl, 367t, 367ca, 368t, 368c, 378b;
BRUCE COLLEMAN COLLECTION: John Cancalosi
21bc; Michael Fogden 20tl; Jeff Foott
Productions 20bl; S. Nielsen 20crb; Pacific
Stock 217cl; John Shaw 20c; CORBIS: Lynsey
Addarid 321c; Jan Butchofsky-Houser 322bl;
Randy Faris 63cr; William Henry Jackson 48cr;
Danny Lehman 66c; Reuters/Henry Romero
352tc; David H. Wells 323bl.

MICHAEL DIGGIN: 33c, 92tr, 92c, 276br.

TOR EIGELAND: 22cb; EMBAJADA DE MEXICO, London:
29br; EMPICS LTD: Santiago Llanquin 352bc.

LUIS FELIX © 1979: 195b; ROBERT FRIED
PHOTOGRAPHY: 20br.

GETTY IMAGES: AFP/Omar Torres 367cr; EVA
MARIA GLEASON, Mexico: 64tl, 64tr, 64bl, 64br,
65b, 141t, 141b, 142t, 142ca, 142b,
143ca, 143b, 367t, 370tl, 370cb, 371c, 376t,
376br, 379clb, 381t; ANDREAS GROSS, Germany:
34tr, 171t, 261cra.

HACIENDA XCANATUN: 290cl; ROBERT HARDING
PICTURE LIBRARY: Robert Freck/Odyssey 51ca,
51c; DAVE G. HAUSER: 164cr, 171c, 219c, 221b;
John Elkins 128t; Susan Kaye Mosaic in
Dolores Olmeda's house Diego Rivera ©
DACS, 1999 218crb, 247b; HUTCHISON LIBRARY:
218t, 232b.

FOTOTECA DEL INAH FONDO CASASOLA: 50t, 50b;
INDEX, Barcelona: 39b, 49b; Mithra *El
Feudalismo Porfirista* Juan O'Gorman 53c.

JUSTIN KERR: 277crb.

DAVID LAVENDER: 29ca, 29cra, 34tl, 35cra, 35crb,
348–9, 348t, 348bl, 349br, 349bl, 349ca, all 350
except bl, all 351; LONELY PLANET IMAGES:
Richard I'Anson 38; John Neubauer 66bl.

MAROMA RESORT AND SPA: 358bl, 359tr; ENRICO
MARTINO: 18t, 19c, 24c, 30c, 30b, 32t, 163c,
175t, 177b, 262ca; MEXICO TOURISM BOARD:
362ca; JOSE LUIS MORENO: 283bl, 283bc.

JUAN NEGRIN: 22–3; NHPA: John Shaw 211b.

G. DAGLI ORTI: 46t, 233cra, 233cr; OXFORD
SCIENTIFIC FILMS: N. Mitchel 246t.

PANOS PICTURES: Mark Henley 10cla; PLANE
PICTURES: Lutz Pfeiffer 373cr; PLANET EARTH
PICTURES: Mary Clay 21crb; Beth Davidow 21cb;
Brian Kenney 21clb; Ken Lucas 20clb; John
Lythgoe 171cr, 216c; Claus Meyer 286ca;
Nancy Sefton 21tr, 283cl; Doug White 21tl.

REX FEATURES: 55c, 374t; Sipa Press/L. Rieder 55b.

EL SANTUARIO: 358tc; Chloe Sayer: 16c, 22cla,
22b, 24cr, 24cra, 29b, 28bl, 28br, 29t, 29crb,
35bl, 330ca, 330br; SEXTO SOL, Mexico: 20cra,
22t, 176t, 353bl; Edn 34ca; Adalberto Rios
Szalay 15t, 33b, 52c, 117t, 170t, 170b, 171bl,
179t, 184t, 225tr, 244–245, 373t, 374b;

Adalberto Rios Lanz 32b; A.M.G. 18c, 354t;
Ernesto Rios Lanz 20cla, 171cra; Bob
Schalkwijk 23br, 49c *Padre Hidalgo*
O'Gorman, 49tr; SOUTH AMERICAN PICTURES: 116r,
54tl, 81b, 110tc; Tony Morrison 221t; Chris
Sharp 41t, 243t; HERI STIERLING: 47b, 233bc.

TERRAQUA: 283cr, 283br; TONY STONE IMAGES:
236t, Richard During 219t.

MIREILLE VAUTIER: 9 (inset), 11tl, 16t, 22c, 23bl,
26tr, 29tl, 29b, 30t, 31t, 33t, 34cl, 35cla, 35c,
40c, 42bl, 42br, 43c *The Conquest* O'Gorman
44t, 44b, 45tr, 51t, 52b, 54c, 54b, 55t, 57
(inset), 92tl, 93cb, 94b, 118t, 127 (inset); 162t,
162b, 185c, 235ca, 264b, 265clb, 277ca, 289
(inset), 347cla, 361 (inset), 353b.

WERNER FORMEN ARCHIVE: Museo Nacional de
Antropología, Mexico 44ca; ELIZABETH WHITING
ASSOCIATES: 25br, 50c; Peter Wilson: 18b, 126–127
WWW.WI-FI.ORG: 371tc; WYSE TRAVEL CONFEDERATION:
363c.

ALEJANDRO ZENTENO: 187b, 248c, 249t, 277b,
277b.

Front endpaper: All special photography.

JACKET Front - GETTY IMAGES: Image Bank/
Carolyn Brown main image; JUAN R.
NEGRIN: bl. Back - DK IMAGES: Linda Whitman
cla,clb, tl; Francesca Yorke bl. Spine - GETTY
IMAGES: Image Bank/Carolyn Brown t; DK
IMAGES: Peter Wilson b.

All other images © Dorling Kindersley. For
further information see: www.dkimages.com

Phrase Book

Mexican Spanish is essentially the same as the Castilian spoken in Spain, although there are some differences in vocabulary and pronunciation.

The most noticeable are the use of *ustedes* (the plural version of "you") in both informal and formal situations, and the pronunciation of the soft "c" and the letter "z" as "s" rather than "th."

Mexicans use *carro* (instead of *coche*) for a car, and often call buses, as well as trucks, *camiones*. Words of indigenous origin are common. A word for market used only in Mexico is *tianguis*, for example, although *mercado* is also employed. Mexicans tend to be fairly formal, and it is good

manners to use *usted* (rather than *tú*) for "you," un–less you know the person well. Always say *buenos días* or *buenas tardes* when boarding a taxi, and address both taxi drivers and waiters as *señor*.

If you wish to decline goods from street vendors, a polite shake of the head and a *muchas gracias* will usually suffice. Adding *muy amable*, literally "very kind," will help to take the edge off the refusal. A term to be handled with care is *madre* (mother), as much bad language in Mexico is based on variants of this word. When referring to someone's mother, use *tu mama* (your mom), or the formal version *su señora madre*, just to be safe.

In an Emergency

Help!	¡Socorro!	soh-**koh**-roh
Stop!	¡Pare!	pah-reh
Call a doctor!	¡Llame a un médico!	yah-meh ah **oon** meh-dee-koh
Call an ambulance!	¡Llame una ambulancia!	yah-meh ah oonah ahm-boo-**lahn**-see-ah
Call the fire department!	¡Llame a los bomberos!	yah-meh ah lohs bohm-**beh**-rohs
Where is the nearest telephone?	¿Dónde está el teléfono más cercano?	dohn-deh ehs-**tah** ehl teh-**leh**-foh-noh **mahs** sehr-**kah**-noh
Where is the nearest hospital?	¿Dónde está el hospital más cercano?	dohn-deh ehs-**tah** ehl ohs-pee-**tahl** mahs sehr-**kah**-noh
policeman	el policía	ehl poh-lee-**see**-ah
Could you help me?	¿Me podría ayudar?	meh poh-**dree**-yah ah-yoo-**dahr**
I've/we've been mugged	Me/nos asaltaron	meh/nohs ah-sahl-**tahr**-ohn
They stole my ...	Me robaron el/la...	meh roh-**bahr**-ohn ehl/lah

Communication Essentials

Yes	Sí	see
No	No	noh
Please	Por favor	pohr fah-**vohr**
Thank you	Gracias	**grah**-see-ahs
Excuse me	Perdone	pehr-**doh**-neh
Hello	Hola	oh-lah
Good morning	Buenos días	bweh-nohs dee-ahs
Good afternoon (from noon)	Buenas tardes	bweh-nahs tahr-dehs
Good night	Buenas noches	bweh-nahs noh-chehs
Bye (casual)	Hasta luego	ah-stah loo-**weh**-goh
Goodbye	Adiós	ah-dee-ohs
See you later	Hasta luego	ah-**stah** loo-**weh**-goh
Morning	La mañana	lah mah-**nyah**-nah
Afternoon/ early evening	La tarde	lah **tahr**-deh
Night	La noche	lah noh-cheh
Yesterday	Ayer	ah-**yehr**
Today	Hoy	oy
Tomorrow	Mañana	mah-**nyah**-nah
Here	Aquí	ah-**kee**
There	Allí	ah-**yee**
What?	¿Qué?	keh
When?	¿Cuándo?	kwahn-doh
Why?	¿Por qué?	pohr-**keh**
Where?	¿Dónde?	**dohn**-deh
How are you?	¿Cómo está usted?	koh-moh ehs-**tah** oos-**tehd**
Very well, thank you	Muy bien, gracias	mwee bee-**ehn grah**-see-ahs
Pleased to meet you	Mucho gusto	moo-choh **goo**-stoh
See you soon	Hasta pronto	ahs-tah **prohn**-toh
I'm sorry	Lo siento	loh see-**ehn**-toh

Useful Phrases

That's fine	Está bien	ehs-**tah** bee-**ehn**
Great/fantastic!	¡Qué bien!	keh bee-ehn
Where is/are ...?	¿Dónde está/están ...?	**dohn**-deh ehs-**tah**/ehs-**tahn**
How far is it to ...?	¿Cuántos metros/ kilómetros hay de aquí a ...?	kwahn-tohs meh-trohs/kee-loh-meh-trohs eye deh ah-**kee** ah
Which way is it to ...?	¿Por dónde se va a ...?	pohr **dohn**-deh seh vah ah
Do you speak English?	¿Habla inglés?	ah-blah een-**glehs**
I don't understand	No comprendo	noh kohm-**prehn**-doh
Could you speak more slowly, please?	¿Puede hablar más despacio, por favor?	pweh-deh ah-blahr mahs dehs-**pah**-see-oh pohr fah-**vohr**
I want	Quiero	kee-**yehr**-oh
I would like	Quisiera/ Me gustaría	kee-see-**yehr**-ah meh goo-stah-**ree**-ah
We want	Queremos	keh-**reh**-mohs
Do you have change (for 50 pesos)?	¿Tiene cambio (de cincuenta pesos)?	tee-**eh**-neh **kahm**-bee-yoh deh seen-**kwehn**-tah peh-sohs
(It's) very kind of you	Muy amable	mwee ah-**mah**-bleh
There is/there are	Hay	eye
Do you have/is there/are there?	¿Hay?	eye
Is there any water?	¿Hay agua?	eye ah-gwah
It's broken	Está roto/a	ehs-**tah** roh-toh/tah
Is it far/near?	¿Está lejos/cerca?	ehs-**tah** leh-hohs/**sehr**-kah
Take care/be careful!	¡Ten cuidado!	tehn koo-ee-**dah**-doh
We are late	Estamos atrasados	ehs-**tah**-mohs ah-trah-**sah**-dohs
We are early	Estamos adelantados	ehs-**tah**-mohs ah-deh-lahn-**tah**-dohs
OK, all right	De acuerdo	deh ah-**kwehr**-doh
Yes, of course	Claro que sí	klah-roh keh see
Of course!/with pleasure	¡Cómo no!/con mucho gusto	koh-moh noh/kohn moo-choh **goo**-stoh
Let's go	Vámonos	**vah**-moh-nohs

Useful Words

big	grande	**grahn**-deh
small	pequeño/a	peh-**keh**-nyoh/nyah
hot	caliente	kah-lee-ehn-the
cold	frío/a	**free**-oh/ah
good	bueno/a	**bweh**-noh/nah
bad	malo/a	**mah**-loh/lah
enough	suficiente	soo-fee-see-**ehn**-teh
well	bien	bee-**ehn**
open	abierto/a	ah-bee-**ehr**-toh/tah
closed	cerrado/a	sehr-**rah**-doh/dah
full	lleno/a	yeh-noh/nah

empty	**vacío/a**	vah-**see**-oh/ah
left	**izquierda**	ees-key-**ehr**-dah
right	**derecha**	deh-**reh**-chah
(keep) straight ahead	**(siga) derecho**	(**see**-gah) deh-**reh**-choh
near	**cerca**	**sehr**-kah
far	**lejos**	**leh**-hohs
up	**arriba**	ah-**ree**-bah
down	**abajo**	ah-**bah**-hoh
early	**temprano**	tehm-**prah**-noh
late	**tarde**	**tahr**-deh
now/very soon	**ahora/ahorita**	ah-**ohr**-ah/ah-ohr-**ee**-tah
more	**más**	mahs
less	**menos**	**meh**-nohs
very	**muy**	mwee
a little	**(un) poco**	oon poh-koh
very little	**muy poco**	mwee poh-koh
(much) more	**(mucho) más**	(**moo**-choh) mahs
too much	**demasiado**	deh-mah-see-**ah**-doh
too late	**demasiado tarde**	deh-mah-see-**ah**-doh **tahr**-deh
farther on/ahead	**más adelante**	mahs ah-deh-**lahn**-teh
farther back	**más atras**	mahs ah-**trahs**
opposite	**frente a**	**frehn**-teh ah
below/above	**abajo/arriba**	ah-**bah**-hoh/ah-**ree**-bah
first, second, third	**primero/a segundo/a tercero/a**	pree-**meh**-roh/ah seh-**goon**-doh/ah tehr-**sehr**-oh/ah
floor (of a building)	**el piso**	ehl **pee**-soh
ground floor	**la planta baja**	lah **plahn**-tah **bah**-hah
entrance	**entrada**	ehn-**trah**-dah
exit	**salida**	sah-**lee**-dah
elevator	**el ascensor**	ehl ah-sehn-**sohr**
toilets	**baños/sanitarios**	**bah**-nyohs/sah-nee-**tah**-ree-ohs
women's	**de damas**	deh **dah**-mahs
men's	**de caballeros**	deh kah-bah-**yeh**-rohs
sanitary napkins	**toallas sanitarias/ higiénicas**	toh-**ah**-yahs sah-nee-**tah**-ree-yahs/hee-**hyeh**-nee-kahs
tampons	**tampones**	tahm-**poh**-nehs
condoms	**condones**	kohn-**doh**-nehs
toilet paper	**papel higiénico**	pah-**pehl** hee-**hyen**-ee-koh
(non-)smoking area	**área de (no) fumar**	**ah**-ree-ah deh (noh) foo-**mahr**
camera	**la cámara**	lah **kah**-mah-rah
(a roll of) film	**(un rollo de) pelicula**	(oon **roh**-yoh deh) peh-**lee**-koo-lah
batteries	**las pilas**	lahs **pee**-lahs
passport	**el pasaporte**	ehl pah-sah-**pohr**-teh
visa	**el visado**	ehl vee-**sah**-doh

Health

I feel ill	**Me siento mal**	meh see-**ehn**-toh mahl
I have a headache	**Me duele la cabeza**	meh doo-**eh**-leh lah kah-**beh**-sah
I have a stomach-ache	**Me duele el estómago**	meh doo-**eh**-leh ehl ehs-**toh**-mah-goh
I need to rest	**Necesito descansar**	neh-seh-**see**-toh dehs-kahn-**sahr**
The child is/the children are sick	**El niño está/los niños están enfermo(s)**	ehl **nee**-nyoh ehs-**tah**/lohs **nee**-nyos ehs-**tahn** ehn-**fehr**-moh(s)
We need a doctor	**Necesitamos un médico**	neh-seh-see-**tah**-mohs oon **meh**-dee-koh
thermometer	**el termómetro**	ehl tehr-**moh**-meh-troh
drug store	**la farmacia**	lah fahr-**mah**-see-ah
medicine	**la medicina/ el remedio**	lah meh-dee-**see**-nah/ehl reh-**meh**-dee-oh

pills	**las pastillas/ pildoras**	lahs pahs-**tee**-yahs/lahs peel-**doh**-rahs

Post Offices and Banks

Where can I change money?	**¿Dónde puedo cambiar dinero?**	dohn-deh **pweh**-doh kahm-bee-**ahr** dee-neh-roh
What is the dollar rate?	**¿A cómo está el dólar?**	ah **koh**-moh ehs-**tah** ehl **doh**-lahr
How much is the postage to...?	**¿Cuánto cuesta enviar una carta a...?**	**kwahn**-toh **kwehs**-tah ehn-vee-**yahr** oo-nah **kahr**-tah ah
and for a post-card?	**¿y una postal?**	ee **oo**-nah pohs-**tahl**
I need stamps	**Necesito estampillas**	neh-seh-**see**-toh ehs-tahm-**pee**-yahs
cashier	**cajero**	kah-**heh**-roh
ATM	**cajero automático**	kah-**heh**-roh ahw-toh-**mah**-tee-koh
withdraw money	**sacar dinero**	sah-**kahr** dee-**neh**-roh

Shopping

How much does this cost?	**¿Cuánto cuesta esto?**	**kwahn**-toh **kwehs**-tah ehs-toh
I would like ...	**Me gustaría ...**	meh goos-tah-**ree**-ah
Do you have?	**¿Tienen?**	tee-**yeh**-nehn
I'm just looking, thank you	**Sólo estoy mirando, gracias**	**soh**-loh ehs-**toy** mee-**rahn**-doh, **grah**-see-ahs
What time do you open?	**¿A qué hora abren?**	ah **keh** oh-rah **ah**-brehn
What time do you close?	**¿A qué hora cierran?**	ah keh oh-rah see-**ehr**-rahn
Do you take credit cards/ traveler's checks?	**¿Aceptan tarjetas de crédito/ cheques de viajero?**	ahk-**sehp**-tahn tahr-**heh**-tahs deh **kreh**-dee-toh/**cheh**-kehs deh vee-ah-**heh**-roh
I am looking for...	**Estoy buscando...**	ehs-**toy** boos-**kahn**-doh
Is that your best price?	**¿Es su mejor precio?**	ehs soo meh-**hohr** preh-see-oh
discount	**un descuento**	oon dehs-koo-**ehn**-toh
clothes	**la ropa**	lah **roh**-pah
this one	**éste**	**ehs**-the
that one	**ése**	**eh**-she
expensive	**caro**	**kahr**-oh
cheap	**barato**	bah-**rah**-toh
size, clothes	**talla**	**tah**-yah
size, shoes	**número**	**noo**-mehr-oh
white	**blanco**	**blahn**-koh
black	**negro**	**neh**-groh
red	**rojo**	**roh**-hoh
yellow	**amarillo**	ah-mah-**ree**-yoh
green	**verde**	**vehr**-deh
blue	**azul**	ah-**sool**
antique store	**la tienda de antigüedades**	lah tee-**ehn**-dah deh ahn-tee-gweh-**dah**-dehs
bakery	**la panadería**	lah pah-nah-deh-**ree**-ah
bank	**el banco**	ehl **bahn**-koh
bookstore	**la librería**	lah lee-breh-**ree**-ah
butcher's	**la carnicería**	lahkahr-nee-seh-**ree**-ah
cake store	**la pastelería**	lah pahs-teh-leh-**ree**-ah
department store	**la tienda de departamentos**	lah tee-**ehn**-dah deh deh-pahr-tah-**mehn**-tohs
fish store	**la pescadería**	lah pehs-kah-deh-**ree**-ah
greengrocer's	**la frutería**	lah froo-teh-**ree**-ah
grocer's	**la tienda de abarrotes**	lah tee-**yehn**-dah deh ah-bah-**roh**-tehs
hairdresser's	**la peluquería**	lah peh-loo-keh-**ree**-ah

jeweler's	la joyería	lah hoh-yeh-**ree**-yah
market	el tianguis/ mercado	ehl tee-ahn-goo-ees/mehr-**kah**-doh
newsstand	el puesto de periódicos	ehl poo-**es**-toh deh pe-**rio**-dee-kohs
post office	la oficina de correos	lah oh-fee-**see**-nah deh kohr-**reh**-ohs
shoe store	la zapatería	lah sah-pah-teh-**ree**-ah
supermarket	el supermercado	ehl soo-pehr-mehr-**kah**-doh
travel agency	la agencia de viajes	lah ah-**hehn**-see-ah deh vee-**ah**-hehs

Sightseeing

art gallery	el museo de arte	ehl moo-**seh**-oh deh **ar**-teh
beach	la playa	lah **plah**-yah
cathedral	la catedral	lah kah-teh-**drahl**
church	la iglesia/ la basílica	lah ee-**gleh**-see-ah/ lah bah-**see**-lee-kah
garden	el jardín	ehl hahr-**deen**
library	la biblioteca	lah bee-blee-oh-**teh**-kah
museum	el museo	ehl moo-**seh**-oh
pyramid	la pirámide	lah pee-**rah**-meed
ruins	las ruinas	lahs roo-**ee**-nahs
tourist information office	la oficina de turismo	lah oh-fee-**see**-nah deh too-**rees**-moh
town hall	el palacio municipal	ehl pah-**lah**-see-oh moo-nee-see-**pahl**
closed for holidays	cerrado por vacaciones	sehr-**rah**-doh pohr vah-kah-see-**oh**-nehs
ticket	la entrada	lah ehn-**trah**-dah
how much is the entrance fee?	¿Cuánto vale la entrada?	**kwahn**-toh vah-leh lah ehn-**trah**-dah
guide (person)	el/la guía	ehl/lah **gee**-ah
guide (book)	la guía	lah **gee**-ah
guided tour	una visita guiada	**oo**-nah vee-**see**-tah gee-**ah**-dah
map	el mapa	ehl **mah**-pah
city map	el plano de la ciudad	ehl **plah**-noh deh lah see-oo-**dahd**

Transportation

When does the… leave?	¿A qué hora sale el…?	ah **keh** oh-rah **sah**-leh el
Where is the bus stop?	¿Dónde está la parada de autobuses?	**dohn**-deh ehs-**tah** lah pah-**rah**-dah deh ow-toh-**boo**-sehs
Is there a bus/train to…?	¿Hay un camión/ tren a…?	**eye** oon kah-mee-**ohn**/trehn ah
the next bus/train	el próximo camión/tren	ehl **prohk**-ee-moh kah-mee-**ohn**/trehn
bus station	la central camionera/ de autobuses	lah sehn-**trahl** kah-mee-ohn-**ehr**-ah/deh ow-toh-**boo**-sehs
train station	la estación de trenes	lah ehs-tah-see-**ohn** deh **treh**-nehs
subway/metro	el metro	ehl **meh**-troh
platform	el andén	ehl ahn-**dehn**
ticket office	la taquilla	lah tah-**kee**-yah
round-trip ticket	un boleto de ida y vuelta	oon boh-**leh**-toh deh **ee**-dah ee voo-**ehl**-tah
one-way ticket	un boleto de ida solamente	oon boh-**leh**-toh deh **ee**-dah soh-lah-**mehn**-teh
airport	el aeropuerto	ehl ah-ehr-oh-poo-**ehr**-toh
customs	la aduana	lah ah-doo-**ah**-nah
departure lounge	sala de embarque	**sah**-lah deh ehm-**bahr**-keh

boarding pass	pase de abordar	**pah**-seh deh ah-bohr-**dahr**
taxi stand/rank	sitio de taxis	**see**-tee-oh deh **tahk**-sees
car rental	renta de automóviles	**rehn**-tah deh aw-toh-**moh**-vee-lehs
motorcycle	la moto (cicleta)	lah moh-toh(see-**kleh**-tah)
mileage	el kilometraje	ehl kee-loh-meh-**trah**-he
bicycle	la bicicleta	lah bee-see-**kleh**-tah
daily/weekly rate	la tarifa diaria/ semanal	lah tah-**ree**-fah dee-**ah**-ree-ah/seh-mah-**nahl**
insurance	los seguros	lohs seh-**goo**-rohs
gas station	la gasolinería	lah gah-soh-leen-er-**ee**-ah
garage	el taller mecánico	ehl tah-**yehr** meh-**kahn**-ee-koh
I have a flat tire	Se me ponchó la llanta	seh meh pohn-**shoh** lah **yahn**-tah

Staying in a Hotel

Do you have a vacant room?	¿Tienen una habitación libre?	tee-**eh**-nehn **oo**-nah ah-bee-tah-see-**ohn lee**-breh
double room	habitación doble	ah-bee-tah-see-**ohn doh**-bleh
with a double bed	con cama matrimonial	kohn **kah**-mah mah-tree-moh-**nee**-ahl
twin room	habitación con dos camas	ah-bee-tah-see-**ohn** kohn dohs **kah**-mahs
single room	habitación sencilla	ah-bee-tah-see-**ohn** sehn-**see**-yah
room with a bath	habitación con baño	ah-bee-tah-see-**ohn** kohn bah-nyoh
shower	la ducha	lah **doo**-chah
Do you have a room with a view (of the sea)?	¿Hay alguna habitación con vista (al mar)?	eye ahl-**goo**-nah ah-bee-tah-see-**ohn** kohn **vees**-tah (ahl **mahr**)
I have a reservation	Tengo una habitación reservada	tehn-goh **oo**-nah ah-bee-tah-see-**ohn** reh-sehr-**vah**-dah
The … is not working	No funciona el/la…	noh foon-see-**oh**-nah ehl/lah
I need a wake-up call at … o'clock	Necesito que me despierten a las …	neh-seh-**see**-toh keh meh dehs-pee-**ehr**-tehn ah lahs
Where is the dining-room/bar?	¿Dónde está el restaurante/ el bar?	**dohn**-deh ehs-**tah** ehl rehs-toh-**rahn**-teh/ehl **bahr**
hot/cold water	agua caliente/ fría	**ah**-goo-ah kah-lee-**ehn**-teh/ **free**-ah
soap	el jabón	ehl hah-**bohn**
towel	la toalla	lah toh-**ah**-yah
key	la llave	lah **yah**-veh

Eating Out

Have you got a table for …	¿Tienen mesa para …?	tee-**eh**-nehn meh-sahpah-**rah**
I want to reserve a table	Quiero reservar una mesa	kee-eh-roh reh-sehr-**vahr oo**-nah meh-sah
The bill, please	La cuenta, por favor	lah **kwehn**-tah pohr fah-**vohr**
I am a vegetarian	Soy vegetariano/a	soy veh-heh-tah-ree-**ah**-no/na
waiter/waitress	mesero/a	meh-**seh**-roh/ah
menu	la carta	lah **kahr**-tah
fixed-price menu	menú del día/comida corrida	meh-**noo** dehl **dee**-ah/koh-**mee**-dah koh-**ree**-dah
wine list	la carta de vinos	lah **kahr**-tah deh **vee**-nohs
glass	un vaso	oon **vah**-soh

bottle	**una botella**	oo-nah boh-**teh**-yah
knife	**un cuchillo**	oon koo-**chee**-yoh
fork	**un tenedor**	oon teh-neh-**dohr**
spoon	**una cuchara**	oo-nah koo-**chah**-rah
breakfast	**el desayuno**	ehl deh-sah-**yoo**-noh
lunch	**la comida**	lah koh-**mee**-dah
dinner	**la cena**	lah **seh**-nah
main course	**el plato fuerte**	ehl **plah**-toh foo-**ehr**-teh
starters	**las entradas**	lahs ehn-**trah**-das
dish of the day	**el plato del día**	ehl **plah**-toh dehl **dee**-ah
rare	**termino rojo**	**tehr**-mee-noh **roh**-hoh
medium	**termino medio**	**tehr**-mee-noh **meh**-dee-oh
well done	**bien cocido**	bee-**ehn** koh-**see**-doh
Could you heat it up for me?	**¿Me lo podría calentar?**	meh loh pohd-**ree**-ah kah-lehn-**tahr**
chair	**la silla**	lah **see**-yah
napkin	**la servilleta**	lah sehr-vee-**yeh**-tah
tip	**la propina**	lah proh-**pee**-nah
Is service included?	**¿El servicio está incluido?**	ehl sehr-**vee**-see-oh ehs-**tah** een-skloo-**ee**-doh
Do you have a light?	**¿Tiene fuego?**	tee-**eh**-nee foo-**eh**-goh
ashtray	**cenicero**	seh-nee-**seh**-roh
cigarettes	**los cigarros**	lohs see-**gah**-rohs

Menu Decoder *(see also pp308–13)*

el aceite	ah-**see-eh**-teh	oil
las aceitunas	ah-seh-**toon**-ahs	olives
el agua mineral	**ah**-gwa mee-neh-**rahl**	mineral water
sin gas/con gas	seen gas/kohn gas	still/sparkling
el ajo	**ah**-hoh	garlic
el arroz	ahr-**rohs**	rice
el azúcar	ah-**soo**-kahr	sugar
la banana	bah-**nah**-nah	banana
una bebida	beh-**bee**-dah	drink
el café	kah-**feh**	coffee
la carne	**kahr**-neh	meat
la cebolla	seh-**boh**-yah	onion
la cerveza	sehr-**veh**-sah	beer
el cerdo	**sehr**-doh	pork
el chocolate	choh-koh-**lah**-teh	chocolate
la ensalada	ehn-sah-**lah**-dah	salad
la fruta	**froo**-tah	fruit
el helado	eh-**lah**-doh	ice cream
el huevo	oo-**eh**-voh	egg
el jugo	ehl**hoo**-goh	juice
la langosta	lahn-**gohs**-tah	lobster
la leche	**leh**-cheh	milk
la mantequilla	mahn-teh-**kee**-yah	butter
la manzana	mahn-**sah**-nah	apple
los mariscos	mah-**rees**-kohs	seafood
la naranja	nah-**rahn**-hah	orange
el pan	pahn	bread
las papas	**pah**-pahs	potatoes
las papas a la francesa	**pah**-pahs ah lah frahn-**seh**-sah	French fries
las papas fritas	**pah**-pahs **free**-tahs	potato chips
el pastel	pahs-**tehl**	cake
el pescado	pehs-**kah**-doh	fish
picante	pee-**kahn**-teh	spicy
la pimienta	pee-mee-**yehn**-tah	pepper
el pollo	**poh**-yoh	chicken
el postre	**pohs**-treh	dessert
el queso	**keh**-soh	cheese
el refresco	reh-**frehs**-koh	soft drink/soda
la sal	sahl	salt
la salsa	**sahl**-sah	sauce
la sopa	**soh**-pah	soup
el té	teh	herb tea (usually camomile)
el té negro	teh neh-groh	tea
la torta	**tohr**-tah	sandwich
las tostadas	tohs-**tah**-dahs	toast
el vinagre	vee-**nah**-greh	vinegar
el vino blanco	**vee**-noh blahn-koh	white wine
el vino tinto	**vee**-noh teen-toh	red wine

Numbers

0	**cero**	**seh**-roh
1	**uno**	**oo**-noh
2	**dos**	dohs
3	**tres**	trehs
4	**cuatro**	**kwa**-troh
5	**cinco**	**seen**-koh
6	**seis**	says
7	**siete**	**see**-eh-teh
8	**ocho**	**oh**-choh
9	**nueve**	**nweh**-veh
10	**diez**	dee-**ehs**
11	**once**	**ohn**-seh
12	**doce**	**doh**-seh
13	**trece**	**treh**-seh
14	**catorce**	kah-**tohr**-seh
15	**quince**	**keen**-seh
16	**dieciséis**	dee-eh-see-**seh**-ees
17	**diecisiete**	dee-eh-see-see-**eh**-teh
18	**dieciocho**	dee-eh-see-**oh**-choh
19	**diecinueve**	dee-eh-see-**nweh**-veh
20	**veinte**	**veh**-een-teh
21	**veintiuno**	veh-een-tee-**oo**-noh
22	**veintidós**	veh-een-tee-**dohs**
30	**treinta**	**treh**-een-tah
31	**treinta y uno**	treh-een-tah ee **oo**-noh
40	**cuarenta**	kwah-**rehn**-tah
50	**cincuenta**	seen-**kwehn**-tah
60	**sesenta**	seh-**sehn**-tah
70	**setenta**	seh-**tehn**-tah
80	**ochenta**	oh-**chehn**-tah
90	**noventa**	noh-**vehn**-tah
100	**cien**	see-**ehn**
101	**ciento uno**	see-**ehn**-toh **oo**-noh
102	**ciento dos**	see-**ehn**-toh **dohs**
200	**doscientos**	dohs-see-**ehn**- tohs
500	**quinientos**	khee-nee-**ehn**-tohs
700	**setecientos**	seh-teh-see-**ehn**-tohs
900	**novecientos**	noh-veh-see-**ehn**-tohs
1,000	**mil**	meel
1,001	**mil uno**	meel **oo**-noh

Time

one minute	**un minuto**	oon mee-**noo**-toh
one hour	**una hora**	oo-nah **oh**-rah
half an hour	**media hora**	**meh**-dee-ah **oh**-rah
half past one	**la una y media**	lah **oo**-nah ee **meh**-dee-ah
quarter past one	**la una y cuarto**	lah **oo**-nah ee **kwahr**-toh
ten past one	**la una y diez**	lah **oo**-nah ee dee-**ehs**
quarter to two	**cuarto para las dos**	**kwahr**-toh pah-rah lahs **dohs**
ten to two	**diez para las dos**	dee-**ehs** pah-rah lahs **dohs**
Monday	**lunes**	**loo**-nehs
Tuesday	**martes**	**mahr**-tehs
Wednesday	**miércoles**	mee-**ehr**-koh-lehs
Thursday	**jueves**	hoo-**weh**-vehs
Friday	**viernes**	vee-**ehr**-nehs
Saturday	**sábado**	**sah**-bah-doh
Sunday	**domingo**	doh-**meen**-goh
January	**enero**	eh-**neh**-roh
February	**febrero**	feh-**breh**-roh
March	**marzo**	**mahr**-soh
April	**abril**	ah-**breel**
May	**mayo**	**mah**-yoh
June	**junio**	**hoo**-nee-oh
July	**julio**	**hoo**-lee-oh
August	**agosto**	ah-**gohs**-toh
September	**septiembre**	sehp-tee-**ehm**-breh
October	**octubre**	ohk-**too**-breh
November	**noviembre**	noh-vee-**ehm**-breh
December	**diciembre**	dee-see-**ehm**-breh
Two days ago	**Hace dos días**	**hah**-seh dohs dee-ahs
In two day's time	**En dos días**	ehn **dohs** dee-ahs
May 1	**El primero de mayo**	ehl pree-**meh**-roh deh **mah**-yoh